Language and Religion

Language Intersections

Volume 2

Language and Religion

Edited by
Robert A. Yelle
Courtney Handman
Christopher I. Lehrich

DE GRUYTER
MOUTON

ISBN 978-1-61451-594-4
e-ISBN (PDF) 978-1-61451-432-9
e-ISBN (EPUB) 978-1-5015-0074-9

Library of Congress Control Number: 2018956865

Bibliographic information published by the Deutsche Nationalbibliothek
The Deutsche Nationalbibliothek lists this publication in the Deutsche Nationalbibliografie; detailed bibliographic data are available on the Internet at http://dnb.dnb.de.

This volume is text- and page-identical with the hardback published in 2019.
Typesetting: Integra Software Services Pvt. Ltd.
Printing and binding: CPI books GmbH, Leck

www.degruyter.com

Acknowledgments

This volume was commissioned by De Gruyter in 2013 for the Language Intersections series. The editors would like to thank Emily Farrell and Alissa Jones Nelson, who commissioned the volume, and Lara Wysong, who has overseen the production, for their advice and assistance. Robert would like to thank Michael Silverstein for early advice; the University of Memphis, New York University Law School, and Ludwig Maximilian University, Munich, where he was employed successively while working on the volume; Wenzel Braunfels for checking the bibliographic references; and his wife, Lynda Sagrestano, for her support. Courtney would like to thank the office of the Dean of Faculty at Reed College for support through the Stillman-Drake Funds of a conference on Religion and Media that brought together the editors of this volume. She would like to thank all of the participants of that conference. She would also like to thank James and Adele Slotta for their love and support. Christopher Lehrich would like to acknowledge the support of his family, and especially to thank his co-editors.

https://doi.org/10.1515/9781614514329-201

Contents

Acknowledgments — V

Robert A. Yelle, Courtney Handman, and Christopher I. Lehrich
Introduction — 1

Part I: **Ritual and language**

Naphtali S. Meshel
To be taken with a grain of salt: Between a "grammar" and a GRAMMUR of a sacrificial ritual system — 31

Robert A. Yelle
Intertextuality, iconicity, and joint speech: Three dialogical modes of linguistic performance in Hindu mantras — 57

Paul Copp
Writing Buddhist liturgies in Dunhuang: Hints of ritualist craft — 68

Leslie Arnovick
The power of Pater Noster and Creed in Anglo-Saxon charms: De-institutionalization and subjectification — 87

Aurélie Névot
Trembling voices echo: Yi shamanistic and mediumistic speeches — 114

Part II: **Ideologies of religious language**

Naomi Janowitz
Speech acts and divine names: Comparing linguistic ideologies of performativity — 139

Mustafa Shah
The word of God: The epistemology of language in classical Islamic theological thought — 158

Paolo Visigalli
Interface with God: The divine transparency of the Sanskrit language — 193

Laurence Wuidar
Ineffability and music in early Christian theology — 215

William Downes
The significance of "the plain style" in seventeenth-century England — 243

Jenny Ponzo
The debate over glossolalia between Conservative Evangelicals and Charismatics: A question of semiotic style — 276

Kocku von Stuckrad
The place of language in discursive studies of religion — 304

Part III: **Media and materiality after the linguistic turn**

Seth L. Sanders
Words, things, and death: The rise of Iron Age literary monuments — 327

Isabel Laack
The (poetic) imagery of "flower and song" in Aztec religious expression: Correlating the semiotic modalities of language and pictorial writing — 349

Patrick Eisenlohr
Religious language and media: Sound reproduction and transduction — 382

Anderson Blanton
The "point of contact": Radio and the transduction of healing prayer — 404

Jon Bialecki
"The Lord says you speak as harlots": Affect, *affectus*, and *affectio* — 418

Contributors — 442

Index — 449

Robert A. Yelle, Courtney Handman, and Christopher I. Lehrich

Introduction

1 Overview and justification

This volume brings together an interdisciplinary group of scholars to survey a field that is of growing importance for both religious studies and anthropology: namely, the study of the religious dimensions of communication and of the linguistic aspects of religion. A few decades ago, to all appearances, the impetus given to the study of religion by insights derived from structural linguistics had all but exhausted itself. Despite the native concern of scholars of religion with problems of historical philology and translation, and apart from the continuing tradition of rigorous analysis of religious and ritual language in the field of linguistic anthropology, disciplined reflection on the intersection of language and religion had moved away from the center of religious studies.

A number of factors account for this change. One is the (often legitimate) critiques of the overly intellectualist, universalizing, and rigidly formalist approaches associated with older models of structuralism. Poststructuralists such as Jacques Derrida and Michel Foucault inherited certain preoccupations of the structuralists, such as their attention to texts and their construction, especially through binary oppositions. Yet they also criticized the power relations and hierarchies of value encoded in the logocentric search for a universal key to knowledge, a search that perpetuated some of the cultural parochialisms of European metaphysics and Christian Biblicism (see esp. Derrida 1976). The focus on structure, while designed to divine a meaning in such denigrated cultural products as myths and rituals, had an unfortunate tendency to privilege *langue* (abstract structure) over *parole* (concrete utterance), writing over speech (or vice-versa), linguistic over non-linguistic forms; indeed, reason over unreason, meaning anything that could not be captured through structural models.

A second, related critique within religious studies, anthropology and allied disciplines reacted against the tendency to turn everything into a text: a move that devalued material, aesthetic, and embodied forms of knowledge and experience. The privileging of texts occluded other modes of expression, with the unfortunate side-effect that iconic, performative, and oral modes often were left out of account. This repression of the material and expressive dimensions of culture

Robert A. Yelle, Ludwig Maximilian University, Munich
Courtney Handman, University of Texas at Austin
Christopher I. Lehrich, Boston, Massachusetts

https://doi.org/10.1515/9781614514329-001

was also a notable tendency of the colonial encounter between Europeans and indigenous peoples. Even later, when material culture became a focus of study, the preferred methodology was to focus on its semantic content, and to treat everything as a symbol to be decoded. The end goal was a written message – an "ethnography" or writing about culture – that would replace the thing itself, as its uncovered essence. Subdisciplines such as material religion and aesthetics of religion, and programmatic movements such as the turn to performance and the iconic turn, have attempted to rectify this imbalance.

Despite these necessary critiques, there are important reasons for now rethinking the connections between language and religion. Historians of religion whose work focuses on the interpretation of texts are necessarily concerned with understanding the role that language plays in forming, expressing, and communicating religious ideas and experiences. Some of the earliest insights in this relatively young discipline came during the 19th century, after the European discovery of Sanskrit and of the Indo-European language family led to comparative historical philology. Friedrich Max Müller's science of religion or comparative mythology built on this basis. Later, Ferdinand de Saussure constructed his structural linguistics on the same foundation. Structuralism in turn influenced the studies of literature, mythology, and ritual. Despite the collapse of some of the grand theories of a few decades ago, there is really no alternative to a comparative approach to religious language if we hope to explain such cross-cultural phenomena as the prevalence of poetry and special, apparently nonsensical "magic words" in spells; the reverence for hieratic, often archaic languages and scripts (see Mustafa Shah's chapter on the language of the Holy Qurʾān in this volume); and the denseness of metaphorical imagery in certain religious traditions. The retreat from a comparative approach to the relative safety of descriptive philology and translation represents a missed opportunity to improve our understanding of both the range and commonalities of human experience and expression.

The Bible, although supposedly a quintessential example of a revealed text, is a human product that uses a number of linguistic forms and stylistic devices commonly found in other cultures. Genesis 1 could be interpreted to mean that God created the world through a speech act, "Let there be light!" (*fiat lux*, Vulgate) (on speech acts, see Naomi Janowitz's chapter in this volume). In the Latin Vulgate text of Genesis 2:16–17, Adam names the creatures "according to their own names" (*nominibus suis*), a statement that eventually precipitated a debate over whether these were already the names of the creatures, or whether Adam as first legislator granted these names by decree, and so established a convention (Yelle 2013a: 90). Acts 2 recounts the first Pentecost, when the Apostles were inspired with the power to preach the Gospel in all languages. This story later was sometimes represented as the (temporary) cure of the diversity or "curse of confusion" of languages that began with the fall of the Tower of Babel in Genesis 11 (Yelle 2013a: 90). Although the Gospels are in Greek, Jesus's spells in Mark 5:41 and 7:34 are left in the original Aramaic, as well as translated, apparently signaling the magical efficacy of the original utterances. Each of these examples invokes the widespread belief in a perfect, inspired, or magically effective language. Aristeas' familiar story of the creation of the Septuagint (or "Seventy"), the 3rd century BCE translation of the Pentateuch into Greek, according to which seventy different translations all miraculously agreed, also comes to mind in this regard.

The language of the Hebrew Bible is also highly poetic. The Psalms especially are replete with parallelisms, which repeat the same idea in slightly different words. We also find chiasmus, or the repetition of the same or similar sounds or words in inverted order. An extended example is Leviticus 24:13–23, described further below. Psalm 119 is an elaborate acrostic of which each verse begins with a different letter of the Hebrew alphabet.

Elsewhere in the Bible we find prohibitions against certain uses of language. The Third Commandment forbids taking the Lord's name in vain (Exodus 20:7 and Deuteronomy 5:11, RSV). This may mean either swearing an oath upon the name of God, forswearing upon such an oath, or perhaps cursing God. God in the Hebrew Bible is often referred to using plural forms (e.g., Elohim), a usage often found with honorifics or modes of addressing superiors through indirect speech. Later in Jewish tradition, it was forbidden to say the personal four-letter name of God or Tetragrammaton, for which one instead substituted either "Adonai" (Lord) or (in modern times) "ha-Shem" (the Name). Such name taboos are common across traditions. Matthew 6:7 was interpreted by English Puritans to prohibit "vain repetitions" in prayer (Geneva and KJV), a prohibition that Roman Catholics supposedly violated with their incessant, mechanical Ave Marias and Pater Nosters. Quakers in particular took to heart two injunctions: Jesus's intensification of the Third Commandment, "swear not at all" (Matthew 5:34, KJV), and Ecclesiastes 5:2 (KJV): "Let your words be few" (Bauman 1983). Paul's statement that such modes of inspiration as glossolalia (speaking in tongues) will "pass away" (1 Corinthians 13, RSV) contributed to the idea in the early Christian church that miracles and prophecies had ceased, and later, during the Reformation, to the foundations of what we call "disenchantment" (Yelle 2013a: 22–24). Reacting against this, some modern Pentecostals and charismatic churches have revived glossolalia (see Jenny Ponzo's and Jon Bialecki's chapters in this volume). Paul further characterized the Gospel as a form of "plain speech" that removed the veil of mystery that occluded Mosaic law (2 Corinthians 3:12–13, KJV). Such ideas interacted with Protestant literalism and influenced movements for the reform of language in 16th- and 17th-century England, as described in William Downes's chapter in this volume.

Many of the above phenomena are commonly found across cultures; parallelism, a common form of the "poetic function" studied by Roman Jakobson (1960: 356, 368–370), is an example. Certain characteristically "religious" uses of language, apart from mythology, appear to occupy a position on a cline or continuum with other, more mundane forms of language. As Michael Silverstein's analyses of the metricalization of discourse imply, one of the characteristic features of ritual language is a heightening of the poetic function, as exemplified by the proliferation of rhyme, alliteration, chiasmus, repetition, etc. (Silverstein 2004; see also Stasch 2011). A study of such extraordinary uses of the utterly ordinary suggests that ritual is a type of communication, attention to which may therefore illuminate language. Through such two-way comparisons, both religion and language emerge into clearer definition, as neither identical nor opposed phenomena, but as linked in their techniques and objectives. One of the reasons for a renewed focus on language and religion should be to advance our understanding of such forms, beyond what can be accomplished through the study of a single linguistic or religious tradition.

Another reason, however, should be to promote awareness of the cultural specificities of ideas and practices concerning language. The Protestant critique of "vain repetitions" in prayer was carried by British colonials to India, where this polemic was used to devalue Indian chants such as mantras (Yelle 2013a: 103–135). In recent decades, anthropologists, including notably Webb Keane (2007) and participants in the Anthropology of Christianity movement, have highlighted the role of theologically based linguistic ideologies in defining modernity vis-à-vis the "primitive." Our increasing recognition of such cultural differences may appear to undermine the earlier search for linguistic universals in which structuralists engaged. However, as the above example shows, sometimes it is precisely by recognizing a cross-cultural phenomenon – such as repetition in prayers and chants – that one is enabled to identify derogations from such patterns, as in the case of the Protestant critique of "vain repetitions." Hindu mantras (or Catholic rosaries) and Protestant "plain speech" mark opposing ends of a cline or continuum defined by degrees of the poetic function. Historical and ethnographic attention to cultural differences in this case complements rather than contradicts the structuralist analysis of the poetic function of language.

It is more than thirty years since Fredric Jameson (1972: vii) said that "a genuine critique of Structuralism commits us to working our way completely through it so as to emerge, on the other side, into some wholly different and theoretically more satisfying philosophical perspective." Yet can it be said even now that such a reappraisal, much less a "complete" one, has occurred? It would be more accurate perhaps to admit that, as concerns the study of religion, the conversation has shifted to other topics. Let us begin by granting the critiques of language and of religion so widely and forcefully articulated over the last generation. We no longer need to argue that religion is not a *sui generis* object "out there" to be examined. We all know that language as deployed under the Saussurean regime was always at base dependent on a reification of language as a system of logical relations, inherently divorced from social life. Postcolonial critiques have long since revealed the many means by which language and religion have been imposed to control and dominate subaltern bodies, mouths, and minds. Suppose we take this all for granted. Have all the old questions regarding the connection between language and religion simply evaporated into so much hot air or *flatus vocis*? How shall we make sense of the continuing talk of religious practitioners and of the patterns to which our scholarly forebears adverted?

What of the Saussurean formulation of language as binary, that profoundly relational conception under which individual human acts and practices (*parole*) are in effect evanescent bodyings-forth of a transcendent, synchronic system that stabilizes and underwrites truth (*langue*)? Some critics, such as Derrida, have argued that this view of linguistic structure depends on metaphysical or even theological presuppositions. Even if this is the case, it would not dissolve the study of language into that of society or culture as a whole, much less exorcise the ghost of metaphysics from our ideological systems. The more recent work of developing scholarship focused on the body (as opposed to language), on the historically particular (as opposed to the structurally universal), on emic practice rather than etic system – all this, however salutary, arguably only defers the question. In negating language, such scholars retain it as a supplement, as an outside, which takes the form of an ethnography or other scholarly writing that purports to distill the "essence" of an embodied phenomenon to words (Silverstein 2004: 622n; Mazzarella 2009). So conceived, this opposition necessarily functions with respect to a system or structure – in Saussurean terms, a *langue*. This merely reconstitutes structuralism without the penetrating reflexivity of the great formalists, such as Vladimir Propp and Viktor Shklovsky.

Religious studies, particularly in Europe in recent years, has seen a rise of interest in discourse analysis (see Kocku von Stuckrad's chapter in this volume), which attends to the social construction of objects through language and communities of conversation – including academic communities, such as scholars of religion. This is certainly a necessary and positive development, which attempts to overcome essentialism and to respond to the fundamental structuralist insight that, language being arbitrary, categories such as "religion" are discursively constituted and shifting. However, many of the practitioners of discourse analysis refrain from deploying the concepts and techniques developed in semiotics and linguistic anthropology for the analysis of language: the poetic function; the typology of signs (icons, indexes, and symbols) distinguished by Peircean semiotics; the idea that many rituals are "indexical icons" or diagrams of the worldly processes to which they refer, according to Michael Silverstein's development of Jakobson and Peirce (Silverstein 2004: 626–627); and so forth. What would be beneficial here is a more systematic engagement with a broader set of concepts and methodologies for the analysis of language. Why not use all of the tools at one's disposal?

Despite the value added by the insights of the iconic and material turn, arguably the same point applies. That is because the most sophisticated and successful examples we have of semiotic analysis are those that have been developed for language. There are obvious reasons why the principles of structural linguistics were carried over first to the study of literary texts and myths; Lévi-Strauss notes already that "myth *is* language," while also recognizing that it must communicate in a way that differs from standard language (Lévi-Strauss 1963: 209). However, on its own terms, Saussure's "sémiologie" was not confined to language, but extended to other sign-systems, including religion. When it comes to the other tradition indispensable for the emergence of semiotics, that of Charles Sanders Peirce, this system grew out of a critique of traditional logic and metaphysics, and thus of philosophical language, but from its beginnings was by no means focused exclusively on the analysis of words. The Peircean "icon" can apply to a pictorial image as well as to a rhyme (Yelle 2016). Although we should not expect that an analysis of other cultural forms will look exactly the same as that of language, this is no reason why we should not begin with a thorough study of the semiotics of language and of texts. To do otherwise would run the risk of leaving out something important, or at least of reinventing the wheel.

New methodologies are opening the way for a rapprochement among structural, historical, phenomenological, and even scientific approaches to the linguistic study of religion. With the decline of *a priori* modes of semiotic theorizing, there are opportunities for using the data – both historical and ethnographic – of religion to further develop some of the foundational questions of linguistics and communication. This Introduction surveys a range of current approaches in the study of language and religion. Among the topics touched upon are the cross-cultural regularities seen in the poetic dimensions of ritual performances; the problem of the apparent non-arbitrariness of linguistic and other signs in many religious traditions, in which the idea of a sacred, magical, perfect, or iconic language creates particular semiotic modalities for the relationship between speakers and their speech; linguistic iconoclasm, or attacks against poetic performance and magical languages, which influenced the semiotic ideology of European modernity, as illustrated by Dutch Calvinist attacks against the "fetishization" of language in colonial Indonesia (Keane

2007: 179–181) and by British polemics against Hindu mythology as idolatry in colonial India (Yelle 2013a: 33–70); the role of materiality – of embodiment, of different semiotic modalities (e.g., gesture, dance, and music), but also of different modes of disseminating the sign such as writing, printing, and electronic media – in enabling and circumscribing different types of religiosity (see Patrick Eisenlohr's and Anderson Blanton's chapters in this volume); the convergences and divergences between written and spoken languages, and of calligraphy and characters as a special mode of religious praxis (see Aurélie Névot's chapter on Yi shamanistic writing in this volume); the question of the relationship between language and other language-like forms, such as music, with which language is often compared and combined in a religious context (see Laurence Wuidar's chapter in this volume); and the possibilities and limits of using language as a metaphor or theoretical rubric for the illumination of ritual and other religious phenomena.

To define either language or religion at the outset of an endeavor such as this one would represent an act of hubris. It would also preempt one of the goals of this work, which is to use both language and religion as metaphors for each other, and so to contribute something toward the general definition of each. We shall, for example, consider (among other topics) what are the special characteristics, if any, of religious language that distinguish this from ordinary language. To pose the question in this way is, to some extent, unavoidably circular, in that it presupposes that we know what "religion" and, therefore, "religious language" is. Yet this does not vitiate the endeavor itself. The goal instead is to build from common-sense understandings (and preconceptions) and customary, lived uses, toward a clearer definition of these categories. The mistake would be to narrow the scope of our inquiry too much before going through such an exercise in hermeneutics or the interpretation of data.

The critical spirit has often taken as its point of departure the critique of language. This was as true of Plato's debate with the Sophists as it was of the early Nietzsche's argument that even the most scientific language is a displaced metaphor (Nietzsche 1989), and of the mature Nietzsche's effort through genealogy and the etymology of moral categories to show that metaphysical oppositions such as "good" and "evil" encode culturally contingent valuations that are provisional and subject to reversal (Nietzsche 1968: 460–492). Recent decades have witnessed an extension of such approaches, which reveal how the "religious" and the "secular" have been invented and propagated, while the poetic has been deprecated persistently as irrational and contemptible. Such approaches have opened up a window on the differences among "semiotic" or "linguistic ideologies" (see Yelle 2013b: 3), and provide a fruitful counterbalance to the earlier structuralist emphasis on universal patterns.

Our return to classic questions about "language and religion" attempts neither iconoclasm nor necromancy. The question is not how to criticize, but how to build critically. The present volume makes a modest gesture toward rethinking, thinking anew, the relations between religion and language. Granted all that we have learned about the impossibility of both of these categories as objects of study, the fact remains that the data commonsensically piled into that intersection is enormous, varied, and complex. Rather than make deterministic claims about these data, the volume sets forth a traditional, some might say old-fashioned cluster of issues for reconsideration, and invites established and emerging scholars from a range of fields, disciplines, and methodologies, to reflect on these issues and the intrinsic difficulties that they pose.

2 Key issues

The set of key issues in the study of language and religion abstracted briefly here and then elaborated more fully below in this section is intended to provoke further reflection, rather than to foreclose discussion. That is why we have raised so many unanswered – and perhaps unanswerable – questions.

Ritual and language: Why are poetic devices (e.g., alliteration, chiasmus, simple repetition) prevalent in religious and ritual language cross-culturally? What is the best explanation for the accumulation of multimodal forms of expression in ritual? For the denseness of symbol and metaphor in religious discourse? Which theories – e.g., performativity, ritualization, religious cognition/transmission – best account for these cross-cultural patterns? What is the range and function of iconicity in religious discourse in general? How is religious discourse distinct from that of secular modernity in this regard?

Ideologies of religious language: What accounts for the tendency toward belief in a "natural," i.e. iconic and/or magical language across religious traditions? How can this tendency be reconciled with the modern rise of the doctrine of the arbitrariness of the sign, whether represented by John Locke or Ferdinand de Saussure? What accounts for polemics against the sign, or linguistic iconoclasm, in traditions such as Protestantism, where restraint rather than exuberance of expression has been enforced? How do we understand the coordination between attacks against plastic and those against verbal images, as detailed by Keane and others? What factors – social and semiotic – are there in common among critiques of poetic form as found in, e.g., Plato's attack on *mimesis*, the Buddha's rejection of Vedic meter (*chandas*) (Kelly 1996), Puritan polemics against vain repetitions in prayer, Counter-Reformation complaints against polyphony in liturgical music (Wegman 2005), etc.? How have

Protestant literalism and Enlightenment rejections of figuration in language contributed to the construction of the semiotic ideology of modernity?

Media and materiality after the linguistic turn: Protestant linguistic iconoclasm affirmed as an aesthetic and moral ideal immediacy and presence: the words of scripture transmit the plain intention of the deity, and the prayers of the worshipper (ideally) express her or his sincere faith; there is no more room for magic words. In most religious traditions around the world, however, semiotic (including linguistic) mediation, meaning the relatively independent role that signs can play in communicating and conforming meaning and practice, is taken for granted (as well as theorized). Prayers, songs, ritual formulas, and entire languages (e.g., Classical Arabic, Biblical Hebrew) are some of the morally valued material resources through which speakers perform and produce religious traditions. Much recent research has focused on the largely Protestant critiques of mediation and ritual, but other questions still need to be considered: How do different practices and regimes of mediation in religious life produce pious subjectivities? How do different religious traditions morally code different media (e.g., audio-visual recordings vs. printed texts, translated vs. untranslated scriptures, music vs. speech)? What are the implications of elaborate and longstanding memorization systems (e.g., Vedic recitation, Talmud study, *ars memoria*, examination study of the Chinese Classics) in relocating sacred texts internally? How does language as a material form (in iconic, natural, sacred, and scriptural senses) relate to the other media of religious practice (e.g., prayer beads, statuary, architecture)? How does the introduction of new media into religious practice alter our understanding of the social function and moral valences of mediation?

After the "linguistic turn" of much 20th-century humanities and social science research, a growing scholarly movement arose that has sought to displace language as affording privileged access to an understanding of both social life and individual experience. In more and less radical versions of this emerging tradition, language is viewed either as unimportant in contrast to a phenomenological truth available directly through studies of the body and bodily practice, or as simply one of many semiotic modalities through which social and ritual life happens. Given the breadth of traditions covered in this volume, how can we characterize the relationship between language and the body, or more broadly the material? Does language – as a particularly dense and structured semiotic system – provide a privileged vantage point from which to study religious life? What are the limits of using language as an analytical rubric for religion, myth, or ritual? Certain behaviors, such as music and gesture, co-evolved with language, and arguably share some of its properties, but not others (e.g., meaning, or semantic content). How does religion look when viewed from the perspective of such para-linguistic phenomena?

2.1 Ritual and language

We often find in ritual or liturgical languages an increase in the poetic function of language, meaning various forms of repetition including alliteration, rhyme, tautology (the repetition of the same phrase), chiasmus (the repetition of similar sounds in an inverted order), etc. The types of repetition deployed vary depending on the cultural tradition in question. Roman Jakobson focused attention on parallelism, or the repetition in succession of two different versions of the same idea. The tendency of the Hebrew Bible to express the identical sentiment using first one set of words, then another that is synonymous, was noted long ago by Bishop Robert Lowth (1787; cf. Kugel 1998). What is the function of such devices? One answer that Jakobson gave was that such poetic features produce a "set toward the message as such" (1960: 356): they alert the listener (or reader) that "Here now is a special form of communication; pay attention!" Although this might be the case with the parallelisms in the Hebrew Bible, another explanation is the desire to make the semantic content of the message absolutely clear by providing synonyms. For example, Psalm 119:105 states: "Your word is a lamp to my feet and a light for my path." The statement of the same idea twice using different but closely related images does some or all of the following: it removes confusion as to what the meaning is in cases where this would otherwise be doubtful or obscure; it contributes to preserving the language of the scripture from corruption, as one half of the parallelism tends to "stabilize" the other; and it reinforces the idea rhetorically, as can happen even when the exact same phrase is repeated more than once. Repetition is commonly used for this purpose in everyday discourse also. Communication theory has recognized that one of the ways of transmitting a message successfully against a background of distortion, is to repeat the message, particularly while varying it. Might this not also apply in the case of biblical parallelisms?

The Bible has other types of poetic features, including the use of chiasmi, some quite elaborate, as at Leviticus 24:13–23, where the basic talionic formula, "eye for an eye" (*ayin taḥat ayin*), which is itself a kind of chiasmus, appears at the relative center of a long chiasmus, the units of which are composed of individual sentences. There are also acrostics in the Bible. Each of the sections of Psalm 119 begins with a different Hebrew letter, in alphabetical order. The Wikipedia article on "Acrostic" claims that "Acrostics prove that the texts in question were originally composed in writing, rather than having existed in oral tradition before being put into writing." However, a Rabbi whom one of us consulted claimed precisely the opposite: namely, that this device enabled the Psalm to be remembered more easily, which is necessary only in an oral tradition.[1] Similarly, such formulas as "life for a life" (*nefesh taḥat nefesh*) may have begun, as Bernard Jackson suggested, as oral maxims in the context of tribunals called to adjudicate disputes (Jackson 2000: 272–274, 283). Complicating matters further, however, the chiasmus in Leviticus 24 is not really audible, but rather visible only upon backward-scanning of a text: it is what Jackson has called a "literary chiasmus" (Jackson 1998: 133). The same is true of some very elaborate chiasmi in the Tantric mantras. So the thesis that such devices have a mnemonic function in an oral culture or subculture, or oral stage of culture, does not explain all of the cases.

The close association of poetry with ritual, which emerges most clearly in magic spells, suggests that ritual is a mode of rhetorical or persuasive performance. "Ritual repetition," then, means more than simply the habitual recitation of conventional formulas according to a received tradition. It means also the repetition of formulas that are thought, by virtue of this repetition, to achieve their desired effect. The belief that poetry has a peculiar power to achieve such effects does not have to be the result of an inherited tradition. We have the case of Wicca, a tradition invented in the middle of the 20th century (although supposedly based on older models), which claims, in one of its key documents, the *Wiccan Rede*, which may date from only the 1960s–1970s: "For tread the Circle thrice about to keep unwelcome spirits out/To bind the spell well every time, let the spell be said in rhyme." Incidentally, this is an example of recursion or reflexivity: a rhyming formula that reflects on the importance of the poetic function.

Several functions of such devices have already been noted: concentrating attention on the symbol, or what Jakobson called "the set toward the message as such"; reinforcing ritual as a mode of rhetorical or persuasive performance; and supporting the mnemonic function, especially in the case of certain poetic formulas deployed in oral cultures. Stanley Tambiah (1985: 128) has noted the coordination of several of these functions in the context of a discussion of the "performative" aspects of ritual. Another theory that has received significant attention in the religious studies literature is "ritualization" (Bell 1997: 81). Influenced by the structuralist emphasis on how meaning is created out of sheer difference, this theory argues that there is no substantive thing called "ritual," but rather a strategy of ritualization that marks off certain behaviors as special. To some extent, this view coincides with Jakobson's argument that poetry highlights its status as a message or communicative event. However, unlike Jakobson, proponents of

1 Rabbi Cantor David Julian, Or Chadash Synagogue, Memphis, TN, personal communication to Robert A. Yelle.

ritualization are often uninterested in conducting a fine-grained analysis of the discursive patterns in ritual, due to their view that any device or distinction is capable of signaling a ritual event.

Whereas each of the examples just mentioned is of a language that in itself has meaning, and is therefore fully "language" as we commonly understand that term, there are also numerous cases in ritual of vocables that are, at least by conventional terms, unmeaning (see Tomlinson 2014: 22–47). The *ephesia grammata* ("askion kataskion," etc.) and other magic words of the *Greek Magical Papyri*, such as "*abracadabra/ablanathanalba*"; the "seed" (*bīja*) mantras of Hindu Tantra; and, one might add, the Latin of the Tridentine Mass for a worshipper who does not understand that language (and has not provided for the syllables a different semantic interpretation) all fall into this category. Although one could dispute, in particular cases, that such formulas lack semantic value, it nevertheless appears undeniable that one of the uses of language in some rituals, particularly of the magical variety, is to obscure, repress, or dispense entirely with the semantic dimension of language. This is part of what Bronislaw Malinowski called the "coefficient of weirdness" in magical language (1935, II: 218–223). Does this represent a desire for mystification? A drive to go beyond the limitations of ordinary language into some supernatural dimension? A mimicry of the idea that a sacred language should be obscure (as in the case of oracular pronouncements)? Each of these explanations has been advanced in different cases.

Rudolf Otto identified such "sacred primal sounds" (*numinose Urlaute*) as "hu!" or "ha(s)!" as the (onomatopoetic?) marks of a primal religious encounter:

> When the ecstatic dervishes of Islam complete their Zikr [chant], they break out in cries such as "Allah Akbar," that finally end in a long-drawn-out, groaning "Hū." This "Hū" is actually explained as the Arabic pronoun for the third person. [...] But whoever has listened to these outbreaks, can hardly believe in pronouns [as an explanation]. This "Hū" creates much more the impression of the sound of discharging one's self of the numinous feeling. [...] Another such primal sound of the feeling of the numinous is the holy syllable Om. It describes likewise no concept at all. It is like the particle "ās" nothing other than a sound. [...] It is actually nothing other than a kind of whispering. (Otto 1923: 11–15)[2]

While recovering some of the aesthetic dimensions of religious interjections and magic words, Otto's phenomenological approach tended to place such sounds – like the holy or "numinous" itself – beyond rational analysis. In some cases, however, a structuralist analysis would be more useful. This

2 Translation by Robert Yelle.

is certainly true in the case of the syllable "oṃ," or the *praṇava*, which represents, not a mere interjection, but a deliberate attempt to diagram the stages of the Hindu cosmogony (Yelle 2003: 26–28; see also Robert Yelle's chapter in this volume).

Some forms of ritual language that appear to lack meaning, such as glossolalia, are supposed to be spontaneous expressions of a divine language. Other forms are clearly a result of the "fixity" of language in much liturgy or ritual, and with this, the idea that only certain precise phonemic combinations may have the desired sanctity or efficacy. When this converges with a worshipper or spectator who does not comprehend the language in question, the result is a heightening of the pragmatic value of language through the reduction of its semantic value. An obvious case is the continued use of the Latin Mass which, after a decline post-Vatican II, is now experiencing a modest increase. Despite the victory of vernacularization represented by the Protestant Reformation, to this day certain formulations in the Bible are given in the original language. The Gospel of Mark, as noted above, contains examples of Jesus's use of Aramaic formulas as magical spells.[3] The fact that these formulas were originally conserved within the Greek text shows that the fixity of magical formulas is nothing new. A larger-scale example of the same phenomenon was the wholesale transmission in Shingon (esoteric) Buddhism of Sanskrit mantras to Japan, where these formulas were left untranslated and pronounced identically – so far as was possible in the phonemes of a very different language – in the evident belief, which was also held by the authors of the Sanskrit Tantras, that the efficacy of such formulas depended on this being done. The tendency of magic to rely on fixed formulas has long been noted. In the 18th century, Conyers Middleton quoted the 3rd century CE Christian theologian Origen's statement that "many of those, who charm or drive out Devils, call upon the God of *Abraham*, without even knowing who *Abraham* was.[...] [I]f a man [...] invoke or exorcise by the name of the God of *Abraham*, *Isaac*, and *Jacob*, the Devils will obey, and do what they are commanded; but if he translate those names, according to their meaning, into any other language, they will have no force at all" (Middleton 1749: 85–86; quoting Origen, *Contra Celsus*, chap. 22–24).

3 Mark 5:41 (RSV): "Taking her by the hand he said to her, 'Tal'itha cu'mi,' which means, 'Little girl, I say to you, arise.' And immediately the girl got up and walked..." With this formula, Jesus raised a girl from the dead. Mark 7:34 (RSV): "And taking him aside from the multitude privately, he put his fingers into his ears, and he spat and touched his tongue; and looking up to heaven, he sighed, and said to him, 'Eph'phatha,' that is, 'Be opened.'" With this formula, Jesus cured a deaf man.

2.2 Ideologies of religious language

Many traditions have employed special or even hieratic (sacred and secret) methods of communication: for example, Egyptian hieroglyphics, Vedic chant, and Latin and Arabic as liturgical languages in countries where such languages are not the vernacular. Such differences in use reflect a range of sociological factors, including the division between priests and laity and the conservatism of codified traditions. They also frequently coincide with a belief in the special sanctity or efficacy of such languages, as well as in their status as a reflection of reality. Sometimes, this coincides with the belief in the power of an original language (*Ursprache*), something like a pre-Babel version of Hebrew, as in the case of Adam's naming of the creatures in Genesis 2. The belief is widespread enough to have made its way into fairy tales such as the Brothers Grimm's *The Willow-Wren* (*Der Zaunkönig*): "In olden times every sound still had its meaning and significance. When the smith's hammer resounded, it cried, "Strike away, strike away."[...] At this time the birds also had their own language which everyone understood. Now it only sounds like chirping, screeching, and whistling, and sometimes like music without words" (Grimm and Grimm 1997: 705).

The idea of a "disenchantment" of language encoded in such nostalgic and fictional accounts is paralleled in a number of early modern narratives, except with a twist: in the latter, the transparency of language, its ability to represent and express reality, represents a precious achievement won by science through the vanquishing of false, unintelligible, purportedly magical speech. Such is the case with the previously mentioned Protestant critique of vain repetitions, and substitution of a mode of plain speech pioneered by the Gospel (Yelle 2013a: 22–29). In some cases, the disappearance of poetic formulas can be directly associated with such polemics. Although Thomas Cranmer's *Book of Common Prayer* of 1549 still retained the ancient formula "to have and to hold" in the marriage oath, which had its own poetry based on parallelism (e.g., "for richer for poorer"), it dispensed with older, more alliterative versions of the oath, such as that in which the wife promised to be "bonny and buxom in bed and at board" or each spouse promised to be true "for fairer for fouler." Cranmer stripped out almost all of these alliterations. This was not likely coincidental, as the preface to the new liturgy declared its intention to streamline and remove "vain repetitions" from the ritual (Yelle 2013b: 127–32).

One possible explanation for the decline of such poetic devices is that, with the advent of printed books, they are no longer needed as mnemonic devices. The contribution of poetry to memorability was noted long before modern scholars such as Eric Havelock (1963) and Jack Goody (1977) took up the issue. Thomas Hobbes, for example, noted that "in ancient time, before letters were in common use, the laws were many times put into verse; that the rude people, taking pleasure in singing or reciting them, might more easily retain them in memory" (Hobbes 1651: chap. 26, sec. 15). But the replacement of such poetic forms, first by writing and then by the printed book, represented more than the simple adoption of a more effective technique of recording and dissemination. This was also a change in mentality, closely associated with disenchantment. Famously, in the 17th century, Royal Society member and folklorist John Aubrey claimed that printing had frightened away the fairies that used to inhabit the Eglish countryside (Aubrey 1881 [1686–87]: 68). In the midst of the Deist period in England, Thomas Morgan identified printing as the instrument of the overthrow of priestcraft:

> [The] Law and History [of the Jews], were at first written in the sacred recondite Language, or *Egyptian* Hieroglossic, where *Moses* had learned it. This Language was a sort of Cypher, or Short-hand, peculiar to the Priests, or sacerdotal holy Order, and was never to be read, understood, or interpreted by any others. And thus this separate, holy, and happy People, were never to be trusted with their own Law, Religion, or History, in the vulgar tongue, but were to take all from the Priests, and believe and do as they directed them.[...] [H]ad it not been for the Increase of natural Knowledge, especially by the Invention of Printing, it must have been the Religion of all Nations still. For though the Heathen Philosophers published their Works in the vulgar Tongue, or own Country Language, yet these could be read and understood, comparatively, but by very few, the Priest and Magistrate both combining to keep the common People as much as possible in a State of Ignorance and Illiterature. (Morgan 1742: 166–67)

In this case, we observe the convergence of two different trends: the arrival of the printed book, and a Protestant bias against poetic, performative language. Whereas the former arguably rendered such types of poetry unnecessary as mnemonic devices, the latter dismissed them as "vain repetitions": at best nothing more than empty rhetoric, and at worst a form of magic or idolatry that impugned God's sovereignty (Yelle 2013a: 103–135; 2013b: 113–136). Both trends converged in Cranmer's *Book of Common Prayer*, which was part of a movement to distribute a uniform printed version of the liturgy. The privileging of semantic content over poetic form, and over ritual performance, that was shared to varying degrees by different early Protestant groups, deeply influenced their view of such practices as the repetition of Hindu mantras (*mantrajapa*), which British similarly condemned as "vain repetitions." The parallelisms in the Hebrew Bible also occasionally came in for condemnation on this charge (Yelle 2013a: 112nn44–45). With the passage of time, some sects within the Protestant umbrella, in the course of moving away from the austere modes of worship of their forebears, turned to more spontaneous and expressive modes of prayer, including glossolalia. It is interesting that, despite deviating from the Puritan path, these forms of practice generally did not attempt to revive the use of the fixed formula. Perhaps the rejection of that type of ritual was too deeply grounded in Protestant theology.

Linguistic iconoclasm partly represents a displacement of many of the poetic, performative, or otherwise pragmatic functions of language in favor of its semantic function. The form and medium of expression were circumscribed and subordinated to its meaning or content. A related dimension of the modernization of language in European traditions concerned the movement toward what we might, broadly speaking, call "transparency" in language. Although clearly associated with the emphases on both literalism and subjective "sincerity" in certain Protestant traditions (Keane 2002), the drive toward linguistic transparency was associated also with the scientific Enlightenment. Thinkers from Francis Bacon and Hobbes in the 17th century to Jeremy Bentham and Friedrich Max Müller in the 19th attempted to reform language so as to make it conform more closely with reality (Yelle 2013a: 33–70; 2013b: 92–112). The quixotic idea of a perfect language or, alternatively, mode of writing also emerged within Baconianism. The basic idea was that words should unambigously pick out something real, whether a fundamental concept, a philosophical idea, or preferably, a concrete object in the natural world. Many of the critiques of language voiced within this tradition were directed against theological or metaphysical categories, as with Hobbes's etymological reduction of the biblical words "angel" and "spirit" to their Greek and Latin roots: namely, "messenger" and "breath," respectively (Hobbes 1651: chap. 34). Together with the attack on poetic, performative language, such polemics against symbolical and metaphorical terminology established a stark divide between scientific and religious language, to the detriment of the latter, as further described in William Downes's chapter in this volume.

Although these developments occurred mainly within parts of Europe (and its colonies) in the past few centuries, other traditions at other times have been concerned with insuring the stability and proper functioning of language. The ancient Confucian idea of the "rectification of names" maintained that "things in actual fact should be made to accord with the implications attached to them by names, the prerequisites for correct living and even efficient government and that all classes of society should accord to what they ought to be" (Steinkraus 1980). This constitutes a recognition of the importance of language for social order. But criticisms of language may be directed instead to the overthrow of hierarchy. The Buddha's refusal to allow his teachings to be transmitted in verse – *chandas*, a term then associated specifically with Brahmanical texts – was perhaps an attempt both to distinguish the new tradition from Brahmanism, and to undermine the rhetorical authority associated with genres of Vedic recitation (Kelly 1996). There were also those skeptical of the power of mantras within ancient India, such as a certain Kautsa, who is noted as a minority opinion in some ancient texts. More recently, the 16th-century Bengali Vaiśṇavite saint Caitanya's effort to dramatically simplify the mantras used for worship, like similar efforts by the Japanese Buddhist Nichiren and the later Soka Gakkai movement based on his teachings, could be understood as an effort to expand the popular basis for worship. None of this necessarily depends on a commitment to iconoclasm. In Islamic traditions, despite the polemic against idolatry, even Muhammad has frequently been portrayed (especially in Persianate Islam), and there also developed a rich tradition of calligraphy and Qur'ānic recitation. Clearly there is no necessary connection between the critique of plastic images and that of poetry or ornament in general.

2.3 Media and materiality after the linguistic turn

Protestant Christianity, as is often said, moved the ritual center of the church from the altar to the pulpit – from the transformation of bodies and materials as the focus of worship to the transformation of thoughts and beliefs. The bogeyman of Protestantism, the Roman Catholic Church, was understood as the place of tradition, of institutionality, of a this-worldly approach to religion, of a fetishism of objects. God is not in a wafer, the Protestants said, nor in a statue. For these polemicists, objects were not the media through which presence with God is possible–they were simply human creations that actually kept one from focusing on the reality of God. In the iconoclastic violence that accompanied the Reformation, statues and other forms of representation were desecrated as so many fetishes. A classic pieta, with Mary cradling Jesus' dead body, was damaged by someone who lopped off Mary's head. God does not reside in the image, this critical gesture argues.

This is because language came to be seen by many Protestants as the only true route to God and his presence. The Bible – according to the Lutheran demand for *sola scriptura* – allowed words to have an access to the soul that images could not because, in this representational economy, words addressed that aspect of the self that was becoming more and more important to definitions of the human. That is, humans were being conceived as entities who have been given reason and, through that, a capacity for self-determination. And reason was exercised through talk, through the process of enumerating arguments. A hierarchy of human attributes placed thinking minds far above feeling bodies. Material representations then came to be seen simply as bodily. To emphasize the bodily would be to overturn the *logos* that brought reasoning minds closer to God, or even worse, to court idolatry by challenging the Puritan insistence on divine transcendence and omnipotence.

As missionaries and later anthropologists went around the world to influence and study local people, they searched for signs of religion then in the spaces of the mind, as a set of beliefs, arguments, or claims. They also imposed a Protestant model that privileged the text as the locus for articulation of belief, contributing both to the recording of oral traditions and to some of the most ambitious attempts to translate the Bible into diverse languages, such as those of the Baptist missionaries of Serampore, north of Calcutta. Various missionary alphabets shared with earlier philosophical proposals for a universal language the utopian or soteriological objective of a unified religion (Yelle 2013a: 71–102). The diversity of languages, and the ways in which they were fetishized by the unconverted, were hindrances to this objective. In places like colonial New Guinea, Lutheran missionaries consistently paired together the categories "heathen" and "Roman Catholic" because both, from this perspective, depended too much on ritual objects and not enough on linguistic statements expressing and valuing human reason. Clifford Geertz arguably reflected a more scholarly version of this religious rationality in his famous article, "Religion as a Cultural System" (1966). Religions for Geertz were semantically coherent perspectives on the world, models of and models for reality. Even if "expressed" (heathen-like) through ritual, any group's religious practices would necessarily point to an overarching cultural meaning. While apparently sympathetic to indigenous worldviews, this type of symbolic anthropology arguably perpetuated a Protestant privileging of the semantic over the pragmatic.

The end of the 20th century saw a major move away from structuralist and linguistic analyses of religious practice. One particularly strong argument against the central role of language in religious studies came from Talal Asad's critique of Geertz's universalist definition of religion, on the grounds that this definition depended upon precisely the genealogy and history outlined in the past few pages (Asad 1993). At the same time, Asad demanded that scholars pay attention to not just the minds but also the bodies of religious people. In his counter-history, he focused on how a connection to God was long assumed in medieval life to be found through pain or bodily discipline, not reasoned debate or assent to creedal claims. At roughly the same time, scholars such as Robert Orsi (1985) and Colleen McDannell (1995) started to look at all of the ways in which objects and material forms perdure as central media of divine presence. Rosaries do not just belong to a distant and superseded past. They embody spiritual biographies. Religious subjectivities are formed in relationship to particular objects. To take an example from Saba Mahmood's influential work on women's piety movements in contemporary Egypt: one learns to be a subject through practices of wearing a *hijab* or Islamic woman's head scarf (Mahmood 2005). Prayers and canonic literature have their place, Mahmood argues, but the Islamic woman's religious subjectivity is not necessarily formed as a product of textual exegesis. The everyday fact and constant reminder of God's presence made manifest in the head scarf produces a subjective relationship to God formed in the very way one moves. More importantly, this turn back to the body also launched a critique of the self-determining and autonomous individual of Western imagination. As Mahmood argues, one does not become a proper subject through the use of autonomous reason alone, but only through a relationship of submission to God. The individual is not the unit of salvation or the unit of emancipation. Rather the subject is constituted only through the recognition and valuation of its connection to another. This critique of the religious subject is part of a larger scholarly trend that seeks to recognize the important role of materiality in social life in a number of different domains. For example, Bruno Latour and other scholars in science studies argue that the realm of "the social" in fact needs to be populated with entities (actants) that collectively produce knowledge (Latour 1987, 2005). In this sense, the seat belt is as important to regimes of responsibility as is the driver or policy maker. To put things back into a religious idiom, the pious woman is a product of her interactions with things like head scarves as much as the Protestant iconoclast is the product of her desecration of a statue or painting.

In pushing scholars toward a recognition of the media of religious life, work in this vein opens up religious studies to much more than belief and its linguistic encoding in scripture or talk. Yet scholarship in this vein often suggests something else: language – long the central site of the autonomous, individual subject and the most transparent of all forms mediating the mind and God – may actually be not a site of freedom, but a site of oppression or occlusion. Language and writing was the tool of colonial oppression, and continues to be so in the ways that historical archives, for example, only seem to allow the literate and those properly disciplined in language to speak across time. Traces of the body are now seen as the site of the really real – of real oppression in the form of violence, but also of real presence in the form of lived experience (Scarry 1987; Biehl 2005). Many authors now find language to be a hindrance to the historical recovery of dominated peoples. Bodies, that is, seem now to be the site of transparent expression in a way that was once only reserved for language.

But the question then is: if we can give up on the Protestant/Enlightened model of religion, of subjectivity, and of autonomy, can't we also give up on Protestant models of language? Can't we conceive of language as something other than just the medium of rational debate? Can't language also be seen as embodied? We do, in fact, have to use our bodies to speak in most cases. Can we then afford to ignore the ways in which language remains a physical entity even in religious modes? Or how language can embody the actual words of God, or how speaking in front of a religious community can cause intense pain or shame? Language does not have to be seen from a purely Saussurean perspective that eradicated the importance of the material (*parole*) in favor of the symbolic (*langue*).

Moreover, the inescapability of language in scholarly discourse means inevitably that those systems of meaning or praxis that are mediated by the body and through concrete objects must, in order to become an object of reflection, be "translated" into words, most commonly in the form of the classic ethnography. This poses a profound methodological challenge for any effort to escape language entirely. Isadora Duncan's famous response, when asked the meaning of her dance, "If I could tell you, then I wouldn't have to dance it," reinforces the independence of physical movement from speech, but does so arguably at the cost of being able to render such movement intelligible, at least in words. What is lost and what is gained when we nevertheless reduce the material to the verbal? In the case of dance, systems such as Labanotation may record the movements more accurately than any verbal gloss could do, just as musical notation records the notes of a song. Kinesics (Birdwhistell 1971) represents an analogous attempt to examine the semiotics of movement or gesture independently of spoken language. Do such systems constitute new languages? Language-like phenomena? Or something else entirely?

Some authors therefore have turned towards scholarship that emphasizes the embodied and actual existence of language via semiotic theories stemming from the American philosopher Charles Sanders Peirce. Peirce placed particular stress on distinguishing different modalities of signs, and especially on how their material qualities are "bundled" together in ways that affect how they might interact with one another (Keane 2003, 2013; Manning and Meneley 2008). In many religious traditions, language is as much an object – a material substance that must be worn, consumed, or touched – as it is a symbolic entrée to a belief or worldview (Fader 2009). The point is not to see this as an either/or opposition, but to expand the universe of media through which religious subjects and communities are formed, and to examine the ways in which different media offer different possibilities for those processes.

Written texts are a special case of the intersection of languages with materiality. The very stability of scripture often entails an idea of sacred certainty, as with the canonical treatment of various texts as definite foundation-points for interpretive elaboration. Such sacred status sometimes insists on the oral dimensions or performance of these writings, or on the sacred character of transcribed sound as distinct from semantic meaning. Examples include the Holy Qur'ān, the Gathas, and the Vedas, as well as the particular status of the Tetragrammaton with respect to Torah scrolls as opposed to ordinary Tanakh texts. As Jonathan Z. Smith (1982: 36–52) argued, such sacred canonicity also appears in relation to texts, perhaps especially divinatory texts, even in the absence of ordinary writing, as with Yoruba *ifa* and Chinese *Zhouyi* (*Yijing*) commentarial or interpretive canons. Writing can thus serve to mediate between divine and human modes of meaning and understanding, grounding the religious structures of semiotic ideology.

Indeed, the origins of writing systems commonly receive mythological formulations that inform the meanings of those systems as well as what is written in them. In other words, the putative origins of a writing system often express or reinforce a semiotic ideology. Egyptian hieroglyphics were held to have been instituted by the gods, which had an undeniable impact on their perceived significance. The religious ideology of such writing also appears to have undergone considerable change over its long history. For example, not a single Greek witness correctly describes the linguistic structure of hieroglyphics, which are usually phonograms but may also be read as logograms or semagrams (determinatives); instead, every Greek description understands the glyphs to be ideographic or pictographic, although there can be little doubt that such writers as Herodotus had some direct contact with literate priests. Since the Greek *hieroglyphikos* (ἱερογλυφικός) apparently translates the Egyptian *mdw·w-nṯr* (*medu-netjer*, "god's words"), it may well be that 5th-century priests, faced with sophisticated conquering barbarians, explicated this sacred system in terms of what was most important about them: their origin from the gods and their unique ability to express and encode divine meaning at many levels. That the glyphs were actually used, linguistically speaking, in a quite different manner may have seemed a relatively trivial or tangential issue. Thus the religious ideology of hieroglyphics during the last thousand years of their usage – the last readable inscription dates from 394 CE – appears to have enshrined writing and language within a divine context that largely disregarded semantic meaning (see Lehrich 2007: esp. 121–122).

Texts point us in one direction, toward the materiality of language. Music – at least when in the form of sound, of an evanescent performance – points us in another, toward disembodiment. Both forms, however, can highlight the sensory and aesthetic dimensions of language over its semantic dimensions. Indeed, when words are absent, music constitutes a special case of man-made sound that is artistic and communicative, yet not meaningful in the same way that language is. Still the analogy between music and language points us toward the limits of what the latter category might mean, as a specifically human phenomenon. Beginning with E. T. A. Hoffmann and continuing with Eduard Hanslick, various individuals have claimed that music, or at least Western art music, was uniquely capable of transcending the limits of ordinary discourse and of serving as an ideal medium of expression. Rudolf Otto found in music the closest analogy to numinous experience (Lehrich 2014a: 22–43). Laurence Wuidar's chapter in this volume traces older variants of this idea in Christian tradition. In many societies, music has been identified as a more powerful means of communication than ordinary language. Plato's violent antipathy to Orpheus, for example, derived from the dangerous transparency that music supposedly had to the gods, such that human musicians could deploy divine power unchecked by rational language and thought (Lehrich

2014b: 136–47). It appears that Mexica (Aztec) culture ascribed a similar power to song: the gods expressed themselves particularly directly in song, and by the same token prayers were most efficacious when communicated musically (see Isabel Laack's chapter in this volume). Confucius consistently related music (*yue*) to ritual (*li*), yet it appears that while both were means of mediation and communication between heaven and humanity, and both required careful, attentive rectification, they were nevertheless not equivalent. Unfortunately, in the absence of the lost *Classic of Music* (*Yuejing*), we may never entirely understand how this distinction operated. Intriguingly, few if any other cultures have a traditional categorical distinction directly comparable to the Western one between music and other forms of sound – a distinction that itself developed in Europe only over the course of the 16th and 17th centuries.

3 Chapter summaries

The volume consists of seventeen chapters and is divided into three parts, each of which focuses on one of the three general themes highlighted above. Part I addresses ritual and language; Part II, ideologies of religious language; and Part III, media and materiality after the linguistic turn. These boundaries are, however, somewhat artificial, as a number of chapters defy any neat classification and also raise additional themes, some of which have been discussed earlier in this Introduction.

The chapters in Part I all engage substantially with the connection between ritual and language. Naphtali Meshel develops the analogy between the rules of grammar that structure natural languages, and the implicit rules governing sacrificial ritual operations. Building from earlier elaborations of the parallels between language and ritual, Meshel tests the limits of this parallel by examining certain rules and constraints – conscious and unconscious – for composing successful sacrifices in biblical and early Jewish ritual texts. Robert Yelle identifies three forms of dialogicality in Hindu mantras: intertextuality, iconicity, and joint speech. Whereas the Tantric *haṃsa* mantra (haṃsaḥ so'ham) reworks older, Vedic formulas to express, in poetic and chiastic form, the identity of the self with God, other mantric practices display distinctive features associated with the practice of chanting in groups. Paul Copp shows how the Buddhist texts discovered at Dunhuang reveal patterns of disjoining and rejoining texts, especially framing invocations and blessings, to create new liturgies. These patterns tell us much regarding not only the ways in which even canonical texts were reworked creatively, but also how they were deployed in ritual performance. Leslie Arnovick looks at the migration of liturgical texts such as the Lord's Prayer and the Creed into medieval Anglo-Saxon charms. The reuse of these formulas is accompanied by "de-institutionalization" or the loss of cultic context and "subjectification" or an intensification of the speaker's agentive role. Aurélie Névot reveals the practices of male and female shamans (*bimos* and *chemas*) in the Yi linguistic minority in China, focusing particular attention on the special writing system of the *bimos*. The characters of their ritual manuals are no ordinary language, but rather an individual code that metaphorically incorporates the blood and breath of a *bimo*, who decodes and gives voice to this strange writing through his chant.

Part II describes various ideologies of religious language. Naomi Janowitz contrasts the well-known theory of speech acts developed by J. L. Austin and John Searle, which focuses on performative utterances and action verbs, with Louis Althusser's theory of divine names, which focuses instead on the power of these proper nouns, as revealed also in name taboos. Examples from Jewish antiquity illustrate how the name of God was invoked, also in its literal absence, as a source of ritual power. Mustafa Shah surveys debates within Islamic tradition over the nature of the word of God as manifested in the Holy Qur'ān. The incomparability of this revealed text led many to claim that it was uncreated and eternal, as well as inimitable. Paolo Visigalli moves from indigenous Indian views of Sanskrit as a perfect language, based partly on the transparency of its morphology, to Friedrich Schlegel's 19th-century deployment of such ideas in pursuit of an Oriental Renaissance that might be accomplished through the recovery of this ancient language. Laurence Wuidar traces the idea in early and medieval Christian theology that music is a divine language capable of expressing even the ineffable. Music was associated with mystical experience, understood as a particular mode of attunement of body and soul to harmonize with God. William Downes recounts the ideal of a "plain style" of speech that arose in 17th-century England and that provided a foundation for modern ideologies. Among the factors in this rise were the Protestant critique of Catholic liturgical language, as well as scientific polemics against poetic, aesthetic, and metaphorical language, which polemics created and policed the border between rationality and irrationality. Jenny Ponzo addresses the contemporary Christian phenomenon of glossolalia, or speaking in tongues, which is based on New Testament accounts of the miraculous gifts received from the Holy Spirit. Practiced by Pentecostals while shunned by conservative Evangelicals, glossolalia marks not only a theological difference concerning whether such miracles have ceased, but also a difference in styles of interpreting the Bible. Kocku von Stuckrad extends the linguistic turn in the study of religion to the newer method of discourse analysis, which eschews the arguably fruitless search for essences in favor of critical reflection on the processes by which our ostensibly scientific categories are formed and disseminated. He makes a forceful case for the wider application of discourse analysis as a solution for our present impasse over how (or indeed whether) to define such concepts as religion, ritual, etc.

Part III looks at religious language in relation to mediation through the material domain. Seth Sanders challenges the scholarly privileging of words over things by returning to the archaeological evidence from the Iron Age Levant. Inscribed stone funerary monuments complemented and interacted with modes of verbal communication with dead ancestors, by concretizing and thereby establishing the presence of these spirits. Isabel Laack takes up the challenge of reinterpreting the Aztecs' enigmatic references to "flower and song," as a kind of self-designation of the power of certain Nahuatl poems. She analyzes the implicit semiotic ideology that the imagery and the sounds of these songs are capable of indexing, directly rendering, and making immanent ultimate reality; and she argues that the visuality of Aztec pictorial writing might have been understood in an analogous way. Patrick Eisenlohr examines the interaction of the medium of cassette tapes with the recitation of *na't* devotional poetry by Muslims in Mauritius. Recorded performances provide an entextualization and standard of recitation that codifies authenticity and, paradoxically, elides the gap between medium and message. Anderson Blanton describes a similar paradox in the American evangelist Oral Roberts's use of the radio as a "point of contact" that could perfectly mediate the healing power of prayer and erase the gap of distance between preacher and congregant/listener. The movement from the revival tent to mass media in this way could extend rather than end the charismatic practice of healing touch. Jon Bialecki grapples with the profound methodological challenge of how to measure affect – which is normally considered a subjective state – objectively in the ethnographic context. Building from Spinoza's distinction between *affectio* and *affectus*, roughly and respectively a force itself and the reaction to that force, he then demonstrates how this distinction helps us to understand the sequence of behaviors in a California Pentecostal congregation.

Taken collectively, these chapters provide a representative sample of some of the sophisticated research that is being done today on the history, anthropology, and philosophy of religious language. Without exhausting the range of important issues raised by the intersection of the categories of language and religion, they open up new resources for thinking productively with and through those categories.

References

Asad, Talal. 1993. The construction of religion as an anthropological category. In *Genealogies of religion: Discipline and reasons of power in Christianity and Islam*, 27–54. Baltimore: Johns Hopkins University Press.

Aubrey, John. 1881 [1686–87]. *Remaines of Gentilisme and Judaisme*. London: Folk-lore Society.

Bauman, Richard. 1983. *Let your words be few: Symbolism of speaking and silence among seventeenth-century Quakers*. Cambridge: Cambridge University Press.

Bell, Catherine. 1997. *Ritual: Perspectives and dimensions*. New York: Oxford University Press.

Biehl, João. 2005. *Vita: Life in a zone of social abandonment*. Berkeley, CA: University of California Press.

Birdwhistell, Ray L. 1971. *Kinesics and context: Essays on body motion communication*. Philadelphia: University of Pennsylvania Press.

Derrida, Jacques. 1976. *Of grammatology*. Translated by Gayatri Chakravorty Spivak. Baltimore: Johns Hopkins University Press.

Fader, Ayala. 2009. *Mitzvah girls: Bringing up the next generation of Hasidic girls in Brooklyn*. Princeton: Princeton University Press.

Geertz, Clifford. 1966. Religion as a cultural system. In Michael Banton (ed.), *Anthropological approaches to the study of religion*, 1–46. London: Tavistock.

Goody, Jack. 1977. *The domestication of the savage mind*. Cambridge: Cambridge University Press.

Grimm, Jacob & Wilhelm Grimm. 1997. *The complete fairy tales*. Ware, Hertfordshire: Wordsworth.

Havelock, Eric. 1963. *Preface to Plato*. Cambridge, MA: Harvard University Press.

Hobbes, Thomas. 1651. *Leviathan*. London.

Jackson, Bernard. 1998. An eye for an I?: The semiotics of lex talionis in the Bible. In William Pencak & J. Ralph Lindgren (eds.), *New approaches to semiotics and the human sciences: Essays in honor of Roberta Kevelson*, 127–149. New York: Peter Lang.

Jackson, Bernard. 2000. *Studies in the semiotics of biblical law*. Sheffield, UK: Sheffield Academic Press.

Jakobson, Roman. 1960. Closing statement: Linguistics and poetics. In Thomas Sebeok (ed.), *Style in language*, 350–377. Cambridge, MA: MIT Press.

Jameson, Fredric. 1972. *The prison-house of language*. Princeton: Princeton University Press.

Keane, Webb. 2002. Sincerity, "modernity," and the Protestants. *Current Anthropology* 17. 65–92.

Keane, Webb. 2003. Semiotics and the social analysis of material things. *Language & Communication* 23(3). 409–425.

Keane, Webb. 2007. *Christian moderns: Freedom and fetish in the mission encounter*. Berkeley, CA: University of California Press.

Keane, Webb. 2013. On spirit writing: materialities of language and the religious work of transduction. *Journal of the Royal Anthropological Institute* 19(1). 1–17.

Kelly, John. 1996. What was Sanskrit for? Metadiscursive strategies in ancient India. In Jan E. M. Houben (ed.), *Ideology and status of Sanskrit: Contributions to the history of the Sanskrit language*, 87–107. Leiden: Brill.

Kugel, James. 1998. *The idea of biblical poetry*. Baltimore & London: Johns Hopkins University Press.

Latour, Bruno. 1987. *Science in action: How to follow scientists and engineers through society*. Cambridge, MA: Harvard University Press.

Latour, Bruno. 2005. *Reassembling the social: An introduction to Actor-Network-Theory*. Oxford: Oxford University Press.
Lehrich, Christopher I. 2007. *The occult mind: Magic in theory and practice*. Ithaca: Cornell University Press.
Lehrich, Christopher I. 2014a. The unanswered question: Music and theory of religion. *Method & Theory in the Study of Religion* 26(1). 22–43.
Lehrich, Christopher I. 2014b. Orphic revenge: The limits of language for a semiotics of religion. *Religion* 44. 136–147.
Lévi-Strauss, Claude. 1963. *Structural anthropology*. Translated by Claire Jacobson & Brooke Grundfest Schoepf. New York: Basic Books.
Lowth, Robert. 1787. *On the sacred poetry of the Hebrews*. London.
Mahmood, Saba. 2005. *The politics of piety: The Islamic revival and the feminist subject*. Princeton: Princeton University Press.
Malinowski, Bronislaw. 1935. *Coral gardens and their magic: A study of the methods of tilling the soil and of agricultural rites in the Trobriand Islands*, 2 vols. New York: American Book Company.
Manning, Paul & Anne Meneley. 2008. Material objects in cosmological worlds: an introduction. *Ethnos* 73(3). 285–302.
Mazzarella, William. 2009. Affect: What is it good for? In Saurabh Dube (ed.), *Enchantments of modernity: Empire, nation, globalization*, 291–309. New Delhi: Routledge.
McDannell, Colleen. 1995. *Material Christianity: Religion and popular culture in America*. New Haven: Yale University Press.
Middleton, Conyers. 1749. *Free inquiry into the miraculous powers*. London.
Morgan, Thomas. 1742. *A brief examination of the Rev. Mr. Warburton's Divine legation of Moses*. London.
Nietzsche, Friedrich. 1968. On the genealogy of morality. In Walter Kaufmann (trans.), *Basic writings of Nietzsche*, 437–599. New York: Modern Library.
Nietzsche, Friedrich. 1989. On truth and lying in an extra-moral sense. In Sander Gilman, Carole Blair & David Parent (eds.), *Friedrich Nietzsche on rhetoric and language*, 246–257. New York: Oxford University Press.
Orsi, Robert. 1985. *The Madonna of 115th street: Faith and community in Italian Harlem, 1880–1950*. New Haven: Yale University Press.
Otto, Rudolf. 1923. *Aufsätze das Numinose betreffend*. Stuttgart: Friedrich Andreas Perthes.
Scarry, Elaine. 1987. *The body in pain: The making and unmaking of the world*. New York: Oxford University Press.
Silverstein, Michael. 2004. "Cultural" concepts and the language-culture nexus. *Current Anthropology* 45(5). 621–652.
Smith, Jonathan Z. 1982. Sacred persistence: Toward a redescription of canon. In *Imagining religion: From Babylon to Jonestown*, 36–52. Chicago: University of Chicago Press.
Stasch, Rupert. 2011. Ritual and oratory revisited: the semiotics of effective action. *Annual Review of Anthropology* 40 (2011). 159–174.
Steinkraus, Warren. 1980. Socrates, Confucius, and the rectification of names. *Philosophy East and West* 30. 261–264.
Tambiah, Stanley. 1985. A performative approach to ritual. In *Culture, thought, and social action: An anthropological perspective*, 123–166. Cambridge, MA: Harvard University Press.

Tomlinson, Matt. 2014. *Ritual textuality: Pattern and motion in performance*. Oxford: Oxford University Press.
Wegman, Robert. 2005. *The crisis of music in early modern Europe, 1470–1530*. New York: Routledge.
Yelle, Robert. 2003. *Explaining mantras: Ritual, rhetoric, and the dream of a natural language in Hindu Tantra*. New York & London: Routledge.
Yelle, Robert. 2013a. *The language of disenchantment: Protestant literalism and colonial discourse in British India*. New York: Oxford University Press.
Yelle, Robert. 2013b. *Semiotics of religion: Signs of the sacred in history*. London: Bloomsbury.
Yelle, Robert. 2016. The Peircean icon and the study of religion: A brief overview. *Material Religion* 12. 241–243.

Part I: **Ritual and language**

Naphtali S. Meshel

To be taken with a grain of salt: Between a "grammar" and a GRAMMUR of a sacrificial ritual system

1 Introduction

The goal of this paper is to offer a brief overview of two rules – selected from a set of several hundred such rules – operative in the "grammar" of a ritual system termed Σ (Sigma), which is described in full in Meshel (2014) and defined briefly below. I will argue that if "grammars" of ritual systems can be composed at all, this can be achieved only by taking a step away from the linguistic analogy and by identifying the nonlinguistic operative categories inherent in the ritual systems under investigation. Once several distinct operative categories are identified, the transformational rules between these operative categories are discovered, and the specific rules comprising each operative category within a given ritual system are formulated, the resultant theory may qualify as a "grammar," perhaps more accurately termed a GRAMMUR: Generative, Rigorously Applied Mathematically Modelled Unconscious Rules. While this paper focuses on two rules from one operative category, it is intended to suggest the potential explanatory power of a full-fledged "grammar" of a ritual system.

In the past half century, the scholarly investigation of ritual has been pursued within a large variety of theoretical frameworks, including linguistics, information theory, systems theory, ethology, and cognition.[1] Of these, linguistics has been the single most important framework for the study of ritual and several of the others employed in this undertaking are modelled upon, or at least inspired by, linguistics.

Within the theoretical framework of linguistics, there has been a tendency among some anthropologists and scholars in comparative religion to liken the structures of ritual systems to the grammars of natural languages. This has resulted in the widespread use of grammatical terminology to describe the struc-

1 See Staal (1979, 1980, 1989), Michaels et al. (2010) (linguistics); Lévi-Strauss (1963) (information theory); Gane (2004, 2005) (systems theory); Burkert (1987) (ethology); and Lawson (1976) and Lawson and McCauley (1990) (cognition). For a sense of the proliferation of such approaches in the past few decades, see Kreinath (2006) and Michaels (2016).

Naphtali S. Meshel, The Hebrew University of Jerusalem

https://doi.org/10.1515/9781614514329-002

tures of ritual systems, with the most radical theory even asserting the existence of an evolutionary relationship between ritual and language[2]; it has also resulted in a conviction that rituals, like languages, have grammars.[3] The literature on this theoretical issue singles out sacrificial ritual as a special case, perhaps because some scholars believe that sacrifice holds a unique place among rituals, as if it were *the* ritual par excellence, to which all other rituals may ultimately be reduced.[4]

The idea that the structures of languages and sacrificial rituals are homologous has its roots in antiquity. As Staal (1989: 40–41) notes, the 2nd century BCE Sanskrit grammarian Patañjali first suggested this homology in the introduction to his *Mahābhāṣya*, a commentary on the classical Sanskrit grammar of *Pāṇini*. To put it somewhat simplistically, Patañjali assumes – though he does not explicitly claim – that sacrificial ritual systems have grammars and aims to convince his readers that languages should have grammars as well. (Incidentally, structuralists often make the reverse claim, using language as a template for ritual rather than the other way around.) In Patañjali's thinking, as Staal understands it – perhaps over-generously, as some recent scholars have argued – the formal homology between language and sacrificial ritual pertains to a specific tension inherent in both systems, a tension between unlimited theoretical possibilities and limited realizable options.[5]

---

2 Staal (1989: 268).

3 See for example Eichinger Ferro-Luzzi (1977), Lawson and McCauley (1990), Payne (1999), Gane (2004), the various contributions to Michaels et al. (2010), and Michaels (2016) for a sampling of a large body of literature from diverse cultural contexts.

4 See Milbank (1995) and the bibliography cited there, to which one might add Evans-Pritchard (1965: 53), Sperber (1975: 110–111), J. Z. Smith (1987: 196–197), and Burkert (1987: 212). For a criticism of the predominance of animal sacrifice (over vegetable sacrifice) in modern scholarship, see McClymond (2008).

5 This reading and the conclusions I draw from it (Meshel 2014: 1–3) have been criticized by Michaels (2016: 76–77), and also by Anand Mishra and Paolo Visigalli (personal communication). Michaels demonstrates that Patañjali, who speaks of thousand-year-long sacrifices, is not concerned with protracted sacrificial rituals that are not performed because they are pragmatically unlikely or unfeasible; but only with protracted sacrificial rituals that are *no longer* performed – thus removing the edge from Staal's reading. If we reject Staal's reading, then we should avoid projecting our views onto Patañjali, and either consider another worthy – such as the medieval Jewish scholar Moses Maimonides, discussed below, or perhaps Patañjali's predecessor Kātyāyana (read very generously by Visigalli) – as *prōtos ergatēs* in the field of "ritual grammar." Alternatively, we must admit that the intuition is a modern one, only faintly adumbrated in ancient and in medieval literature (see Meshel 2014: 7–18). While certainly deferring to Michaels, Mishra and Visigalli on this matter, I would like to offer one argument in defense of Staal's reading of Patañjali: It is quite possible that Patañjali sincerely believed that in the mythic

While Staal's work has inspired a large body of literature on "ritual grammar," current discussion in the field of comparative religion about the theoretical underpinnings and possible implications of the grammar of ritual greatly outweighs descriptive accounts of the ritual systems themselves, although such accounts ought to serve as the foundation for the broader theoretical discussions. This situation has led Michaels to state that previous work on the grammar of ritual has generally been "more programmatic than proto-grammatical."[6] In fact, despite the relative abundance of detailed discussions of grammatical features within particular rituals, a systematic outlay of even a single ritual system's grammar has been entirely lacking in the literature, until very recently.[7] It is striking that there has even been some discussion of a "universal grammar" of sacrificial ritual – rules that may be applicable to all sacrificial systems in diverse human societies – even before one complete grammar of a specific sacrificial system exists.

An example will help illustrate what would constitute a "grammar" of a ritual system and what such a grammar could contribute to our understanding of ritual systems. In the 12th century, the Jewish scholar Moses Maimonides formulated several general rules about the sacrificial laws in biblical and rabbinic traditions. One cluster of these abstractions, consisting of Maimonides' own generalizations as well as generalizations culled from earlier rabbinic literature, appears towards the end of his introduction to tractate Zebaḥim, in his Commentary on the Mishna (Kafaḥ 1963: 19):

---

past individuals could live long enough to perform thousand-year-long sacrificial rituals, but in the non-mythic world of Patañjali's audience, these rituals are necessarily imagined and unperformed; therefore Patañjali himself recognized that each protracted ritual ought to be imparted not by means of direct exposure to the entire ritual but by means of a combination of a limited set of building blocks and a limited set of rules. I admit, however, that such a combination would be "generative" only by very generous usage of the term.

6 See Michaels (2007: 241). Michaels (2016: 78n9) claims that to date, only two attempts have been made to compose a "grammar" of a ritual system – one on Newar life-cycle rituals (Michaels 2012) and one on ancient Israelite and early Jewish sacrificial rituals (Meshel 2014).

7 This is not to diminish in any way from the importance of a large body of literature relevant to our discussion – for example, Sebeok (1966); Bourdieu (1977); Staal (1979) etc.; Lawson and McCauley (1990); Humphrey and Laidlaw (1994); Gane (2005); Payne (1999); Yelle (2003). For a particularly insightful analysis of palindromes in ritual, see Yelle (2013: chap. 2, "The Poetics of Ritual Performance", esp. 46–50). Whether a particular theory qualifies as a "grammar" of a non-linguistic system depends, of course, on how one defines "grammar" in this context. As shall become clear in due course, the restrictive definition offered here requires that an analysis be comprehensive, sensitive to different operative categories and to transformational laws between them, that it account for diachronic change, and be amenable to mathematical modelling. The number of operative categories and specific rules will, naturally, vary from one "grammar" to another.

> And if you consider all of the abovementioned sacrifices, you will find that there is not a single female among all of the public offerings. [...] Similarly you will find that every lay-person's purification offering is a female animal. [...] Similarly it will become evident to you that there is not among all of the public offerings an ovine [i.e., sheep] purification offering, nor a caprine [i.e., goat] wholeburnt offering...

Note that several of the generalizations in Maimonides' introduction are found nowhere in the ancient sources he had at his disposal; they are Maimonides' own abstractions, designed to accord with several examples of sacrifices within the biblical text (as interpreted by the early rabbinic authorities) and with a number of sacrificial combinations newly introduced in rabbinic traditions but not found in the biblical text. Yet of the many dozens of sacrificial combinations found in literature from the turn of the era, including Qumranic literature, Josephus, Philo, and a large body of apocryphal and pseudepigraphic literature[8] – combinations that differ substantially from the instructions of the Pentateuchal law – not a single one substantially violates these rules formulated by a 12th-century Spanish-North African rabbi. Most of these texts were unavailable to Maimonides, so we can only suppose that he has hit upon certain rigorous, underlying rules, the same rules which the authors of the late Second Temple period had internalized as a result of their exposure to the biblical text, and which guided them when generating their own new sacrificial combinations.

Consider a common linguistic analog: young children hear grammatical utterances from their parents. The children are exposed to numerous – but finitely many – grammatical utterances. The fact that these children regularly acquire fluency in a language on the basis of that finite number of utterances, and in particular that they can then produce grammatical but as-yet-unheard utterances, demonstrates that they have internalized grammatical rules from a limited input. A linguist can compose a grammar for that language on the basis of those utterances of one speaker, a grammar that would then prove valid for the utterances of other speakers as well even though the linguist had not heard them.

So too, Jewish authors writing in antiquity derived their understanding of sacrifice from (roughly) the same Pentateuchal text, and some of them presumably also witnessed a shared set of Temple practices. These authors describe rituals that do not appear in the sources they would have encountered but that nevertheless accord with rules they had internalized from their exposure to a finite set of rituals. Writing in the 12th century, Maimonides (like the aforementioned

8 For a partial list, see below at 52. For the Temple Scroll, see Yadin (1983). For the Aramaic Levi Document (ALD), see Greenfield et al. (2004). For Josephus, see primarily Flavius Josephus, Judean Antiquities 1–4, in Feldman (2000). For Philo, see for example Philo (1937).

linguist) postulated generalizations in order to characterize the Pentateuchal and rabbinic literature, but his rules also prove valid for other rituals to which he could not have been exposed. In short, Maimonides was describing a "grammar" of rituals that earlier practitioners and authors had internalized.

Whereas Maimonides only discusses a few internalized grammatical rules, a full "grammar" of ritual should map out a system of these rules in a comprehensive fashion. Such a grammar would delineate the generalized principles that govern the formation of ritual sequences. For an analysis to constitute a "grammar" – as defined here – it would not be sufficient for it to offer a full and systematic listing of an inventory of building blocks for the "praxemic" description of a robust ritual system[9]; and to identify general rules that determine which combinations of building blocks are licit and which are not – though such a description is in and of itself no small task by any standard. It would also have to be: (1) generative, in the sense that a small set of rules inferred from a large set of data can be shown to govern the formation of new sequences; (2) rigorously applied, in the sense that exceptions to the rules might be allowed (as in a grammar of a language) – but fewer exceptions would produce a simpler and more successful grammar; (3) amenable to mathematical modelling – this is not a requirement of the grammar, but rather an indication of its explanatory power: a successful grammar ought to be describable concisely and parsimoniously in abstract terms, and should be representable in simple graphic or formulaic terms; (4) unconsciously internalized – as in a language, it should be demonstrated that some of the rules are not explicit in the ritual manuals (and competent practitioners need not be consciously aware of them); lastly, (5) rules must to be grouped into discrete operative categories in such a way that the theory of the ritual system is sensitive to differential levels of abstraction, clearly describing specific transformational rules between these levels. The existence of different operative categories is analogous to linguistics, which includes operative categories such as phonetics, phonology, morphology, syntax and semantics. Instead of imposing these same categories on ritual systems, however, one might expect to find a different set of operative categories unique to ritual systems, and which need to be discovered inductively, "from the ground upwards", by careful examination of each ritual system.

9 Sequences of ritual action are composed of smaller building blocks (let us call these building blocks "praxemes," and their analysis – "praxemics"; see discussion below) that combine in clearly defined, perhaps even predictable, structures. This systematic listing, of course, should not be merely a list of grammatical combinations, which the ancient legal texts themselves supply, and which represent only a subset of all grammatical combinations.

Finally, an empirical "experiment" should be devised to examine the "predictive" value of the "grammar" – as in the diachronic testing of Maimonides' generalizations described above, wherein they are tested against texts which he could not have known – and its explanatory power ought to be explored. In the case of Σ, described below, a successful grammar would assist in the solution of philological problems, and would aid in the understanding of passages that may have otherwise been misconstrued.

The Grammar of Sacrifice, and most specifically in "A Grammar of Σ," which is included in it (Meshel 2014; Appendix), aims to provide such an analysis – in other words, to formulate one grammar for one particular ritual system. The ritual system under investigation is the ancient Israelite sacrificial system (referred to as Σ) as represented in a set of detailed sacrificial texts found in the books of Exodus, Leviticus, and Numbers, and which, as we shall see, is applicable to a host of post-biblical texts as well – pseudepigraphic, Qumranic and Jewish Hellenistic – such as Jubilees, the Temple Scroll, the Aramaic Levi Document, Josephus, and Philo, to name but a few, and a very large body of early and medieval rabbinic literature. These texts depict a system of ritual activity that retains a highly unchangeable "grammar," in the sense of a rich set of unstated, simple, rigorous underlying sacrificial rules. The degree to which these rules apply to actual ritual practice (that is, actual Israelite and Jewish practice, outside the texts that describe them) is hotly debated, and will not be discussed in detail here.[10] The degree to which Σ's operative categories apply to other, non-Israelite ritual systems depends on empirical findings that are only beginning to surface; as a preliminary note it should suffice to generalize that some of Σ's operative categories have strong explanatory power for non-Israelite (ancient Near Eastern and perhaps South Asian) sacrificial systems, whereas others appear to be entirely irrelevant outside Σ (see Appendix).

10 Of the four most extensive ancient Israelite and early Jewish sources on ritual sacrifice – Pentateuchal law, Ezekiel 40–48, the Temple Scroll, and the early rabbinic literature – three are at least partially imaginary in the sense that they were composed either several generations after the destruction of the Temple (the rabbinic sources in their present form) or because they are self-professedly utopian (Ezekiel, the Temple Scroll). For example, Ezekiel and the Temple Scroll from Qumran both depict a sacrificial system that is to take place in an imagined architectural structure. Since the details of the sacrificial procedures in the Temple Scroll and in Ezekiel are in many cases dependent on the precise structure of the building, and since the "more perfect" Temple described in detail in these texts is self-professedly imaginary, it follows that the sacrificial system itself is also at least partially utopian, rather than merely descriptive of any actual historical practice. With regard to the Pentateuchal texts, matters are more contested; see Meshel (2014: 24–27).

The Grammar of Sacrifice identifies several operative categories, which it names using the neologisms *zoemics, jugation, hierarchics,* and *praxemics*, as well as a fifth operative category that concerns the meaning of the sacrifice. Zoemics concerns the classification of animals according to certain biological traits such as species, gender, and age. Jugation, which will be further discussed below, concerns the manner in which various sacrificial materials are joined to create large sacrificial complexes. Hierarchics examines the relation between different and sometimes overlapping terms used to designate sacrificial types, terms such as "wholeburnt offering," "purification offering," and "reparation offering." Praxemics concerns discrete ritual acts and the ways in which these acts can and cannot be combined.

The present essay treats an atypical example from the operative category of jugation. *The Grammar of Sacrifice* primarily investigates "real" instantiations of ritual in Σ, that is, ritual sequences that are, at the very least, laid out in a straightforward manner in the texts describing them. This paper, however, considers an example of "imaginary" ritual practice, i.e., one that is not textually explicit but is nevertheless permitted in the logic of the system. Due to the nature of our texts, we will be doubly removed from the world of sacrifice, both because some texts that serve as the basis of the grammar postdate the destruction of the Temple and the resulting end of Jewish sacrifice and sometimes describe a non-existent, utopian world of Jewish sacrificial practice; and because all of the texts only allow for, but do not envision, one of the following examples of sacrificial patterns.

Although certainly not the primary objective of the creation of a comprehensive grammar, exploring these more recondite examples bears upon the scope of the system: just as the construction of a syntactically precise yet semantically unintelligible sentence is an important aid in understanding the English language, the identification of sacrificial patterns is essential for an understanding of Σ.

2 Examples

2.1 Serial cereal offerings

We will focus on an example pertaining to the potential outcomes of laws depicting a system of "standalone" grain (or "cereal") offerings, that is, grain that is not subordinate to a meat offering.

In the sacrificial system reflected in the Pentateuch, an animal is rarely to be offered in isolation. An animal offering often entails accompanying non-animal materials, such as grain offerings and libations of wine. Cereal offerings, too, often entail other non-animal materials, such as oil and salt. We shall refer to such supplementary offerings as "subordinate jugates" (from Latin *jugare*, 'to join'), and the subject of inquiry, therefore, will be termed "jugation." Note that jugation is only one of several operative categories in Σ: if one were to resort to the linguistic analogy (an analogy which, one must stress, should be used very cautiously), then jugation would be comparable to adjoining nouns to nouns in order to create compounds (a system which is very robust in some languages, e.g., Sanskrit). Other components, such as verbs, subordinate clauses, etc., would find no parallel in this operative category.

In order to discuss the relationships between primary and supplemental sacrificial materials, we use the following convention: a primary sacrifice receives the subscript letter "A," each jugate that is immediately ancillary to it receives the letter "B," and so on. We will also use the term "co-jugates" to refer to two or more jugates at the same level that are not jugated to different elements. The definition is a subtle but useful one: two or more B-level offerings (such as semolina and wine) jugated to the same A-level offering (such as flesh, in Figure 1) are co-jugates, for example, but so are two or more A-level offerings that are offered together under specified conditions. These somewhat abstract definitions will become clearer in meaning through a few concrete examples given below.

Judging from the priestly biblical texts and from post-biblical material, the most common type of jugation in Σ is the adjoining of a grain offering (also termed

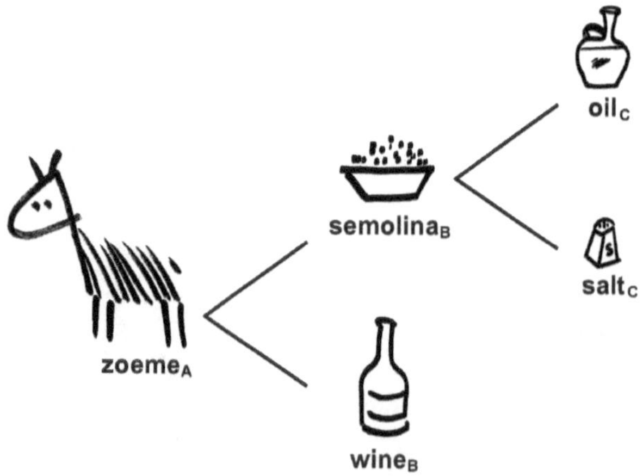

Figure 1: Basic jugational scheme of meat offering.

"cereal offering" or "meal offering")[11] and a libation to an animal offered on the altar. This combination appears to be a legacy from ancient Levantine sacrificial practice and is couched in human *realia*: like the offerers themselves, the gods are assumed to prefer a starch and an alcoholic beverage along with their meat.[12] Similar condimentary practices may explain, to some extent, the requirement to add salt to portions of certain offerings.

This elementary jugational structure in priestly law is governed by a small set of specific constraints, some of which are quite simple and intuitive, while others are more nuanced. An analogy to fast-food menus will help demonstrate the nature of these constraints. In addition to orders of a lone burger, a lone soda, and lone fries, one may choose from combinations of food that together constitute a meal. A burger with fries (a starch prepared in oil and often salted) and a soda is common, and a burger with fries or a burger with a soda are also not unheard of – hence the typical adage, "Would you like fries with that?" However, a combination of only fries and a soda is not licit: that is, while it is not illegal to order fries and a drink separately, they do not constitute a meal. This is reflected in the absence of such an option from most "combo" menus. So, too, note that the subordination of fries and sodas to burgers is one-way: ordering a drink does not typically evoke "Would you like a burger with that?" Such is the precise nature of jugational subordination in Σ.[13]

In addition to subordinate cereal offerings, such as are described in Numbers 28–29, the priestly literature in the Pentateuch also mentions independent cereal offerings, or jugations that pertain to entirely non-animal offerings. For example, Leviticus 2 describes several voluntary offerings of semolina that do not accompany animal sacrifices. In the case of raw semolina, frankincense is required as well. Thus, the voluntary A-level (i.e., standalone) offerings of raw semolina (Leviticus 2:1–3) are as in Figure 2.

While Leviticus 2 clearly describes standalone offerings, modern scholars have debated whether these laws concerning standalone freewill grain offerings were also meant to apply to the case of grain offerings that are themselves

11 These terms translate the Hebrew term *minḥâ*. For its etymology and various denotations, see Snaith (1967); Levine (1974: 7n9, 17n38); Eberhart (2002: 78–79); Anderson (1987: 30); and Marx (1994: 1–28).

12 See 1 Sam. 1:24, 10:3. See Urie (1949), Wenham (1979: 128), and, for example, Fleming (2000: 233–293).

13 On the combination of grain (in the form of bread) and wine in the Eucharist, modelled after rituals associated with the Jerusalem Temple, see Marx (1994: 163–165).

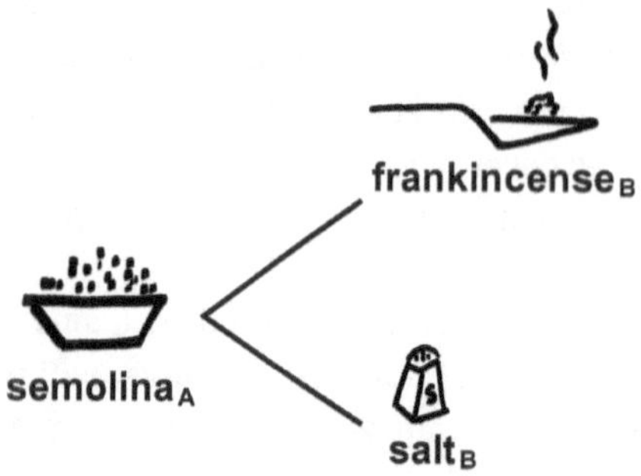

Figure 2: Basic jugational scheme of grain offering.

subordinate to animal offerings.[14] This controversy also finds precedent in antiquity and will be examined in more detail below.[15]

2.2 Jugation affected by jugation

Before we turn to our example of practicably impossible but grammatically permissible jugational patterning, let us examine a case of practicably possible, grammatically permissible, but counterintuitive jugational patterning. This example should assist in demonstrating that practical, economic or culinary considerations – while undoubtedly important and operative in the formation of sacrificial norms – are insufficient as explanations for the internal rationale of some of Σ's laws. Rather, we shall claim, a rationale is to be sought elsewhere – within the logical patterns of its "grammar."

---

14 E.g., Knobel (1861: 76); Seebass Numeri 2.139 holds a middle position: the laws in Leviticus 2 would pertain to subordinate grain offerings as well, to the exclusion of the requirement of frankincense. Priestly law does not explicitly require the jugation of frankincense to a cereal offering that is itself jugated to an animal offered as a calendric offering (see, however, Haran 1978: 230). Several late Second Temple texts suggest that such jugation did in fact take place. See Aramaic Levi Document 8:6, where the frankincense is physically added on top of the flesh-cereal-wine complex; Genesis Apocryphon 10:15–16, Schiffman (2005: 197–198), and Himmelfarb (2004: 116–121). Rabbinic tradition in this case adhered to the letter of the text and, like the Priestly law, exempted frankincense from subordinate cereal offerings (mishna Menaḥot 5:3).

15 Jubilees, Josephus, the Temple Scroll and early rabbinic tradition seem to agree that Leviticus 2:2b–3 pertains to A-Level offerings only, whereas B-Level grain offerings are turned to smoke in their entirety upon the altar. However, the Sadducean halacha referred to in the scholion to Megillat Ta'anit suggests that some authorities in antiquity viewed this law as pertaining to B-Level grain offerings as well. See Regev (1996), and cf. Noam (2003: 250–254); concerning Miḳṣat Ma'aśe ha-Torah see Qimron and Strugnell (1994: 150–152).

We have already mentioned in passing the requirement to add salt to certain offerings. As we shall see in the following section, some controversy existed in antiquity also concerning the scope of the requirement to salt various offerings (see Leviticus 2:13, discussed in detail below). However, even if one posits that all offerings must be salted, the salting of wine need not seem especially awkward: one might claim that, since the wine is offered physically alongside the meat and the cereal offering, which are salted, the wine is not itself actually salted except through proximity to these salted sacrifices.[16] In rabbinic tradition, however, wine would not in every case automatically be salted in this way through being joined with meat, since wine may be offered independently (wine$_{A}$). Moreover, even when offered as a B-Level jugate subordinate to a meat offering, wine$_{B}$ may be physically separate, as it may be offered at a time and place that are different from the flesh and grain components.[17] Thus, a problem of salting arises: should wine$_{A}$ and wine$_{B}$ be salted?

One rabbinic tradition decrees that the subordinate jugation of salt to wine depends on the location of the libation within a larger jugational scheme.[18] According to this tradition, wine$_{A}$ requires salt$_{B}$, but wine$_{B}$ (a libation offered as a subordinate jugate of a flesh offering) does not require salt$_{C}$ (see Figures 3 and 4). Hence the following rule can be formulated:

> Rule 1: subordinate jugation of salt does not apply to wine libations that are themselves subordinate jugates of a zoeme.

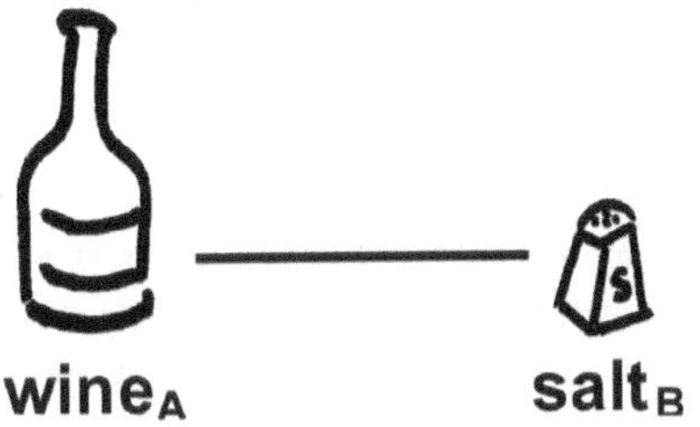

Figure 3: Wine$_{A}$, salted.

16 Such a procedure is reflected in Aramaic Levi Document 8:6.

17 See also Sirach 50:15 and the evidence discussed in Meshel (2014: 83–84).

18 See Babylonian Talmud Menaḥot 21a and Maimonides, Hilchot Ma'aśe Ha-Qorbanot 2:1, 16:14, with the commentaries, and contrast Maimonides, Hilchot Issure Mizbeaḥ 5:11. The formal reason for this is that although neither is offered on the altar fire, wine$_{A}$ is considered "fit for the [altar] fires" – it is only due to certain external restrictions that it is not poured on the fire (to refrain from extinguishing the altar fire), whereas subordinate wine$_{B}$ is not considered "fit for the fires" in the first place.

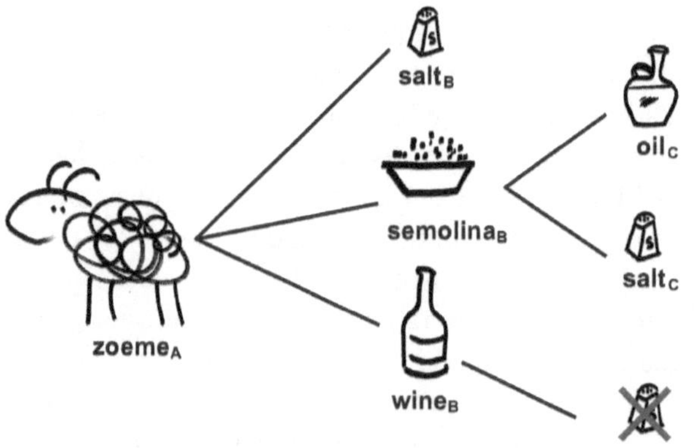

Figure 4: Wine$_B$, unsalted.

This rule can hardly be explained on practical grounds. The very fact that what is at stake is the salting of wine suggests that we are dealing here with implicit jugational patterning, a development within the grammar of sacrifice that departs from the usual use of condiments in a meal, since wine is not salted when used for ordinary consumption. Recalling the fast-food analogy, it is natural to salt one's burger or one's fries, or both, but the beverage is not normally salted.

Moreover, if one were to argue that wine$_B$ is exempt from the jugation of salt$_C$ because it is somehow conceived of as salted along with the flesh and cereal offering that it accompanies, even if it is not in physical contact with them, this would be refuted by the fact that in the rabbinic system, grain$_B$ offerings still require salt, even though the flesh that they accompany is also salted.

Considering the fact that the salting of wine is mentioned only in texts composed after actual sacrificial procedures in Israel were a matter of the distant past, it is quite possible that such a custom was never carried out in practice. However, it demonstrates the potential of jugational patterning inherent in Σ, even after the sacrificial procedures ceased to be performed. This example will therefore prove useful in demonstrating how Σ is conducive to extrapolation from the practical to the imaginary.

2.3 The salt of the hearth

Having examined a case of practicably possible, grammatically permissible, but somewhat counterintuitive jugational patterning, let us turn to an example of practicably impossible but grammatically permissible jugational patterning.

Inherent jugational patterning permits not only the generation of ritual combinations never previously prescribed (such as the salted wine$_{\mathrm{A}}$ of the rabbinic tradition), but also the generation of theoretically permissible ritual combinations that are not actually practiced. These "unreal" jugations are analogous to grammatical sentences that have never been expressed, either due to pragmatic reasons or because they have never come up in conversation. Consider sentence A, of the latter class:

A. "Xavier Klugman is sitting under that banyan tree."

This sentence has likely never occurred to anyone before, not because of any practical difficulty involved in its production, but purely because the topic of Mr. X. Klugman under a banyan tree has probably never arisen in conversation.

Among the more informative cases are sentences that cannot be expressed, either because they are of unlimited length (sentence B), or because they are too complicated for most speakers to follow (sentence C):

B. "Here is the buffalo that sees the god who sees the buffalo that sees the god...."

C. "Do you know what the reason he can tell what the color of the buffalo whose horn this is is is?"

Sentence B can be exceedingly long (though it must be finite): it is grammatical but literally ineffable (one is reminded of Patañjali's mention of sacrificial sequences that would last a thousand years).[19] Sentence C is grammatical but pragmatically unlikely, since it is too Dr. Seussesque to follow.

The distinction between "real" and "unreal" jugational patterns resembles both the distinction between *parole* and *langue* as conceived by Structuralists and the distinction between performance and competence as conceived by Generativists.[20] The "real" jugational patterns are the sum total of all sequences that have ever been expressed (either in text or in practice) in Israelite sacrifice; the "unreal" ones exist only potentially, inasmuch as they are grammatical, licit patterns. Let us now turn to one such example.

---

19 Mah. 1.94 (Kielhorn 1878–1885: 9), see discussion in Meshel (2014: 1–3)
20 See Saussure (1966: 7–15); Chomsky (1957, 1981).

Leviticus 2:13 reads, "You shall salt every cereal offering; you shall not omit from your cereal offering the salt of your covenant[21] with your God; with [or: "upon"] all your offerings you must offer salt." Several difficulties present themselves in this verse: first of all, it is unclear how many discrete instructions the verse contains.[22] Grammatically, it consists of two (13a, 13b), or possibly three (13aα, 13aβ, 13b) discrete sentences.[23] However, these sentences may all express a single ruling, formulated in a pleonastic fashion found elsewhere in biblical law.

The solution to this first problem is linked to another problem, the scope of "all your offerings" (or, "each of your offerings," Hebrew כָּל־קָרְבָּנְךָ) in 13b. If taken literally as referring to every single offering, then the verse contains at least two discrete commands: salt every cereal offering (13a), and salt every offering (13b). This redundancy may be resolved in part by a hypothesis of diachronic accretion: 13b may be a later interpolation, attempting to broaden the scope of 13a to include other offerings as well.[24]

However, since this diachronic reconstruction does not solve the problem but only transfers the responsibility from the author to the interpolator, we will consider the verse in its final form, bearing in mind that this may also have been the original form. As it stands, the verse allows for at least three possible readings of the phrase "with/upon all your offerings you must offer salt":

(a.) a contextually limited reading: only cereal offerings mentioned in the section to which this law is appended (Leviticus 2 – so only freewill cereal$_{\text{A}}$ offerings) require salting;

(b.) a less contextually restricted reading: all cereal offerings require salting (including statutory and freewill cereal$_{\text{A}}$ and cereal$_{\text{B}}$ offerings);

(c.) a more literal reading: all offerings, including all meat offerings as well as all cereal offerings, require salting.

Since the law of Leviticus 2:13 appears in a passage pertaining to cereal offerings, it is most likely, though not provable, that the law in 13b was intended to

21 Concerning this "covenant," see Schwartz (2004: 210).

22 From a literary perspective, of course, this multiplicity of discrete grammatical sentences does not necessary imply a multiplicity of discrete legal injunctions. Stylistic variation and repetition of the sort found in v. 13 are found even in the prose of the Priestly literature (see Paran 1989: 49–73, 163–164).

23 The former is probably more correct, with a subordinate clause, "lest you omit from your cereal offering the salt of your covenant with your God." Compare the phrase "lest x die" in Leviticus 16:2, Numbers 18:32 et passim.

24 For a brief philological discussion of Leviticus 2:13, see Meshel (2014: 97–99 and nn. 124–131).

refer only to cereal offerings, in contrast to a more literal sense of "each of your offerings."

The earliest traditions reflect a reading somewhere between (b.) and (c.). From Ezekiel (who may or may not have been aware of this priestly injunction), one may deduce that the salting of sacrificial meat was known in some ancient priestly circles (see Ezekiel 43:24). However, Ezekiel mentions the salting of meat only once, in the context of the wholeburnt offering. A careful reading of the (late Second Temple) Aramaic Levi Document 9:6–9, which specifies the precise amounts of salt for each animal, may similarly lead to the conclusion that only the wholeburnt offering requires salt, a notion which the 1st-century historian Josephus also implies (Antiquities 3.227).[25] The requirement to salt the show-bread, found already in the Septuagint (Greek) version of Leviticus 24:7, probably reflects a rejection of reading (a.) in favor of reading (b.) or (c.).

Rabbinic traditions are even more inclusive in their reading of "all your offerings" in Leviticus 2:13b,[26] offering an extremely literal reading:

(d.) an ultra-literal reading: all offerings – not only meat offerings and cereal offerings, but also such offerings as wine and oil – require salting.

In Pentateuchal law, there is hardly any practical difference between readings (c.) and (d.). Sacrificial materials that are neither cereal offerings nor meat offerings (such as wine, oil, or frankincense) are hardly discussed as independent A-level offerings in Pentateuchal law, and when wine, oil, or frankincense are offered as B-level jugates, they are offered along with salt (the meat itself or the cereal offering is salted; this is particularly true if salt is sprinkled on the top of the whole offering).

However, later traditions contain such structures for which readings (c.) and (d.) play out differently. Since the list of offerable materials was gradually expanded in post-biblical texts, several materials that are not found in priestly law as independent offerings re-entered the sacrificial repertoire of Second Temple and post-biblical sacrificial texts as acceptable A-level offerings: wine$_A$, oil$_A$, frankincense$_A$, wood$_A$, and even salt$_A$ offerings all appear to be acceptable offerings according to later traditions.[27]

---

25 For a discussion of the late Second Temple and early rabbinic sources referred to in this section, see Meshel (2014: 100–103nn132–146).

26 See also Mark 9:49 and Schiffman (2005: 194 and n68).

27 See, for example, Nehemiah 10:35, 13:31; Jubilees 21:12–13; Aramaic Levi Document 8:7; Temple Scroll 20:14, 21:14–16, 23:9–24:16, tosefta Zebaḥim 1:11, 10:4, tosefta Menaḥot 12:10, 15, Sifra (Weiss 12a); Babylonian Talmud Zebaḥim 91b; and the discussion in Meshel 2014: 100–1.

This led to the possibility of a much wider application of the phrase “all your sacrifices,” which now included the salting of materials that had not been conceived of as offerings in Pentateuchal law. Thus, in rabbinic literature, the law of Leviticus 2:13b came to be regarded much more inclusively as a generic law covering diverse materials, and in fact rabbinic sources refer explicitly to the question of salting oil$_A$, frankincense$_A$, wood$_A$, and wine$_A$.[28] Let us therefore depart for the time being from the original intention of Priestly law and examine the development of Σ within the rabbinic traditions pertaining to the subordinate jugation of salt. From these rabbinic texts, it appears that an offering can be exempt from salt as a subordinate jugate only under the following conditions: (1.) it is not considered fit for the altar fire in the first place, (2.) it is exempted by a specific verse, or (3.) it is exempted by an explicit, otherwise unrecorded divine decree.[29] This implies that, in this (obviously fantastic) system, wherever an *ad hoc* divine exemption is absent, anything that is considered an “offering” (roughly, קָרְבָּן) in theory requires a subordinate jugate of salt.

There is one possibility that the classical rabbinic texts did not entertain, though a consistent application of the logic of sacrifice would require taking it into account: since salt$_A$ is a “grammatical” offering in the rabbinic system – as noted above, rabbinic tradition viewed salt as a sacrificial material in its own right and not as an additive[30] – and since no special divine (scriptural or oral) decree exists for exempting salt$_A$ from salt$_B$, it appears that the jugation of salt$_B$ to salt$_A$ is not only possible but necessary.

This in itself causes no serious rupture in the system, as one can imagine an offering of the form depicted in Figure 5:

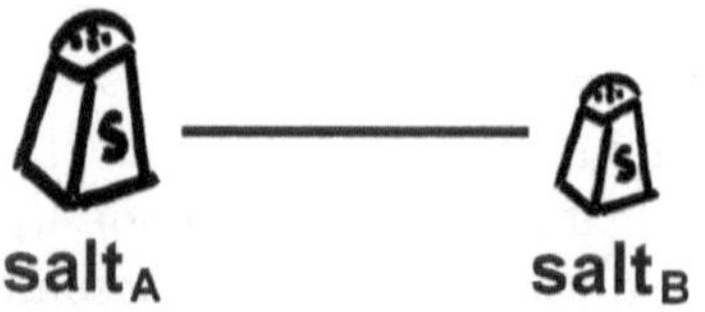

Figure 5: Salting salt.

However, in the rabbinic system, subordinate B-level jugates also require salting (with the exception of wine$_B$, which – as we have seen – is exempt). Now, since there is no divine decree exempting salt$_B$ from the subordinate jugation of salt$_C$, it

28 See Sifra (Weiss, 12a–b), Babylonian Talmud Menaḥot 20a, Maimonides, Hilchot Issure Mizbeaḥ 5:11, and the commentaries. Surprisingly, Rashi on Leviticus 2:13 (Chavel 1982: 326) does not reflect the maximalist rabbinic reading, but rather reading (b.).

29 See Meshel (2014: 101 n. 143).

30 Moreover, the offering of salt is referred to as תקריב (“you shall offer,” Leviticus 2:11), see Meshel (2014: 102n144).

appears that – if the generativity of the “grammar” of ritual is taken to its extreme limits – a sacrifice of salt would be a never-ending enterprise of the form (salt$_A$ (salt$_B$ (salt$_C$ (..., as in Figure 6:

Figure 6: Infinitely long chain of salt.

This would be in accordance with a rule of Σ, also from the operative category “jugation,” according to which:

> Rule 2: every offering entails an immediate subordinate jugate of salt.

In fact, having established this rule, it should now be possible to state that *every* sacrificial material in the rabbinic system – not necessarily a salt$_A$ offering – should entail an endless chain of subordinate jugates as soon as it requires one subordinate jugate of salt.[31] This situation would create a serious rupture in sacrificial procedures, since it might essentially prevent any sacrificial rite from being completed – entangling our imaginary priests in a form of Zeno’s paradox.

This loophole reveals either a loose end in the rules or a rupture, marginal but potentially fatal, in the sacrificial system. Of course this loophole is a mental game, and it still remains to show what it can teach us about the grammar – not to mention the meaning – of ritual as it is presented in Σ. Yet although it may lie at the fringes of the greater project at hand, this far-fetched example is nonetheless critical to understanding the comprehensive nature of a complete “grammar.” Moreover, these “unreal” sequences have, in a sense, logical precedence over those we call “real.” As Staal realized, the formal homology between language and ritual is useful precisely to account for the pragmatically unlikely sequences that both systems necessarily generate. Thus, in order for a generative grammar to be comprehensive, it must allow for every conceivably possible grammatical form and prevent the generation of all ungrammatical forms. The subordinate jugation of salt to any offering is a rule that must be part of this “grammar,” even though – like many rules in the grammars of natural languages – it allows for the production of pragmatically impossible sequences.

---

31 The same situation may be found even in Leviticus 2:13b, if this is understood according to reading (d.) above. See Meshel (2014: 103n146).

3 Conclusion

3.1 The limits of language

The homology between a grammar of language and that of ritual requires, as noted in the title of this article, a grain of salt. Unlike natural languages, Σ clearly has no phonetics, nor is it governed by morphological or syntactic rules analogous to those of natural languages.[32] Instead, in Σ one finds at least the four operative categories of zoemics, jugation, hierarchics, and praxemics, as enumerated above. Furthermore, if the Israelite sacrificial rituals bear any meaning, it is unlikely that this meaning relates to the formal structure of ritual in any way comparable to the linguistic relationship between morphology, syntax, and semantics.[33]

For this reason, little evidence has been found that would justify a high-resolution analogy between language and ritual. Much less should one expect to find a particular affinity between the grammars of languages spoken in particular cultures and the ritual systems found in those same cultures.[34] In fact, the use of the term "syntax" for non-linguistic systems now seems inappropriate. The present study thus calls into question Staal's central thesis, according to which ritual systems display formal properties that closely resemble the syntactic properties of natural languages. The grammar of Σ only resembles linguistic grammars inasmuch as both are generative, rigorous, and amenable to concise formulation; both are partially unconsciously internalized, and include operative categories located on discrete levels of abstraction, as well as rules of transformation between these categories; and both have some relation to meaning. In this respect, the analogy between the formal structure of ritual and the formal structure of language has proven fruitful. However, the operative categories in the grammars of this ritual system are different from the operative categories in the grammars of natural languages.

---

32 Contra Eichinger Ferro-Luzzi (1977); Staal (1979, 1989); Lawson and McCauley (1990); and Michaels (2007). Nor would one expect a diachronic study of ritual "grammars" to reveal anything analogous to a "Grimm's law for the equivalent of ritual dialects" (see Goody 1993: 42).

33 See Meshel (2014: chap. 6, pp. 174–197).

34 See Eichinger Ferro-Luzzi (1977).

3.2 The sacrifice of grammar

Since the grammars of rituals and the grammars of natural languages are fundamentally dissimilar, the term "grammar" is not truly suitable for sacrificial systems. It is merely beneficial to speak of a grammar of sacrifice in the sense of a finite set of generative rules that are unconsciously internalized, applied rigorously, and amenable to concise, formulaic notation. These rules determine what is acceptable ("grammatical") within a particular ritual system and place certain constraints on the system's development over the course of time.

We are forced to wonder whether the term "grammar" should be avoided in the case of ritual, since perhaps following the analogy to language too rigorously has been detrimental to the study of sacrificial systems. Therefore, having identified the categories of Σ and having coined terms for them, it might now be wiser to discard this misleading term. For example, one might propose the acronym GRAMMUR – Generative, Rigorously Applied, Mathematically Modelled, Unconscious Rules – in order to avoid the linguistic analogy, which has by now become more misleading than fruitful for the study of ritual.

Nevertheless, aside from the term's widespread use in non-linguistic contexts,[35] there is one substantial reason to retain the term "grammar." Few systems that are neither linguistic nor ritual are describable in terms of generative rules. This does not mean that other systems do not have grammars (in fact, it is highly likely that other systems like music, dance, and certain games are based on "grammars" of their own),[36] but very few systems are as rigorously rule-governed, and at the same time as complex and well-documented over several millennia (allowing for the analysis of diachronic processes within the "grammars") as ritual and linguistic systems.

Thus, in order to speak of a ritual system's grammar, it is necessary to sacrifice the narrow denotation of "grammar." In sacrifice, one gives up some of one's possessions in order to obtain a higher objective; here, one must give up the narrow denotation of a term in order to be granted an entry into the inner workings of an ancient culture, as well as a more accurate interpretation of its formative texts.

---

35 See OED s.v. *grammar* (6.a), which reflects the expanded use of "grammar" to denote the "fundamental principles or rules of an art or science."
36 See for example Lerdahl and Jackendoff (1983).

4 Postscript: Response to Michaels

It is both a pleasure and a most welcome challenge to have a leading voice from a different field critically engaging with one's own work. I therefore wish to respond briefly to Michaels' critique of *A Grammar of Sacrifice* in his recent masterful book, *Homo Ritualis*.[37]

In doing so, I in no way wish to detract from the approach advocated by the Heidelberg school of ritual dynamics (*Ritualdynamik*) in their various publications – which I have always found inspiring, but only to demonstrate how a Σ-type grammar differs from an R-type grammar (R for *Ritualdynamik*), and where the two approaches may converge.[38] Of course, the method one adopts depends on the kind of information one has at hand (practiced or textual), on the explanatory power one requires of one's "grammar" (philological, anthropological), and on one's perception of what constitutes a "grammar" of a nonlinguistic ritual system (see my own definition above). Thus, one may expect to find situations in which an R-type "grammar" may have greater explanatory power, and situations where a Σ–type "grammar" is preferable. The two approaches are not mutually exclusive, and one might attempt attacking the same set of data with two grammatical models.

One criticism raised by Michaels is (I will state it more harshly here for the sake of clarity) that the three operative categories invented for the sake of describing Σ – zoemics, jugation (one aspect of which has been discussed in this paper), and hierarchics – are not at all necessary for the construction of a "grammar," nor are they truly "grammatical" properties, since "zoemics and jugation actually concern the classificatory or cognitive system underlying the *materia sacra* and 'hierarchies' in Meshel's sense. They are just two 'syntactical' rules of many. The supposed reduction of a 'grammar' of rituals to acts [in the case of Σ, the category 'praxemics'] is justified by the fact that simply thinking something is not a ritual, but utterances are already a form of action [...]."

This critique is, in my opinion, not valid due to two main considerations, quantitative and qualitative. The first, quantitative objection is that the laws of zoemics, jugation, and hierarchics include several dozens of formulas (not counting the graphic representations), each of which represents a host of licit combinations and explains the restriction of a multitude of others (in zoemics alone, the number is in the order of 2 to the power of 20; see the section "A Grammar of Σ,"

37 Michaels (2016: esp. 76–86 and 92–3).

38 In the footnotes above, I have responded to some of the more specific criticisms raised in Michaels (2016) – see notes 5 and 7.

appended to *The Grammar of Sacrifice*, primarily pp. 1–9). Terming these operative categories "two syntactical rules" of many would be equivalent to stating that the laws of *sandhi* in Sanskrit are "one phonetic rule" according to which "sometimes assimilation occurs," or that entire operative categories (not syntax), such as phonology and morphology, are merely two "syntactic" rules of many, in the grammar of a particular language.

The second objection is qualitative. I wholeheartedly accept Michaels' insight that hierarchics and zoemics are properties of the mind engaged in ritual, not properties of the bodies and *materia sacra* involved in its implementation (I leave aside jugation, where matters are more complex, as jugation is clearly expressed in the physical conjoining of *materia sacra*). Yet, I am of the opinion that it is precisely for this reason that they are so cardinal for the grammatical description of Σ, and possibly of other ritual systems as well. Just as in the description of a language, many categories are only represented (e.g., audible) as properties of actual linguistic utterances – consider "unvoicedness," "zero morpheme," and even "subject," for example – so zoemic and hierarchic properties are discernible not in a void, but as properties determining the accompanying *materia sacra*, the agent to be selected, and the manner in which the flesh will be distributed.

Here I reiterate my criticism of previous approaches to the "grammar" of ritual, once again by analogy to the grammars of languages: If one were to limit oneself to composing a grammar of a linguistic system on the basis of phonetics alone, the resulting "grammar" would have a very low explanatory power. Similarly, composing a grammar on the basis of praxemics alone would have a very low explanatory power. While it is tempting to turn most of one's attention to praxemics – since it is an operative category that has long been recognized in the literature, and is immediately discernible in any ritual system (South Asian or Mediterranean, textual or practical) – it is important to recognize what can be gained by turning one's gaze away from praxemics and toward completely different operative categories, such as those identified in Σ, and perhaps others that have not been discovered yet.

A second criticism raised by Michaels – more precisely, a degree of skepticism – pertains to the scope and nature of Σ. Michaels remains cautious about "the possibility of developing a deep structure or a deep grammar of rituals" because "the example Meshel has given is based on a very limited and solely textual ritual, the sacrifice of Σ, that is, the ancient Israelite Priestly sacrificial system as presented in the Pentateuch" (Michaels 2016: 80 and n13).

My response to this point is again twofold – first, with regard to Σ's scope, second, with regard to its textuality. Regarding its scope: there is no question that in Σ the set of data is not only finite – pertaining as it does to a system no longer in practice – but also, within the world of ritual texts, exceedingly small in relation to any rough equivalent in South Asia (not to mention the complexities and variations of rituals practiced in living traditions). As in the case of the study of other complex phenomena, it may be advisable to begin with a relatively small and manageable set of data: resorting to a biological analogy à la Staal, one might say that the genome of *C. elegans* and the nervous system of fruit flies – or even of laboratory-engineered forms of these species not found in nature – are better points of departure for a biologist than their equivalents in more complex organisms. Therefore, I hope that the findings in Σ – a "laboratory case," so to speak – offer some fruitful directions for the study of systems that are vastly more complex and more heterogeneous, such as South Asian and ancient Anatolian ritual systems.

That said, a minor correction is called for, as I suspect that Michaels (2016: 80n13) misrepresents the workings of Σ. Its grammar is operative not only in the Pentateuch but also in a much larger and more diverse set of works, spanning nearly two millennia of continuous textual data, from the first half of the first millennium BCE to the first half of the second millennium CE: biblical, Qumranic, Jewish Hellenistic, apocryphal and pseudepigraphic, rabbinic and Karaite literature. In terms of genre, too, the variety is remarkable, covering texts as diverse as Leviticus, Ezekiel, Jubilees, the Aramaic Levi Document, Philo, Josephus, the Temple Scroll, Mishna and Tosephta, the Sifra, the Babylonian Talmud, Maimonides, and a host of commentaries, as well as many more minor sources containing information about Σ, such as the Genesis Apocryphon, Megillat Ta'anit, and a multitude of others.

Thus, there are undoubtedly tremendous disadvantages – from the anthropologist's point of view – in working with texts that are themselves idealized versions of rituals that may or may not have taken place as prescribed. However, working with ancient texts from a period spanning such a long period of time offers a window into the diachronic aspect of the grammar – a *sine qua non* in the Σ-approach to the "grammar" of ritual, which might also be applied to South Asian systems.

Finally, it remains to ask whether the operative categories of Σ have any explanatory power for non-Israelite systems, perhaps even for non-textual systems. Preliminary work on ancient Near Eastern and Mediterranean sacrificial systems, such as the Ugaritic sacrificial system (a similarly small corpus of textual data pertaining to sacrificial practices in the late 2nd millennium BCE Levant) suggests that at least some of Σ's operative categories have strong explanatory power for that system as well: zoemics, hierarchics, (unsurprisingly) praxemics – but interestingly not jugation. This situation may be the result of historical, even cladistic affinities, between Israelite and other ancient Levantine systems. A preliminary exploration of the explanatory power of Σ's operative categories to the *Āpastamba-Śrautasūtra* suggests that jugation and hierarchics may be operative in South Asian sacrificial rituals as well. On the other hand, the operative category zoemics – perhaps counterintuitively, considering the complexity of the distinctive features of *materia sacra* in the *Śrautasūtra*s – has little explanatory power for the texts examined. While the comparative task that lies ahead is formidable, the initial findings are unequivocal: empirical and inductive categories such as "zoemics," "jugation," "hierarchics," and "praxemics" – and possibly others not yet recognized – are likely to have more explanatory power for the study of sacrificial ritual in the future than imported categories such as "syntax" and "morphology." Regarding this point, the Σ- and R- approaches may converge.

Acknowledgments: I wish to express my gratitude to the editors and to the following scholars for reading and commenting on previous drafts of this paper: Martha Himmelfarb, Axel Michaels, Anand Mishra, Paolo Visigalli, Rebecca Khalandovsky, and Ayelet Wenger.

References

Anderson, Gary A. 1987. *Sacrifices and offerings in ancient Israel: Studies in their social and political importance* (Harvard Semitic Monographs 41). Atlanta: Scholars Press.
Bourdieu, Pierre. 1977. *Outline of a theory of practice*. Cambridge: Cambridge University Press.
Burkert, Walter. 1987. The problem of ritual killing. In Robert G. Hamerton-Kelly (ed.), *Violent origins*, 149–176. Stanford, CA: Stanford University Press.
Chatterji, Kshitish Chandra. 1964. *Patañjali's Mahābhāṣya: Paspaśāhnika*, 3rd edn. (Usha Memorial Series 7). Calcutta: A. Mukherjee.
Chavel, Charles B. (ed.). 1982. *Perushei Rashi 'al ha-Torah: 'al-pi defus rishon, ketav-yad Oksford u-mahadurat Berliner.* Jerusalem: Mosad ha-Rav Kuk.
Chomsky, Noam. 1957. *Syntactic structures* (Janua linguarum 4). The Hague: Mouton.
Chomsky, Noam. 1981. On cognitive capacity. In Ned Block (ed.), *Readings in philosophy of psychology*, vol. 2, 305–323. Cambridge, MA: Harvard University Press.
Eberhart, Christian A. 2002. *Studien zur Bedeutung der Opfer im Alten Testament: Die Signifikanz von Blut- und Verbrennungsriten im kultischen Rahmen* (Wissenschaftliche Monographien zum Alten und Neuen Testament 94). Neukirchen-Vluyn: Neukirchener Verlag.
Eichinger Ferro-Luzzi, Gabriella. 1977. Ritual as language: The case of South Indian food offerings. *Current Anthropology* 18(3). 507–514.
Evans-Pritchard, Edward E. 1965. *Theories of primitive religion*. Oxford: Clarendon.
Feldman, Louis. 2000. *Flavius Josephus: Translation and Commentary* 3. Leiden: Brill.
Fleming, Daniel E. 2000. *Time at Emar: The cultic calendar and the rituals from the diviner's archive.* Winona Lake, IN: Eisenbrauns.
Gane, Roy E. 2004. *Ritual dynamic structure* (Gorgias Dissertations 14.2). Piscataway: Gorgias.
Gane, Roy E. 2005. *Cult and character: purification offerings, Day of Atonement, and theodicy.* Winona Lake, IN: Eisenbrauns.

Girard, René. 1987. Generative scapegoating. In Robert G. Hamerton-Kelly (ed.), *Violent origins*, 73–105. Stanford, CA: Stanford University Press.
Goody, Jack. 1993. Knots in May: Continuities, contradictions, and changes in European rituals. *Journal of Mediterranean Studies* 3. 30–45.
Greenfield, Jonas C., Michael E. Stone & Ester Eshel (eds.). 2004. *The Aramaic Levi Document: Edition, translation, commentary* (Studia in Veteris Testamenti pseudepigrapha 19). Leiden: Brill.
Humphrey, Caroline & James Laidlaw. 1994. *The archetypal actions of ritual: A theory of ritual illustrated by the Jain rite of worship*. Oxford: Clarendon.
Joshi, S. D. & J. A. F. Roodbergen (eds. and trans.). 1986. *Patañjali's Vyākaraṇa-Mahābhāṣya, Paspaśāhnika, Introduction, text, translation and notes.* Poona: Publications of the Centre of Advanced Study in Sanskrit.
Haran, Menahem. 1978. *Temples and temple-service in ancient Israel: An inquiry into the character of cult phenomena and the historical setting of the priestly school*. Oxford: Clarendon.
Himmelfarb, Martha. 2004. Earthly sacrifice and heavenly incense: The law of the priesthood in Aramaic Levi and Jubilees. In Ra'anan S. Boustan & Annette Yoshiko Reed (eds.), *Heavenly realms and earthly realities in late antique religions*, 103–122. Cambridge: Cambridge University Press.
Kafaḥ, Yosef David. 1963. *Mishna im perush Mosheh ben Maymon: Maḳor ve-targum*. Jerusalem: Mosad ha-Rav Ḳuḳ.
Kielhorn, Franz (ed.). 1878–1885. The *vyākaraṇa-mahābhāshya of Patañjali*. Bombay: Government Central Book Depot.
Knobel, August. 1861. *Kurzgefasstes exegetisches Handbuch zum Alten Testament. Dreizehnte Lieferung. Numeri, Deuteronomium und Josua*. Leipzig: S. Hirzel.
Kreinath, Jens. 2006. Semiotics. In Jens Kreinath, Jan Snoek & Michael Stausberg (eds.), *Theorizing rituals*, 429–470. Leiden & Boston: Brill.
Lawson, E. Thomas. 1976. Ritual as language. *Religion* 6(2). 39–123.
Lawson, E. Thomas & Robert N. McCauley. 1990. *Rethinking religion: Connecting cognition and culture*. Cambridge: Cambridge University Press.
Lerdahl, Fred & Ray S. Jackendoff. 1983. *A generative theory of tonal music*. Cambridge, MA: MIT Press.
Levine, Baruch A. 1974. *In the presence of the Lord: A study of cult and some cultic terms in ancient Israel* (Studies in Judaism in Late Antiquity 5). Leiden: Brill.
Lévi-Strauss, Claude. 1963. Structural analysis in linguistics and anthropology. In *Structural anthropology*, 31–54. Translated by C. Jacobson & B. G. Schoepf. New York: Basic Books.
Marx, Alfred. 1994. *Les offrandes végétales dans l'Ancien Testament: Du tribut d'hommage au repas eschatologique*. Leiden & New York: Brill.
McClymond, Kathryn. 2008. *Beyond sacred violence: A comparative study of sacrifice*. Baltimore: Johns Hopkins University Press.
Meshel, Naphtali S. 2014. *The "grammar" of sacrifice: a generativist study of the Israelite sacrificial system in the priestly writings;* with *A "grammar" of Σ*. Oxford: Oxford University Press.
Michaels, Axel. 2007. 'How do you do?': Vorüberlegungen zu einer Grammatik der Rituale. In Heinrich Schmidinger & Clemens Sedmak (eds.), *Der Mensch—ein "animal symbolicum"? Sprache—Dialog—Ritual*, 239–258. Darmstadt: WBG.

Michaels, Axel. 2012. A preliminary grammar of Newar life-cycle rituals. *The journal of Hindu studies* 5(1). 10–29.
Michaels, Axel. 2016. *Homo ritualis: Hindu ritual and its significance to ritual theory*. New York: Oxford University Press.
Michaels, Axel et al. 2010. *Grammars and morphologies of ritual practices in Asia* (Ritual Dynamics and the Science of Ritual 1). Wiesbaden: Harrassowitz.
Milbank, John. 1995. Stories of sacrifice: From Wellhausen to Girard. *Theory, Culture and Society* 12(4). 15–46.
Milgrom, Jacob. 1979. The offering of incense in second temple times. In *Sefer Ben-Zion Luria: Meḥqarim ba-Miqra᾿ uve-Toledot Yisra᾿el*, 330–333. Jerusalem: Kiryat Sefer (in Hebrew).
Milgrom, Jacob. 1991–2001. *Leviticus: A new translation with introduction and commentary*, 3 vols. New York: Doubleday.
Noam, Vered. 2003. *Megilat Ta'anit: Ha-nusaḥim, pishram, toldotehem: Be-tseruf mahadurah biḳortit*. Jerusalem: Yad Yitsḥaḳ Ben-Tsevi.
Paran, Meir. 1989. *Forms of the priestly style in the Pentateuch: Patterns, linguistic usages, syntactic structures*. Jerusalem: Magnes Press (in Hebrew).
Payne, Richard K. 1999. The Shingon Ajikan: Diagrammatic analysis of ritual syntax. *Religion* 29(3). 215–229.
Philo. 1937. *On the special laws* (De specialibus legibus). Translated by F. H. Colson (Loeb Classical Library, Philo 7). London: W. Heinemann.
Qimron, Elisha & John Strugnell. 1994. *Miḳṣat ma'aśe ha-Torah* (Discoveries in the Judaean Desert 10). Oxford: Clarendon.
Regev, Eyal. 1996. The controversy regarding the eating of the cereal offering of the well-being sacrifices and the thanksgiving cakes in 4QMMT, the Temple Scroll, and the Scholion to *Megillat Ta'anit*. *Tarbiẓ* 65. 375–388 (in Hebrew).
Saussure, Ferdinand de. 1966. *Course in general linguistics*. Translated by Wade Baskin. New York: McGraw-Hill Book Co.
Schiffman, Lawrence H. 2005. Sacrificial Halakhah in the fragments of the Aramaic Levi Document from Qumran, the Cairo Genizah, and Mt. Athos Monastery. In E. G. Chazon, D. Dimant & R. A. Clements (eds.), *Reworking the Bible: Apocryphal and related texts at Qumran* (Studies on the Texts of the Desert of Judah 58), 177–202. Leiden: Brill.
Schwartz, Baruch J. 2004. Leviticus. In Adele Berlin & Marc Zvi Brettler (eds.), *The Jewish Study Bible*, 203–280. New York: Oxford University Press.
Sebeok, Thomas A. 1966. The structure and content of Cheremis charms. In Dell Hymes (ed.), *Language in culture and society: A reader in linguistics and anthropology*, 356–371. New York: Harper and Row.
Smith, Jonathan Z. 1987. The domestication of sacrifice. In Robert G. Hamerton-Kelly (ed.), *Violent origins*, 191–205. Stanford, CA: Stanford University Press.
Snaith, Norman H. 1967. *Leviticus and Numbers*. London: Nelson.
Sperber, Dan. 1975. *Rethinking symbolism*. Translated by Alice L. Morton. Cambridge: Cambridge University Press.
Staal, Frits. 1979. The meaninglessness of ritual. *Numen* 26(1). 2–22.
Staal, Frits. 1980. Ritual syntax. In Masatoshi Nagatomi (ed.), *Sanskrit and Indian studies: Essays in honour of Daniel H. H. Ingalls* (Studies in Classical India 2), 119–142. Dordrecht: D. Reidel.

Staal, Frits. 1989. *Rules without meaning: Ritual, mantras, and the human sciences* (Toronto Studies in Religion 4). New York: Peter Lang.
Urie, D. M. L. 1949. Sacrifice among the west Semites. *Palestine Exploration Quarterly* 81(1). 67–82.
Wenham, Gordon J. 1979. *The book of Leviticus* (New International Commentary on the Old Testament 3). Grand Rapids, MI: Eerdmans.
Yadin, Yigael (ed.). 1983. *The Temple Scroll*. 2 vols. Jerusalem: Israel Exploration Society.
Yelle, Robert A. 2003. *Explaining mantras: Ritual, rhetoric and the dream of a natural language in Hindu Tantra*. New York: Routledge.
Yelle, Robert A. 2013. *Semiotics of religion: Signs of the sacred in history*. London: Bloomsbury.

Robert A. Yelle

Intertextuality, iconicity, and joint speech: Three dialogical modes of linguistic performance in Hindu mantras

1 Introduction

When we say "dialogue," we usually think first of the situation in which two people are exchanging ideas, possibly though by no means necessarily in the form of a debate. This standard sense is not the one under discussion here. My essay will instead extend the term metaphorically, to different communicative situations in which there is an attempt to bring two different modes of expression into alignment: *intertextuality*, or the reference to and reworking of verbal formulas within a single, historical linguistic tradition; *iconicity*, or the manner in which language is often made to map onto its pragmatic context, in order to converge with – and perhaps bring about – a certain result; and *joint speech*, a mode of spoken language in which groups coordinate their utterances in real time. The body of data from which the bulk of my illustrations will be drawn consists of mantras from the Vedas through the Tantras, in particular the *haṃsa* mantra. Although all of these dialogical modes are found in different cultures, the particular form that they take in Hinduism is unique to that tradition, and in fact describes a difference from modern European traditions, which have adopted a linguistic ideology that can be markedly hostile to such phenomena. Consequently, a study of intertextuality, iconicity and joint speech in Hindu traditions can contribute to a different sort of dialogue: the one that comparative disciplines such as the history of religions, anthropology, and general linguistics aim to develop.

2 Intertextuality

The *haṃsa* mantra – *haṃsaḥ so'ham* – is common in a number of Tantric texts, and appears as early as the *Vijñāna Bhairava* (ca. 500 CE).[1] The literal

1 For a discussion of Tantras describing the *haṃsa* mantra, see Yelle (2003: 28–30).

Robert A. Yelle, Ludwig Maximilian University, Munich

https://doi.org/10.1515/9781614514329-003

meaning of the mantra is plain enough: "The (divine) swan, that I am." The swan (*haṃsa*) has been a symbol of the deity since the Vedas (Padoux 1990: 140; 2011: 43). The terseness of the formula conceals a density of symbolism, however, as the two syllables "ha" and "sa" out of which it is composed are glossed as standing for the god Śiva and his consort Śakti, respectively; and the entire mantra therefore represents the movement from male to female, and then from female back to male again. The *haṃsa* mantra is an example of intentional chiasmus, a poetic device that depends upon an inversion of syllables. This chiastic structure appears to be an attempt to diagram various processes of creation, including the movement of the breath in and out of the body, and the act of sexual reproduction, which involves the rhythmic exchange between the sexes.

I shall say more about such forms of iconicity below. What I wish to stress now is the manner in which the *haṃsa* mantra also represents a deliberate effort to invoke and redeploy – perhaps even to perfect – several earlier mantras. First of all, through euphonic combination, the second half of the *haṃsa* mantra (*saḥ* + *aham*) becomes "*so'ham*," which is explicitly stated to contain the praṇava, *oṃ*. Some late Vedic texts prescribe that one append this syllable at the beginning and end of a mantra, thus converting the mantra into a kind of chiasmus. The *haṃsa* mantra may be invoking this precedent.

There are more direct precedents for the *haṃsa* mantra. This can be shown most conveniently by laying out the parallels:

Rig Veda 10.90.5[2]:
"From him [Puruṣa] Virāj was born; again Puruṣa from Virāj was born."

> *tasmād virāl ajāyata virājo adhi puruṣaḥ*
>
> *Atharva Veda* 14.2.71[3]:
> I am he (*ama*), you are she (*sā*); you are she, I am he.
> I am the Sāman chant, you are the Ṛg verse.
> I am the sky, you are the earth,
> Come, let us unite,
> deposit the seed,
> to get a son,
> a male child.
> *amo'ham asmi sā tvaṃ sā tvam asy amo'ham*
> *sāmāham asmi ṛk tvaṃ dyaur ahaṃ pṛthivī tvam...*

2 Text in van Nooten and Holland (1994). Translation in Griffith (1896).

3 Quoted in *Bṛhadāraṇyaka Up*. 6.4.20. Text and translation in Olivelle (1998).

Rig Veda 10.90.5 and *Atharva Veda* 14.2.71 already reflect the idea of a movement from male to female, then back again. The latter formula, which is quoted in *Bṛhadāraṇyaka Upaniṣad* 6.4.20 (Staal 1989: 83), is also close in sound to the *haṃsa* mantra. Each of these earlier hymns appears to serve as a model for the *haṃsa* mantra, although the latter was invented more than a thousand years after.

Another intertextual reference encoded in the *haṃsa* mantra is to the so-called "Great Sayings" (*mahāvākya*) that were distilled by later Vedantic tradition as the essence of the philosophy of the Upaniṣads. The *haṃsa* mantra resembles such formulas as "ahaṃ brahmāsmi" (*Bṛhadāraṇyaka Up*. 1.4.10) and "tat tvam asi" (*Chāndogya Up*. 6). The phrase "puruṣaḥ so'ham" is found in *Īśā Up*. 16. Simply by substituting another epithet for the deity – namely, *haṃsa* – for *puruṣa*, one would produce the *haṃsa* mantra. But what would be the reasons for doing so? Presumably, this substitution was motivated by the opportunity to convert the formula into a chiasmus that repeats "ha" and "sa" in inverted order.

In the same way that the *mahāvākya*s were conceived by later Vedantic tradition as the distillation of the Upaniṣads, the *haṃsa* mantra, which on my reading is also a kind of *mahāvākya*, both distilled and perfected the combination of two ideas adumbrated already one thousand years or more earlier: that the Ātman or individual self is identical with the Brahman or supreme principle; and that this liberating knowledge comes about through a combination of masculine and feminine.

These two ideas could be interpreted as inconsistent with each other, as the first points to monism, the second to dualism of the Sāṃkhya variety. Without forcing the interpretation too far, one could suggest that the *haṃsa* mantra incorporates dualism within an overarching monism, in a manner common in Śaivite Tantra. This is supported by comparison with *Rig Veda* 10.90, which describes the creation of the universe through the sacrifice and dismemberment of a giant man who contains everything within himself. As we have seen, verse 5 describes this process of creation as involving a male being (*puruṣa*) giving birth to a female being (*virāj*), who then gives birth to the male being again. There is a similar pattern in *Bṛhadāraṇyaka Up*. 1.4.3, where the world consists of a single being called both "ātman" and "puruṣa," until this being splits itself into male and female halves, which then copulate to produce the various creatures. The first utterance of this primal being is, "so'ham asmi."

In this context, it is highly significant that the two syllables that correspond to Śiva and Śakti, namely "ha" and "sa," are created through the (literal!) dismemberment of the word *haṃsa* that represents Brahman. The chiasmus of the *haṃsa* mantra performatively demonstrates the splitting and recombination of this single word, thus mirroring the manner in which the entire universe emerged through the sacrificial redistribution of a single, divine substance.

As my goal is not merely to exegete a particular tradition, but also to point to more general phenomena in the history of language and religion, I should like to note how closely the mythology that unites these formulas is to that described by Claude Lévi-Strauss in connection with the Oedipus story (Lévi-Strauss 1963). The primary tension in the Greek myth – and perhaps in myth in general – stems from the apparent contradiction between autochthony and sexual reproduction, or "birth from one" versus "birth from two." In the Oedipus myth, this tension is expressed through the protagonist's crimes of parricide, which denies sexual reproduction, and incest, which returns us to autochthony. This erasure of normal sexual reproduction, however, produces an instability that resolves itself tragically. Although we observe empirically that humans are produced through relations between the sexes, there is a logical parsimony in the idea of auto-generation, an idea found in numerous myths from the creation *ex nihilo* of Genesis 1 (and, arguably, the creation of Eve from Adam in Genesis 2) to *Bṛhadāraṇyaka Up.* 1.4. The *haṃsa* mantra encapsulates a long tradition of containing dualism (sexual reproduction) within monism (autochthony).

One last point regarding the intertextuality of the *haṃsa* mantra: the common supposition that the Tantras represent a completely different dispensation from the Vedas should be qualified by our recognition of the convergences between these traditions. It is clear that, at least in the case of such formulas as the *haṃsa* mantra, the Tantras deliberately reworked the language of the Vedas, while remaining close to those texts in both form and content. The fact that the Vedas were oral compositions that were transmitted orally and learned by heart would have encouraged such poetic reworkings. A helpful metaphor for a modern, bookish audience is a library where printed copies of the Vedas, Upaniṣads, and Tantras sit on contiguous shelves. The gap of more than a thousand years between the *Rig* and *Atharva Veda*s, on the one hand, and our first evidence of the *haṃsa* mantra, on the other, is meaningless in this cultural context.

3 Iconicity

Iconicity is the effort to model language on reality through imitation of the latter. Found not only in onomatopoeia or sound symbolism, iconicity extends also to syntactic and grammatical structures that diagram the process of communication itself. The use of inverted word order in the case of actual dialogical exchanges, such as question-and-answer or call-and-response, is a case in point. Some Hindu mantras, such as the *haṃsa* mantra (haṃsaḥ so'ham), deliberately employ inversion in order to diagram the exchange between male and female, and between the other world and this one.

An icon, according to the semiotic typology of Charles Sanders Peirce which has now become widely accepted, is a type of sign that depends upon a resemblance between sign (representamen) and referent (object) (see Yelle 2016). The iconicity of an iconic sign can be based on any resemblance to its referent, any shared quality whatsoever. In the case of the *haṃsa* mantra, this is supposed to represent the in- and out-breaths. The claim is that one is always already saying this mantra while breathing, 21,600 times in the course of a day. The *haṃsa* mantra is ostensibly natural and spontaneous, the "unchanted" (*ajapā*) or "unstruck" (*anāhata*) mantra (Padoux 1990: 141). "Ha" and "sa" are asserted to be onomatopoeias, or "sound symbolism" as contemporary linguistic theory labels such things (Hinton, Nichols, and Ohala 1994). This claim carries some plausibility, especially in the case of an aspiration such as "ha."

Scientifically speaking, the role of iconic or sound symbolic words in language is very limited. However, it is interesting that many traditions, and not only Hinduism, often identify ritual language as iconic in this way. The view that one's own language (Sanskrit, Hebrew, English) somehow represents the world better (perfectly?) is a tempting bit of cultural chauvinism. The Tantras take this much further. Chiastic patterns are not unique to the *haṃsa* mantra. As I demonstrated in an earlier work, the Tantric practice of "enveloping" (*saṃpuṭa*) or surrounding the central part of a mantra with different *bīja*s, or even the entire Sanskrit syllabary, arranged in forward and reverse order, extends an earlier practice of appending the *praṇava* at the beginning and end of a mantra (Yelle 2003: 23–47). Enveloping converts the sequence of vocables in a mantra into imitative diagrams of various processes of creation, such as the cosmogony and sexual reproduction, as well as breath, as we have seen in the case of the *haṃsa* mantra. All of these processes are represented as in-and-out, or back-and-forth, and thus as chiasmi. Arguably, the syllable *oṃ* already diagrams the three stages of the cosmogony – namely, creation, preservation, and destruction (*sṛṣṭi-sthiti-saṃhāra*) – and the path of speech from the back of the throat to the front of the lips. Using the entire alphabet, as is done in some cases, makes this diagram more explicit.

Despite the indigenous claim that the *haṃsa* mantra is natural, spontaneous, and onomatopoetic, the real mode of resemblance between such mantras and the world is based on what linguists call "sequential iconicity": an analogy in structure, rather than a direct resemblance in quality. In Peircean terms this is called a "diagram" or "diagrammatic icon." A good example of such an icon is a map, where the resemblance to its referent (e.g., a city) is not in terms of size (small vs. large), or material (paper vs. concrete, dirt, metal, etc.), or even number of dimensions (two vs. three or four), but rather in terms of relative proportions and the arrangement of parts.

Another helpful analogy in the case of the *haṃsa* mantra is a mirror, which shows the same image, only inverted. The *haṃsa* mantra is actually an icon of itself, in the sense that it consists (supposedly) of the same sounds repeated twice, the second time in reverse order. The recursiveness of the formula expresses the relation of identity between Brahman and Ātman. Although monadological, this identity is expressed dialogically, through chiasmus or inversion. Such chiastic formulas are used not infrequently in real-world events of dialogical communication (Yelle 2013b: 48–49). In many Indo-European languages, a question may be formed by inverting the order of subject and verb ("Do you know her?"), which is then put back in normal order in the answer ("I do [not] know her."). Similarly, in the case of the *haṃsa* mantra, inversion expresses a kind of back-and-forth between God and the world, or the individual self. The overall message is panentheism, or radical monism.

It is interesting to compare this theology with that expressed in a chiasmus in the Hebrew Bible. In Exodus 3:14, Moses asks God his real name, and receives the following answer: *ehyeh asher ehyeh*. This is normally translated "I am who I am" or "I am that I am." On its face, this statement appears to refuse to answer the question, to engage in real dialogue. The response itself (if we can call it that) is a tautology, which may imply that God is incomparable – except to himself – and unnameable. We know that there were indeed other names given to God in the Bible, but later Jewish tradition prohibited the pronunciation of God's four-letter name. This prohibition appears to have been connected with that announced already in the Pentateuch against idolatry. God can neither be represented by an image, nor (adequately) named. From a theological perspective, this complex of ideas expresses a radical monotheism. Unlike with the *haṃsa* mantra, there is no hint of dualism or of the identity of human beings with the divinity.

Like similar chiastic formulas in Tantric mantras, especially when deployed in ritual praxis, the *haṃsa* mantra may also be what Michael Silverstein has called an "indexical icon," as through its structural resemblance to various modes of creative action it also points to (indexes) these modes and (virtually speaking) brings these about:

> Dynamic figuration in ritual, then, depends upon a tight metricality within the "literal" or denotational text to effect its goal or end, to bring about something in the field of socially deployed symbols.[…] The literal form of ritual text is always such an iconic index – a picture made real in the here-and-now – of that which it accomplishes, patently or transparently mapping the diagrammatic figuration of its denotational language in what we might appreciate as its "literal" interpretation into its interactional import, or effect. (Silverstein 2004: 627)

Silverstein exemplifies this concept through the Roman Catholic Eucharist, by which the congregant is incorporated into the body of the Church through his or her own incorporation of Christ's body, in the form of the Eucharistic wafer. As Silverstein notes, this double incorporation is explicitly chiastic, and mirrors the crucifix, which is "dynamically figurated by reciprocal action, a back-and-forth whereby a small ingestion figurating incorporation is tantamount to (i.e., results in) a large counterdirectional incorporation into a mystical corporate union or fellowship" (Silverstein 2004: 627). It is no accident that this ritual is called "Holy Communion," as it represents a moment of profound communication, both among the members of the congregation and between the individual congregant and the deity.

Despite the vast cultural differences between Catholic Christianity and Hinduism, we observe here a rather precise convergence between the Eucharist and the *haṃsa* mantra in their use of chiastic forms to describe a moment of (figurative) incorporation of the deity into the believer, and vice-versa.[4]

4 Joint speech

According to the standard model, communication consists of the transmission of a single, discrete message from one speaker (addresser) to at least one listener (addressee) (see, e.g., Saussure 1966: 11). This standard model is monadological, in the sense that it regards a speech act as the production of a single speaker that is ideally also univocal, i.e., clear in both expression and content (meaning). The problem is that the standard model is inadequate as an account of certain forms of speech that do not conform to such presuppositions. The cognitive scientist Fred Cummins has investigated the neglected phenomenon of "joint speech," meaning the coordination of oral performance in groups:

> "Joint speaking" is an umbrella term I have coined to cover all occasions in which the same words are uttered by multiple people in unison. This includes many practices of collective prayer, the chants of both protest demonstrators and sports fans, the recitations of young school children, performances of choral speech, and the swearing of collective oaths in secular contexts. (Cummins 2014a)

According to Cummins, joint speech exhibits distinctive characteristics, including "phonetic distortions,[...] prosodic stylizations, and [...] recurring patterns" (Cummins 2014b):

4 See Pelkey (2018) further regarding the semiotics of chiasmus.

> [J]oint speech [is] frequently, almost inevitably, characterized by repetition: the same phrase or short verse is repeated tens, or even hundreds of times over.[...] Repetition is undergirded by physical actions such as fist pumping, bead twiddling, or arm waving. While bead manipulation is relatively private, the more macroscopic actions further serve to facilitate synchronization among participants. Repetition also serves to accentuate and exaggerate the rhythmic properties of utterances, while repetition of a short phrase can also induce a change in perception from speech to song. In repeated spoken chants, the form of speech that arises thus blends seamlessly into the musical domain, establishing a continuity between speech and music. (Cummins 2014a)

The phenomenon of joint speech, as described by Cummins, converges with that of work songs or *Arbeitslieder* described by earlier scholars such as Karl Bücher (1909) and, more recently, Ted Gioia (2006; see also Boas 1955: 303, 314–17). For purposes of coordinating their movements, workers often keep time through singing. Common examples of such coordination include marching, rowing, and working on chain gangs.

Cummins (2016) mentions Catholic repetitions of the Hail Mary and Hindu Vedic chants as examples of joint speech. Indeed, many instances of Hindu chanting involve groups rather than individuals. A documentary recording a modern reconstruction of a Vedic ritual, *Agni: Altar of Fire* (1976, Robert Gardner and Frits Staal) appears to confirm Cummins's identification of Vedic chant as joint speech. During certain moments in the film, an older Brahmin moves a younger Brahmin's head rhythmically back and forth while they coordinate their chanting. Presumably, this serves as a kind of visceral metronome or even bodily aide-mémoire of the proper chant.

There is something else that such forms of language have in common. Together with Catholic repetitions of the Ave Maria, the Pater Noster, etc., Vedic *svādhyāya* and Tantric *mantrajapa* were condemned by many British Protestants as "vain repetitions" (Yelle 2013a: 103–35; Yelle 2013b: 113–36). These polemics originated in Calvinist tradition and were carried to India during the colonial period, where they were deployed against indigenous South Asian practices. The Protestant critique of vain repetitions in prayer reflected a linguistic ideology that privileged sense over sound and that condemned certain forms of language as rhetoric, magic, and idolatry. This critique was also associated with the ascendance of print culture over earlier forms of oral praxis.

While writing about these Reformation- and colonial-era developments, I was unaware of Cummins's account of joint speech, which suggests another perspective on the intercultural encounter between British Protestants and Hindus. Some of the Protestant polemics associate vain repetitions with gestures, just as we should expect if the practices condemned were forms of joint speech. The English Puritan theologian Richard Baxter, for example, condemned Catholics for their "spells and mimical irrational *actions*. [...] Ignorant, rude, unseemly words, or unhandsome *gestures*[...] pray[ing] irrationally, incoherently, confusedly, with vain repetitions [...]" (Baxter 1673: 179; emphasis added). Already in 1630, Henry Lord condemned Indian Brahmins who "straine their bodies into certaine mimicall *gestures*. [...] They must never reade of the booke delivered to Bremaw [Brahman], but it must be by a kinde of singing, and quavering of the voice" (Lord 1630: 72–73; emphasis added). Stripped of their pejoratives, these sound rather like descriptions of joint speech, which, as Cummins states, incorporates gesture with oral performance.

What was so objectionable about these forms of ritual performance? As Cummins suggests, joint speech appears to violate certain expectations regarding speech as, ideally, the transmission of a clearly demarcated, and plainly enunciated, message from one speaker to one or more listeners:

> Joint speaking appears to be a rather bizarre activity if we view speech as a specialization of language, and language as the means by which we exchange encoded propositions. In joint speech, everybody is speaking, and nobody is listening. Utterances are repeated over and over, frequently with associated body movements, but it is unclear who, if anybody, is being addressed. (Cummins 2014b)

Cummins (2014a) characterizes our view of language as "Cartesian," as it is "fundamentally committed to an ontological split between mind and world," and between verbal and other types of action. He identifies this view as more appropriate to written than to spoken language, and he suggests that its rise may have been associated with that of print culture. All of this agrees with what I have argued previously regarding the Protestant critique of vain repetitions. Following Cummins's investigations, we should add that part of what seems to have incensed certain Protestants was the manner in which such performances violated the injunction to take individual responsibility for one's own speech, an injunction that valued the semantic over the performative aspects of language, and that idealized sincerity in communication (Keane 2002). This sometimes accorded with a monadological model of communication that was ill-equipped to acknowledge the value of joint speech. The contrast between joint speech and Protestant (or Cartesian?) sincerity parallels, to some extent, that described by Mark Porter (2017) as the distinction between "resonance" and "authenticity" in the liturgical context.

5 Conclusion

This chapter has outlined three different modes of linguistic performance observable in Hindu mantras: intertextuality, iconicity, and joint speech. Each of these modes exemplifies what we may call, without straining the sense of the term unduly, a different form of dialogicality. Each of these modes is also found in other cultures, and has been the subject of comparative investigation. A study of the manner in which such modes have been deployed in South Asian traditions, however, reveals as many differences from as similarities to the linguistic ideology and associated forms of language practice found in modern, European cultures. These differences describe contrasting theologies of language, in which a salient part of the contrast concerns the nature or even the possibility of dialogue between the human and the divine. Broadly speaking, some older modes of dialogue, such as iconicity and joint speech, have been marginalized in the contemporary West. Consequently, it appears imperative for scholars of South Asian traditions to approach their topic with an understanding of the comparative science of linguistics, not only to open up new readings of old texts, but also to challenge our inherited models of language, which in some cases reflect biases imported from earlier theological debates.

Acknowledgements: For advice and assistance on this article, I would like to thank Alberto Pelissero and Gianni Pelligrini of the University of Turin; Fred Cummins of University College, Dublin; and Tim Lubin of Washington & Lee University. An earlier version of this paper was presented at "The Dialogical Indian" conference held at Lancaster University in July 2017; I would like to thank the participants at this conference and especially the organizers, Brian Black and Ram-Prasad Chakravarthi, for their helpful comments. All errors of commission and omission are my own.

References

Baxter, Richard. 1673. *A Christian directory*. London.

Boas, Franz. 1955. *Primitive art*. New York: Dover.

Bücher, Karl. 1909. *Arbeit und Rhythmus*. Leipzig & Berlin: Teubner.

Cummins, Fred. 2014a. Voice, (inter-)subjectivity, and real time recurrent interaction. *Frontiers in psychology: Cognitive science*, 5.760. doi: 10.3389/fpsyg.2014.00760 http://pworldrworld.com/fred/?page_id=14 (accessed 6 July 2018).

Cummins, Fred. 2014b. The remarkable unremarkableness of joint speech. *Proceedings of the 10th International Seminar on Speech Production*, 73–77. Cologne. http://pworldrworld.com/fred/?page_id=14 (accessed 6 July 2018).

Cummins, Fred. 2016. On vain repetitions: The enactment of collective subjectivities through speaking in unison. Unpublished paper dated August 16, 2016. http://pworldrworld.com/fred/?page_id=14 (accessed 6 July 2018).

Gioia, Ted. 2006. *Work songs*. Durham & London: Duke University Press.

Griffith, Ralph T. H. (trans.). 1896. *Rig Veda*. Benares: E. J. Lazarus & Co.

Hinton, Leanne, Johanna Nichols, & John J. Ohala (eds.). 1994. *Sound symbolism*. Cambridge: Cambridge University Press.
Keane, Webb. 2002. Sincerity, "modernity," and the Protestants. *Cultural anthropology* 17. 65–92.
Lévi-Strauss, Claude. 1963. The structural study of myth. In Claire Jacobson & Brooke Grundfest Schoepf (trans.), *Structural anthropology*, 206–231. New York: Basic Books.
Lord, Henry. 1630. *A display of two forraigne sects in the East Indies*. London.
Nooten, Barend A. van & Gary B. Holland. 1994. *Rig Veda: A metrically restored text* (Harvard Oriental Series 50). Cambridge, MA: Harvard University Press.
Olivelle, Patrick. 1998. *The early Upaniṣads*. New York: Oxford University Press.
Padoux, André. 1990. *Vāc: The concept of the word in selected Hindu Tantras*. Translated by Jacques Gontier. Albany, NY: SUNY Press.
Padoux, André. 2011. Japa. In *Tantric mantras: Studies on mantraśāstra*, 24–53. New York: Routledge.
Pelkey, Jamin. 2018. *The semiotics of X: Chiasmus, cognition, and extreme body memory* (Bloomsbury Advances in Semiotics). London: Bloomsbury.
Porter, Mark. 2017. Sounding back and forth: Dimensions and directions of resonance in congregational musicking. *Journal of the American Academy of Religion* 85(2). 446–469.
Saussure, Ferdinand de. 1966. *Course in general linguistics*. Translated by Wade Baskin. New York: McGraw-Hill.
Silverstein, Michael. 2004. "Cultural" concepts and the language-culture nexus. *Current Anthropology* 45(5). 621–652.
Staal, Frits. 1989. Vedic mantras. In Harvey Alper (ed.), *Mantra*, 48–95. Albany: SUNY Press.
Yelle, Robert. 2003. *Explaining mantras: Ritual, rhetoric, and the dream of a natural language in Hindu Tantra*. New York & London: Routledge.
Yelle, Robert. 2013a. *The language of disenchantment: Protestant literalism and colonial discourse in British India*. New York: Oxford University Press.
Yelle, Robert. 2013b. *Semiotics of religion: Signs of the sacred in history*. London: Bloomsbury.
Yelle, Robert. 2016. The Peircean icon and the study of religion: A brief overview. *Material Religion* 12. 241–243.

Paul Copp

Writing Buddhist liturgies in Dunhuang: Hints of ritualist craft

1 Introduction

Manuscripts surviving from the eastern Silk Road site of Mogao, located near the city of Dunhuang in what is today China's Gansu Province, make possible, among many studies, close explorations of the ways Chinese Buddhists of the 9th and 10th centuries CE and earlier constructed ritual programs.[1] Focusing on rituals for the chanting of Buddhist scriptures and spells, this study attempts to answer the following question: What can the structures and contents of Chinese manuscript liturgies for such rites suggest about the nature of the ritual cultures in which they were produced? The study examines three features of the liturgies: the natures of the frames by which texts were made the focuses of recitation rites, the borrowings and adaptations of existing materials of which those frames were made, and the understandings of the nature of scriptural language implicit in these practices.

Chanting has always been at the center of Buddhist practice in China (as elsewhere). Taken in the abstract, we might think of the practice as simply one version of a basic procedure of Buddhist ritual practice wherein the "body" of the Buddha is manifested in some form, whether textual, visual, or otherwise. The great blessings, or "merit," attendant on such manifestations, according to Buddhist doctrine, are then acknowledged and directed toward chosen recipients, whether those performing the ritual themselves or, more usually, their sick or deceased family members, the state, or "all beings." Chinese manuscript evidence from Dunhuang suggests that, in the case of scriptural texts, they were rarely if ever simply chanted by themselves without the kind of framing preparations noted in this study. Nor, again based on this evidence, do the canonical liturgies – whether in the form of incantation scriptures or the ritual programs associated with the eminent monks of the great monasteries – appear to have been followed strictly. Few if any of these texts appear among the manuscripts in forms suggesting they were used in ritual practice exactly as they are found

1 For an introduction to Dunhuang and the manuscripts found there, see Hansen (2012: 167–198), and Rong (2013: 51–136).

Paul Copp, University of Chicago

https://doi.org/10.1515/9781614514329-004

in the later printed canonical collections. Instead, new liturgical frames were created, usually following a basic structure: invocation and invitation, recitation of empowering prayers or spells, main event (recitation of a scripture or long *dhāraṇī*), and then a closing act of some kind, often further spells and/or the announcement of merit gained and directed.

Perhaps because they were not associated with famous priests or high monastic lineages – and likely because of their sometimes idiosyncratic natures – the manuscript versions of this basic practice examined here were only very rarely included in the printed canonical collections that have made up the main textual sources for Chinese Buddhism of this period, though evidence dating from the 11th through 14th centuries from the ancient Tangut "Black City" of Khara-Khoto (Ch. *Heicheng* 黑城 or *Heishuicheng* 黑水城), located in what is now western Inner Mongolia, makes clear that certain of the liturgical forms found on the manuscripts were indeed later transmitted in individual printed forms (Institut vostokovedeni͡ia 1996). This fact, along with a range of other evidence, both excavated and transmitted, strongly suggests that the Buddhist cultures that produced these ritual forms made up significant parts of the history of Buddhist practice in this period. Yet until the Dunhuang manuscripts were discovered at the turn of the 20th century, this was to a great extent a lost history, glimpsed mainly in tale literature and in the sometimes-disapproving comments of monastic censors. New studies of these materials, and of others found in Central Asia and China – and, more and more, of those in newly available Japanese temple collections – reveal a richer Buddhist (and Daoist, Manichaean, Christian, and "popular") religious history in the 9th and 10th centuries, and indeed through to the 13th century, than we had known (Mollier 2008; Copp 2011; Lieu 1998; Riboud 2015).

Within the region now encompassed by the People's Republic of China, the 9th and 10th centuries CE began in the final calamitous period of the Tang empire (618–907), and stretched through the decades of contending polities that began with the collapse of the Tang – principally, the Khitan-ruled Liao (907–1125) and the mainly Chinese-ruled "Five Dynasties" and "Ten Kingdoms" – and ended with the early reunifying decades of the Song state (960–1279). In this age, Dunhuang, given its geographical location far to the northwest, beyond or at the distant margin of the Tang and Song states, was in many ways remote from these wider political travails. Rather than the fall of the Tang and rise of the Song, the age there saw the end of a period of Tibetan rule (787–848), in which the Dunhuang region was spared the anti-Buddhist ravages of the Huichang suppression of 842–846, which in the lands to its east dealt sometimes fatal blows to a range of Buddhist traditions and institutions, and brought the return of Chinese control in the progressively independent rules of the Zhang clan (848–914) and then the

Cao clan (914–1036) (Taenzer 2012; Rong 2013: 38–46). It was during this final local reign that the inner branch cave filled with manuscripts, prints, paintings, and other objects – the source of the Dunhuang trove – was sealed, at some point shortly after the year 1000, to be discovered and re-opened 900 years later in a very different world.

The 9th and 10th centuries also saw the beginnings of the transition from manuscript culture to print culture in China, a history in which Buddhist ritual composition played a central role, and for which it offers key evidence.[2] The Dunhuang materials, our best source of this evidence, contains both manuscripts (the vast majority of the collection) and a small but significant number of block-printed texts or xylographs, including, famously, the scroll edition of the *Diamond Sutra*, a text central to the analyses of this essay, that has come to be known as the "world's earliest dated printed book" (Wood and Barnard 2010). Importantly, as well, one printed edition of the *Diamond* from Sichuan, a center of the nascent printing technology to the south of Dunhuang, appears to have influenced at least the local course of Buddhist manuscript culture at Dunhuang, providing a standard, or "true," edition within the welter of manuscript variety.[3] Among the texts in both formats are the short liturgical works that are the subject of this study: handwritten scrolls and booklets, and stand-alone printed sheets prescribing relatively short rites for the enactment of cultic texts centering on icons (as well as manuscripts that, as we will see, stored the components of such rites for the construction of new liturgies).

Buddhist ritual practice, at all levels, from that of the grand liturgies of the ultra-elite priests of the capitals (some of which, as noted, entered the transmitted tradition of the imperially printed canons), to the smaller and relatively ephemeral devotional rites preserved on manuscripts and xylographs at sites like Dunhuang, in part centered on the construction of new frames for popular cultic figures (such as bodhisattvas or protective deities) or texts (usually incantations and narrative scriptures). These new frames enabled new forms of worship, healing, protection, and/or spiritual transformation. To take one example, new ritual programs were written to fit an existing incantation into an originally unrelated ritual system, or to integrate it into new styles of ritual enactment, such as mental eidetic contemplation (as opposed to visual contemplative regard), a phenomena that, as Koichi Shinohara has recently noted, was perhaps especially

2 On the place of Buddhist (and Daoist) practices in the rise of printing in China see, for example, Barrett (2012).

3 This was the famous edition made of the blocks held by a certain Guo 過 clan, numerous copies of which were made in the Dunhuang region in the early 10th century. See, for example, the discussion in Teiser (1994: 97–99).

central to the growth of esoteric Buddhism, not only in Buddhist China but in India before it (Shinohara 2014). To take another example, new programs were put together in order to tap, and make more widely available, the cultural potencies of a widely revered spell or scripture.

This essay focuses on these latter practices. It explores two aspects of the making of ritual programs: the creation of new ritual frames and the adaptation of existing texts, and parts of texts, in this process. The Dunhuang ritual xylographs and manuscripts allow us to examine these latter practices at various stages of development. This is especially true of the manuscripts. The xylograph liturgies we have were, by nature, finished products; whatever processes led to their composition are lost. Many of the manuscripts, in contrast, allow us to examine the compositions of rites in detail, and offer insights into how those who composed them – for the purposes of this study simply called "ritualists" – understood the natures of the texts they adapted and the language of those texts, as well as the ways they could be reframed, and to an extent remade, according to local needs.

The printed iconic liturgies were single-sheet devotional programs, apparently distributed by monasteries and the printers they either controlled or patronized. Some were quite simple: for example, narrow sheets printed with an image of the Bodhisattva Guanyin, his name, and the single sentence, "Make a thousand vocal offerings every morning with a pure mind" – meaning, chant the name of the bodhisattva one thousand times every morning while contemplating the image on the xylograph.[4] Others are more elaborate and larger sheets in two visual zones. The upper zones contain an icon of a buddha, bodhisattva, or protective deity, while the lower have texts prescribing a somewhat more complex ritual program centering on the icon, typically including a spell and descriptions of the powers of the rite.[5]

The rituals prescribed in these xylographed sheets, naturally, did not vary over their many instances – a well-known feature of texts in print culture. What was carved on the block, assuming skilled execution of the print, was repeated perfectly in every impression made of it. Further, we have no evidence, at least in this material, that those who received and (presumably) enacted these rites

4 See, for example, Stein Painting 240, available in the digital database of the International Dunhuang project (http://idp.bl.uk/), under the search value "1919,0101,0.240". On printed texts at Dunhuang, see Tsiang (2010). Note that in the materials preserved at Dunhuang, as far as I am aware, Guanyin is always a male figure. On his transformation into a female figure, see Yü (2001).

5 See, for example, Stein Painting 233 (Ch.00150.b), a printed sheet providing an icon and chanting rite, called the "Simplified Rite for the Chanting of the Mantra of Holy Bodhisattva Guanyin." For an image of the xylograph, search the digital database of the International Dunhuang Project (http://idp.bl.uk/) under the search value "1919,0101,0.233".

improvised their own versions based on the sheets. None of them contain handwritten notes, reading marks, or changes of the kind common on manuscripts. Though as always we must be careful about arguments from silence, or from limited evidence, the xylographs – from their carving on the blocks to what we can see of their reception – suggest a local top-down, or center-out, style of ritual practice in which all devotees, at least in theory, practiced in precisely the same ways, following the programs prescribed by the temples that had the sheets printed and distributed.[6]

The composers of both the printed and manuscript liturgies discovered at Dunhuang, however, were alike in that they treated the received textual and ritual traditions as raw material to be re-framed, altered, and otherwise reworked according to their own styles and needs. The greater variety evidenced in the manuscript liturgies, again, allows us to see more of the processes of adaptation and improvisation that lay behind finished products such as the xylographs. Doing so gives the sense of a much more open, and at least relatively centerless, style of Buddhist ritual practice and liturgical composition, in which ritualists saw themselves as having considerable freedom in terms of what they could borrow, adapt and juxtapose.[7]

I will examine two versions of the basic liturgical structure for the framing of cultic texts in Chinese Buddhist ritual. The first I will call "internal" and the second "external." The key differences between them are the sources of the paratexts that make up the frames and the relations of those paratexts with the main text that is framed. By "paratexts," I mean primarily those texts that play roles ancillary to the main textual event, whether spell or scripture (though in principle I also mean broadly anything in the physical manuscript or xylograph that frames and shapes the presentation and reception of the main text, including images, reader's marks, and the visual layout and physical format of the object). In the first liturgical style, described here in cases of chanting spells drawn from scriptures, specifically chanting programs for the *Dabei zhou*, the *Incantation of Great Compassion*, central elements of the paratexts were internal in the sense that they were drawn from within the main text itself, and in fact served to remake the scripture they were drawn from in more briefly – and perhaps more focused – chantable form. The paratextual frames of the second style are seen here in cases of chanting scriptures as wholes. Though these frames came by

6 The evidence for the spread of such sheets is as yet thin, but we can point to an example of an incantation amulet printed in Chengdu that was found in a tomb in the Chang'an (modern Xi'an) area. See Tsiang (2010), and Copp (2014: 59–140).

7 For a treatment of another body of evidence suggestive of this mode of ritual improvisation, see Copp (2011: 193–226).

tradition and convention to have close practical relations with the central cultic text, they were wholly adventitious to it in the sense that they had no inherent relation to its content and did not serve to rework its structure. They were drawn entirely from external sources, and the cultic texts they framed remained more or less whole (scribal errors or omissions aside). For examples of this style I take, briefly, a liturgy for the recitation of the *Scripture of the Incantation of Great Compassion* as a whole, and in somewhat more detail a program for the chanting of the *Diamond Sutra*, one of the most famous works of Mahāyāna Buddhist philosophy in the Chinese scriptural canon and one of the most storied cultic texts in Chinese Buddhist legend and practice.

2 Internal frames: Liturgies for the *Incantation of Great Compassion*

We begin by examining the texts that frame the *Incantation of Great Compassion* in certain of its liturgies. As a case study, I take the version included on a scroll, 259 centimeters in length, held today in the British Museum, where it is known as "Stein [hereafter "S."] 2566." The manuscript also contains a copy of a liturgy for the chanting of the "extended" version of the *Foding zunsheng zhou* 佛頂尊勝呪, the *Incantation of the Glory of the Buddha's Crown* that, like the *Great Compassion* liturgy, draws from the content of this spell's source text (Copp 2014: 165–6). A colophon at the end of the scroll announces that the texts had been copied in the Guanyin inner chapel of the Sanjie Monastery (*Sanjie si* 三界寺) near Dunhuang by the monk Huiluan 惠鑾 (d.u.). Interestingly for our purposes, he refers to both liturgies simply as "*dhāraṇīs*" – the name for a genre of Buddhist incantation that is discussed further below – suggesting, perhaps, that their liturgical settings had come to be seen, at least in certain contexts, as to an extent built-in to the incantations themselves.[8]

The *Great Compassion* liturgy begins with an interlinear note – itself adapted from the scripture – telling the devotee that before he chants the spell and its accompanying invocation, he should prepare himself by contemplating and vocalizing the name of the Buddha Amitabha three times with a focused mind. The text notes that "the Buddha Amitabha is the root teacher of Guanyin," the bodhisattva instantiated in the spell. Then follows the invocation, incantatory prayers, and assertions of power drawn from the scripture:

8 I have consulted the transcription of the colophon found in Shi (2000: 78a–b).

[invocation:]

We beseech Guanzizai of the Moon Wheel,
His vast perfect body of purple gold,
His thousand arms always outstretched into this world,
His thousand shining eyes ever illuminating all,
His twelve-hundred spells and gestures fulfilling the prayers of all beings,
His face peaceful with its three eyes and pervasive majesty,
Bearing on its brow Amitabha with his jeweled scepter.
Speaking holy spells and their mystic teachings,
He realizes in full the awakening of buddhas.
His intelligence utterly unimpeded, he saves humans and gods;
Among all bodhisattvas he alone is chief.
Catching even the faintest strains [of his incantation], one's karmic dust and sand is cleansed;
Chanting it, one completes the causes of buddhahood.
The power of the Great Compassionate One's vow is inconceivable.
Thus we now chant it in praise.

[incantatory prayers adapted from scriptural passages:]

Veneration to the Great Compassionate One, Guanshiyin!
May we swiftly comprehend all things!
Veneration to the Great Compassionate One, Guanshiyin!
May we soon attain the Eye of Wisdom!
Veneration to the Great Compassionate One, Guanshiyin!
May we swiftly save all beings!
Veneration to the Great Compassionate One, Guanshiyin!
May we soon attain Skill in Means!
Veneration to the Great Compassionate One, Guanshiyin!
May we swiftly board the Ship of Insight!
Veneration to the Great Compassionate One, Guanshiyin!
May we soon pass beyond the Ocean of Suffering!
Veneration to the Great Compassionate One, Guanshiyin!
May we swiftly attain the Way of Ethics and Meditation!
Veneration to the Great Compassionate One, Guanshiyin!
May we soon scale Nirvana Mountain!
Veneration to the Great Compassionate One, Guanshiyin!
May we swiftly gather in the Hut of the Unconditioned!
Veneration to the Great Compassionate One, Guanshiyin!
May we soon become one with the Body of the Dharma Nature!

[assertions of power adapted from scriptural passages:]

If we encounter the Mountain of Swords the Mountain of Swords will break!
If we encounter the Bath of Flames the Bath of Flames will vanish!
If we encounter the Hells the Hells will wither!
If we encounter Hungry Ghosts the Hungry Ghosts will be sated!

> If we encounter the evil hearts of Asuras [demons] they will of themselves be vanquished!
> If we encounter beasts they will of themselves attain the Great Wisdom![9]

This text, which was put together from various sources (note for example that the bodhisattva is named both Guanzizai and Guanshiyin, which elsewhere usually mark separate ritual/textual traditions), contains most of the features of invocations and the texts that extend them that are relevant to this investigation. It begins with the devotional invocation of the deity, focusing on his attributes, his golden body and thousand arms extended to save beings in the world, and especially the many spells associated with him. Next, in a passage drawn from one translation of the *Incantation*'s scripture, it moves to assertions of the miraculous powers of the chief of these spells, which those engaging in the rite will soon chant. Finally, it gives a set of prayers and ritual assertions – themselves very much like spells found in a range of cultures, including in the Daoist traditions of China – taken from the same translation of the scripture that contains the version of the spell to be chanted. In brief, "we worship the bodhisattva, may he grant us blessings," and, "after chanting his spell we will be so powerful that should we be reborn either in a hell or in the realms of hungry ghosts or animals, those conditions will shatter of themselves."

The incantation that follows these lines on the manuscript is a *dhāraṇī*, a genre of spell that in Chinese Buddhist contexts consisted of the transliterated syllables of an original Indic incantation, a text that, a few commonly occurring Sanskrit words aside, was incomprehensible to all but a small elite within the Chinese Buddhist community (Copp 2012). Dhāraṇīs were famed for their spiritual powers, which were said in a range of texts and contexts to be able to cure all physical and spiritual ailments and to speed one along the path to ultimate transformation as a Buddha. As such, they were among the most popular of all Buddhist texts in Tang and Song China, where they were worn as amulets, inscribed on stone to protect the living and the dead, and – most importantly for this essay – chanted in a range of ritual contexts, from grand ceremonies in monasteries to smaller rites engaged in alone or in small groups, the contexts evidenced by the scrolls and booklets from Dunhuang studied here. Their impenetrability as texts made them utterly malleable in terms of reception and use, and in fact in need of an accompanying discursive (and often material and behavioral) frame. To put it simply: without such frames of assertion and behavior, in

---

9 S. 2566. The translation is my own. I have followed the printed edition found in Takakusu and Watanabe, et al. 1924–1932 [Hereafter "*Taishō Collection*," or "*T*"], where it is number 2843; vol. 85: 1295b-1296a. Note that the editors of *T* mistakenly identify the source as S. 2560.

China the spells quite literally meant nothing; with them, as we see here, they could shatter hells.

The frame is closed with a final section, called "Transferring the Blessings of the *Dhāraṇī*," which reads, "May the blessings of this recitation/Pervade all sentient beings./May we and all beings/Accomplish together the Buddha Way" (S. 2566; quoted from *T* 2843; vol. 85: 1296b).

Thus, a version of the standard frame of Buddhist ritual is created. Spirits are invited to empower and protect a space for the enactment of the cultic object. Here, a single sovereign figure is invoked – the Bodhisattva Guanyin – but as we will see in other cases a number of lesser divinities are called upon instead. Next, devotion to the object and its powers to fulfill the desires of the participants is asserted. That object – here, the *dhāraṇī* incantation – is then brought forth within this new divine realm. Finally, the success of the enactment and its blessings are announced and those blessings are sent into the world to transform it.[10]

The second part of the Dunhuang liturgy for the *Incantation of Great Compassion*, the framing expressions of devotion and desire, is particularly revealing of the method by which new ritual programs were made. They are a quotation from a translation of the *Incantation* attributed to the 7th-century monk Bhagavaddharma. Examining the passage in its original context, we see that the composers of the new rite stayed true, in general terms, to the dictates of the scripture (Reis-Habito 1993: 97–117). In it the Bodhisattva teaches that all those who wish to practice his *Incantation* must make this set of ten petitionary or aspirational prayers and vows (*yuan*), all of which, as we saw, take the form "Veneration to the Great Compassionate One, Guanshiyin! May we [quickly accomplish X]."

> Should any monks or nuns, male or female donors, boys or girls, wish to chant and keep [this *dhāraṇī*], they should arouse the mind of compassion and kindness within them and make the following vows along with me.[11]

The Bodhisattva further instructs that, immediately following the recitation of the vows, those who would chant the *dhāraṇī* should next:

---

10 The disassembling of the ritual space is rarely described in such liturgies.

11 *Qianshou qianyan Guanshiyin pusa guangda yuanman wu'ai dabeixin tuoluoni jing* 千手千眼觀世音菩薩廣大圓滿無礙大悲心陀羅尼經, tr. Bhagavaddharma (d.u), *T* 1060; 20: 106c.

call out my name with full concentration and then wholeheartedly contemplate my root teacher Amitabha, the Thus-Come One. They can then properly chant this *dhāraṇī* incantation.[12]

The makers of the liturgy reproduced on S. 2566 appear to have treated this portion of the text's ritual instructions as a module that could be lifted from its scriptural context and, with the addition of a *qiqingwen* 啟請文, or ritual invocation, and an announcement of blessings as framing bookends, taken as a stand-alone ritual program. The liturgy provided a way to carry out the primary ritual action of the scripture – the chanting of the *Incantation of Great Compassion* – in the way the scripture prescribes it. The importance of this practice in Chinese Buddhist history is impossible to overstate. With the exception of the simple and ubiquitous recitation of the name of the Buddha Amitabha, it became probably the single most widely enacted practice in all of Chinese (or, indeed, East Asian) Buddhism. For this reason, the scholar Chün-fang Yü has characterized its source text, the translation attributed to Bhagavaddharma, as "by far the most important of all the esoteric scriptures in China" (Yü 2001: 59). This version of the scripture did circulate in something approaching complete form in the period treated in this essay (at least six manuscripts found at Dunhuang contain all or parts of it),[13] but more importantly for this essay the abbreviated liturgical passage centered in S. 2566 had life of its own as a ritual module in a geographic region stretching from Dunhuang, through the Chinese cultural heartland, to Japan. It is featured, for example, in a ritual manual for the chanting of the incantation attributed to the great Song Dynasty Tiantai priest Zhili 知禮 (960–1028)[14] and in a late Japanese printed edition, dated 1801, of another manual for the chanting of the spell, attributed to the Tang priest Amoghavajra (Bukong 不空, 705–774) but otherwise unattested, that is held in the Hasedera Temple 長谷寺 in Kamakura, Japan.[15]

12 *Qianshou qianyan Guanshiyin pusa guangda yuanman wu'ai dabeixin tuoluoni jing*, 107a.

13 Stein numbers 1210, 1405, 4512, 4543, 5460, and Pelliot chinois 3912.

14 *Qianshouyan dabei xinzhou xingfa* 千手眼大悲心呪行法, T 1950; 46: 975c-976a. See also Yü (2001: 69).

15 This text is also contained in the *Taishō Collection. Qianshou qianyan Guanshiyin pusa dabei xin tuoluoni* 千手千眼觀世音菩薩大悲心陀羅尼, *T* 1064; 20: 115c.

3 External frames: Liturgies for the *Diamond Sutra*

Frames for the chanting of scriptures in their entireties appear to have been much simpler. When the *Scripture for the Incantation of Great Compassion* in something like complete form is found in liturgical settings on Dunhuang manuscripts, for example on the booklet known as S. 5460, it is set up by a simple invocatory *qiqingwen*-like prayer, called here a *fayuanwen* 發願文. The manuscript is no longer complete (and I have not yet been able to find the rest of it in any of the Dunhuang collections), but it appears that it once held the entirety of the scripture. As it stands, following the brief opening prayer, it gives the title and the name of the translator of the Bhagavaddharma text, and then provides most of the opening section of the scripture, with a number of apparent scribal errors – miswritten characters and occasional line omissions – through the ten vows translated earlier and up to the line "If we encounter the Bath of Flames the Bath of Flames will vanish!" The prefaced *fayuanwen* goes as follows:

> We bow our heads to the Lords of the Triple World:
> Endless Buddhas of the ten directions.
> Now we make our great vow
> To chant this *Scripture of Great Compassion*.
> Above, the treasure of the four forms of kindness,[16]
> Below, salvation for those suffering the three dark paths.
> All who experience [the chanted scripture]
> Will make the vow to awaken.
> When this single karma-given body is exhausted,
> We will be born together in the Land of Ultimate Bliss.

Simply in terms of its content, this is an utterly conventional Buddhist ritual statement. What makes it important for a study of ritual framing and modular improvisation is that it is also found, with one significant difference, as the introduction to a liturgy for the chanting of the *Diamond Sutra* contained on the manuscript S. 1846. The difference, of course, is that at the key moment it reads "to chant this *Diamond Sutra*."[17] The prayer, at least in its basic structure, appears to have been part of the common store of texts that ritualists drew upon when

---

16 There are various versions of the four. One of the most common is the kindness of one's parents, that of all sentient beings, that of rulers, and that of Buddhism itself.
17 Another difference (as we will see later) is that in line 9, as it is translated here, the text reads not "karma-given body" (*baoshen* 報身) but "treasure body" (*baoshen* 寶身).

fashioning new ritual settings for the main cultic texts of the tradition. Turning to the setting for the *Diamond* on S. 1846, we find invocations and spells drawn from the common stock, and, most notably, a set of previously minor deities – the Eight Great Diamond Spirits (*Ba da jin'gang* 八大金剛) – who came to be closely associated with the scripture in its ritual enactments. Given their importance and unique historical connection with *Diamond* liturgies, I will focus on this last set of figures and texts, taking them as emblematic of the structural differences between "internal" and "external" frames.

Although they have only faint presence in the transmitted tradition of printed canons, the Eight Great Diamond Spirits were prominent in Buddhist practices of the Dunhuang region around the turn of the 10th century. They are paired with the scripture on a number of manuscripts – all but one of them liturgies – and are painted, as well as named, on at least three manuscripts.[18] Zhai Fengda 翟奉達 (fl. 902–966), a locally prominent official and lay Buddhist practitioner who was a productive patron of the religion at Dunhuang – copying numerous sutras and overseeing, in 925, the reconstruction of his family's ancestral Buddhist cave-shrine, known today as Cave 220 – attached a text to a copy of the *Diamond* he had made that is the sole non-liturgy among the manuscript sources for the eight figures. It makes clear the importance with which Dunhuang locals (or at least Zhai himself) viewed the connection between the Diamond Spirits and the scripture it is in their nature to protect.[19] The added text, which Zhai may have compiled and not merely copied, is the "Record of the Spiritual Efficacy and Blessings Gained from Chanting the *Diamond Sutra*" (*Chisong Jin'gangjing lingyan gongde ji* 持誦金剛經靈驗功德記), a collection of tales extolling the miraculous powers of the sutra. After the tales are two more texts concerning the potency of the scripture and the proper manner of its enactment: the "Hymn on the Blessings Bestowed by the *Diamond Sutra*, composed by the Kaiyuan Emperor" (*Kaiyuan huangdi zan Jin'gangjing gongde* 開元皇帝讚金剛經功德) (see Teiser 1994: 119), or verses attributed to the Tang Emperor Xuanzang (r. 712–756), and finally an untitled prescription for the chanting of the *Diamond* that features the Eight Great Diamond Spirits.

18 Pelliot chinois 4095, 4096 (which may be fragments of a single book), and 4098. S. 5669 contains a painting of the first of the eight.

19 P. 2094. The scripture and its prefatory text are on differently colored papers pasted together. For a microscopic analysis of these papers undertaken by Ryukoku University in collaboration with the Bibliothèque nationale de France, see http://www.afc.ryukoku.ac.jp/pelliot/htmls_MA/P2094MA.html (accessed 8 February 2015). On Zhai, see for example Teiser (1994: 102–121). On his management of the reconstruction of Cave 220, see Ning (2004: 9, 76–77), etc.

This final portion of the text begins, "Anyone who wants to chant the *Diamond Prajñā Pāramitā Sutra* must first invoke the names of the Eight Great Diamond Spirits, be of perfect sincerity in mind, and only then chant the sutra. These Eight Great Diamond Spirits will come to protect those who chant this sutra" (P. 2094; *T* 2743; 85: 159c). Following two mantras that are discussed below, the text then gives the standard list of the eight, along with their powers and principalities.

> First, summon the Green Diamond Spirit Who Dispels Disaster. He dispels all karmically-held disasters and eliminates all catastrophes. He is lord of the Great Sea.
>
> Second, summon the Diamond Spirit Who Removes Poisons. He dispels all the poisons and illnesses of beings. He is lord of dispelling poisons and disasters.
>
> Third, summon the Yellow Diamond Spirit of Wish-Fulfillment. He enables beings to attain their wishes. He is lord of the vessel overflowing with blessings.[20]
>
> Fourth, invite the White Diamond Spirit of Pure Water. He dispels all afflictions and sufferings of beings. He is the lord of all treasures.
>
> Fifth, invite the Red Diamond Spirit of the Voice. He lights up the luminosity of beings such that they have visions of the Buddha. He is lord of that which arouses the wind.
>
> Sixth, invite the Meditative Disaster-Expelling Diamond Spirit. He dispels the suffering of the Three Disasters and Eight Hardships. He is lord of lapis lazuli.
>
> Seventh, invite the Purple Worthy Diamond Spirit. He makes beings minds awaken in understanding and express the bodhi-mind. He is lord of the firm and stable storehouse.
>
> Eighth, Invite the Great Numinous Diamond Spirit. He makes all beings accomplish their wisdom teeth and be complete in the power of wisdom. He is lord of the dragon kings.

It is rare to have direct evidence that ritual prescriptions like this one were actually carried out in history. But, as we have seen, a number of the liturgies examined here feature the Eight Great Diamond Spirits in precisely the place that Zhai's text says they should be. S. 1846, which bears the *qiqingwen* found, in slightly different form, also within the *Incantation of Great Compassion* liturgy on S. 5460, is one of the most complete.[21] Its chanting program, echoing Zhai's own preface to the *Diamond*, begins with a legend of the scripture's history in China, here the "Preface to Great Master Fu's Verses on the *Diamond Sutra*" (*Liangchao Fu Dashi*

20 A highly tentative translation of *gangsa gonde* 堈灑功徳.

21 Another, slightly different, version of this liturgy is found on the manuscript *yun* 云 99, held in the national Library of China, in Beijing, and collected in volume 9 of Fang (1995), where it is number 73f.

song Jin'gangjing xu 梁朝傅大士頌金剛經序). This work was said to have been drawn from a semi-legendary commentary to the *Diamond Sutra* attributed to Fu *Dashi* 傅大士, (Fu Xi 傅翕, 497–569) – Great Master (or "Mahāsattva") Fu – a layman who, legend tells, was responsible for the conversion to Buddhism of the famous Emperor Wu of the Liang Dynasty (r. 502–549), one of the greatest patrons of the religion in Chinese history. The text, although it does not survive in any transmitted edition, clearly achieved a degree of popularity well beyond Dunhuang. Aside from S. 1846, portions of the text survive in Uighur translation on manuscripts from Turfan, and a Chinese version was listed by the Korean monk Gihwa 己和 (a.k.a. Hamheo Deuktong 涵虛得通, 1376–1433) as one of the five principal commentaries on the *Diamond* in his "Commentaries of Five Masters of the *Diamond Sutra*" (*Kŭmgang panya paramilgyŏng ogahae sŏrŭi* 金剛般若波羅蜜經五家解說誼).[22]

Immediately following this text in the program on S. 1846 is the injunction, quoted above, that those who would chant the *Diamond* must first invoke the Eight Great Diamond Spirits. Following this, before their eight names, are (as previously mentioned) two spells. The first is a mantra in 15 syllables called the "Mantra for the Purification of Spoken Karma" (*jing kouye zhenyan* 淨口業眞言), a spell intended to rid the chanter of the ill-effects of past misdeeds committed with words. The next is called the "Mantra of Offerings to the Bodhisattva Xukong [Ākāśagarbha]" (*Xukong pusa gongyang zhenyan* 虛空菩薩普供養眞言).[23] Next comes an especially interesting example of the kind of adaptation of classical sources common in these materials. After the statement "*yun he fan*" 云何梵 – which is difficult to interpret, but perhaps means: "One asks, 'How to chant it?'" – the liturgy contains lines on the "diamond-like" nature of the Buddha's true body, and thus of reality itself, that are clearly drawn from Dharmakṣema's (385–433) 5th-century Chinese translation of the *Mahāparinirvāṇa Sutra*. In their original context, the lines are the first in a series of questions asked of the Buddha by the Bodhisattva Mahākāśyapa.

> I ask, how did [the Buddha] attain his immortal state, his diamond[-like] indestructible [true body]? By what means did he attain the power of great solidity [i.e., perfect reality]?

---

22 On the Uighur text, see Hazai and Zieme (1971). On the Gihwa text, see the entry by Charles Muller in the online *Digital Dictionary of Buddhism* (accessed 8 February 2015). A lecture on the *Diamond* said to have been given by Fu at the Liang emperor's court is recounted in the Chan collection known as the "Blue Cliff Record," *Foguo Yuanwu chanshi biyan lu* 佛果圓悟禪師碧巖録 (*T* 2003; 48: 197a–b).

23 A version of a mantra found associated with Ākāśagarbha in a range of texts. See, for example the "Ākāśagarbha mantra" (*Xukongzang zhenyan* 虛空藏眞言) in the *Dari rulai jianyin* 大日如來劍印 ("Sword Seals of the Great Sun Tathāgata"), *T* 864a; 18: 197a.

> I ask, how can one completely reach the other shore [of liberation] by means of this sutra? Would the Buddha open the sublime [gate] and explain it for all beings? (S. 1846; *T* 2732; 85: 1b)[24]

On the manuscript, after this quotation, the nature of "the diamond" – here not only reality but also the text of which it is now an emblem – is asserted and further clarified, which leads to the prayer noted earlier, adapted it now seems from common stock:

> We bow our heads to the Lords of the Triple World:
> Endless Buddhas of the ten directions.
> Now we make our great vow
> To chant this *Diamond Sutra*.
> Above, the treasure of grace for our grave sins,
> Below, salvation for those suffering the three dark paths.
> All who experience [the chanted scripture]
> Will make the vow to awaken.
> When this single treasure body is exhausted,
> We will be born together in the Land of Ultimate Bliss.

By this paratextual language – legend, prescription, assertion, incantation, and prayer – all of which we might, again, characterize as external, or adventitious (in contrast to the internal, or intrinsic, language featured in liturgies of the *Incantation of Great Compassion*) the scripture at the heart of the rite was framed as a cultic object of great power.

The liturgy next has the ritualists seal the space in which the rite takes place. The invocation of the Diamond Spirit protectors of the action and its object is introduced with the simple title, "Invitation of the Eight Diamond Spirits" (without the descriptive "Great"). Then the eight are named and characterized in precisely the words seen earlier, though without the final assertion of the "lordship" of each figure. Added to them, without comment or introductory title, are invocations of four more figures[25]: "First, invite the Bodhisattva of the Diamond Lasso (*jin'gang juan* 金剛羂). Second invite the Bodhisattva of the Diamond Cord (*jin'gang suo* 金剛索). Third invite the Bodhisattva of Diamond

---

24 The lines are found both in Dharmakṣema's translation of the *Mahāparinirvāṇa Sutra* and in Huiyan's 慧嚴 (363–443) "southern" revision of it. The former at *T* 374; 12: 379c and the latter at *T* 375; 12: 619b. On Huiyan's revision, see Liebenthal (1955: 287n15).

25 Note that the version on *yun* 99 in Beijing does give a separate title here: "Invite the Four Bodhisattvas" (*fengqing si pusa* 奉請四菩薩).

Love (*jin'gang ai* 金剛愛). Fourth Invite the Bodhisattva of Diamond Speech (*jin'gang yu* 金剛語)."[26]

After this six-fold preface (as I count it here) comes finally the main event itself, the chanting of an edition of the *Diamond Sutra*. After giving its edition of the scripture, the liturgy then closes with two sets of texts. The first consists of three verses that appear to be unattested outside the two versions of this liturgy: one each for the "Three Natures" of reality described in "Consciousness-Only" Buddhist philosophy (imagined, dependent, and perfect). The second are three final spells that, as Neil D. Schmid has noted, in slightly different versions close out other *Diamond Sutra* liturgies, as well as Zhai Fengda's edition of the text (Schmid 2011: 370). The three spells, each shorter than the last, are named the mantras of "the Great Body" (*dashen* 大身), "Wish-Fulfillment" (*suixin* 隨心), and "the Heart of the Heart" (*xinzhongxin* 心中心).

4 Conclusion

In the scriptures of Buddhism and in its devotional rites, the words of the Buddha are asserted to be inviolable, sacred, supremely potent – the very essence of reality itself. In such ritual contexts, they are to be worshipped and worshipfully reproduced as perfectly as possible; they cannot be altered, edited, or otherwise treated as normal human speech. But, behind the curtain, as it were, in the practices of Buddhist ritualists, another view of these words becomes clear. In these practices, the speech of the Buddha was fully open to transformation, re-framing, and re-use; props employed to stage the Real and kept afterwards as the makings of new and different performances later. The practices, indeed, recall Evans-Pritchard's description of the contextual transformation in Nuer practice of the "sacred pole, associated with God, the spirits of their lineage, and also with its ghosts," back into a simple object on which to hang things (Evans-Pritchard 1956: 234).[27] Such a view of religious language, which is widely evidenced in Dunhuang Buddhist liturgical manuscripts, was

26 All but the first of these figures is well attested. The first, *jin'gang juan*, as far as I can determine appears only here, and might be a case where a two-syllable word, *juansuo* – "cord" or "lasso," often translating the Sanskrit *paśa* – common in names of deities in Buddhism (Amoghapaśa, Vajrapaśa, etc) has been split to create a second figure. Compare with the creation of three buddhas (Piluzhena 毘盧遮那, Luzhena 盧遮那, Zhena 遮那) out of the single Vairocana (Piluzhena).

27 I borrow the term "contextual transformation" in regards to this practice from Morton (2009: 269).

inherent to the work of the ritualists whose job it was to stage, and re-stage, the potent cultic objects of their tradition in ways appropriate to the needs of the moment. It is only when properly framed – with language, behavior, bodies, and objects arranged carefully in space – that words, spoken or inscribed, take on the kinds of heightened status they have in religious practice.

Beyond what they suggest about the nature and conventions of Buddhist ritualist practice in the China of the 9th and 10th centuries, the preliminary investigations of this study also shed light on the *history* of this practice, in Buddhist China and beyond. First, the manuscripts, as so often, appear to be evidence for an important layer of Chinese Buddhist history that was largely ignored, even suppressed, by the compilers of the canonically transmitted (that is, printed, often with imperial support) textual tradition. But with closer examination we can begin to see further details of this history. Although the practices explored here were often strongly shaped by the particular needs of their times and populations, we have seen that they were not entirely "local." In some cases, indeed, there appear to have been close connections within a (temporally as well as geographically) far-flung body of Buddhist manuscripts, stretching from Dunhuang to Japan, many of which constitute our earliest editions of Chinese Buddhist texts. Strikingly, these connections in certain cases appear to have been closer than were those linking the manuscript and the imperially printed editions, which have typically been taken as the standard and best editions of texts in Buddhist East Asia. Such evidence suggests that the "subterranean" history of ritual practice and textual transmission glimpsed in the Dunhuang liturgies was important indeed. In fact, though it is far beyond the scope of this study, comparison of its preliminary findings with those of Koichi Shinohara's recent book, *Spells, Images, and Mandalas: Tracing the Evolution of Esoteric Buddhist Rituals* (2014), which explores very similar cultures of ritual practice and composition in India in fine detail, suggests the possibility that the "local" culture of ritualist craft sketched here may in fact have stretched across Buddhist Asia.

Acknowledgments: This research was undertaken as part of the international Silk Road arts project, ' 丝绸之路艺术数据库基础研究 17LZUJBWZD001'.

References

Barrett, T. H. 2012. *From religious ideology to political expediency in early printing: An aspect of Buddho-daoist rivalry*. London: Minnow Press.

Copp, Paul. 2011. Manuscript culture as ritual culture in late medieval Dunhuang: Buddhist talisman-seals and their manuals. *Cahiers d'Extrême-Asie* 20. 193–226.
Copp, Paul. 2012. Anointing phrases and narrative power: A Tang Buddhist poetics of incantation. *History of Religions* 52(2). 142–172.
Copp, Paul. 2014. *The body incantatory: Spells and the ritual imagination in medieval Chinese Buddhism*. New York: Columbia University Press.
Evans-Pritchard, E. E. 1956. *Nuer religion*. Oxford: Clarendon.
Fang, Guangchang 方廣錩. 1995. *Zangwai Fojiao wenxian* 藏外佛教文獻 [Buddhist documents from outside the canons]. Beijing: Zongjiao wenhua.
Hansen, Valerie. 2012. *The Silk Road: A new history*. Oxford: Oxford University Press.
Hazai, György & Peter Zieme. 1971. *Fragmente der uigurischen version des Jin'gangjing mit den gāthās des Meister Fu*. Berlin: Akademie-Verlag.
Institut vostokovedenii͡a (Rossiĭskai͡a akademii͡a nauk), Sankt-Peterburgskoe otdelenie (eds.). 1996. *Eluosi kexueyuan dongfang yanjiusuo Sheng Bidebao fensuo cang Heishuicheng wenxian* 俄羅斯科學院東方研究所聖彼得堡分所藏黑水城文獻 [Documents from the city of Khara-khoto held at the Institute of Oriental Studies of the Russian Academy of Sciences (St. Petersburg branch)]. Shanghai: Shanghai guji.
Liebenthal, Walter. 1955. A biography of Chu Tao-sheng. *Monumenta Nipponica* 11(3). 284–316.
Lieu, Samuel N. C. 1998. *Manichaeism in Central Asia and China* (Nag Hammadi and Manichaean studies 27). Leiden: Brill.
Mollier, Christine. 2008. *Buddhism and Taoism face to face: Scriptural, ritual, and iconographic exchange in medieval China*. Honolulu: University of Hawaii Press.
Morton, Christopher. 2009. Fieldwork and the participant-photographer: E. E. Evans-Pritchard and the Nuer rite of *gorot. Visual Anthropology* 22(4). 252–274.
Ning, Qiang. 2004. *Art, religion, and politics in medieval China: The Dunhuang cave of the Zhai Family*. Honolulu: University of Hawaii Press.
Reis-Habito, Maria. 1993. *Die Dhāraṇī des grossen Erbarmens des Bodhisattva Avalokiteśvara mit tausend Händen und Augen: Übersetzung und Untersuchung ihrer textlichen Grundlage sowie Erforschung ihres Kultes in China*. Sankt Augustin: Steyler Verlag.
Riboud, Pénélope. 2015. Le christianisme syriaque à l époque Tang. In Pier Giorgio Borbonne & Pierre Marsone (eds.), *Le christianisme syriaque en Asie centrale et en Chine*, 41–62. Paris: Geuthner.
Rong, Xinjiang. 2013. *Eighteen lectures on Dunhuang*. Translated by Imre Galambos. Leiden: Brill.
Schmid, Neil D. 2011. Dunhuang and Central Asia (with an appendix on Dunhuang manuscript resources). In Charles D. Orzech, Henrik H. Sørensen & Richard K. Payne (eds.), *Esoteric Buddhism and the Tantras in East Asia*, 365–78. Leiden: Brill.
Shi, Pingting 施萍婷 (ed.). 2000. *Dunhuang yishu zongmu suoyin xinbian* 敦煌遺 書總目索引新編 [General index of Dunhuang texts, new edition]. Beijing: Zhonghua.
Shinohara, Koichi. 2014. *Spells, images, and mandalas: Tracing the evolution of esoteric buddhist rituals*. New York: Columbia University Press.
Taenzer, Gertraud. 2012. *The Dunhuang region during Tibetan rule (787–848): A study of the secular manuscripts discovered in the Mogao caves*. Wiesbaden: Harrassowitz.

Takakusu, Junjirō & Watanabe Kaigyoku, et al. (eds.). 1924–1932. *Taishō shinshū daizōkyō* 大正新修大藏經 [Taishō-era new edition of collected Buddhist scriptures], 100 vols. Tokyo: Taishō issaikyō kankōkai.

Teiser, Stephen F. 1994. *The Scripture on the Ten Kings and the making of purgatory in medieval China*. Honolulu: University of Hawaii Press.

Tsiang, Katherine. 2010. Buddhist printed images and texts of the eighth-tenth centuries: Typologies of replication and representation. In Matthew T. Kapstein & Sam Van Schaik (eds.), *Esoteric Buddhism at Dunhuang: Rites and teachings for this life and beyond*, 201–252. Leiden: Brill.

Wood, Frances & Mark Barnard. 2010. *The Diamond Sutra: The story of the world's earliest dated printed book*. London: British Library.

Yü, Chün-Fang. 2001. *Kuan-yin: The Chinese transformation of Avalokiteśvara*. New York: Columbia University Press.

Leslie Arnovick

The power of Pater Noster and Creed in Anglo-Saxon charms: De-institutionalization and subjectification

1 Introduction

Because Anglo-Saxons had faith in its efficacy, prayer was commonly used in many circumstances outside of religious services, especially in healing rituals like those prescribed in charms. This is especially true of the Pater Noster or Lord's Prayer, and the Creed, which is not exactly a prayer, but an assertion of belief. Ælfric of Eynsham (ca. 955–1010 CE) expects all believers to memorize, understand, and use the Lord's Prayer and Creed, and he requires priests to expound them for the people. Evidence from early medieval charm collections like the 9th-century *Leechbook* and 10th- or 11th-century *Lacnunga* indicate the success of the church's educational campaign:

> Gif wænnas eglian mæn æt þære heortan: gange mædenman to wylle þe rihte east yrne 7 ehlade ane cuppan fulle forð mid ðam streame, 7 singe þæron "Credan" 7 "Pater noster"; 7 geote þon(ne) on oþer fæt, 7 hlade eft oþre 7 singe eft "Credan" 7 "Pater noster", 7 do swa þ(æt) þu hæbbe þreo; do swa nygon dagas; sona hi(m) bið sel. (*Lacnunga* clxxvi)[1]
>
> [If "wens" (cysts) afflict a person at the heart: let a virgin go to a spring which runs directly east and draw up a cupful in the direction of the current, and sing thereon the Creed and the Our Father; and then pour it into another vessel, and again draw up a second (cupful) and sing again the Creed and the Our Father, and continue until you have three; do so for nine days; he will soon be better]. (Pettit 2001, 1: 121)

When we assess both the Pater Noster and the Creed in light of what Anglo-Saxons knew about them and how the utterances behave in extant charms, we come closer to reconstructing each text's force as an incantation (or spell) and the power it conveys. An explication of the two reveals a fundamental difference in the function of each within the charms. This essay contrasts the use of the Creed – particularly the Apostles' (or baptismal) Creed – with that of the Pater Noster to argue that the borrowing of the Creed from liturgy is essentially

1 I cite Pettit's (2001) edition and translation of the *Lacnunga* throughout.

Leslie Arnovick, University of British Columbia

https://doi.org/10.1515/9781614514329-005

different from the use of the Lord's Prayer. Besides its utterance in congregational worship, the Lord's Prayer was used primarily for personal prayer, the inherently subjective prayer of a private individual.[2] When we find the Pater Noster in charms, we need not classify it as a liturgical loan. Rather, both charms and liturgy are recipients of a biblical loan which preserves the essence of the Lord's gift. It may elicit liturgical echoes in charm performance, but the Lord's Prayer belongs to the people and by extension to the realm of the folk and the domain of charms.[3] The church tells us through sermon texts and penitential handbooks that the praying of the Pater Noster in charms proves in no way inconsistent with its commission by Jesus.

While also permitted in folk remedies, the use of the Creed outside sanctuary or baptistry, in contrast, represents systematic de-institutionalization of its liturgical context. The sacred force of the liturgical and sacramental celebration is lost in the transfer: only its resonance remains in charms. Yet that de-institutionalization is fore-grounded when we scrutinize its results in the charm incantations, for along with this de-institutionalization comes subjectification, an increase in the speaker's subjective state or attitude toward the proposition. Identifying as "I," the charm performer, patient, or anyone else uttering a charm incantation recites the Creed in order personally to direct its power for the purpose of healing or other restoration.[4]

This chapter begins by locating Anglo-Saxon charms within the purview of church teaching and then reconstructs the distinct oral-traditional contexts for Pater Noster and Creed charm incantations. By placing Lord's Prayer utterances side by side with those for the profession of faith, in the third part of this essay, we can identify institutional (i.e., sacramental) loss and concomitant pragmatic gain. Both the Lord's Prayer and the Apostles' Creed exhibit subjectification when used in the Germanic folk context of charm performance. A subtle but significant difference in the degree and nature of the subjectification belonging to each comes to light in the final analysis.

2 Church proscription and prescription

The Lord's Prayer and Creed play a significant role in the native English medical institution recorded in charm rites, whether or not sacred forms sanctify

2 *Oxford English Dictionary*, 3rd edn., s.v. *personal*.

3 I use the term *folk* in the sense of the compound noun *folklore*, i.e., the "traditional beliefs, legends, and customs, current among the common people" (*Oxford English Dictionary*, 3rd edn., s.v. *folklore*).

4 My discussion of Pater Noster charms represents a revision of sections of Arnovick (2006).

superstitious acts banned by the church. Both texts function as incantations (or parts of incantations) in oral-traditional charm performances, although only written records survive. Early medieval sermons and penitential handbooks speak to the persistence of pagan folk traditions throughout Europe well after the widespread adoption of Christianity. Missionaries and clergy like Eligius (ca. 588–660 CE), Bishop of Noyon-Tournai, order superstitious activities to cease:

> Before all things [...] I declare and testify unto you, that you should observe none of the impious customs of the pagans, neither sorcerers, nor diviners, nor soothsayers, nor enchanters; nor must you presume for any cause, or any sickness, to consult or inquire of them; for he who commits this sin immediately loses the sacrament of baptism. In like manner, pay no attention to auguries and sneezings; and when you are on a journey, do not mind the singing of certain little birds. Let none trust in, or presume to invoke, the names of demons. [...] Let no Christian place lights at the temples, or at stones, or at fountains, or at trees, [...] or at places where three ways meet, or presume to make vows. Let none presume to hang amulets on the neck of man or beast; even though they be made by the clergy, and called holy things, and contain the words of Scripture; for they are fraught, not with the remedy of Christ, but with the poison of the Devil. Let no one presume to make lustrations, nor to enchant herbs, nor to make flocks pass through a hollow tree, or an aperture in the earth; for by so doing he seems to consecrate them to the Devil. Let no woman presume to hang amber beads on her neck [...] to invoke Minerva, or the other ill-omened persons; but let her desire the grace of Christ to be present in every work, and confide with her whole heart in the power of His name. [...] Let no man have his fate or his fortune told, or his nativity, or what is commonly called his horoscope. [...] Moreover, as often as any sickness occurs, do not seek enchanters, nor diviners, nor sorcerers, nor soothsayers, or make devilish amulets at fountains, or trees, or cross-roads. (Maitland 1969 [1889]: 169–172; see also Grendon 1909: 143)

As for the Germanic Christians in England, the Anglo-Saxons still held to older ways, as Ælfric (ca. 955–c. 1010), priest and abbot, laments: "It shameth us to tell all the shameful sorceries,/ which ye foolish men practise through the devil's lore,/ whether in wiving, or in traveling,/ or in brewing, or if a man pray for anything,/ when they begin anything or anything is born to them" (Skeat 1881: 371). Quoting Augustine of Canterbury's 6th-century sermon against such "witchcraft," he concludes that a "person who behaves this way is not Christian, but "apostate" (*wiðer-saca*):

> Nu alyse ic me sylfne wið god and mid lufe eow forbeode
> þæt eower nan ne axie þurh ænigne wicce-cræft
> be ænigum ðinge oððe be ænigre untrumnysse
> ne galdras ne sece to gremigenne his scyppend
> forðan se ðe þys deð se forlysð his cristen-dom
> and bið þam hæðenum gelic þe hleotað be him sylfum
> ðæs deofles cræfte þe hi fordeð on ecnysse

> [Now I deliver myself as regards God, and with love forbid you,
> that any of you should enquire through any witchcraft
> concerning anything, or concerning any sickness,
> or seek enchanters to anger his Creator;
> for he that doeth this, he letteth go his Christianity,
> and is like the heathen who cast lots concerning themselves
> by means of the devil's art, which will destroy them for ever]. (Skeat 1881: 369–371)

It were better, St. Eligius stresses, that he "who is sick trust only in the mercy of God, and receive the sacrament of the body and blood of Christ with faith and devotion; and faithfully seek consecrated oil from the church, wherewith he may anoint his body in the name of Christ, and according to the apostle, the prayer of faith shall save the sick, and the Lord shall raise him up" (Maitland 1969 [1889]: 169–172; see also Grendon 1909: 143).

Christianity nevertheless failed to offer equivalent alternatives for divination and healing, and, as a result, pagan techniques became incorporated into local Christian practice (Klingshirn 1994: 219). Where it could, the church tried to accommodate folk practices that did not contradict Christian precepts. In recognition of the very human impulse toward such unorthodox treatments and cures, or perhaps in hopes of sanitizing practices it could not eradicate, the church proposed modifications if not alternatives to charm rites. The influential Penitential of Theodore (668–690, with later additions) cautions against the saying of spells or other magic words altogether. In cases like demon possession (*daemonium sustinenti*), the manual concedes, though, that the victim "may have [gem] stones and herbs [applied] without [the use of an] incantation" (Book 2, X.5; McNeill and Gamer 1990: 207). If speech was deemed absolutely essential, orthodox prayers could be substituted for pagan utterances.[5]

As the Penitential attributed to Archbishop Ecgbert (ca. 750) specifies, "truly it is not allowed for any Christian man [...] to gather herbs with any charm, except the Our Father and the Creed, or with some prayer that pertains to God" (Raith 1933: 30). Ælfric advises his flock similarly: "he who wishes to journey any whither, let him sing his Paternoster and Credo, if he know [them], and cry to his Lord, and cross himself and travel without care through God's protection, without the devil's sorceries" (Skeat 1881: 368–371).

Those who violate prohibitions on charms could only do penance for the sin. As Ælfric reminds the English: "unless he offer alms and much penance/to his Creator, he shall be lost eternally" (Skeat 1881; 368–371). Targeting the pagan

5 I use the term *orthodox* to mean, "Of, belonging to, or in accordance with the accepted theological or ecclesiastical doctrines of a particular religion, etc.; (also) designating practices or beliefs conforming with these" (*Oxford English Dictionary*, 3rd edn., s.v. *orthodox*).

supernaturalism of Germanic folklore in his Decretum (ca. 1008–12), Burchard of Worms counsels ready reparations, "Hast thou collected medicinal herbs with evil incantations, not with the Creed and the Lord's prayer, that is, with the singing of the "credo in Deum" and the paternoster? If thou hast done it otherwise thou shalt do penance for ten days on bread and water" (Book 19, "The Corrector," Chapter V, 65; McNeill and Gamer 1990: 39–40, 330–331). Stronger penalties were meted out for infractions regarded as more severe. Theodore's manual stipulates, for instance, that when "a woman performs diabolical incantations or divinations, she shall do penance for one year of the three forty-day periods, or forty days, according to the nature of the offence" (Penitential of Theodore, Book 1, XV, 4; McNeill and Gamer 1990: 198). Even the patient might be guilty:

> If anyone sings enchantments for infatuation or any sort of chantings except the holy symbol [i.e., the Creed] or the Lord's Prayer, he who sings and he to whom he sings shall do penance for three forty-day periods on bread and water. (St. Hubert Penitential; McNeill and Gamer 1990: 294)

Given that the charm habit was ingrained in social and linguistic tradition, the Pater Noster and Creed could safeguard those who participated in charm rites, especially because of their familiarity to the people. Laity knew well the Pater Noster and Creed, for both were the birthrights of baptism. Adult candidates for membership, such as Danes who were converting, received instruction on the mysteries of the Eucharist during the Lenten period preceding their Easter baptism. The words and the meaning of the prayers were imparted by the bishop, who would later test his pupils' memories. Most everyone else, baptized as infants, would be taught the Pater Noster and Creed by their god-parents. Confirmation presented a second opportunity for older children to be reminded of the prayers' form and significance.[6] For those who had difficulty understanding the Latin, Ælfric and Wulfstan (Bishop of London, Worcester, and Archbishop of York, d. 1023) recommend that each be learned and prayed in English. Variation in the extant versions of the Old English Lord's Prayer reveals pastoral emphasis on the words' meaning instead of fidelity to the Vulgate Latin based in Matthew 6:9–15 (Forbes 2013: 42). Ælfric provides this text of the Lord's Prayer at the end of his Catholic Homilies:

> Ðu ure Fæder, þe eart on heofenum,
> sy ðin nama gehalgod.
> Gecume þin rice.

6 The emergence of parochial culture out of minster culture sustained the church's ministry in both town and countryside. See further Blair (2006: 161–181) on clerical, monastic, and episcopal visits to laity both during and after the time of Bede.

Sy ðin willa swa swa on heofenum swa eac on eorðan.
Syle us to-dæg urne dæghwomlican hlaf,
and forgif us ure gyltas swa swa we forgyfað þam ðe wið us agyltað.
And ne læd þu na us on costnunge,
ac alys us fram yfele. Sy hit swa. (Thorpe 1971 [1844], II: 596)

[Thou our Father, who art in heaven, be thy name hallowed. Thy kingdom come. Be thy will as in heaven so also on earth. Give to us today our daily bread, and forgive us our sins as we forgive them that sin against us. And lead us not into temptation, but deliver us from evil. Be it so.] (Thorpe 1971 [1844], II: 597)

At least once a year, priests were obliged to preach on the meaning and significance of both prayers. Sermons delivered in English were to reinforce the message, as Ælfric insists:

Ælc cristen man sceal cunnan his Pater noster and his Credan. Mid þam Pater nostre he sceal hine gebiddan, and mid þam Credan he sceal his geleafan getrymman. Se lareow sceal secgan ðam læwedum mannum þæt andgit to ðam Pater nostre and to þam Credan, þæt hi witon hwæs hi biddan æt Gode, and hu hi sceolon on God gelyfan. (Thorpe 1971 [1844], II: 604)

[Every Christian man shall know his Pater Noster and his Creed. With the Pater Noster he shall pray, and with the Creed he shall confirm his belief. The teacher shall explain to the laity the sense of the Pater Noster and of the Creed, so that they may know what they pray for to God, and how they shall believe in God.] (Thorpe 1971 [1844], II: 605)

Along with the people's knowledge of their words and meaning, their authorization by the church for healing leads to the use of both Pater Noster and Creed in charms. Even the way in which prayers are cited in charms like *Lacnunga* clxxvi, "sing thereon the Creed and the Our Father," follows from their integration into the ritual actions of charm performance.[7] The words themselves are typically not provided in the charm text. Instructions simply state a title, unless the prayer proves unique, having, for instance, been composed for a particular charm. Similarly, the performer is expected to sing a "litany," a "Gloria," and a "Sanctus." The scribal abbreviation of these texts rests on the assumption of their familiarity.

Before discussing the use of the Pater Noster and Creed in charms, it is necessary to account for a key aspect of performance pragmatics, namely the role of the performer who practices charm healing. If prayers like the Lord's Prayer posed no problem for laity, the elaborate liturgical selections found in some charms – like the Sanctus from the Mass or the Benedicite from Morning Prayer – presupposes a celebrant who can recite them (Niles 1980:49). However heathen-looking Anglo-Saxon charms appear, many must have been intended for use by a churchman of

7 Both the dual form, *Pater Noster*, and the singular form, *Paternoster*, occur in the charms.

some learning, as John Niles (1980: 50) recognizes. Indeed, some charms stipulate that a Mass be sung over medicinal ingredients, a qualification signaling at least the cooperation of clergy.

What other qualifications were required? We will return to the question of what, if any, institutional charm authority a speaker needed, but we can attempt an answer by focusing on the mechanics of oral performance from an oral-theoretical and pragmatic-linguistic perspective. Early medieval manuscripts are silent about who performed charms in the majority of cases, be they local clergy, trained leech, layman, or laywoman (see further Jolly 1996). On the whole, the "scanty" evidence historians can garner suggests that professional doctors were most likely laity rather than clergy (Jolly 1996: 103). While priests could deliver incantations or entire charms, so could lay or monastic practitioners who were not priests. We should not forget, moreover, that many charms must have been communal property in the oral world of the early English. Recipes and incantations circulated through oral tradition. People learned charm formulas from others who learned them from others.

In order to flesh out our portrait of the healer, we can turn to charm texts to help us reconstruct the pragmatics of oral-traditional performance. Typically charm texts state a malady to be addressed with an *if* clause, as in, "If cattle be privately taken away"; a *then* clause follows, providing, where appropriate, an herbal recipe and/or an incantation to be delivered over the preparation or the patient, as in "[then] sing on the foot spoor" (MS Cotton Tiberius A.113, fol. 103; Cockayne 1965 [1865], III: 286). As the healer initiates the charm ritual, his or her actions construct a special performance arena or frame of reference wherein the cure takes place. Utterances "sung" within this arena are claimed as ritualized rather than everyday language. While we do not know precisely how healers "sang," we assume that incantations were either chanted or sung. In other words, the healer adopted a special performance register to mark the spell as a spell. Prosodic features like rhythm and intonation communicate the nature of the utterance to the audience. By virtue of vocal and other physical actions, the speaker assumes the role of the leech. Taking on this institutional voice, the speaker encodes his or her personal attitude to empower a charm and effect its healing.

3 The Lord's Prayer in charms

A look at traditional associations and the means by which they are brought to bear during charm performance sets the foundation for analyzing Pater Noster incantations. Because incantations partake in oral-traditional performance, the prayers chanted or sung in oral rituals partake in oral-traditional signification. Aural reference generates a particular kind of allusion that oral theorists label "traditional referentiality." Through this sign system, the communal knowledge of an audience informs performance. This oral construct can be likened to the model of literary allusion from which it derives, i.e., intertextuality. John Miles Foley (1991) introduces the concept in order to describe the dynamic nature of oral-performative and oral-traditional texts. These texts and the rhetorical structures they contain refer to and echo within a larger extra-textual context. Reciprocally, the text is informed and enriched by a tradition that may reach back in time as far as communal memory exists or resound within a more contemporary orality (Foley 1991: 7). Hearing the Pater Noster in charms, the audience would hear related liturgical performances in their mind's ear. They would simultaneously recognize the biblical tradition at the core of liturgy. When the healer prays the Lord's Prayer, as a result, his or her speech belongs neither to the Eucharistic liturgy nor to that of the Last Rites, although it resonates within those traditions. Ultimately, the traditional referentiality of the Lord's Prayer is based in a Christian's individual right to make requests of the Father.

Learned in childhood or at initiation into the church, the Lord's Prayer is to be prayed several times a day. Inside a church or out, Anglo-Saxons could pray the Pater Noster with a sense of entitlement. Theirs to pray in His name, the Lord's Prayer is given to the people directly by Christ. Teaching His followers to pray, He authorizes people to address God as "Father." The only prayer Jesus gives His disciples, perhaps on more than one occasion, survives in two versions and in three texts (Thurston 2003 [1910]). By tradition of its origin it serves as the vehicle for special requests of the Father. Because it is personal and individual as well as ecclesiastical, the praying of the Lord's Prayer outside of church represents the subjective desires of the speaker. The prayer's presence – even dominance – in folk rites reflects the commonness of its use outside of Catholic liturgy.[8]

The English were used to hearing the Pater Noster in church, as well, every time they attended, which they were expected to do on Sundays and feast-days.[9] Whether or not individuals themselves received Communion, they repeated

---

8 I use the term *liturgy* as it is defined in the *Oxford English Dictionary*: "a form of public worship, esp. in the Christian Church; a collection of formularies for the conduct of Divine service." Note that the use of *liturgy* to mean "public worship conducted in accordance with a prescribed form" is obsolete and is not used here (*OED*, 3rd edn., s.v. *liturgy*). The ritualized act of charm performance is not liturgical, even when a charm contains incantations taken from liturgy.

9 The evaluation of actual participation in church ceremonies and sacraments is complex. For a review of the English church's high expectation for and discussion of attendance at Mass and Confession, see further Forbes (2013: 45–48).

the Lord's Prayer publically, at least in part, when they were present at Mass. Because the Lord's Prayer allowed the faithful to receive the Sacrament, it is thought fitting that all of the faithful should participate in saying it (Jungmann 1961: 468). Directions in early service books tell us that the whole congregation was meant to join in its repetition. "Oremus," the priest begins: "let us pray." Whereas some prayers are said by the priest alone, and other prayers are said by the priest on behalf of the people, the Pater Noster is apportioned between priest and people. It requires audience participation. By the 8th century, for instance, rubrics specify that the prayer must conclude "by all answering": "but deliver us from evil" (Jungmann 1961: 468). Audience participation is more than symbolic; it is essential in the public praying of the Lord's Prayer. After all, it is the personal – albeit communally performed – prayer that is recited during the liturgy. Whether the assembly speaks the prayer's final plea, or whether choir speaks in their place, "the people say the Our Father along with the celebrant" (Jungmann 1961: 468).

Its role in the Eucharistic liturgy is ancient. Because the request for daily bread had been taken in the figurative sense as a plea for spiritual sustenance, the Lord's Prayer has long been used as a Communion prayer. Said before the distribution of the Sacrament, the Pater Noster was thought to bind together, through God's presence, the society of the faithful (Jungmann 1961: 464, 462). In this location in the official service since the 5th or 6th centuries, the Lord's Prayer summarizes and recapitulates the Eucharistic prayer while initiating the Communion. For this reason, the Lord's Prayer is used whenever Communion is celebrated outside the larger Mass, for example, on Good Friday and at Communion for the Sick. The prayer, in short, prepares a Christian for Communion and for the reception of the Sacrament and the fellowship of the Holy Spirit.

When a person was gravely ill or dying, it was the Lord's Prayer that was brought along with the Host by visiting clergy. One wonders whether the sick might have come to expect the praying of the Pater Noster in a solemnity performed at their sickbeds. The praying of the Lord's Prayer within charm rituals might have offered a particular comfort because of its association with the Eucharist brought into the home. The Pater Noster is incorporated into charms not merely because everybody knows it, but because people recognize its centrality to supplication and worship, private or communal.

If Anglo-Saxons knew this prayer by heart they also knew its power. When we look at the internal operation of charms – *Lacnunga* clxxvi is typical – we see that the Pater Noster plays an integral role in curative formulas. It is clear that the prayer does not merely Christianize a heathen rite. In this *Lacnunga* charm for a cardiac affliction, the Lord's Prayer transforms water taken from a stream into a cure for heart disease. Here, as in the other charms in which it appears, the Pater Noster wields an exclusive power that the Anglo-Saxon charms exploit. As I have shown elsewhere, of the 111 containing incantations, 28 rely on the Pater Noster (24 are in Old English, 4 in Latin; Arnovick 1999: 69). The Pater Noster constitutes an utterance that is more fundamental than decorative in the corpus, which, though small, indicates larger patterns of use. The prayer functions consistently in this manner throughout the corpus. When this prayer represents the sole incantation in the charm it effects the desired results, to bless or to transform:

> Gif se wyrm sy nyþergewend oðð[e] se blendenda fic, bedelf ænne wrid cileþenigan moran 7 ni[m] mid þinum twam handum upweard[e]s, 7 sing þærofer VIIII Pater nostra; æt þam/ nigeðan æt "libera nos a malo" bred hy þon(ne) up; 7 nim of þam ciðe 7 of oþrum þ(æt) þær sy an lytel cuppeful, 7 drinc[e] hy þon(ne); 7 beðige hine mon to wearman fyre; him bið sona sel. (*Lacnunga* lxxvii)
>
> [If the "worm" (i.e., anal fistula) is turned downwards or the bleeding hemorrhoid: dig round a (?) bundle of shoots (growing from) the root of greater celandine and grasp it with your two hands, (palms) upwards, and sing thereover nine Our Fathers; at the ninth, at "deliver us from evil", wrench it up; and take from the shoot and from (?) others (or other parts?) so that there is a little cupful, and then let him drink it; and warm him in front of a warm fire; he will soon be better.] (Pettit 2001, I: 69)

Crucial to the treatment, the phrase "deliver us from evil" accompanies the extraction of the plant. Uttered over the celandine root as it is wrenched out of the ground, the Pater Noster fortifies its natural medicinal qualities. Blessed thus, the shoots should deliver the sufferer from the evil of the protruding vein or fistula. Despite the decree that only the Pater Noster and Creed were acceptable for use in the collection of medicinal herbs, the Pater Noster does not merely stand in for a pagan incantation here. One verse from the prayer explicitly states the charm's proposition that the patient be delivered from disease. Beseeching supreme authority, the Pater Noster is used to effect therapeutic change.

Often the Pater Noster appears with other liturgical formulae in charm incantations. Along with the celebration of the Mass, the singing of one or more of the following prayers blesses or otherwise transforms an object (for example, an herbal substance) for use in the remedy:

"Alleluia"
Benedicite
Creed
"Deus in nomine tuo"
"Deus misereatur nobis"
"Domine Deus, inclina domine"
"Gloria in excelsis Deo"
"In nomine patris"
Litanies
Psalms (e.g., Psalms 68, 91, 119)
Magnificat
"Miserere mei"
Tersanctus

The Lord's Prayer is combined, for instance, with Psalm 115 (Vulgate) along with gibberish (used here in the neutral sense of unintelligible locutions used to address spirits) and Latin in *Lacnunga* charm clii, for a horse who suffers a sprain:

> "Naborrede unde uenisti" tribus uicibus; "Credidi propter" tribus uicibus; "Alpha et O, initium et finis"; "Crux mihi uita est et tibi mor, inimici"; "Pater noster".
>
> ["Naborrede whence you came" three times; "I believed therefore" (Vulgate Psalm 115) three times; "Alpha and Omega, beginning and end"; "the cross is life to me and death to you, enemy"; the Our Father.] (Pettit 2001, I: 105)

Each biblical and liturgical form – psalm, Mass, litany – holds great power in and of itself; when these are performed with Creed and Lord's Prayer, their strength becomes formidable.

Prayed alone or in the kind of collaboration just seen, the Pater Noster must have been considered good medicine. Employed in one fourth of all incantations, the prayer predominates among the official church prayers used in charms. Even the positioning of the Our Father with respect to other verbal formulae in the corpus reflects its dominance among incantations. In approximately seventy percent of the occasions in which the prayer is used, the Lord's Prayer follows other incantations in sequence. Either the Pater Noster appears last within a set of prayers or other verbal formulae, or it is prayed after all other utterances or sets of utterances.

The predominance of prayers in final position is noteworthy. Perhaps it was convenient to insert the Lord's Prayer after other utterances, to emend pagan charms. Yet this is also its standard liturgical position; numerous ceremonies end with the saying of the Pater Noster. Operations fundamental to the charm indicate that its placement was never gratuitous. Set in order in the charm, the Christian prayer symbolically subsumes or claims other incantations. More generally, the prayer takes up rhetorically-marked positions. On a religious level, both the first and the last of many have significance, a fact which does not diminish their contribution as signs. The first and final position of the Pater Noster in twenty-three of twenty-eight charms accord with its unique status and special prominence as Christ's prayer, echoing structurally the Alpha and the Omega. In the last analysis, though, proximity to the other incantations proves more important than their particular order. When the Pater Noster accompanies another incantatory plea, it sanctions that performative utterance.

To ascertain the force of Pater Noster incantations, we can classify them as requests. Requests belong to a type of speech act called "mands," a subclass of directives that includes commands, demands, requests, and entreaties (Lyons 1977, II: 745–746). The final petition of the Lord's Prayer, "deliver us from evil," encompasses perfectly all needs of the afflicted. Often an accompanying incantation like an exorcism – "death to you, enemy" – reiterates the desired effect of eliminating harm. More specific requests are established by the charm's stated purpose: against "fever" or the "half-dead disease" (epilepsy), for example. Nevertheless, the explicit mands ("deliver us," etc.) indicate that the Lord's Prayer proves a direct request, proposing a course of action favored by a speaker confident in the Lord's ability to grant the adjuration.

In the Father's name, the Pater Noster conveys an adjacent request to Him, asking that God effect its proposition. A *Lacnunga* charm against glandular swellings has a dual appeal to the supernatural, for example, combining gibberish with nine Pater Nosters and an Alleluia:

> Ecce dolgula medit dudu(m) beðegunda breðegunda elecunda eleuachia mottem mee renu(m) orþa fueþa letaues noeues/ terre dolge drore uhic All(eluia).
>
> Singe man þis gebed on þ(æt) se man drincan wille nygan siþan, 7 "Pater noster" nigan siþan. (*Lacnunga* clxiv)
>
> [Ecce dolgula medit dudum beðegunda breðegunda elecunda eleuachia mottem mee renum orþa fueþa letaues noeues terre dolge drore uhic Alleluia.
>
> Let this prayer be sung nine times upon that which the person wants to drink, and the Pater Noster nine times.] (Pettit 2001, I: 115)

Arcane and borrowed lexica in the gibberish not only differentiate the ritual of the charm from the discourse of the everyday but also lend great flexibility to the practical, performative ends of the charm. Void of lexical content, incantatory gibberish utterances order, direct, command, and adjure the spirits according to the charm's purpose. Evoking the supernatural, gibberish intimidates, for it seems to the audience to possess a secret lexical meaning only the charmer (and the spirits) understand. Gibberish performs word magic (Arnovick 2006: 51). One might deduce a strategic redundancy in *Lacnunga* clxiv: should the gibberish fail, perhaps the Pater Noster will work. "It is almost as if the magician [is] ... hedging his bets," M. L. Cameron suspects (1993: 134). However legitimate that observation, if left unqualified, it underestimates the force of the Christian prayer used as part of an incantation. Pragmatically as well as rhetorically in *Lacnunga* clxiv, the nine Pater Nosters sanctify the gibberish, propelling the performative along with it to the Lord. To regard the Pater Noster as an orthodox stamp of approval implies that it is perfunctory. Far from being the case, that implication denies the power attributed to the Pater Noster by those who pray it.

To look further at this behavior from a discursive point of view, we can observe that the prayer has, in a sense, been dislocated from its previous pragmatic contexts, whether personal or liturgical, and redeployed to provide structure for a charm. Such behavior, which previously I have called "discursization," represents a kind of "pragmaticalization," wherein an utterance takes on a new function, namely an organizational role, in discourse. It is not unlike the pragmatic transformation of the parting blessing, *God be with you*, which accompanies its formal lexical change to *Good-bye*. *Good-bye* no longer serves as a blessing at parting but has come to act as a polite conversational close, its purpose to recognize the interlocutor while structuring the discourse (Arnovick 1999: 95–118). Alternatively, we can understand the phenomenon as "entextualization," a meta-discursive action whereby "various dimensions of contextualized 'interpretive meaning' [are] added to those seemingly inherent in the text" (Silverstein and Urban 1996: 2).

In the case of the Lord's Prayer, the prayer gains a new function within charm performance. Not only does it beseech and direct the power of the Almighty, but also the mand gives shape to the charm. To see this from the perspective of charm composition, we may imagine that a healer who writes a new charm might place Pater Nosters in these standard positions in the charm, following a textual model or oral formula. In short, the Pater Noster request has gained a new pragmatic-linguistic use when it occurs in the speech context of a charm ritual. This is not to say that the linguistic use supersedes the religious meaning of the prayer, but rather to say that the Pater Noster has gained a discursive function. It structures the charm that deploys its uniquely sacred power. Charm users, of course, need not be aware of these precise functions for them to operate. Confidence in the prayer would comfort hearers. Said first or last, the beloved prayer would reassure both patient and audience. While we do not know how and when the prayer became part of a charm text, we do, in fact, discover an intrinsic rationale for its inclusion and location there.

4 The Creed in charms

We have seen the productivity of the Pater Noster in charms. In contrast, when the Creed is borrowed from liturgy, both its dislocation and the effect of its dislocation are more profound, as we shall see after examining its Christian contexts. The Bible tells us that Jesus healed the faithful simply because they believed. As Rufinus of Aquileia (340/45–410) reminds Christians, "the preaching of the Cross is to those who perish, foolishness, but to those who are saved, that is, to us, it is 'the power of God'" (Freemantle 1892; http://www.newadvent.org/fathers/2711.htm). Declarations of belief taking either form of official Creed are included in Anglo-Saxon healing rituals, for this reason. While the Creed takes the locutionary form of an affirmation of belief, its illocutionary force as a speech act in charms is that of an indirect request for help.

Because the Creed is part of the audience's communal knowledge, traditional referentiality offers a semiotic pathway for the Creed's contribution to charms. Apart from the Mass, we find the Creed, or credal statements, appearing most prominently in the Christian rite of initiation; the sacrament of baptism; and other ceremonies, including exorcisms, making use of "materials," not only water but also oils and salt. There were two Creeds used in the early church. First is the 4th-century Nicene Creed, also called the Mass Creed for its use in the Eucharist within the declaration of fellowship which begins the Mass of the Faithful. It enters the Roman Rite after 1014 CE. Beginning "Credo in unum Deum," the Nicene Creed stresses the nature of the Triune God. The other Creed is the so-called Apostles' Creed, also known as the minor or baptismal Creed. The appellation derives from the medieval legend of its origins: the Apostles were supposed to have written this Creed collectively on Pentecost when under the inspiration of the Holy Spirit. Although each of the doctrines espoused in this Creed can be correlated with statements current in the apostolic period, the legend itself dates from the 6th century. The Apostles' Creed ("Credo in Deum") was used by the Anglo-Saxons for baptism, instruction, and in monastic liturgies, especially those at Easter.

For the charm performer, his or her patient, and for any onlookers, charms could derive great power from the recitation of the Creed. As a confession of faith, the Creed was undoubtedly seen as wielding the implicit power of faith as a force for healing. When the Creed is prescribed in charms, the forms "Credo" or "Credan" generally appear without specification of which Creed, if either, is required (nor how much of it was to be recited).[10] Only twice does the opening line distinguish the form. "I believe in God the Father" identifies the Apostles' Creed in one charm, and "I believe in one God" indicates the Nicene Creed in another.[11] Because the essential affirmation of faith is the same for both Creeds, it may not actually matter which Creed is repeated as an incantation. Ælfric's sermon on the Creed, for instance, begins with the Apostles' Creed but then evolves into an exploration of the Nicene Creed's statements on the nature of the Trinity. Although ambiguous in most of the charms, evidence from the individual texts

---

10 Six out of eight times the title alone signals the credal incantation.

11 Nevertheless, although the charm relying on the Nicene Creed uses holy water in its preparation, neither running water nor the baptismal font is mentioned.

themselves, along with cultural context, nevertheless suggests that the default was the Apostles' Creed: charms that employ the Creed frequently include elements associated with baptism.

The one Creed learned by every Christian was the Apostles' Creed. The Anglo-Saxon church stipulated that "all catechumens memorize the [...] [Lord's Prayer and Apostles' Creed] before receiving baptism and that children baptized as infants be taught the prayers as soon as they were able to learn them" (Lionarons 2010: 87). Because the Creed protects the faithful, St. Augustine of Hippo advises its daily use:

> Receive, my children, the Rule of Faith, which is called the Symbol (or Creed). And when you have received it, write it in your heart, and be daily saying it to yourselves; before ye sleep, before ye go forth, arm you with your Creed. (Augustine 2009 [1892]; "A Sermon to Catechumens on the Creed," http://www.newadvent.org/fathers/1307.htm)

Typically the Apostles' Creed was prayed in Latin, but even as early as the 8th century, Bede (672/673–735) recommended its translation into English along with the Lord's Prayer. To the same end, Ælfric, and Wulfstan after him, went so far as to provide an Old English translation of both. Eadwine's 12th-century Canterbury Psalter contains both the Latin text and English translations of the Apostles' Creed:

> Credo in deum patrem omnipotentem creatorem caeli et terra; Et in Iesum Christum filium eius unicum dominum nostrum qui conceptus est de spiritu sancto Natus ex Maria uirgine, Passus sub Pontio Pilato Crucifixus, mortuus et sepultus, Descendit ad inferna tercia die resurrexit a mortuis, Ascendit ad caelos sedet ad dexteram dei patris omnipotentis Inde uenturus (est) iudicare uiuos et mortuos. [the rest is missing from ms.] Credo in spiritum sanctum sanctam aecclesiam catholicam sanctorum communionem remissionem peccatorum carnis resurrectionem uitam aeternam. Amen. (Harsley 1889: 264; https://archive.org/details/eadwinescanterbu00cathrich)

> Ic gelefe on gode fædera ælwealend/ ealmihtig sceppend heofones 7 eorðan 7 on helende crist suna his anlich drihten ure. Syo þe akynned is of ðam halig gaste boran of M [aria uirgine]. [Þolode under Pontius] pilate 7 on rode ahangen dead 7 beberiged. He adun astæh to hellæ. Ðriddan degge he aras fram deaþa. He astah to heofone. Sit on swi[ð]ran healfe godes fæderes ealmihtig. Þanen he is to comene 7 to demenna quiche 7 deade. Ic gelefe on halig gast 7 on halig gesomnunge fulfremede [7] halegan himennesse [7] forgyfenysse synne [7] flecsces uparisnesse [7] lif eche. Beo hit swa. (Harsley 1889: 264; https://archive.org/details/eadwinescanterbu00cathrich)

For the sake of comparison, here is the Apostles' Creed said today:

> I believe in God the Father Almighty, Creator of heaven and earth; And in Jesus Christ, His only son, our Lord, Who was conceived by the Holy Ghost, born of the Virgin Mary, Suffered under Pontius Pilate, was crucified, died and was buried. He descended into hell; the third

> day He rose again from the dead. He ascended into heaven, sitteth on the right hand of God the Father almighty; from thence He will come to judge the living and the dead. I believe in the Holy Ghost, The Holy Catholic Church, the communion of saints, the forgiveness of sins, the resurrection of the body, and the life everlasting. Amen. (www.catholic.org/prayers)

In order to account for the baptismal elements present in Creed charms, let me remind you about the sacrament of baptism as the Anglo-Saxons knew it. Baptism cleansed individuals from the guilt of original sin and its main penalty, damnation to hell. Other rites performed at baptism helped to mitigate further consequences of original sin, as Augustine (2009 [1892]) explains: "as you know, even little children undergo exsufflation, exorcism; to drive away from them the power of the devil their enemy, which deceived man that it might possess mankind." Although they were performed throughout the year, baptisms ideally took place at the Easter vigil, sometime on Holy Saturday. By the 10th century, infant baptism was common practice in western Christianity, including the Anglo-Saxon church (although immigrants from Scandinavia might be received as adults). Baptism begins with a series of exorcisms which culminate with the candidate's being asked to renounce Satan, all his works, and all his pomp, as we see in the rite for Holy Saturday baptism as set forth in the Sarum Missal (Legg 1969: 130–131).

After candidates or godparents (on their behalf) renounce the devil, the candidate is then anointed with the oil of unction. A triple interrogation subsequently takes place. As we also see in the Gelasian Sacramentary (a Gallicanized Roman Rite from the 7th or 8th centuries), during the climax of the rite, the candidate or those acting on his or her behalf is asked to affirm belief in the Father, Son, and Holy Spirit:

> Dost thou believe in God the Father almighty?
>
> Resp. I believe
>
> Dost thou believe also in Jesus Christ His only son our Lord, Who was born and suffered?
>
> I believe
>
> Dost thou believe also in the Holy Spirit, the holy church, the remission of sins, the resurrection of the flesh?
>
> I believe. (Wilson 1894: 86)

Just as the response "I believe" is given to each of the three questions, so the candidate is plunged in the water, three times in all. Finally, the priest proclaims, "I baptize thee in the name of the Father, the Son, and the Holy Spirit." The baptismal rite ends with the catechumen's first communion (Wilson 1894: 86). At the kernel of the rite of baptism is, in the words of Cyril of Jerusalem, the confessing of the "saving confession" (Kelly 1950: 39).

In addition to this interrogatory Creed, much earlier in the service or even in the course of the ceremonies preparatory to the baptism, there was another occasion to affirm belief on behalf of candidate and community. This time it was the case of reciting a declaratory Creed, the verbal content of which was in large measure adopted from the baptismal interrogations (Kelly 1950: 52). Rubrics in the Gelasian Sacramentary enjoin the priest to pronounce the Creed "with his hand on the children's heads" outside of the baptistery (Kelly 1950: 38). According to the Sarum Manual's later medieval form for "the making of the catechumen," in the prelude to baptism, the priest must ask parents, godparents, and others assembled to say the Pater Noster, Ave Maria, and Common Creed (i.e., the Apostles' Creed). The priest himself then recites these prayers out loud for everyone to hear (Collins 1960: 30).

After children were baptized, their godmothers and godfathers were duty-bound to teach them the Apostles' Creed. For Wulfstan, that should occur just as soon as the child was able to talk. It became the clergy's responsibility to teach and explicate the Creed, often in sermons preached during Lent. Wulfstan warns that adults who do not know the prayers are not good Christians and cannot be "baptized, confirmed, receive the eucharist, or be worthy of a consecrated grave" (Lionarons 2010: 129).

If there are spiritual penalties for failing to know and say the Creed, there are benefits for the baptized who affirm their faith. The Creed has a transformative effect upon speakers: in a recursive fashion, faith strengthens faith. As Augustine states, "these few words are known to the faithful, to the end that in believing they may be made subject to God; that being made subject, they may rightly live; that in rightly living, they may make the heart pure; that with the heart made pure, they may understand that which they believe" (http://www.newadvent.org/fathers/1304.htm). The saying of the Creed served also as a corrective to the "foolish customs" that imperiled the people. According to Bede, St. Cuthbert (635–687) traveled the English countryside "to convert the neighbouring people far and wide. [...] For many of them profaned the creed they held by wicked deeds and [...] in times of plague, would forget the sacred mysteries of the faith into which they had been initiated and take to the false remedies of idolatry [...] by means of incantations or amulets or any other mysteries of devilish art" (Bede 2009: 223).

Within this context of the Creed's familiarity and significance, we can now scrutinize the Anglo-Saxon charms in which it appears. At least eight charms in the *Leechbook* and *Lacnunga* prescribe the utterance, "credo," probably the declaratory Apostles' Creed, given the larger context of each charm. Although ancillary to baptism here, the Creed transports the liturgical traditions associated with it into the charm. Whether actually said or merely cited, the presence of the Creed brings to the healing rite the confidence of catechetical instruction and the certainty of church membership. The healer who repeats the Creed claims his or her baptismal birth right as a Christian, his or her soul sealed and marked as God's own.

In addition to the Creed, numerous baptismal elements appear in the charms. In popular healing rites we find the Creed used in very specific ritual environments. Frequently when the Creed appears in charms, so too does water, so too does exorcism, so too does Trinitarian blessing. Although subjective expressions of belief (posed as indirect requests) are crucial to the success of the charm, a larger constellation of elements in these charms call upon baptism as a healing rite. While not every Creed charm also contains water and exorcism and Triune blessing, the presence of some or all of these elements in combination with the Creed invoked the baptismal liturgy. As a result of their associations with baptism, Creed charms convey the very power of the sacrament itself.

Let us begin with water, as it is a common element in charm remedies. Restorative waters prove an important tool for the Anglo-Saxon leech. Sometimes water from a stream is used; on other occasions, holy water or "font water" is required. Frequently, water blessed by the priest is poured over solid ingredients such as herbs, as a medicinal medium. Actions performed with water are just as important as the water itself. In several charms we find a kind of immersion akin to that performed in baptism. In a charm against elf disease, the leech is directed to "bind all the worts in a cloth; dip it thrice in hallowed font water" (*Leechbook* III. lxii; Cockayne 1965, III: 345). In another case, perhaps recalling ancient baptisms by the river, a virgin must stand in a stream, to "fetch in silence against the current half a sextarius of running water" (*Lacnunga* xxix; Pettit 2001, I: 17; see also the previously cited *Lacnunga* clxxvi against wens). The water she scoops will make a holy drink against "elfish magic and [...] all the temptations of the Devil." Accompanied by prayer and proclamation, water washes away sin and disease.

In addition to aqueous immersion and the Creed, we find exorcism. Because ailments were attributed to demonic (spiritual) agency, only forceful words and rituals could vanquish them (Jolly 1996: 123). In as much as exorcism cast out the devil during baptism, it cast him out during charm rites; vanquishing him vanquished his afflictions. Formulas from baptismal exorcism were readily borrowed into charm incantations, as a result. *Lacnunga* lxiii, for a holy salve, thus purifies the sick person by commanding Satan:

> Lord, holy Father, omnipotent and eternal God, by the application of my hands may the Enemy, the Devil, flee from the hairs, from the head, from the eyes, from the nose from the

> lips, from the tongue, from the epiglottis, from the neck, from the breast, from the feet, from the heels, from the whole framework of his members, so that the Devil may have no power over him, neither in speaking, nor in keeping quiet, nor in sleeping, nor in rising, nor by day, nor by night, nor in touching, nor in rest, nor in going, nor in sight, nor in laughter, nor in reading; so be it in the name of the Lord Jesus Christ, who redeemed us by his holy blood, who lives and reigns with the Father, God forever and ever. Amen. (Pettit 2001, I: 33)[12]

This exorcism is not unique to the charms. In fact, it comes directly from the baptismal liturgy. Compare the pre-baptismal exorcism from the Stowe Missal, a late 8th- or early 9th-century Irish sacramentary:

> Holy Lord, almighty Father, eternal God expel the devil [...] from this man, from his head, hair, crown, brain, forehead, eyes, ears, nose, mouth, tongue, under-tongue, throat, jaws, neck, breast, heart, from his whole body on the inside, from outside, from his hands, feet, all members, the joints of his members, from his words, works, and all activity now and to come, through you, Jesus Christ, who reign. (Kelly 1985: 240)

The same baptismal exorcism is repeated elsewhere in the charms, this time in the *Leechbook*, in a cure for cardiac ailment. Note the triple formula which is chanted over a potion to give it efficacy:

> My Lord, I ask you, Father; I entreat you, Son; I implore you, Lord and Holy Spirit; that by all your powers, Holy Trinity, you obliterate all the works of the Devil from this man [...] so that he may confess all his sins and all the inequities which he has [...]. (*Leechbook* III: xviii)[13]

Then the Creed is to be repeated. The washing away of evil through water and exorcism is finally effected by the statement of belief in the Creed. In *Lacnunga* we find a similar triple formula after various prayers, psalms, and the Creed are intoned over a potion made with holy water. The consecration – akin to that for baptism – is pronounced:

> In the name of the Father and of the Son and of the Holy Spirit let it be blessed. (*Lacnunga* xxix; Pettit 2001, I: 17)

The presence of Creed, exorcism, immersion in water, and Trinitarian blessing partially or altogether in a charm, is – to offer an analogy from linguistics – not unlike the presence of certain linguistic features that collectively characterize a particular dialect. The features may not be unique to that dialect, but when a critical number of them appear together they identify the speaker as belonging to

12 For a detailed account of exorcism at baptism, see Dendle (2014: 107ff).
13 Note the complete enumeration of body parts and actions, a special, ritual kind of lexical accumulation which Robert Yelle terms "exhaustion" (2013: 36).

a particular speech group. Similarly the presence of multiple elements so closely associated with baptism lead us to acknowledge its invocation for the purpose of healing.

The use of the Creed in Anglo-Saxon charms speaks to the success of the church's mission to teach the basic tenets of the Christian faith. Sermons preached in the English vernacular taught the Anglo-Saxons the Creed's form and meaning, as did religious poetry. The use of the Creed in folk medicine suggests that Christians understood both the confession they uttered and the potency of baptism. In fact, given the importance of baptism to Anglo-Saxon Christians, perhaps we might have been surprised not to find the Apostles' Creed and the sacrament of baptism harnessed in their healing rites.

5 De-institutionalization and subjectification

Having assessed the Pater Noster and Creed in charms, we can explore further the perlocutionary effect or results of the de-institutionalized incantations. We have seen that the Pater Noster acts as a building block or design element for the charm as a discursive performance. Sanctioned for use in private devotion, the Lord's Prayer is deployed within the folk tradition of the charm. Individual healers seize the agency humanity was given and put the prayer to use in healing. The Pater Noster participates in a folk rite even while it retains its Christian force. Its new discursive function does not diminish its religious meaning. Yet the pragmatic-linguistic gain is clear. Re-deployed in a native healing tradition, the Pater Noster imports its Christian power to that genre.

When the Lord's Prayer occurs in charms, the prayer contributes both liturgical and personal traditions to the incantation. To the extent that healer and audience experience its liturgical references, we can deduce a priori the de-institutionalization of the Pater Noster. The invocation or reminder of its place and role in the Eucharist speaks to the absence of the sacrament itself in charm rituals. The effects of the Pater Noster's de-institutionalization are difficult to isolate, however, for they are overshadowed by the tradition of individual entitlement granted God's children. The prayer already belongs to the folk. The healer's subjectivity is inherent in Pater Noster requests.

A very different situation holds when the Creed finds its way into charms. The Creed may have been recited by the Anglo-Saxons privately to help them remember their faith, as Augustine recommends, but, having been composed for the purpose of initiation, it is primarily liturgical. Even though the Creed represents a personal expression of belief, its context is clearly liturgical. When credal language operates in charms, de-institutionalization is equally clear. But the use of the Creed in charms does not constitute a decline in supernatural instrumentality. Rather, that instrumentality has been transformed and appropriated. The same words are now said through personal rather than institutional prerogative, through healing rather than sacramental force:

Table 1: The de-institutionalization and subjectification of the Creed said in charms.

Creed said at baptism	**DE-INSTITUTIONALIZATION and SUBJECTIFICATION→**	**Creed said at healing**
Christian		Christian and/or pagan
orthodox		not orthodox
sacrament		not sacrament
liturgical		folk-traditional (not liturgical)
performed before audience		performed before audience (even if only patient)

Like the Pater Noster, the Creed is inherently subjective. Yet it belongs to an institutional setting, the exclusion of which increases speaker subjectivity. On one level, the de-institutionalization of a sacramental structure like baptism represents a loss. When an act is de-institutionalized, the cultural tradition formerly associated with it is altered or disappears. Viewed within its linguistic context, any "loss" subsequently entails pragmatic consequences and supports discursive ends. The coopting of the Creed into folk ritual proves consistent with linguistic changes seen in subjectification, the pragmatic-semantic process through which "meanings become increasingly based in the speaker's subjective belief state, or attitude toward what is said" (Traugott 1989: 35; 1997: 185). The speaker expresses his or her individual intention for healing rather than participating in the ritualized events of baptism or the Eucharist. In this way, Creed charms re-focus perspective on the speaker, saying to hearers, in effect, "these are my good intentions for you." Collectively, then, the movement from liturgy to charm favors an orientation internal to the speaker at the expense of one external to him or her (see further Traugott 1995: 47).

Subjectivity, the "capacity of the speaker to posit himself as a 'subject'" manifests in incantations as second-person commands and first-person directives (Benveniste 1971: 224). When charm texts prescribe an utterance like, "In the name of the Father and of the Son and of the Holy Spirit let it be blessed," the voice of the leech is clear from the second-person imperative, *let*, even while appealing to the Lord's authority (Pettit 2001, I: 17). Similarly, we recall exorcisms with such commands as, "obliterate all the works of the Devil from this man" (*Leechbook* III: xviii). Against scabies: "take this evil and depart with it" (Grendon 1909: 196). Elsewhere we hear, "I adjure you" (*Lacnunga* xxv; Pettit 2001, I: 15). All these incantations convey the speaker's directives. Then, too, the accumulation of such deictic devices, to which pragmatic indexical force has been attributed, especially in magic, "enhances the overall force of the spell as an index of its goal" (Yelle 2013: 31).

As opposed to second-person directives, incantations with first-person declaratives are more explicitly subjective, for the "manifestation of subjectivity does not stand out except in the first person" (Benveniste 1971: 229). The first-person form is the indicator of subjectivity that characterizes "the attitude of the speaker with respect to the statement he is making" (Benveniste 1971: 229). "I will help you now," chants the healer in a *Leechbook* charm against a sudden sharp pain (charm cxxvii; Pettit 2001, I: 91). Several of the charms discussed previously possess incantations in which the speaker makes a direct appeal to supernatural or divine forces. As we saw above in *Lacnunga* lxiii for a holy salve, the speaker entreats the Trinity to heal the patient:

> My Lord, I ask you, Father; I entreat you, Son; I implore you, Lord and Holy Spirit. (Pettit 2001, I: 35)

Some additional examples highlight the subjectivity of the first-person voice. For water-elf disease, an incantation from *Leechbook* is chanted over a potion of holy water, ale, and herbs:

> Ic benne awrat betest
> beado wræaða fra benne
> Ne burnon ne burston [...]. (*Leechbook* III.lxiii)
>
> [I have wreathed round the wounds
> The best of healing wreaths,
> That the baleful sores may
> Neither burn nor burst.] (Cockayne 1965, II: 351–2)

For delayed birth or to prevent stillbirth, a pregnant woman is to step over her husband, reciting these words:

> Up ic gonge, ofer þe ic stæppe
> mid cwican cilde, nalæs mid cwellendum
> mid fulborenum, nalæs mid fægan. (*Lacnunga* clxi)
>
> [Up I go, over you I step;
> With a live child not with a dying one,

> With a child brought to full-term, not with a doomed (i.e., premature) one.]
> (Pettit 2001, I: 113)

Consider the Credidi propter, Psalm 115, mentioned above in *Lacnunga* clii, with its first-person statement: "I have believed, therefore have I spoken." The profession of faith that is the Creed must also be understood within this context of clear subjectivity:

> I believe in God the Father Almighty, Creator of heaven and earth [...].

What is more, highly subjective, first-person credal statements increase the subjective force of incantations. As Émile Benveniste explains, "By saying, I believe (that ...), I convert into a subjective utterance the fact asserted impersonally" (1971: 228). In a sense, the subjectivity of the charm performer, the person who recites each incantation, is strengthened reciprocally through the uttering of the Creed. This is the voice who invokes Christian liturgy in order to exorcize the forces of illness and trouble. But the voice and its personal source remain clear. From a linguistic perspective, Creed charms manifest, above all, speaker instrumentality. As a result, the charmer who repeats the Creed is not the neophyte who confesses, "I believe." Nor is he the godparent or priest who makes an affirmation by reciting the Creed in its entirety. He or she is the folk healer whose Creed stands as an indirect request: "I believe; therefore, please heal or restore." Subjectivity lies at the foundation of Karen Jolly's observation that, "the speaker or healer speaks with his or her own authority or power"; and it is through the "power of the speaker's words and actions that changes took place" (1996: 127, 109).

6 Conclusion

Incantations delivered within a healing rite, as opposed to a liturgical rite, reveal not only the agency behind these spoken words but also the exercising of that agency. The charm speaker whose voice is firmly rooted in subjectivity can be differentiated from the priest or bishop who observes the liturgy, as a brief counter example reveals. Within the Mass the celebrant plays several roles, none of them subjective. He blesses and he praises. He speaks for and with the people as he prays. He narrates the events leading to the institution of the Eucharist. At the appropriate time, he quotes the words of Jesus, and in so doing, he transforms earthly bread and wine into Christ's Body and Blood. The officiate's speech at the liturgy of baptism is similarly non-subjective. When a bishop or another clergyman baptizes, his role in the celebration of the sacrament is clearly stated with the first-person pronoun, *ego*, and the first-person singular verb, *baptizo*. Although the priest baptizes with the first-person, he does so in the name of the Father, the Son, and the Holy Spirit. His personal voice is subordinated as he invokes the deity who receives the baptized person as His own. When clergy baptize, moreover, just as they consecrate bread and wine, they do so through the authority given them at ordination. Through the laying on of hands, in an act passed down through centuries of apostolic succession, the church grants a man who will speak as priest the license to perform binding actions through his words. The cleric who speaks the words of baptism speaks with and through the voice of ancient tradition as it is encoded by the church.[14]

When Pater Noster and Creed incantations are uttered as subjective representations in charm performance, alternatively, the liturgical and sacramental institutions are present as echoes. Even if the healer is a priest, his otherwise productive ecclesiastical authority has been rendered symbolic. Symbolic authority is not nugatory, however. The semblance of authority reinforces subjectivity in the delivery of incantations typically associated with clergy.

Let me return to the question of who it was that performed charms. It is probable that the healer or anyone else using a charm (with the exception of those requiring a Mass) did so without special authorization beyond that based on their knowledge and skill. The voice that speaks is therefore the personal voice of the charmer. The addition of Pater Noster and Creed to charms reinforces the subjective speech of the healer through the texts' traditional referentiality and the subjectification that follows from the de-institutionalization of sacramental institutions.

The presence of Lord's Prayer and Creed in Anglo-Saxon charms bears witness to the power of the charm, and especially the incantation, as a discursive act. The adaption of both Pater Noster and Creed sustains new linguistic functions even while it facilitates the charm's salutary effect. The Pater Noster acts as a frame for incantations. As such it offers a kind of formula for the composition of incantatory utterances within charm performances. Credal charms also operate in an arena of the subjective rather than the sacramental. The de-institutionalization of liturgical speech acts yields a charm empowered by the healer himself, the speaker whose utterances invokes the liturgical in the context of healing.

---

14 This discussion of the de-institutionalization of the Pater Noster from the Eucharistic rite applies to the majority of charms in which the prayer occurs; for the most part these charms do not include the saying of the Mass as part of the healing. Yet the Mass is also required in some charm prescriptions. Sometimes it sanctifies a remedy after or during its preparation. On other occasions it constitutes an incantation in itself. We do not know how charms with Mass incantations were actually performed in Anglo-Saxon England.

When we study Anglo-Saxon charms, as Patrick Wormald reminds us, we acknowledge a "force of habit" which binds a society to its past (1978: 69). Charms offered the early English a practical instrument for controlling the world through divine assistance (see Nöth 1977). Christian and traditional elements function synthetically in charms. When Pater Noster and Creed are appropriated into English folk rites, they empower the healer who uses them to target illness or loss.

References

Arnovick, Leslie K. 1999. *Diachronic pragmatics: Seven case studies in English illocutionary development*. Amsterdam & Philadelphia: John Benjamins.

Arnovick, Leslie K. 2006. *Written reliquaries: The resonance of orality in medieval English texts*. Amsterdam & Philadelphia: John Benjamins.

Augustine. 2009 [1892]. A sermon to catechumens on the creed. In Philip Schaff (ed.) & H. Browne (trans.), *Nicene and post-Nicene fathers*, first series, vol. 3. Buffalo, NY: Christian Literature Publishing Co. 1892. Revised and edited for New Advent by Kevin Knight. http://newadvent.org/fathers/2711.htm (accessed 28 October 2016).

Bede. 1896. *Venerabilis Baedae Historiam ecclesiasticam gentis Anglorum, Historiam abbatum, Epistolam ad Ecgberctum una cum Historia abbatum auctore anonymo, ad fidem codicum manuscriptorum denuo recognovit*. Edited by Charles Plummer. 2 vols. Oxford: Clarendon Press. http://www.archive.org/stream/venerabilisbae.

Bede. 2009. *The ecclesiastical history of the English people*. Edited by Judith McClure & Roger Collins. Oxford & New York: Oxford University Press.

Benveniste, Émile. 1971 [1966]. *Problems in general linguistics*. Translated by Mary Elizabeth Meek. Coral Gables, FL: University of Miami Press.

Blair, John. 2006. *The church in Anglo-Saxon society*, revised edn. Oxford: Oxford University Press.

Cameron, Malcom L. 1993. *Anglo-Saxon medicine*. Cambridge: Cambridge University Press.

Cockayne, Thomas Oswald. 1965 [1865]. *Leechdoms, wortcunning, and starcraft of early England*, vol. 2. London: Kraus Reprint Ltd.

Collins, A. Jefferies. 1960. *Manuale ad usum percelebris ecclesie Sarisburiensis: From the edition printed at Rouen in 1543 compared with those of 1506 (London), 1516 (Rouen), 523 (Antwerp), 1526 (Paris)*. London: Henry Bradshaw Society.

Dendle, Peter. 2014. *Demon possession in Anglo-Saxon England*. Kalamazoo, MI: Medieval Institute Publications.

Foley, John Miles. 1991. *Immanent art: From structure to meaning in traditional oral epic*. Bloomington: Indiana University Press.

Forbes, Helen Foxhall. 2013. *Heaven and earth in Anglo-Saxon England: Theology and society in an age of faith*. Farnham, Surrey: Ashgate Publishing.

Freemantle, W. H. (trans). 1892. Rufinus, Commentary on the Apostles' Creed. In Philip Schaff & Henry Wace (eds.), *Nicene and post-Nicene fathers*, second series, vol 3. Buffalo, NY: Christian Literature Publishing Co. Revised and edited for New Advent by Kevin Knight. http://newadvent.org/fathers/2711.htm (accessed 28 October 2016).

Grendon, Felix. 1909. The Anglo-Saxon charms. *The Journal of American Folk-lore* 22 (84). 105–237.
Harsley, Fred (ed.). 1889. *Eadwine's Canterbury Psalter*. Early English Text Society. London: N. Trübner & Co. https://archive.org/details/eadwinescanterbu00cathrich (accessed 28 October 2016).
Jolly, Karen Louise. 1996. *Popular religion in late Saxon England: Elf charms in context*. Chapel Hill: University of North Carolina Press.
Jungmann, Josef Andreas. 1961 [1951]. *The mass of the Roman rite: Its origins and development (Missarum Sollemnia)*. Translated by Francis A. Brunner and revised by Charles K. Riepe. New York: Benziger Brothers.
Kelly, Henry Ansgar. 1985. *The devil at baptism*. Ithaca: Cornell University Press.
Kelly, J. N. D. 1950. *Early Christian creeds*. London: Longmans and Green.
Klingshirn, William E. 1994. *Caesarius of Arles: The making of a Christian community in late antique Gaul*. Cambridge: Cambridge University Press.
Legg, J. Wickham. 1969. *The Sarum missal: Edited from three early manuscripts*. Oxford: Clarendon Press.
Lionarons, Joyce Tally. 2010. *The homiletic writings of Archbishop Wulfstan: A critical study*. Woodbridge: D. S. Brewer.
Lyons, John. 1977. *Semantics*, vol. 2. Cambridge: Cambridge University Press.
McNeill, John T. & Helena M. Gamer (eds.). 1990. *Medieval handbooks of penance*. New York: Columbia University Press.
Maitland, Samuel Roffey. 1969 [1889]. *The dark ages*, 2 vols. Port Washington, NY: Kennikat Press.
Niles, John D. 1980. *Old English literature in context: Ten essays*. Cambridge: D. S. Brewer.
Nöth, Winfried. 1977. Semiotics of the Old English charm. *Semiotica* 19(1/2). 59–84.
The Oxford English dictionary. 2010-present. 3rd edn. Oxford: Oxford University Press. http://dictionary.oed.com/entrance.dtl (accessed 25 October 2016).
Pettit, Edward (ed.). 2001. *Anglo-Saxon remedies, charms, and prayers from British Library MS Harley 585: The Lacnunga*, 2 vols. Lewiston, NY: The Edwin Mellen Press.
Raith, Josef (ed.). 1933. *Die altenglische Version des halitgar'schen Bussbuches (sog. Poenitentiale Pseudo-Ecgberti)*. Hamburg: Henri Grand.
Skeat, Walter W. (ed.). 1881. Ælfric's lives of saints. Early English Text Society. London: N. Trübner & Co.
Silverstein, Michael & Greg Urban (eds.). 1996. *Natural histories of discourse*. Chicago: University of Chicago Press.
Thorpe, Benjamin. 1971 [1844]. *Homilies of the Anglo-Saxon church*, 2 vols. London: Johnson Reprint Corporation.
Thurston, Herbert. 2003 [1910]. The Lord's Prayer. *Catholic encyclopedia*. http://www.newadvent.org/cathen/09356a.htm (accessed 25 October 2016).
Traugott, Elizabeth Closs. 1989. On the rise of epistemic meanings in English: An example of subjectification in semantic change. *Language* 65 (1). 31–55.
Traugott, Elizabeth Closs. 1995. Subjectification in grammaticalisation. In Dieter Stein & Susan Wright (eds.), *Subjectivity and subjectivisation*, 31–54. Cambridge: Cambridge University Press.
Traugott, Elizabeth Closs. 1997. Subjectification and the development of epistemic meaning: The case of promise and threaten. In Toril Swan & Olaf Jansen Westvik (eds.), *Modality in German languages: Historical and comparative perspectives*, 185–210. Berlin: Mouton de Gruyter.

Wilson, H. A. (ed). 1894. *The Gelasian sacramentary. Liber sacramentorum Romanae ecclesiae: Ed. with introduction, critical notes & appendix*. Oxford: Clarendon Press.
Wormald, Patrick. 1978. Bede, Beowulf and the conversion of the Anglo-Saxon aristocracy. In Robert T. Farrell (ed.), *Bede and Anglo-Saxon England: papers in honour of the 1300th anniversary of the birth of Bede, given at Cornell University in 1973 and 1974*, 32–90. Oxford: British Archaeological Reports.
Yelle, Robert. 2013. *Semiotics of religion: Signs of the sacred in history*. London: Bloomsbury.

Aurélie Névot

Trembling voices echo: Yi shamanistic and mediumistic speeches

In memory of Anne-Marie Christin

1 Introduction: Masters of psalmody (*bimos*) and women who give voice to the dead (*chemas*)

*Bimo*s are male religious specialists of Yi nationality (*Yizu* 彝族) which, at around 8 million, is the largest Chinese Tibeto-Burman-speaking population. Scattered over the Yunnan, Sichuan, Guizhou, and Guangxi Provinces, these ritualists use special writings that have to be read aloud in the form of chants. Not only are these writings different from Chinese writing but they also change from one province to another and, as far as *bimo*s belonging to the Sani branch of Yi nationality – a branch that numbers around 78,000 and resides in the Stone Forest district of Yunnan Province, are concerned, their writings even change from one village to another.

Numbering a little over one hundred individuals, these *bimo*s (which means 'Masters of psalmody' in their own language) use a secret writing that has to be melodized – when they chant, they read directly from a script. By doing so, they are said to travel through the cosmos to encounter divinities and to discuss with them solutions to the problems of humans. In each village, besides exorcisms and domestic rituals, notably funerals, a *bimo* who is elected by the community may worship at the annual territorial cult *midje* – the most important festival – alongside the rotating chief. The Sanis' local religion is indeed closely associated with autochthonous political leadership (Névot 2008a, 2013).

The ritual language in question, which is thus exclusively mastered by initiated persons, is esoteric and differs from the vernacular language. More specifically, the syllabic writing with which it is closely associated – numbering 1,200 characters according to official data, or 3,000 according to the missionary Paul Vial (1855–1917)[1] – was not created in order to transcribe the local idiom.

1 This last number seems more accurate because it takes into account the written forms used by this shamanistic tradition before their standardization by the Chinese state (Névot 2008a, 2008b, 2011, 2012, 2014).

Aurélie Névot, Centre National de la Recherche Scientifique, Paris

https://doi.org/10.1515/9781614514329-006

This "oral/sung writing" is entirely independent of the everyday way of speaking: it does not respect the latter's five tones, and its laconic style is based on pentasyllables. However, at the same time, it shares certain characteristics with the everyday way of speaking: most of the script characters, when read but not chanted (during a non-ritual setting such as a teaching session), correspond to syllabo-semantic units from the Sani idiom. In this way, the *bimos*' speech, when not chanted and thus outside a ritual context, is not completely meaningless for laypersons, but it is ambiguous and literally "extra-ordinary," i.e., out of the ordinary speech. It has the "coefficient of weirdness" that Malinowski discussed (1935: 220). A certain equivocity occurs. This may be explained by the small number of phonemes that daily speech makes available. As for the shamanistic chant itself, which has to be sung during a ritual session, it is actually said to be 'secret speaking' (*ka di dje di bé*). It is unintelligible by laypersons who, moreover, compare it to caterwauling. While the secret is kept by speech, it is also etched in the written character, which is totally indecipherable by common people.[2] These features are linked to the nature of the exclusive communication which is supposedly established between the *bimo* and the spirits, communication which requires no understanding – hence no attention – from the audience.

Ritual lineages reinforce the secret nature of this speech. Indeed, on the whole, *bimos* possess texts that are quite similar in content from one lineage to another, although with differences in their characters. They do not have precisely the same writing because the scripts they master are intimately related to what passes through (and thus what is shared by) the generations of religious specialists belonging to the same (patrilineal) lineage: blood, *se* – containing (vital) breath, *sè*.[3] Writing – the quintessence of power – is so closely connected to the trans-corporeality of the Masters of psalmody that "written character" and "blood" are concepts signified by the same character, even though this character may differ from one shamanistic lineage to another. A *bimo* inherits this *se* (writing-blood) by what might be seen as "incorporation", that is to say by copying his master's texts (a master who is preferably his father or his grandfather, with whom he is supposed to share the same bones).[4]

---

2 I received training among a few *bimos* who gave me the opportunity to learn their shamanistic writing and thus to have access to their secret written language, and to question their scriptural metaphysics.

3 Read [sə] and [sɛ] respectively, both pronounced in the first tone – the Sani language having five tones. Indeed, as a shaman I met in the field said, "without blood no breath and without breath no blood" (*bimo* Li, village of Dalaowa).

4 This link established between the inner body of a *bimo* and his writings is metaphorical: *bimos* do not write by using their own blood but by using black ink. More generally, in China, the

Thus, not only is sharing the agnatic substance of an initiated lineage essential to become a *bimo*, but so too is sharing blood, conceived as the unique shamanistic transmission support. Each lineage belongs to a village-territory and to a larger geographic space that refers to a stem-family; three original shamanistic "areas" are more clearly identified. Therefore, each Master of psalmody expresses through his texts, on the one hand, his lineage particularities through the prism of a few writing-blood characters that are his own – that constitute his full shamanistic identity – and on the other hand, characters specific to each of the "areas" previously mentioned. Nevertheless, let us underline that the very large majority of scripts are common to the whole *corpus* of the Stone Forest district. Hence four identity levels are combined: on the lineage identity is grafted the identity of the *bimos* of the Stone Forest, another referring to a *bimo* cultural subarea and, lastly, a form of village identity.

The disciple is believed to give birth to the shamanistic chant from this embodiment of the writings of his master under the auspices of the spirits of psalmody. In other words, a man becomes a Master of psalmody by singing his own chant at the end of an initiation based on the copying of secret writing: to use the vocabulary of Vandermeersch, the *bimos*' characters are "graphical vocalizations" (*vocalises graphiques*) (1990: 192), but not written speech. They therefore constitute graphical melodies. When copying, disciples learn that certain characters are omitted and therefore remain invisible in order to preserve the secrets of the lineage. Though truncated visually, the versification is not truncated orally: the unwritten characters are communicated from master to disciple. Characters are thus visually absent but orally present, and only speaking *realizes* them (in the sense of making them become effective). Consequently, here psalmody gives flesh to the character, which nevertheless remains invisible. Visible characters generate speaking, while invisible characters are generated by speaking. Vision gives voice, though voice never gives vision.

Consubstantial to each group of initiated individuals, having to be copied from one generation to another for it to be incorporated by each disciple, linked to the personal voicing of each initiated man and referring at the same time to the idea of a shared identity, the writing-blood – which creates distinctions – lies at the core of *bimos*' shamanic metaphysics, and is effective only if it is both chanted *and* accompanied by blood sacrifices. In short, this writing *is* blood and chant in one. The *bimos*' ritual language is sacrificial, written and bloody, metaphorically speaking, as it is actually written in black ink; or if not sacrificial, it is regarded at

intimate relationship established between characters and the body of any writer is well known: for instance, writings are supposed to beat to the same rhythm as a calligrapher's arteries.

least as a written body substance. This scriptural shamanism thereby allows one to rethink the relationship between orality and writing. The *bimos*' perspective of *se* ('writing-blood') not only challenges the deceptive opposition that is often thought to exist between "oral traditions" and "written traditions," between written and oral speech, but it also incites us to move beyond the mistaken conception of writing as a simple scriptural representation of language, and moreover to move beyond the idea of immaterial speech as far as the latter is conceived (by *bimos*) as having a written, bloody origin, i.e., a substantiality.

In the first phase of analysis, I focus on the *bimos*' oral writing and on the way each of them acquires their own ritual voice linked to their secret speaking, which is based on consubstantiality between their body and their text. I then argue that this written language is not conceived as a mere recording of or mnemotechnic for ritual language, but instead as a "developing agent" of shamanistic and divine speech that is progressively incorporated by the disciple during his learning. Writing is the *substrate* of *bimo* ritual language. The focus is also on speech that helps to convey the message of the sacrificer to the god through the blood of the sacrificial victim, which is inscribed as a bloody text, and which is supposed to speak (*bé*) directly to the spiritual entity. It is indeed through blood that human speech is passed on by the sacrificial victim (*mo*), the 'spokesanimal' that enables transmission of shamanistic speech. Secondly, I introduce the notion of "psalmodic chimera," as far as the shaman shares the language of the gods when he chants his manuscripts, which reflects the oral proximity between the *bimos* and the gods. Correlatively, reflexivity represents an essential part of *bimo* ritual speech, and we examine its parallel structures in order to focus on the relationship that is established between psalmody and the shaman's textual walk into the beyond. This analysis would not be complete without ultimately referring to female mediums of the Sanis called *chemas*, which literally means 'dead (*che*) women (*ma*).' I propose to concentrate on their specific ritual language, a mirror-language of the *bimos*, by referring to Achema, the heroine of a myth that suggests that she is turned into a *chema* at the end of a long journey.[5] After an aborted sacrifice, Achema becomes consubstantial with the cave of ancestors (*fei*) and an echo that sends back the words of her brother, who is a *bimo*. Thus, according to mythology, the original *chema* speech echoes the original *bimo* speech. The analysis of this mutual voicing, which could be seen as a "co-dehiscence" or joint, spontaneous flowering or rupture (see below), gives a more comprehensive vision of the ritual uses of language from a Yi-Sani perspective.

5 For more details about ritual practices of *chemas*, see Névot (2017).

2 Through bones and blood: The utterance of the *bimo* writing

When he chants, the *bimo* moves to and fro, generally in a crouched position, in rhythm with the verses he psalmodizes. During this poetic performance, he is accompanied by a small bell and has to take a breath at the end of each verse – each of which is, let us recall, in pentasyllabic meter. Although this posture is not described as such in ritual texts, it is metaphorically introduced through specific verses depicting the shaman whirling like a spinning top, jumping like a grasshopper, or leaping like a deer.

A shamanistic verse stipulates that *bimo*s who are unable to psalmodize (*bi*) or ritual practitioners who 'do not speak the script characters' (*ma sebé*) are not Masters of psalmody of the Sanis. As mentioned before, in this cultural context, shamans' chants are based very specifically on writing; orality and writing are intricately interlinked in their ritual practices.

2.1 Oral writing

Let us refer to a term used in *bimo* texts (Névot 2013: 195): *teu*, which means 'read and talk at the same time', in other words: 'read aloud'. This expression evokes writing *and* speaking, as well as the word *bi*, psalmody. The fact that a *bimo* is defined as an enunciator, as somebody who speaks/chants texts, is fully relevant. And this *teu* implies offerings of alcohol:

bi mi geu teu teu	The *bimo teu* in the village,
dje ku ga chla chla	The noise of the alcohol flowing, is it heard?
(Névot 2013: 148)	

The link established between the textual chant and the sacrificial offering is more obvious through the expression *michi*, *mi* meaning 'melody' and *chi* 'sacrifice,' which is part of the *bimo*'s teaching vocabulary. The *bimo*'s psalmody and celestial whirling are also respectively likened to the song and the flight of a migratory duck, *vébi*, *bi* meaning 'to move,' 'to jump,' 'to dance,' and homophonous with *bi*, 'to psalmodize' (Névot 2013: 230). To be more precise, the chant is called *tso* or *tso che*, *che* being written either like 'dead/death' or like 'snake': thus, *tso che* may be translated either as 'the chant of dead/death' or as 'the chant of snake,' expressions that are clarified by the myth of Achema, a snake-woman who becomes a dead-woman echoing the speech of her shaman-brother.

Bimo chants are visual. Speaking here is 'archi-writing' (*archi-écriture*) according to Christin's meaning, which uses Derrida's expression (1967): "verbal and yet visual, definitive without giving any orders but devoted in advance to readings that alone are able to invigorate it" (Christin 2009 [1995]: 189).[6] In a European context, Ingold (2007: 12–13) reminds us when referring to de Certeau (1984: 136–137) that, in the Middle Ages, writing was perceived as something that speaks. As for the Sanis, a shaman's task is to make the writing speak.

This interdependence of parole, sound, and writing during rituals is manifest in a myth about a mute shepherd who undertakes an apprenticeship with a male monkey and a female pheasant. These animals teach him to write, the former perched on a tree (thus linked to the sky) mastering speech, which the latter transcribes on the ground (thus linked to the earth).[7] Writing is thus conceived as the "depository" of speech,[8] but if speech and writing mirror each other, they refer both to two sexual halves and to animals from very remote species. This myth seems to illustrate the mixed nature of writing described by Christin: "because its system is based on two registers at the same time, the verbal register and the graphic register, but also because those two registers themselves are fundamentally heterogeneous from one another" (Christin 2009 [1995]: 15).[9] This duo of original masters coming from the wild world makes sky and earth cooperate through their teaching. Celestial speech is anchored on earth, and it is this writing and its pronunciation that the shepherd is said to learn. And at the end of his initiation, he does acquire speech. As for the shamanistic initiation which may be observed among Sanis, it supposes that a disciple first learns to read while copying characters, before being able to psalmodize.[10]

6 Translated from the French: "Verbale et pourtant visuelle, définitive et cependant ne donnant pas d'ordres mais vouée par avance aux lectures qui seules peuvent la vivifier."

7 This myth was collected in 1928 in Sichuan (Daliangshan) by Young (1935: 17). Although it does not come from Sani *bimo*s but from Nosu *bimo*s (another group of Yis), these data seem vital for understanding the relationship between orality and writing in *bimo* shamanistic traditions.

8 Which refers to a very ancient Chinese conception, see Levi (1997).

9 Translated from the French: "Parce que son système s'appuie sur deux registres à la fois, celui du verbe et celui du graphisme, mais aussi parce que ces registres sont eux-mêmes foncièrement hétérogènes l'un à l'autre."

10 Here I refer to the apprenticeship which, Great Masters of psalmody (*bimomomas*) say, is the most "traditional."

2.2 Write then enunciate by transmission of bones and blood

It is the "agnatic ideology," to use the expression of Sahlins (1965: 104), which prevails among Sanis. In other words, patrilineality prevails. As for the Hans – the majority population of China – the father is said to transmit his bones to his descendants, while the mother transmits her blood and her flesh.[11] Let us recall that in Chinese patrilineages, father and son are perceived as the "same body": they share the same bones and only males are believed to have the capacity to transmit identicalness. It is said that a *bimo* transmits his bones to his sons; in addition, if he belongs to a shamanistic lineage, he is likely to transmit his blood, linked to flesh, to one of his sons. This ritual apprenticeship indeed implies what might be seen as a slow incorporation of the blood and breath of a *bimo* master-father, as a body-to-body process, or as an imbibing of poetical texts through reading and copying – a process that I qualify as a *transubstantial process*. This adjective has to be understood in the words of Merleau-Ponty, that is to say in reference to the notion of flesh, of the living body, in the sense that it describes a sharing between substances. This is about capturing the intrinsically productive power of the texts, inherited from *bimo* ancestors. This transmission is the result of an acquired writing technique, not of enunciation. A *bimo* does not learn how to chant: he learns how to write texts from his ancestor's lineage by copying them as many times as possible. He is said to be able to express his voice, *do*,[12] and to psalmodize, *bi*, at the end of this writing initiation. In other words, his voicing is seen not as being learned but as coming out by itself. Hence, a shaman has to improvise if his voicing is to be consecrated. He has of course heard other ritualists psalmodizing and therefore knows what chanting is like.

Thus, if it is necessary to share the bones of a shamanistic lineage in order to become *bimo*, blood is seen as the unique transmission basis of the shamanistic identity. Onto the kinship filiation established at birth is grafted a textual filiation established, as it were, under the aegis of the spirits of psalmody which are said to be the reason for the desire to follow an apprenticeship. To put it another way, after having embodied ritual texts containing blood and breath from his lineage, a *bimo* acquires the chant. As de Sales writes about the Kham-Magar shaman, "he has undergone an ontological transformation that makes him different from ordinary human beings, and that gives him the exclusive power to negotiate with the spirits" (2016: 250). Little by little, he may also acquire the capacity to memorize

---

11 "While '*bones* and flesh' were both the image of death and the ground of mortality, they were also the substance of kin ties. They were the bodily element common to all kin who shared what in the West are called 'blood ties'" (Lewis 2006: 58).

12 *Do* is also linked to the idea of extraction, of a coming out.

his texts. Nevertheless, the *bimos* I met have always clearly said that learning texts by heart is not a goal, but that certain passages may spontaneously be memorized because they recur in each ritual. Indeed, very rare are shamans who have the capacity to psalmodize without having to read their texts. In this cultural context, what comes first is not rote learning but the total incorporation of the master's writings. When characters do not have to be read anymore, one might believe they are now internal, in the shamanistic self, expressing themselves directly through the breath of the voice. Ultimately, therefore, when they know their texts by heart, some *bimos* do not have to have their manuscripts in front of them. But, as far as their discipleship is concerned, they pursue their own textual immersion, i.e., manuscripts remain chanted in the ritual lineages. Hence, almost paradoxically for Western observers, the prevalence of orality demonstrates an extreme interiorization of writing. This presupposes, with regard to this tradition, an extraordinary vocation and a shamanistic ancestral background that dates back many generations, i.e., an outstanding textual imbibation to which only 'Great *bimos*' (*bimomomas*) have access.

Pragmatically, putting aside our ethnocentric biases privileging writing, we may suggest that the memorization of texts is subordinate to the multiple copies of texts and the intensive practice of rituals. Poetry and parallelisms are of undeniable neuronal mnemonic efficiency. Yet this shamanistic writing is not conceived as the transcription of a ritual language that should be recited. It is not so much the apprenticeship vector of the latter as a substance that helps to generate this language and to integrate a lineage power inscribed inside the writing-blood. Hence, writing is not treated here as a "construction method of the memorable" (*un mode de construction du mêmorable*) to use Severi's expression (2007) about Kuna shamanistic iconography.

2.3 A speaking process: The sacrificial animal

In order to convey chants as far away as where the spirits reside, and thus to pass on to the world beyond the message contained in the texts, the chanting of the ritual book is always accompanied by blood sacrifices. In singing his ritual text, the shaman at the same time expresses the need to sacrifice an animal as well as what is asserted through this sacrifice. The texts specify that by its blood, *se* (pronounced in the first tone), and its breath, *sè*, the sacrificial victim carries the message conveyed in the chanting, to the spirits, *se* (pronounced in the second tone). Now as we know, this chanting is based on written characters, *se*, and it is connected to the blood, *se*, and by extension the breath, *sè*, of the shaman. Thus, the vital essences of the sacrificial animal carry what is dictated by the writing-blood: chanting the characters, *se*, is conveyed by the continual course of the animal's blood (*se*) that is spilled on the altar. The *bimo*'s words addressed to the spirits therefore pass by the underlying theme *se*, and the animal's *se* together with the *se* of the writing contributes to the ritual effectiveness. The blood sacrifice is indeed the missing link between what is written and what is said, and this transubstantiation, which is necessary to transform the writings of the shaman into words addressed to the spirits, enables the transfer of *se* from the body of the shaman to the body of the sacrificial animal. In other words, the message from human beings is transmitted to the spirits through the shaman (human-spirit speaker); his psalmody turns this human message into words that the spirits can understand thanks to the transubstantial process. The word has to emerge from the writing and the sacrifice at the same time.

These words belong to the sacrificial animal, which speaks like humans but not like the shaman. The animal acquires the words through its own sacrifice, in keeping with the pattern, sacrificing–sacrificed–spirits. The shaman explicitly asks the animal to speak, *bé*, while he himself is said to 'read aloud,' *teu*, to psalmodize, *bi*. Thus, the sacrificial victim masters the human language and, through the shaman as an intermediary, is able to speak to spirits. If the sacrificial animal *bé* (speaks) and the shaman *bi* (psalmodizes), and if this psalmody enables the former to make sacrificial utterances – a substitute for human words – it is because the previously mentioned bodily relationship unifies the shaman and the animal. This solid link is established through ritual texts and their voicing. Such a "body to body"/"blood to blood" connection is an "incarnated" link between the shaman and the animal. The vocabulary used by Masters of Psalmody may allow us to pursue this interpretation further. The sacrificial animal is called *mo* in the shaman's secret language, and the character used to write this word is the same as the second character that appears in the term that designates the *bimo*. Thus, if ritual texts reveal a bodily relationship between the shaman and the sacrificial animal through the substance *se* (writing, blood), the names of these two ritual components further underline their consubstantiality. In this sense, the sacrificial animal is "partly" shaman, when the *bi* has been taken away: *mo* is the *bimo* without the psalmody but with human words added, since it is capable of speech, *bé*. It is the sacrifice of the *mo* that brings forth these words.

3 Psalmodic chimera

We have just seen that becoming a shaman means learning to read and write in order to integrate the power of the manuscripts and then to be able to intone the chants that give access to the invisible world of the spirits. The prosody of this chant, accompanied by sacrifices that pursue the speaking process from texts to spirits, will always be the same, whatever the linguistic form (dialogue, narrative, etc.). For instance, the shaman will sing:

ma di neu dje dja	I cry out three times. (Névot 2013: 140)

The *bimo* constantly uses the same singing tones he pronounced to close his initiation ritual without therefore respecting the tonalities of the word that may be used in the vernacular language.

3.1 The *bimo* speech: A divine language?

A *bimo* may chant cultic records that provide explanations of the various ritual stages, texts that accompany the odyssey of the shaman through the cosmos, descriptive texts that determine the religious calendar by announcing, for example, the dates of rituals, and recitative texts that evoke the Sanis' cosmogony and mythology. These different registers are not separated from each other: in the same text, a *bimo* may successively read verses associated with several of these topics.

By psalmodizing, the ritual specialist goes on cosmic odysseys. By investing his body with the voicing of his writings – which are indeed in resonance with his blood and his breath – he celebrates the ritual. By peeling away the chanted words, he addresses the spirits. For instance:

neu nya neu Gedze	You, venerable Gedze,[13]
Gedze gu che se	the spirit of the harvest,
gu che gu t'a ba	don't put the years or the crop upside down.
	(Névot 2013: 78)

Spirits may also speak through the shaman's ritual speech. In this sense, the Master of psalmody has multiple identities, whereas his chanting does not change according to the context of enunciation: he keeps his own vocal identity. His chant remains the same, whoever the being is that is supposed to speak through him. How are we to understand such a speaking community?

In a particular section of the *midje* manuscript which is sung during the harvest festival (as discussed in the introduction of this chapter), a few verses

13 The most important spirit in the Sani pantheon, living within the ninth stratum of the sky.

evoke different dialogues between the shaman in charge of the ritual and the spirits which speak through the chant:

se che gu cho ko	The golden old man is ploughing.
dze li la yi t'i	Are you the one who leads the livestock to us?
jo dze sa se ga	I am the venerable spirit who leads them to you.
yi t'i dza ko Pu ga ga	Isn't it Pu[14] who leads the livestock to us and takes charge of the food? (Névot 2013: 139)

The first question is put by the ritualist to the spirit, who answers in return. The last question is also asked by the *bimo* who doubts the spirit's claim, the spirit whose aim is to send the shaman off in the wrong direction. Contrary to what I analyze later, there is no reflexivity here in the ritual speech-writing. The *bimo*'s discourse and that of the god (the golden old man) are intricate – and without the help of a Master of psalmody, I would not have known who was speaking to whom.

Severi states that "it [ritual enunciation] makes the enunciator a complex figure, made up by the condensation of contradictory entities" (2002: 37). Although a *bimo* is the vehicle of divine speech, he is very different from Amerindian shamans who change their human status through ritual songs, for instance integrating animal speech into their human persona (Severi 2002: 35). A *bimo*, by contrast, never uses any animal language, only spiritual speech. He has an analogical connection with wild animals, but he is never actually supposed to give voice to these animals. In this cultural context, a *bimo* may only give voice to spirits, without changing his ritual voice at all. In this case, both of these entities (human and divine) speak using the same tone. We could say that the shaman sings like the spirits or that his ritual speech is that of the spirits. His voice is the same as the spirits' voice: all of them speak the same language. Through the embodiment of writings, a kind of co-tonal identity between the shaman and the divine is thus created, or one may say a kind of "psalmodic chimera" is created, which reflects the dual nature of these shamans who are capable of penetrating the invisible and of sharing its language, while officiating in the visible world. By singing his texts, the *bimo* also emerges into landscapes that he alone sees. Perhaps that is why the community in fact never listens to his chanting. His psalmodies always seem to concern him alone and the world beyond, which prompts some patients/clients to chat, play cards, or even interrupt during a ritual speech which is supposed to take place within other strata of the world.

14 The Great Ancestor.

3.2 Reflexivity in the *bimo*'s speaking

Severi underlines (2002: 27) that reflexivity is a constitutive part of the ritual itself. Similarly, de Sales suggests that a "reflexive dimension may be the formal feature that distinguishes shamanistic speech from the bard's oral poetry" (2017: 36), and shows that the strong reflexive dimension of ritual speech "sets up the conditions for the emergence of a transcendent authority" (2016: 243). During the harvest festival, the *bimo* in charge of this collective ritual always starts to sing about himself worshipping, and about himself as the son of a *bimo*:

dje Pu leu bi li	The *bimo* who performs the sacrifice for Pu comes,
leu pu bi za li	the son of a *bimo* of the happy community comes.

In another passage in the *midje* text, reflexivity is even more obvious:

bi ju se neu de u	When a *bimo* is born,
se neu du ma ga	he doesn't do the same job as everybody.
o lo la reu li	On his head, he wears a felt turban,
la reu né ju ju	the turban is black.
va la va teutu	When the *bimo* reads aloud,
va teu tyé beubeu	when the *bimo* is powerful, the village gathers around him.
vé lo bi né cha	With his hand, the *bimo* sees and searches.
bi teu miche ga	He is the *bimo* who reads out a melody.
bi teu che deu deu	His voice is like the wind.
jo m' jo ma m'	Am I the officiating *bimo*? (Névot 2013: 204)

Reflexivity also occurs when the *bimo* speaks about the construction of the altar, which is considered to be directly connected to the sky:

mu u bi na lo	In the sky, the *bimo* goes to observe (Névot 2013: 108)

Let us refer once more to Severi: "Reflexivity appears no more [...] as a 'comment' on ritual effectiveness made from the point of view of daily life. It becomes rather an essential part of the way in which ritual actions are made to become meaningful for the participants of a ritual celebration. Reflexivity is, in this case, situated within the ritual context" (Severi 2002: 27). But how can this statement apply if ritual speaking is unintelligible for the non-initiated, as is the case in the Sani cultural context?

It has been suggested that spirits and *bimo*s share the same speech. Hence, reflexivity could be analyzed as being understood by the spirits. It might be an estrangement, as it were, to affirm the shamans' power before the gods, rather than before the earthly community. The reflexivity of Masters of psalmody is made by themselves, on themselves, and maybe also for themselves, that is to say for the coming *bimos*. Indeed, we have to consider that these textual songs are always incorporated in a transmission process. Therefore, this I/*bimo* pair that we read in the texts may pertain to the nature of the books and writings which always have to be copied/rewritten "in secret" by the disciple for whom ritual actions become meaningful thanks to the many reflexive forms in his master's text. The recurrence of the verse "the son of a *bimo* of the happy community" confirms that reflexivity here concerns the disciple, the lineage and the transmission process. In other words, this reflexivity may be linked to learning, and all the more so because texts also evoke the specificities of the *bimos* who are said to be the only ones to have the capacity to psalmodize books (*bi sebeu*) (Névot 2013: 81), and it may recapitulate the title of the melodies that have to be sung (Névot 2013: 199). As Severi points out for Amerindian shamans, reflexivity may reflect the problem of doubt – not the client's doubt in the present context, but the disciple's. Reflexivity may thus assert *bimos*' power before the gods *and* the *bimos* to be.

3.3 Walking in the world beyond

According to the abridged version of the Yi-Han dictionary (1984), 'dance/to dance' is pronounced the same way as 'psalmody/to psalmodize,' *bi*, but is written differently. In the dictionary published in 1909 by the missionary Vial (1855–1917), who lived among the Sanis from 1887 to 1917 (Névot 2010, 2012), the word 'to dance' – that he writes using a different written form from the one in the Yi-Han dictionary – is associated with the first character of the word *bimo*, which would therefore be translated as 'Master of dance.' I myself have never seen this written form in the ritual texts I have studied so far. And the character *bi*, as the French missionary writes it, would not mean – according to the aforementioned Yi-Han dictionary – 'dance/to dance' but 'step' (with the idea of walking). From a diachronic perspective, psalmody, dance, and step are thus combined, recalling the constant movement of the Master of psalmody before the altar and in the universe he visits through his chant.

'There is not a single area that I can't reach,' *ma tche deu ma tche*; 'The place that I haven't reached yet, I reach,' *ma tche deu nè tche* (*nè* underlining the idea of exit, of extraction, linked to the movement of the *bimo* on his way to a territory that remains untouched by his passage). The shaman tirelessly repeats these two verses, as well as other formulas also based on forms of parallelism, in order to give rhythm to his psalmodies and to mark progress on his journey through the spirit world. Little by little, in the course of the pentasyllabic verses he chants, he invests the cosmos with his blood through blood sacrifices. It is said that the *bimo* rides a horse to reach the different strata in the sky. There, he meets the spirits, ancestors, wandering souls, and plants which are necessary to perform the ritual. Hence, *by lending his body to his writing through chants, the Master of psalmody transforms the writing into the ritual space in which he is able to travel.*[15]

Yet, as Houseman and Severi emphasize, "the main focus of ritual action in the case of shamanism is not 'cosmological exploration' but a particular process of metamorphosis implied by the 'travel pattern,' as well as symbolic predation of the evil spirit ritually enacted by the shaman. [...] The ritual word is no longer seen as a fragment of an imaginary discourse about the nature of the universe but as an instrument of this magic predation" (Houseman and Severi 1998: 272). Let us come back to the *bimos*' "travel pattern" which is inscribed in their speech and is thus essential to their writing.

Narrative structures are not present in all shamanic traditions; Severi shows that parallelism in particular is relevant to learning, poetry, linguistic techniques, but also to the transformation process (Severi 2002: 28–32):"It becomes a way to construct a supernatural dimension that is thought of as a possible world, possessing an existence parallel to that of the ordinary world." In the *bimo* context, it is all the more important that this parallelism as a linguistic form is inscribed in the text; parallel lines of writing trace the way that gives access to the world beyond.

The bookish space of *bimos* is indeed unusual: writing is inscribed on paper from top to bottom and from left to right, in the form of vertical columns of characters that may be separated by vertical lines. Such a pattern is said to be associated with the fact that this writing is not calligraphic, unlike Chinese which moves from right to left, but implies an inscription in/on the page. It is very similar to embroidery. There is a saying in the vernacular language that is common to writing and to embroidery, their respective characters being almost the same. Moreover, the lines making up a character are said to be threads, while the vertical lines that ensure that the text stands upright are associated with the uprightness of a thread. Writing would therefore be comparable to the weft, drawing a pattern on the paper: a book is called 'mountain (of) writing-blood'

15 The chiasmus established between the painter and the world in Merleau-Ponty's thoughts about painting helps to develop our analysis of the relationship between writing and the body. The philosopher notably writes that "by lending his body to the world, the painter changes the world into painting" ("C'est en prêtant son corps au monde que le peintre change le monde en peinture") (Merleau-Ponty 2006 [1964]: 16).

(*sebeu*), and the two pages that face a *bimo* during his psalmodies are called "two versants," i.e., mountain slopes.

Mountains, axes between the sky and the earth, play a fundamental role during shamanic journeys because they support the *bimo* on his ascent, the ascent itself being supported by the voicing of the written characters, the black color (*né*) of which refers not only to soot from the hearth – associated to a mountain – but also to vision (*né*). By psalmodizing written parallel lines, the shaman opens a space through which he walks (*gh'eu*). Therefore, the book itself, which is an interface between the world of humans and that of the spirits, makes up the space where the *bimo* starts moving through psalmodies. A *bimo* no doubt undergoes a metamorphosis by chanting his ritual texts which contain the blood and breath of his lineage, making his way through the lines of writing, climbing mountains to contact spirits and to access the sky.

4 Achema: the mutual dehiscence of male and female ritual languages

Contrary to Masters of psalmody, among *chemas* the transmission process is matrilineal, and these women only perform domestic rituals, do not use any writings, and are not allowed to perform any sacrifices. Like Masters of psalmody, they sing pentasyllabic verses to contact spirits, but unlike their male counterparts, they are not supposed to acquire any knowledge. They dance without being able to travel in the cosmos, whereas their helping spirits do travel.

Note that *chemas*, whose exact number is unknown,[16] are the only religious specialists capable of "hosting" ancestors – the deified dead[17]– who are supposed to speak through their bodies. Like matrices crossed by ancestors, they are repositories that allow the latter to express themselves, to voice their complaints, and to enable a human being to hear their grievances. What a *chema* says is in fact called 'the speech of the dead' (*che do*).

A tormented woman may go to a senior medium to seek a solution to her health or psychic problems. This *chema* may then tell her (if the latter has ancestors who were mediums) that she must accept her condition and herself become

16 They have not yet been officially listed for the whole district, unlike *bimos* whose practices are now more or less controlled by the Chinese state (Névot 2008b, 2009, 2011, 2012, 2014, 2017).
17 A dead person turns into an ancestor (*puse*) on the last day of their funeral. They are then deified and called *se*: *se* is a generic name to designate the divinities. I use the words 'divinity,' 'god,' and 'spirit' indifferently to translate this vernacular expression.

a *chema* in order to get better, i.e., to connect with her forebears' spirits. These mediumistic auxiliary spirits have to be called upon during the initiation ritual to make the woman a medium. Their invocation occurs in front of a cave (*fei*[18]) that is supposedly the dwelling-place of the future *chema*'s line of ancestors, among whom there was a former *chema* (it may have been her mother, her maternal grandmother, or the latter's mother).

Whereas *chemas* and *bimos* may sometimes make up couples,[19] they do not mix their respective practices: the shaman remains the specialist of an "oral writing" associated with sacrifices, whereas the medium does not master this writing nor does she sacrifice animals; instead she dances and sings to the spirits to lend her voice to ancestors. The complementary relationship between *chemas* and *bimos* (the first one dancing, *bi*, the second one psalmodizing, *bi*, these two terms being homophonous and graphically very similar) clearly emerges in the myth of Achema. The latter features a human sacrifice that results in the concomitant arrival – dehiscence – of the two religious Sani specialists, the mediumistic speech echoing the shamanistic speech. I use the notion of *dehiscence* here because it helps characterize the phenomenon of the corporal opening of Achema. Indeed, although the word "dehiscence" refers to the idea of an opening, of a blooming at the end of a maturation process, this term comes more specifically from the Latin *dehiscens*; it is the present participle of *dehiscere*, which is made up of the prefix *de*-and the verb *hiscere* 'to open,''to open your mouth (in order to speak),''to talk,''to say,''to speak,''to sing (something on the lyre)'(Dictionary Gaffiot 1934: 749).

4.1 From snake-woman to dead-woman

Ma, the second syllable of the word *chema*, means 'woman', and the first one, *che*, refers to death or to a dead person. Local *bimos* write this word *che* using the writing character which means 'death/to die' and more generally refers

18 Read [fɛj]. This cave is a recurrent element in Sani mythology where it is described as a kind of matrix which generated primordial ancestors; it is materialized outside each village, each patrilineage having its own cave that contains the anthropomorphic representations of couples of ancestors from the fourth to sixth generations prior to the generation of the actual lineage chief – the first three generations of ancestors have to stay on the wall of his house facing the front door. When he dies, his elder son purchases the same duties, and the great-great-grandfather and grandmother of his father are eliminated from the ranks: they do not have the right to receive individual offerings. They then have access to the *fei*.

19 For instance, three *chema-bimo* couples live in Dalaowa.

to 'corpse.' As for Father Vial, he wrote the word *chema* with *che* which has a written form that means 'snake' (Vial 1909: 308). In this case, *chema* would mean 'snake-woman.' This written form directly refers to Achema, the original mythical medium.

Born the year, month, and day of the snake sign, the name "Achema" is indeed written with *che* that corresponds to the written character for snake.[20] In the *bimo* ritual text entitled *Achema* belonging to *bimo* Ang (who died in 2006) from Bantian village, the name of the heroine is truncated in certain verses and appears as Chema (still written with the written character for "snake"). However, when the heroine enters the ancestral cave (*fei*[21]), she undergoes a bodily transformation concomitant with a change in name: thereupon *che* is written in the ritual text using the written form that corresponds to the meaning 'death/dead.' Let us focus on this episode to help us understand this point.

At the end of a long journey that takes her from her native home to her husband's, Achema escapes with the help of her brother to return to their parents' home – the idea of "turning back" is quite explicit in the text. On the way, a bee – an insect that has a sexual connotation for the Sanis – urges them both to venture into the cave, *fei*, which is also, in mythology, the matrix where a brother and a sister are said to have given birth to the ancestors of the Sanis. Only Achema ventures into the *fei*. By touching its wall, so the ritual text says, she becomes stuck to it. At the same time, she is no longer called Achema, nor is her name truncated to Chema, but to *chema*. The written character for 'snake' is therefore replaced by the written character that means 'death/dead.' Hence Achema, previously the 'snake-woman,' becomes the 'dead-woman' in the cave where she undergoes a corporeal transformation and simultaneously becomes the echo of her brother's speech – a brother who is a *bimo* himself.

In other words, the body of Achema is petrified inside the *fei* and the heroine becomes *chema* in the form of a cave. However, according to another sequence in the myth, the place usually given to ancestors inside this cave is vacant. The original matrix is empty: ancestors no longer live there. Achema replaces them by also becoming what contains them. She is both the content and container, consubstantial with the *fei*. The original and mythical *chema* is thus capable of holding ancestors in her body-cave.

---

20 The snake features in the Chinese calendar's twelve-year cycle. For the Sanis, a snake is an inauspicious animal. With "snake" and "death" being homophonous, to see a reptile is said to announce death; to counter such a bad omen, a *bimo* or a *chema* has to be summoned to perform an exorcism.

21 See note 18.

4.2 *Bimo* speaks, *chema* "speaks in return"

In order to be freed, Achema asks her brother (a *bimo* disciple[22]) to make offerings to the cave: she specifies that a white pig, a white sheep, and a white cockerel have to be sacrificed.[23] However, her brother fails to find a white pig. He therefore decides to cover a (black) pig with white earth. Because of this link between black and white, he connects the earth and the sky with which these colors are associated, and engenders a return to primordial times when the earth and the sky were not yet separate and when the world was upside down and no rules applied.[24] Thereupon there is a torrential downpour which reveals the true color of the animal, consequently ensuring the separation between the sky and the earth, top and bottom, male and female, etc.,[25] while Achema remains consubstantial with the *fei*. Although the sacrifice proves unsuccessful, it is paradoxically thanks to this cultural failure that the balance of the cosmos is re-established and that the *bimo*'s "speaking/parole in answer (*do ku*)"[26] pronounced by Achema becomes *chema*.

Mythology therefore suggests that the original medium, who was immobilized and was transformed into a "dead-woman" after having been a "snake-woman," is associated with a hollow that reflects speech, a kind of cave of echoes: Achema is transformed into the reverberated voice of her brother – this emblematic figure among the Sanis is regarded as the echo. The last three verses of our ritual text of reference specifically state: "The *fei* totally sends back (*gu*) what is said (*bé*). The brother [of Achema] comes to pronounce a sentence (*tchi*), his sister replies (returns, *gu*) a sentence (*tchi*)."[27] The term *tchi* also refers to the idea of trembling, shivering.

In other words, at the end of her epic, Achema, *bimo*'s sister, becomes *chema*: consubstantial with the cave, she pronounces a parole (*do*), she speaks (*bé*) 'in return' (*gu*). This speaking is born from an aborted sacrifice dedicated to the

---

22 See Névot (2009) to follow the complete analysis of the myth.

23 In the same way as white is the color that refers to celestial spirits, the cave is connected to the sky.

24 And especially in the absence of the prohibition of incest. The myth also implies a ban on incest between brother and sister, see Névot (2009).

25 For Sanis, as well as for Chinese culture in general, correspondences have been established between the different elements that make up the world, and more especially between elements that are said to be connected to the sky (*yang*) or those connected to the earth (*yin*).

26 This is the expression used in the published version of Achema in both *bimo* and Chinese writings by Ma (1985).

27 Ritual text (not published) of *bimo* Ang, from the village of Bantian, previously introduced.

sky – her brother *bimo* is unable to organize it despite his attempt to mask this ineptitude. Yet, as mentioned above, during contemporary rites orchestrated by *bimos*, the sacrificial animal (*mo*) is said to speak (*bé*) to the spirit(s) for whom the ritual is organized in the name of the sacrifiers, sacrificial blood being ritually essential to transmit the *bé* from the world of human beings to that of the spirits.

Therefore, by acquiring the *bé*, Achema/*chema* finally becomes the substitute for the animal victim of the sacrifice that she asked her brother to perform in her name. From sacrifier she thus becomes sacrificial victim, while her brother is the sacrificer. But her blood does not flow, for her body turns into stone; she carries the *bé* as an echo. As the cave of the ancestors, she is able to return speech from the world beyond (from the matrix she has become an ancestral cave linked to the sky). Her speech, which comes from the world of the dead, addresses the human world, not that of the spirits – hence the idea of "return," with *gu* also referring to the idea of inversion.

We now may understand why *chema*s, like the ones that might be observed in the field, do not perform any blood sacrifices. They do not have to find a substitute to contact the gods because they themselves are regarded as sacrificial and to be those who carry the *bé*, speech that comes directly from ancestors.

4.3 Altered voice

As the echo – the return of speech, the trembling voice that comes back – Achema does not acquire human speech. She reflects the human tone of voice without being a human voice. She is therefore comparable to a vibration, a quivering; she mirrors our own voice. Hence Achema is *convocata* and *convocans*, called and caller (appelant); a hollow body, a receptacle. She "gives voice back" by altering it.

Achema can thus incorporate all voices, a *chema* can create an intimate alliance with the dead. What prevails is not so much the components of the woman's body as the voice she expresses. We may take into account, for the *chema*, what Loraux writes about the Greek oracle: she is "a body that becomes voice [*voix*] ('a voice that has no body'), but also a body that becomes a way [*voie*]: 'a passage for the speech of the god. A way for speaking, the woman is erased, the god speaks'" (Loraux 1987: 8).[28] Let us refer as well to Sissa who also writes about the

28 Translated from the French: "un corps qui se fait voix ('une voix qui n'a pas de corps'), mais un corps aussi qui se fait voie: 'voie de passage pour la parole du dieu. Voie pour une parole, la femme est effacée, le dieu parle.'"

prophetess: "In a woman's body that has become a place, an icy wall, an empty page, speaking does not find a symbolic order: it emerges like a flash of light" (Sissa 1987: 29).[29]

One difference is nevertheless worth noting between what may be observed for a *chema* and for a prophetess – who, inspired by a god, expresses her answers herself (Loraux 1987: 52). In the *chema*'s case, because this speech is ancestral, it is analogous, not to a ray of light – such as that which, according to the ancient Greeks, was produced by Apollo and reflected by the Delphic oracle – but instead to the echo of a voice, that of the original *bimo* in Sani mythology, and of the ancestors who pass through her, during rituals. She therefore becomes altered speech – a trembling. The medium is a spokesperson, an errant voice. It is a hollow, sepulchral, and cavernous speech from beyond the grave.

Ancestors may be heard through a medium, but they are only seen in the appearance of the latter: their identity is thus only perceived through voicing. The medium contains another self, another entity to whom she lends voice, whereas a medium may also mime gestures of the dead (she is allowed to smoke cigarettes if the ancestor is a man, for instance). In fact, villagers believe they recognize the voice of their ancestors when a *chema* speaks; thus the voice of their ancestors – not the voice of the "trans-gender" medium – prevails. Here we observe a transfiguration of the ancestor inside the *chema* who turns herself inwards (she closes her eyes) in order to open herself to the other world and exteriorizes a voice which is different from her own. The mouth of the medium could thus be regarded as the orifice *par excellence* of an opening onto the other world, the space for the passage from the external to the internal.

By incorporating an ancestor, the *chema* engenders an alteration which does not affect the divine but the human, because the medium has to leave room for the ancestor in her (sacrificial) insides while remaining human. This internal division makes her body a space at the interface between human *and* divine. The mediumistic body, the voicing body, is thus altogether human and divine. In this cultural context, it is all about ancestors speaking, not about an embodiment, and about audibility not visibility, unlike in the case of the *bimo*'s voicing of written characters. Voice is what substantially links a medium to ancestors and, furthermore, the human being to the deceased.

29 Translated from the French: "Dans un corps de femme devenu lieu, paroi de glace, page vide, la parole ne trouve pas un ordre symbolique: elle surgit comme un éclat de lumière."

5 Conclusion

Yi shamanistic and mediumistic ritual speech occurs in half-way worlds, "voices between" that allow the passage of substances to relate to a shamanistic verse: "the mouth is moving, the breath is passing" (Névot 2013: 189). They emerge after bodily transformations: that of the *bimo* through the incorporation of texts connected to writing-blood, that of the original *chema* petrified in the cave.

As the echo, the voice of the original *chema* traces the voice of the original *bimo* which is not therefore factual, stuck in a particular moment in time, but which lasts into the world beyond and has access to the sky; it is an altered voice. The idea here is of an "after voicing," a voicing that is transmitted and transformed. Leaving mythology aside, observations in the field have shown that by using writing, *bimo*s have not erased voice or the breath of language from their rituals, but have on the contrary based their worship on a speaking writing.[30] Thanks to bones and blood transmission from master to disciple, then thanks to sacrifices that accompany their chants and their cosmic odysseys, Masters of psalmody are said to listen to the spirits' grievances and to discuss these with them by sharing the same language. As for the *chema*s, transmission occurs between women, thus also through the blood they are said to distribute directly through their bodies. Therefore, they do not need a medium, such as writing for the *bimo*s, to contact spirits. They are symbolically seen as sacrificial victims who integrate by echo the shamanistic voice. They mirror the Masters of psalmody by staying on earth, because they are, through their bodies, directly connected to the beyond, whereas shamans make this connection by journeying through their manuscripts. Nevertheless, shamanic and mediumistic bodies are both thought to be sonorous. Male and female voicings help to cross separate worlds and create vibrations, tremblings and shiverings through which entities of different nature may be linked together. In them is concentrated the essence of the beings.

Acknowledgments: My warm thanks go to Bernadette Sellers for correcting the style of my English and to Anne de Sales, Robert Yelle, Chris Lehrich, and Courtney Handman for reading through this article and giving me precious advice.

30 Contrary to what Kawada writes: "Language is primarily vocal and, by erasing the voice, the breath of language, it has been possible to fix writing in space and to assume its continuity" (*le langage est avant tout vocal et c'est en effaçant la voix, le souffle du langage, que l'écriture a pu se fixer dans l'espace et s'approprier la continuité*) (1998: 11).

References

Certeau, Michel de. 1984. *The practice of everyday life*. Trans. S. Rendall. Berkeley, CA: University of California Press.

Christin, Anne-Marie. 2009 [1995]. *L'image écrite ou la déraison graphique*. Paris: Flammarion [Champs].

Derrida, Jacques. 1967. *De la grammatologie*. Paris: Éditions de minuit.

Dictionary Gaffiot. 1934. Latin-français. Paris: Hachette.

Houseman, Michael & Carlo Severi. 1998. *Naven or the other self: A relational approach to ritual action*. Leiden, Boston & Cologne: Brill.

Ingold, Tim. 2007. *Lines: A brief history*. London: Routledge.

Kawada, Junzo. 1998. *La voix. Étude d'ethno-linguistique comparative*. Paris: Éditions de l'École des hautes études en sciences sociales.

Levi, Jean. 1997. Langue, rite et écriture. In Viviane Alleton (ed.), *Paroles à dire, paroles à écrire. Inde, Chine, Japon*, 157–182. Paris: Éditions de l'École des hautes études en sciences sociales.

Lewis, Mark Edward. 2006. *The construction of space in early China*. Albany: State University of New York Press.

Loraux, Nicole. 1987. Préface. Un secret bien gardé. In G. Sissa, *Le corps virginal: La virginité féminine en Grèce ancienne*, 7–16. Paris: J. Vrin.

Malinowski, Bronislaw. 1935. *Coral gardens and their magic: A study of the methods of tilling the soil and of agricultural rites in the Trobriand Islands*, vol. 2. London: Allen & Unwin.

Merleau-Ponty, Maurice. 2006 [1964]. *L'oeil et l'esprit*. Paris: Gallimard [Folio essais].

Névot, Aurélie. 2008a. *Comme le sel je suis le cours de l'eau. Le chamanisme à écriture yi des Yi du Yunnan (Chine)*. Nanterre: Société d'ethnologie.

Névot, Aurélie. 2008b. Une écriture chamanique bonne pour gouverner. Du processus de nationalisation des caractères d'écriture *ni* en caractères d'écriture *yi*. In Brigitte Baptandier & Giordana Charuty (eds.), *Du corps au texte. Approches comparatives*, 293–323. Nanterre: Société d'ethnologie.

Névot, Aurélie. 2009. Chamanes et intellectuels d'état: les transcriptions de la mémoire écrite des Nipa (Yunnan/Chine). In Gisèle Krauskopff (ed.), *Les Faiseurs d'histoire, Politique de l'origine et écrits sur le passé*, 217–246. Nanterre: Société d'ethnologie.

Névot, Aurélie. 2010. Paul Vial (1855–1917) – le père des esprits. L'inculturation d'un prêtre catholique en Chine. In Paul Servais (ed.), *Christianisme et Orient, 17e–21e siècles*, 153–175. Louvain-La-Neuve: Bruylant-Academia.

Névot, Aurélie. 2011. Une écriture secrète sur la scène publique en Chine, *Revue de l'histoire des religions*, 228 (2), Religion, secret et autorité: Pratiques textuelles et culturelles en clandestinité. 227–243.

Névot, Aurélie. 2012. Literate shamanism in Southwestern China: Bimo religion, the state and Christianity. *SHAMAN: International Journal of Shamanistic Research* 20(1). 23–54.

Névot, Aurélie. 2013. *Versets chamaniques. Le livre du sacrifice à la terre (Yunnan)*. Nanterre: Société d'ethnologie, coll. Écritures.

Névot, Aurélie. 2014. The politics of ethnicity in China and the process of homogenization of the Yi nationality. In Marine Carrin, Pralay Kanungo & Gérard Toffin (eds.), *The politics of ethnicity on the margins of the state: Adivasis/Janjatis in India and Nepal*, 279–300. Delhi: Primus.

Névot, Aurélie. 2017. Danse cosmique et voix en écho. La déhiscence des Chema. In Brigitte Baptandier (ed.), *Le battement de la vie: le corps naturel et ses représentations en Chine*, 189–211. Nanterre: Société d'ethnologie [Recherches sur la Haute Asie 22].

Sahlins, Marshall. 1965. On the ideology and composition of descent groups. *Man* 65. Art. 97, 104–107.

Sales, Anne de. 2016. The sources of authority for shamanic speech: examples from the Kam-Magar (Nepal). *Oral Tradition Journal* 30/2. 243–262. Special issue, Marie Lecomte-Tilouine & Anne de Sales (eds.), Words of Truth. Authority and Agency in Ritual and Legal Speeches in the Himalayas.

Sales, Anne de. 2017. Ramma the husband, Suwa the wife: the consecration song of a Kham-Magar shaman (Nepal). In Martin Gaenszle (ed.), *Ritual speech in the Himalayas: oral texts and their contexts* (Harvard Oriental Series 93), 15–38. Cambridge, MA: Harvard University Press.

Severi, Carlo. 2002. Memory, reflexivity and belief: Reflections on the ritual use of language. *Social Anthropology* 10(1). 23–40.

Severi, Carlo. 2007. *Le principe de la chimère: Une anthropologie de la mémoire*. Paris: Éditions rue d'Ulm-musée du quai Branly, coll. Aesthetica.

Sissa, Giulia. 1987. *Le corps virginal: La virginité féminine en Grèce ancienne*. Paris: J. Vrin.

Vandermeersch, Léon. 1990. Compte-rendu sur L'art chinois de l'écriture de Jean-François Billeter (1989), Études chinoises, vol. 9(1). 191–192.

Vial, Paul. 1909. *Dictionnaire Français-Lolo. Dialecte Gni*. Hong Kong: Imprimerie de la Société des Missions Étrangères.

Yi-Han abridged dictionary. *Yi Han jianming cidian* 彝汉简明词典. 1984. Kunming 昆明: *Yunnan minzu chubanshe* 云南民族出版社.

Young, Ching-chi. 1935. *L'écriture et les manuscrits Lolos* (Publication de la bibliothèque sino-internationale, No.4). Geneva: Imprimerie et Éditions Union S.A.

Part II: **Ideologies of religious language**

Naomi Janowitz

Speech acts and divine names: Comparing linguistic ideologies of performativity

1 Introduction

Discourse is said to create kinship systems, gender, and (according to some) even the world of nature, replicating the power attributed to the deity's utterance "Let there be light" in Genesis. Speech act theory in turn explains the creative power of language, providing the "performative" engine for social construction.[1] J. L. Austin (1962) famously argued that certain first person statements were not so much truth claims as speech acts that "do things" (such as, "I now pronounce you man and wife" and "I give and bequeath my watch to my brother"). Austin's theory continues to dominate debates about effective language. This dominance excludes other ideas about how words relate to their contexts of use.

As one example, in *Excitable Speech*, Judith Butler favors Austin's model over what Louis Althusser called the "Christian Religious Ideology" of naming (Butler 1997: 31–37). Althusser was interested in "social interpellation," how a person becomes a subject (in this case of the state) (Althusser 1994). In Christian divine naming, as briefly presented by Althusser, the deity calls out a name, such as "Peter," and thereby turns Peter into a subject. Althusser's primary example of Christian naming ideology is taken from Exodus 3, where Moses replies to God's summons, "It is I." Moses' reply is followed by the deity's revelation of his name (Exodus 3:4, 14). For Althusser, the deity presents himself as the "subject par excellence" just as Moses recognizes that he is a subject of the deity (Althusser 1994: 134).[2]

From Butler's point of view, divine naming is a model of limited value since it depends on the possession of sovereign power by the speaker. This power occurs very rarely in general society. Equivalent linguistic power operates only in those situations where speech is backed by state forces. She explains, "Human speech rarely mimes that divine effect except in the cases where the speech is backed by

1 For revolutionary social-constructivists, nothing exists beyond discourse (Hacking 1999: 9–12).
2 The naming creates a subject who is subsequently subjected to a greater subject. These mutually recognize each other and also guarantee that "everything is really so" (Althusser 1994: 135).

Naomi Janowitz, University of California, Davis

https://doi.org/10.1515/9781614514329-007

state power, that of a judge, the immigration authority, or the police, and even then there does sometimes exist recourse to refute that power" (Butler 1997: 32).

However, Butler dismissed Althusser's insights into effective language too quickly. Althusser has revealed another way in which language effects the context of use, one that is not based on the verbs that dominate Austin's theory. Instead divine naming presents a very different concept based on something about the power of names and naming in general. Both ideologies, speech act theory and divine naming, offer partial windows into the multi-functionality of language. They differ in the way that language uses are plumbed in search of context-relating social efficacy. After examining the linguistic function of names, we will look at several examples of divine names in detail. It will then be possible to see how the distinct ideologies capture different aspects of the social role of language.

2 How personal names name

Austin included christening a boat as one of his speech acts (Austin 1962: 5). He did not, however, discuss names in general at all, since his emphasis was on certain self-reflexive verbal forms. Althusser turned to Exodus because of the importance of naming ideologies in biblical and post-biblical texts. He introduced, but only briefly, some of the issues involved in not only divine names but also naming in general, putting his finger on something important about the social use of names. Althusser was interested in the deity's name "I am who I am," and its role in establishing him as the ultimate subject. But this enigmatic answer also shows hesitancy on the part of the deity to reveal his name. Uttering personal names is subject to widespread taboos. As Luke Fleming explains, "Verbal taboo is a domain of ethnolinguistic study uniquely amenable to cross-cultural study" (Fleming 2011: 143). Something about personal names elicits tremendous interest and concern on the part of speakers. Using a name seems to have implications beyond reference. Hence the widespread taboos against uttering personal names in diverse cultures, all with different nuances. These taboos carefully delineate the social permission needed to refer to people and the ways in which names can and cannot be used in both oral and written form.[3] The special functionality of personal names appears as widely in languages other than English, unlike Austin's first-person verbal phrases.

3 Butler (1997: 33) is correct that a name can be refused. But the baptismal event plus rigid reference makes it harder to say, "who me?"

This special functionality is based on the distinct linguistic role of personal names. Names do not simply refer to individuals. Benjamin Lee explains, "[...] the semantics of proper names is based not on a description model – nor can it be reduced to such a model – but rather on an initial indexical specification backed up by a sociohistorically constructed and transmitted meta-indexical chain of reference" (Lee 1997: 90). In other words, as explained in the classic work by Kripke, personal names refer based on a "baptismal" event when a name is first "fixed" by ostension as referring to a specific person (Kripke 1972: 4). Every name is closely related to the social context in which it is conferred, encoding all sorts of information about the speakers who endow the name and the addressee who is named. Thus a personal name is also a unique symbol for that person, indexically connected with the person at the moment it is given. The relationship is even stronger when part of a one-time event, e.g., baptism. In sum, as an "inherently inferring noun-phrase type," a personal name (whether one word or several) refers uniquely and irrevocably to the person named even as it stands symbolically for that person (Fleming 2011: 146).

At the same time, this "pointing to" or indexical capacity of names is familiar from other context-dependent linguistic units such as the oft-discussed deictics ("this," "then," etc.).[4] Unlike the noun "car," for example, which can be easily redefined in different contexts, a personal name carries the same reference cross-context (Fleming 2011: 149). A personal name functions both referentially and indexically, as if stating, "This very specific car and only this unique car."[5] The "rigid" reference means that personal names cannot be casually employed without invoking social implications, leading to the social restrictions (Kripke 1972: 4). For all these reasons a personal name functions context-free, being "resistant to recontextualization" (Fleming 2011: 149). Citation, for example, cannot diffuse contextual implications. It is hard to talk "about" a name without seeming to "use" it.

The source of what we might call a name's "rigid performativity" is the formal and context-related (indexical) capacity of language.[6] The indexical (contextual) implications of names are contagious and carry over to other lexical units that resemble names. For example, "Homophone and near-homophone avoidance represents an essentialization of the performative effect of verbal taboos as adhering in the material sign-form itself" (Fleming 2011: 157).

4 In other words, "Personal names function in a manner quite distinct from these other denotational indexicals" (Fleming 2011: 148).

5 Personal names combine "the constant denotation of the truly symbolic nouns with the indexical denotation of shifters, anaphoric pronouns and denotation" (Fleming 2011: 151).

6 Fleming (2011: 151), following Silverstein.

Divine names, not surprisingly, compound the problems of rigid reference and indexical implications of personal names, and offer particularly rich examples of deference and taboos. As a mode of "performativity," divine names are particularly instructive because unlike Austinian speech acts, they highlight the role of indexical icons as motivators of efficacy.[7] Their seemingly "natural" performativity contrasts with the conventional performativity of speech acts. At the same time, divine name ideologies implicate other types of signs (writing, art, etc.), opening up the issue of cross-modal efficacy, that is, how signs other than language also have contextual implications (efficacy). As we will see in the examples below, a natural form of performativity also has a contagious potential that conventional, verb-based performativity does not.

Example 1: Divine name and human form

The first example is two Iron Age drawings on storage jars found at Horvat Teman, an ancient crossroads on the Judah-Sinai border.[8] The fragmentary drawings with inscriptions, a striking archeological find, have elicited extensive discussion. Schmidt (2016) argues that the drawings are a practice study for a larger wall drawing. In the first drawing (A), an ornate humanoid male and female couple is placed between two musicians and a cow with calf.[9] A formula inscription overlaps the figures as follows (Inscription 3.1): "Speak to Yaheli, and to Yose and to [] I bless you before/to Yahweh of Shomron and his Asherah."

Scene A has elicited the greatest furor because the humanoid depiction of Yahweh contradicts Biblical injunctions against some types of divine images.[10] Similarly, strands of Israelite theology condemned Yahweh's consort Asherah even as she was the focus of Israelite ritual practices.[11] The male deity's crown is similar to the one worn by the deity Bes; divine attributes were shared between cults in both verbal and artistic presentations. Brian Schmidt judiciously identifies the male figure as Yahweh. He follows the label and opts for a reading that "requires far less convoluted arguments than any alternative interpretation

7 On indexical icons see the discussion in Parmentier (1997: 37–42).
8 The evidence, along with speculative interpretation, is presented in Meshel (2012).
9 The drawing can be found in Meshel (2012: 87).
10 For a summary of these issues see Halbertal and Margalit (1992).
11 Among the many discussions of Asherah, see the classic works by Olyan (1988) and Ackerman (1992).

offered to date" (Schmidt 2002: 107).[12] The drawing correlates with the use of statues in urban cultic centers. In this setting the "statue" is a small drawing.

The second drawing (B) includes a small crowd of worshippers near a cow, also overlapped by an inscription as follows (Inscription 3.9): "before/to Yahweh of Teman and his Asherah [...] whatever he shall ask of anyone, may He grant it [...] and may Yahweh give him according to his heart."[13]

A vertical inscription from the same scene reads (Inscription 3.6): "Thus say Amaryaw, Say to my lord Are you at peace? I have blessed you before Yahweh of Teman and his Asherah. May he bless and keep you and may He be with my lord [...]."

In an astute interpretation, Schmidt argues that Scene B is an example of "empty space aniconism" (Schmidt 2002: 114), in which a crowd of worshippers being blessed can point towards the divine source of the blessing. The place the deity might be (the sky), as a statue "before them," is empty even as the worshippers direct their prayers to that "empty" space in the sky. This use of empty space aniconism "highlights for the ancient viewer, the transcendence of Yahweh and his Asherah who invisibly dwell in the heavens exercising their power to bless those who send homage to them" (Schmidt 2002: 122 and 114; following Mettinger).

Both cultic models are depicted; that is, the urban temples with statues (Scene A) and the open-air "empty space" sanctuaries (Scene B). Both drawings employ an aesthetic of "overlapping perspective" (Schmidt 2002). Understanding this mode of representation is necessary for the viewer to correctly interpret the scenes (a problem for modern viewers). Objects are portrayed from more than one direction at the same time in order to give them three-dimensionality. Viewers know this social convention and use it to interpret the pictures.

Another overlapping layer of the formulas with the drawings then extends this overlapping portrayal. Overlapping connects the two modalities, verbal (inscription) and non-verbal (drawing). The blessing literally happens "before" Yahweh, in the nexus of the words and drawings "before" the viewer.[14]

---

12 Ahituv, Esehel and Meshel disassociate the drawings from the inscriptions in order to preserve an "image-free" ancient Israelite religion. See Meshel (2012: 129). They state, "There is no support for the idea that the people of Ajrud tried to represent the effigy of YHWH. The drawings on the pithoi do not challenge the accepted view of the non-iconographic character of Yahwistic cult and theology" (Meshel 2012: 129).

13 The drawing can be found in Meshel (2012: 92).

14 The modern insistence that Asherah is not a reference to the direct name of a divinity but only to a secondary object of divine representation (following the model of rabbis praising the Ark as a secondary representation of Yahweh) is another example of representational prohibition in action.

The inscriptions call upon the deity and his Asherah to bless specific individuals. The act of blessing joins representations of divinity (figures and names) in space and time with the worshippers who are formal (figures and names) models of the "blessed." Who exactly is speaking the blessing is not clear; there is no evidence that the blessing has to be delivered by some special authority, since the blessing comes from the deity. Humans declare other humans, and sometimes the deity, blessed as a way of marking the exalted status of the deities and drawing attention to the activity of the deities in the human world.

It is with these verbal forms that Austinian speech act theory comes into play. As for the formulas, "I bless you" comes the closest to a "performative" speech act.[15] As Seth Sanders has demonstrated, in West Semitic languages, the perfect form will be the closest equivalent to the performative, since it is the "morphologically and semantically minimal verbal category" (Sanders 2004: 170; see also Hasselbach-Andee 2015).

The phrase "I blessed you" is glossed in the archaeological report by Ahituv, Eshel, and Meshel as a parallel to Judges 17:2, where a mother declares, "Blessed of/to YHWH [be] my son" (Meshel 2012: 127).[16] She calls attention to the status of her son as being in a particular state in relation to the deity. This is a very common pattern found in biblical texts. Blessings as well as curses are automatically effective speech that is spoken by the deity but conveyed via human speakers (and even animals). We are far from Austin's speech acts here. The primary force of blessings is not based on any verbal form but located in a broader ideology of blessing that correlates with naming.

The deity is always referred to in the third person (by the personal name Yahweh and by "he"). Unlike the later standard blessing formula ("Blessed are you God"), second-person references are only made to the person seeking the blessing. The specific name "Yahweh" is necessary since the word "god" does not function as a proper name when there are many gods. Deities are connected to locations, so the full name of the deity is Yahweh of Shomron/Teman. Divine names clarify exactly which divinity will be personally responsible for the blessing. The figure alone is not sufficient since deities, like kings, share standard insignia.

Later biblical texts adapt some of these ancient modes of blessing, including the idea of inscribing a deity's name as a means of making a site holy. Deuteronomy 12:11 states: "Then to the place the Lord your God will choose as a dwelling place for his name, there are you to bring everything I command you."[17] The deity's name

---

15 Blessing formulas are discussed in Meshel (2012: 127–129).

16 While some English translations offer "by" the Hebrew is not agentive and is better glossed as blessed "in relation" to the deity.

17 For a general discussion of the Deuteronomic source in the context of the documentary hypothesis see Baden (2012: 129–148).

"dwells" in a specific location by means of a statue, by inscribing the name on a monument, and by a foundation sacrifice in which the divine name was deposited (baptismally!) in a temple foundation in written form (Richter 2002: 127–205). In all these cases the specific name of the deity is central since it explains exactly which deity is sacralizing the Temple, supporting the king or laying claim to territory. The "dwelling" formula is glossed in several places in Deuteronomy as "to place in," as a clarification of what it means for a name to "dwell" centuries after the ancient practices had lost their original setting.[18]

Some scholars argue that the Deuteronomic name ideology represents the withdrawal from the Temple by the deity, replacing an immanent theory of divine representation with a transcendent one.[19] The implication of the theology, however, is not that the deity has left *only* his name in the building.[20] Instead the issue is the specific form that divine representation takes in a specific cultic setting. The contrast between a notion of the name "dwelling" somewhere and "placing the name" somewhere pales against the general point that both tie the tightest possible knot between the two modalities, verbal and non-verbal: nothing can stand for the deity more directly than his name and thus his building. In both cases the name is an indexical icon that spatially connects divinity with a specific place. Like the Iron-Age drawings with their inscriptions, the "dwelling" name ideology is another example of cross-modal representation. The linguistic model is used to calibrate the sacredness of the Temple building.[21] The value of the Building-as-name ideology is the special functionality of names.[22] As discussed above, a name has a special relationship with what it names. Each reminder about the in-dwelling name "baptizes" the Temple in a re-naming event that is itself a repetition of the primordial naming of the deity. Baptism, and re-baptism, is always indexical, sanctifying the building directly as it makes the connection between divine name and place.

Treating the building, or a name, as a formal representation of divinity may seem like an idolatrous move. Idolatry is not a type of cultic practice as much as an interpretive claim made, often by outside opponents or internal reformers, about some contested representation (how something is understood, or misunderstood,

18 New meanings for a name "dwelling" in a place will develop in the first centuries C.E. as discussed in the next example.
19 For a critique of this interpretation see Richter (2002). It incorporates later interpreters, starting with the translators of the scriptural texts into Aramaic in the first centuries C.E. into the Deuteronomic text. See Example #3 below.
20 And no longer, presumably, his body.
21 The ideology permits many ideas about names, as Hundley (2009) enumerates: name as legally-binding, as making de facto owner, as obligating someone.
22 Hundley (2009: 549) claims a special connection between name and what is named in the ancient, as opposed to the modern, setting.

to stand for something else). The building "is" the deity no more and no less than his name "is" him and the humanoid figure from Scene A "is" the deity.

In the ancient examples, as continued in the biblical texts, Yahweh's name can be directly employed. Deference does not demand avoiding the name when it is possible to name more than one deity. As pointed out by Morton Smith, etiquette demanded describing each deity as if he were the greatest and the only really important one (Smith 1952). The use of "my Lord" for example by Abraham when greeting the angelic messengers shows another deferential mode of discourse used with people who may be of higher status. The same deference was used with deities by combining the deferential phrase with their personal name.

All of this will change with the rise of monotheistic theology. When God becomes a personal name for the deity since there is only one, the rules of address will change drastically. Deference will make new demands.

Example 2: Divine name as form (X)

The mid-3rd-century Dura Europos synagogue, on the Roman-Parthian border, is famous for its floor-to-ceiling paintings of biblical scenes.[23] The building was miraculously preserved when, during a war between Persia and Rome, it was filled with dirt to buttress the city walls. The dramatic paintings depict numerous biblical scenes and characters, including a woman wearing only a necklace taking Moses out of the bulrushes.[24] Throughout the synagogue the deity is represented in four different modalities, including the divine name form.

First, several panels include a hand of God reaching down into a scene. The hand is a sign of the deity as the source of divine agency, as the hand formally activates the scene. The deity is responsible for the parting of the waters for the Israelites in Exodus and the resurrection of the dry bones in Ezekiel. The potentially ambiguous source of miracles is clarified with the dramatic hands literally reaching into the stories from outside the frames.

Second, other scenes point to the deity more indirectly, presenting stories in which he is a central, if indirect character. No hand appears in the scene where the Israelite king is being anointed; however, this is the deity's chosen representative on earth. An image can direct attention towards something

23 For the earlier analysis see Goodenough and Neusner (1988) and Kraeling (1979) and for more recent discussion and bibliography see Fine (2005) and Fine (2014: 101–121).

24 The paintings are so complex that Weitzman and Kessler (1990) argue they must be based on lost illuminated manuscripts, though no such manuscripts have ever been found.

subject to restricted representation.[25] A throne can "point to" the absent being presumed to sit upon it. In Scene B, a name written in the sky and worshippers can point to the heavenly deity. In the Jerusalem Temple panel, Aaron stands as chosen representative of the deity, dressed in his holy robes with his name inscribed next to him in front of the Temple building.[26] Inside the "closed portal," as the Temple scene is called, is the divine presence. Just above the Torah niche the deity is invoked by an arrangement of the elements from the story of the near-sacrifice of Isaac in Genesis 22 (back of man, knife, animal, etc.).[27]

The Torah scroll, stored in the Torah niche, is a third material representation of the divine presence, sanctifying the synagogue by their presence.[28] Prayer takes place "before" the niche, directed towards the sacred scrolls.

Fourth and finally, another formal divine representation and common mode of invoking divine presence is liturgy. A liturgical fragment was found among the ruins of the synagogue. The prayer includes a fascinating blessing formula with a previously unknown version of the divine name.[29] The fragment reads (following Fine's translation):

> Fragment A:
> Blessed is X, king of the world/eternity
> apportioned food, provided sustenance
> sons of flesh cattle to [...]
> created man to eat of [...]
> many bodies of [...]
> to bless all cattle [...]
>
> Fragment B:
> pure (animals) to (eat?)
> provide sustenance
> small and large
> all the animals of the field
> [...] feed their young
> and sing and bless.

25 Biblical texts include numerous examples of thrones and throne-bearers pointing towards the one sitting on the throne, or being carried off in a chariot.
26 Many other scenes indirectly point to the deity, such as the anointing of the king.
27 A shift familiar from the many other examples in which sacrifice is replaced by discourse about sacrifice.
28 In other cases, the Torah was stored in another room and brought in to be read.
29 For a discussion and bibliography see Fine (2005).

The exact purpose for the prayer is not known; the imagery fits a blessing after meals but other settings are also possible (Fine 2005: 56–57). This phrasing is similar but not identical with the standard rabbinic blessing formula: Blessed are you, Lord our God, king of the world.[30] The two striking differences are the use of an "X" shape and the lack of a direct 2nd person addressee "you."[31] The unusual formula is evidence that the liturgical formulas have not yet been standardized.

The Hebrew alphabet does not include a letter shaped like an "X." The character used appears to be a Greek Chi. In the context of the prayer it is a substitute for a divine name, but still an indexical icon. The striking usage is evidence of taboos against writing the name down too distinctly.[32] It is unclear what the setting for using the name might have been at the Dura synagogue, that is, whether it could be said out loud and when. In a later rabbinic formulation, the divine name can be said when ten men are present. It is hard to imagine that it was not possible to use the name liturgically, though again, how and when it could have been used is not clear.

The blessing is not addressed to the deity ("you"). The formulation parallels the earlier declarations of the blessed state of the deity, again pointing to a different kind of performativity from a speech act.[33] Once again prayer takes place in a site sanctified by multi-modal formal representations of the deity, including drawings and the divine name. All of these divine representations overlap in the synagogue, jostling with each other. Any name now refers to the only deity as taboos demand a substitution of the name at least in written form. This complex spectrum of representation discounts any abstract scale of idolatry.[34] Instead, what is acceptable seems to rely very much on what other practices are current at any given time. The Biblical scenes with the hand of the deity, for example, are a type of "iconic aniconism." The hand is permitted, but not the rest of the body. A throne is permitted to discreetly point to the being that sits on it long after the direct portrayal of the one sitting on the throne is forbidden. Not writing down the deity's name, surrounding it with careful restrictions, casts a shadow over

30 Kimelman (2005) dates the emergence of the standard rabbinic formula to the mid-3rd century, close to the period of the destruction of the Dura synagogue.

31 This version is different from the rabbinic divine name ideology, as our next example demonstrates. In their ideology, the name could be written since it was not the true, unspeakable name.

32 As argued by Fine, who cites a similar usage in the 7th century Munich Palimpsest (Fine 2005: 52).

33 So too in the Dead Sea Scrolls standardization occurs internal to a single text rather than across texts (Nitzan 1994: 77).

34 Including the one found in Halbertal and Margalit (1992), which is a brilliant elevation of Israelite polemics to the level of theory.

any direct utterance of the name as heresy or magic. The deity is both hidden and available according to the divine name ideology.

Example 3: Divine name as circumlocution and text

In the rabbinic divine name ideology, in a baptismal naming event hard to top, the Genesis creation story is given a new interpretation: the deity created the world by speaking his name (Janowitz 1993). The divine name, as a synthesis of all creative ability, is itself given a name that refers in shorthand both to the fact that it is a name and to its complex content. The name used to create the world is given the name Shem Ha-Meforash, an obscure and hard to translate term that can be glossed as "the Exceptional Name."[35]

This ideology plays out in numerous variations in all sorts of secondary theological points.[36] As a name for the divine name, the term signals that this name itself is now an object of speculation and investigation, a mini-text in itself. The name can, indeed must, be interpreted in order for it to reveal its secrets. The power of the name means that its use must be highly restricted, limited by a fundamental taboo. Endless formal and functional substitutes are created that supply, within carefully delineated parameters, the transformational efficacy of all speech (including prayer). Somewhat ironically, the name that was avoided in earlier blessing can now be written out, since it is not really the true, hidden name anyway.

We will briefly trace two examples of how this ideology extends in all directions. The name ideology is read back into the biblical text in the Aramaic translations by means of circumlocutions for the divine name. The new name extracts the implicit idea of God's creative speech from Genesis and substitutes a timeless framework. The name swallows the Biblical text as the entire text becomes an extended divine name. Exodus 3:14–15 includes the famous revelations of the divine name: "Moses asked the Lord, Who should I say sent me? And the Lord said to Moses, I am who I am. And he said, This you will say to the children of Israel: I am sent me."

35 Bacher (1905) argues that the term basically sets this name apart from all other names.

36 Christian theologians also eagerly adopted these ideas. For example, Jerome lists the ten names of the deity, nine of which can be spoken while the tenth is "ineffable" (Jerome, Letter 25 to Marcella, *Patrologia Latina* 22, 429).

In Targum Neofiti, an Aramaic translation of the Torah, God, instead of giving the short version of his name, replies to Moses:

> This you will say to the children of Israel: The one who spoke and the world was there at the beginning, and who is to speak to it "Exist" and it will exist, sent me.[37]

The text in Exodus already contains a short meditation on the meaning of God's name, playing with the connection between the name "YHWH" and the root "to be" (HYH). The interpretation is then extended in the Aramaic translation. God not only exists, he is also the source of all existence as the creator of the world. Thus in order to refer to him and to explain who he is – to answer the question, what is your name? – the simplest way is to describe him in his unique role as the speaker who creates. The deity's creative act of speaking has become his proper name.

This new version of cross-modal representation of divinity mixes a very delicate, deferential avoidance of the divine name with a very dramatic materialization of it in the form of the physical text. The name is entextualized into a text that becomes one extended name (Silverstein and Urban 1996: 1–6 and passim). While the entire world is a materialization of the deity, the text (the written divine name) is a much more direct materialization. Divine speech, in the objectified state of the text itself, embodies the deity on earth. The Divine-name-form is not the "human" form of Pithoi drawings or the Dura painting, but it is just as "idolatrous" since the material representations appear magical to outsiders and the scroll can be misunderstood and misused.

The name is a report of a report of a reported speech (Moses reports what the deity told Moses to say, and that in turn is the report that the deity told Moses to say). But due to the rigid reference of naming, the text as name can become problematic. The second line of development dilutes the text-as-name, equating divine speech more generally with "word." This is a more indirect sanctification than divine name, with fewer implications.[38] The words by which the world was created are found in the document, along with many other examples of divine speech (words). Each "Thus says the Lord" is an utterance of divine speech and the text is a collection of all such "words."

This linguistic ideology is once again read back into the text via the Targumic translation. The Aramaic word for 'word' (*memra*) is added in the translation, as for example "I will be there, my *memra*, with you" (Neofiti to Exodus 3:12).

---

37 Targum Neofiti is dated anywhere between the 2nd century to the 5th century CE.

38 The introduction of the Gospel of John, for example, has to explicitly equate the word (*logos*) with the name (*logos*) in order to achieve the rigid reference of name.

It only takes a slight equation of word with name to bring us back to the name ideology, but that slight difference of emphasis leaves open additional linguistic ideologies.

Example 4: Divine name as secret form

Our final two examples take us to the medieval elaborations of divine naming (12th to 13th century).[39] These articulations do not present new theories so much as spin out many of the implications of the ideologies we have already encountered. They both focus on the name as secret and powerful, an old idea but one that gains its own special emphasis in these examples.

First, *The Book of the Name*, written by Eleazer of Worms at the beginning of the 13th century, presents secret doctrines he hoped to preserve in the face of the death of his teacher and attacks on the Jewish community.[40] The text begins, "With the Name Was, Is, and Will be, I begin the Book of the Name" (1.1).[41] The name is both the subject of the text and also invoked at the outset. In a sense, the book could end here. As repeated explicitly throughout the treatise, "his name is his reality." If we could see immediately into the name, if we could uncover its structure, all the rest of the text would be commentary. But since we cannot do this, the author explicates the name for us. "Why is the Yod at the start of the name?" The answer Eleazer gives is that "Aleph is above, Beth is below, etc., Yod is afterwards." His name begins with "afterward" in order "to teach that the existence after the world is like that before the world" (2:10).

The book details a ritual for passing on the secret divine name from Rabbi to student. Based on Psalm 27:3, "The voice of God is over the waters," the teacher and his students are told to fast and then stand in water up to their ankles.

The Rabbi then recites the blessing:

> Blessed are you, our God, the king of the universe, the Lord God of Israel. You are one and your name is one. You have commanded us to keep your name hidden because it is so terrifying. Blessed are you and blessed is your glorious name forever, the numinous name of the Lord our God. The voice of the Lord is upon the waters. Blessed are you our Lord who reveals His secret to those who worship him, the One who knows all secrets.

---

39 Both of the examples are hard to date because the texts preserve earlier ideas. The nuances of debates about dating the ideas are beyond the scope of this paper.

40 For information about Eleazer of Worms see Dan (1995) and (Dan 2002).

41 This text is not available in English translation or even in a critical Hebrew edition. For a general introduction with some translations, see Dan (1995). Translations are my own, in some cases adapted from Dan's translations.

The ritual builds in numerous formal (iconic) representations of the deity. In the Genesis creation story, the deity hovered over the water in the act of creation. In this version Eleazer uses his secret name, which is hidden from everyone in the world except for those to whom it is passed on. In the ritual a close identification is made between the divine presence hovering over the waters to create the world and the Rabbi with his disciples standing in the water and uttering the same word. The disciple who participates in the ceremony also knows the name, hearing it just as it was spoken at the moment of creation. This is a wonderful example of building not only a cosmology but also a cosmogony into a ritual. Recreating the primordial moment of creation transforms the human speaker.

The fact that the deity has a secret name was widely disseminated. A secret has no social valence if it is not known to exist and to be available to certain people. A rich set of stories elaborate a "history" for the secret name passed on by priests and then worthy rabbis. Eleazer of Worms only revealed this secret due to the dire circumstances of his life.

The text also describes a mini-version of the ritual carried out after the water ritual at the synagogue, with the divine name recited over a glass of water.[42] This recitation of the name "over water" brings the creative divine power directly into the synagogue, sanctifying it in yet another modality.

Our second example of the secret name comes from Pedro Alfonso, an early 12th-century Jew who converted to Christianity.[43] He wrote many theological treatises in Latin, including a "Dialogue against the Jews."[44] In the dialogue, Petrus is trying to convince his Jewish interlocutor about the truth of the Trinitarian deity using various types of textual evidence. He discusses the Hebrew divine name as proof of the superiority of Christian theology. For example, he points to the use of a plural "gods" in several biblical citations. When the Jewish interlocutor Moses replies that these citations include singular verb forms, Petrus counters with his knowledge about a secret divine name. He explains that, "the very subtle name of God, which is found explained in the *Secrets of Secrets*, is a name I say, of three letters (although it is written with four characters [*figurae*], for one of them is

42 For the combination of a divine name and water see the medieval versions of the *sotah* (suspected adultress rite) discussed in Janowitz (2014).

43 In the case of Eleazer of Worms, he wrote about the divine name because he hoped to preserve them. Peter converted to Christianity, and so revealed the form of the divine name as part of his argument in support of Christian theological doctrine.

44 Among other activities, he is said to have been a doctor to Henry I of England (Petrus and Resnick 2006).

written twice, doubled)."[45] He then makes three names out of the four letters as shown in a "geometric illustration [*figurae*]."

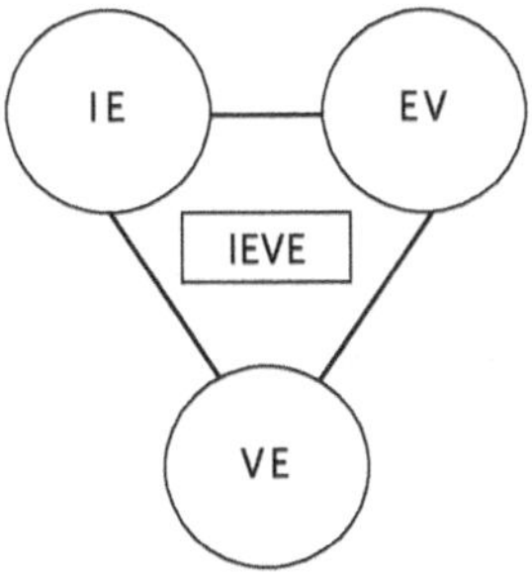

Figure 1: Alfonso's original model of the Divine Name.

Later versions of the text include a different figure:

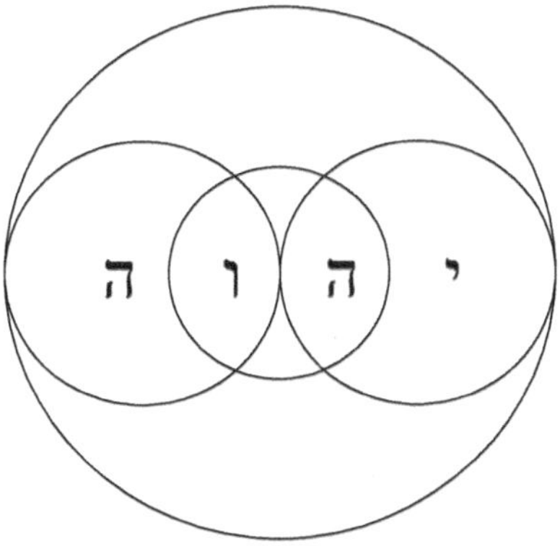

Figure 2: Alternate version of Alfonso's model.

The four letters of the divine name include three different letters (*yod*, *hay* twice, and *vav*), thereby representing the Trinity and proving that it is the true theology. Both diagrams are formal representations of the deity of yet another new type. Something about the explanation of the name leads Petrus to shift to a diagram, offering as it were, a map of the name outlined for the reader. This move might seem to be breaking a taboo since it involves writing down the name. However, diagrams of names appear in later Jewish texts as well, including the names of

45 Pedro Alfonso, *Dialogus contra Judaeos* PL 157,611. The drawing also appears in Maurer (1979: 978). The drawing is included in the Latin text but not in the English translation by Resnick (Petrus and Resnick 2006).

the deity mapped out in the form of a human body. When such proof is needed, then the form can be unveiled.

This example employs a coordinated dual-modality for the name, as, following an example explored by Cale Johnson (2013), when the word "fish" is portrayed in the form of a fish. Dual-modalities may be used as "material representation of otherwise intractable ideas" (Johnson 2013: 8). For example, in order to convey the idea of silence, a modern poem encircles many instance of the word "silence" around a blank inner circle. While it is easy to understand how a hand can represent the hand of God, in our example the problem is representing a divine name. The use of the drawing is an attempt to both contain and exploit the full implications of the formal relationship between the name and what is named. This inner form is part of the "reality" of the name and must be put on display in order to make that reality clear. At the same time the name as a representation is increasingly thought to be only a partial representation of what is ultimately an unknowable secret.

3 Conclusion: Comparing ideologies

The two linguistic ideologies overlap and differ in striking ways. From one point of view, speech act performatives could be thought of as a kind of "naming" themselves: the verbs "transparently" name the type of action being enacted: "I baptize" is *eo ipso* a "baptism." It is this very self-naming which drew Austin's attention in the first place, and since they name an action done by language are the model for Silverstein's explicit metapragmatics (Silverstein 1976).[46]

Austin's dependence on the self-naming verbs means he has to incorporate enough of the context to demonstrate how a particular verb was understood to encode social action in a particular setting. He had to add felicity conditions in an attempt to locate the context in which a verb is effective and the "naming" of the action successful. Thus speech act theory "emerges from a sociohistorically specific formulation from within a culture caught at a particular happenstance moment of lexicalization of certain metapragmatic verbs (verbs used to denote discursive interactional event types) which, as lexical primes, come into and go out of general use" (Silverstein 2010: 344).

On the other hand, names, with their rigid reference, supply a different model of indexical summoning of the divine presence. No felicity conditions are needed

46 This is why speech acts cannot model all the various functionalities of language but are limited to "nameable" action.

here. Automatic efficacy is taken for granted and extreme caution must therefore be observed. This ideology does not always play out in the same manner. Evolving constraints necessitate a constantly shifting calibration of the iconic presentation, ending up with the need to completely obscure the name. As a mediator between humans and their deity, the divine name is under constant pressure. As Leone and Parmentier note, "Cross-cultural investigations suggest [...] that the greater the assumed unbridgeability of the gap between earthly and transcendent realms[...] the more difficult becomes the task of traditional 'semiotic mediators' between realms, mediators that can now become increasingly open to intense ideological critique and political attack" (Leone and Parmentier 2014: 58).

Yet even as the ideological critique unfolds, the necessary indexical connection that is at the heart of the naming ideology continues to depend upon a material form in order to successfully invoke a divine presence. The material formal representation is always iconically connected to the divine referent. The formal "shape" is assumed to have a natural rather than conventional link to the divine. Thus all our examples of divine name rituals are built from not only words but other iconic signs as well.

One person's shape is another person's idol, even as all representations refer to the deity indexically as they cross-contextually manifest the divine presence in a particular location. The contagion of the "natural" connection of a name is harder to contain than the efficacy of a conventional speech act, easily dethroned by the mere shift in the verbal form. Both ideologies capture something speakers sense about the power of language, the capacity of names to invoke a presence and of self-reflexive verbs to describe the very action they enact.

Acknowledgments: I would like to thank Richard Parmentier and the editors of this volume for helpful comments.

Bibliography

Ackerman, Susan. 1992. *Under every green tree: Popular religion in sixth-century Judah* (Harvard semitic monographs 46). Atlanta, GA: Scholars Press.

Althusser, Louis. 1994. Ideology and ideological state apparatus (notes towards an investigation). In Slavoj Žižek (ed.), *Mapping ideology*, 100–140. London: Verso.

Austin, J. L. 1962. *How to do things with words*. Oxford: Clarendon Press.

Bacher, W. 1905. Shem ha-meforash. *Jewish Encyclopedia* 11. 262–264.

Baden, Joel S. 2012. *The composition of the Pentateuch: Renewing the documentary hypothesis*. New Haven: Yale University Press.

Butler, Judith. 1997. *Excitable speech: A politics of the performative*. New York: Routledge.

Dan, Joseph. 1995. The book of the divine name by Rabbi Eleazer of Worms. *Frankfurter judaistische Beiträge* 22. 27–60.
Dan, Joseph. 2002. *The heart and the fountain: An anthology of Jewish mystical experiences.* Oxford & New York: Oxford University Press.
Fine, Steven. 2005. Liturgy and the art of the Dura Europos synagogue. In Ruth Langer & Steven Fine (eds.), *Liturgy in the life of the synagogue: Studies in the history of Jewish prayer*, 41–71. Winona Lake, IN: Eisenbrauns.
Fine, Steven. 2014. *Art, history, and the historiography of Judaism in Roman antiquity* (Brill reference library of Judaism 34). Leiden: Brill.
Fleming, Luke. 2011. Name taboos and rigid performativity. *Anthropological Quarterly* 84(1). 141–164.
Goodenough, Erwin Ramsdell & Jacob Neusner. 1988. *Jewish symbols in the Greco-Roman period* (Bollingen series). Abridged edn. Princeton: Princeton University Press.
Hacking, Ian. 1999. *The social construction of what?* Cambridge, MA: Harvard University Press.
Halbertal, Moshe & Avishai Margalit. 1992. *Idolatry*. Cambridge, MA: Harvard University Press.
Hasselbach-Andee, Rebecca. 2015. Explicit performative utterances in Semitic. In Lutz Edzard (ed.), *Arabic and Semitic linguistics contextualized: Festschrift for Jan Retsö*, 448–485. Wiesbaden: Harrassowitz.
Hundley, Michael. 2009. To be or not to be: A reexamination of name language in Deuteronomy and the Deuteronomistic history. *Vetus Testamentum* 59(4). 533–555.
Janowitz, Naomi. 1993. Re-creating Genesis: The metapragmatics of divine speech. In John A. Lucy (ed.), *Reflexive language: Reported speech and metapragmatics*, 393–405. Cambridge: Cambridge University Press.
Janowitz, Naomi. 2014. Water, word and name: The shifting pragmatics of the sotah/suspected adulteress ritual. In Leonhard Clemens & Helmut Löhr (eds.), *Literature or liturgy? Early Christian hymns and prayers in their literary and liturgical context in antiquity*. Tübingen: Mohr Siebeck.
Johnson, J. Cale. 2013. Indexical iconicity in Sumerian belles lettres. *Language and Communication* 33(1). 26–49.
Kimelman, Reuven. 2005. Blessing formulae and divine sovereignty in rabbinic liturgy. In Ruth Langer & Steven Fine (eds.), *Liturgy in the life of the synagogue: Studies in the history of Jewish prayer*, 1–39. Winona Lake, IN: Eisenbrauns.
Kraeling, Carl H. 1979. *The synagogue: The excavations at Dura-Europos augmented edition* (final report 8, part 1). New York: Ktav Publishing House.
Kripke, Saul. 1972. Naming and necessity. In Donald Davidson & Gilbert Harman (eds.), *Semantics of natural language*, 253–355, 763–269. Dordrecht: D. Reidel.
Lee, Benjamin. 1997. *Talking heads: Language, metalanguage, and the semiotics of subjectivity*. Durham, NC: Duke University Press.
Leone, Massimo & Richard J. Parmentier. 2014. Representing transcendence: The semiosis of real presence. *Signs and Society* 2 (S1). S1–S22.
Maurer, Armand. 1979. The sacred tetragrammaton in medieval thought. In Asociación Española de Filosofia Medieval (ed.), *Actas del V Congreso Internacional de Filosofia Medieval* 2. 975–983. Madrid: Editora Nacional.
Meshel, Zeev. 2012. *Kuntillet Ajrud (Horvat Teman): An Iron Age II religious site on the Judah-sinai border*. Jerusalem: Israel Exploration Society.
Nitzan, Bilha. 1994. *Qumran prayer and religious poetry* (Studies on the texts of the desert of Judah 12). Leiden & New York: Brill.

Olyan, Saul M. 1988. *Asherah and the cult of Yahweh in Israel*. Atlanta, GA: Scholars Press.
Parmentier, Richard J. 1997. The pragmatic semiotics of cultures. *Semiotica*, special issue 116 (1). Berlin: Mouton de Gruyter.
Petrus, Alfonsi & Irven Michael Resnick. 2006. *Dialogue against the Jews* (Fathers of the church mediaeval continuation 8). Washington, D.C.: Catholic University of America Press.
Richter, Sandra L. 2002. *The Deuteronomistic history and the name theology: L^{e}šakkēn š^{e}mô šām in the Bible and the ancient Near East* (Beihefte zur Zeitschrift für die alttestamentliche Wissenschaft 318). Berlin & New York: Walter de Gruyter.
Sanders, Seth. 2004. Performative utterances and divine language in Ugaritic. *Journal of Near Eastern Studies* 63(3). 161–181.
Schmidt, Brian B. 2002. The Iron Age pithoi drawings from Horvat Teman or Kuntillet Ajrud: Some new proposals. *Journal of Ancient Near Eastern Religions* 2(1). 91–125.
Schmidt, Brian B. 2016. *The materiality of power: Explorations in the social history of early Israelite magic*. Tübingen: Mohr Siebeck.
Silverstein, Michael. 1976. Shifters. Linguistic categories and cultural descriptions. In K. Basso & H. Selby (eds.), *Meaning in anthropology*, 11–55. Albuquerque: University of New Mexico.
Silverstein, Michael. 2010. "Direct" and "indirect" communicative acts in semiotic perspective. *Journal of Pragmatics* 42(2). 337–353.
Silverstein, Michael & Greg Urban (eds). 1996. *Natural histories of discourse*. Chicago: University of Chicago Press.
Smith, Morton. 1952. The common theology of the ancient Near East. *Journal of Biblical Literature* 71(3). 135–147.
Weitzmann, Kurt & Herbert L. Kessler. 1990. *The frescoes of the Dura synagogue and Christian art* (Dumbarton Oaks studies 28). Washington, D.C.: Dumbarton Oaks Research Library and Collection.

Mustafa Shah

The word of God: The epistemology of language in classical Islamic theological thought

1 Introduction

One of the striking characteristics of early classical Islamic theological thought is the frequency with which language-based topics dominated arguments and discussions. This is evident in the medieval debates about the uncreated status of the Qur'ān, to deliberations about the concept of the Qur'ān's linguistic inimitability, and even to theories about the origins of language. This chapter will offer an examination of the gestation of the various discussions, investigating what was at stake in the disputes, and the wider ramifications of their impact within the sphere of theological and linguistic thought.

The Qur'ān defines itself as the veritable speech of God revealed in a flawlessly lucid Arabic diction.[1] According to traditional Muslim sources, it was revealed to the Prophet Muḥammad piecemeal during the periods of 610 CE and 632 CE. Initially preserved on palm-leaf stalks, scattered parchments, shoulder blades, and limestone, and memorized in the "hearts of men," these sources state that it was eventually collated into a fixed written text, not in the lifetime of the Prophet, but during the rule of the third caliph ʿUthmān (d. 656 CE). Consisting of over 6,000 verses and divided into 114 chapters of differing length, the organization of the text is neither chronological nor indeed thematic. Lengthier chapters tend to be placed at the beginning of the text, with the exception of the opening chapter. In fact the structure of its individual chapters and segments within them seemingly intimates overriding liturgical influences and the importance attached to the Qur'ān as a recited text: key narratives and exempla are repeated in different chapters with slight and subtle variations, and many of the narratives are allusive. Additionally, individual verses within chapters adhere to intricate patterns of rhyme and cadences, all of which accentuate the aesthetic and aural countenance of the text. Interestingly, in Arabic the very etymology of the

1 The concept of God's absolute unity (*tawḥīd*) serves as the primary theological doctrine of Islam, providing the axial basis of the faith's teachings and this is consistently emphasized in the Qur'ān.

Mustafa Shah, School of Oriental and African Studies, University of London

https://doi.org/10.1515/9781614514329-008

term Qur'ān connotes the act of "recitation," and Semiticists speak of a semantic nexus with the Syriac equivalent *qeryana*; and even the Qur'ān frequently refers to the fact that it is a text to be recited and rehearsed. Certainly, embedded within the text was a distinctive range of theological, legal, eschatological, and ethical teachings; yet its arrangement underlines the significance attached to its role as a devotional text and a book of guidance. Moreover, whatever the form of address in the Qur'ān – namely, whether the text is relating God's speaking directly and issuing commands or whether the text is recounting dialogues, including the direct quotes of the Prophet's Meccan opponents or the prophets of the Biblical scriptures – the traditional belief is that it is God who is the author of all aspects of the book's composition.

Significantly, the Qur'ān stresses the uniqueness, transcendence and incomparability of God, but it also extends this sense of exceptionality to the very composition of the Qur'ān.[2] Indeed, so cogent was the idea of the text's linguistic inimitability and distinctiveness as the veritable speech of God that it is exclaimed in the Qur'ān that "Had humans and jinns (spirits) come together to replicate this Qur'ān, they would not have been able to do so, even if they were to work assiduously together in that task" (Q. 17:88).[3] In classical theological thought, arguments about the status of the Qur'ān as the speech of God, its linguistic inimitability, and broader questions about the origins of language came to dominate rational and dialectical discourses. The resolve with which scholars attempted to flesh out the issues and contextualise the arguments underlines not only the importance of perceptions of language to the discussions, but also the originality of the scholarship. The discipline within which the rational import of theological topics was expounded upon is referred to as *kalām*, a term which

---

2 Likewise, equally reflective of the Qur'ānic conception of God's uniqueness and transcendence is the declaration that, "Verily, they (the Arabs) have no real appreciation of God's true measure: for on the Day of Judgement the earth and the heavens will be rolled up and held in his right clutch. Glory to him for He is above the partners whom they ascribe to Him"; and "Say (to them oh Prophet): 'who will provide for you from the heavens and earth; and who has control over your hearing and sight? Who is that brings forth the living from the dead and the dead from the living? And who is it that arranges matters (of the world)?' They will say 'it is God' so why do they act without refrain?" (Q. 10:3 2)

3 The first revelations are said to have occurred at Mecca and the final ones in Medina, the city to which the Prophet had migrated in 622 CE. The traditional accounts teach that the archangel Gabriel served as God's intermediary, delivering the verses of revelation to the Prophet. Despite the fact that Islam adopts unique perspectives and standpoints with regard to its prescription of doctrine and praxis, its teachings are not simply offering an entirely new system of beliefs and practices, but are essentially constellated around also reviving a "primitive" tradition of monotheism; pre-Islamic conventions and customs are subject to either repeal or revision.

literally denotes speech. These rational theological approaches to the explication of doctrine emerged in the early 8th century CE, turning on the use of logical and dialectical strategies and premises to defend religious doctrine and dogma (see Shah 2015; van Ess 1996; El-Bizri 2008). In later years these dialectical techniques formed just one of the many aspects of *ʿilm al-kalām* (the science of theology), which came to represent the sum and substance of rational and speculative theological discourses.[4] Within the realm of *kalām*, the panoply of topics pored over by theologians included subjects such as atomism; causality; arguments for the existence of God; occasionalism[5]; moral agency; theodicy; reward and punishment; eschatology; the historical efficacy of the transmission of knowledge; political leadership; the status of God's speech; the inimitability of the Qur'ān; the nature of the divine attributes; the origins of language; and even quantum leaps (Sabra 2009; Dhanani 1994).

Historians of early Islam remain divided regarding the overall reliability of the extant literary sources.[6] Questions have been raised about their fragmentary nature, a fact that contributes to the challenge of historically dating and authenticating materials purported to be of an early provenance.[7] Texts and epistles produced later were often attributed to historical figures who lived in earlier periods; some were flagrant examples of pseudepigraphy. In some instances, the historical gaps between the extant texts and the periods to which they refer have led some to conclude that these texts offer a highly idealised and heavily redacted version of the inception of ideas and practices, one that is colored by later prejudices and presuppositions. Texts and treatises on key theological issues were in many cases composed after doctrines had passed through subtle processes of evolution. These sources may reveal more about the periods in which they were

---

4 Other terms are often used to refer to the treatment of issues of faith, including *uṣūl al-dīn* (the fundamentals of belief), *ʿilm al-naẓar wa'l-jadal* (the science of disputation and polemics), *ʿilmal-tawḥīḍ* (the science of God's unicity).

5 This doctrine stresses the absolute efficacy of God in all the affairs of the created world to the extent that he is perpetually intervening in creation and is the one true efficient agent of cause and effect.

6 For a summary of the issues see Humphreys (1995); Donner (1998). The authenticity of the poetry has been questioned; the Qur'ān certainly censures practices and ideas associated with the pre-Islamic period but it also condones values which it deems consistent with the Islamic ethos. Other than the Qur'ān, the pre-Islamic poetry intimates an interaction between the ideas presented in the Qur'ān and those preserved in early literary sources. The poetry often betrays a society pre-occupied with polytheism.

7 In many ways this reminds one of Michael Cook's reference (1981: 156) to "the indefinite tolerance of the source-material for radically different historical interpretations."

composed than those to which they refer. Where arguments turn on the issue of historically dating doctrines and identifying their founders, caution is warranted. However, when we move away from narrower historical questions, these texts assume importance and interest. The quality and sophistication of their arguments about the status of the Qur'ān, notions of its compositional qualities and inimitability, and the origins of language dramatically animated early and medieval thought, providing a fascinating window into attitudes to language and its analysis within the classical Islamic tradition.

2 Religious movements and sects: The dominance of rational theology

Surveys of Islamic history routinely divide its religious movements into two principal ideological branches: on the one side there are the Sunnis (*ahl al-Sunna*), who make up the majority following of the faith; while, on the other side there is the Shīʿī branch of the faith.[8] Disagreements as to who was the rightful successor to the Prophet have historically divided Sunni and Shiʿī strands of Islam, although other doctrinal distinctions eventually emerged. Within Shīʿī thought it was argued that the choice of leader (*imām*) was a divinely determined process: it was not something that could be left to the fiat of humans (see Halm 2004). The idea of the infallibility of the *imām* also became a cornerstone of the Shīʿī branch of Islam, which further divided into Ismāʿīlī, Zaydī, and a number of other groups, including the Druze. Likewise, the Sunni label encompassed a broad spectrum of groups and movements holding diverse views on theological matters and on approaches to the exposition of doctrine. Included among these were arch-traditionalists or *ahl al-ḥadīth*, who frowned upon the use of dialectical strategies and the rational explication of doctrine, as well as the Ashʿarīs and the Māturidīs, who were avid advocates of rational theological thought and its attendant strategies. However, there are also key doctrinal differences which separate the *ahl al-ḥadīth* from the Ashʿarīs and Māturīdīs, and these principally turn on

8 The worldview presented by the Qur'ān is one in which a spiritual heritage is shared with Judaism and Christianity. Within the Islamic context, ancient Arabian religions are presented as reprehensibly promulgating the cult of polytheism. Although the Qur'ān refers to the fact that the pre-Islamic Arabs had recognized that God was the sole creator and sustainer of the universe, it censures them for associating lesser deities with him, and for advocating that these were able to interpose on their behalf (De Blois 2010; Berg 2003; Donner 2010; Berg and Rollens 2008; Brock 1982).

arguments about the nature of the divine attributes. The pre-eminence of Sunni theological discourses as a default position of traditionalism within histories of Islamic theology has been challenged by a number of researchers (Reinhart 2010; Wilson 2007). The inference of these researchers is that there were many movements during the formative years of Islam, each of which extolled its own brand of what it believed represented orthodoxy. Although the historical predominance of the Sunni movement and the sheer volume of its contribution to Islamic intellectual thought remains colossal, the Shīʿī, Ismāʿīlī, and Zaydī theologians, together with all the other groups and movements, contributed immensely to the evolution and expansion of the discourses of *kalām*.

Rational theological disputation comes of age with the contributions of the religious movement referred to as the Muʿtazila, who would have envisaged themselves as adherents of the Sunni movement, although hostility towards their brand of theology and the doctrines they supported led to their being rejected by the other Sunni groups.[9] Influenced by Greek philosophical ideas, they were champions of the view that reason must be the prime arbiter of truth and they assiduously used this axiom to guide their exposition of religious doctrine. It is important to bear in mind that they were not promoting a rejection of traditional doctrines but simply disapproved of absolute fideism.[10] It would be wrong to claim that the Muʿtazila were a doctrinally homogenous movement: differences

---

9 A political explanation can be sought for the appearance of the puritanical movement referred to as the seceders (Khawārij). In the aftermath of the civil war of Ṣiffīn (35/657) between the fourth caliph ʿAlī ibn Abī Ṭālib (d. 40/661) and his rival for power, Muʿāwiya ibn Abī Sufyān (d. 60/680), sharp disagreements resulted due to the caliph's acceptance of arbitration. Having fought alongside ʿAlī, the Khawārij disputed the legitimacy of his decision, arguing that it contravened God's divine decree, they withdrew from among the ranks of his supporters. The incident later led to much speculation about the status of sinners and whether they were eternally damned. The Khawārij remained influential throughout the formative years of the Islamic polity with the state having to contend with their fractious and insurrectional activities; but their doctrines and views across a range of issues were preserved in various theological and exegetical works.

10 Traditionally, a figure by the name of Wāṣil ibn ʿAṭāʾ (d. 131/749), an Iraqi from Basra, is identified as the founder of the school. Although he seems to have been involved in disagreements about the status of sinners, an issue stirred by the Khawārij, he is said to have been influenced by philosophers in terms of his dismissing the idea that God possessed substantive attributes. He is reported to have been a frequent visitor to the study circle of the celebrated ascetic figure, al-Ḥasan al-Baṣrī. It is recounted that during a lecture in the mosque, a question was posed to al-Ḥasan about the status of sinners. While deliberating upon his response, he was interrupted by Wāṣil who declared that a sinner could not be defined as being an absolute believer nor indeed an absolute disbeliever, but rather such an individual occupied an intermediate station between two stations (*al-manzila bayna al-manzilatayn*). See also Madelung (1997); Crone and Hinds (1986).

on points of doctrine among its theologians were often stark and vigorous. Still, essentially, within the Muʿtazilī cosmology, God was not only considered noble and just, but it was also argued that he acted in accordance with the dictates of reason: in their view good and evil were determined by rational criteria linked to their intrinsic properties. When referring to themselves, the Muʿtazila proudly employed the epithet "the upholders and divine justice and unity." This was on account of their strident rejection of the doctrine of predestination and their denial of anthropomorphic conceptions of the divine being.[11] Such was the scale of their contribution to Islamic rational theological thought that for centuries they dominated its discourses.[12] The Sunni rationalists who emerged in opposition to the Muʿtazila were individuals who took it upon themselves to develop critiques of standard Muʿtazilī beliefs and those of other theological adversaries. An advocate of such approaches was al-Ashʿarī (d. 936 CE), who was a "convert" from the ranks of the Muʿtazila, having been trained by their cynosures. His name became eponymous with the most prominent school of scholastic theology, the Ashʿarīs (Frank 1991; also van Ess 2010). Centuries of Islamic thought were defined by discussions among these various camps, with the traditionalists disavowing and excoriating Muʿtazilī doctrine across a range of theological issues.[13] The Māturidīs, whose founder was Abū Manṣūr al-Māturīdī (d. 944 CE), were the dominant school of theology in Transoxania and beyond, developing a distinguished school of thought which was as active and productive as the Ashʿarī school.[14]

---

11 Intriguingly, despite conceiving of the divine being in terms of his unmatched quiddity, they did concede that humans were able to draw conclusions about the nature of the divine essence through intuitive reasoning: using the physical world as a reference point, it was argued, the nature of God's attributes and acts could be logically inferred. It was classified as "inferring the invisible from the visible" (*qiyās al-ghā'ib ʿalā al-shāhid*).

12 The Muʿtazila did take the view that it was the moral responsibility of humankind, by virtue of the intellectual capacities created in them by God, to recognize his existence and unity prior to the advent of revelation.

13 Traditionist scholars (*ahl al-ḥadīth*) tended to be those who devoted themselves to the study and codification of the Prophetic traditions and avoided all speculative theology. Traditionalists are those individuals who pay due deference to such sources but also argue that the techniques of rational theology and *kalām* can be used to defend traditional doctrines and dogma. Arch rationalists favoured the primacy of *kalām*-driven approaches.

14 Within the Sunni camp, there did develop a stream of rationalism which favoured making use of dialectical and rational strategies and methodologies for the defence of Sunni doctrine much to the opprobrium of the arch-traditionists. The proto-Sunni movement defined itself through its critique of the doctrines which it held to be in contravention with the body of beliefs and practices substantiated by the Prophetic sunna or custom. In fact many of the points of dispute are the corollary to "reactionary" discourses with doctrines being refined in order to qualify or refute refractory arguments.

Tensions within the Sunni camp between rationalists and arch-traditionalists on questions of methodology and issues of dogma were often as strained as those that defined relations with the Muʿtazila.

3 Discussions of the status of God's speech and the episode of the *miḥna*

The 8th and 9th centuries CE witnessed the efflorescence of Muʿtazilī theological thought, and it is during these historical periods that defining the status of God's speech became a subject of much debate and controversy. The question of whether the Qur'ān was created or uncreated later became entwined with notions of the text's eternal status. The Muʿtazilī adopted the doctrine that the Qur'ān was a created text as a cardinal belief, arguing that to suggest otherwise compromised the concept of God's unity. The notion that the Qur'ān was created and contingent was initially floated by an individual who is presented in the traditional biographical sources as a somewhat heretical figure: Jahm ibn Ṣafwān (d. 745 CE) (Schöck 2016; also see Frank 1965).[15] It is reported that Jahm was an ardent proponent of determinism and someone who inveighed against the idea that humans possessed either capacity or volition. In ways which anticipate some of the current discussions on "religious language," he also adopted the principle that it was incorrect to describe God in terms which are used when speaking of created entities: only God could be exclusively described as being the "creator," the "agent," the "originator," and the "determiner of life and death."[16] Claiming that God was the effective agent behind all actions, Jahm pronounced that humans are defined as actors in a metaphorical sense only: although one might describe the fact that "the sun is declining" or that a "tree is moving," essentially it is God who is the veritable agent who brings this about. Turning his attention to the nature of divine speech, and with the aim of accentuating the idea of God's transcendence, Jahm posited that his speech was created in time (*muḥdath*) as was his knowledge, and that God could not be designated as being a speaker in any literal sense.[17] These critical standpoints furnished threads of

---

15 It is even mooted that there were antecedents for these sorts of ideas explored by individuals such as Maʿbad al-Juhanī (d. 705 CE) and Ghaylān al-Dimashqī (d. 743 CE). See Judd (1999).

16 For more general background discussions on this see Alston (2005).

17 An outline of Jahm's views is presented in the heresiographical literature whose accounts of his opinions are largely complimentary. An English translation of one of these classical texts is provided in Kazi and Flynn (1984).

thought which informed later deliberations on this very subject. There are no extant sources that intimate Jahm's position or views on the actual composition of the Qur'ān or indeed its language or quality as a literary text. However, Mu'tazila luminaries were to expand on these standpoints, integrating them into discussions about the status of the Qur'ān that were informed by their conception of God's transcendence. They dismissed the view that God possessed separate divine attributes such as knowledge, power, speech, and will in any substantive sense. They were not denying the belief that God was "knowledgeable and powerful," but simply rejecting the notion that these attributes possessed an entitative status within the divine essence: namely, that they existed as separate and discrete entities in the Godhead; in their estimation such a view seemingly implied the existence of a plurality in the divine essence which was implausible. They explained that speech was the "attribute of an act"; it was by no means eternal nor did it subsist in him. Guided by their explication of this doctrine, they posited that God was not a speaker in the literal sense of the word, but rather his speech was temporal in that it existed contingently in a substrate; and with this in mind they insisted that the Qur'ān as God's revealed text must be considered created (*muḥdath* or *makhlūq*) (Peters 1976). The Mu'tazila employed the maxim: "there was a point at which it (the Qur'ān) did not exist, then it came into existence." The implications of this doctrine were portentous, leading to centuries of debates about the status of the text and its relationship to the divine essence. Initially, the traditionalists and rational theologians dismissed the use of the term *makhlūq*, which was viewed as a pejorative innovation, but were soon critiquing the assertion that God did not speak in a real sense. Moreover, the Qur'ān refers to God as speaking and listening in what was seemingly a veridical sense and uses the phrase, "the speech of God"; it even describes God's speaking to Moses (Q. 4:164). Defenders of the Qur'ān's uncreated status were soon promoting maxims such as "From him it began and to him it shall return" (Madelung 1974). They insisted that his speech was a divine attribute that was, like God himself, eternal. Literary sources that preserve the related discussions include a plethora of references to Qur'ānic verses that were adduced by the opposing theological groups to support their standpoints.

The doctrine of a created Qur'ān was not simply an abstract concern of theologians. In fact the issue took on political significance when the Abbasid caliph al-Ma'mūn (r. 813–833 CE) dramatically imposed the doctrine as the official state creed in 198/833 CE, an episode referred to as the *miḥna* (inquisition). The medieval scholar al-Ṭabarī (d. 923 CE), renowned as one of Sunni Islam's most celebrated historians and exegetes, devotes a section to the controversy in his voluminous universal history of the Islamic world, citing from the correspondence between the caliph and the governor of Baghdad, Isḥāq ibn Ibrāhīm, on the subject (Al-Ṭabarī 1969: vol. 8, p. 639).[18] In it al-Maʾmūn declared that God has made it obligatory upon those whom he has charged with the welfare of his subjects that they should strive to uphold the teachings of the faith. He insisted that while it was the case that a majority of the state's subjects might be crude and common people who were unable to fathom not only his signs and guidance, but also the essence of the nature of his unicity, such a situation could not be condoned for those who occupy positions of authority. Lamenting this state of affairs, al-Ma'mūn identified some of the perceived menaces which result from drawing an equivalence between God and his revealed scripture, noting that common folk actually believed that the Qur'ān was an eternal (*qadīm*) and primordial document. Al-Ma'mūn mentioned various proofs that he claimed pointed to its created status, among which was a Qur'ānic verse stating, "And so we relate to you of that which has passed" (Q. 20:99), intimating that the Qur'ān was referring to events of the past and that sequentially it must have come into existence thereafter. In other instances simple lexical arguments were advanced: the Qur'ān states: "Verily; we have *made* this an Arabic Qur'ān" (Q. 12:2). Elsewhere it also employs the same verb "made" when describing the creation of the universe: "Praise be to he who created the heavens and the earth and who also '*made*' darkness and light" (Q. 6:1). The reasoning is that darkness and light were created *ex nihilo* and therefore the use of the same verb when referring to the Qur'ān indicated that it too belonged to the genus of created phenomena, as the verb "made" denotes the act of creation. A separate verse does mention that the Qur'ān existed on a heavenly "preserved tablet" (Q. 85:22), but al-Ma'mūn skilfully adduced this verse to argue that its being on a physical tablet confirmed its finite and created status. In Maʾmūn's discussions, mention is also made of the notion of an uncreated Qurʾān ominously resonating with the Christian doctrine of the *logos* in Christ. In his correspondence he went on to castigate those who profess to be true followers of the "Sunna" and the people of faith and consensus. He states that they spend their time excoriating adversaries, depicting them as deviants, apostates and renegades, while leading the common folk to espouse egregious views on the Qurʾān. In correspondence al-Ma'mūn eventually instructs his chief jurist-consult to have his letter read to all judges, decreeing that they along with the "people of *ḥadīth*" should all have their beliefs "tested" with regards to their acceptance of the doctrine of the created status of the Qur'ān. The point is made that al-Ma'mūn refused to countenance placing in a position of authority those whose faith does

18 The whole history was translated into English. The volume covering the *miḥna* was translated in Bosworth (1987). See also van Ess (1967); Hurvitz (2001); De Gifis (2014).

not meet the criterion for the true doctrine of unity. He insists that anyone who refuses to assent to this doctrine should not be allowed to issue legal edicts nor engage in the instruction of the scriptural sources, adding that the testimony of such persons was deemed invalid.

Some have argued that the episode of the *miḥna* was an attempt on the part of the caliph to assert his religious authority, and that the theological gravity of the disputes was not his main motivation.[19] Others have claimed that al-Maʾmūn was not the main instigator of this policy, but that various jurists within the court of the caliph were its true architects (Zadeh 2011: 61–62; see also Madelung 1974; Crone 2005: 131). Indeed, this led to the view that the imposition of the *miḥna* was an attempt to circumvent the textual authority of the Qurʾān and thereby increase the political power of the caliph and indeed his ministers in ways that undermined the role of scholars in interpreting the law. Yet there is little evidence to suggest that such a doctrine was espoused with such intentions in mind. Besides, neither al-Ma'mūn nor indeed leading Muʿtazilī theologians and jurists were seeking to attenuate accepted legal conventions and norms for interpreting the law; the Muʿtazilī commitment to the authority of the law and the sources used to determine juridical judgements and rulings appears unswerving. Al-Maʾmūn passed away in 218/833 CE, immediately following the imposition of the doctrine, but despite his passing, the policies of the *miḥna* were pursued by a number of his successors, including al-Muʿtaṣim (ruled 833–842 CE) and al-Wāthiq (ruled 842–847 CE), before they were eventually discarded by the caliph al-Mutawakkil in 847 CE (see Nawas 1994: 615–629). The relinquishing of the doctrine is seen as a victory of sorts for a traditionalist brand of orthodoxy. However, despite the fact that the turn of events marked a waning of the political influence of those with Muʿtazilī sympathies, the strength of this movement's contributions to intellectual thought was sustained over successive centuries.[20] Indeed, in all major areas

19 The correspondence is analysed at length by Turner (2013: 12–13). Martin Hinds concluded that the *miḥna* was simply about the authority of the caliphate and the role of caliphs as interpreters of the faith, suggesting that Muʿtazilite interests coincided with those of the state. In Hinds' estimation the episode was important because the caliphate lost the religious authority it had aspired to hold (Hinds 1996: 232–245).

20 The Sunni hero of the *miḥna* was the traditionist figure Aḥmad ibn Ḥanbal (d. 855 CE), who became the eponym of one of the four conventional schools of law in Islam. He is renowned for his stern opposition to *kalām*, protesting against its reliance on premises and presuppositions for the defence of doctrine which had no precedent in the Prophetic Sunna. Whatever the actual reasons for the *miḥna*, it undoubtedly marked a turning point in the consolidation of Sunni orthodoxy as the failure of the policy meant that traditionalist theological positions were eventually consolidated.

of Islamic thought, including the linguistic sciences, law, exegesis and theology, the Muʿtazilī contribution remained seminal.

There was one simple issue at the heart of the Muʿtazila's concerns: namely, if it were posited that the Qurʾān was the literal speech of God, one might infer that he possessed a physical organ with which to articulate speech; there were clear parallels with Jahm's position. Placing the Qurʾān in the realm of created entities avoided such an inference. The correspondence of al-Maʾmūn certainly provides a sense of the intricacies of the arguments and a measure of the passion with which he justified his convictions. The striking observation about the discussions is that al-Maʾmūn and the Muʿtazila were not using the arguments about the created status of the Qurʾān to question the composition of the text, its authority or indeed literary merits. These were indisputable, as evidenced by the profusion of literary works composed by Muʿtazilī theologians in which the linguistic superiority of the Qurʾān is extolled. When interpreting select Qurʾānic verses that made references to God's speaking or other physical attributes or actions, rational theologians were keen to obviate apparent anthropomorphic imagery implied by the scriptural sources. In order to achieve this, they assiduously resorted to metaphorical instead of literal interpretation. This can be witnessed in the exegesis of Qurʾānic verses such as "And indeed God spoke to Moses directly" (Q. 4:164) in addition to, "And a voice beckoned him from the right flank of the valley, from a tree on hallowed soil and said, 'Moses, I am God, the Lord of the worlds'" (Q. 28:30). Certain rational theologians were quick to dismiss the idea that these verses intimated that God physically spoke; rather, they asserted that the manifestation of this speech was materially contingent. At stake in the arguments over the question of the Qurʾān's created or uncreated status were simply competing conceptions of God's transcendence.

One of those in attendance at the debates during the period of the inquisition was the Sunni rationalist scholar Ibn Kullāb (d. 855? CE), who rigorously defended the view that the text was uncreated.[21] In the periods of the gestation of the arguments about the Qurʾān's status, the debates were mainly about the createdness versus the uncreatedness of the Qurʾān. However, in later years the discussions turned on whether the text was both uncreated and eternal (*qadīm*). Ibn Kullāb has an interesting set of views on the subject. He posits that God remains eternal with his attributes and names.[22] Ibn Kullāb also refers to speech as being one of

21 He is viewed as the progenitor of Sunni *kalām* discourses, inspiring the Ashʿarī school which became one of the main proponents of rational theology in the Sunni tradition.

22 Madelung (1974: 515). Underscoring the unity of identity within the essence, he uses the formula that his attributes are not him nor are they something other than him. Madelung argues that the issue in the pre-Miḥna period was not simply the question of temporality versus

the attributes of God that subsists within his eternal essence in the same way that knowledge and power inhere eternally within him. His point is that the attributes should not be deemed hypostatically eternal but that God is eternal and his attributes are with him eternally.[23] It is in this vein that he refers to an eternal Qur'ān, although he holds that this does not consist of letters or sounds, nor can it be fragmented, divided, segmented or parted, as it exists as an indivisible entity within God's essence. Ibn Kullāb states that the physical trace and impression (script) of the Qur'ān are constituted in its various letters and consonants and in its very recitation.[24] He therefore distinguished between the speech of God in its abstract sense within the essence of the eternal Qur'ān, and its physical "expression" or "substrate" (*'ibāra*), which can differ and be at variance with the former. The analogy Ibn Kullāb chooses to drive home these distinctions is the liturgical act of remembering God: individuals' remembrance of him can differ, but the subject of remembrance remains immutable (Wolfson 1976: 248–9). Ultimately, he states that God's speech is called an Arabic Qur'ān because its trace or vestige (*rasm*), in terms of its form of expression and recitation (*qirā'a*), occurs in Arabic. Ibn Kullāb even says that this is equally true of the revealed biblical scriptures whether they be in Syriac or Hebrew. Conclusively, when one hears a recital of the Qur'ān, one is actually experiencing this "expression" of his eternal speech.[25] Ibn Kullāb dismissed the idea that God is speaking in the literal or historically contingent sense of the word, for the simple reason that he derided the inference that accidents like speech can subsist within the divine essence, although within his schema all the divine attributes, including speech, exist primordially in that God is eternally with them.[26] The 10th-century bibliophile Ibn al-Nadīm, author of a

---

eternality, and that traditionalists objected more to the abstract presentation of God which strips him of his personal interaction with man. Madelung (1974: 508) claims that it was Ibn Ḥanbal whose position chiefly led to the adoption of the doctrine of an eternal Qur'ān.

23 Al-Ash'arī (1987: 357). For more on the divine attributes see Josef van Ess's entry on the Mu'tazila in the *Encyclopedia of Religion* (1987: 6322). He explains Abū Hāshim's 'theory of states' based on a grammatical solution to a theological problem. It was the jurist Abū Ḥanīfa who are reported to have stated that an oath sworn on the Qur'ān was not binding as the text was created and something other than God (Zadeh 2011: 61–62).

24 For the suggestion that Christian ideas were being borrowed see Wolfson (1976), who devotes a chapter to inlibration (1976: 235–247); more recent studies of a critique of *kalām*-driven views are found in Mayer (2014) and Gimaret (1988).

25 He was the author of a lost apologia on the subject of the divine attributes to which al-Ash'arī probably had access.

26 This was in deference to the Islamic theory of atomism: it maintains that the universe is made up of atoms; the smallest of these is represented by a corporeal particle which is essentially indivisible. The substances (*jawāhir*) of the world are formed from a conglomeration of atoms and accidents (*'araḍ/a'rāḍ*), which inhere in them; the latter possess no capacity for infinite

work which integrates biographical information with an inventory of the literary works of the first four centuries of the Islamic tradition, includes an anecdote of a debate between Ibn Kullāb and a Mu'tazilī protagonist who, having heard Ibn Kullāb propose that "the speech of God is God," responded by stating that "by virtue of this doctrine, he is a Christian,"suggesting that he sensed equivalences with the doctrine of the *logos* (Ibn al-Nadīm 1988: 230).

While Ibn Kullāb was positioning himself to counter the arguments of the Mu'tazila who contended that the Qur'ān was created, in later years traditionalist as well as rational theologians disavowed some aspects of the doctrines he put forward to explain the status of the Qur'ān.[27] Incidentally, the Ash'arī school was built upon the edifices of Ibn Kullāb's theological ideas, methods, and arguments. They argued that God's speech was one of the attributes of his essence, like his knowledge and power, and was neither created nor originated. Indeed, Qur'ānic verses were frequently adduced by them to underline the fact that the sacred text fell into the category of uncreated phenomena. Yet while many Ash'arī scholars censured Ibn Kullāb's use of the term *'ibāra* (expression) or *ḥikāya* (replication or reproduction), when referring to the revealed text, the fact is that even these Ash'arī theologians, like Ibn Kullāb, offered sophisticated distinctions between the material manifestation of God's speech and its unarticulated species which inhered in the divine essence; within their schema, this eternal form of the text was referred to as the *kalām nafsī* (internal speech) (al-Rāzī 1987: 1.244). To underpin their arguments, Ash'arī luminaries were soon offering sophisticated distinctions between the act of recital and the subject of recitation; they also distinguished between the graphemic representation of the spoken word and its actual referent.

Such distinctions about the nature of God's speech were given definitive resolution in the work of the Ash'arī theologian, al-Bāqillānī (d. 1013 CE). When dealing with a range of objections raised by Mu'tazilī opponents, one of the propositions that he singles out in his refutation is the contention that essentially the Qur'ān consists of chapters, verses, words, letters and phonemes, which all indicate that it is temporal and contingent. This is based on their view that

---

endurance (*baqā'*) but God sustains them through his constant and direct intervention in the world: this is the doctrine of occasionalism. The Mu'tazila employed the term *ḥikāya* (physical representation or emulation) when referring to the physical exemplification of the Qur'ān.

27 There were some theologians who were uneasy with the idea of an eternal Qur'ān and accused Ibn Kullāb of playing an inadvertent role in the promulgation of the doctrine, claiming that when the pious ancestors challenged this view, they had never intended to state that the Qur'ān was eternal. This is Madelung's point about Ibn Taymiyya's view, which was hostile to Ibn Kullāb's reasoning but equally dismissive of the line taken by followers of the founder of the Ḥanbalī school of thought (Madelung 1974: 524–55).

the structural parts and segments of the text were materially finite and subject to enumeration as they are regimented by points of inception and termination. Responding to this, al-Bāqillānī states that these observations apply to the external act of recitation and its outward characteristics and not the divine speech of the almighty, which was an attribute of his essence. Al-Bāqillānī explained that this is because the voiced reading of the text required mechanisms of expression: namely, organs such as a tongue and larynx for the production of speech; whereas, in contradistinction, God as an absolutely transcendent being had no need for such organs. Thus, the aforementioned physical divisions and delineations of chapter and verse did not apply to the uncreated speech of God (*kalām nafsī*), which was neither finite nor subject to enumeration. Al-Bāqillānī then cites a Qurʾānic verse to drive home the distinction: "Had the ocean served as ink for the words of your Lord, it would have run dry before the words of your Lord ever finished, even if thou were to bring forth reserves the like thereof" (Q. 18:109), and "Had the trees of the world been used as pens and seven oceans been used to supply them (with ink), the words of your Lord would still not expire" (Q. 31:28). He then adds that it is recognized that a copyist is able to transcribe a number of Qurʾānic parchments using one inkwell and also that a reciter of the sacred text may complete a set number of recitations, and that these acts of devotion are defined by material finiteness and limits: they are subject to having a beginning and an end in the sense that they are but attributes of our recitation, transcription, and memory of the text. However, the concrete attribute of God's speech cannot be described as ceasing or being confined to limits. Having followed a line of argumentation in which proofs are dexterously extracted from the Qur'ān to drive home the abstract distinction between the divine speech as an eternal attribute and its worldly form, al-Bāqillānī then refers to a Prophetic tradition (*ḥadīth*) in which the story is told of a group of companions, Arabs and non-Arabs, reciting the Qur'ān in the presence of the Prophet, who proceeded to encourage them despite an apparent disparity between the quality of their recitations. Al-Bāqillānī explains that the Arabs' recitation is seemingly flawless, while the recitation of the non-Arabs is marked by a stuttering and a lack of fluency, demonstrating the genuine distinction between the act of recitation and the subject of recitation, the act of reading and the subject of what is being read. The point made here is that infelicities of language do not impinge upon the primeval immaculateness of God's eternal speech. Referring to additional proofs, al-Bāqillānī states that following the destruction of Jerusalem in 586 BCE by Nebuchadnezzar II, the Prophet Ezra prayed to God that punishment be visited upon those who sacked the city and burned sacred scripture. Al-Bāqillānī recounts that the divine response to this plea explains that only the covers, parchment, and script of the Torah had been burned, and that "my speech was not consumed." Taking his cue from this anecdote, al-Bāqillānī insists that had a tyrant taken a copy of the Qur'ān and set about igniting it and reducing it to ashes, would one say that the eternal speech of God has been consumed by combustion and has perished? Or would one simply say that his speech is enduring and permanent, and that it has neither been consumed by flames nor perished, but that only the parchment and script have been destroyed? Continuing this line of argumentation, al-Bāqillānī provides a cogent example of the difference between "recitation" and the "subject of recitation" by stating that had one hundred readers recited the text of the Qur'ān, would that not represent one hundred recitals with each reader being rewarded individually for the recital, making the total number of rewards one hundred? He then declares that there is only one Qur'ān that is the subject of recitation. Interwoven through the various proofs and counter-proofs, the position taken by al-Bāqillānī is one that endeavours to locate a middle path between the Muʿtazilī position of denying the uncreated nature of God's speech and the arch-traditionalist one, which refused to compromise the divine and eternal quality of the worldly version of the text in its physical form, and which viewed such formulae such as the *kalām nafsī* as representing a specious attempt to concede the doctrine of the eternal nature of God's speech (see Al-Bāqillānī 2007: 116).

Separately, a number of arch-traditionists were associated with adopting what was defined as a schema of "inlibration," which was used to explain the relationship between the divine heavenly prototype of the Qur'ān and its physical counterpart.[28] They eschewed the elaborate arguments set out by rational theologians and stated that what is between the two covers of the Qur'ān is the word of God—and that, concomitantly, that which is read, heard, and written is the veritable "Word of God." Moreover, it is suggested that in the same way that the "Word of God" is uncreated and eternal, so too are the intonations heard through an act of recitation: Qur'ānic scripture and God's speech were incontrovertibly identical. Dismissing the notion that accidents could not occur within the divine essence, they contended that God as a speaker was not confined to an eternal substrate but he could speak if and when he chose to do so. Intriguingly, a number of key mystical movements were sympathetic to such views. For example, the Sālimiyya, adherents of the mystic Muḥammad ibn Aḥmad ibn Sālim, had been passionate advocates of the belief that the physical letters and sounds of the Qur'ān were eternal (*azaliyya*). Figures linked with the movement were trenchantly opposed to the Ashʿarī notion of *al-kalām nafsī*. Indeed, members even composed diatribes

---

28 Wolfson (1976: 235–55, esp. 252–253). A detailed account of this concept is provided. It has been suggested that this resonates with the Christian doctrine of "incarnation," which described the relationship between the different persons of the Trinity.

against al-Ashʿarī and Ibn Kullāb (Ibn Taymiyya: 499). Ultimately, in the quest to enshrine the sacred cachet of God's speech, theologians of all persuasions had attempted to devise all sorts of formulae and syntheses of data that would conceptually safeguard the fact that in simple terms God's speech was embodied between the two covers of the Qurʾānic codex. However, such treatments, which were articulated with specific theological premises and perspectives in mind, never quite managed to solve the aporia created by the attempts to draw distinctions between the eternal word and its worldly manifestation. Although there is no evidence to suggest that the debates about whether the Qurʾān was created or uncreated affected the course of applied exegetical, literary and legal approaches to the contents of the text, the disputes about the nature of the language of the Qurʾān, God's role as a speaker, and the divine attributes inexorably spilled over into deliberations about the doctrine of the text's linguistic inimitability and composition, and likewise impinged upon ideas about the role of divine agency in the origin of language. The ensuing debates, and the tensions which issued from them, dominated theological discourses for centuries, inspiring a fecund body of literature and thought.

4 The doctrine of *iʿjāz*

Over the centuries, the conceptual quandaries originating from the attempts to explain the relationship between the eternal word of God which inhered in the divine essence, on the one hand, and its physical manifestation, on the other, brought into sharper focus the literary merits of the Qurʾān. This study of the compositional, rhetorical, and aesthetic distinctiveness of the Qurʾān was fleshed out under the rubric of *iʿjāz al-Qurʾān*, which, although literally denoting the act of "rendering incapable," came to represent the concept of the text's linguistic inimitability insofar as it validated the claims of Muḥammad's prophethood. Indeed, it would appear that the Muʿtazilīs may have first coined the technical use of the term *iʿjāz*, which took on greater significance in the 9th century CE, when works connected to the subject of *iʿjāz* first appeared. Although the minutiae of the concept had yet to be fully systematised, it was key theologians who were avidly engaged in the composition of such treatises (Boullata 1988; Kermani 1996; Larkin 1988; Martin 1980; Rahman 1996). Historically, the roots of the doctrine were to be found in the Qurʾān, which grandly lauds the supreme and matchless nature of its own literary arrangement. In a range of allusive narratives that preserve dialogues between the Prophet and his Meccan opponents, reference is made to their allegations that the Qurʾān consisted of "the mere words of a mortal" (Q. 74:25); "the words of a poet" (Q. 69:41); "the mutterings of a soothsayer" (Q. 69:42); "sorcery passed down" (Q. 74:24); and even "ancient fables recounted to him" (Q. 46:17). Condemning the charges, the Qur'ānic rejoinder to this appears in the form of a challenge, insisting that if they allege that its contents are fabricated utterings, then let them and their cohorts produce a chapter the like thereof. The challenge is laid down at separate junctures in the Qur'ān; at Q. 52:33–34, the accusation that the Prophet is "manufacturing words" is mentioned, followed by a denial which asks those who truly claim so to produce a "speech similar to it." Elsewhere in the Qur'ān this challenge is expressed much more explicitly: "They will say: 'He has concocted this': say to them: 'Come forth with ten forged chapters the like thereof and call upon whomsoever you desire [to help you in this endeavor] other than God, if you are truthful'" (Q. 11:13). In a separate chapter the scale of the challenge is seemingly reduced: "They say: 'He has concocted this.' If you are in doubt concerning that which was revealed to our servant, then produce a single chapter the like thereof, calling upon your supporters other than God if you are really truthful" (Q. 2:23–24). These verses were interpreted in conjunction with the aforementioned Qur'ānic verse that defiantly declares,"Had humans and jinns [spirits] come together to replicate this Qur'ān, they would not have been able to do so."

Building on the edifices of these Qur'ānic declarations, over successive historical periods, the constellation of arguments adduced to support the idea of *iʿjāz* brought together a confluence of theological as well as literary perspectives and proofs, all of which were employed to underpin the lexical sublimity of the text. Among these was the claim that its inimitability resided in the Qur'ān's prediction of unseen events; other proofs referred to the supposed illiteracy of the Prophet which intimates the text's divine origins.[29] The irony of this was all too obvious in the context of the challenge issued by the Qur'ān to its Meccan opponents: they presented themselves as the paragons of linguistic eloquence and questioned the authenticity of the Qur'ān and its message, and yet they were unable to rise to the Qur'ānic challenge of producing a single chapter, despite the fact that the text they were actually disparaging was allegedly authored by an "unlettered individual." In the literature on *iʿjāz*, closely aligned with this line of argument is the view that it was the convention that Prophets were bestowed with specific miracles which substantiated their missions; it was even alluded to in the *ḥadīth* literature.[30] It is argued that Moses was granted powers to perform

29 It is argued that the idea of the Prophet's illiteracy is not borne out by the Qur'ān or the tradition. The inference is that this notion was developed in the later discourses (Gunther 2002).
30 This is recorded in the tradition cited by al-Bukharī, the renowned *ḥadīth* scholar in a section within his collection of traditions devoted to the virtues of the Qur'ān.

wizardry and outwit Pharaoh's sorcerers, validating his mission; this was in an era when magic was the predominant science of the day. Likewise, in an age when medicine was hailed as ground-breaking, Jesus was bestowed by God with the power to heal the sick, cure the leper, and raise the dead. In the Islamic context this miracle was not restricted to a specific moment in time but was seemingly enduring, as it turned on the inimitability of the Qur'ān, and was linked to its unceasing rhetorical pre-eminence and eloquence.

One Muʿtazilī theologian who played an important role in advancing the discourses on *iʿjāz* was al-Naẓẓām (d. 836 CE). Arguing that the miracle did not reside in the linguistic matchlessness of the text, he proffered a dissenting view on *iʿjāz,* which contended that the inimitability of the text emanated from the fact that God had prevented the Arabs from rising to the challenge set out in the Qur'ān. The concept was called *ṣarfa*, which literally denotes deflection; namely, the Arabs could quite easily have matched the linguistic marvels of the text but were deflected and bound from doing so by divine intervention. Other Muʿtazilī cynosures dismissed this dissenting view on the basis that it contravened the central tenets of human freewill and responsibility: the idea of God's intervention in such matters was inconsistent with their theology. Other criticisms of this view argued that if God had indeed deflected the will of the Arabs at the time of the challenge, the period of deflection would have expired, allowing later generations of Arabs to mount a subsequent challenge. *Ex hypothesi*, the fact that this had not occurred proved the fallaciousness of the doctrine of *ṣarfa*. It was the Muʿtazilī belle-lettrist al-Jāḥīz (d. 855 CE), a figure connected to al-Naẓẓām, who proposed the theory that the *iʿjāz* of the Qur'ān rested in the text's select choice of vocabulary or *lafẓ*. Al-Jāḥīz developed the idea that the ancient Arabs reckoned themselves the veritable masters of linguistic excellence, constantly boasting of their literary ability and flair, yet were unable to rise to the literary challenge set out in the Qur'ān. Other scholars soon weighed in with their views, including the traditionalist al-Khaṭṭābī (d. 998 CE), who sought to focus on the importance of *naẓm*, i.e., the Qur'ān's unique textual composition and lexical configuration; and the Muʿtazilī scholar al-Rummānī (d. 994 CE), who blended literary as well as theological arguments in his conspectus of *iʿjāz*.[31] Building upon the rich vein of ideas on the sacred text's inimitability, the seminal text on *īʿjāz* was written by an Ashʿarī scholar, ʿAbd al-Qāhir al-Jurjānī (d. 1078 CE), who definitively fleshed out the concept of *naẓm*. His text appeared to be designed to criticise views on *iʿjāz* outlined by a Muʿtazilī scholar, ʿAbd al-Jabbār (d. 1025 CE), the author of the

31 The Muʿtazilī theologian al-Rummānī identified eight features of *iʿjāz*, among which he included *ṣarfā*.

Kitāb al-Mughnī, a multi-volumed theological summa which included a volume devoted to *iʿjāz*. As a result, theological, linguistic, and rhetorical characterizations of the text dominated discussions in the *iʿjāz* literature.[32]

It is unsurprising that al-Bāqillānī, an active participant in the discussions about the status of God's speech, also composed a text that dealt with the subject of the Qur'ān's inimitability. Refuting many Muʿtazilī views on *iʿjāz*, he put forward the thesis that "the aspect of its inimitability resides in its unique literary arrangement, composition and the compactness of its style." He explained that this broke with all the established linguistic conventions of composition with which the Arabs were familiar, including even their conventional forms of speech; and he added that for these reasons they were unable to respond to the challenge of competing with the text. Al-Bāqillānī's defence of the doctrine of *iʿjāz* included a lengthy comparison between select verses of the Qur'ān and an ode written by Imrū' al-Qays, considered the greatest pre-Islamic poet of the Arabs, seeking to illustrate the chasms between the two in terms of style, composition, and clarity of expression (Grunebaum 1950). The focus on poetry was interesting for the simple reason that the Qur'ān actually pours scorn on the claim by the Prophet's adversaries that he himself was a possessed poet and soothsayer, including the accusation that the Qur'ān was being dictated to him by someone with knowledge of ancient scripture (Q. 16:102). One does need to bear in mind the fact that poetry was a sophisticated medium of literary expression in pre-Islamic Arabia. There was a range of intricate meters and thematic formats for the composition of poetry; tribes appointed resident poets who would be called upon to defend their honour, satirise opponents, compose eulogies, and entertain. Even the Prophet installed a prominent Arab poet, Ḥassan ibn Thābit, as his advocate, a figure who declared that through his composition of poetry he would extricate the Prophet from his Meccan polytheistic peers in the same way that a baker pull outs a thread of hair from kneaded dough. Yet in the Qur'ān, in a chapter aptly entitled "the Poets," they are described as being "followed by those who err," and that "their actions do not match their words" (Q. 26:226). Those who sought to defend poetry and its relevance as a literary medium simply explained that such dicta were designed to condemn poets among the polytheists who satirised the Prophet. Nonetheless, on the issue of format, throughout the Qur'ān an attempt is made to place distance between the style of the Qur'ān and that of poetry, and at one juncture in the text it is pronounced that "we have

---

32 Literary devices such as hyperbaton, paronomasia, grammatical shift, ellipsis, metonymy, metaphor, synecdoche, simile, assonance, and alliteration were exemplified with reference to Qur'ānic expressions.

not taught him poetry, nor is it fitting for him but rather this is a lucid Qurʾān" (Q. 36:69). Likewise, there was a concerted effort within the classical literary tradition to draw clear distinctions between the form of rhyme (*sajaʿ*) as featured in the Qurʾān and the various rhyme patterns employed by ancient Arabian soothsayers. Distinctively, al-Bāqillānī categorically states that it was incorrect to imply that the Qurʾān employs (poetic) rhyme for the simple reason that within the literary schema of conventional rhyme and assonance, meaning is subjugated to word form; whereas in the Qurʾān, meaning dictates and determines the use and choice of words. Moreover, he notes that the patterns of rhyme that feature in the Qurʾān do not conform to models of ancient rhyme with which the Arabs were familiar: he concedes that there might exist select areas of the text's composition that appear to follow a scheme of verse, but on closer inspection, the Qurʾān's rhythmic structure is *sui generis*.

As has been suggested, the concept of the Qurʾān's linguistic inimitability and its related discussions did provide a useful channel through which scholars could move away from complicated arguments about the epistemological status of the Qurʾān as God's speech, and turn their attention to shedding light on the distinctive and exceptional qualities of its composition. However, these sorts of debates about the aesthetic and theological qualities of the language of the Qurʾān in no way undermined the importance attached to the use of pre-Islamic literary sources, including poetry and prose, to authenticate and flesh out theories of language developed by grammarians and lexicographers. And poetry was used not only for linguistic justification and exemplification in grammatical argumentation, but also within the sphere of Qurʾānic commentary (Ibn al-Anbārī 1971). Grammarians were sometimes accused of granting "poetry epistemological primacy in the interpretation of the Qurʾān," a charge they dismissed by appositely referring to the fact that the Qurʾān itself speaks of its being revealed in a clear Arabic diction with which the Arabs were familiar. Accordingly they argued it made sense to consult their poetry, the preferred medium of literary expression, in order to fathom axioms and standards of language usage to which the text adhered. There were also dicta which could be invoked to support such practices: one of the Companions of the Prophet reportedly declared that "Poetry is the (literary) register of the Arabs" and that "should a specific Qurʾānic expression escape your comprehension, then seek it in their (Arabs') poetry (*diwāns*)" (Ibn al-Anbārī 1971: 99–102).[33] Despite this use of poetry, grammarians were always eager to point out that, in terms of its linguistic traits and features, the Qurʾān

33 It has been argued that the production of such anecdotes was part of a contrived attempt to secure support for methodologies which were viewed with suspicion. See Wansbrough (1977).

was "a stronger proof for (grammatical) citation than poetry." Still, this did not diminish the enthusiasm with which "non-scriptural" sources were espoused within the traditions of exegesis and linguistic thought, as a functional approach to explaining the features of language prevailed. Thus, while the debates about the status of the word of God continued in their various theological formats and contexts, they did not hinder or impede the independence and inquisitiveness with which the study of language was avidly broached not only as an intellectual endeavour, but also in the service of the Qur'ān.

5 The debates about the origins of language

It might be expected that the gravity of the discussions about the status of the Qur'ān and even aspects of *iʿjāz* would have an enduring impact upon the treatment of the subject of the origins of language. However, these discussions developed much later within rational theological discourses of the 9th century CE, and the association with the whole debate about the created status of the Qur'ān and *iʿjāz* appears to have been eclipsed by the broader issue of the divine attributes. Early grammatical treatises and philological manuals made no mention of the subject; however, it gradually began to be expounded upon in a number of later theological, grammatical, and legal treatises in which the epistemology of language was expounded upon. Two principal opposing theses came to dominate the discussions: these were respectively referred to in Arabic as *tawqīf* (revelationist) and *iṣṭilāḥ* (conventionalist). Within the former, God was assigned a prominent role in the imposition of language; the latter implied that the establishment of language was entirely arbitrary, being the product of common convention and agreement among humans. Other views existed that combined elements of each of these main theses, but in general it is the antithesis between *tawqīf* and *iṣṭilāḥ* positions around which the different perspectives were finely calibrated. The doctrine of *tawqīf* was based on a reading of the Qur'ānic verse that states, "And indeed God taught the names (*asmāʾ*) of all things to Adam; then, he presented '*them*' to the angels and announced 'inform me of the names of these if you are truthful'" (Q. 2:31). Although the verse is allusive in its treatment of the subject, it did become the *locus classicus* adduced by proponents of *tawqīf* to defend the role of divine agency in the inception of language. In their view "the names" encompassed all the elements of language as the later conceptual classification of the parts of speech was simply a grammatical construct. Interestingly, Genesis 2:19–20, which serves as a *locus classicus* for Christians regarding the question of the status – whether arbitrary or natural – of language, states that "Out of the ground the LORD God formed every beast of the field, and every fowl of the air; and brought them unto Adam to see what he would call them: and whatsoever Adam called every living creature, that was the name thereof." In the *tawqīf* thesis, it is not Adam but God who is the agent behind the process of naming, and of assigning meanings to words, although it was held that the nature of the relationship between words and meanings remained entirely arbitrary: there is no natural affinity or intrinsic connection between specific words and their meanings. In this sense it is important to distinguish between debates in the Islamic context and those which occurred in Greek philosophical thought. Plato's *Cratylus* offers a debate about whether there exists a natural or an arbitrary connection between words and their meanings; these two positions are expressed respectively by the concepts of *phúsis* (φύσις) and *thésis* (θέσις) (Sedley 2003; Barney 2001; Ibn al-Anbārī 1971). In the Islamic setting, however, the issue turns on the identification of the original designator of language, although both the concepts of *tawqīf* and *iṣṭilāḥ* are essentially conventionalist perspectives, for they stress the arbitrary nature of the relationship between words and sounds. Despite the fact that the dialogue in Plato's *Cratylus* presents its arguments with reference to nouns, it is the general elements of language which are the focus of attention.[34] This is also the case for the Islamic debates, for although the Qur'ānic verse refers to God's teaching "the names" to Adam, these names were identified as connoting the totality of the elements of language. The author of the first Arabic lexicographical dictionary, al-Khalīl ibn Aḥmad (d. 777 or 791 CE), is reported to have proposed an onomatopoeic theory to explain the origin of a confined number of words, but such a view gained few adherents. However, in the 9th century, one theologian who subscribed to a radical version of this view was the Muʿtazilī scholar ʿAbbād ibn Sulaymān, who, it should be remembered, engaged in disputations about the createdness of the Qur'ān with Ibn Kullāb during the period of the *miḥna*. ʿAbbād argued that "a natural affinity existed between the collective phonemic constitution of words and their signified meanings," even hypothesizing that a change in the name of an entity predicates a change in its constitution (Shah 2011; also Shah 2000). He was castigated for his views by his Muʿtazilī cohorts, who described them as utterly senseless.

In opposition to *tawqīf*, the thesis of *iṣṭilāḥ* postulates that language was established via a process of commonly agreed conventions (*muwāḍaʿa*),

34 Socrates is the individual who appears in the dialogue as an arbiter between the two protagonists, fleshing out the ramifications of each of their theses through reference to etymology and other related concepts, although it is maintained that the views of Plato lie at the heart of the dialogue.

whereby humans assigned words to meanings. During the formative years of the Islamic tradition, opinions on the two theses were polarized between scholars who endorsed *tawqīf* on the one hand, and those who were proponents of *iṣṭilāḥ*. It is difficult to trace the historical gestation and origins of the different elements of the doctrine of *tawqīf*. However, once the thesis of *iṣṭilāḥ* was advocated, *tawqīf* was invoked as a counter doctrine. Loyalty to either doctrinal position was influenced by different factors. It is generally agreed that the architect of the concept of *iṣṭilāḥ* was a Muʿtazilī theologian by the name of Abū Hāshim (d. 933 CE), who was renowned for developing a defence of the Muʿtazilī doctrine of the divine attributes using the Arabic grammatical concept of "states" (*ḥāl*) as an analogue for this theory.[35] Significantly, the chief opponent of *iṣṭilāḥ* was al-Ashʿarī, who is identified in the sources as one of the first individuals to espouse the opposing doctrine of *tawqīf*, adducing traditional proofs to counter Abū Hāshim's thesis, although a number of leading Muʿtazilī scholars actually supported *tawqīf*.[36] Why Abū Hāshim devised the thesis of *isṭilāḥ* is not quite clear, but the subject seems to have been informed by discussions about "the names and divine attributes of God." This is evident from the fact that Abū Hāshim's thoughts on the subject appear under such headings in various theological treatises, including ʿAbd al-Jabbār's *Kitāb al-Mughnī*.[37] In a section of his text which deals with the attributes and the process of naming, he explains that a given name (*ism*) can represent its named entity or referent (*al-musammā*) only through the concomitant processes of intention (*qaṣd*), choice (*irādā*) and gesticulation (*ishāra*), following which names are assigned to entities and meanings (see the discussion in Shah 2011). In this argument, intention serves as the *sine qua non* for the validation of the connection between a name and its referent, and without an awareness of this intention among interlocutors, no process of establishing language conventions and usage is possible. Had the relationship between words and meanings been determined by God, the *qaṣd*, which was intrinsic to setting up the conventions of language, would need to have been divulged through

35 His father was a leading mentor within the school; indeed, he was the teacher of al-Ashʿarī, a figure who later defected from the Muʿtazilites.

36 The basic theological arguments for *tawqīf* attributed to al-Ashʿarī are preserved in the literature of later Ashʿarite luminaries. One such work is the *Mujarrad maqālāt al-shaykh Abī ʾl-Ḥasan al-Ashʿarī* ('The essential theological doctrines of Al-Ashʿarī') composed by Ibn Fūrak (d. 1015 CE), a later adherent of the school (Ibn Fūrak, Abū Bakr Muḥammad ibn al-Ḥasan 1987). Abū Hāshim was a prolific author but none of his works has survived; his views are dispersed across a range of later theological texts.

37 It remains an important source of early Muʿtazilī thought.

acts of gesticulation. This would have entailed God's disclosing to humans knowledge of his intentions by engaging in gesture, which is inconceivable. There is a simple logic at work in the discussions: if humans are acquainted with the "intention" of God, the notion of religious obligation becomes invalid for within Muʿtazilī systems of thought it was incumbent upon mankind to seek knowledge of God's existence independently, relying on the faculties of reason. This is explained by ʿAbd al-Jabbār who comments that, "It is inconceivable that we should necessarily know God's intention in the state of obligation, just as it would be inappropriate to know necessarily His essence at the time before obligation comes into existence" (ʿabd al-Jabbār 1965: 164; Shah 2011: 321). The same form of argument appears in other theological texts where it is stated that "knowledge of the attribute of an entity," which in this context would be God's imposition of language, "would *a fortiori* necessitate knowledge of the essence of that entity, namely God" (Asnawī 1999: vol. 1, p. 302; Shah 2011: 321). Consequently, the whole doctrine of human responsibility and obligation would be without foundation. Separately, there is even an argument attributed to Abū Hāshim in which he cited a verse of the Qurʾān that declares, "never did we dispatch a Prophet except that he conversed in the language of those to whom he was sent in order to make (matters) plain for them" (Q 14:4). Abū Hāshim explains that for *tawqīf* to be viable, God would have to provide an intelligent individual with an intuitive knowledge of language. However, he dismisses this possibility by stating that this would entail such an individual's instantaneously recognizing the existence of God, consigning to irrelevance the concept of religious obligation. Hence, his argument is that the existence of a language based on common agreement and convention must by necessity precede the advent of revelation (see the detailed arguments in Shah 2011: 321ff.).

The nexus between *iṣṭilāḥ* and the divine attributes becomes evident from debates in the early tradition about distinctions between the name (*ism*) and its referent (*musammā*). A number of Muʿtazilī theologians had propounded the notion that from eternity, God had neither name nor attribute, and that these were derived through a process of *iṣṭilāḥ* and *qiyās* (analogical reasoning); consequently, they adopted the view that the *ism* (*nomen*) and the *musammā* (*nominatum*) were not ontologically one. Sensing that the concept represented an insidious attempt to assail the doctrine of the essential nature of the divine attributes, theologians affiliated to the Ashʿarī school countered by arguing that the *ism* and *musammā* were nominally one and unified; and this became a standard refrain among many later rational Sunni theologians. Al-Ashʿarī is reported to have argued that the divine names of God and His attributes can be determined only by way of *tawqīf*. This tension between the perspectives raises the possibility that *tawqīf* may have been gone through several phases of distillation and review to counter the Muʿtazilī position on the divine names (see Shah 2013).

In the defence of the doctrine of *tawqīf*, al-Ashʿarī is reported to have resorted to the argument of infinite regress to dismiss *iṣṭilāḥ*: namely, that every stage of the assigning of meaning to words by humans would require a preceding process *ad infinitum*, which is logically absurd. Therefore *tawqīf* must be the only viable explanation for the origin of language. The attestation of proofs from the Qur'ān is fascinating, as proponents of *tawqīf* and *iṣṭilāḥ* were astute at extracting from such evidences data that supported their specific explanations. For example, the Qur'ān condemns the Meccan polytheists' practice of instituting names for their deities by stating, "These are merely names that you and your forebears invented and for which God has provided no sanction" (Q. 12:41) and (Q. 53:23). Advocates of *tawqīf* would argue that this represents an example of God's denouncing the artificiality of the polytheists' practice of "naming," which constitutes an implicit indictment of *iṣṭilāḥ*. Supporters of *tawqīf* had other verses they could adduce from their armoury of arguments: in Q. 30:22 it is pronounced that: "And among his signs are that he created the heavens and the earth; and (also) the diversity of your tongues (languages) and colors," a verse which firmly hinted at the role of divine agency in the inception of language. Still, the import of such verses was contested by those who subscribed to *iṣṭilāḥ*, as they countered that the verse was merely referring to the physical anatomy and constitution of the tongue! Correspondingly, while Q. 2:31 was identified as the *locus classicus* for the thesis of *tawqīf*, defenders of *iṣṭilāḥ* argued that the verse does not stipulate that God taught Adam "the names of all things," but rather that God empowered Adam to establish the conventions of language usage. It is therefore evident that even when presented with Qur'ānic citations, both camps were able to adapt these to support their respective standpoints. Ultimately, scriptural proofs were hostages to the various doctrinal perspectives and outlooks which were the key drivers of the discussions. In a 10th-century manual of philology, the Kufan grammarian Ibn Fāris subscribed to a particularly rigorous doctrine of *tawqīf*, making the daring assertion that Arabic orthography, grammar, and the science of prosody were the products of *tawqīf*. Historically, it was commonly accepted that within the biographical dictionaries of Arabic linguistic thought, the institution of the systematic study of grammar and the articulation of a theory of language were first formulated in the work of a Basran grammarian by the name of Sībawayhi (d. 793 CE), whereas the study of lexicography and prosody, in the form of the meters of the poems of the ancient Arabs, was refined by al-Khalīl ibn Aḥmad (d. 791 CE). However, Ibn Fāris claimed that these pioneers had merely uncovered and discovered ancient disciplines of learning eroded by the passage of time. He even included in his final section on the topic of *tawqīf* an apocryphal anecdote which states that Adam was the first person to invent all written scripts, including Arabic and Syriac, and that he did this 300 years prior to his death. According to one Prophetic tradition (*ḥadīth*), Adam lived for one thousand years. The report goes on to state that, having inscribed these scripts on clay, he baked them and had them buried. Following the great deluge, each race discovered one of these scripts and used it. The Arabic script was unearthed by Ismael.[38]

While clear linkages appear to exist between discussions on the divine attributes and the concept of *iṣṭilāḥ*, the idea that the doctrine of an uncreated Qur'ān initially led scholars to defend the thesis of *tawqīf* is less obvious. This argument was advanced in the work of Bernard Weiss (1974), who emphasized that the debate between al-Ashʿarī and Abū Hāshim represented the truly classic Muslim discussion on the origins of language. Weiss spoke of an affinity between the revelationist view of language's origin and the pre-speculative, orthodox understanding of the doctrine of the uncreated Qur'ān, adding that by accepting that "the Koran is the Eternal Speech of God" a climate of thought had been created in which "it is hardly appropriate to make man the ultimate author and inventor of language" (Zadeh 2008, 2009). He posed the question: "How can there be an Eternal Divine Speech, identifiable with the actual words of the Koran, if man be the originator of that instrument through which speech is possible?" Weiss explained that the controversy was short-lived because of the intervention of al-Bāqillānī, who declared the issue could not be resolved and that both *tawqīf* and *iṣṭilāḥ* were entirely plausible. Weiss referred to the fact that certain followers of al-Ashʿarī came up with the theory that defined divine speech as an abstract quality (*ṣifa* or *kalām nafsī*) inhering in the divine essence, raising it above the level of ordinary speech.[39] He claimed that, as a result, in Sunni intellectual circles the debate was brought to an end, although he did concede that the issue persisted in the works of proponents with a stern orthodox outlook. In Weiss's view, the revelationist theory was ideally suited to buttress the doctrine of an uncreated Qur'ān, especially during the time of Ashʿarī and Abū Hāshim, when the debate was at its most intense. But it seems Weiss has entirely overlooked the fact that one of the earliest exponents of rational Sunnite theology, Ibn Kullāb, had already formulated the notion of God's speech existing eternally and essentially in his essence as a *maʿnā* (entity), drawing a distinction between this speech and its temporal expression (*iʿbāra*) in the form of revealed scripture.[40] Thus, such a distinction about the status of divine speech was already outlined

---

38 In his book Ibn Fāris (n.d.) surveys the virtues and traits of the Arabic language.
39 See Al-Shahrastānī ([1931]–1934: 320–21).
40 Kopf (1956) previously mentioned his use of the term ʿibāra was criticized by a number of scholars, including al-Bāqillānī.

well before the debate on the origin of language intensified, intimating that the desire to defend the doctrine of the uncreated status of the Qurʾān initially had little to do with the espousal of *tawqīf*.

The tendency to associate *tawqīf* with the doctrine of an eternal, uncreated Qurʾān has persisted in modern scholarship, despite inconsistencies in this association.[41] First and foremost, there is no clear evidence that the proponents of *tawqīf* principally linked their stance to the doctrine of an uncreated Qurʾān. In addition, even the suggestion that the doctrine of *isṭilāḥ* could serve as an expedient accessory to the arguments for the created status of the Qurʾān is less than categorical. It is true that the Muʿtazilī theologian ʿAbd al-Jabbār stipulates that the establishment of language by human convention has to be in place before it can be used by God (ʿabd al-Jabbār 1965: 164). It is also the case that some later medieval scholars did countenance a link between the doctrine of a created Qurʾān and *iṣṭilāḥ*, but this is by no means decisive as far as the early debates are concerned. Indeed, there was an extended period of intense discussions on the topic before al-Bāqillānī's supposed intervention, and in these a number of Muʿtazilī theologians were identified as fervent supporters of *tawqīf*, including one of the most important figures in the movement's history, al-Jubbāʾī (d. 915 CE). If the corollary to this doctrine were that the Qurʾān was an uncreated text, they would hardly have been among its most enthusiastic supporters; yet many were. Weiss has also claimed that the reason why the grammarians came down on the side of *tawqīf* was out of loyalty to a strong tradition of Qurʾānic exegesis (*tafsīr*), but the latitude with which such verses could be interpreted indicates that there were other factors driving the discussions.

The view that a distinct correlation existed between the thesis of *iṣṭilāḥ* and the doctrine of a created Qurʾān was supported by Michael Carter. He concluded that "If language could be proved to be a mere human institution, it would follow that the Qurʾān was created and consequently subject to all the limitations of human endeavour, thus enabling the Muʿtazilites to claim that dogma and law should be constructed on the basis of reason only" (Carter 1983). Again, there is no evidence to suggest that proving language to be a human institution was decisively linked to the debate about the created status of the Qurʾān. Furthermore, the Muʿtazilī approach to the synthesis of law was neither contingent upon nor driven by the idea of a created Qurʾān. Additionally, many later Ashʿarites endorsed the plausibility of *iṣṭilāḥ*: would they have been among its enthusiastic adherents given the implications suggested by Carter? It seems far more likely

---

41 See the views of Kees Versteegh (1996) who located the debate about the created-uncreated status of the Qurʾān as inspiring the positions of *iṣṭilāḥ* and *tawqīf*.

that key theologians from among the Muʿtazila and other rational theologians supported *tawqīf* because it added weight to the notion of the Qurʾān's inimitable qualities. Certainly, the crystallization of the thesis of *tawqīf* was redolent of an impulsive reaction to counter *iṣṭilāḥ*. Ashʿarī's objection to *iṣṭilāḥ* was probably initially out of concern that it could be manipulated to undermine the teaching on the divine attributes and be cited to draw distinctions between the *ism* (*nomen*) and the *musammā* (*nominatum*). One recent writer has proffered the opinion that the final victory on the subject belonged to the Muʿtazila, for they succeeded in bringing about the destruction of the orthodox view of *tawqīf*, which was superseded by *iṣṭilāḥ* (Versteegh 1996). This view appears to overlook the fact that many within the ranks of traditionalist orthodoxy still maintained that *tawqīf* was presumed to be more probable (*maẓnūn*); and more significantly, the theological doctrines that engendered *iṣṭilāḥ* were never condoned within traditionalist circles, particularly the thesis that God's divine names could be determined by a process of analogy (Asnawī 1999). Thus in many respects it was *tawqīf* that won the day. It is therefore not surprising that in a seminal medieval compendium devoted to philology, its author chose to begin his survey with the statement: "Praise be to God the creator of tongues and languages; the one who established words for meanings," which inevitably confirms the esteem in which the doctrine of *tawqīf* continued to be held within the Sunni camps (Suyūṭī 1970).

Despite such rigid interpretations of the doctrine of *tawqīf*, philologists often subscribed to theories that seemed to be in contravention of the idea of a language in which the relationship between words and their meanings was primordially defined and set. This was true of the theory of etymology, antonyms, synonyms, homonyms and even the concept of metaphor. There were even scholars who composed treatises refuting the existence of such philological phenomena. For example, Ibn Fāris, when discussing etymology, acknowledged the reality that Arabic was subject to certain patterns (*qiyās*) based on the fact that Arabs derived parts of their speech from other related parts. However, he warned that discussions about the subject had to bear in mind that language was revelationist (*tawqīf*) in terms of its inception. Likewise in the case of antonyms, which in the Arabic context relate to a single word possessing two antithetical meanings, some scholars disputed their very occurrence in the language of Arabic on theological grounds. They argued that such a phenomenon could lead to ambiguities, implying a flaw in the design of language; this was deemed inconceivable if one were to accept that language was established by the process of divine agency as implied by the doctrine of *tawqīf*. Still, philologists devised ingenious ways of rationalizing the existence of such phenomena. Indeed, a circumspect glance through some of the seminal classical dictionaries of Arabic shows that their authors included lengthy sections devoted to collating such linguistic materials and even identifying practical reasons, such as dialectal usage and language development, to explain their incidence in the language of Arabic.[42] This is also the case for arguments about whether foreign vocabulary featured in the language of the Qur'ān: some scholars denied the possibility, insisting on the pure Arabic character of the text; others stated that although it is plausible, it could be explained by a theory of concurrence and the fact that such lexical elements had entered the vocabulary of Arabic and were used and understood by the Arabs despite their featuring in or even originating from other languages.

Although the doctrinal hegemony of *tawqīf* held sway within traditionalist circles, scholars were still able to express opinions about the status of different languages. This fact is evident in the treatise devoted to the synthesis of the principles of law by the famous representative of the literalist legal school of thought in Andalusia, Ibn Ḥazm (d. 1064 CE). Discussing whether a specific language could be considered the finest of languages, he remonstrates that some people are under the misguided illusion that their native languages are unsurpassed; he explains that such views were meaningless in the context of language. Referring to the Qur'ānic verse which states that never was a Prophet dispatched, except that he conversed in the language of those to whom he was sent, he insists that nothing in the sacred sources decrees that one language was superior to another tongue; adopting an empirical approach, he stressed that language was essentially a medium of communication that was viewed in relative terms. He then moves on to criticize the Greek physician and philosopher Galen (d. 210 CE) for allegedly stating that Greek was the finest languages and that all other idioms resembled "the barking of dogs or the croaking of frogs." Ibn Ḥazm explains that one would find that speakers of different languages held similar views when hearing vernaculars with which they were not familiar. Having made the case that the appreciation of language was a relative experience, Ibn Ḥazm turns his attention to those who professed the view that Arabic is the finest of languages on the basis of its being the diction in which God's speech was revealed. Describing such views as equally implausible, he refers to the Qur'ānic verse that spoke of the dispatch of Prophets conversing in the indigenous languages of the people to whom they were sent. He then points out that the linguistic medium of God's own revelation varied, as evidenced by the revelation of the Torah, the Psalms, the Gospels, the scriptures of Abraham, and the fact that God conversed with Moses in Hebrew. He concluded that all of this confirmed that these languages

---

42 On a related note, for theological reasons some scholars questioned the existence of metaphor in the language of Arabic on the basis that it might be used to circumvent the literal language of the Qur'ān and other textual sources for theological gain. See Shah (2000).

were equal in terms of their prestige and rank, despite the fact that Ibn Ḥazm firmly endorsed the doctrine of *tawqīf*. Conversely, there were scholars who took an entirely different view: Ibn Fāris, the author of the *Ṣāḥibī* and an unswerving supporter of *tawqīf*, declared that Arabic was the finest and most refined of languages. He even asserted that it was not possible for a translator to accurately render the Qur'ān into another language, due to its unique rhetorical and stylistic features, in the way that scholars had translated the Gospels from Greek to Ethiopic and Syriac and indeed the Torah and the Psalms into Arabic. Distinctively, conflicting opinions and views were held by scholars, despite the overall loyalty to *tawqīf*. Interestingly, in an influential article published in the 1950s, Lothar Kopf suggested that within the classical tradition it was religious dogma that hindered the development of key aspects of Arabic linguistic thought (Kopf 1956). Kopf claimed that this was evident in areas such as discussions relating to the origins of language; approaches to aspects of the interpretation of the Qur'ān; the issue of the existence of foreign vocabulary in the Qur'ān; discussions on the Qur'ān's syntax; and even musings about the linguistic ascendancy of the dialects of the Meccan Arabs. However, it has been shown that the treatment of such topics reveals not only that there was a receptivity to the analysis of different perspectives and standpoints, but also that remarkable levels of resourcefulness and creativity prevailed within the attendant scholarship. Certainly, religious doctrine was not a hindrance to the articulation and synthesis of thought but rather served as an accelerant.

6 Conclusion

Arguments about language have played a dominant role in classical theological discourses. From the initial debates about whether the Qur'ān was created or uncreated, to the disputes about the nature of the attribute of speech in the divine essence, linguistic constructs and theories have been key to the elaboration of doctrines and views. The strength and intensity of the discussions stimulated intellectual activity across a range of supplementary areas, as evidenced by the scholarship devoted to the issue of the inimitability of the Qur'ān and indeed the question of the origins of language. Yet one of the striking features of the various discourses is the fact that such an eclectic range of views and arguments was accommodated within them. Clearly, deference to religious doctrine did not prevent scholars from tackling topics objectively and openly; the rich repository of theological and linguistic literature that exists within the classical Islamic tradition bears testimony to that fact.

References

Alston, William. 2005. Religious language. In William J. Wainwright (ed.), *The Oxford handbook of philosophy of religion*, 220–244. Oxford: Oxford University Press.

Barney, Rachel. 2001. *Names and nature in Plato's Cratylus*. New York & London: Routledge.

Berg, Herbert (ed.). 2003. *Method and theory in the study of Islamic origins*. Leiden & Boston: Brill.

Berg, Herbert & Sarah Rollens. 2008. The historical Muḥammad and the historical Jesus: A comparison of scholarly reinventions and reinterpretations. *Studies in Religion/Sciences Religieuses* 37(2). 271–292.

Bosworth, C. E. 1987. *The history of al-Ṭabarī: The reunification of the ʿAbbāsid caliphate: The Caliphate of al-Maʾmūn A.D. 813–833/A.H. 198–218*, vol. 32. Albany, NY: SUNY Press.

Boullata, Issa. 1988. The rhetorical interpretation of the Qurʾān: *Iʿjāz* and related topics. In Andrew Rippin (ed.), *Approaches to the history of the interpretation of the Qurʾān*, 139–157. Oxford: Clarendon Press.

Brock, Sebastian. 1982. Syriac views of emergent Islam. In G. H. A. Juynboll (ed.), *Studies on the first century of Islam*, 9–21, (f/ns 199–203). Carbondale & Edwardsville: Southern Illinois University Press.

Carter, Michael. 1983. Language control as people control in medieval Islam: The aims of the grammarians in their cultural context. In Ramzi Baalbaki (ed.), *Arab language and culture*, 65–84. Beirut: American University of Beirut.

Cook, Michael. 1981. *Early Muslim dogma: A source-critical study*. Cambridge: Cambridge University Press.

Crone, Patricia & Martin Hinds. 1986. *God's caliph: Religious authority in the first centuries of Islam*. Cambridge: Cambridge University Press.

Crone, Patricia. 2005. *Medieval Islamic political thought*. Edinburgh: Edinburgh University Press.

De Blois, Francois. 2010. Islam in its Arabian context. In Angelika Neuwirth, Nicolai Sinai & Michael Marx (eds.), *The Qurʾān in context: Historical and literary investigations into the Qurʾānic milieu*, 615–624. Leiden: Brill.

De Gifis, Vanessa. 2014. *Shaping a Qurʾānic worldview: Scriptural hermeneutics and the rhetoric of moral reform in the Caliphate of al-Maʾmūn*. Abingdon: Routledge.

Dhanani, Noor. 1994. *The physical theory of kalām: Atoms, space, and void in Basrian Muʿtazilī cosmology*. Leiden: Brill.

Donner, Fred McGraw. 1998. *Narratives of Islamic origins: Beginnings of Islamic historical writing*. Princeton: Darwin Press.

Donner, Fred McGraw. 2010. *Muhammad and the believers: At the origins of Islam*. Cambridge, MA & London: Belknap Press.

El-Bizri, Nader. 2008. God: essence and attributes. In Tim Winter (ed.), *The Cambridge companion to classical Islamic theology*, 121–140. Cambridge: Cambridge University Press.

Ess, Josef van. 1967. Ibn Kullāb und die Miḥna. *Oriens* 18/19. 92–142.

Ess, Josef van. 1987. Muʿtazila. In Mircea Eliade (ed.), *Encyclopedia of Religion*, 6322. New York: Macmillan.

Ess, Josef van. 1996. Verbal inspiration: Language and revelation in classical Islamic theology. In Stefan Wild (ed.), *The Qurʾan as text*, 177–194. Leiden, New York & Köln: Brill.

Ess, Josef van. 1991–7. *Theologie und Gesellschaft im 2. und 3. Jahrhundert Hidschra*, 6 vols. Berlin: Walter de Gruyter.
Ess, Josef van. 2010. *Der Eine und das Andere. Beobachtungen an islamischen häresiographischen Texten*, 2 vols. Berlin: Walter de Gruyter.
Frank, Richard. 1965. The Neoplatonism of Jahm ibn Ṣafwān. *Le Muséon* 78. 395–424.
Frank, Richard. 1991. Elements in the development of the teaching of al-Ash'arī. *Le Muséon: Revue D'Études Orientales* 104. 141–190.
Gimaret, Daniel. 1988. *Les noms divins en Islam: exégèse lexicographique et théologique*. Paris: Cerf.
Grunebaum, Gustave E. 1950. *A tenth-century document of Arabic literary theory and criticism: The sections on poetry of al-Bāqillānī's I'jāz al-Qur'ān. Translated and annotated.* Chicago: University of Chicago Press.
Günther, Sebastian. 2002. Muḥammad, the illiterate prophet: an Islamic creed in the Qur'ān and Qur'ānic exegesis. *Journal of Quranic Studies* 4.1. 1–26.
Halm, Heinz. 2004. *Shi'ism*. Edinburgh: Edinburgh University Press.
Humphreys, R. Stephen. 1995. *Islamic history: A framework for inquiry*. London & New York: I. B. Tauris.
Hurvitz, Nimrod. 2001. *Miḥna* as self-defense. *Studia Islamica* 92. 93–111.
Judd, Steven C. 1999. Ghaylān al-Dimashqī: The isolation of a heretic in Islamic historiography. *International Journal of Middle East Studies* 31(2). 161–184.
Kazi, A. K. & J. G. Flynn (trans.). 1984. *Muslim sects and divisions: The section on Muslim sects and divisions by Muḥammad b. 'Abd al-Karīm Shahrastānī (d. 1153)*. London, Boston, Melbourne & Henley: Kegan Paul International.
Kermani, Navid. 1996. Revelation in its aesthetic dimension. In Stefan Wild (ed.), *The Qur'ān as text*, 214–224. Leiden: Brill.
Kopf, Lothar. 1956. Religious influences on Mediaeval Arabic philology. *Studia Islamica* 5. 33–59.
Larkin, Margaret. 1988. The inimitability of the Qur'ān: Two perspectives. *Religion and Literature* 20(1). 31–47.
Madelung, Wilferd. 1974. The origins of the controversy concerning the creation of the Qur'ān. In Félix M. Pareja Casañas (ed.), *Orientalia Hispanica: Sive studia FM, Pareja octogenaria dicata*, 504–525. Leiden: Brill.
Madelung, Wilferd. 1997. *The succession to Muḥammad: A study of the early caliphate*. Cambridge: Cambridge University Press.
Martin, Richard C. 1980. The role of the Baṣrah Mu'tazila in formulating the doctrine of the apologetic miracle. *Journal of Near Eastern Studies* 39(3). 175–189.
Mayer, Toby. 2014. The cosmogonic word in al-Shahrastānī's exegesis of *Sūrat al-Baqara*. *Journal of Qur'anic Studies* 16(2). 1–41.
Nawas, John A. 1994. A re-examination of three current explanations for al-Ma'mūn's introduction of the *Miḥna*. *International Journal of Middle East Studies* 26(4). 615–629.
Peters, J. R. 1976. *God's created speech: A study in the speculative theology of the Mu'tazilī Qāḍī al-Quḍāt Abū l-Ḥasan 'Abd al-Jabbār ibn Aḥmad al-Hamadānī*. Leiden: Brill.
Rahman, Yusuf. 1996. The miraculous nature of Muslim scripture: Astudy of 'Abd al-Jabbār's *I'jāz al-Qur'ān*. *Islamic Studies* 35(4). 409–424.
Reinhart, Kevin. 2010. Sunni sectarianism. In Yasir Suleiman (ed.), *Living Islamic history: Studies in honour of Professor Carole Hillenbrand*, 209–225. Edinburgh: Edinburgh University Press.

Sabra, Abdelhamid. 2009. The simple ontology of *kalām* atomism: an outline. In Edith Dudley Sylla & William R. Newman (eds.), *Evidence and interpretation in studies on early science and medicine*, 68–78. Leiden: Brill.
Schöck, Cornelia. 2016. Jahm b. Ṣafwān (d. 128/745–6) and the "Jahmiyya" and Ḍirār b. ʿAmr' (d. 200/815). In Sabine Schmidtke (ed.), *The Oxford handbook of Islamic theology*, 55–80. New York: Oxford University Press.
Sedley, David. 2003. *Plato's Cratylus*. Cambridge: Cambridge University Press.
Shah, Mustafa. 2000. The philological endeavours of the early Arabic linguists: Theological implications of the *tawqīf-iṣṭilāḥ* antithesis and the *majāz* controversy, Part II. *Journal of Qur'ānic Studies* 2(1). 43–66.
Shah, Mustafa. 2011. Classical Islamic discourse on the origins of language: Cultural memory and the defense of orthodoxy. *Numen: International Review for the History of Religions* 58(2/3). 314–343.
Shah, Mustafa. 2013. Al-Ṭabarī and the dynamics of *tafsīr*: Theological dimensions of a legacy. *Journal of Qur'ānic Studies* 15(2). 83–139.
Shah, Mustafa. 2015. *Kalām:* rational expressions of medieval theological thought. In Houari Touati (ed.), *Encyclopedia of Mediterranean Humanism*, Spring 2014. http://www.encyclopedie-humanisme.com/?Kalām (accessed December 2016).
Turner, John P. 2013. *Inquisition in early Islam: The competition for political and religious authority in the Abbasid empire*. London: I. B. Tauris.
Versteegh, Kees. 1996. Linguistic attitudes and the origin of speech in the Arab world. In Alaa El-Gibali (ed.), *Understanding Arabic: Essays in contemporary Arabic linguistics in honor of El-Said Badawi*, 15–31. Cairo: The American University in Cairo Press.
Wansbrough, John. 1977. *Qur'ānic Studies: Sources and methods of scriptural interpretation*. Oxford: Oxford University Press.
Weiss, Bernard. 1974. Medieval Muslim discussions of the origin of language. *Zeitschrift der deutschen morgenländischen Gesellschaft* 124(1). 33–41.
Wilson, Brett. 2007. The failure of nomenclature: The concept of orthodoxy in the study of Islam. *Comparative Islamic Studies* 3(2). 169–194.
Wolfson, Harry Austryn. 1976. *The philosophy of the Kalām*. Cambridge, MA: Harvard University Press.
Zadeh, Travis. 2008. Fire cannot harm it: Mediation, temptation, and the charismatic power of the Qur'ān. *Journal of Qur'ānic Studies* 10(2). 50–72.
Zadeh, Travis. 2009. Touching and ingesting: Early debates over the material Qur'ān. *Journal of the American Oriental Society* 129(3). 443–466.
Zadeh, Travis. 2011. *The vernacular Qur'ān: Translation and the rise of Persian exegesis*. Oxford: Oxford University Press.

Arabic sources

ʿabd al-Jabbār, al-Qāḍī Aḥmad al-Asadabādī. 1965. *Al-Mughnī fī abwāb al-tawḥīdwa'l-ʿadl* [Enrichment in the categories of divine unity (of God) and justice], vol. 5. Edited by Maḥmūd Muḥammad al-Khuḍayrī. Cairo: al-Dār al-Miṣriyya li'l-Ta'līf wa'l-Tarjama. The discussions on the origins of language feature in the text devoted to sects and movements.

Asnawī, Jamāl al-Dīn ʿAbd al-Raḥīm. 1999. *Nihāyat al-sūl fī sharḥ minhāj al-wuṣūl ilā ʿilm al-uṣūl* [The ultimate aspiration in the exposition of (the work) of methodology in achieving proficiency in the science of (legal) fundamentals], 2 vols., vol.1, 302ff. Edited by Shaʿbān Muḥammad Ismāʿīl. Beirut: Dār Ibn Ḥazm.This is essentially a book on the principles of jurisprudence.

Al-Ashʿarī, Abū'l-Ḥasan. 1987. ʿAlī ibn Ismāʿīl. *Maqālāt al-Islamiyyīn* [Doctrines of Islamic religious sects and movements], 2 vols. Edited by Muḥammad ʿAbd al-Ḥamīd. Cairo: Dār al-Maʿārif. This represents al-Ashʿārī's renowned doxography on sects and movements, noted for the highly objective tone of the author.

Al-Bāqillānī, Abū Bakr, Muḥammad b. al-Ṭayyib. 2007. *Al-Insāf fī mā yajibu iʿtiqāduhu wa lā yajūz al-jahl bihi* [Equitableness regarding the requisite matters of religious belief and concerning which ignorance is not permitted]. Beirut: Dār al-Kutub al-ʿIlmiyya. This is one of al-Bāqillānī's many theological works. The biographical tradition asserts that his oeuvre comprised around 56 works.

Al-Bāqillānī, Abū Bakr Muḥammad b. al-Ṭayyib.1954. *Iʿjāz al-Qurʾān* [Inimitability of the Qurʾān]. Edited by Aḥmad Ṣaqr. Cairo: Dār al-Maʿārif.

Ibn al-Anbārī, Abū Bakr Muḥammad ibn al-Qāsim. 1971. *Kitāb īḍāḥ al-waqf wa'l-ibtidāʾ* [Book of elucidation concerning points of pauses and inception], 2 vols. Edited by Muḥyī al-Dīn ʿAbd al-Raḥmān Ramaḍān. Damascus: Majmaʿ al-Lugha al-ʿArabiyya. This is a text devoted to defining conventions for the recitation of scripture.

Ibn al-Nadīm, Muḥammad. 1988. *al-Fihrist*. Edited by R. Tajaddud, 3rd edn. Beirut: Dār al-Masīra.

Ibn Ḥazm, Abū Muḥammad ʿAlī ibn Aḥmad. 1984. *al-Iḥkām fī uṣūl al-aḥkām* [The consolidation of the principles of law], 2 vols., parts I-VIII. Cairo: Dār al Ḥadīth.

Ibn Fāris, Abū ʾl-Ḥusayn Aḥmad b. Zakariyyāʾ. N.d. *al-Ṣāḥibī fī fiqh al-lugha ʾl- ʿarabiyya wa-sunan al-ʿArab fī kalāmihā* [The treatise on the subject of the comprehension of language of Arabic and the conventions of the Arabs in their speech]. Edited by Aḥmad Ṣaqr. Cairo: Dār Iḥyāʾ al-Kutub al-ʿCairo.

Ibn Fūrak, Abū Bakr Muḥammad ibn al-Ḥasan. 1987. *Mujarrad maqālat al-shaykh Abī'l-Ḥasan al-Ashʿarī* (exposé de la doctrine d'al-Ashʿarī). Edited by D. Gimaret. Beyrouth: Dar el-Machreq. Ibn Furāk was not a pupil of al-Ashʿarī, but studied with the latter's students.

Ibn Taymiyya, Aḥmad ibn ʿAbd al-Ḥalīm. *Minhāj al-Sunna al-Nabawiyya fī naqḍ kalām al-Shīʿa al-Qadariyya* [Procedure with regards to the prophetic practice of refuting the discourse of the Shīʿa and the Muʿtazila], 9 vols. Edited by Muḥammad Rashād Sālim. Riyadh, n.d. As its title indicates this is a polemical treatise written by a scholar renowned for his allegiances to traditionalist orthodoxy.

Al-Rāzī, Fakhr al-Dīn, Muḥammad ibn ʿUmar. 1987. *Al-Arbaʿīn fī uṣūl al-dīn* [The Forty Tenets of Religious Faith]. Edited by Aḥmad al-Ḥijāzī al-Saqqā, 4 vols. Cairo: Maktabat al-Kulliyāt al-Azhariyya.

Al-Rummānī, Abū'l-Ḥasan ʿAlī ibn ʿĪsā. 1991. *al-Nukat fī iʿjāz al-Qurʾān* [Musings on the topic of the Qurʾān's inimitability]. (Published with two other monographs on the inimitability of the Qurʾān by al-Jurjānī and al-Khaṭṭābī.) Edited by Muḥammad Khalafallāh Aḥmad and Muḥammad Zaghlūl Salām. Cairo: Dār al-Maʿārif. Rummānī was a hugely influential Muʿtazilī scholar who lived in the 10th century.

Al-Shahrastānī, ʿAbd al-Karīm. [1931]-1934. *Nihāyat al-iqdām fī'l-ʿilm al-kalām* [The *summa philosophiae* of al-Shahrastānī]. Edited with a translation from manuscripts in the libraries of Oxford, Paris, and Berlin by Alfred Guillaume. London: Oxford University Press.

Suyūṭī, Jalāl al-Dīn ʿAbd al-Raḥmān. 1970. *al-Muzhir fī ʿulūm al-lugha wa-anwāʿihā* [Efflorescence in the sciences of language and theirsub-divisions], 2 vols. Edited by Jād al-Mawlā, A. M. al-Bajāwī & M. A. Ibrāhīm. Cairo: Dār Iḥyāʾ al-Kutub al-ʿArabiyya.

Al-Ṭabarī, Muḥammad ibn Jarīr. 1969. *Taʾrīkh al-rusul wa'l-mulūk* [The history of prophets and kings], 11 vols. Edited by Muḥammad Abū'l-Faḍl Ibrāhīm. Cairo: Dār al-Maʿārif. This is the seminal history written by the author in the 10th century.

Paolo Visigalli

Interface with God: The divine transparency of the Sanskrit language

Just like an enamored wife, in beautiful attire, uncovers herself to her husband, in the same way speech uncovers herself to the knower of speech – so that speech may uncover herself to us, grammar should be studied.

– Patañjali, *Great Commentary* (*Mahābhāṣya*) (2nd century BCE)

La Grammaire des Brahmanes peut être mise au rang des plus belles sciences; jamais l'Analyse & la Synthése ne furent plus hereusement employées... Il est étonnant que l'esprit humain ai pû atteindre à la perfection de l'art, qui éclatte dans ces Grammaires: les Auteurs y ont réduit par l'Analyse la plus riche langue du monde, à un petit nombre d' élements primitifs.

[The grammar of the Brahmins can be reckoned amongst the most beautiful sciences. Never were Analysis and Synthesis employed more felicitously. It is stunning that the human spirit had attained the perfection of the art which shone through these Grammars: therein, through Analysis the Authors have reduced the richest language of the world to a small number of primitive elements.]

– Jean François Pons, *Richesse et énergie de la langue Samskret* (1743 [1740]: 222[1])

[D]iese Sprache [i.e., Sanskrit], die selbst in ihren ersten und einfachsten Bestandtheilen die höchste Begriffe der reinen Gedankenwelt, gleichsam den ganzen Grundriß des Bewußtseins nicht bildlich, sondern in unmittelbarer Klarheit ausdrückt...

[This language [i.e., Sanskrit], which in its first and simplest components expresses – not figuratively, but with unmediated clarity – the highest ideas of the pure conceptual world, the layout of consciousness, as it were...]

– Friedrich Schlegel, *Über die Sprache und Weisheit der Indier* (1808)

1 Introduction

In the first chapter of Patañjali's *Great Commentary* (2nd century BCE), the seminal text of Sanskrit philosophy of language, we read about Indra's attempt to learn Sanskrit. His teacher Bṛhaspati, "the lord of the holy utterance," deploys the teaching method adopted by Brahmins to memorize the sacred Vedas, a word-by-word

1 Pons (1743) is partly reprinted in Staal (1972).

Paolo Visigalli, Shanghai Normal University, College of Humanities and Communication

https://doi.org/10.1515/9781614514329-009

repetition. Although their recitation of Sanskrit words lasted for one thousand divine years (each year being infinitely longer than its human counterpart), the "teaching session did not reach its conclusion."[2] The fact is that the Sanskrit vocabulary is extraordinarily "copious," as was noted, among others, by William Jones, one of the fathers of modern Indology.[3] Clearly, men should require a short-cut method to master Sanskrit within their limited life-span. Such a method, Patañjali informs us, is provided by the traditional discipline of Sanskrit grammar (*vyākaraṇa*) as codified in its foundational work, Pāṇini's *Eight Lectures* (ca. 4th century BCE). This work, taking for granted the analysis of Sanskrit words into the basic building blocks of language, the morphemes of modern linguistics, teaches a limited number of generative rules in virtue of which one can combine such blocks and produce an unlimited number of correct Sanskrit words and sentences. It is only through this method that "the huge streams of words can be learned with little effort."[4]

This anecdote introduces the main theme of this chapter: the idea that the Sanskrit language is more regular and morphologically transparent than other languages, i.e., many Sanskrit words can readily be analysed into discrete, basic linguistic units. I call this the *transparency* of Sanskrit. Two points require clarification: first, is Sanskrit's transparency a function of the grammatical analysis carried out by the Indian grammarians, or was this analysis made possible only because of the inherent morphological transparency of Sanskrit? Scholars' opinions differ: some consider the morphological transparency of Sanskrit words as an objective feature depending on language typology, and regard it as a prerequisite for the development of the indigenous grammatical analysis (Deeg 1995: 54–57). Others tend to consider Sanskrit's transparency to be, to a large extent, "an illusion," due to the fact that the first European Sanskritists studied the language through the sophisticated analytical tools provided by Sanskrit traditional grammar (Rocher 1995: 191). For the purposes of this chapter, it is not necessary to

---

2 *Mahābhāṣya* 5.27. Unless noted otherwise, all translations are my own. According to indigenous commentators, the Indra-Bṛhaspati anecdote should not be taken literally, but as a "merely illustrative passage" (*arthavāda*) showing the unfeasibility of learning Sanskrit in such a way. See Chatterji (1957: 41) and Joshi and Roodbergen (1986: 75).

3 William Jones, cited by Rocher (1995: 189). The citation is from a famous paragraph in Jones' "Third Anniversary Discourse, On the Hindus," pronounced at the Asiatic Society at Calcutta on 2 February 1786 and published in 1788. For a brief contextualization of Jones' "overquoted passage" see Collinge (1995: 197) and Davies (1998: 65–66). By Jones' time, the richness of the Sanskrit vocabulary had already been noted by several writers and had become a bit of a trope. See Rocher (1995: 188–189).

4 *Mahābhāṣya* 6.3–4.

adjudicate between these two views; it is enough that for the Indian and Western thinkers, whose speculations we will consider hereafter, transparency was real.

Second, Sanskrit's morphological transparency should not be regarded as a category that pertains to the grammatical domain only, but, as we will see, it reveals a series of intersections with the domain of religion. In India, transparency coordinates with emic descriptions of ritual and with the conviction that language has a magic, generative power. In the West, the Indian idea of transparency, which was picked up by the first European Sanskritists, morphed into new forms: it prompted the emergence of the discipline of historical linguistics, but also stimulated speculations about Sanskrit being the bearer of a primordial patrimony of religious knowledge.

The chapter explores two kinds of evidence: the Indian emic interpretations of transparency, and 19th-century European authors' pronouncements on Sanskrit's "wonderful structure."[5] For India, I will concentrate on Patañjali's *Great Commentary*. For Europe, I will focus on Friedrich Schlegel's hugely influential *On the Language and Wisdom of the Indians* (1808). My aim is twofold: first, to provide a brief yet accurate description of such speculations on the transparency of Sanskrit in their respective contexts. Second, to show that the idea of transparency, though construed differently by Indian and European thinkers, was likewise regarded as the defining characteristic of Sanskrit, indeed, as the ultimate reason for Sanskrit's superior status as a sacred and perfect language.

Before we begin, two examples will help clarify what I call transparency. Take the Sanskrit word for 'Sanskrit', *saṃskṛta*. For the Indian and modern grammarians alike, this word can readily be analyzed into three distinct components: *sam*-(*s*)-*kṛ*-*ta*,[6] each component or morpheme conveying a semantic or grammatical information (*sam* 'together', *kṛ* 'to do', *ta* is the marker of the past particle). The components' cumulative meaning yields something like "that which has been done, i.e., put together [in the proper way]," which meaning is commonly taken to denote Sanskrit's role as the perfected language of ritual and religion, as opposed to other, lesser languages.[7] As we will discuss below, Sanskrit's high status as the sacred language and its ritual fitness are seen as being intimately related to its artificially codified grammatical nature. Now, consider the Chinese

5 This phrase is Jones', taken from the same paragraph cited in note 3. Here, too, Jones follows a well-established trope among writers on things Indian. As we will see below, the structure of Sanskrit was first praised in an important letter written by the French missionary Jean François Pons in 1743, which is quoted in the epigraph above.

6 For convenience's sake, we can ignore the "s" here, the so-called "s-mobile" that occurs in some form of the root *kṛ*, but not in others.

7 On the meaning of "Sanskrit," see Thieme (1982: 11) and Cardona (1988: 655).

word for 'Sanskrit,' *fànwén* 梵文. The two characters mean something like 'India' and 'language,' respectively.[8] Each character stands for one word, each word constituting one morphological and semantic block that is not susceptible to further analysis. In this respect, Chinese *fànwén* differs from Sanskrit *sam-(s)-kṛ-ta* – to stick to our terminology, Chinese is not transparent.[9]

2 Indian transparency

From early times, Indian thinkers analyzed the Sanskrit language with a linguistic acumen and precision unparalleled elsewhere in the premodern world. A deep linguistic awareness of the features of poetic diction is already evident in the *Rigveda*, India's earliest literary monument. Its authors were skillful artisans of the poetic word who conceived of language as a magical, generative power, "a causal force behind even the gods and the universe" (Scharfe 1977: 77). Further, driven by the conviction that only texts that are pronounced properly are ritually effective, Brahmins faced the problem of how to ensure a reliable transmission of the Veda. As a consequence of the powerful role ascribed to language and as a response to the concerns of preserving and transmitting the Vedic texts, ancient Indians refined their linguistic analytical skills and advanced a number of linguistic disciplines, the most sophisticated of which is Sanskrit indigenous grammar or *vyākaraṇa*.

Lying at the basis of this discipline is the method of 'concomitant presence' (*anvaya*) and 'concomitant exclusion' (*vyatireka*). Explicitly formulated by the comparatively late grammarian Kātyāyana (ca. 3rd century BCE), such a way of reasoning must have also shaped earlier Indian attitudes toward language. The

---

8 I am simplifying here a bit; originally, *fàn* seems to have been the abbreviated transcription of the Indic word Brahmā, *fànmó* 梵摩 (see Wilkinson 2015: 385), and *wén* may have meant 'writing' rather than language as such.

9 Chinese is not chosen randomly. In his book (1808: 45, 49), Schlegel contrasts Sanskrit's grammatical structure with that of Chinese, which he sees as the language that is typologically most distant from Sanskrit. Such a contrast was taken up and further elaborated by Wilhelm von Humboldt in his correspondence with French sinologist Abel Rémusat. On this correspondence, published in 1827, see Rousseau and Thouard (1999). In his posthumous and most influential work, Humboldt (1988 [1836]: esp. 230–236) continues to speculate on the differences between Sanskrit and Chinese. For a synopsis of Humboldt's view on these two languages, see Aarsleff's introduction to this work (xxvi, xxxi). I build on the traditional comparison between Sanskrit and Chinese only in order to clarify what I mean with Sanskrit's morphological transparency. I am not concerned here with considering the implications that were drawn from this comparison.

method consisting in determining the constant co-occurrence of a linguistic item and its corresponding meaning is described by George Cardona (1967–1968: 45) as follows: "a meaning is not understood unless the item expressing it occurs; if an item occurs a meaning is understood, and when that item is absent the meaning attributed to it is also absent." As a result of deploying this analytic method, Indian thinkers soon came to appreciate the morphological transparency of Sanskrit. They conceived of Sanskrit propositions as further analyzable into words, and these latter as consisting of smaller units, the morphemes.

The awareness of the transparency of Sanskrit is already adumbrated in Vedic texts antedating the Common Era by several centuries. The following passage from the *Taittirīya Saṃhitā* is a case in point, and was read by later commentators as something like a myth of origin of Sanskrit grammar.

> Speech used to speak turned away, inarticulate.[10] The gods said to Indra: "Do articulate this speech for us" [....] Indra stepped down in the middle [of speech] and made it articulate. Thus this speech here is pronounced as articulate. (*Taittirīya Saṃhitā* 6.4.7.3)

The passage gives the etiological account of why Indra partakes of one of the libations of the sacred *soma* juice, the hallucinogenic beverage widely used in ritual in ancient India. It tells us that Indra is granted this libation as a reward for having made speech articulate.

Sāyaṇa, a prolific commentator active in 14th-century Vijayanāgara, reads this passage as a foundational account of the discipline of grammar. In his interpretation, speech "formerly [used to speak] turned away, like the roaring of the ocean, similar to a stick, in that it was an [inarticulate] unity."[11] Indra then made this undifferentiated, unanalyzable roar articulate, by apportioning it into a series of ever smaller units, the sentences, the words, and the grammatical bases and affixes. Sāyaṇa's interpretation is problematic in that it anachronistically presupposes the existence of a fully developed discipline of grammar exhibiting the grammatical concepts of bases and affixes by the time of the composition of the *Taittirīya Saṃhitā*. Nonetheless, he is most probably correct in identifying what is at stake in the Vedic passage: the close connection between Sanskrit's status as the perfect language of ritual and its grammatical codification. (In this respect, we must add that "articulate" in the *Taittirīya Saṃhitā* passage is expressed with

---

10 In this passage speech seems to be likened to the indistinct mumbling of a person who speaks to someone while facing the opposite direction.

11 *Taittirīya Saṃhitā Bhāṣya* 538. "Similar to a stick" (*daṇḍāyamāna*) probably conveys the idea that speech was one single entity, without internal subdivision, like a stick made of one single block of wood. Possibly, the image of the stick contrasts with the bamboo or reed (*kāṇḍa*), whose cane is segmented into parts.

forms of *vyākṛ*, the Sanskrit base from which *vyākaraṇa*, the Sanskrit name for "grammar," is derived.) Indeed, the passage suggests that Sanskrit must undergo a process of grammatical analysis in order to become truly articulate, that is, to achieve its grammatical transparency. In this view, grammar is not, therefore, merely an extrinsic, accidental feature of Sanskrit, but an essential determinant. In other words, the fact of being grammaticalized and the resultant transparency set Sanskrit apart from all other unarticulated forms of speech (forms which, it is fair to guess, include all other languages, according to the Sanskrit grammarians).

The most thorough discussion of the relationship between Sanskrit and its grammatical codification is articulated in the first chapter of Patañjali's *Great Commentary*, the seminal text of Indian grammar and philosophy of language which I mentioned at the outset. Patañjali discusses a dazzling variety of topics, condensing arguments and counterarguments in a dialectical maelstrom. I focus only on a few selected aspects, those that are most germane to our concerns.

One of the major questions addressed by Patañjali is "what is Sanskrit grammar good for?" ("Grammar" must here be understood as the discipline of grammar, the system of rules governing the formation of Sanskrit words formulated in Pāṇini's *Eight Lectures*.) A critical voice argues that the Vedic words are learned through the memorization of the Veda, and ordinary words are learned from common speech. What, then, is the point of learning the difficult discipline of grammar?[12] Patañjali is too fine a philosopher of language not to recognize the validity of such a criticism. He is fully aware of the fact that grammar's role is negligible regarding the employment of words in ordinary speech. Grammar does not establish the relation between a word and its meaning,[13] nor does an ordinary speaker resort to the rules of Sanskrit grammar when he needs to produce a word. Rather, words come to people naturally: they do not go to the grammarian to ask for words when they need them, as they would go to a potter when needing a pot (Joshi and Roodbergen 1986: 115–116). Moreover, Patañjali has no illusions as to the role of Sanskrit as a privileged medium of communication superior to other languages. He readily admits that there is no difference between using the correct Sanskrit word for "cow" or the corresponding vernacular forms: both serve the communicative purpose equally, conveying the meaning "cow" successfully (125).

In order to muster robust arguments for establishing a raison d'être for the discipline of grammar, Patañjali draws attention to grammar's role as a tool for

---

12 *Mahābhāṣya* 5.10; translation Joshi and Roodbergen (1986: 68). Hereafter references in the body of my chapter are to this translation.

13 One of the assumptions of grammar is that "the relation between a word and (its) meaning has already been established on account of the usage of people." *Mahābhāṣya* 7.28; Joshi and Roodbergen (1986: 90).

the preservation and interpretation of the Veda (26–31). Further, and more interesting to us, he elaborates on the connections between grammar and the sphere of ritual and religion. For Patañjali, knowledge of grammar not only enables the grammarian to perform the rituals effectively through the perusal of the proper ritual formulas, but also provides him with a means for self-divinization – "So that we should have similarity with the mighty god, grammar must be studied" (53). Although Patañjali does not elaborate on this tantalizing point,[14] other passages develop the links between Sanskrit grammar and religious ideas further. Thus, for example, in citing and commenting on a Rigvedic verse, Patañjali argues that the goddess of speech reveals herself to grammarians only, thereby perhaps suggesting that the grammarian's analytical skills are the only means of attaining to the divine core of language (57–58).[15] Most notably, Patañjali contends that speaking Sanskrit is an act that produces 'religious merit' (*puṇya*) and is conducive to 'bliss' (*abhyudaya*) and *dharma*.[16] This is an arresting idea, but how exactly is grammar supposed to achieve that? I explore below two salient aspects in Patañjali's discussion, and supply the context in which they can best be understood.

First, Patañjali emphasizes that it is only through abiding by the restrictive rules of grammar, that is, by using the correct Sanskrit words, that one gains religious merit. The basic idea behind this claim is the recognition that grammar does for language what other normative disciplines do for other domains. Patañjali illustrates this with a vivid example: while the sexual drive is equally satisfied by engaging in sexual intercourse with a licit or illicit partner, it is only the former case that is sanctioned in the traditional lore and, therefore, produces an increase in religious merit (122). *Mutatis mutandis*, the same applies to language. Although, as we saw above, Sanskrit and non-Sanskrit words alike produce a successful communication, only the former is seen as producing merit. On a deeper level of analysis, this strand of Patañjali's argumentation seems to be premised on the idea that for any action to be appropriate it needs first to be based on, and comply with, a preexisting normative code. In this connection, it is worth recalling that the *Great Commentary* is considered to be one of the earliest representatives of *śāstra*. This term refers to an Indian literary genre, or, perhaps better, a form of discourse, which emphasizes how any form of correct praxis – and such texts

---

14 Discussed by Shulman (2005: 376).

15 See Visigalli (2017: 1162–1163). See also the first epigraph of this chapter.

16 *Mahābhāṣya* 10.21 [*abhyudaya*], 8, 3 [*dharma*]; Joshi and Roodbergen (1986: 117). "Bliss" appears to have a twofold sense, referring to both an increase in wealth and social status in this world, and to a blissful state in the afterlife. For a perceptive discussion of Patañjali's idea in the context of Indian attitudes towards language, see Cardona (1990: 10–11).

cover a wide variety of topics, including love-making, stealing and, of course, language – must ultimately be based on a corresponding theoretical description that is preexisting and is embodied in the respective *śāstra* text.[17]

Second, in order to gain a fuller understanding of Patañjali's speculations, we also need to probe into their connections with earlier Vedic ideas about ritual and the magical power of language. To this end, consider that section in which Patañjali discusses whether religious merit acquired through speaking Sanskrit derives from the acquaintance with the grammatical knowledge (*jñāna*) that helps discriminate between grammatically correct and incorrect words, or from the consequent employment (*prayoga*) of the former only (145–158). For one thing, this passage follows the *śāstra* model in emphasizing the predominance of a preexisting "theory" over a dependent "praxis." For another, it points to the influence exerted by earlier Vedic ideas which may have paved the way for the formation of the later full-fledged *śāstra* model. Specifically, Patañjali's discussion of the interdependency of knowledge and praxis can be seen as the continuation of a discussion on the efficacy of ritual articulated in earlier Vedic texts. Central to these texts was the question whether a ritual is effective because it is performed properly, or, as several (but by no means all) Upaniṣadic passages claim, proper praxis does not suffice, but needs to be premised on the knowledge of the ritual acts' symbolic meaning – a knowledge that is sometimes regarded as the true ritual engine and thus capable of replacing the actual ritual praxis. In short, Patañjali's discussion of the relation between grammar and the acquisition of religious merit appears to be in continuity with the earlier speculative trend centering on the so-called internalization of ritual.

What are the similarities between a ritual performance and grammar? We have already noted how the dialectic between theory and praxis plays out in similar terms in both domains. At a deeper level, the sophisticated Indian disciplines of ritual and grammar seem to share a fundamental epistemic assumption: they conceptualize their respective domains of inquiry, ritual performance, and language, as complex systems that are ultimately analyzable into basic fundamental units. While, as we saw, grammarians conceived of language as ultimately consisting in morphemes, ritualists likewise conceived of rituals as different

17 For a fuller discussion of *śāstra*, see Pollock (1985). It is imperative to notice however that in Patañjali's thinking the dynamic between theory and praxis is complicated by his emphasis on linguistic usage (*prayoga*) as the basis for grammatical analysis. Central to Patañjali's thesis is the notion of *śiṣṭas* or qualified speakers, a community of virtuous and learned Brahmins residing in the Gangetic basin; their correct linguistic usage is independent from grammar. On the *śiṣṭas* in Patañjali's and other early grammarians' thinking, see Deshpande (1992).

arrangements of basic building blocks.[18] In short, a similar model seems to underlie both disciplines, a model that rests on the same basic assumption, that which I called *transparency*. In addition, another similarity between ritual and grammar is that, just as a ritual performer gains religious merit when all his ritual actions converge to produce a cohesive ritual event, so too does a grammarian by generating the correct Sanskrit words and sentences through the juxtaposition (*saṃskṛ*, 'to put together [in the proper manner]') of the basic building blocks of language.[19]

Patañjali's speculations on ritual and grammar articulated in the first chapter of the *Great Commentary* have gained a certain prominence in modern scholarship on ritual. Patañjali has been credited with being the first to observe that ritual and language have a formal homology, both have "grammars" (Staal 1989: 40–41; Meshel 2014: 1–3; Michaels 2016: 74). As Naphtali Meshel notes in his contribution to this book, the thesis that ritual systems have a "grammar," and can thus be analyzed with the analytical tools and categories derived from, or at least inspired by, linguistics, has been "the single most important framework for the study of ritual" in the past decades. In his contribution, Meshel problematizes this thesis, perceptively arguing that the analogy between the formal structure of language (grammar) and the formal structure of rituals should be taken with a grain of salt.

Although I find Meshel's general argument convincing and intriguing, I do not fully agree with his interpretation of Patañjali's position. A systematic critical review would take us too far afield.[20] The following general observations will suffice to indicate the main dissimilarity between Meshel's and my own interpretation of Patañjali's thinking.

Meshel opines that Patañjali implicitly assumes a formal homology between Sanskrit and sacrificial ritual: both systems have "grammars," in the sense of a finite inventory of building blocks and a finite set of rules that can be used to generate an unlimited array of combinations. I think this is basically correct, but not for the reasons adduced by Meshel. Indeed, those passages of the *Great Commentary* that Meshel (and Staal) interpret as revealing Patañjali's view about

18 On Indian ideas about rituals as consisting of basic units, see Staal (1982, 1989); see also Michaels (2010). On ritual as the paradigm-setting discipline of ancient India, see Smith (1989); on the relation between ritual and grammar, see Renou's (1942) classic study.
19 See Thieme (1982), Smith (1989: 101). Both scholars emphasize the ritual usage of forms *saṃskṛ*; e.g., *saṃskāra* 'ritual.'
20 See however Michaels' critical comments (2016: 74–77).

the homology between ritual and Sanskrit can best be interpreted as illustrating a different affinity between these two domains.[21]

In my view, Patañjali does not discuss their formal homology, but rather, as mentioned above, he focuses on the following intersections between ritual and Sanskrit: 1) the dynamic between theory (*śāstra*) and praxis (*prayoga*) plays out in analogous terms in both domains; 2) both ritual and linguistic practice needs to conform to restrictive rules (*dharmaniyama*), which, we may say, are aimed at preserving the social and linguistic *status quo* (see Michaels 2016: 74–77); and 3) the employment of ritual and words sanctioned by such rules is supposed to bring about merit and bliss.

However, even though for different reasons, I agree with Meshel's thesis according to which Patañjali assumed a formal homology between the structures of ritual and Sanskrit. In fact, I think the point can be made more forcibly. Even though I cannot find decisive evidence in the *Great Commentary*, I think it is highly likely that Patañjali took for granted (which is not the same as to consciously formulate) that ritual and Sanskrit have a structural homology. This claim is supported by what several scholars have observed[22]: the Indian indigenous disciplines of ritology and Sanskrit grammar (*vyākaraṇa*) share several technical terms, concepts, and methods of analysis. Indeed, as I suggested above, at a deeper level of analysis, both indigenous disciplines appear to share an analogous epistemic model based on the notion of *transparency*. Considering these affinities, I think that the title of founding father of "ritual grammar" should not be given to Patañjali, but, collectively, to his anonymous predecessors whose analyses straddled the boundary between ritual and language; they not only recognized the affinity between these two domains, but systematically worked out their intuition to produce highly sophisticated indigenous disciplines.

3 Western transparency

Twenty centuries after the *Great Commentary* the idea of the transparency of Sanskrit reemerged, metamorphosed into a new shape, in Friedrich Schlegel's *On the Language and Wisdom of the Indians* (1808) (hereafter "*LW*"). An eminent

---

21 The two main passages are: 1) *Mahābhāṣya* 5.26–6.7; Joshi and Roodbergen (1986: 74–77 [Bṛhaspati-Indra episode; need of an economic system of rules for describing grammar]); 2) *Mahābhāṣya* 9.6 ff.; Joshi and Roodbergen (1986: 136–137 [discussion of "unused" (*aprayukta*) words and rituals]).

22 See Meshel (2014: 3) and Michaels (2016: 74n3) with references to literature.

literary critic and philosopher, Schlegel was also Germany's first Sanskritist. The connections with India ran deep in the Schlegel family. Friedrich's eldest brother, Karl August, served as a soldier under British command in India and, before his premature death in Madras in 1789, devoted himself to the study of the "Indian culture [*Geist*]" (xiii). His older brother, August Wilhelm, took up Sanskrit upon Friedrich's suggestion and became Germany's first professor of Sanskrit in Bonn in 1819.

LW is a complex, fascinating, and hugely influential text, and as such can be approached from many different perspectives. Many commentators have emphasized the role Schlegel's discussion of the linguistic affinities between Sanskrit and other languages had played in igniting scholarly interest in Sanskrit and birthing the discipline of historical comparative grammar.[23] Scholars have also unraveled some of the ways in which *LW* is reflective of Schlegel's religious convictions (his conversion from Protestantism to Roman Catholicism)[24] as well as his political and ideological convictions (Schlegel's emphasis on a spiritual and historical connection between Vedic India and contemporary Germany has been correlated with his increasing nationalism, nurtured by Germany's political and military humiliation at the hand of Napoleonic France[25]). In addition, commentators have also noted the "reactionary implications" of Schlegel's linguistic thought, in particular his classification of languages as inferior or superior, "which continued to influence much of the 19th-century linguistics" (Timpanaro 1977: xiii).

Here, I want to draw attention to Schlegel's discussion of the grammatical transparency of the Sanskrit language and make two proposals. First, Schlegel's idea of transparency appears to be indebted to Indian linguistic speculations of the kind outlined above. This historical link has so far gone unnoticed. Second, I submit that such an idea of transparency is key to understanding Schlegel's vision as advanced in *LW*.

Briefly, Schlegel seeks to use *LW* to boost Indian studies. He contends that a more thorough understanding of Sanskrit and its literature will not only cast

23 See, *inter alia*, Lehman (1967: 22); Struc-Openberg (1980); Koerner (1987); and Collinge (1995). Most notably, Schlegel popularizes the term "comparative [*vergleichende*] grammar." Contrary to what is sometimes stated, this term was not coined by Schlegel, but was first used, among others, in one letter sent to him by his brother August Wilhelm; see Struc-Oppenberg (1980: 425n44). See also Timpanaro (1977 [1972]: xxx–xxxv).

24 See Tzoref-Ashkenazi (2006). Already Heinrich Heine had sarcastically noted that "These gentlemen [i.e., the Schlegel brothers] considered India the cradle of Catholicism"; cited from Timpanaro (1977: xxvii).

25 See Tzoref-Ashkenazi (2006) and Dusche (2013). For a more charitable interpretation of Schlegel's thought, see Handwerk's (1998) perceptive study.

light on the "as yet so dark history of the primeval world" (iii). It will also bring about a cultural and spiritual change – a "second Renaissance," as Schlegel puts it, using a term that was becoming current among early 19th-century German and French Indophiles, and was later to find sanction in Arthur Schopenhauer's work (see Cross 2008).

Schlegel's passionate concern for Sanskrit and ancient India must be understood in relation to the intellectual milieu of early 19th-century Germany. Dominated by Romanticism, this milieu proved fertile ground for assimilating the newly "discovered" Sanskrit literature. As Stephen Cross (2008: 61) puts it, at that time:

> A wave of enthusiasm and fervent hope swept through the rising generations in the [German] universities. It was felt that brilliant new possibilities heralding the beginning of a great cultural renewal, a rebirth of both spiritual life and poetry, had suddenly become available.

Like many other thinkers of his generation, Schlegel regarded ancient India as the cradle of civilization, the home of a primordial wisdom that was now beginning to be unlocked through the translations of the Calcutta-based civil servant-scholars of the East India Company. Sanskrit was heralded as the ancestral language, and its literature was expected to play a key role in bringing about the much-awaited spiritual reformation.

In *LW*, Schlegel portrays the study of Indian antiquity in terms of a battle between darkness and light. By "illuminat[ing] the entirely unknown domains of earliest antiquity," such study will recuperate the "vestiges of truth, [...] of divine truth" (203) that are scattered everywhere, but predominantly in the oldest Oriental literary monuments. Although Schlegel contends vigorously that Sanskrit literature has to offer "rich treasures" (219) in the field of poetry and philosophy, he is nonetheless anxious to emphasize its inherent limits:

> [The] Indian documents show the origins of the error, the first monstrous products which the Spirit [*Geist*] increasingly fabricates and counterfeits, once it has abandoned and lost the simple purity [*Einfalt*] of the divine insight; of this latter, however, even in the midst of superstition and night, the splendid vestiges of its light [*Lichtspuren*] still remain. (198)

The ideas advanced in this passage require further scrutiny. On the one hand, Schlegel ascribes a great value to Sanskrit literature. Because of their putative extreme antiquity, Sanskrit texts are presumed to provide the closest links to the primeval moment in history, which is characterized by the highest spiritual clarity and closest proximity with the divine (*das Göttliche*) (e.g., 219). On the other, Schlegel underscores that such texts do not offer a direct link with the divine; in them the primordial light is mixed with later errors:

> [N]o one will ever find the surest separation of the commingled error but through Christianity, which alone provides information about the truth and insight, which are higher than all the knowledge and fancies of reason. (204)

And yet, even though Schlegel relativizes the *content* of Sanskrit literature in relation with the Christian revelation, he appears to identify what he calls the "innermost structure" or "grammar" of the Sanskrit language as the surest carrier of the primordial divine revelation. It is here that the idea of *transparency* plays a crucial role.

Before we turn to it, we need to briefly consider Schlegel's thought about the distinct origins of languages and their different grammatical structures, two topics closely related to the idea of transparency.

Countering the thesis of the monogenesis of languages, Schlegel argues that different languages exhibit radically different grammatical structures, which must be seen as proof of their distinct origins. With respect to grammar, he identifies two major groups of languages: the 'flectional' [*Flexion*] group, and all the rest. Elaborating on the findings of William Jones, Schlegel contends that all languages belonging to the flectional group derive from Sanskrit. Such flectional languages are Latin, Greek, Persian, and, most notably, Greek and German, which bear the closest resemblance to Sanskrit. Although Schlegel is wary of identifying Sanskrit as the parent language of the flectional group, he believes that Sanskrit must be fairly close to that *Ursprache* or "original language." However, only further investigation of the (then) only insufficiently known Veda, the earliest Indian texts, will decide the relation between classical Sanskrit and the *Ursprache* (66–67).

For Schlegel, there is one essential difference between the grammar of the flectional languages and that of the others; this difference he describes in terms of an opposition between 'organic' [*organisch*] and 'generative' [*fruchtbar*] on the one hand, and on the other 'mechanical' [*mechanisch*] and 'barren' [*unfruchtbar*] – that is, ultimately, in terms of a distinction between what is naturally alive and what is not.[26] In the flexional languages, and preeminently so in Sanskrit, the "roots" are what the name itself suggests: a 'living germinal nucleus' [*lebendiger Keim*] (50). It is through internal modifications of the root sounds that the root meaning evolves into all possible meanings, in a process of unfolding of unlimited expansive power. Conversely, the grammar of the other languages consists in

---

26 Schlegel outlines the difference between the two groups of language most thoroughly in *LW* at 41–42 and 50–51. For a reconstruction of the contemporary controversy about polygenesis versus monogenesis, which provides the background for Schlegel's speculations, see Timpanaro (1977 [1972]: xx). On the difference between "organic" and "mechanical", see Timpanaro (1977 [1972]: xix–xx) and Davies (1998: 71–74). For the use of organicist ideas and terminology by Schlegel and his near-contemporaries, see Davies (1998: 73, 86).

the mechanical juxtaposition of external affixes, and the root is not a "generative seed, but only a heap of atoms, as it were" (50).

Schlegel describes the putatively perfect flexional nature of Sanskrit grammar with two seemingly antonymic terms, 'artistic' [*kunstreich*] and 'simple' [*einfach*]. The grammatical processes through which the Sanskrit roots undergo internal modifications are highly sophisticated, yet remain naturally simple, devoid of all the mechanical trappings burdening the grammars of the other inferior languages.

For Schlegel, the 'artistic simplicity' [*kunstreiche Einfachheit*] (44) of Sanskrit grammar is a result of its transparency. This latter is the expression of the superiority of the mental and spiritual powers of the primeval peoples who produced Sanskrit. Sanskrit grammar retains traces of these peoples' psychic life, a life characterized by "the clearest and most intimate sobriety [*Besonnenheit*]" (63), the "deepest sensations," and "spiritual/mental clarity [*Geistesklarheit*]" (64). Most fundamentally, the primeval speakers of Sanskrit had unmediated access to the "primeval divine revelation [*ursprüngliche Offenbarung*]" (105), and, consequently, they could grasp the "ancestral natural meanings [...] of letters, root-sounds, and syllables" (42). An almost sacred status is thus ascribed to Sanskrit grammar, which is regarded as the site in which the primordial, divine revelation can be glimpsed. Sanskrit, "in its first and simplest components [i.e., its roots and sounds] [...] expresses – not figuratively [*bildlich*], but with unmediated clarity – the highest ideas of the pure conceptual world, the layout of consciousness, as it were" (63).[27]

In short, Schlegel's notion of the transparency of Sanskrit grammar is twofold. First, transparency refers to the natural and organic way in which ever-new meanings are formed through the internal modifications of the root sounds. Second, and most importantly, this grammatical structure stems from and preserves the purest modes of thought of ancestral people, their heightened spiritual and mental clarity, and their unmediated link with the divine.

A number of different influences inform Schlegel's idea of transparency. Most noticeably, echoes of Reformed theology, the Romantic concern with origins, and the concomitant idealized view of ancient India as the cradle of a pure, primeval civilization, coordinate with German Idealism (Schelling) and Herder's ideas of

---

27 As a foil for Schlegel's position, it may here not be out of place to refer to Friedrich Max Müller's claim in his essay "Semitic Monotheism" (1868 [1860]: 362–363); namely, that Semitic languages such as Hebrew clearly show the derivation of words from three-letter-roots, thus reducing the chance of reifying words and producing mythology (and idolatry). Sanskrit and other Indo-European languages supposedly do the opposite. See Yelle (2013: 64).

universal history.[28] I will not try to pick apart all such influences, but focus on two other major ones: Cratylism and the Sanskrit indigenous grammar.

Cratylism refers to the idea, most famously advanced (alongside different views) in Plato's *Cratylus*, that sounds are meaningful basic units of language and are not conventional, but have an intrinsic link with reality. As Gérard Genette has shown most thoroughly, Cratylism has been pervasive in Western traditions. Broadly speaking, Cratylism is the belief in a "perfect" or "natural" language, the idea that a given language enjoys a direct connection with reality.[29] In *LW*, the influence of Cratylism is most evident in Schlegel's speculations on the link between Sanskrit and the "the original natural meaning [...] of letters, root-sounds, and syllables" (42) and "the natural meanings of things" (64). It is also clear, however, that Schlegel's revisitation of the Cratylean notion of a perfect language differs from those held by most of his predecessors. While most of these latter, in line with Plato's *Cratylus*, stress the link that words, syllables, and sounds have with their natural origins, Schlegel identifies the site of the interface between language and (divine) reality at the level of grammar.

Schlegel's emphasis on grammar has been perceptively discussed by Genette in relation to the "Copernican revolution" in the domain of language in the early 19th century, a revolution brought about by the discovery of Sanskrit and the emergence of historical comparative linguistics (Genette 1995: 259–266). As Genette observes, grammar – understood as morphology – became the focus of attention of early 19th-century linguists.[30] This revolution impacted Cratylism, posing a serious challenge to one of its basic assumptions, namely, that languages are in essence nomenclatures. As Genette argues, it was no longer possible to retain the by-then-naïve conviction that languages simply consist of words – in particular "nouns" – bearing a relation of similarity (*mimesis*) with the things denoted; languages came to be conceived at a further remove of abstraction as morphological systems.

We must stress that Schlegel appears to be the first to emphasize the role of morphology as the central defining issue for linguistic value. As I will show shortly, a few pronouncements praising the grammatical structure of Sanskrit can be found in earlier authors; however, none of these comes close to foreshadowing the unprecedented crucial role ascribed to Sanskrit morphology in *LW*.

28 For the influence exerted by these thinkers on Schlegel, see Timpanaro (1977: xvii; xviii), with references.

29 On the "perfect" and "natural" language, see Genette (1995) [1976]; Eco (1995) [1993]; and Yelle (2003).

30 A special place among them must be accorded to Wilhelm von Humboldt; see Genette (1995: 265).

From what source did Schlegel draw inspiration for his technical description of Sanskrit morphology, and for his ideas regarding morphology's importance? I believe that the most likely answer is: from indigenous Indian speculations on language, specifically the Indian grammatical tradition.[31]

Before discussing the evidence supporting this claim, the new ways in which Schlegel reworked the Indian idea of transparency must be emphasized. Although Schlegel, like the ancient Indian grammarians, conceived of transparency as intersecting the domains of grammar and religion, his understanding of what counted as "religious" was radically new. Though not expressly asserted anywhere, a belief in the soteriological dimension of Sanskrit morphology is taken for granted in several passages of *LW*. In Schlegel's thinking, Sanskrit morphology – transparency – constituted a perfect structure that retained the traces of the purest, primeval clarity of the men of yore, who faced the divine squarely, without intermediary. By implication, Schlegel must have regarded the study of Sanskrit morphology as a spiritual exercise of sorts, which could enable contemporary man to backtrack the course of history, and come as close as possible to the primordial moment of divine revelation. In Schlegel's grammatical mysticism, Sanskrit morphological transparency was the bearer of primordial religious knowledge in that it was the locus – the transparent interface – through which one could obtain glimpses of the divine.

Robust evidence supports my proposal that a defining influence on Schlegel's notion of morphological transparency stems from the Indian indigenous grammatical tradition. To begin, Schlegel was exposed to Indian linguistic ideas in the very process of learning Sanskrit. In their endeavor to learn the language, early Sanskritists had to rely, more or less directly, on the Sanskrit grammarians' linguistic analyses. Rosane Rocher describes the general situation as follows:

> Sanskrit was first taught to Europeans – directly or mediately – according to the enduring tradition of rigorous analysis by Pāṇini and other Indian grammarians and phoneticians. The identification of the root as the smallest common denominator of derived forms, vocalic alternation, derivational and inflectional suffixes, substitution rules, zeroing, etc., and the description of articulatory processes were the procedures according to which Europeans learned Sanskrit from pandits. (Rocher 1995: 191)

We can be more precise in assessing the influence that Indian grammatical models exerted on Schlegel's linguistic training. In the preface to *LW* (v), Schlegel tells us that he acquired his knowledge of Sanskrit from two sources: the oral

---

31 To the best of my knowledge, this line of influence has not been pointed out before. Thus, for instance, no reference to the Indian tradition is found in Timpanaro's (1977) and Davies' (1998) masterly discussions of Schlegel's *LW*.

instructions of Alexander Hamilton (a Scotsman who had studied Sanskrit in India with paṇḍits),[32] and perusal of manuscript No. 283 of the French Imperial Library, compiled by an "unnamed missionary."

Jean Filliozat has studied this manuscript (now catalogued as *sanscrit 551*) and identified its compiler as Jean François Pons (1698–1752), a Jesuit missionary active in Bengal. As Filliozat has shown, the manuscript was sent to France in 1738 and contains, among excerpts from other texts, the outline of a Sanskrit grammar. Written in Bengali script and translated into Latin, this grammar must have resulted from the cooperation between Pons and local Brahmins. Based on Indian grammatical models, it contains a list of the Sanskrit roots with the main conjugational forms, as well as a complete paradigm of the root *kṛ* ('to do, make') and an incomplete one of *bhū* ('to be, become'). Besides Schlegel, two other eminent orientalists, Abraham Hyacinthe Anquetil-Duperron and Antoine-Léonard de Chézy – respectively, the translators of the Avesta and of the Upaniṣads (the latter from a Persian version), and the first professor of Sanskrit at the Collège de France (1814) – learned the rudiments of Sanskrit from this grammar (Filliozat 1937). It is plausible that this grammar exerted a shaping influence on Schlegel's notion of the morphological transparency of Sanskrit. Specifically, the list of Sanskrit roots and the conjugational paradigms that are contained therein may have informed Schlegel's notion of "root" and of the grammatical structure of flectional languages.[33]

Schlegel was not the first European to become fascinated by Sanskrit grammar; indeed, he had an influential predecessor in Pons, the "unnamed compiler" of the Paris manuscript. In a letter sent on 23 November 1740, first published in 1743, Father Pons praised the *perfection de l'art* attained by the Sanskrit grammarians, who "through Analysis have reduced the richest language of the world to a small number of primitive elements, which one can regard as the *caput mortuum* of the language" (Staal 1972: 30). As Pons elaborates, from a "root or primitive element" one can derive by means of the rules of grammar "many thousands of proper Sanskrit words."[34] Pons' letter was

---

32 On Hamilton, see Rosane Rocher's entry in *Oxford Dictionary of National Biography*, available online at http://www.oxforddnb.com/view/article/12044 (accessed 5 February 2016).

33 In addition, it is conceivable that a direct influence by this grammar can be detected in the third book of *LW* (36), where Schlegel illustrates some features of Sanskrit grammar with examples from the paradigms of *kṛ* and *bhū*, that is, the same paradigms employed in the manuscript. It should be noted that Schlegel does not provide a precise definition for 'root' [*Wurzel*], but uses it in different senses. See Rousseau's (2006: 1415) pertinent remarks. On how early 19th-century linguists understood the notion of 'root,' see Alfieri (2014).

34 It may be worth noticing that Pons illustrates this point by adducing several forms of the root *kṛ*. Recall that a complete paradigm of this root occurs in the grammatical outline that Pons sent to France in 1738, two years before writing this letter.

translated into several languages and exerted an enduring and wide-ranging influence, echoes of which, as mentioned above, are visible in William Jones' famous discourse on the genetic relation between Sanskrit and other languages.

Under Pons' direct or indirect influence, many other European writers became attracted to Sanskrit grammar. I give here one example. In his article on Sanskrit in the *Encyclopédie méthodique* (Beauzée 1786: 356), Nicolas Beauzée (1717–1789) cited, along with other sources, lengthy excerpts from Pons' letter. Entirely reliant on his sources for describing a language he did not know, Beauzée believed that Sanskrit was an artificial language that had been invented by the Brahmins. He found support for this in the fact that Sanskrit was "so regular, energetic, rich, and harmonious." Because of such qualities, Beauzée proposed that Sanskrit should be adopted as an international scholarly language, if only the notoriously recalcitrant Brahmins could be convinced to teach it to Europeans.

Although Schlegel's fascination with Sanskrit grammar must thus be understood in relation to a number of forerunners, his assessment differed from his predecessors' in one crucial respect. Pons and Beauzée, despite their differences in interpretation, recognized that the grammatical transparency of Sanskrit was the result of the Brahmins' analyses. Beauzée went so far as to claim that grammar was the means by which Brahmins deliberately created the extraordinarily difficult Sanskrit language, with a view to concealing the mysteries of their religion from the inferior castes.[35] Conversely, Schlegel did not recognize the role played by Indian grammarians in highlighting Sanskrit's morphological transparency. He seemed to forget the grammar contained in the Paris manuscript, which he used as his Sanskrit primer and which, as I argued above, may have informed his linguistic ideas. Instead, he conceived of the transparency of Sanskrit as something entirely unrelated to man-made grammatical analysis. By factoring out human intervention, Schlegel could raise Sanskrit grammar to a super-human level, as the liminal site wherein glimpses of the divine could be obtained.

---

35 Similarly, the missionary Paulinus a Sancto Bartholomaeo (1804 [1790]: 21), one of the first to publish a grammar of Sanskrit, felt bound to recognize the 'admirable cunning of the Devil' (*admirabilis Diaboli calliditas*), which induced the ancient Brahmans to create the rich and complicated Sanskrit language. See also Dugald Stewart's claim that Sanskrit was an artificial language created by Brahmins for secrecy, a hybrid of native Indian words and Greek endings and syntax, invented after Alexander's conquests of northwest India; in Trautmann (1997: 124–127).

4 Concluding remarks

This chapter has examined the idea that Sanskrit is a morphologically transparent language. It has emphasized the role played by transparency as the defining category by which Indian and Western thinkers conceptualized Sanskrit as a superior, even perfect language. The complex nature of transparency has been emphasized; far from being a merely grammatical notion, it lies at the intersection between linguistic and religious concerns. Specifically, in India, the notion of transparency as advanced in the *Great Commentary* must be understood in relation to the traditional commitments to the efficacy of ritual and the generative power of magical language. In Friedrich Schlegel's vision, Sanskrit's transparency is testimony to a primeval divine revelation, the vestiges of which are retained in, and thus accessible through, Sanskrit grammar.

In addition, this essay proposed that the Indian linguistic tradition may have informed Schlegel's speculations in *LW*. While, as neatly summarized in Rocher's citation given above, it is commonly admitted that Sanskrit grammar provided the nascent discipline of historical linguistics with some of the fundamental intellectual tools for language analysis, the complex nature of such a transmission of ideas is perhaps not fully realized. Schlegel's case strongly suggests that this transmission cannot only be studied in terms of a transfer of grammatical knowledge. Rather, as I argued above, the Indian grammatical ideas were part and parcel of a complex language ideology, and were received and grafted upon a likewise complex and composite intellectual milieu. In both contexts, there was no evident, clear-cut boundary between what counted as linguistics and what as religion. In particular, we saw that, together with the intellectual tools that enabled him to carry out his linguistic analysis of the flectional languages, Schlegel seems also to have borrowed, directly or indirectly, from his Indian sources the notion – or the illusion – of Sanskrit as the perfect language. If it was just an illusion, it turned out to be an incredibly productive one, which would lead to a revolution in how we look at language and human history.

References

Alfieri, Luca. 2014. The arrival of the Indian notion of root into Western linguistics: From Colebrooke (1805) to Benfey (1852). *Rivista Italiana degli Studi Orientali* 87. 59–85.

Beauzée, Nicolas. 1786. Samskret. In *Encyclopédie méthodique*, tome 3, *Grammaire et littérature*. 355–359. Paris.

Cardona, George. 1967–68. *Anvaya* and *vyatireka* in Indian grammar. *Adyar Library Bulletin* 31. 313–352.

Cardona, George. 1988. *Pāṇini, his work and its traditions*, vol. 1, *Background and introduction*. Delhi: Motilal Banarsidass.
Cardona, George. 1990. On attitudes towards language in ancient India. *Sino-Platonic Papers* 15. 1–19.
Chatterji, K. C. (ed. and trans.). 1957. *Patañjali's Mahābhāṣya: Paspaśāhnika edited with English translation, notes and commentaries*. Calcutta: A. Mukherjee & Co.
Collinge, Nevil Edgar. 1995. History of comparative linguistics. In E. F. K. Koerner & R. E. Asher (eds.), *Concise history of the language sciences from the Sumerians to the cognitivists*, 195–202. London & New York: Elsevier.
Cross, Stephen. 2008. Schopenhauer in the context of the Oriental Renaissance. In Barua Arati (ed.), *Schopenhauer and Indian philosophy: A dialogue between India and Germany*, 58–80. New Delhi: Northern Book Centre.
Davies, Anna Morpurgo. 1998. *History of linguistics*, vol. 4, *Nineteenth-century linguistics*. London & New York: Longman.
Deeg, Max. 1995. *Die altindische Etymologie nach dem Verständnis Yāska's und seine Vorgänger: Eine Untersuchung über ihre Praktiken, ihre literarische Verbreitung und ihr Verhältnis zur dichterischen Gestaltung und Sprachmagie*. Dettelbach: Joseph H. Röll.
Deshpande, Madhav M. 1992. The changing notion of śiṣṭa from Patañjali to Bhartṛhari. *Asiatische Studien/Études Asiatiques* 47(1). 95–115.
Dusche, Michael. 2013. Friedrich Schlegel's writings on India: Reimagining Germany as Europe's true oriental self. In James Hodkinson, John Walker, Shaswati Mazumdar & Johannes Feichtinger (eds.), *Deploying Orientalism in culture and history: From Germany to Central and Eastern Europe*, 31–54. Martlesham, Suffolk: Boydell & Brewer.
Eco, Umberto. 1995 [1993]. *The search for the perfect language*. Translated by James Fentress. Oxford: Blackwell.
Filliozat, Jean. 1937. Une grammaire sanscrite du XVIIIe siècle et les débuts de l'indianisme en France. *Journal Asiatique* 229. 275–284.
Genette, Gérard. 1995 [1976]. *Mimologics*. Translated by Thaïs E. Morgan, with a foreword by Gerald Prince. Lincoln & London: University of Nebraska Press.
Handwerk, Gary. 1998. Envisioning India: Friedrich Schlegel's Sanskrit studies and the emergence of romantic historiography. *European Romantic Review* 9(2). 231–242.
Humboldt, Wilhelm. 1988 [1836]. *On language: The diversity of human language-structure and its influence on the mental development of mankind*. Translated by Peter Heath, with an introduction by Hans Aarsleff. Cambridge: Cambridge University Press.
Joshi, S. D. & J. A. F. Roodbergen (eds. & trans.). 1986. *Patañjali's Vyākaraṇa-Mahābhāṣya: Paspaśāhnika, Introduction, text, translation and notes*. Poona: Publications of the Centre of Advanced Study in Sanskrit.
Koerner, Konrad. 1987. Friedrich Schlegel and the emergence of historical-comparative grammar. *Lingua e Stile* 22. 341–65.
Lehmann, Winfred (ed.). 1967. *A reader in nineteenth-century historical Indo-European linguistics*. Bloomington & London: Indiana University Press.
Mahābhāṣya. Cited in the edition by Franz Kielhorn. 1880–1885. *The Vyākaraṇamahābhāṣya of Patañjali*, 3 vols. Bombay: Government Central Book Depot. Numbers refer to page and line of the first volume.
Meshel, Naphtali. 2014. *The grammar of sacrifice: A generativist study of the Israelite sacrificial system in the Priestly writings, with A grammar of Σ*. Oxford: Oxford University Press.

Michaels, Axel. 2010. The grammar of rituals. In Axel Michaels et al. (eds.), *Ritual dynamics and the science of ritual*, vol. 1, *Grammars and morphologies of ritual practices in Asia*, 7–29. Wiesbaden: Harrassowitz.

Michaels, Axel. 2016. *Homo ritualis: Hindu ritual and its significance for ritual theory*. New York: Oxford University Press.

Müller, F. Max. 1868 [1860]. *Semitic monotheism*. In *Chips from a German workshop*, vol. 1, *Essays on the science of religion*, 342–380. London: Longmans, Green, and Co.

Paulinus. 1804 [1790]. *Vyàcarana seu Locupletissima samscrdamicae linguae institutio in usum fidei praeconum in India Orientali et virorum letteratorum in Europa, adornata a p. Paulino a S. Bartholomaeo*. Romae: typis S. congreg. de propag. Fidei.

Pollock, Sheldon. 1985. The theory of practice and the practice of theory in Indian intellectual history. *Journal of the American Oriental Society* 105(3). 499–519.

Pons, Jean François. 1743 [November 23, 1740]. Lettre du Père Pons, missionaire de la Compagnie de Jesus, au P. Du Halde de la même Compagnie. In *Lettres édifiantes et curieuses, écrites des missions étrangères, par quelques Missionaires de la Compagnie de Jesus, XXVI Recueil*, 218–256. Paris. Partly reprinted in Frits Staal (ed.). 1972. *A reader on the Sanskrit grammarians*, 435–69. Cambridge, MA: MIT Press.

Renou, Louis. 1942. Les connexions entre le rituel at la grammaire en Sanskrit. *Journal Asiatique* 233. 105–65. Reprinted in Frits Staal (ed). 1972. *A reader on the Sanskrit grammarians*, 435–69 Cambridge, MA: MIT Press.

Rocher, Rosane. 1995. Discovery of Sanskrit by Europeans. In E. F. K. Koerner & R. E. Asher (eds.), *Concise history of the language sciences from the Sumerians to the cognitivists*, 188–191. Cambridge: Elsevier.

Rousseau, Jean. 2006. La classification des langues au début du XIXe siècle. In Sylvain Auroux, E. F. K. Koerner, Hans-Josef Niederehe & Kees Versteegh (eds.), *History of the language sciences/Geschichte der Sprachwissenschaften/Histoire des sciences du langage*, 1414–1426. Berlin & New York: Walter de Gruyter.

Rousseau, Jean & Denis Thouard (eds.). 1999. *Lettres édifiantes et curieuses sur la langue chinoise: un débat philosophico-grammatical entre Wilhelm von Humboldt et Jean-Pierre Abel-Remusat (1821–1831)*; avec une correspondance inédite de Humboldt présentée par Jean Rousseau. Villeneuve-d'Ascq: Presses universitaires du Septentrion.

Scharfe, Harmut. 1977. *A history of Indian literature: Scientific and technical literature*, vol. 2, *Grammatical literature*. Wiesbaden: Harrassowitz.

Schlegel, Friedrich. 1808. *Über die Sprache und Weisheit der Indier. Ein Beitrag zur Begründung der Alterthumskunde*. Heidelberg: Mohr und Zimmer.

Shulman, David. 2005. Axial grammar. In Árnason, Jóhann Páll, S. Shmuel Noah Eisenstadt & Björn Wittrock (eds.), *Axial civilizations and world history*, 369–396. Leiden: Brill.

Smith, Brian. 1989. *Reflections on resemblance, ritual, and religion*. New York & Oxford: Oxford University Press.

Staal, Frits (ed.). 1972. *A reader on the Sanskrit grammarians*. Cambridge, MA: MIT Press.

Staal, Frits. 1982. Ritual, grammar, and the origins of science in India. *Journal of Indian Philosophy* 10(1). 3–35.

Staal, Frits. 1989. *Rules without meaning: Ritual, mantras and the human sciences*. New York: Peter Lang.

Struc-Oppenberg, Ursula. 1980. Friedrich Schlegel and the history of Sanskrit philology and comparative studies. *Canadian Review of Comparative Literature* 7(4). 411–437.

Taittirīya Saṃhitā. In N. S. Sonatakke & T. N. Dharmadhikari (eds.). 1970–1999. *The Taittirīyasaṃhitā with the Padapāṭha and the commentaries of Bhaṭṭa Bhāskara Miśra and Sāyaṇācārya*. Pune: Vaidika Saṃśodhana Maṇḍala.

Thieme, Paul. 1982. Meaning and form of the "grammar"of Pāṇini. *Studien zur Indologie und Iranistik* 8–9. 1–34. Reprinted in Renate Söhnen-Thieme (ed.). 1995. *Paul Thieme: Kleine Schriften*, vol. 2, 1170–1201. Wiesbaden: Franz Steiner.

Timpanaro, Sebastiano. 1977 [1972]. Friedrich Schlegel and the beginnings of Indo-European linguistics in Germany. Introduction to Friedrich Schlegel, *Über die Sprache und Weisheit der Indier. Ein Beitrag zur Begründung der Alterthumskunde. New edition with an introductory article by Sebastiano Timpanaro (translated from the Italian by Peter Maher) prepared by E. F. K. Koerner*, xi–xxxviii. Amsterdam: John Benjamins. First published as Timpanaro, Sebastiano. 1972. Friedrich Schlegel e gli inizi della linguistica indoeuropea in Germania. *Critica Storica* 9(1). 72–105.

Trautmann, Thomas. 1997. *Aryans and British India*. Berkeley, CA: University of California Press.

Tzoref-Ashkenazi, Chen. 2006. India and the identity of Europe: The case of Friedrich Schlegel. *Journal of the History of Ideas* 67(4). 713–734.

Visigalli, Paolo. 2017. Words in and out of history: Indian semantic derivation (*nirvacana*) and modern etymology in dialogue. *Philosophy East and West* 67(4). 1143–1190.

Wilkinson, Endymion Porter. 2015. *Chinese history: A new manual*, 4th edn. Cambridge, MA: Harvard University Asia Center.

Yelle, Robert A. 2003. *Explaining mantras: ritual, rhetoric, and the dream of a natural language in Hindu Tantra*. London: Routledge.

Yelle, Robert A. 2013. *The language of disenchantment: Protestant literalism and colonial discourse in British India*. New York: Oxford University Press.

Laurence Wuidar

Ineffability and music in early Christian theology

1 Introduction

Throughout the ages, theologians and philosophers, poets and mystics of all religions have had one crucial problem in common and that is, how to express the inexpressible; how to speak the unspeakable; how to tell the transcendent. Throughout the ages, music has been a possible answer to this problem even if for many religions, music has also been considered a dangerous medium – perhaps even one to be prohibited.

This chapter explores, on the one hand, the possibilities offered by music – both actual and metaphorical music – to speak to God and to express spiritual experiences; and on the other hand, the limits of music as a language for expressing the inexpressible transcendence of God.

The analysis is based on texts of the Jewish hellenistic philosopher and theologian Philo of Alexandria (*De opificio mundi; Vita Mosis; De mutatione nominum; Quis rerum divinarum heres sit*), and the Christian philosophers and theologians Clement of Alexandria (*Protrepticus; Paedagogus*), pseudo-Dionysius the Areopagite (*De caelesti hierarchia; De divinis nominibus; De mystica theologia*), Athenagoras of Athens (*Legatio pro Christianis*), Athanasius of Alexandria (*Oratio contra Gentes*), Origen (*Contra Celsum, Tractatus in Psalmos*) and Augustine (*Enarrationes in Psalmos, Confessiones*).[1]

As is well known, music is a language ruled by mathematics: music is made by sounds that are based on immutable mathematical *ratios*. That is why music is part of the *quadrivium*, next to astronomy, geometry and arithmetic.[2] Astronomy and music are the sciences of number in movement, geometry and arithmetic the

1 Many of these texts are available in translation at http://www.earlychristianwritings.com. Translations of Clement of Alexandria, Justin, and Origen are from this source. Translations of Athenagoras and Athanasius are from Skeris (1976). Translations of Philo are from http://www.earlyjewishwritings.com/text/philo/book1.html. Translations of Dionysius are from Parker (1897). Other translations used are indicated below.

2 Among numerous contributions on this subject, see Vendrix (2008) and Gozza (2000), which contains some classical essays as the one by Daniel P. Walker, "The Harmony of the Spheres," in Gozza (2000: 67–77).

Laurence Wuidar, Fonds National Scientifique, University of Geneva

https://doi.org/10.1515/9781614514329-010

sciences of number that is immobile. Music is the science of sounding number. But music is also the sister of rhetoric, as its goal is to promote affects[3]: it brings the listener to experience affect and is the vehicle for speaking to the heart (see Cochrane, Fantini, & Scherer 2013; Palisca 2000). From the age of Pythagoras to the beginning of the 18th century (e.g., Andreas Werckmeister 1707), music has been regarded as a mathematics, rich in cosmological speculations,[4] and as a powerful language (*musica practica*). Boethius (470–524), in his *De institutione musica*, formulated the classical threefold division of music: *musica mundana* or *universalis* is the higher type (the music of the celestial spheres, of the seasons, of the four elements: this is the immutable dimension of music); *musica humana* is the middle type (the harmony of the faculties of the human soul, of the body, and of their combination: this is the mutable dimension of music); and *musica instrumentalis* is the music made by voice or musical instruments (that is mutable and valuable thanks to its analogy with the two previous types). When dealing with early Christian texts, we have to keep this division in mind, as the very definition of music in these texts is quite different than the one we inherited from the 18th century.

While the above is nothing new, one more general observation is necessary about music and religion. Jewish, Christian and Islamic theologians dealt with the distinction between good (sacred) and bad (profane and pagan) music: with the power of music and thus its good use to bring the soul closer to God, or to unite the individual in the divine cults, and with its bad use, to bring the body to luxurious experiences, which they condemned (Pons 1955: 30–42). Music can be one of the best spiritual medicines, and the singing of psalms has all virtues: it brings joy to man and woman from their childhood to their death; it keeps the soul temperate and positively affects the body; it is the best protection against night time temptation; all devils run away when they hear sacred music; it helps the mind to understand the sacred doctrine and the memory to conserve this understanding.[5] The Church Fathers and their followers offer panegyrics of music that present music as the most wonderful medium for the believer, as music contains

---

3 Isidore of Seville, *Etymologiae*, III, XVII: "Musica movet affectus, provocat in diversum habitum sensus."

4 Already in Plato's *Timaeus*, the cosmic order is a musical order. This theme, while old, has been much investigated since Haar (1960) and Spitzer (1963).

5 The most complete texts that celebrate the praise of sacred music are Basil of Caesarea, *Homeliae in Psalmos*, 1, 1; John Chrysostom, *Expositio in Psalmos*, 41, 1–2; Athanasius, *Epistula ad Marcellinum de interpretatione psalmorum*, 27–29; Ambrose of Milan, *Explanatio Psalmiv*, 1. See also Nicetas of Remesiana, *De utilitate hymnorum*, 5. On the specific mention of memory see Chrysostom, *Interpretatio in Isaiam Prophetam*, I, 1.

every perfection and bring everything to perfection.[6] Obviously this wonderful power of music may also be used in ways that contravene religious and licit aims. That is why the same Fathers list the dangers of music, and that is why pagan and profane music are to be banished: they act as a poison for the soul, they corrupt morality bringing the listener into luxurious experience, and they deform the soul which becomes effeminate and vulgar; while the sensual sonorousness of musical instruments is the rubbish of the devil.[7]

Whether they deal with legitimate or prohibited music, theologians and mystics also deal with another musical classification: the distinction between internal and external, or spiritual and corporeal music. Music (*musica practica*, *musica instrumentalis*, and corporeal music are synonymous; it is the music that enters the ear and touches the soul) may help the believer to experience God, as it has an impact on the soul. But the believer is also invited to listen to an internal music and to sing in his heart.[8] This constitutes another division of music, parallel to the Boethian one. This internal music is an experience of the divine that cannot be easily translated into words. Moreover, like the prophets, the mystic transcends the limits of usual discourse and reaches a new form of language that enables him or her to speak with God. The mystic experiences a *raptus* ('rapture, ecstasy'), and this transportation out of his or her rational and bodily condition is often due to music (both *musica practica* and internal music).[9] From early Christian times, the internal music heard by the heart was thought to have different manifestations: an internal music from unknown origin that transports the person in ecstasy (as we will see in some medieval texts), the voice of God that sings to the internal ear (as we will see in Augustine), or the music of the angels (Jerome,in his letters "Ad

---

6 Isidore of Seville, *Etymologiae*, III, XVII: "Itaque sine Musica nulla disciplina potest esse perfecta."

7 John Chrysostom, *In Epistulam I ad Corinthios*, 12, 5; *De Davide et Saule*, III, 3.

8 As recommended by Paul in Ephesians 5:19.

9 This idea finds echoes in Sufi tradition, which considers music as one of the most perfect ways to reach Allah. While Medieval Western mystics were writing about sacred (lawful) and lascivious (prohibited), spiritual (mystical) and corporeal (liturgical) music, Eastern Sufis of the 11th and 12th Centuries were dealing with the same questions of legitimacy and power of music within mystical practices. For some Eastern (Indian) medieval sources and treatises on music within the Sufi tradition, see Aquil (2012: 22). Mystical treatises concerned with musical questions are of course to be read in parallel with juridical and moral discussions about music within religious and spiritual contexts. It is enough to record the intent of Al-Gazali (1058–1111): "we will give [...] the law of good conduct related to the hearing of music and singing internally and externally." Al-Gazali, *Ihya Ulum ad-Din*, in MacDonald (1902: 1). For a discussion about the different views on music in Islamic theology in the medieval times (including al-Gazali), see During (1988); Lewisohn (1997: 1–33).

Eustochium," on the model of saint Paul's *raptus*, states that he had an auditory vision of the angel choir, but he can't tell what the music was like). The mystic will then translate these internal musical experiences into some external medium: a text, an image or a musical composition. He wants to give a material sign and an external expression of his internal musical experience, even if he knows perfectly well that this expression can only tell part of his experience, and that very imperfectly. For our concern, this is a crucial type of document: mystics are the ones most acutely aware of the limits of language's ability to speak about supernatural experience, whether divine, visionary, or musical. Apart from the internal experience of music, a different kind of experience, that is not originally musical, can be translated by means of music, i.e., represented through musical metaphor in texts or compositions. This happened, as is well known, in the case of Hildegard von Bingen, who translated her visions into music.[10] Such historical material is very rich, and still remains to be studied, as little has been written on these antique and medieval sources, with some exceptions, for example Hildegard or Francis of Assisi (Guilloux 2010, 2012: 29–75).

Finally, in addition to the belief that supernatural experiences are impossible to translate into words, Jewish and early Christian authors inherited from neo-Platonism (e.g. Plotinus) the philosophical position that the simplicity of God is ineffable because language testifies to reality in a fragmentary way and is thus a complex, not a simple process. Whereas language affirms something and consequently excludes something else, God embraces everything and excludes nothing. There is an irreducible difference between the names of God and his secret nature. Words are too limited and grammar too constrictive to express God's infinity and His secret nature, which transcends all that human beings can think or say. And this is true also for music, which cannot perfectly express the nature of the deity.

Historically, on the one hand, music – *musica practica*, musical mathematical ratio and musical metaphor – had been ascribed the faculty to express the universal beauty and the divine creator, to express human experience of the divine, and to help humans to reach the divine. On the other hand, although music as a language has been considered too limited to speak about God, musical sounds without words, like silence, has been seen as the mirror of apophatic (negative) theology. It is the possibility of music to embody both the cataphatic and the apophatic paths, to speak about God and to speak to God that the texts selected in this chapter illustrate.

The texts selected for this illustration are not the usual sources in music history nor in the history of philosophy of music; they offer a range of fresh perspectives,

---

10 Iversen (2000: 37–63); Pfau (2005); Sequeri (2005) is a generic volume that runs from ancient India to contemporary music.

and invite us to reconsider the importance of music for early Christian theologians, not only from a moral or pastoral point of view.[11] If the cosmological dimension of music is very well known, having been studied since at least 1960, what has been less investigated is how, according to these texts, nature and man can be metaphorically transformed into musical instruments, or even how the deified man was conceived as a divine melody. Another theme that has not been studied is how musical sounds became the mirror of negative theology. Both these dimensions stressed a particular relationship among the divine, music, and language.

2 The musical creator and his creation

2.1 Divine language

The God from the Bible creates all things through His divine speech (*Genesis* 1:3–26). He is the one who knows how to speak, the one who has a performative language. A human being has only an informative language that tends to translate into words the world of sensations and ideas. God is the architect, the builder of the universe as a perfect city: the City of God made by the divine geometer (Epistle to the Hebrews 11:10; Philo of Alexandria, *De opificio mundi*, 17–22). If God is a geometer, as stated in the Epistle to the Hebrews, He is also the divine musician who creates and maintains the universal harmony. In 1617, Robert Fludd still described this divine musician as creator and conservator of celestial and terrestrial harmony. In a famous engraving of his *Utriusque Cosmi, maioris scilicet et minoris metaphysica* published by Johann Theodor de Bry, Fludd shows God's hand that tunes the planetary and elementary monochord, the famous musical instrument that was the basis for physical and theoretical tuning. This engraving represents the end of a long tradition that was born with Plato's *Timaeus*. This is not the place to write the history of Pythagorean-Platonic and Christian *Harmonia Mundi* one more time[12]; we need only recall that Plato's divine maker,

---

11 Unfortunately, the statement made by Routley (1950: 45) has not yet been the object of a serious reevaluation: "The subject of music in these writings (with the conspicuous exception of those of Augustine) will not be expected to occupy a very large space." There are three fundamental anthologies of early Christian extracts on music: Gerold (1931); Skeris (1976); and McKinnon (1987). These are the starting point of any research on these sources. The collection of papers from McKinnon (1998) is of course of fundamental importance. Clavin (2007) has an engaging starting point: to serve contemporary liturgical music.

12 See footnote 4 above.

who built the universe according to musical numbers, later became the Jewish and Christian God who created the world's harmony.

Through his performative language, God creates everything in weight, measure and order (*Book of Wisdom,* 11: 21), and this order is a perfect musical composition. He is thus the model and perfection: every musician or architect, musical composition or building that comes after God will only be able to reproduce, in an imperfect, earthly way, His divine music and architecture.

2.2 Musical creation

If God is the perfect musician, Nature is his musical score (e.g., Philo, *De virtutibus*, 72–74; *De opificio mundi*, 78). The Book of Nature is a second scripture after the Holy Bible. God expresses himself through both of these writings, and to respond to Him, the creation sings to the Lord (Psalm 148). Each celestial and terrestrial entity has a particular song, and all together they form a chorus in praise to the divine choir master.

The Christian apologetic Athenagoras of Athens (ca. 133–190 CE) offers a perfect summary of the old motif of thanking God for His divine tuning of the universal instrument:

> If then the world is a tuneful instrument struck rhythmically, I reverence the one who put it in tune and plucked the strings and sang the harmonious accompaniment, but not the instrument itself. The steward of the games does not pass over the lyre-players in the contest and go and crown their lyres. If, as Plato says, this world is God's craft, then, marveling at its beauty, I go to worship the craftsman. (Athenagoras 1956: 16)

Apostolic as well as Greek and Latin Fathers of the Church developed the classical pagan and Jewish thematic of universal harmony integrating the chorus of all creatures, the rhythmical order of earthly time (day and night; spring, summer, autumn, and winter),[13] and Christ. From the Apostolic Fathers, the *harmonia* topos finds its achievement in the Savior: the Creator governs the physical universe, but the Incarnation of the eternal Logos restored the universal harmony that man's sin had turned into discord.[14] The Divine Logos playing the lyre of the universe

13 See for example *Letter of Clement of Rome to Corinthians*, XX, 1; Clement of Alexandria, *Protrepticus*, I, 5, 1; Origen, *Tractatus in Psalmos*, 91, 5; Gregory of Nyssa, *In Inscriptiones Psalmorum*, I, 3; Hilary of Poitiers, *Tractatus super Psalmos*, 68 e 148; Ambrose, *Explanatio Psalmi*, 1, 2; *Hexameron*, III, 2, 6–7.

14 On the term "logos" in Greek Pagan culture and Greek Christianity, see Radice and Valvo (2011).

became then a classical theme within early Christian literature. Athanasius of Alexandria, for example, gives one more musical metaphor:

> Just as a musician, tuning his lyre and skillfully combining the bass and the sharp notes, the middle and the others, produces a single melody, so the wisdom of God, holding the universe like a lyre, draws together the things in the air with those on earth. (Athanasius of Alexandria, *Oratio contra Gentes*, 31)

Music offers words to express the perfect order created and maintained by God. It differs from the static harmony and perfection of visual arts, such as painting or architecture. Musical harmony has to be continuously searched and reached, as God continuously holds and helps, tunes and adjusts the creation. In the same way, man, as the image of God, is not a static visual image, but a musical one, as man has to go in search of perfection and has to tune himself throughout his whole life. That is why, as we will see, man appears in early Christian literature as an echo of the universal stringed instrument.

For many Fathers of the Church, creation was thus a musical instrument tuned by the invisible hand of God. Man has the duty to sing to this instrument, as he has the duty to sing in gratitude for the redemptive mission of Christ.

2.3 The New Song

The New Song is Christ and the Christians, his virtuous life and the harmony between what he says and what he does. The New Song is placed on the lips of the Messiah, but also of those who love him (*Ode of Solomon*, 41:16–17). Apostolic Fathers and Church Fathers such as Clement of Alexandria (ca. 150–ca. 215) developed the power of this New Song in comparison with the power of mythological music: the new Singer, the Word of God is much more powerful than all mythological singers and musicians such as Orpheus, Amphion, or Arion, while Orpheus's song is just the prefiguration of the power of the Word (see Vieillefon 2003 and Jourdan 2010). The Logos sings the New Song not "in Phrygian or Lydian or Dorian mode; but in the new music, with its eternal strain that bears the name of God" (*Protrepticus*, I, 2, 3). This new music transposed all Orphic powers of music onto man: the new song "has made men out of stones, and men out of wild beasts. [...] They who were otherwise dead, who had no share in the real and true life, revived when they but heard the song" (I, 4, 5). Origen (ca. 185–253), one of the most influential exegetes of the early Church in both its Western and Eastern divisions, who was born in Alexandria and knew quite well the writings of Philo of Alexandria, also compares Christ to a choirmaster: "our chorus-leader and teacher came forth from the Jews to control the whole world by the word of his teaching" (*Contra Celsum*, V, 33). Music represents the excellence of speech: the Word of God that creates and governs the word is a musical one, and the Savior appears as a choirmaster who directs both universe and human beings.

God is the Perfect Musician and the whole creation is his tuneful instrument. Angels and Man have nevertheless a particular role in this symphony. Symmetrically to God's creative language, Genesis presents Adam as naming the various creatures to fulfill the creative process (Genesis 2:19–20). This role God gave to humanity shows the fundamental importance of human logos – language and reason – as the mirror of divine Logos. God gave to human beings the responsibility to achieve His creation by giving a name to the created realities. And the human being is the only one who has an articulated language. Logos, as language and reason, establishes the unique relationship between God and Humanity, and explains why human beings are in God's image (Genesis 1:26–27). To thank and glorify God, man wants to go beyond his daily speech and introduces music: he thus both turns his inside sight to the angels' chorus and transforms himself into a musical instrument.

3 Angelic and musical discourse

The human being has the consciousness of the impossibility for normal discourse to speak about God. However, he wants to praise Him and His creation, to speak to Him and to say the Unknown, even if he knows he can do it only in an imperfect way. In the introduction of *De opificio mundi*, Philo of Alexandria (ca. 30 BCE–45 CE) gives a perfect synthesis of this crucial tension we find in Jewish and Christian authors, from the Fathers of the Church to medieval mystics.

> Accordingly no one, whether poet or historian, could ever give expression in an adequate manner to the beauty of his ideas respecting the creation of the world; for they surpass all the power of language [...]. That, however, is not a reason for our yielding to indolence on the subject, but rather from our affection for the Deity we ought to endeavour to exert ourselves even beyond our powers in describing them: not as having much, or indeed anything to say of our own, but instead of much, just a little, such as it may be probable that human intellect may attain to, when wholly occupied with a love of and desire for wisdom. (*De opificio mundi*, I, 4–6)

Philo, whose acute research on language and its limits indicates the path for Christian authors, made a first mediation between a neo-Platonic, inexpressible transcendence of the divine and a religion of the Book. First of all, Philo shows in an exemplary way how musical language provides the words to describe indescribable realities: his use of musical metaphor to speak about God and to testify to the experience of the divine (e.g., in *Quis rerum divinarum heres sit*, as we will see at the end of this chapter) opens the way to the emphatic use of musical terms to speak about God in early Christianity.[15] But the Jewish Hellenistic philosopher also inherits the Platonic notion of the radical transcendence of the One, and thus the impossibility for human language to speak properly about Him. This brief quotation underlines the tension between these two positions.

Augustine (354–430) expresses the same tension: the wish for language but also the consciousness of its insufficiency and vanity to express the beauty of God and his creation (*Enarrationes in Psalmos*, 26, II, 12). Human language is unable to testify, not only to the Unknown, but also to the material and contingent world. For Augustine, mortal speech is even unable to praise God and to offer Him the right prayer. That is why Augustine asks man to listen to God's music, to know how to produce a song consonant to His divine ears.

3.1 God's musical discourse to the soul

Music is an earthly perfection of discursive language as it brings together words, which are specific to humanity, and musical sounds, which birds also possess. In a famous passage, Augustine makes the fundamental distinction between the songs of irrational beings, such as birds, and the songs of human beings (*Enarrationes in Psalmos*, 18, II, 1)[16]: only the latter, thanks to God's will, have the consciousness of music. But if man has the consciousness of music, this must have its origin in God.

Augustine echoes Philo's question to God. In his *Life of Moses*, the Jewish philosopher and theologian had asked what kind of musical language he may use to pray to God:

> O! Master how can anyone sing your praises adequately, with what mouth, with what tongue, with what organization of voice? Can the stars become a chorus and pour forth any melody which shall be worthy of the subject? Even if the whole of the heaven were to be dissolved into voice, would it be able to recount even a portion of your virtues? (*Vita Mosis*, II, 43, 239)

Christian authors turned their spirit and mind to God in the same way and asked Him to teach them the song. For Justin (ca. 100–165 CE), Christ himself taught man

15 Although I refer only to music here, it is obvious that Philo also stood as a forerunner of later Christian typological interpretations of the imagery of the Bible.
16 Migne, *Patrologia Latina*, 36 available at http://www.augustinus.it.

to sing and "to offer thanks by invocations and hymns for creation" (*Apology*, I, 13, 2). So did he assert again in his *Dialogue with Trypho the Jew*, 74, 3: "The Holy Spirit bids the inhabitants of all the earth, who have known the mystery of this salvation [...] sing and give praise to God the Father of all things." Christ and the Holy Spirit are the mediators who offer man the possibility to know how to sing to the Father. The "historical" model is Christ himself singing the Halleleuia with his disciples: "He stood in the midst of His brethren the apostles [...] and when living with them sang praises to God" (*Dialogue with Trypho the Jew*, 106, 4–7).

Augustine tells man that he can't by himself transform material sounds into a musical form consonant to God's hearing (*Enarrationes in Psalmos*, 32, II, 1, 8).[17] To know the song that will please God, man should listen to God's song.[18] The Lord himself put the New Song on human lips (see Psalm 39:4). He took man out from the abyss and gave him His song. Man must be able to listen in order to be able to sing.

Music establishes the individual relationship between man and God in a musical dialogue. Augustine imagines a God who is singing to the soul of each Christian so that each one can rightly sing to Him. Music sets up a circular process: from God, to man, back to God. A first possibility to find a convenient language to speak to God is thus indicated by Augustine in his Psalm commentaries. It echoes a long tradition from Philo to various martyrs and Fathers of the Church: to know what musical language will please God, man has to ask God to sing to his soul, and has to listen to God's music to be able to sing to God – internally but also externally.

Enarrationes in Psalmos, 32 has thus a meaning for devotional practice. It has to be read in parallel to the much more famous influence that Augustine's views on music had on public liturgical practice. As is well known, in his *Confessions*, Augustine states how he has been traumatized by music: when he was in Church in Milan, he has been turned away from divine scripture and sacred words by the emotional power of melody and its capacity to generate sensuous pleasure. That music generates pleasure is an old Aristotelian and Stoic theme well known to Philo[19] and very often criticized by Christian

---

17 A similar question had been raised by Cyprian (Carthage, ca. 200–258 CE) in *De dominica oratione*, 4; available at http://earlychristianwritings.com. Man must please God through his speech and song and must remember that he is standing in God's sight while using his voice; as Cyprian says: "We must please the divine eyes both with the habit of body and with the measure of voice," especially the voice and song of the heart as God is the hearer of the heart. My translation.

18 I deal with this issue in a more detailed way in Wuidar (2014: 56–61) and (2010: 66–84).

19 Philo, *Legum Allegoriae*, II, 18, 75: "The aulos, the kithara, and every kind of instrument please the hearing, so do the tuneful sounds of creatures without reason – swallows, nightingales,

philosophers and theologians such as John Chrysostom.[20] Augustine narrates in a dramatic way this physical and emotional power of music. He was listening to the melody and was seduced by the beauty of purely material sounds: his free will was alienated by sounds and he felt pleasure listening to a melody not being aware any more of words (*Confessiones*, X, 33, 49–50). A melody is made of material sounds: it is the physical dimension of music. Text is the rational part of music and Augustine should have listened to it. From this personal experience, the bishop was hesitating to admit music in Christian liturgy. But, as he also notes, music has also a magnificent power to introduce sacred words into the heart of listeners and singers. Music will always keep this ambiguous nature, and theologians from antiquity until today are aware of its ambiguity. Like every discourse, music has a rhetorical, psychical, and physical power that can bring the listener into God's hands or into the devil's hands. It depends on the content of the music but even more on the listener's mental disposition. Musical discourse, like every rhetorical discourse, is potentially pernicious, but if it is well used, it helps the believer to reach God more effectively than other forms of language.

3.2 Angelic chorus as a model for liturgical music

A second possibility to access a language to speak to God and to praise Him is found in Pseudo-Dionysius (5th century), the most important theoretician of the limits of language, even a metaphorical one, to speak about God. The Greek author offers the first systematic exposition of the gap between human language and God within Christian philosophy and theology. Pseudo-Dionysius also offers a theological justification for the use of music in liturgy: musical language is part of divine language that comes to earth through the mediation of the procession of the celestial hierarchy. So on the one hand, from Greek philosophers (Plotinus or Pseudo-Dionysius), the most obvious answer to the Ineffable has been the silence of the apophatic path, or of negative theology: silent prayer, silent veneration, silent adoration of His mysteries and secret essence. On the other hand, the Ineffable, the simple and unique, proceeds down to the human

---

and other birds that make music – and the euphony of rational being, singing to the kithara in comedy, tragedy, and other theatrical production." For the thematic of effects of music and practical use of music in Philo see Ferguson (2003: 391–426).

20 See e.g., John Chrysostom, *De Davide et Saule*, III, 3; *Interpretatio in Isaiam Prophetam*, V, 5; *Expositio in Psalmos*, 41, 2.

realm of perceptible complexity and plurality. Creation, scripture and liturgy are receptacles of God's words and thoughts. Participation of creatures in the divinity gives them the possibility to express the Inexpressible even in an imperfect way. As Psalm 148 sings: water and fire, birds and fishes are all singing the glory of Lord. Among the creatures two of them have a special role and status: angels and humans, both of which are theorized in Dionysius's *The Celestial Hierachy* and *The Ecclesiastical Hierarchy*.

Human language is radically maladjusted to testify to God: it can give a list of its attributes and tell His name, but those are only words. Not to remain completely hermetic to human beings, God manifests Himself through both scripture and the procession of the celestial hierarchy that together indicate God's self-manifestation and disclosure under the veil of earthly symbols.

> And so it is that the transcendent is clothed in the terms of being, with shape and form on things which have neither, and numerous symbols are employed to convey the varied attributes of what is an imageless and supra-natural simplicity. (*The Divine Names* 1, 592B, 20–27)

God reveals Himself through creation, scripture and liturgy: through a procession of thearchies – the Trinity as well as the entire celestial sphere with its inhabitants – He comes into the realm of time, space, and sense perception. At this point, we have to consider Dionysius's view on music as part of the procession.

Since the book of Isaiah, the angels' chorus is the model of the song in praise of the Lord (Isaiah 6:3).[21] The chorus is singing *Sanctus, sanctus, sanctus*, and this triple exclamation will be interpreted both by theologians and theoreticians of music as the prophetic announcement of the Christian Trinity (Chrysostom, *Interpretatio in Isaiam Prophetam*, VI, 3). The man who recognizes the New Song and who is redeemed by it becomes part of the angelic choirs (Clement of Alexandria, *Paedagogus*, I, 6, 45, 2). Before redemption, the imitation of angelic choirs is possible within liturgical music. Dionysius shows how the angelic hierarchy is a model for human laudatory music. His idea about music as a language that participates in God's thearchy will influence medieval musical mysticism, such as that of Richard Rolle d'Hampole (ca. 1300–1349 CE).

Hierarchies participate in and reflect divine harmony and proportion, and following these they are hierarchically led up to the super-primal principle and end of all orders.

> Each Order is the interpreter and herald of those above it, the most venerable being the interpreter of God who inspires them, and the others in turn of those inspired by God. For

21 For a classical iconographic study, see Hammerstein (1962).

> that superessential harmony of all things has provided most completely for the holy regulation and the sure guidance of rational and intellectual beings by the establishment of the beautiful choirs of each Hierarchy. (*The Celestial Hierarchy*, X)

The Celestial Hierarchy deals with the divine harmonies in the hierarchies and the beauty of the angelic choirs as the echo of God's order and musical order. It also deals with the knowledge, including musical, of the angels: they receive their knowledge from God, and each hierarchy transmits its knowledge to the next lower one as "He also divided each rank in the same divine harmonies, and on this account the Scriptures say that the most divine Seraphim cry one to another, by which, as I think, it is clear that the first impart to the second their knowledge of divine things." Angelic speech and knowledge have been much investigated by medieval theologians (see, e.g., Suarez-Nani 2002). For example, Thomas Aquinas, a subtle commentator on Dionysius, dedicates several chapters to it. Angels offer theologians the model for a non-discursive, immediate, purely spiritual and immaterial language. They communicate one to another in a silent discourse – *per silentium verbi* – that does not move the air (Thomas Aquinas, *Quaestiones disputatae*, "De Veritate," 9, 4, 9–7). Angels know the perfect music to sing praises to God, they have the perfect language to speak one to the other and they know the main things to transmit to human beings: they are announcers of the divine silence ("enuntiatores divini silentii," Thomas Aquinas, *In Dionysii*, 4, 1). All the limits of human language are transcended by angelic language. This is true even though angels, like human beings, lack access to the perfect knowledge of God: they are still creatures and will never have the full understanding of divine essence.

Knowledge and musical knowledge then descend through the hierarchies and reach the ecclesiastical hierarchy, where angelic music is embodied in liturgical music. In *The Ecclesiastical Hierarchy*, Dionysius considers protagonists, names, and functions of this angelic song as transmitted to the ministries of Christ.[22]

> The all-holy ministers [...] sing in an universal Hymn of Praise the Author and Giver of all good, from Whom the saving mystic Rites were exhibited to us, which divinely work the sacred deification of those being initiated. Now this Hymn some indeed call a Hymn of Praise, others, the symbol of worship, but others, as I think, more divinely, a Hierarchical thanksgiving, as giving a summary of the holy gifts which come to us from God. (*The Ecclesiastical Hierarchy*, III, 8, 436C)

22 As far as I know there is no complete study on Dionysius and music. See however Jeck (1998: 125–140).

The ecclesiastical hierarchy imitates the celestial one to give human beings the possibility to reach immaterial contemplation through material and sensitive figures (*The Celestial Hierarchy*, I, 2, 3, 121C-D). In the liturgy, perfumes are figures of the intelligible diffusion, lights are images of divine light, and music, as part of the "sacred discursive disciplines" (*The Celestial Hierarchy*, 121D), is the figure of contemplative fulfilment. Music is one of several media that touch the sensitive part of man to elevate his soul to divine contemplation and divine participation, proportionate to human capacity. In Dionysian definition, music sung by ministries and assembly is not only a sensitive medium for spiritual elevation, but also a symbol and a hierarchical action. Like every Dionysian hierarchy, it has its achievement in the human participation in the divine, and ends in the divinity of man. Action and content confer its value to liturgical music and explain the divine origin and finality of musical language. In the ascendant movement that conducts human beings to God, music transforms man until he is assimilated to God. In the descendent movement, God fills musical language with His gifts and the celestial hierarchy illuminates the Ecclesiastical Hierarchy that imitates angelic music. The descendent illumination through music and human beings' ascendant participation in celestial music both converge on human deification, even though music as language is unable to speak properly about God.

4 Musical metaphor in mystic and negative theology

4.1 Negative theology and musical sound

In *The Divine Names*, Dionysius establishes that the only way to express God is through metaphor: analogies and metaphors invite the reader to see the occult harmonies between two different realities. Metaphor goes beyond words because it tells things by the veil of analogy. It is the only appropriate language to speak about human and divine secrets (*Epistle*, IX, 1, 1105C). From this capacity to look inside the things through the metaphorical discourse, man is elevated to the capacity to sing to God (*The Divine Names*, V, 8, 824A). He intends the cause and is able to celebrate it as the author of all things.

This song ends in silence as the most excellent song, but silence is also the condition for the soul to be illuminated and thus to be able to sing the divine hymns. Every prayer and every discourse about God ends and reaches its perfection in the silent veneration of the transcendental nature of God (*The Celestial Hierarchy*, XV, 9, 340B; *The Divine Names*, I, 4, 589B; Psalm 64:2).[23] But, if silence is opposed to word and music, it is also the complement and the condition of every sacred music because the internal silence guides man to divine hymns (*The Divine Names*, I, 4, 589B).

The *Corpus Dionysiacum* represents the theoretical model for the use and usefulness of metaphor to speak about God. Dionysius records what Plotinus was saying: "The One, to tell the truth, is ineffable; anything you say is already and always something. [...] He doesn't have any name as we can't say anything about Him" (Plotinus, *Enneads*, V, 3, 13; see Carabine 1996). Neither the name of Creator nor the name of Jesus will change this radical otherness between human language and divine essence. It is possible to give Him the name of all existing reality because everything comes from Him, but to do this is to indicate the cause through its effects.

In this case, as reaffirmed by one of the most precocious and brilliant followers of Dionysius, Johannes Scotus Eriugena (ca. 815–877), God "is truth, goodness, essence, light, justice, sun, star, spirit, water, lion, bear" (*Periphyseon*, I, 458B).[24] Metaphor is the only way to speak about God: metaphorically one can give all names to the divine being who remains beyond any name.[25] If *The Divine Names* lists and comments on all of these names, *The Mystical Theology* denies the possibility to attribute any name to God and reduces every human word to silence (it is not by chance that *The Mystical Theology* is one of the most influential theological and philosophical treatises of history):

> As even now, when entering into the gloom which is above mind, we shall find, not a little speaking, but a complete absence of speech, and absence of conception. In the other case, the discourse, in descending from the above to the lowest, is widened according to the descent, to a proportionate extent; but now, in ascending from below to that which is above, in proportion to the ascent, it is contracted, and after a complete ascent, it will become wholly voiceless. (*The Mystical Theology*, III, 1033C)

As Scotus reaffirms, "the ineffable nature can't be indicated in a proper way by any verb, any name, any sensible sound" (*Periphyseon*, I, 460B). At this point, music also becomes silence: when words have been abandoned, only musical

---

23 Silence's eloquence has often been studied, most frequently independently of music. Some recent researches have to be mentioned: Williamson (2004: 527–544); De Andia (2011: 371–387) and Somenzi (2012: 71–89). For a rich bibliography on silence in antique philosophy and early Christian literature see Kunz (1996: 817–825) and the anthology of Lilla (2013).

24 Text in Jeauneau (1996). My translation.

25 *Periphyseon*, I, 460C: "Non enim proprie sed translative dicitur essentia, veritas, sapientia caeteraque huiusmodi."

sounds remain[26] before being dissolved in silence.[27] Both musical sounds and silence are languages beyond the limits of words.

Early Christian and mystical literature consider the value of musical sounds – melody without words. In various passages of his *Enarrationes in Psalmos*, Augustine defines jubilation as a divine experience.[28] Joy is so intense that no word can express it. Thus only musical sound remains: when words cannot explain what the inner man experiments, only sound remains. When articulated language encounters its limits, the jubilation in musical sounds remains, a melody without words to express the exultation and thus all experience of divinity.

Musical sound has its own semantics and signification. More than that, it is independent from articulated language and free from the limitations imposed by words. That is why musical sound is a non-discursive language more adapted to describe realities that transcend human reason and the limited, fragmentary language that is human discourse.

4.2 Medieval mystics: Musical metaphor as a way to express divine experience

Medieval mystics will develop this idea. For Bernard of Clairvaux or Richard Rolle for example, "musical eructation" (Bernard, *Sermone super Cantica Canticorum* LXVII, 3–4) is the answer to the violence of divine love (Rolle, *Melos amoris*, XLII, 130, 15–18; XLV, 138, 19).[29] Musical sound speaks about divine love in a language able to transcend the grammatical order. In that sense, my hypothesis is that melody without word is the musical echo to negative theology. When human reason understands that it will never understand God, when the human being recognizes that he can only tell the names of God but not His essence, nor can

26 Augustine, *Enarrationes in Psalmos* 32, II, 1, 8: "Etenim illi qui cantant, sive in messe, sive in vinea, sive in aliquo opere ferventi, cum coeperint in verbis canticorum exsultare laetitia, veluti impleti tanta laetitia, ut eam verbis explicare non possint, avertunt se a syllabis verborum, et eunt in sonum iubilationis."

27 See for example Gregory the Great, *Moralia in Iob*, XXVII, 74. For a general reflection on silence as a divine attribute within research on music and theology, see Ernetti (1980: IX–XVII).

28 See McKinnon (1990: 61–70); Zorzi (2002: 383–413).

29 On Rolle and music there is no complete study. See, however, Maisonneuve (1980: 409–423); Boenig (1995: 75–86); Fuhrmann (2008: 35); Wuidar (2015a: 186–225; 2015b: 11–42; and 2015c: 5–48). For a study of a similar case see Schroeder-Sheker (1989: 133–139), which deals with a 13th-century German woman, Mechtild of Hackeborn (1241–1298), and the writings of her sister Abbess Gertrude (d. 1291).

he tell completely by means of language His infinite love, then man exults in a sonorous jubilee without words.

> The intellect cannot express the glory of the Delighted One, it has been taken in the song and from it praise germinated, joyful. Man is wrapped in virtues, he cannot go away from the light's embrace, he is in an immutable splendour, he remains in the melody. (*Melos amoris*, XXXIII, 101, 7–10)[30]

In his mystical writing *Melos amoris*, Richard Rolle expresses it with a thousand musical metaphors that tend to describe his internal musical experience of divinity. The English mystic is converted into an endless and ineffable song. His rational discourse and mental activity find a new perfection in being transformed into music (*Melos amoris*, XIV, 43, 35–36).[31] His contemplation of divine realities becomes a musical contemplation: he can hear the music from the sky and listening to it he is transfigured into a divine melody (*Melos amoris*, VI, 17, 14, 27–28). He has access to celestial music made by angels and saints. These musics are the joy of the mystic who is listening to an internal and divine song.

> I grab the song of glory that angels admire, I consume the sweetness of the heavenly harp and to my ears echoes the song of those who chant forever. (*Melos amoris*, III, 9, 15–16)[32]

Like Augustine, who was listening to God's song to be able to sing properly to Him, Rolle listens to an internal and divine music to be transfigured into a divine melody and thus to musically assimilate to God. Rolle transposes Dionysius' concepts of assimilation and musical procession (descendent angelic music and ascendant liturgical music) and puts Christ in the centre of the process (*Melos amoris*, XXXI, 99, 15–16):

> His acid death vivified me and gave me a real life, transforming malediction into melody and maledicted into musician. (*Melos amoris*, XL, 125, 3–4)[33]

Christ died on the Cross in order to transform human beings into an eternal song. The soul reaches perfection when it is able to receive the divine melody and

---

30 In Rolle (1971). My translation, as for all of Rolle's texts: "Exprimere non potest gloriam Dilecti dum capitur in canticum et germinat ingenter in genere iubileo. Natura nimirum involvitur virtute et nequit iam nudari a nexu nitente; micat immutabilis, nam manet in melos."
31 See also *Incendium amoris*, 5, 32: "Quippe cogitacio convertitur in canticum."
32 "Canorem glorie carpo angelis admirandum, suavitas saciat cithare superne et melos resonat psallencium sempiterne."
33 "Sua amarissima morte ut viverem veraciter me vivificavit, malediccionem merencium mutans in melodiam musicorum."

when it is converted by this divine music. The soul then becomes song in God. The man perfectly converted by the divine melody turns into a melody himself (*Melos amoris*, XXVIII, 83, 16–18; XXXVIII, 119, 23–24). Rolle represents one of the richest examples of the mystical description of a divine, internal, and spiritual experience of music, as well as one of the most accomplished expressions of this experience by musical metaphor. The mystical transformation of Rolle finds its roots in the metaphor of man being transformed into a musical instrument, a metaphor that has existed since the 1st century, as it is presented in a poetic way already in the *Odes of Solomon*:

> As the hand moves over the harp, and the strings speak, so speaks in my members the Spirit of the Lord, and I speak by His love. (*Odes of Solomon* 6:1–2)[34]

5 Man as a musical instrument

Jewish and early Christian literature presents one more musical way to speak to God and to celebrate Him. The very particular metaphor of man being transformed into a musical instrument is one of the literary ways that theologians have found to describe the earthly perfection of man and the relationship between God and man.[35]

5.1 Body and soul as a musical instrument to reach God

If the world is a musical instrument tuned by God, who plucked the strings, the human being also becomes this musical instrument, being tuned by the Word of God that tenses and relaxes the cords of his body and soul, following a Stoic image. Clement of Alexandria presents the Word of God playing on the world and on human beings so as to produce pneumatic music.[36]

> By the power of the Holy Spirit He arranged in harmonious order this great world, yes, and the little world of man, too, body and soul together; and on this many-voiced instrument of the universe He makes music to God. (*Protrepticus*, I, 5, 3)

34 Harris (1911: 96).
35 I dedicate Wuidar (2016) to this theme.
36 For more details on this see Ferguson (1993: 266–283, 268–269 [about the musical man]) and (1985: 15–23).

Macrocosm and microcosm are both musical instruments played by the Word of God. The Son uses the mediation of a musical instrument to celebrate the transcendent nature of the Father.

> By the lyre is meant the mouth stuck by the Spirit, as it were by a plectrum. [...] Our body He calls an organ, and its nerves are the strings, by which it has received harmonious tension, and when stuck by the Spirit, it gives forth human voice. "Praise Him on the clashing cymbals." He calls the tongue the cymbal of the mouth, which resounds with the pulsation of the lips. (*Paedagogus*, II, 4, 41, 4–5)[37]

The Holy Spirit is the one that transformed human language into a language capable of praising God. Clement of Alexandria is commenting on the musical hyperbole of Psalm 150:3–5. The reader/singer is invited to praise the Lord through all instruments: "Praise Him on the psaltery, and praise Him on the lyre," sings the psalm. And many early Christian authors, such as Clement, give an allegorical interpretation of this injunction. Usual language is unable to praise the Lord, but linguistic organs – mouth, nerve, tongue, lips – once transformed in musical instrument by the action of the Spirit, are able to sing to God. The incarnated musician will find the way to sing to the Immaterial in his body that has been transfigured by the presence of the Spirit.

Body is part of the perfect man – body and soul will take part in the resurrection and no operation of the soul would happen without the participation of the body. If he acts virtuously, a man celebrates God by his actions; this idea will be developed by Origen, mainly in his *Tractatus in Psalmos* 97, 5.[38] Gregory of Nyssa will also develop it: he underlines that a musical instrument/life is never tuned once and for ever but has to be continuously harmonized. Each time the chord has an excessive tension or each time it is too relaxed, the "musical man" must tune his instrument. As for Clement or Origen, the tuning is about the bodily activities, the external attitudes and virtues as well as the inner attitudes and habits (Gregory of Nyssa, *In Inscriptiones Psalmorum*, I, 3). The musical metaphor not only transforms the body into a musical instrument, each organ having a role in the celebration of the Lord, but also takes into account the relationship between body and soul. "The senses in the body are tuned like a lyre" (Athanasius, *Oratio contra Gentes*, 31) if intelligence is their guide. For Athanasius of Alexandria

37 See also *Protrepticus*, I, 5, 4: "The Lord fashioned man a beautiful, breathing instrument, after His own image; and assuredly He Himself is an all-harmonious instrument of God, melodious and holy."

38 See also Origen, *Tractatus in Psalmos*, 32, 2–3: "The body can also be said to be the psaltery of ten strings, since it has five senses, and the soul five faculties, each one of which arises from one of the senses."

(ca. 295–373), the senses are related to the intelligence as the lyre is related to the accomplished musician. The harmony and the balance between the different pitches of the lyre, the deep sound of one string, the higher one of another, the medium sound of yet another, can be achieved only by a skilled musician and will need to be tuned again and again ever. This musical metaphor is developed again in the *Epistola ad Marcellinum*, 27: the harmonizing of the double pipe produced a *symphoniae*, which is the instrumental echo of the soul and the body's symphony brought about by reason. Soul, body, mind and senses, reason and intelligence are all concerned with language, but they have to become themselves a musical language to testify to God.

> "Praise the Lord with the kithara, make melody to him with the psaltery of ten strings, etc." The kithara is the practical or active soul moved by the commandments of God, the psaltery is the pure mind moved by pneumatic knowledge. [...] Figuratively, the body can be said to be a kithara, and the spirit a psaltery, which (to continue the musical image) resemble the wise man who uses correctly and properly the limbs of the body like strings, as well as the powers of the spirit. He who sings with his mind sings beautifully, reciting pneumatic psalms and singing in his heart to God. (Origen, *Tractatus in Psalmos*, 32, 2–3)

The musical and thus perfect man, the only one able to reach and please God, balances active and contemplative life. He is the one who lets himself be guided by the Lord: the ten strings of his soul are moved in accordance with the Ten Commandments. He is the one both active and passive: he is an open receptacle ready to receive the presence and the words of God, and in this maximal passivity to reach the most active prayer. To find words to speak to God, he has to abandon himself to the divine plectrum: he is not the player but the instrument played by God. And when God plays on the musical man, the latter sings in his heart to God.

This is the most perfect language a man can speak on earth: the silent music of the heart. Origen, Augustine, Richard Rolle: early Christians and medieval mystics all reach the same conclusion, namely, that the inner song is the language that pleases God and is at the same time the language that opens the main channel of communication between man and the divine. One figure actualizes the circular relationship between human musical discourse and God's discourse in an exceptional way: the Prophet.

5.2 The prophet as God's musical instrument

A first mature reflection on the union between musical and prophetic discourse has its roots in the philosophy of language of Philo. Christian authors will then develop it. In various treatises as for example *De mutatione nominum* and *Quis rerum divinarum heres sit*, Philo offers a first detailed account of the prophet as a musical instrument played by God. Transforming the figure of the musical man found in Plato's *Phaedon* (85e–86c) and developing the biblical figure of Elisha (2 Kings 3:15), Philo stresses the relationship between prophetic language and musical.[39]

In *De mutatione nominum* he notes that the prophet Hosea's discourse is "the voice of the Invisible One whose invisible hand plays on the instrument of the human voice" (*De mutatione nominum*, 24, 139). The words of the prophet are not his own words but rather the words of God. The prophet is only an instrument used by the divinity to express Himself. And in Jewish as well as in Christian writings this instrument is described as a musical one, to emphasize the exceptional nature of the discourse pronounced by the prophet, whose words are neither usual nor human words. In *Quis rerum divinarum heres sit*, the prophet is transformed into a musical instrument which is played by God and which, because of this, is capable of any kind of musical harmony. The treatise begins with some consideration on the limits of language: humans' usual language is unable to express intense joy, just as it is unable to express intense pain. In his prayer the believer nevertheless uses language, but the language of the soul. For Philo, the soul expresses itself through the musical ratio of the octave: the perfect musical interval reflects the perfect prayer which is both silent and musical, as the octave contains potentially all musical sounds. God is listening to the soul that cries to him in music (*Quis rerum divinarum heres sit*, 15). Some human beings not only express themselves by musical silent-sounds that come out of their soul, but their body becomes a musical instrument. While they are transported in ecstasy, these elected people abandon their own body and mind to become entirely at the service of God's speech. The prophet turns subsequently into God's instrument: every phonetic organ is now part of a complex musical instrument that God plays with his invisible art (*Quis rerum divinarum heres sit*, 266). Every human language has to be rooted in the divine Logos in order to tend to perfection, but when the Logos itself talks through a human body and transforms it into its musical instrument, then the supernatural language that comes out of this body is already perfect. God is the only one who possesses the perfection of language, and He sometimes makes man participate in it (see also *De confusione linguarum*, XI, 40).

Early Christian authors continue to use the musical image of the prophet. Tertullian considers the relationship between music, ecstasy and prophecy

39 A complete study on the prophets and music has yet to be written, although the theme has attracted attention for more than a century: see Müller (1896: 247). For an interesting illustration of it in Renaissance times, see Roth (2010: 45–76).

starting from a different point of view than the one exposed by Philo. Music (the singing of psalms) can bring man and woman into ecstasy,[40] and in his or her enthusiastic ecstasy, he or she will have visual and sonorous visions as mysterious communications and gifts of divine revelation (Tertullian, *De anima*, 9, 4). Thus, as for the prophet Elisha, music is the way to reach mentally and bodily states that will allow the person to become God's instrument. Music helps to reach *excessus mentis* – ecstasy – and to receive God's secret words, revelations, and communications.

Next to the role of practical music in disposing the person to receive prophetic language and knowledge, Christian authors very often re-propose the metaphor of the prophet as a musical instrument played by God. Athenagoras of Athens, in his apology to Marcus Aurelius, uses several musical images. Some are dealing with the Spirit that plays the prophets as His instruments:

> The Spirit of God [...] moves the lips of the Prophets as if they were musical instruments. [...] For example, Moses, Isaias, Jeremias, and the rest of the prophets, when the Divine Spirit moved them, spoke out what they were in travail with, their own reasoning falling into abeyance and the Spirit making use of them as a flautist might play upon his flute. (Athenagoras, *Plea for the Christian*, 7, 9)[41]

In a spurious work attributed to Justin (Donaldson 1866: 96–116), the author proposes exactly the same description of the prophet as a musical instrument and the nature of prophetic language.

> For neither by nature nor by human conception is it possible for men to know things so great and divine, but by the gift which then descended from above upon the holy men, who had no need of rhetorical art, nor of uttering anything in a contentious or quarrelsome manner, but to present themselves pure to the energy if the Divine Spirit, in order that the divine plectrum himself, descending from heaven, and using righteous men as an instrument like a harp or lyre, might reveal to us the knowledge of things divine and heavenly. (*Hortatory Address to the Greek*, 8)

During the prophet's experience of being an instrument in God's hands, reason and common language are not any more in use. Rhetorical art, grammar, the usual structure of discourse, reason, and mental activity are abandoned: the prophet becomes a channel to receive another kind of language and knowledge.

40 The antique idea that music leads the person to ecstasy will be a constant in Western philosophy of music and religion. For some 17th-century examples in English literature, see Finney (1947a: 153–186 and 1947b: 273–292). About the relationship between ecstasy and prophetic speech, see for example Wilson (1979: 321–337).
41 Translation from Athenagoras (1956: 37–39).

Maximum passivity means maximum activity, because it means maximal opening to the supernatural activity. The prophet becomes an active-passive receptacle in which supernatural knowledge is reversed. To express the knowledge God gives to the prophet, the last one needs a new language: his words are inspired by the Holy Spirit, which transforms his tongue and his mouth into a musical instrument. The prophet is the harp, the lyre, or the flute of God: in any case he is played by the Spirit.

6 Conclusions

Because of its nature, musical language has a particular status in theological reflection on the limits of language. Texts presented here from Jewish tradition to early Christian and medieval writings all deal with this peculiar nature of music and with the use of music as a metaphor for communication with the divine.

As Philo notes, music cannot be an appropriate language to speak about God because of its composite nature. Words and discursive language are fragmentary and too limited. The same is true of music, as harmony is a mixture – of different sounds, pitches, voices – thus its nature is to be multiple and not simple. Harmony is made with different parts joined together, so these parts are also potentially separable. That is why music cannot be a language to express properly God's simplicity. Even if musical laws are mathematical and thus immutable, their sensible embodiment makes music a temporal reality, and part of the phenomenological world. That is why music cannot be a language to express properly God's immutability and transcendence. Philo concludes by saying that every human language will be like the harmony produced by a musical instrument. Musical harmony unites low and high sounds, this fusion produces an artistic composition, but this composition will never be able to testify to the simplicity of God (*De mutatione nominum*, XIII, 87).

Nevertheless, music is also regarded in this tradition as the sensuous element that helps believers to reach contemplation of and even assimilation with God, the sensuous element that disposes the prophet to receive the divine gift of supernatural knowledge, as well as grants him the language to express it. And music is the common metaphor to describe the particular relationship between God and his earthly instrument. This musical metaphor has a special status when authors have to describe the exceptional nature of language.

The very nature of man is to be a mixture, a composition, or even better: a musical composition. The nature of man is to be a mixture of angelic and animal nature, an entity composed of spirit and matter. This peculiar nature of human beings stresses their unique analogy with music, which is also a mixture or harmony of opposed qualities. The human being must harmonize the diverse faculties of his soul, and as well his soul with his body, to reach harmony with the divine; he thus has to follow the perfection that music shows him, in order to actualize himself. Once man has reached this perfection, he can attain to God, as he experiences the peace of the soul and of the bodily passions, enters a world without words, and is transformed into a spiritual man, who hears only a musical discourse. The internal and spiritual musical experience is a divine experience, because its attributes are those of God: melodious and harmonious, in a continuous motion that mirrors that of God in the human soul. Music is both a temporal (internal and external) experience and a perpetual one, as reflected in the angels' choirs that sing continuously. These two dimensions of music are not strictly divided, as Dionysius shows: sacred music incarnates the movement from perpetual music to phenomenal music. If sacred and liturgical music is the phenomenal transposition of the perpetual and immutable music of the angels, man as an instrument is also the musical transposition of human nature: eternal (harmony and the immortal soul) and contingent (instrument and the body).

The metaphor of man transformed into a musical instrument offered the theologians a privileged paradigm to explore both human language and the relationship of human beings with God. When man is played by the spirit, when he has reached the perfection of contemplative life and has abandoned his active life, he joins the most excellent activity in the maximum passivity, and becomes the musical instrument within God's hands. Man thus echoes the divine harmony, and his speech – both internal and external – is no longer imperfect. The perfection of human language for Jewish as well as for early Christian theologians was expressed by the musical metaphor: man is transfigured by the presence of the Holy Spirit that plays upon His human instrument, enunciating a perfectly consonant discourse that ascends beyond language.

The purely musical sounds in mystical contexts are then no longer a dangerous medium that may lead men to succumb to the temptations of physical pleasure. They instead become the mirror of the Ineffable: beyond the limits of discursive language, beyond the limitations of grammar and words, the musical sound expands itself without measure and thus expresses the Immeasurable. *Melisma* – musical sound that has abandoned words to move among several tones on one single syllable – as well as internal musical experience of an indescribable celestial music (made by God, angels, or saints), are both musical languages that enable us to speak about God and to listen to Him. The musical sound that has renounced words is the counterpart of negative theology or the apophatic way to express God, which renounces any possible positive word.

References

Aquil, Raziuddin. 2012. Music and related practices in Chishti Sufism: Celebrations and contestations. *Social Scientist* 40(3–4). 17–32.

Athenagoras. 1956. *Plea for the Christian* (Ancient Christian writers 32). Westminster: Newman Press.

Boenig, Robert. 1995. St. Augustine's *Jubilus* and Richard Rolle's *Canor*. In Bartlett Anne Clark & Thomas H. Bestul (eds.), *Vox mystica: Essays on Medieval mysticism in honor of Professor Valerie M. Lagorio*, 75–86. Cambridge: Brewer.

Carabine, Deirdre. 1996. *The unknown God: Negative theology in the Platonic tradition, Plato to Eriugena*. Leuven: Peeters Publishers.

Cochrane, Tom, Bernardino Fantini & Klaus Scherer (eds.). 2013. *The emotional power of music: Multidisciplinary perspectives on musical arousal, expression, and social control*. Oxford: Oxford University Press.

De Andia, Ysabél. 2011. L'au-delà de la parole: le silence et l'Ineffable. In Roberto Radice & Alfredo Valvo (eds.), *Dal logos dei greci e dei romani al Logos di Dio: Ricordando Marta Sordi*, 371–387. Milano: Vita e Pensiero.

Donaldson, James. 1866. *A critical history of Christian literature and doctrine from the death of the Apostles to the Nicene Council*, vol. 2, *The apologists*. London: MacMillan.

During, Jean. 1988. *Musique et extase: L'audition mystique dans la tradition soufie*. Paris: Albin Michel.

Ernetti, Pellegrino. 1980. *Principi filosofici e teologici della musica*. Roma: Edi-pan.

Ferguson, Everett. 1985. The contemplative and active lives: The Patristic interpretation of some musical terms. *Studia Patristica* (16). 15–23.

Ferguson, Everett. 1993. Towards a Patristic theology of music. *Studia Patristica* (24). 266–283.

Ferguson, Everett. 2003. The art of praise: Philo and Philodemus on music. In John T. Fitzgerald, Thomas H. Olbricht & L. Michael White (eds.), *Early Christianity and classical culture. Comparative studies in honor of Abraham J. Malherbe*, 391–426. Leiden: Brill.

Finney, Gretchen L. 1947a. Ecstasy and music in seventeenth-century England. *Journal of the History of Ideas* 8(2). 153–186.

Finney, Gretchen L. 1947b. "Organical musick" and ecstasy. *Journal of the History of Ideas* 8(3). 273–292.

Fuhrmann, Wolfgang. 2008. "Melos amoris": Die Musik der Mystik. *Musiktheorie: Zeitschrift für Musikwissenschaft* 23(1). 23–44.

Gerold, Théodore. 1931. *Les Pères de l'Église et la musique*. Strasbourg: Imprimerie Alsacienne.

Gozza, Paolo (ed.). 2000. *Number to sound: The musical way to the scientific revolution*. Dordrecht: Kluwer Academic Publishers.

Guilloux, Fabien. 2010. *Saint François d'Assise et l'ange musicien: Thème et variations iconographiques dans les collections du Museo Francescano de Rome*. Roma: Istituto storico dei Cappuccini.

Guilloux, Fabien. 2012. Saint François d'Assise et l'ange musicien: Un topos iconographique et musical chrétien. *Imago Musicae: International Yearbook of Musical Iconography* 25(1). 29–75.

Haar, James. 1960. *Musica mundana: Variations on a Pythagorean theme*. Cambridge, MA: Harvard University Press.

Hammerstein, Reinhold. 1962. *Die Musik der Engel. Untersuchungen zur Musikanschauung des Mittelalters*. Bern & München: Francke.

Harris, J. Rendel. 1911. *The odes and psalms of Solomon*. Cambridge: Cambridge University Press.
Iversen, Gunilla. 2000. Réaliser une vision: La dernière vision de *Scivias* et le drame *Ordo virtutum* de Hildegarde de Bingen. *Revue de musicologie* 86(1). 37–63.
Jeauneau, Édouard. 1996. *Iohannes Scottus Eriugena: Periphyseon*, 5 vols., vol. 1 (Corpus Christianorum, Continuatio Mediaevalis 161). Turnhout: Brepols.
Jeck, Udo Reinhold. 1998. Mystische kontemplation und sakrale Musik bei ps.-Dionysios Areopagites und seinen Kommentatoren. In Frank Hentschel (ed.), *Musik und die Geschichte der Philosophie und Naturwissenschaften im Mittelalter. Fragen zur Wechselwirkung von "musica" und "philosophia" im Mittelalter*, 125–140. Leiden: Brill.
Jourdan, Fabienne. 2010. *Orphée et les chrétiens: La réception du mythe d'Orphée dans la littérature chrétienne grecque des cinq premiers siècles*. Paris: Les Belles Lettres.
Kunz, Claudia Edith. 1996. *Schweigen und Geist: Biblische und patristische Studien zu einer Spiritualität des Schweigens*. Freiburg im Breisgau: Herder.
Lewisohn, Leonard. 1997. The sacred music of Islam: Samā' in the Persian Sufi tradition. *British Journal of Ethnomusicology* 6(1). 1–33.
Lilla, Salvatore. 2013. *Il silenzio nella filosofia greca (presocratici – Platone – Giudeo-ellenismo – Ermetismo – Medioplatonismo – Oracoli Caldaici – Neoplatonismo – Gnosticismo – Padri greci): Galleriadi ritratti e raccolta di testimonianze*. Roma: Institutum Patristicum Augustinianum.
Lindsay, Wallace Martin (ed.). 1911. *Isidori Hispalensis episcopi Etymologiarum sive Originum Libri XX*. Oxford: Oxford University Press.
MacDonald, Duncan B. 1902. Emotional religion in Islām as affected by music and singing. *Journal of the Royal Asiatic Society of Great Britain and Ireland* 34. 1–28.
Maisonneuve, Roland. 1980. La musique et le divin chez les mystiques anglais du XIVè siècle. In Danielle Buschinger & André Crépin (eds.), *Actes du colloque 24–29 mars 1980: Musique, littérature et société au Moyen Age* (Université de Picardie, Centre d'études médiévales), 409–423. Paris: Champion.
McKinnon, James. 1987. *Music in early Christian literature*. Cambridge: Cambridge University Press.
McKinnon, James. 1990. The patristic jubilus and the Alleluia of the Mass. *Cantus Planus* 1. 61–70.
McKinnon, James. 1998. *The temple, the church fathers, and early Western chant*. Aldershot: Ashgate Variorum Collected Studies.
Müller, David Heinrich. 1896. *Die Propheten in ihrer ursprünglichen Form. Die Grundgesetze der ursemitischen Poesie erschlossen und nachgewiesen in Bibel, Keilinschriften und Koran und in ihren Wirkungen erkannt in den Chören der griechischen Tragödie*. Wien: A. Hölder.
Palisca, Claude V. 2000. Moving the affections through music: Pre-Cartesian psycho-physiological theories. In Paolo Gozza (ed.), *Number to sound: The musical way to the scientific revolution*, 289–308. Dordrecht: Kluwer.
Parker, John (ed. and trans.). 1897. *The works of Dionysius the Areopagite*. London: James Parker and Co.
Pfau, Marianna. 2005. *Hildegard von Bingen: Der Klang des Himmels*. Köln: Böhlau.
Pons, André. 1955. Le droit de la musique et du chant sacré dans l'écriture sainte. *Revue de Musicologie* 37. 30–42.

Radice, Roberto & Alfredo Valvo (eds.). 2011. *Dal logos dei greci e dei romani al Logos di Dio: Ricordando Marta Sordi*. Milano: Vita e Pensiero.

Rolle, Richard. 1971. *Le chant d'amour (Melos Amoris)*. Latin text edited by E. J. F. Arnould, with introduction and notes by François Vandenbroucke, o.s.b., translated by les Moniales de Wisques. Paris: Les éditions du Cerf.

Roth, Marjorie. 2010. Prophecy, harmony, and the alchemical transformation of the soul: The key to Lasso's Chromatic Sibyls. In Laurence Wuidar (ed.), *Music and esotericism*, Aries Book Series, 45–76. Boston & Leiden: Brill.

Routley, Erik. 1950. *The church and music: An enquiry into the history, the nature, and the scope of Christian judgment on music*. London: G. Duckworth & Co.

Schroeder-Sheker, Therese. 1989. The use of plucked-stringed instruments in Medieval Christian mysticism. *Mystics Quarterly* 15(3). 133–139.

Sequeri, Pierangelo. 2005. *Musica e mistica: Percorsi nella storia occidentale delle pratiche estetiche e religiose*. Città del Vaticano: Libreria Editrice Vaticana.

Skeris, Robert A. 1976. *Chroma Theou. On the origins and theological interpretation of the musical imagery used by the ecclesiastical writers of the first three centuries, with special reference to the image of Orpheus*. Altötting: Alfred Coppenrath.

Somenzi, Chiara. 2012. *Vocibus et cordibus*: la dialettica voce-silenzio nel canto cristiano: Dibattito e molteplicità di soluzioni tra IV e V secolo. In *Silenzio e parola nella patristica: XXXIX Incontro di Studiosi dell'Antichità Cristiana (Roma, 6–8 maggio 2010)*, 71–89. Roma: Institutum Patristicum Augustinianum.

Spitzer, Leo. 1963. *Classical and Christian ideas of world harmony. Prolegomena to an interpretation of the word "Stimmung."* Baltimore: Johns Hopkins Press.

Stapert, Clavin. 2007. *A new song for an old world: Musical thought in the early Church*. Cambridge: Eerdmans.

Suarez-Nani, Tiziana. 2002. *Connaissance et langage des anges, selon Thomas d'Aquin et Gilles de Rome*. Paris: Vrin.

Vendrix, Philippe (ed.). 2008. *Music and mathematics in late medieval and early modern Europe*. Turnhout: Brepols.

Vieillefon, Laurence. 2003. *La figure d'Orphée dans l'antiquité tardive: Les mutations d'un mythe: Du héros païen au chantre chrétien*. Paris: De Boccard.

Werckmeister, Andreas. 1707. *Musicalische Paradoxal-Discourse*. Quedlinburg, Calvisius.

Williamson, Karina. 2004. From heavenly harmony to eloquent silence: Representations of world order from Dryden to Shelley. *The Review of English Studies*, New Series 55(221). 527–544.

Wilson, Robert R. 1979. Prophecy and ecstasy: A reexamination. *Journal of Biblical Literature* 98(3). 321–337.

Wuidar, Laurence. 2010. Parola segreta e trasporto gioioso: la metafora musicale nel commento agostiniano al salmo 32 e nel *De venatione sapientiae* di Cusano. *Divus Thomas, Commentarium de Philosophia et Theologia* 113(3). 66–84.

Wuidar, Laurence. 2014. *La simbologia musicale nei commenti ai salmi di Agostino*. Milano: Mimesis.

Wuidar. Laurence. 2015a. La teologia musicale di Richard Rolle (+1349): *Raptus* canoro e visioni sonore nel *Melos amoris*. *Divus Thomas, Commentarium de Philosophia et Theologia* 118(3). 186–225.

Wuidar, Laurence. 2015b. Conversione ed *ebrietas* musicali: il potere d'alterazione della musica in alcuni mistici medievali e rinascimentali. *Rivista internazionale di musica sacra* 1–2. 11–42.
Wuidar, Laurence. 2015c. La metafora teologico-musicale. Nomi divini ed esperienze mistiche nella tradizione del *Corpus Dionysiacum*. *Rivista di ascetica e mistica* 40(1). 5–48.
Wuidar, Laurence. 2016. *L'uomo musicale nell'antico cristianesimo: Storia di una metafora tra Oriente e Occidente*. Turnhout: Brepols.
Zorzi, Benedetta. 2002. *Melos* e *Iubilus* nelle *Enarrationes in Psalmos* di Agostino: Una questione di mistica agostiniana. *Augustinianum* 42(2). 383–413.

William Downes

The significance of "the plain style" in seventeenth-century England

1 Introduction: What is plain style?

This essay seeks to understand the nature and significance of the English "plain style." This became a new norm for written English by the late 17th century and remains highly significant. It is a vast topic. I will confine myself to the implications, influences and consequences for an understanding of religious language, analyzing plainness using modern linguistic pragmatics. I will propose that the domination of plainness causes a problem with respect to what people can readily believe is true. And I will show how multiple historical factors such as the rise of the modern nation-state with its own developed standard language, printing and spreading literacy, the innovative thinking of the New Philosophy and rapid economic, political and administrative change, conspired to affect the understanding of religious language in England.

Plainness as a style in language has been an issue in European culture since antiquity. In the *Orator,* Cicero distinguishes three contrasting styles available for use in a law court or legislature: "the plain style for proof, the middle style for pleasure, the vigorous style for persuasion" (Bizzell and Herzberg 2001: 340–341). The first style is "short and concise [....] plain and clear [....] Only one quality will be lacking [...] the charm and richness of figurative ornament." In Book IV of *On Christian Doctrine*, Augustine adapts Cicero for Christian purposes (Bizzell and Herzberg 2001: 469–485). He correlates the styles with both the significance of the topic and the function. A plain "subdued" style is most appropriate for teaching. The point is that plainness was in the tradition long before it applied to English. For written English, emerging in a context where Latin was the prior written language, plainness was always an option.

Style is the patterning of choices on all levels of language where alternatives are available. Contrasting styles make available alternative ways to put into words intentions and attitudes with respect to semantic content. Style is one dimension in which language creates social situations – a culture or form of life. This concept of style applies to other semiotics; for example, to ritual, music, art, and architecture. In linguistics, functional varieties are called *registers*, distinguished from other variables such as dialect (Downes 1998: 308–322). To

William Downes, University of East Anglia

https://doi.org/10.1515/9781614514329-011

understand registers and their appropriate styles gives us deep access to contexts of situation and culture – the minds of language users. To the degree that registers enable thought, I call them *cognitive registers* – styles of thought. Cognitive registers enacted in the generic mode of plain style cognitively enable some ways of thinking while disabling others. (I have analyzed petitionary prayer in this way in Downes 2018.)

Plainness is not a thing, but a norm or ideal. It is how one ought to write appropriately in cases where it accomplishes the function of that particular register. The plain style in written English becomes normative in the 17th century for many new registers. Today it is the hegemonic prescribed style of written English. We ought to use this style in a register unless there is a reason not to. For example, if plain style is the norm for a report, then it is needed to accomplish that use, what the report is for, how it functions. To write in this required way is part of learned communicative competence. Plain style is also a more-or-less affair, relative to context. A text is only relatively plain. There are also diverse types of plainness in different domains.

Plainness has two main dimensions. First, it refers to the relative transparency with which a writer's sincere intention to inform the reader of the truth is conveyed or obscured. The more difficulty the reader has in inferring a determinate reading which is assignable to the writer, the more the interpretation is the responsibility of the reader and the less plain is the style. The other dimension is the objectively measurable inferential directness with which the semantic content of the sentences can be retrieved. Plain style certainly admits of stylistic elaboration, but only when it is relevant to the function being served in the context. The hegemony of plainness discourages situations where elaborate rhetorical styles are needed.

Elaborate style has been contested throughout western linguistic self-consciousness. The Sophists taught rhetoric: how to use language to achieve intended political and legal effects. The poets sang complex, beautiful language – linguistic art. Thus Plato divides stylistic elaboration into two distinct domains: rhetoric and poetics. Sophistic practice is at issue in the former; Homer in the latter. Both are analyzed unfavorably, in the *Gorgias* (Books II and X) and *Republic* (Books II, III and X), and more favorably in the *Phaedrus* and in later neo-Platonism, respectively. What today would be called style still falls into these two distinct domains. Both are treated as departures from the literal or the plain.

With respect to rhetoric, Socrates' charge is that stylistic elaboration is not used to seek truth rationally, the project of philosophy. Instead, it is used to arouse prejudices and manipulate audiences and is therefore morally corrupting (Herrick 2013: 52–60). This negative sense of rhetoric is still current today. By contrast, in the later *Phaedrus*, Plato's analysis is more subtle. All we need to note here is that, properly deployed, style in language is also of the essence in rational, logical inquiry, the dialectical search for truth. Inquiry is not simply non-linguistic reasoning.

With respect to poetics, in Plato's *Republic* poets are famously excluded from the ideal polity. Truth about reality is only accessible through the dialectic of rational dialogue – philosophy as practiced by Socrates, simulated in Platonic dialogue. Philosophical method uses reason: to question, to answer, to develop and assess arguments. By contrast, poetic language is dangerous. It seductively misrepresents the gods. But again, there are alternative positive views: not only does Aristotle recognize positive functions of poetry, but neo-Platonism, both in antiquity and in the Renaissance, explores the idea that poetic language is revelatory – truth in riddling form. Heath (2013: 104–179) describes this neo-Platonism in chapters aptly entitled "Ways to find truth in falsehood" and "The marriage of Homer and Plato." In Italian Renaissance neo-Platonism typified by Marsilio Ficino (1433–99), the transcendental can be accessed. In a general model of this spiritual form of magic, D. P. Walker (1975: 75–84) recognizes four ways, "*Vis imaginative*," in which this reading of reality occurs: "meaning and beauty in the visual arts, and figures like talismans [...] in poetry and oratory and words as essences of things as in incantations [...] in music and song; proportion and number (harmony of spheres and sympathetic magic)," and finally, in the occult properties of objects. (The word "occult" here means real but not causally explicable.) These have psychological effects on imagination and physical effects in natural magic.

This vision takes a more rationalized form in Nicholas of Cusa (1401–64), who "saw in neo-Platonism a doctrine which implied a way of knowing or intuition which can go beyond reason, the latter being bounded by the principle of non-contradiction. Although we are finite, we have a way of thereby getting to the infiniteness of God, to which reason cannot attain" (Hamlyn 1989: 124). We can view this as a form of *poetic-aesthetic* cognition, which is believed to be revelatory. It can also be communicated in ritual action and liturgy. This use of language and other semiotic systems underlie a family of cognitive registers. Poetic-aesthetic stylistic elaboration is contrasted with its opposite, the plainness of rational inquiry, or *dialectic*. In the 16th and 17th centuries, in accord with its neo-Platonic and hermetic origins, revelatory ways of thinking and writing had become associated with magic so treated as marginal to rational inquiry.

Herrick (2013: 153), quoting J. G. Burke (1974), also aligns neo-Platonism with magic: "[...] according to the magical view of language, (words) are not just verbal symbols attached to things by conventional usage, there is a direct correspondence between a word and the divine idea it expresses." Herrick continues, "People and events could literally be brought under the control of the highly skilled orator, a theme explored in Renaissance works, including Shakespeare's *The Tempest* and Marlowe's *Dr. Faustus.*"

We can contrast a modern analysis of poetic-aesthetic style in a famous account of the functions of language, Roman Jakobson's "Closing statement: Linguistics and poetics" (1960). Every text is poetical to some degree. To be poetic-aesthetic is to be oriented to language itself. The poetic function is for a text to draw attention to its own form. But it also functions simultaneously in other ways. It is oriented to the state of affairs it represents, the *referential function* and the *expressive function* (orientation to the writer themselves); the *conative function* (orientation to the hearer); the *phatic function* (orientation to social contact); the *meta-representational function* (orientation to the text); and, of course, the *poetic function* described above. Each function determines some of the linguistic choices that form the text. So every text manifests all the functions, which differ only in their order of priority. Thus every text is necessarily mixed according to the hierarchy of its functions. Plainness is dominated by referentiality. It is not so oriented to conative-expressive rhetoric, and is minimally poetic, so not drawing attention to its own linguistic form. Therefore, plain language seems transparent. We are not conscious of it. Thinking in terms of a phenomenology of language, a plain text is like a window through which we view reality directly as the writer believes it to be. Although the poetic function remains present, it has no referential function, no truth-relevant role. Therefore, its role must be aesthetic or ornamental.

2 The linguistics of plain style

We turn now to the linguistic analysis of plain style. I will employ the pragmatic theory of language use in context developed by Sperber and Wilson (1995). I will merely sketch what we need from relevance theory for plainness, using the 17th-century physician-philosopher Sir Thomas Browne as an illustration.

Sperber and Wilson (1995: 260) propose a *cognitive principle of relevance*, such that human cognition is geared to maximize relevance. This is then more specifically applied to *ostensive-inferential communication*. How does the mind process a text intended to communicate a specific message? The starting point is an utterance which is ostensive; i.e. to be relevant at all it must be taken as an attempted communication. It conveys a *communicative intent*. This, in turn, guarantees that the actual message, the *informative intent*, is *optimally relevant*.

How then does the reader determine this optimal relevance? Relevance theory claims that the reader creates a context from which to make deductive inferences, called *contextual implications*, about the linguistic input. Lexical and grammatical input is very skeletal, just a set of cues about what to construct. The premises for the deductions are generated *ad hoc* and called the context. This context is constructed employing just that information from the reader's mental encyclopaedia which is the most accessible then and there. Using this new context, guided by relevance, readers deduce the intended message – the informative intent – that which is optimally relevant. This is just that which produces adequate positive cognitive effects and is derived with least cognitive effort. This must be the first conclusion that the reader reaches, given that input and their own most accessible context created to derive it. This is due to the fact that the writer has produced their input assuming automatically that their own most accessible context is the same as the reader's. This works most of the time, since intentional communication, although fallible, is mostly successful.

The act of comprehension guided by relevance involves: first, constructing a context and inferring a fully determinate *proposition* based on the words the writer has provided. Since the actual words are only skeletal to the content that the writer intended to convey in the context, the intended proposition must be contextually inferred or *explicated*, by drawing *explicatures*. When a proposition is derived, if it alone does not fully achieve relevance, the reader further expands the context and uses this to contextually infer *implicatures*, adding these to the writer's informative intent. (It is easy to see how a more complex style will generate more explicatures and implicatures than a plainer style.) When the reader is satisfied that they have accounted for the input, they stop. They have calculated optimal relevance, and thus inferred the author's informative intent.

2.1 Thomas Browne's contrasting styles

Sir Thomas Browne (1605–1682) is an acknowledged master of elaborate English Humanist prose. At that time, language was central to education. For example, Erasmus' influential programme for education consisted mainly of learning Latin through total immersion. In Stephen Greenblatt's (2004: 24) words, this was "rote memorization, drill, text analysis, elaborate exercises in imitation and rhetorical variation" and exposure to "literary composition and rhetorical flourish from the start." Educated persons would be bilingual in Latin and English and versed in rhetoric and poetics to a degree unimaginable today. This was a prerequisite for university education, which largely consisted of immersion in the ancients. This is evident in Browne, who, before his medical training on the continent, attended Winchester College and Pembroke College, Oxford, graduating as M.A. in 1629.

Although his *Religio Medici* is better known, I will illustrate high style with Browne's *Hydriotaphia, Urne-Buriall: or a discourse of the sepulchral urnes lately found in Norfolk*, published in 1658. This is a reflection on mortality occasioned by Roman burial urns. The poetic function, in Jakobson's sense, is very prominent in Browne's prose rhythms, grammatical and semantic parallelisms, Latinate vocabulary and learned allusions. It typifies English Humanist high style.

Urne-Buriall begins:

> In the deep discovery of the Subterranean world, a shallow part would satisfie some enquirers; who if two or three yards were open about the surface, would not care to rake the bowels of *Potosi* [Brownes' italics], and regions towards the Centre. Nature has furnished one parte of the earth, and man another. The treasures of time lie high, in Urnes, Coynes, and Monuments, scarce below the roots of some vegetables. (Browne 1906: 95)

The first phrase, "In the deep discovery of the Subterranean world [...]" consists of the two prepositional phrases, the second dependent on the first, with the rhythmic pattern of the five syllables of the first phrase "deep discovery" and the parallel, equally rhythmic pattern in the second phrase, "Subterranean world" which ends with the stressed syllable "Sub-." The first phrase has its alliterative "d," the second consists of the Latinate learned word "Subterranean." These introduce the topic of the sentence: reflection on what is found under the earth. "Deep" and "subterranean" need explication. I infer that "deep" is potentially ambiguous between physically under the ground and intellectual depth, and "Subterranean world" has connotations of the classical post-death underworld.

The main verb "would satisfie" has two arguments, "some enquirers" and "a shallow part," which we infer refers to the "Subterranean world" just introduced. Logically, the proposition is that an unspecified subset of enquirers is satisfied with that shallow part of what is under the ground, and that since these enquirers would be satisfied with that – a few yards deep – they wouldn't dig either to the centre of *Potosi* (a footnote tells that this refers to a "rich mountain of Peru") or any region nearer the centre (of the earth). But the proposition doesn't say why! To achieve relevance, we must expand context and draw some implicatures. The "deep discovery" of new material for enquiry about the post-death underworld can implicate that deep reflection about death can be occasioned by evidence found just under the ground and furthermore that this reflection is a treasure comparable to the wealth of Peru. We conclude that this is Browne's informative intent.

This elaborated prose requires effort to determine the underlying propositions and the implicatures needed to grasp its relevance. First sentences normally introduce the theme of a treatise. I conclude that Browne's book aims at deep discovery and therefore – in the humanist tradition – is a reflection on these newly found objects. Why is Browne using so many poetic devices? His rhetoric is not only an ornament to thought but also, because of its analogies, allusions and complexity, it enables his particular “style” of reflective cognition. His style is not revelatory in the neo-Platonic sense discussed above, but learned. This shows that what high style is doing can vary by context. We will see below that the same is true of plainness.

But Browne is equally capable of plain style, shown in a report to the Royal Society. It is one of the first archaeological descriptions, “Concerning some urnes found in Brampton-Field, in Norfolk, Anno: 1667” (Browne 1906: 142–143): “In a large Arable Field, lying between Buxton and Brampton, but belonging to Brampton, and not so much more than a Furlong from Oxnead Park, divers Urnes were found [....] In the Colours also there was great Variety, some were Whitish, some Blackish, and inclining to a Blue, others Yellowish, or Dark Red, arguing a variety of their Materials [...].” Further on, he describes some objects found adjacent, and makes other inferences: “There were also found some pieces of Glass, and finer Vessels, which might contain such Liquors as they often Buried in or by, the Urnes; divers Pieces of Brass, of several Figures [...].” It is clear that this linguistic input can be developed into determinate propositional forms with a few inferential steps and there is no reason to think that Browne is not sincere and truthful. In principle, the content could be truth-evaluated. There are no implicatures. The style is plain.

2.2 Principles of plainness

Our first task is to describe plainness in linguistic terms using relevance theory. I propose that to be plain makes two preliminary normative demands: a sincerity condition and a truth evaluation condition. The first norm is to intend to say exactly what you mean in the sense of sincerely intending to communicate what you actually do believe and feel. This demands a transparent, non-Machiavellian communicative intent, with no hidden intents. The second norm is that these transparent intents be communicated in the clearest and most direct way possible: ideally that a truth-evaluable proposition be derived with the least cognitive effort.

This demands that the writer’s intention with respect to both propositional content and attitude is achieved as clearly and directly as possible. Therefore, it must be formulated in the most relevant way available. In creating a context, the text must trigger the most readily accessible premises and use the fewest deductive steps to arrive at the intended proposition. But this is no more than a re-statement of the principle of optimal relevance which governs all communication. So what else do we need to distinguish plain from elaborated style? The informative intent must also be such as to be made manifest in a clear and direct way. *Clear* means that the proposition must be understood: if not fully, at least to the satisfaction of participants. *Direct* demands that the steps needed to achieve this are objectively few.

2.2.1 On difficulty and simplification

There are perhaps cases where this is not possible. What if there is no objective way that the intended content could either be clear or directly derived in a few obvious steps? The intent is to convey something which is difficult. Let's assume there are messages – for whatever reason – whose plainest written expression must be inferentially either very complex, indeterminate or mysterious. These are complex, vague or difficult topics. In these cases, there is no use complaining that the text isn't plain: that the information could have been better formulated or that the text is badly written. But what if that intent could not be communicated in any other way? The text's very difficulty is an outcome of its optimal relevance. Thus, in plain style as a norm there is a reason to avoid intrinsically difficult, indeterminate, or vague topics. (If we must be plain, are there legitimate ways to simplify our thoughts and language?)

2.2.2 Maxims of plain style

What we generally mean by plainness is the following. The first maxim concerns writers' attitudes: Don't hide your real motives and intentions. Given this, the text can be fully grasped in a few, clear steps. The underlying principle is that the writer aims – in absolute, not relative terms – for *low complexity* with respect to the reader's interpretation. Low complexity demands few inferential steps. Inferential steps are fewer in number if information is compressed. This occurs when premises are both general and true, because knowledge of general truths about a topic is a measure of how well it is understood. A difficult topic is one that is not well understood. It follows that the second maxim is: Avoid difficult topics, those that can't be represented without complexity. This reduces the amount of information in plain style, making it easier to process. Next, the propositional content must be readily discoverable. This requires it to be close to literal meaning, which is known by everybody because it is knowledge of language, not knowledge of the world. So the third maxim is: Be literal. Since all implicatures require access to background information and more deductive steps, don't use them unless it is absolutely necessary. Therefore, the fourth maxim is: Avoid implicatures. Since figures produce implicatures, this excludes figures of speech. Similarly, to express attitudes and affectivity also adds to complexity. A fifth maxim might be: Only aim for affective effects in cases where they are necessary to understand the informative intent. Plain style texts will have flat affect. This is the sort of communicable content and attitude you must intend, if you are to be plain. Eschew everything else.

What is the point of this plainness? We must be sincere and, in spite of simplification, truthful. Thus, a plain text is designed so that the reader can develop the words into a full proposition, one with fully determinate truth conditions. For a reader, this can be stated as an instruction: "When reading a text in plain style, process until you arrive at the first fully determinate proposition, i.e., that with explicit truth conditions, then stop." If the text is well written, this is what the writer both intended to convey and believes to be true. A consequence of this dependence on truth is that plainness is relative to whatever epistemological authority the writer and reader are willing to defer, the criteria for evaluating the truth.

3 Varieties of authority and of plainness

Belief is an attitude to propositions; namely, that they are true or probably true. For truth-evaluation to be made, truth conditions must be satisfied in a real world. But how can this be known? There are differing grounds for belief, different sources of epistemological authority.

Beliefs can be "compelled" by both reason and evidence. They can be accepted on the authority of individual validating experience: sensory data, *a priori* "gut feeling," mystical experience, personal study, and so on. Alternatively, beliefs can also be accepted on faith in authority of a social, historical nature. This can be *endoxa*, the axioms/premises that everybody takes for granted, or more institutional: pressure from one's unique social network, current science, political movement, philosophical school or church tradition, scholastic interpretation. Within these categories, there are yet other distinctions. We have *role authority*, such as presidential, priestly or parental authority; *textual authority* of sacred books; or *charismatic authority*, where leadership derives from personal authority. But any epistemological authority is open to scepticism. We also often think of authority in terms of power. However, to be genuine, authority must not be coercive. It is impossible to genuinely believe something solely because coerced, although one might assent in public, and even act accordingly, in bad faith (Arendt 1961). Genuine authority instead resides in history and forms of life.

My hypothesis is that linguistic parameters interact with situation and source of authority to produce varieties of plain style. The conclusion is that there is no one plain style. What counts as plain depends on context and the source of authority. With respect to source of authority, we can distinguish two general types. First, if individual sensory input and reason is the source of authority, the proposition must have fully determinate truth conditions and be truth-evaluable in principle solely on these grounds. This is *empirical or scientific plainness*. In a secular world-view, this generates the hegemonic cognitive register.

A second type is *literalist plainness* in which mysterious semi-propositions – no matter how irrational or unempirical – are accepted as plainly true on the basis of authority alone. In literalism, mysteries can remain partially understood, and never truth evaluable, but be nevertheless the plain truth because of a validating source who does know the truth. Such literalism is compatible with elaborate, poetical language as the most relevant expression of mysterious revealed truth; for example, the concept of the Trinity. We can contrast Protestant literalism, resting on scripture, and interpreted by reformers like Luther and Calvin, with Catholic sacramental religion depending on church authority, derived from tradition. How rationalized this is depends on the philosophy of the source of authority. In later secular world-views, literalist plainness dominates popular and political culture. Plain style also varies according to historically changing situational type. For example, the description of Browne's urns differs from plainness in a legal document, a record of plague deaths, a political or economic pamphlet, or even poetry.

4 Disablement of poetic effects and relevant mysteries

Plainness remains hegemonic for written English. Unless there is special reason to the contrary, writers ought to be plain. I propose that this hegemony is cognitively disabling with respect to any disposition to take revelatory poetic-aesthetic mysteries seriously, as true. This includes much religious language. Many claim that they find orthodox religions incredible or unintelligible. Why is this so?

There are a number of ways in which general poetic-aesthetic cognition is disabled by plainness. Poetic language entails the reader's inability to determine any one message clearly intended by the writer. The intent is indeterminate. Plainness finds this intolerable. Indeterminacy is the result of the poetic-aesthetic attempt to represent complex, hard to articulate experiences. Relevance theory describes this by saying that in these cases relevance is only achieved by a "wide array of weak implicatures," or poetic effects (Sperber and Wilson 1995: 222). A *weak implicature* is one for which the reader must take responsibility. This contrasts with the non-poetic, single strongly implicated informative intent. In poetic-aesthetic style, interpretation has been problematized and largely turned over to the reader. Therefore, to the degree that a text achieves its relevance through poetic effects, it cannot be plain. Plain style – whether scientific or literalist – cannot do this because it insists on a unique determinate meaning. By contrast, the poetic-aesthetic puts into words the ineffability of a thought. That said, this very indeterminacy enables each reader, in the context of their life, to use a unique personal reading in a regulative or interpretative way.

A second way in which plainness disables aesthetic-religious thinking lies with the fact that many important and widespread concepts are difficult in the sense that they cannot contribute to determinate truth conditions. Ordinary concepts can be used to construct fully determinate propositions without difficulty. From "the water in this pan is now boiling," it is easy to derive a fully formed determinate proposition, which is also truth-evaluable. But when there are concepts within a proposition such that its truth conditions cannot be fully grasped, we face a mystery. The form remains incomplete or *semi-propositional*. Nevertheless, just as we saw with respect to poeticalness, the semi-proposition, in spite of the mystery it contains, usually has enough logical character to warrant inferences needed to achieve relevance. The concept is relevant, even though the reader does not fully grasp it, nor can they empirically or practically evaluate its truth. (The idea of relevant mysteries originates with Sperber 1996 and Recanati 1997; for a fuller account see Downes 2011: 133–162.)

Some religious concepts can never lead to a full proposition in all contexts. These are incorrigible mysteries, and can never be fully grasped. Nevertheless, such mysteries can be highly relevant: for example, Kant's transcendental SELF or the Cartesian EGO. A major class of incorrigible mysteries are rationalized universals – Platonic ideas: FREEDOM, EQUALITY, LOVE, JUSTICE, GOODNESS, etc. Most fundamental religious concepts are incorrigible mysteries: GOD, INCARNATION, THE ABSOLUTE, BRAHMAN, EMPTINESS, TAO, etc.

Yet such abstract concepts have a property which is key to understanding mysteries. In context, *ad hoc* applied versions of the concept can be readily constructed that do achieve relevance and so contribute to a fully propositional form, but only in that context. The mystery is useful. Because of this, the incorrigibility of these mysteries may not seem important. But it does matter when one tries and fails to understand or justify them for their importance in law, morality, politics or religion: FREEDOM of the WILL, the greatest HAPPINESS of the greatest number, LOVE is HIS MEANING. Incorrigible mysteries are crucial in another way. Since we can never definitively tell corrigible from incorrigible mysteries and both are useful, they motivate inquiry. This generates relevant new *ad hoc* applications in practice and motivates open-ended inquiry exploring their meaning.

5 Poetic-aesthetic realism in religion

We can illustrate the poetic-aesthetic within Roman Catholic literalism in the mystery of TRANSUBSTANTIATION. This is an epistemological commitment based on church authority crucial to its Mass and of great historical importance. The consecration and communion is the defining liturgical act of the pre-modern Christian social order. The words of consecration repeat scripture word for word. The doctrine is a scholastic interpretation of these words. Scholastic philosophies translate the poetic-aesthetic and mysterious into the somewhat plainer terms of an authoritative, but more rationalized, system as far as this is possible. The words and their interpretations together trigger endless further implicatures. But the concepts remain mysteries. This illustrates the potential inferential richness of the poetic-aesthetic.

The interpretation in question is that the substance of both consecrated bread and wine, but not the accidents or attributes, are utterly transformed. They become "in reality" Christ's body and blood. This is constituted by the words. There is literalist plainness with respect to the scripture. However, to be properly understood, this first interpretation needs further theological interpretation in the light of church tradition. The priestly role is to perform the whole congregation's offering of itself to God. This is – in reality – the ongoing enactment of Christ's offering of himself on the cross as the unique atoning sacrifice – the Lamb of God – through which humanity is, once and for all, reconciled with God.

In this reconciliation, CHRIST'S BODY is taken into the communicant's body, which is but one part of the collective unity of the church – which is in fact THE ONE BODY OF CHRIST with Christ as its head. In this respect, there is no distinction between people, but absolute equality of "Jew and Greek, male and female, free and slave," etc. (Galatians 3:28). God literally resides within each individual and simultaneously the individual resides literally within God. (See *Catechism of the Catholic Church* 1994: 368–396.) These thoughts are indeed a relevant mystery. Even when theologically interpreted and grasped in the somewhat plainer language of Aristotelian philosophy, they remain a profoundly mystical theology. In this theology, gospel literalism is modified by the church authority. How much and variously the poetic-aesthetic richness of both concepts and language is developed, and applied by individuals in their own spiritual devotions, depends on how liberal their Catholicism is.

But in a way, we are missing the point. In liturgy, people are doing, not interpreting. Words spoken in a public, communal performance have a different, more direct, impact than written text. Relevance arises through the very participation. Everyone present is repeatedly performing the same mystery. To witness oneself with others automatically strengthens belief, although that isn't the theological point of the act. The point is to timelessly and actually relate the redeemed individual to God through Christ in the liturgy of the church, the new Israel. These acts simply cannot be performed on the basis of the individuals' own authority. They logically require institutional, traditional authority. Thus, the sacramental-liturgical form of religion is intrinsically collectivist. This is implicit in Eamon Duffy's (1992) description of the social order of Catholic England in the late pre-Reformation period: its liturgical year, its epistemologically unproblematic collective devotions. Catholic liturgy remains mysterious but true, understood only by God and accepted on the basis of church authority. To the reforming mind, its mysteries are superstitions. To those who embrace empirical-scientific plainness, the Mass is myth. A religious myth isn't literally true but is "a vast work of poetry" (Carse 2008). Like any poetic fiction, it could be viewed as false but relevant. Mythic religion can be taken as referring to something real only when it is unriddled, reduced to plain language which reveals its true significance. By contrast, in literalist plainness, whether Protestant or Catholic, religious mysteries, although never fully understood, are not myths, but truths.

5.1 Neo-Platonism revisited

But could anything philosophically justify realism with respect to poetic-aesthetic styles? In discussing Ficino and Renaissance neo-Platonism (section 1), the claim was made that the aesthetic-poetic, including music and action, could imaginatively provide access to transcendental realities. The Catholic tradition is of this type. The empirical-scientific plain style disables this understanding, placing it in a specialist ghetto. The literalist plain style also disables this, considers it a superstitious over-interpretation, politically motivated by power, and imagines each individual returning instead to their own inspired reading of the authoritative texts.

With respect to the Catholic tradition, D. P. Walker (1975: 36), discussing the source of mediaeval and Renaissance magic, explicitly links the Church with poetic-aesthetic representation. He writes, "the most important (source) [...] is the mass, with its music, words of consecration, incense, lights, and supreme magical effect – transubstantiation. This [...] is a fundamental influence on all mediaeval and Renaissance magic, and a fundamental reason for the Church's condemnation of all magical practices. The Church has its own magic." In much Protestantism, the Catholic understanding of liturgy is classified as superstition.

Of course, the ancient question is how rhetoric, or poetic effects in our analysis, could be revelatory of transcendental reality, as metaphysically real. What truths can be gained to serve as premises for deduction? In his aptly titled book on Italian humanism, *Rhetoric as Philosophy* (1980), Ernesto Grassi argues that such premises are produced by the *inventio* or 'ingenious' basis of rhetoric. Underlying premises for deductive "rationality" are in fact "imagined" archaic metaphors. The analogical system of neo-Platonism, a rationalization of the primitive "folk Platonism" underlying human supernaturalism, is such a system. If such premises are real, that is, input to the deductions central to a form of life, then rhetorical, poetic-aesthetic language is revelatory. Grassi writes:

> Language is divided into two [...] different forms of expression. One is purely rational, which serves to prove and provide the reasons for something. It is considered to be the measure of science, since it vouches for the objectivity of its statements with reasons [....] In ancient times the language was considered to be [...] *unrhetorical.* We said that proofs in this rational language must, in the traditional view, be free of metaphors [....] The final consequence of this rational speech is the demand for a mathematical symbolic language in which the consequences can be drawn from the premises that we assume. Because its "scientific" nature consists in its strictly deductive character, its essence is that that it can possess no *"inventive" character.* Such a language must restrict itself to finding what is already contained in the premises that are not yet explicit or obvious [....] The second form of language is the one that determines the premises themselves which, since they cannot be proven, are the *archai*, the principles [....] we see that the language that is appropriate to metaphors has the characteristic of an "archaic" language. It is only able to make manifest and not to demonstrate. By virtue of its immediate structure this language "shows" us something [...] and hence is "imagistic" [...] it has a theoretical character and yet has the metaphorical character we have discussed. (Grassi 1980: 96–97)

In the theory of Gianfrancesco Pico della Mirandola (1469–1533), after Ficino the most important neo-Platonist of that time, this creativity arises in the images of "fantasy." These are then read in the light of reason. A similar view reappears throughout literary tradition, for example, in Coleridge's Romantic theory of imagination and in theories of symbolism (Wimsatt and Brooks 1962: 384–411, 583–569).

In my own view, imagination is the exploration of possible worlds developed through a concentrated interrogation of the phenomenal world, a disciplined "reverie" or "musement." There are many ways that what is imaginatively possible both in inner perception and/or inner speech can be innovatively relevant in an ad hoc way to what actually exists and happens. It can be construed as true explanatory hypotheses, as predictions, as motivating goals or ideals, as pervasive models and metaphors mapping onto the actual world, or as abstract realities that actually create and interact with what happens. The articles in Vickers (1984) trace the incompatible Platonic and scientific frameworks that co-exist in the same minds in 17th-century England. The mix varies from individual to individual, the most famous case being Newton. Similarly, Brooke (1991: esp. chap. 2) demonstrates an uneasy, mental co-existence of theological and naturalistic concepts. They are only fully separated later.

6 How and why did plain style emerge?

Why did the new emphasis on plainness emerge during this historical period? How did plainness contribute to relevance as sources of authority and situations of language use changed? First, it embodied a new insistence on fully grasping and evaluating truth conditions. Second, there is a new questioning self-consciousness about the legitimacy of sources of authority.

Plain style is only one aspect in a larger cultural reorientation. Charles Taylor (1989) traces a new instability in this "inescapable framework" underlying a western European sense of reality. Among influential circles, the ancient assumption of the "ontic logos," the metaphysical reality of Platonic universals accessible to reason, loses conviction. Neo-Platonism and the Italian Renaissance appropriation and modernization of the "ancients," including their expertise in rhetoric, lose credibility, especially in the rising nation-states of northern Europe. This contributes to a modern attitude that Taylor calls "the affirmation of ordinary life" – a reorientation of "conceptions of the good." Plainness is the language correlate of this.

But how can we account more systematically for the emergence of plain style at this time? A concept appears as an innovation within one or a few individuals, beginning life as an *ad hoc* concept in a new context. If it spreads, it becomes a *cultural* innovation. This early adoption by a core group then spreads only if it has become relevant to a wider population. Sperber calls this "the epidemiology of representations." I view conceptual innovation and diffusion as a level of language change like historical sound change (Downes 2011: 227–241; Downes 1998: 233–274). But how did PLAINNESS as a concept become newly relevant?

Innovation becomes likely when there is increased variability from which to choose and when people are stressed. Increased cultural variability itself is stressful, because it automatically increases the number and range of challenges by providing new contexts. Stress elicits an emotional-motivational response because it activates the innate exploratory "seeking" system of the brain in response, trying to overcome it (Panksepp 1998: 144–163). Variability increases opportunities for innovation, while stress makes seeking change urgent.

There was much in the 16th- and 17th-century context that provided stresses which spread the norm of plainness. Although they are not easily disentangled, I will consider inter-locked domains of variability and stress. These are the causal contexts of our normative change. Although any change is multi-factorial, I won't rank factors in order of importance. First is the rise of the modern nation-state and how it plays out as a crisis in Christian authority. Second is the post-humanist change in philosophical orientation that leads to the early Enlightenment and the rise of science. Related to both is the new secular economy, its transactions, institutions, technical innovations, and global geographical reach. How do these conspire to promote normative and linguistic innovation?

6.1 The nation state, religion and national languages

It is commonplace that the early modern period in northwestern Europe witnesses the consolidation of the modern state – a new concept originating "no earlier than the 16th century" (Morris 2011: 548). Morris cites Skinner's definition of the state as "a form of public power separate from both the ruler and the ruled, and constituting the supreme political authority within a certain defined territory" (Skinner 1978: 353). This is an abstraction, a legal entity separate from either government or its actual personnel. It rationalizes political power, exercises intense normative social pressure, applies within well-defined boundaries and constitutes a legal identity for its subjects. It also has a complex bureaucratic apparatus, claims a monopoly of coercion, and is part of a system of competing states. A key notion is autonomy, as opposed to heteronomy. A state is autonomous: a province or colony is heteronomous, subject to a larger entity.

To understand this change, consider the situation from which it emerged. Morris writes that mediaeval Europe was organized in "complex cross-cutting jurisdictions of towns, lords, kings, emperors, popes, and bishops, without clear hierarchies of political authority or unitary systems of law" (Morris 2011: 553). The institutional organization of the mediaeval church was more developed, and ecclesiastical authority took theoretical precedence over that of royal actors. The emergence of the early modern state "*consisted of the victory of kings and other political actors over their rivals – the Church and the Holy Roman Empire on the one side, the nobility and the independent towns on the other*[...]. *[This] led to the* [...] *institutions and practices that give us our states*" (my emphasis).

In England, these changes invoked enormous stresses, political and personal. The 16th-century Tudor victory over the church and nobility was first achieved when Henry VIII seized supremacy, claiming the ecclesiastical role of supreme head of the church in England. The church's wealth was expropriated. Most of the remaining feudal autonomy of the aristocracy was suppressed. Aristocrats became courtiers. Through the English civil wars, Restoration, and Glorious Revolution, an ever more abstract English state emerged to gain supreme power over individuals in its territory. But the very struggle over control of the state had weakened authority. In its final form, it becomes a limited monarchy, officially Protestant, with a parliament of the propertied, which by the time of the Glorious Revolution controlled the monarchy itself. This nation-state was limited in another way: its authority was undermined by an emergent money economy. Joyce Oldham-Appleby (1978) traces how contemporaries came to understand the systemic properties of markets, the nature of money, and the very concept of an economy separate from both state and society.

Our understanding of this rise of the state is ideologically controversial. The orthodox view is that once the Reformation repudiates papal authority because of its abuses and corruption, religion is the main source of sectarian violence. In Hobbes' *Leviathan* (1651), the first English book of modern political theory, voluntary submission to state supremacy in religion is logically necessary to suppress this religious conflict. Stephen Toulmin (1992) contrasts the systemic violence of religion with a lost humanism – an ideology of tolerant, exploratory scepticism. He writes: "Whether for pay or from conviction, there were many who would kill or burn in the name of theological doctrines that no one could give any conclusive reason for accepting [...]. All that mattered, by this stage, was for supporters of Religious Truth to believe, devoutly, in *belief itself*" (Toulmin 1992: 54; emphasis original). The modern state is justified because it protects from religious violence.

By contrast, William Cavanaugh (2002) argues that the above view is simply the "soteriological foundation myth" for the early modern state. His revisionist view is that the European religious wars represented the birth of the various modern states working out their form and consolidating their positions against all rival sources of power. It is in fact the victory of kings mentioned above. Leviathan supersedes the Body of Christ. In England, the imagined community defined by the claims of the state takes precedence over all other commitments. This reverses the relation of the state and Roman church, in which religion traditionally had theoretical precedence with respect to authority. (To impose their doctrines, Reformers needed state help. Cavanaugh suggests that it was in those

European polities where state authority already adequately controlled the Roman church and didn't need reformers that the Reformation failed.)

Cavanaugh argues that the deeper issue behind the wars of religion is a question of redefinition – "the creation of 'religion' as a set of beliefs which is defined as personal conviction." He continues, "The creation of religion, and thus the privatization of the church, is correlative to the rise of the state" (Cavanaugh 2002: 31). Religion is no longer the unquestionable liturgical realization of an imagined non-state community, but a matter for each individual, who submits at the same time to the coercive but contested power of the state alone. The transformed social order opens up the conscious self to difficult questions about its proper relation to authority – political and epistemological – and hence to the supernatural realm. This is a profound change in thinking and language. The new concept of religion designates something within each individual, separated from its ecclesiastical context. The "shift in the meaning of the term religion [...] through the late 16th and 17th centuries, is towards religion as a system of beliefs. Religion moves from a virtue to a set of propositions" (Cavanaugh 2002: 33). Differences in private belief are tolerable, but only when they pose no threat to state supremacy. By the time of Elizabeth I, Roman Catholics were persecuted not for beliefs *per se*, but as traitors.

If true, this is significant for the rising plainness norm. In the longer term, religion becomes an epistemological problem for individuals. The unquestioned legitimacy of Roman authority and its liturgical religion is repudiated. If individual reason becomes the source of authority, in phenomenological terms, church-warranted mysteries can'tbe experienced as true on that collective basis. For Hobbes, to avoid conflict in religious matters, authority must reside with the sovereign, who alone determines interpretations of scripture and thus its meaning. If that comes to lack legitimacy, then the individual mind depends on its own rationality and on its own interpretation of the authority of scripture: thus plainness becomes crucial because it promises to give individuals unmediated access to truth. In deciding what is true, the underlying stress consists in the fact that each individual must ultimately choose their own source of authority, textual or otherwise, on pain of bad conscience. They can choose their own unassisted faculties, and/or other sources of authority in a religious marketplace. The deeper problem is that because of relevant mysteries, truth-evaluation in fact remains undecidable on purely rational grounds, however plain a text may be believed to be. Belief in plainness opens the door to irrational literalism.

Furthermore, another possibility arises, which comes to full fruition only gradually in later centuries. In principle, free individuals could feel that the problem of religion was not relevant to them at all. They will interact with others in brand-new contexts, vastly enabled by the new state and its economy, where privatized religious belief has little relevance. We have the future potential for the general irrelevance of religion and wholesale secularization of the English form of life.

The modern state sees the parallel creation of national languages from a continuum of regional dialects. The emergence of *Standard English* in this period is a major topic in English sociolinguistics (see Downes 1998: 16–45; Graddol et al. 1996; Milroy and Milroy 1991). The triumph of Standard English is exactly parallel to Cavanaugh's victory of the king. Both are superordinate and nationally unifying. They cognitively separate people from both foreign nation-states and the universal church. Standard English itself, as opposed to Latin, becomes a symbol of this nation-state and enacts and embodies national feeling. On another dimension, Standard English expands as it develops innovative registers to serve new socio-economic functions.

However, as Robert Yelle (2013b: 6) suggests, the origin of such change partly lies within Christianity itself. Protestants in England and elsewhere – notably following Luther's example – championed the plain style on theological grounds. Biblical literalism underpinned not only vernacular translations of the Bible and the liturgy but also supported attacks on poetic and mysterious language, as described further below. Printers like William Caxton provided another motivation towards fixing a nationwide standard accessible to a more widely literate public throughout the state. The history of Bible translation into English presupposes this and also aids its development (see Yelle 2013a: chap. 5). Translation, literacy and printing all conspire to enable the growing importance of the Bible's textual authority over and against the supra-national authority of Rome. Bible reading becomes another route to the newly individualized religion. This logically demands the easiest possible access to God's revealed truth. This favors treating the text as though it can be grasped without specialist linguistic or theological training, can be understood to be plainly and literally true.

The vast expansion of the non-religious situations where written Standard English is used makes both Latin and humanist elaborated style less relevant. Inhabiting these new situations, there is a growing, non-clerical, educated class, freed enough from religious norms to act in their own interest. For a few, there is intense rational seeking for understanding nature; for many others a new freedom to seek their own interests, to act innovatively. For example, the new men acquired property, amassed wealth, enclosed common land, and promoted new technologies. *Chancery English*, developed to meet the bureaucratic demands of the state, is an early case of standardization required to develop technical and economic registers. An institution like Gresham College in the Strand hosts lectures relevant to practical navigators and merchants. New situations with their new language, practices, and institutions include those of centralizing government, production, trade, finance, and the pamphleteering which was the precursor of journalism. In summary, innovative situations are only possible through innovative register change. Plain style Standard English is the mode of most of these new uses of literacy.

6.2 Religion and reformation in England

The linguistic cleavage between high Anglo-Catholic and the reformed stylistic strands has long been recognized. In her study of 17th-century Anglican preaching styles, Morrissey (2002: 687) writes: "The division between 'plain style' Puritan and 'metaphysical' Laudian preachers, owes most to the influences of Perry Miller and W. Fraser Mitchell. It was they who tied this distinction to the intellectual prejudices and theologies of each group." In 1932, Mitchell distinguished a "metaphysical" style of Anglican preaching consisting of rhetorical imagery derived from "the treasures of patristic and mediaeval Catholic tradition" – akin to the complex religious poetry of Donne or Herbert, as a turning away from the "barren logic of Calvin's *Institutes*" (cited in Morissey 2002: 687). Miller also distinguished an anti-rhetorical Puritan "plain style" opposed to Laudian rhetoric. He claimed that the former worked "in terms of logic" and "divorced thought from expression" (cited in Morrissey, 2002: 689).

A similar distinction is drawn by Yelle (2013b: 22–32), who distinguishes the deeper origins and significance of contrasting "linguistic ideologies." The Reformation inspired a *Protestant literalism* which is "a valorization of the semantic content of language and a devaluation of its poetic and magical functions, which contributed to the rise of polemics against both ritual and mythological language" (Yelle 2013b: 25). Yelle makes a crucial point when he notes that in Protestantism, the scriptures, in spite of their actual form, are considered plain. In fact, the phrase "plain style" or "plain way" was first used by Protestants to refer to the gospels. We attempted above to show linguistically how these forms of literalism follow from the reorganization of authority and the rejection of Roman liturgical religion at the heart of the Reformation. The new textual authority of 'scripture alone' (*sola scriptura*), as distinguished from a tradition of interpretation, demands taking sacred text literally, while the individualist authority of reason demands the rejection of the poetic-aesthetic in other religious registers – for example, sermons. This religious imperative conspires with political interests. Yelle shows how the same literalism used against Catholicism was re-deployed against the language of Indian religion as an imperialist strategy of control through the devaluation of "superstitious" indigenous culture. He cites the anthropologist Webb Keane as distinguishing the same clash of linguistic ideologies in the literalism of Dutch Calvinist missionaries against native Sumbanese, which emphasized the repetitive "formal, textual characteristics of ritual language" and its efficacious or magical effects.

Our task is to position plain style within the complex English religious situation in the 17th century, which witnessed a crisis of religious authority. Once Henry VIII makes the state supreme over religion, politics automatically becomes a matter of contesting religious positions. The Roman church is suppressed, and within the Church of England there are three main strands: Anglo-Catholic or high church; Evangelical or low church, more influenced by the continental reformers; and Latitudinarian or broad church, which promotes, within Protestantism, a tolerant rationality. The Puritans – English Presbyterians – fought to establish Calvinism in England, but ultimately failed. There are other non-conformist, Protestant strands, such as Quakers.

With respect to style, both Catholicisms (Roman and Anglo-Catholic) are the home of poetic-aesthetic language and liturgical action warranted by an institutional authority. By contrast, Anglican Latitudinarians emphasize individual authority, rational scholarship, and empirical-scientific plainness in the interpretation of the poetic-aesthetic tradition. Finally, low church Evangelicals and Puritans are literalists, dependent on the authority of individual inspiration in their confrontation with scripture, and thus embrace plainness. In English religion, both rhetorical and plain English have political and theological significance.

Morrissey (2002: 694) shows that *both* styles are used in preaching in the English Reformed tradition. "Unfigured, expository style" is used for the didactic aspect of demonstrating scripture, while a more "figured style" serves to exhort and apply. The historians Kroll, Ashcroft and Zagorin (1992) argue that in the Restoration, anti-rhetorical stylistic caution was a function, not of science, but of "a nexus of political motives." They write that "[...] it is evident that the Restoration did recognize that language was important as a cultural and political issue." It was not only a means of referring to the world but controlling it. (Its later imperialist use illustrates this.) Negative attitudes to rhetorical style ultimately emerge from "anti-enthusiasm," a rejection of religious dogmatism within Anglican Latitudinarianism. What unites all Anglicans is the poetic-aesthetic English of *The Book of Common Prayer* and the *Authorized King James Version* of the Bible.

6.3 Language and the New Philosophy

It was once orthodoxy among historians to explain plain style almost solely in terms of the rise of science. This approach originated with R. F. Jones (1963) and

Robert Merton (1936). Yet, as we have seen already, scientific plain style was not the source of the normative change, but only one of its multiple manifestations. The real key to modernity is the reorganization of epistemological authority. Kroll, Ashcroft and Zagorin (1992: 16) suggest that Jones' and Merton's "scientism" obscures "the way contemporary attitudes to language might provide access to the cultural shift occurring between 1640 and 1660." The hypothesis implies that science promotes "an active *dislike* of words, resulting in the cultivation of a plain style [...] an anti-rhetorical ideal of transparent referentiality" (emphasis original). Since "science" requires a "utilitarian" grasp of things, language must be forced more radically to "*refer*" to objects in the world. This, they claim, reflects Jones' and Merton's projection of their *own* "scientistic ideals of knowledge and language [...] onto their evidence (Sprat's *History* being a classic case) derived less from a Restoration than a modern, industrial 'utilitarian' bias." It is questionable whether "science required an anti-poetical, anti-metaphorical purge of aesthetics" (Kroll, Ashcroft and Zagorin 1992: 16–17).

Nevertheless, the relation of the New Philosophy to plainness remains crucial to our story. This is because scientism, such as that of Jones and Merton, ultimately provides the biggest intellectual barrier, or stumbling block, to poetic-aesthetic language and provides an intellectual underpinning for ever-increasing secularization. Adolph provides a "list of works [...] in which the utilitarian plain style of the 17th century is defended or at least described" (1968: 359–362). The most famous formulation of plain style in the context of the New Philosophy is in Thomas Sprat, *History of the Royal Society* (1667). In the section entitled "Their manner of discourse," Sprat clearly states the plainness norm:

> THE SECOND PART Sect. XX. Their manner of discourse.
>
> But lastly, in these, and all other businesses, that have come under their care; there is one thing more, about which the Society has been most sollicitous; and that is, the manner of their Discourse: which, unless they had been very watchful to keep in due temper, the whole spirit and vigour of their Design, had been soon eaten out by the luxury and redundance of speech.... They have therefore been most rigorous in putting in execution, the only Remedy, that can be found for this extravagance: and that has been, a constant Resolution, to reject all the amplifications, digressions, and swellings of style: to return back to the primitive purity, and shortness, when men deliver'd so many things, almost in an equal number of words. They have exacted from all their members, a close, naked, natural way of speaking; positive expression; clear senses; a native easiness; bringing all things as the Mathematical plainness, as they can: and preferring the language of Artizans, Countrymen, and Merchants, before that of Wits, or Scholars.

Such explicitness and simplicity are common within the New Philosophy. For example, in Robert Boyle's *On the excellency and grounds of the mechanical hypothesis* (1991 [1674]: 139), we find that the "first thing that I shall mention [...]

is the *intelligibleness* or *clearness* of Mechanical principles and explications." He recommends the clarity of its basic categories of "local motion, rest, bigness, shape order, situation and contexture" and the simplicity of its two Hobbesian physical principles, matter or "material substance" and its motions (1991: 153). All these categories are clear enough to be handled mathematically.

Sprat's norm aims for "primitive purity, and shortness." This happens when "things" and "words" correspond, one to one. In modern terms, to understand a proposition is to understand its truth-conditions – what states of affairs in a world would make it true. Sprat's sharp distinction assumes an intended *correspondence* relation between words and things. To conform to the plain style is to clearly represent the truth conceived in this way. Sprat uses two analogies. First, plain language has the clarity of mathematics. Style, if elaborated for other linguistic functions, unnecessarily makes the relation of language and proposition more complex. The strength of Boyle's categories is that they lend themselves to almost mathematical explicitness; most indeed can be quantified. Sprat's second analogy consists of practical language. Three models are mentioned: "Artizans," "Countrymen" (farmers), and "Merchants." The model is the functioning of language for practical purposes.

As Kroll, Ashcroft and Zagorin remarked, in the science-based picture of the emergence of the plain style, since the whole function of language is to refer, writers ought to suppress linguistic choices that don't explicitly serve this function. To achieve this, it must be explicit. When a natural process can be fully spelt out step by step, it can be represented by an *algorithm* of the steps,a fully explicit procedure. This is a definition of a machine. In the New Philosophy, there is a "mechanization of the world picture" (Dijksterhuis 1969). Because machines are algorithmic, this enables mathematical explicitness. Nature is mathematized (Husserl 1970). This picture implies a *corpuscular philosophy* of mechanical systems consisting only of matter in motion, arranged in a hierarchy of constituents from largest to smallest. Atoms are the smallest indivisible units of law-governed matter out of which everything in the world ultimately consists. In principle, all such mechanisms can be measured and quantified. This concept of reality is the antithesis of Renaissance neo-Platonism, where insight can be gained into a spiritual (i.e. abstract) underlying reality through the analogies of revelatory poetic-aesthetic language.

Sprat's normative characterization of stylistic plainness does not appear from nowhere. It is but one reflection of a deeper philosophical questioning of how language relates to reality, and how it therefore gains its authority. One side of this is empiricist, concerned with input; the other side has to do with certainty in reasoning, with logic and therefore mathematics. This is directly reflected in the two aspects of Sprat's account of plainness: the empirical connection of words and things exemplified by practical activities and the emphasis on the clarity of mathematical reasoning. These are popular linguistic correlates of empiricism and rationalism, of the two sides of the new naturalized philosophy.

The truth and therefore the authority of these new methods of representation must depend on how language works. This leads in turn to a critique of reference and truth. We will look first at the empiricist strand that influenced Sprat. The referential reliability of undisciplined language comes to be viewed with suspicion as the empiricist tradition develops. Like many, Sprat was inspired by Francis Bacon (1561–1626), for whom language itself blocks inquiry in two ways. If we become ensnared in it rather than the world it represents, "when men study words and not matter," it becomes "a distemper of learning" (Bacon 1974: 26–27). Second, language is one of the "idols of the market-place" which distorts understanding (Bacon 1960: 56–58; *The New Organon*, aphorisms I, LX, LIX, LX): "The idols imposed by words on understanding are of two kinds. They are either names of things which do not exist (for as there are things left unnamed though lack of observation, so likewise are there names which result from fantastic suppositions and to which nothing in reality corresponds)." This can be seen as an attack on vain metaphysical notions. Or they are of the second kind: " [...] names of things which exist, but yet confused and ill defined." Examples of the former are Fortune, the Prime Mover, Planetary Orbits, the Element of Fire, and fictions "which originate in false and idle theories." The second class "springs out of a faulty and unskilful abstraction." Bacon's response is to focus attention on matter through an inductive method of systematic observation to establish facts. The Baconian ideal for language is referential transparency with respect to these facts, where the words correspond to classes of things, and learning is advanced. The ideal of a perfect script, or universal language, motivates John Wilkins' *Essay towards a real character and a philosophical language* (1970 [1668]) in the context of the Royal Society.

Sprat was also influenced by the spirit of Hobbes (1588–1679), who formulated the first modern materialist philosophy. Thought is derived from sense experience and reality consists wholly of singular bodies whose substance is matter. Substance equals matter. Everything else, such as universals, consists of merely mental objects generated by language: "Incorporeal body is not a name but an absurdity of speech." We gain knowledge solely through our mechanical interaction with matter. "By the impact of external objects on our organs of sense, 'seemings' or 'phantasms' are produced in the brain and these constitute the ultimate data" (Mintz 1962: 23). Misused, language generates figments motivated by vanity which cause dogmatism that causes civil conflict. Although language naturally misleads, we need it to order sensory input. Hobbes' method is scrupulous linguistic reasoning modeled on Euclid's deductions. This determines truth, derived by reason solely from the impact of matter on our senses.

It was immediately recognized that Hobbes' metaphysics had the potential to undermine faith. Even as his ideas spread, Hobbes was widely considered a *bête noir*. A neo-Platonic defence and alternative was brilliantly formulated by the Cambridge Platonists,in particular Ralph Cudworth and Henry More. Mintz (1962: 80) writes that "criticism of Hobbes [...] [was] written against the background of an idealist philosophy derived from platonic and neo-platonic sources [...]."

However, it is on the continent, not in the inductive Baconian method, that the absolute centrality of the deductive, mathematical, aspect of natural philosophy becomes clear. In natural philosophy, it is in Galileo's method that mathematics first marries observation to yield serious results: to demonstrate how mathematics makes explicit the formulation of the lawful regularities that govern nature. His empiricism takes the form of careful measurement of selected observations yielding quantitative data. Hypotheses from which these can be mathematically deduced are experimentally tested. His empiricism is not purely Baconian or taxonomic, but ultimately experimental. The more rationalist, deductively oriented response to the crisis of authority is most fully articulated by Descartes, who philosophically develops the logical, mathematical aspect of the new philosophy. We have already seen that same aspect both in Sprat's use of mathematics as the key model for plainness in language and Hobbes' stress on Euclidian deductivism.

In fact, it is in England, with Newton, that the mathematicization of nature achieves its first fully modern form, replacing Cartesian science. But, in considering Descartes, we can examine in detail the deeper implications of this mathematical model when it is then applied to the messiness of natural language in various registers – its use in the doctrine of plain style. Like all innovators, Descartes assembles what is available in a new way. As we have seen, the demonstrative nature of explanation was well understood. The theorems of a deductive system depend, first, on its initial axioms, and secondly, on the truth of the premises of each deductive step. Certainty demands proofs, and if one is seeking certainty, this is where to look. In Euclidean geometry, the role of axioms and theorems in constructing proofs was available to every educated person; indeed, as we saw, Hobbes was inspired by Euclid, and Galileo's use of mathematical proportionality is conducted in these terms. The latter's thought, like that of Greek science, remained in the language of geometry: spatial relationships between points, curves, surfaces, and figures. This strongly constrained what could be imagined and reasoned about. When Galileo thinks of quantitative relationships more abstractly, he uses rhetorical algebra, couched in ordinary language, hard to grasp, which limits complexity.

Descartes understands that axiomatic systems are the only way for reason to guarantee propositional truth. All the truths in any mathematical system are implicit in its axioms. The theorems are the non-obvious truths deducible from the axioms, explicit step by explicit step. As Descartes says, each step can be simple, but the result is surprising and complex, and certainty is guaranteed. If the axioms are true, the conclusion must be true. Through reason, each individual mind is compelled to assent. We gain reliable authority. It is within ourselves.

Descartes' own great innovation is algebra. Algebra had recently, in France, reached a new level of abstraction in the recognition that it was not just a method of calculation but a language for which a notation needed to be developed. With such a notation, one could reason with guaranteed results about anything that could be analyzed into the abstract relationships of numbers. Descartes' algebraic notation, more or less the one used today, greatly enables this new kind of abstract thinking. In addition, by inventing analytic geometry, Descartes showed how those geometric figures called conic sections (such as curves, ellipses, and parabolas), literally constructed by geometric procedures by the Greeks, can be represented algebraically. In principle, one can use algebra to reason about anything that can be put into rational numbers. And, if the axioms of the mathematical system are true, one arrives of necessity at new truths which are certain.

The power of this new algebraic language is extraordinary, so we must exemplify it in more detail (my example is from Tabak 2004: 60). Consider the quadratic equation of second degree:

$$ax^2 + bx + c = 0.$$

The letter x represents an unknown *variable*. The number or numbers that, when placed in x, make the equation true, are called the *roots* of the equation. Our aim is to find these roots. That *solves* the equation. On the other hand, the letters a, b, and c represent the *coefficients*. These are the numbers that we know, which serve as input. When we put these numbers into a, b, and c, and solve the equation, we determine the unknown x. We gain new knowledge and this knowledge is certain. The next step is to develop explicit step-by-step methods, computations which can solve each type of equation. These are called *algorithms*. There is indeed an algorithm that can be used to solve this kind of equation, called the *quadratic formula*.

In this context, the real significance of corpuscular philosophy and Hobbes' metaphysics now become clear. To be relevant to algebra, reality *must* be expressible as coefficients from which the roots can be determined. If, as Hobbes asserted, all reality is "matter in motion," it is expressible this way. Reality is comprehensible and perhaps, in principle, technically and politically controllable. In the new philosophy, there is but one substance: matter. It is available to the senses to measure, both on the parameters mentioned above and in terms of motion or change. This is the significance of Hobbes' materialism, and why it was relevant enough to reach cultural levels of dissemination. We then have knowledge – beliefs much more certain than ever achieved before – within reach of reason, not faith. As the origin of reality, Hobbes’ real and therefore “material” God is simply the initiator of motion. Since natural philosophy can be grasped with certainty, and mysteries cashed out empirically, then if God’s activities can be discerned in or behind it, rational natural theology becomes available, unmediated by authority.

Algebra is Descartes’ keystone, as matter in motion is Hobbes’. These are the two pillars of the method, which reaches its fruition in Newton. These define the scientific versions of plainness. First, there is the logical clarity and deductive certainty of axiomatic systems; and second, systematic empirical observation and experiment. These exactly map the two aspects of a new concept of truth for plain style. The pieces lock together inferentially in the new conceptual scheme, creating a new norm of language-use. However, as we saw, this normative ideal segregates expressive, conative, and poetic uses of language. This new version of truth is inexpressible in registers like religion, which employ features that are excluded by plainness.

The new cultural system reflects a deeper cognitive change than simply a method for inquiry into nature. This is illustrated by the striking analogy between Cartesian science and the market economy. Plainness as a cognitive register manifests itself equally in both areas, showing clearly that this is a general change in thinking: in natural philosophy, in economics, as well as in religion. I will briefly sketch out this illuminating relationship.

Market capitalism is also an axiomatic system whose players are possessive individuals (MacPherson 1962). These are free owners of property, initially only their bodies and labor. Just as the new philosophy grows knowledge, the new economy grows wealth, increasing the amount of each possessive individual’s property. Capital investment is a form of hypothesis formation, based on deductions about returns and requiring agents to conform to its axioms. Return on investments is a form of empirical testing. Competition tests alternative hypotheses. All the information and communications used in gathering information, reasoning about the future, making predictions, and writing contracts must be “clear and distinct.” Empirical information, so crucial to business, is the equivalent of Baconian science, defining the economic version of plainness. Successful accumulation leads to ever more successful accumulation. Innovative technologies result in rising productivity, thus more accumulation feeding further investment and returns. Motivation for constant exploratory inquiry, inventiveness, and hence constant change is built into a virtuous circle of rewards. A second secular “soteriology” emerges along with that promised by the nation state: economic salvation, which aligns with religious salvation.

6.4 The problem of scepticism regarding language in Cartesian rationalism and Hobbesian materialism

Just as capitalism demands submission to its axioms, and religion demands faith in its chosen authority, so Descartes must protect this new rationalist cognitive register from scepticism. He does this by treating, not just mathematics, but his whole philosophy as an axiomatic system. Cartesianism is vulnerable to scepticism because it presupposes that what is phenomenologically available to introspection can, in principle, be authoritative – a basis of certain knowledge. But Descartes also realized that the mind is fallible, can be deceived by its senses; that the objective world to be described is only a presupposition of his system. In Euclid, axioms were treated as obvious truths, specifically truths which any inquirer was compelled by reason simply to accept. They are not hypotheses or conjectures. Descartes wants to provide similar indubitable axioms for the new method. These will provide metaphysical assumptions for a newly emergent cultural system, consistent with religion, which would compel reason.

Descartes' method of doubt experimentally commits itself to a sceptical strategy in order to find its limits – things that must be certain. These will form the first premises, the *archai*, of his axiomatic system, philosophical but modeled on mathematics. If these are also certain, then any conclusions involving "clear and distinct ideas" which are deduced step-by-step from them must be true. I will not rehearse Descartes' famous *cogito* and his ontological argument for the existence of a perfect God who guarantees that he is not deceived in his subsequent deductions (Descartes 1960 [1637]).

The problem is that Descartes' axioms are relevant mysteries. In this sense they are rhetorical. They are the very things that cannot be fully grasped, although they have enough logical character to warrant inferences: e.g., if God is perfectly good, then God cannot deceive me. But if their truth conditions cannot be fully grasped they are precisely what is excluded by the plain style. The alternatives are two-fold: either plainly-written religion must be made consistent with naturalism; or there must be segregation of plain and poetic styles representing two different kinds of truth. But from within the plain cognitive register, there appears to be no such thing as "poetic truth" (see Stace 1961: 185–194).

Therefore, we depend on the naturalization of theology. This minimally entails that core religious concepts don't contradict naturalism. But if religion is by definition supernaturalist/Platonist and natural reality is Hobbesian, as it became in England in spite of the Cambridge Platonists, this is impossible. Alternatively, naturalization might demonstrate that nature itself provides evidence for supernaturalism, for example, in its design. This remained the empiricist project. If this lacks credibility, as it came to do in England after the Darwinian revolution, scepticism appears inevitable for empiricists too. There is no rational intellectual barrier to the growing irrelevance of religion. And plain religious language must be irrationalist and literalist.

The 17th-century metaphysical *endoxa* remains common sense today, especially in England. As Heisenberg (1958: 169) pointed out, "[...] the nineteenth century developed an extremely rigid frame for natural science which formed not only science but *the general outlook of great masses of people*. This frame was supplied by the fundamental concepts of classical physics, space, time, matter and causality; the concept of reality applied to the things we could perceive by our senses or that could be observed [....] *Matter was the primary reality*" (emphases mine). Heisenberg's point was that this world-picture is no longer viable.

7 Conclusion: Rhetoric as philosophy and its consequences

Thus, we have inherited the 17th-century sceptical problem. If relativism is embraced and realism abandoned, science as well as religion collapse into solipsism – the relative authority of your culture or just your arbitrary will: a free decision.

Axiomatic systems depend on premises, in which all their truths are implicit. These appear to be of two kinds. The first are *ad hoc* hypotheses, proposed solutions to specific scientific problems, from which testable predictions are mathematically deduced. There is no agreed word for how these arise in the mind: "hypothesis formation," "conjecture," scientific "insight," "imagination," etc. What is increasingly clear is that the structures of underlying premises are rhetorical, as the humanists argued (Grassi 1980). Yet rhetoric today dissipates into many disciplines: literary criticism, linguistics, philosophy, anthropology, sociology, cognitive psychology, theology, and so on. The consensus appears to be that scientific and religious explanations ultimately rest on premises drawn from underlying metaphorical systems: "models and metaphors," to use the title of a seminal book by Max Black (1981). As Harré (1985: 171) puts it, "The generation of the concept at the heart of a theory is [...] a matter of analogy. Building a theory is a matter of developing an appropriate concept by analogy" (see also Black 1979; Hesse 1966; Ortony 1979; and in religion, Soskice 1985). This is the normal pragmatic process of semantic change governed by relevance. Paradigm shifts in science involve the sudden wholesale replacement of one underlying metaphorical system with another: a new rhetoric.

The second kind of premise is the metaphysical and moral presuppositions on which theories rest. These are the rhetorical *archai* – mysteries. It is these deeper premises that have their origin in the poetic-aesthetic taken as revelatory of reality. A theory in which primitive metaphorical systems have a bodily basis – which also provides the conceptual scheme underlying language itself – has been developed by cognitive linguists (Johnson 1987; Lakoff and Johnson 1999). This is an attempt to naturalize the "archaic" source of metaphors behind both non-scientific and scientific premises. But there are also Platonic alternatives and metaphysical interpretations of science based on insights arising from more poetic-aesthetic thinking – a growing convergence at the boundary between metaphysics and science (see the featured articles in *New Scientist* 231, issue 3089 (2016): 29–39).

Historically, the new hegemony of plainness cognitively disabled the phenomenological sense of truth in the poetic-aesthetic language of religion, privatizing and placing it in a progressively less relevant ghetto, labelled irrationality. Conversely, to re-think the metaphysical, moral or religious basis of scientific inquiry in terms of poetic transcendentalist imagination became ever more implausible. On the other hand, "literalist" interpretations of the poetic-aesthetic as "the plain truth" strengthened revelatory fundamentalism, devaluing scientific-empirical inquiry. Lacking such a mode of inquiry, literalists can't de-riddle language. They can't rethink religion because they already know the truth, a truth plainly revealed by authority. In both cases, the hegemony of plain cognitive registers disables inquiry. Each makes the other truth hard to take seriously, as each remains irrelevant to the other's context.

Acknowledgments: An earlier version of this paper was delivered in October 2014 while a Fellow at the Institute of Advanced Study, Durham University. I am grateful to the Institute for supporting the research and to the many others, especially my wife Magdalen, who have responded with insightful criticism and support.

References

Adoph, Robert. 1968. *The rise of modern prose style*. Cambridge, MA: MIT Press.

Arendt, Hannah. 1961. What is authority? In Hannah Arendt, *Between past and future: Six exercises in political thought*, 91–141. London: Faber and Faber.

Bacon, Francis. 1960. *The New Organon and related writings*. Edited by F. Anderson. New York: Liberal Arts Press.

Bacon, Francis. 1974. *The Advancement of Learning and New Atlantis*. Edited by A. Johnston. Oxford: Clarendon Press.
Bizzell, Patricia & Bruce Herzberg (eds.). 2001. *The rhetorical tradition: Readings from classical times to the present*. Boston: Bedford & St. Martin’s.
Black, Max. 1979. More about metaphor. In Andrew Ortony (ed.), *Metaphor and thought*, 19–43. Cambridge: Cambridge University Press.
Black, Max. 1981. *Models and metaphors: Studies in language and philosophy*. Ithaca: Cornell University Press.
Boyle, Robert. 1991 [1674]. About the excellency and grounds of the mechanical philosophy. In M.A. Stewart (ed.), *Selected philosophical papers of Robert Boyle*, 138–154. Indianapolis: Hackett Publishing.
Brooke, John H. 1991. *Science and religion: Some historical perspectives*. Cambridge: Cambridge University Press.
Browne, Thomas. 1906. *The Religio Medici and other writings*. Edited by H. Sutherland. London: J. M. Dent.
Burke, John G. 1974. Hermetism as a renaissance world-view. In Robert S. Kinsman (ed.), *The darker vision of the renaissance: Beyond the fields of reason*, 95–118. Berkeley, CA: University of California Press.
Carse, James P. 2008. *The religious case against belief*. London: Penguin.
Cavanaugh, William. 2002. *Theopolitical imagination: Discovering the liturgy as a political act in an age of global consumerism*. New York: T & T Clark.
Chapman, Geoffrey. 1994. *Catechism of the Catholic Church*. London: Continuum International Publishing.
Descartes, René. 1960 [1637]. *Discourse on method*. Translated by A. Wollaston. Harmondsworth: Penguin.
Dijksterhuis, E. J. 1969. *The mechanization of the world picture*. Translated by C. Dikshoorn. London: Oxford University Press.
Downes, William. 1998. *Language and society*. Cambridge: Cambridge University Press.
Downes, William. 2011. *Language and religion: A journey into the human mind*. Cambridge: Cambridge University Press.
Downes, William. 2018. Prayer as a cognitive register. In Paul Chilton & Monika Kopytowska (eds.), *Religion, language and the human mind*. Oxford: Oxford University Press.
Duffy, Eamon. 1992. *The stripping of the altars: Traditional religion in England c.1400–c.1580*. New Haven & London: Yale University Press.
Graddol, David, Dick Leith & Joan Swann (eds). 1996. *English: History, diversity and change*. London & New York: Routledge and the Open University.
Grassi, Ernesto. 1980. *Rhetoric as philosophy: The humanist tradition*. University Park & London: Pennsylvania State University Press.
Greenblatt, Stephen. 2004. *Will in the world*. London: Norton.
Hamlyn, David W. 1989. *The Penguin history of Western philosophy*. Penguin: London.
Harré, Rom. 1985. *The philosophies of science: An introductory survey*. Oxford & New York: Oxford University Press.
Heath, Malcolm. 2013. *Ancient philosophical poetics*. Cambridge: Cambridge University Press.
Heisenberg, Werner. 1958. *Physics and philosophy*. London: George Allen and Unwin.
Herrick, James A. 2013. *The history and theory of rhetoric: An introduction*. Boston: Pearson.
Hesse, Mary. 1966. *Models and analogies in science*. Notre Dame, IN: University of Notre Dame Press.

Hobbes, Thomas. 1651. *Leviathan*. London.
Husserl, Edmund. 1970. *The crisis of European sciences and transcendental phenomenology*. Translated by David Carr. Evanston, IL: Northwestern University Press.
Jakobson, Roman. 1960. Closing statement: linguistics and poetics. In Thomas Sebeok (ed.), *Style in language*, 350–377. Cambridge, MA: MIT Press.
Johnson, Mark. 1987. *The body in the mind: The bodily basis of meaning, imagination and reason*. Chicago & London: University of Chicago Press.
Jones, Richard Foster. 1963. The rhetoric of science in England of the mid-seventeenth century. In C. Camden (ed.), *Restoration and eighteenth-century literature: Essays in honor of Alan Dugald McKillop*. Chicago: University of Chicago Press for William Marsh Rice University.
Kroll, Richard, Richard Ashcroft & Perez Zagorin. 1992. *Philosophy, science and religion in England 1640–1700*. Cambridge: Cambridge University Press.
Lakoff, George & Mark Johnson. 1999. *Philosophy in the flesh: The embodied mind and its challenge to Western thought*. New York: Basic Books.
MacPherson, Crawford B. 1962. *Political theory of possessive individualism: Hobbes to Locke*. Oxford: Clarendon.
Merton, Robert K. 1936. Puritanism, pietism and science. *The Sociological Review* 28(1). 1–30.
Milroy, James & Lesley Milroy. 1991. *Authority in language: Investigating Standard English*. London: Routledge.
Mintz, Samuel I. 1962. *The hunting of leviathan: Seventeenth-century reactions to the materialism and moral philosophy of Thomas Hobbes*. Cambridge: Cambridge University Press.
Morris, Christopher W. 2011. The state. In George Klosko (ed.), *The Oxford handbook of the history of political philosophy*, 544–560. Oxford: Oxford University Press.
Morrissey, Mary. 2002. Scripture, style and persuasion in seventeenth-century English theories of preaching. *Journal of Ecclesiastical History* 53(4). 686–706.
New Scientist. 2016. Vol. 231, issue 3089.
Oldham-Appleby, Joyce. 1978. *Economic thought and ideology in seventeenth-century England*. Princeton: Princeton University Press.
Ortony, Andrew (ed.). 1979. *Metaphor and thought*. Cambridge: Cambridge University Press.
Panksepp, Jaak. 1998. *Affective neuroscience: The foundations of human and animal emotions*. New York: Oxford University Press.
Plato. 2004. *Gorgias*. Translated by W. Hamilton. London: Penguin.
Plato. 2005. *Phaedrus*. Translated by C. Rowe. London: Penguin.
Plato. 2012. *The Republic*. Translated by C. Rowe. London: Penguin.
Recanati, François. 1997. Can we believe what we do not understand? *Mind and Language* 12(1). 84–100.
Skinner, Quentin. 1978. *The foundations of modern political thought*, vol. 2, *The age of Reformation*. Cambridge: Cambridge University Press, 1978.
Soskice, Janet. 1985. *Metaphor and religious language*. Oxford: Clarendon Press.
Sprat, Thomas. 1959 [1667]. *History of the Royal Society*. London: Routledge and Kegan Paul.
Sperber, Dan. 1996. *Explaining culture: A naturalistic approach*. Oxford: Blackwell.
Sperber, Dan. 1997. Intuitive and reflective beliefs. *Mind and Language* 12(1). 67–83.
Sperber, Dan & Deirdre Wilson. 1995. *Relevance: Communication and cognition*. Oxford: Blackwell.
Stace, W. T. 1961. *Mysticism and philosophy*. London: MacMillan.

Tabak, John. 2004. *Algebra: Sets, symbols and the language of thought*. New York: Facts on File.
Taylor, Charles. 1989. *Sources of the self: The making of the modern identity*. Cambridge: Cambridge University Press.
Toulmin, Stephen Edelston. 1992. *Cosmopolis: The hidden agenda of modernity*. Chicago: University of Chicago Press.
Vickers, Brian. 1984. Analogy versus identity: The rejection of occult symbolism, 1580–1680. In Brian Vickers (ed.), *Occult and scientific mentalities in the renaissance*, 95–164. Cambridge: Cambridge University Press.
Walker, Daniel P. 1975. *Spiritual and demonic magic: From Ficino to Campenella*. Notre Dame & London: University of Notre Dame Press.
Wilkins, John. 1970 [1668]. An essay towards a real character, and a philosophical language. In *The mathematical and philosophical works of the Right Rev. John Wilkins*. London: Frank Cass.
Wimsatt, William K. & Cleanth Brooks. 1962. *Literary criticism: a short history*. New York: Alfred A. Knopf.
Yelle, Robert A. 2013a. *Semiotics of religion: Signs of the sacred in history*. London: Bloomsbury.
Yelle, Robert A. 2013b. *The language of disenchantment: Protestant literalism and colonial discourse in British India*. New York: Oxford University Press.

Jenny Ponzo

The debate over glossolalia between Conservative Evangelicals and Charismatics: A question of semiotic style

1 Introduction

The thesis informing this paper is that religious linguistic (or pseudo-linguistic) phenomena like glossolalia are part of a broader process of meaning-making (i.e., of semiosis: see Peirce 1931–1966; Eco 1995) that defines the semiotic identity of religious groups and that involves a plurality of factors, such as doctrinal and theological presuppositions, interpretative styles, non-linguistic practices, and argumentative and rhetoric styles. This paper studies Christians' glossolalia in the context of a broader semiotic style.[1] To this end, it does not tackle the practice of glossolalia from an ethnographic, anthropological, or linguistic perspective, as numerous studies have done, but it rather centers on the discourse about glossolalia, and especially on the role that the interpretation of some key biblical verses has played in the definition and in the evaluation of this practice.

The analysis focuses in particular on the controversy raised over glossolalia between two religious groups characterized by semiotic styles that are antithetical in many aspects: Charismatics and Conservative Evangelicals. A sample of American and European apologetic texts from both sides will be compared in order to show how the condemnation or the justification of the practice of glossolalia implies broader semiotic issues, and especially different ways to interpret the same biblical verses.

2 Glossolalia and Christianity

Glossolalia is practiced in many religious traditions.[2] In the Christian domain, it is also called "speaking in tongues" and it is considered one of the gifts

1 This paper references the results of broader research discussed in Ponzo (2012).

2 Forms of glossolalia were present for example in ancient Egypt, India, and China, and they are present in many different contemporary cultures (e.g., in shamanic rituals); see Carlyle (1956),

Jenny Ponzo, University of Turin

https://doi.org/10.1515/9781614514329-012

(*charismata*) of the Holy Spirit, consisting in the ability to speak in an unknown language. In Christian literature, the term glossolalia often indicates the ability to speak "spiritual" languages (e.g., angelic languages), in contraposition to xenoglossia, i.e., the ability to speak human foreign languages never learnt by the speaker. Glossolalia has been studied by numerous scholars (e.g., Samarin 1972; Goodman 1969; de Certeau 1996), and the general conclusion is that it cannot be labeled as language. From the point of view of linguistics, glossolalia consists of "strings of syllables, made up of sounds taken from among all those that the speakers know, put together more or less haphazardly but which nevertheless emerge as word-like and sentence-like units because of realistic, language-like rhythm and melody" (Samarin 1972: 227). Moreover, linguists have never attested actual xenoglossia.

The New Testament contains several references to speaking in tongues.[3] The verses about this charisma open numerous interpretative problems that have been solved in different ways by different religious groups. The most controversial issues are the relationship between glossolalia and baptism, the relationship between glossolalia and the other charismata, and the question of the tongues' intelligibility.

In Mark 16:17–18, Jesus lists the signs that will accompany the believers: besides casting out demons and performing other prodigious actions, "they will speak in new tongues."[4] In the episode of Pentecost (Acts 2:1–13), after the manifestation of supernatural signs (a sound from heaven like "the rush of a violent wind" and "Divided tongues, as of fire"), the disciples are "filled with the Holy Spirit" and start to "speak in other languages." This passage entails both the comprehensibility of the tongues, which are recognized by native speakers witnessing the miracle, and their enthusiastic character ("But others sneered and said, 'They are filled with new wine'"). In Acts 10:44–48, while Peter is preaching in Cornelius's house, the Holy Spirit falls upon all the bystanders: not only upon the Hebrews, but also upon the Gentiles, who start "speaking in tongues and extolling God." Since these Gentiles have received the Spirit, Peter orders that they receive the baptism with water as well. In Acts 19:6, Paul baptizes his Ephesian disciples with the imposition of his hands, and they immediately receive the Spirit and start speaking in tongues and prophesying.

Spittler (1996). Analogies with glossolalia can also be found in the apparently nonsensical Hindu mantras (on which, see Yelle 2003).

3 For an extensive historical-critical analysis of the verses concerning the tongues, see Scippa (1982).

4 All the quotations of the Bible in English refer to the NRSV.

In the apostolic age, during an assembly, several believers, seized up by inspiration, intervened, praising God or exhorting their coreligionists by speaking in their native language (prophecy), or in unknown languages (xenoglossia), or in nonsensical languages (glossolalia). Paul warns the Corinthians against the overestimation of the spectacular manifestations and states that the most useful charismata are the ones aimed at the edification of the community, and that the exuberance accompanying the Spirit must be disciplined. In 1 Corinthians 12:7–11, 28–31, Paul lists the charismata and places the tongues in an inferior position. Then, the apostle teaches how to gain the charismata, especially through love, which is the subject of 1 Corinthians 13. 1 Corinthians 13:1 is one of the verses usually quoted by Conservative Evangelicals who criticize the incomprehensibility of glossolalia: "If I speak in the tongues of mortals and of angels, but do not have love, I am a noisy gong or a clanging cymbal." Finally, 1 Corinthians 14 is particularly important in the debate that is our focus, because Paul provides instructions on how to use and to evaluate the gift of tongues, which once more is placed in an inferior position with reference to prophecy. 1 Corinthians and Acts show that glossolalia was rather common among the first Christian communities, but after Paul's critique this practice was gradually abandoned and only survived in single individuals and groups.[5] However, from the very beginning of the 20th century, glossolalia has become one of the main traits characterizing Charismatic groups that, from the U.S., proliferated worldwide.

Charismatics hold that each of the faithful must be baptized with the Holy Spirit, and that this baptism is tied to the reception of the gifts described in the New Testament. The first Charismatic movement was the Pentecostal movement. One of its founders was Charles Parham, who began associating baptism with glossolalia. In 1900, Parham and the students of his biblical school (in Topeka, Kansas) were persuaded that today's believers should live an experience analogous to the Pentecost as it is represented in Acts, where the descent of the Spirit on the disciples was confirmed by the sensible sign of tongues. Although the first Pentecostal communities originated among conservative Protestants in the U.S., the "speaking in tongues" practice soon fueled debates within Evangelical denominations and, as a consequence, some left to found independent communities, called "historical Pentecostal churches." Even though the mainstream Conservative Evangelicals would not approve the doctrine that baptism could only be granted after conversion and sanctification by the tongues, they shared most of the other doctrinal positions of the Pentecostals. For example, they

5 E.g., the Montanists, who originated in Phrygia in the 2nd century and spread across the Roman Empire in the following centuries (Trevett 1996).

believed in the Trinity and in salvation through faith, they practiced the Lord's Supper and, most of all, they considered the Bible as the unique, inspired, and inerrant Word of God.

In the second half of the 20th century, a new Charismatic revival took place. This Neo-Pentecostal movement was characterized by a strong interdenominational and international character. In the last thirty years, a third wave of Charismatic movements has flourished worldwide (see Robeck 2014; Kay 2011). Given their independent and transversal nature, the new Charismatic generations display a wide range of doctrinal positions. In this paper, our focus is restricted to a sample of American and European literature defending and criticizing Charismatic doctrine concerning the practice of glossolalia.

3 Charismatics versus Conservative Evangelicals

According to William James (1902: 1–25), the analysis of the extreme poles of a wide spectrum of religious positions is the most instructive, because it shows in a neat chiaroscuro the traits that in more moderated expressions are more difficult to single out. For this reason, our analysis will study Charismatics' and Conservative Evangelicals' interpretations of glossolalia against each other in some of their most articulated, representative, and extreme expressions.

The main doctrinal difference between the two groups concerns experience. Charismatics stress the importance of direct experience and they encourage the active search for the spiritual gifts received by the first Apostles.[6] Conservatives, on the contrary, tend to affirm that miracles and charismata ceased in the apostolic age, to criticize the ecumenical spirit of many Charismatic movements (mainly because of the doctrinal compromises that ecumenism implies), and to claim that the stress on experience is a carnal weakness challenging the centrality of the Bible, i.e., the principle of *sola scriptura*. Conservative Evangelicals are among the most radical opponents of Charismatics, and this rivalry has led to abundant apologetic literature from both sides. In this apologetic-propagandistic literature, glossolalia is a central issue. As we will see, opposed positions concerning glossolalia are connected to different interpretations of the same biblical verses, different argumentative styles, and the use of different genres of communication.

6 For an updated study of the experience of God's presence in American Charismatic Evangelical communities (and more specifically in the Vineyard Church), see Luhrmann (2012).

Both Conservative Evangelical and Charismatic movements originated in the U.S. but spread widely across Europe.[7] The semiotic style characterizing these groups is therefore very widespread. For example, in his influential book *Fundamentalism*, James Barr (1977) presents an exhaustive study of Conservative movements. Although he focuses on Great Britain, Barr chooses to call these British faithful "Fundamentalists," a term that evidently recalls the U.S. movement founded with the publication of *The Fundamentals* (Dixon and Torrey, 1910–1915). In the introduction, Barr justifies this terminological choice with several reasons, the main one being the doctrinal homogeneity between American and British groups. As our analysis will show, this doctrinal homogeneity extends well beyond English-speaking countries and can be found, for example, in Italy as well. The same is true for Charismatics. Indeed, most of the leaders of both Conservative Evangelical and Charismatic communities in Europe have had direct contacts with the respective movements flourishing in the U.S. and in Great Britain (see e.g., Introvigne and Zoccatelli 2016; Standridge 2001).

In order to study the Charismatic and the Conservative Evangelical semiotic styles, we will focus on the discourse about glossolalia in a sample of three works. The first is *They Speak with Other Tongues* by John Sherrill, published in the U.S. in 1964. This book is still reprinted and easy to find today in both the U.S. and Europe, and it is considered one of the most important texts of Charismatic literature (Introvigne and Zoccatelli 2016; Ponzo 2012; Goodman 1972). Sherrill (1923–1917) was a journalist and a prolific writer. Together with his wife Elizabeth, he founded a publishing house of religious books.[8] The second work is *The Charismatics: A Doctrinal Perspective*, published in 1978 by John F. MacArthur Jr. (born 1939).[9] MacArthur is a minister of the Grace Community Church (California) and an active broadcaster. He holds Conservative Evangelical positions, such as young-earth creationism,[10] literalism, inerrancy,[11] and cessationism.[12] MacArthur is

7 And also in Africa and Asia. On the origins and diffusion of Fundamentalist and Conservative Evangelical denominations, see Barr (1977), Marsden (1980), Harding (1991), Harris (1998), Ruthven (2007).

8 The Sherrills' website is http://www.elizabethsherrill.com/ (last accessed on 16 July 2016).

9 MacArthur's website is https://www.gty.org/ (last accessed on 16 July 2016).

10 Young-earth creationism is a doctrine based on a literalist interpretation of the Genesis and according to which the whole universe was created by direct acts of God between 5,700 and 10,000 years ago. See MacArthur (2001), Numbers (2006).

11 Inerrancy is a doctrine stating that the Bible, the inspired Word of God, is completely without error. See Barr (1977); Youngblood (1984); Jelen (1989); Jelen, Wilcox and Smidt (1990); Bartkowski (1996).

12 Cessationism is a doctrine stating that the miracles and charismata ceased in the Apostolic age.

a strenuous opponent of Charismatics. His book contains an exhaustive and representative catalogue of all the doctrinal arguments used by Conservative Evangelicals against Charismatics, and it clearly states Conservatives' interpretative principles. Sherrill's book is one of the numerous targets of MacArthur's critique. The third work is *Carismosofia: paralleli fra occultismo e carismaticismo* 'Parallels between Charismaticism and Occultism' by Nicola Martella (1995).[13] Martella is an Italian author. He is a former member and teacher of the Italian Evangelical Bible Institute, a blogger,[14] and the founder of a small publishing house. He professes conservative principles; for example, he rejects evolutionism and any interpretation of the Bible that "excessively" stresses symbolic meanings, while he believes in verbal inspiration and in the inerrancy of the "original" scriptures. Martella's book is a radical critique of Charismatics, and its arguments are fully coherent with the arguments and the principles articulated by MacArthur, thus proving that the semiotic styles we are focusing on are not confined to the U.S. nor to the English-speaking countries, but have a much broader diffusion in western culture.

4 Instances of the authors

According to the theory of enunciation, each empirical author disseminates traces of his or her identity in the text and builds an avatar that can be more or less similar to his or her actual self (Benveniste 1966). In apologetic literature, in order to build a persuasive discourse, the author has first of all to convince the reader of his or her competence, experience, and authority. The strategies for the construction of an effective instance significantly vary between Charismatic and Conservative Evangelical authors.

They Speak with Other Tongues is an autobiographical narrative in which Sherrill tells how he received the gift of tongues and the baptism of the Spirit. The protagonist's spiritual and intellectual itinerary is similar to a journalistic report of an inquiry, based on biblical sources and on first-person testimonies of Charismatic believers. The story, set in New York in 1959, begins with a doctor diagnosing John with cancer. Shocked, John enters a church, where a seminarian is reading the verses concerning Nicodemus (John 3). The seminarian comments: "as long as Nicodemus was trying to come to an understanding of Christ through his logic, he could never succeed. It isn't logic, but

13 No English version of the book is available. All translations from this book are my own.
14 Martella's blog is http://www.puntoacroce.altervista.org/ (accessed 7 May 2018).

an experience, that lets us know who Christ is" (Sherrill 2004 [1964]: 14). The narrator observes: "I didn't know it then, but this brief address was to hold the key to the most astonishing experience of my life" (Sherrill 2004 [1964]: 14). Indeed, two days later John undergoes a difficult operation and, during a painful night, Christ appears to him as a light, leaving him in a state of extraordinary well-being.

This *ouverture* contains some important elements characterizing Sherrill's semiotic style. Firstly, by quoting his own experience and using an informal language, the narrator triggers the reader's empathy. The beginning of the religious experience is connected to illness, to a state of weakness from which religion can offer relief, thus appealing to people sharing a similar pain. Secondly, a strong emphasis is put on the individual subject: the whole text is built as a personal discourse. Thirdly, the affirmation that experience is more important than logical reasoning is one of the key concepts in Sherrill's Charismatic perspective. Fourthly, doctrinal principles and other important concepts are not reported by Sherrill using the first person, but they are attributed to different characters in the course of the narrative. The narrator does not want to present himself as a doctrinal authority, but wants to create a feeling of complicity with the reader by sharing his experience. For example, Sherrill (2004 [1964]: 15) builds up the credibility and authority of his own character by attributing to one of his neighbors the following sentences: "I'm going to talk to you [John] about your religious life, and I have no right to assume that it lacks anything. After all, you've been writing for *Guideposts* for ten years; you respect religion, you've studied it from many angles [...]."

Although McArthur's work opens with a direct reference to the reader (the first chapter is entitled "Are you one of the have-nots?"), in the rest of the book the style is more impersonal and consists in rational argumentation based on a set of doctrinal principles clearly stated. Conservative authors communicate the idea that they intend to guide the faithful who have been led astray by the proliferation of Charismatic practices. For example, in the presentation of Martella's book we read, "By publishing his books, Nicola Martella affirms that one of the main needs of our times is the development of biblical discernment. Indeed, there are various attacks and challenges directed against the church that must be known and contrasted" (Martella 1995: 4). Martella warns the Christians against Satan's deceit and he expresses "love towards all those who endorse these imperatives: only Christ is the Lord and savior! Only the Bible is the word of God! Only by grace, and through faith, we can be saved!" Martella makes numerous references to his in-depth studies of the Bible and to his experience as a spiritual advisor, thus demonstrating his competence and authoritativeness in the treated subject.

5 Charismatic interpretative style

5.1 Argumentative style and interpretative principles

Sherrill makes narrative his main argumentative strategy. His text reports the experiences of numerous Pentecostal and Charismatic leaders like Charles Parham and David Du Plessis. These stories, narrated either in first or in third person, have a similar structure, which we can describe using a narratological scheme (Propp 1968; Greimas 1970–1983; Greimas & Courtès 1979):

a) Initial situation of equilibrium: the protagonist is generally an average believer, belonging to a mainstream religious community.
b) Rupture of the equilibrium (lack): the protagonist starts feeling a lack in his religious life. The passage to this second phase can happen in two distinct ways:

> The protagonist starts feeling unsatisfied with his religious life, mainly because of the comparison with the biblical narratives of the first Christians' deeds and experiences. For example:
>
> [...] Harald Bredesen, although he'd been busily involved in the work of his church, had also been a dissatisfied young man. It seemed to him that his religious life had no vitality to it, especially when he compared his experiences with those of the earliest Christians. "There was an excitement, a stirring of life in the young Church," Bredesen said. "The Church today, by and large, has lost this. You've felt it, I'm sure. Where are the changed lives? Where are the healings? Where is the belief that men will die for?" (Sherrill 2004 [1964]: 24–25)
>
> [...] Parham, decided he must do something about his religious life. He had been reading the Book of Acts and the letters of Paul and comparing the feebleness he found in his own ministry with the power reflected there. Where were his new converts? Where were his miracles? His healings? Surely, he said to himself, the Christians of the first century had a secret that he and his church no longer possessed. (Sherrill 2004 [1964]: 44)

The sense of lack can also derive from a dramatic event. In Sherrill's case, the dramatic events are his illness, which breaks the order of his "normal" life, and the subsequent supernatural apparition of Jesus at the hospital. Illness and miracle work as liminal experiences bringing the individual in a state of unusual proximity to a supernatural dimension, which momentarily irrupts into ordinary life. The cessation of this contact with the divine, the exit from this liminal status, and the return to the normal routine leave the subject with a feeling of lack and frustration inciting him to undertake a new quest. By becoming aware of a lack in his religious life (note the recurring series of rhetorical questions), the subject identifies his "object of value," i.e., the goal of his quest. In order to obtain the spiritual gifts, the subject has to unveil a mystery or a secret lost many centuries ago.

c) Competence: the first step in the subject's quest for a superior religious life is the acquisition of a "competence" or knowledge, i.e., a know-how that will enable him to successfully accomplish his decisive performance. Dialoguing with other people in a similar position and learning their stories are important components of this phase. Nevertheless, its main element consists in an intense study of the Bible, aimed at deciphering the secret allowing human beings to perform miracles, to receive charismata, and to keep in direct touch with the deity. The interpretation of the scriptures must be accompanied by prayer, which promotes a good understanding of the texts and fosters the reception of the gifts. For example:

> [...] Bredesen had begun to read the biblical accounts of the early churches with these questions in mind, and almost instantly he fell upon a clue. The more he read, the more he became convinced that the first-century Christians received their vitality from [...] the baptism in the Holy Spirit. Bredesen determined that he was going to have this experience for himself, and went about it by taking a vacation. He [...] ensconced himself in a mountain cabin and there began to pray around the clock. He made up his mind to stay in that cabin until he reached a new level of communication with God. (Sherrill 2004 [1964]: 25)

d) Performance and sanction: when the subject has reached the necessary competence, he is ready to undertake his performance, i.e., speaking in tongues. The gift of tongues is the tangible proof of the positive "sanction": the reception of the baptism in the Holy Spirit. The acquisition of the ability to use glossolalia and xenoglossia is described sometimes as a spontaneous flow, sometimes as the result of a willing effort. For example:

> With a sudden burst of will I [Sherrill] thrust my hands into the air, turned my face full upward, and at the top of my voice I shouted:
>
> "Praise the lord!"
>
> It was the floodgate opened. From deep inside me [...] came a torrent of joyful sound. It was not beautiful, like the tongues around me. [...] I didn't care. It was healing, it was forgiveness, it was love too deep for words and it burst from me in wordless sound. After that one shattering effort of will, my will was released, freed to soar into union with Him. No further conscious effort was required to me at all, not even choosing the syllables with which to express my joy. (Sherrill 2004 [1964]: 160)

> At last one morning while he was standing outside the cabin praying aloud, a stillness seemed to settle over the hills. Every fiber of Bredesen's body tensed, as if his whole being were entering into a new plane of awareness. He stopped speaking for a moment. and when he began again, out of his mouth came [...] "the most beautiful outpouring of vowels and consonants[...]." [Later Bredesen finds out he was speaking Polish, a language he did not know at all.] (Sherrill 2004 [1964]: 25)

Bredesen's example is exceptional because, in his case, the reception of the tongues happens in solitude, while most of the accounts report that it takes place in presence of the community. Indeed, the tongues work not only as a sign sent to from the Spirit to the individual, but also as a proof that the individual actually belongs to the community (see § 7).

Christ's apparition (see above) completely changes Sherrill's approach to the sacred text. Reading the Bible after this supernatural event, John discovers a new kind of interpretation, enlightened and vivified by his personal and direct experience: "Reading the Bible was a brand-new experience, because I could understand for the first time a lot that had puzzled me. How Jesus, for instance, could have recruited disciples simply by saying: 'Follow me.' That was easy to believe now: that Presence I'd felt was something you'd follow to the ends of the earth" (Sherrill 2004 [1964]: 21).

Nevertheless, the miraculous apparition is not followed by other supernatural experiences. John finds out that the stagnant and frustrating phase following the first encounter with Christ is common among Christians. The emotional impact of the experience fades away, but according to John memory is not enough, and hence a quest for new experiences starts. The success of this quest is represented by the achievement of tongues, which determines a radical change in John's life: he is joyful, patient, and open-minded; he has a better relationship with the others; he is not shy any more; and he reaches a heightened level of comprehension of the scriptures. As the narrator says, the Spirit can make a hero out of an ordinary man. This affirmation represents an explicit promise of personal fulfilment and self-realization. Charismatic religion grants the individual a special status, a privileged spiritual dimension and an extraordinary personal and direct relationship with God (Samarin 1972: chap. 12; Csordas 1997: chap. 2).

Although glossolalia also exists outside Christianity, what distinguishes the Christians' glossolalia is its relationship with a sacred written text. In the stories of the Pentecostal and Charismatic leaders reported by Sherrill, a series of practices are experimented with in order to make the sacred written text live, to put it "on stage," to act it. Indeed, even the lack of contact with Jesus is lived by John in terms of a personal identification with the biblical narrative: "And was this all, now, that I would ever have? I felt a little as the disciples must have felt when, after Christ had walked beside them for a while, He was suddenly gone" (Sherrill 2004 [1964]: 21). In Sherrill's work, the sacred text is a source guiding action and promoting the experience of the divine.

5.2 The interpretation of the biblical text

After meeting members of Charismatic movements and after his first experiences (Jesus's apparition, participation in services with people speaking in tongues), John starts studying the Bible searching for answers and guidance. Sherrill's book reports several quotations from the scriptures. Sherrill's interpretation can be summarized in the following scheme:

Table 1: Speaking in tongues in the Bible.

SIGN that the Holy Spirit has entered a believer		**GIFT** continual, long-lasting, healing	
Mark 16:17	**Acts**	**1 Corinthians**	**Romans**
– First attestation of the tongues as a sign.	– Proof of the descent of the Spirit on someone (10:45–46). – Expression of the Holy Spirit through men (2:4). – Ordinary practice among believers (11:15).	– Tongues help the believer in self-edification and prayer. – Tongues edify the Church granting her the ability to communicate with God.	– Tongues help the believer when he/she prays without knowing exactly what to ask for.

One of Sherrill's most developed and significant hermeneutical reflections is presented in the episode narrating the story of Charles Parham. Dissatisfied with his religious life, Parham opens a school where he and his disciples study the scriptures trying to understand the "secret" of the fullness of the first Christians' religious life. His disciples analyze the episodes in which the believers encountered the Holy Spirit, and they point out five passages in which the experience of the Spirit seems to be connected to the gift of tongues. Sherrill includes in his text the direct quotation of Acts 2:1–4 (tongues at Pentecost in Jerusalem); Acts 8:14–19 (imposition of hands and reception of the Spirit in Samaria); Acts 9:17–18 (baptism of Paul in Damascus); Acts 10:44–46 and Acts 19:1–6 (descent of the Spirit in Cornelius's house and at Ephesus).

The selection of the passages is based on the keyword "baptism" (in the case of Pentecost, the reference would be Acts 1:4–5), and more specifically on "the baptism being received for the first time" (Sherrill 2004 [1964]: 47). Actually, even in the Greek texts it is not easy to distinguish the passages narrating conversion, baptism with water, baptism with imposition of hands, baptism in spirit, and effusion or descent of the Spirit. Such a distinction is not pertinent for the Charismatic interpreters,[15] who show therefore a certain terminological vagueness. Parham

15 It is instead very important for some conservative commentators, e.g., Standridge (2001).

recognizes that the tongues are surely present in the accounts of the three baptisms, but not in the case of Paul and in Samaria. Surely the interpretative style proposed by Parham's group is far from literalism. Indeed, the theory concerning the tongues in Paul's conversion and in Samaria appears weakly founded on a scriptural basis, but it is presented only as an interpretative hypothesis.

What is interesting is the way in which this hypothesis is verified. After the biblical study, the group starts to make empirical experiments. They intensely but unsuccessfully pray for a whole day, then a woman reminds them that in many of the episodes described in the scriptures prayer was accompanied by one action: the imposition of hands. She therefore asks Parham to lay his hands upon her. Immediately after this "baptism," she starts speaking in tongues.[16] Thus, the confirmation of the interpretative hypothesis derives from the enacting of the biblical narratives, from the reconstruction of a "magical" ritual that has to be performed in a precise way in order to bring about some specific effects. Only the success of the practical experiment can sanction the correctness of the interpretation of the Bible. Sherrill's reader, therefore, has to cope with two different but interdependent and almost equally powerful sources of authority. The first is of course the Bible, the second is the testimony of the experimenters of the Word.

Sherrill's text, by gathering the stories of a number of personal experiences, presents a clear narrative model, an *exemplum* to follow in order to undergo a process of conversion and to obtain a more satisfying religious life. In this sense, this apologetic genre could be compared to traditional hagiography.[17] Since Sherrill's work intends to be first of all a persuasive testimony, it is difficult to identify a coherent and precise interpretative style in it. Sherrill is not tied to a strictly literal interpretation of the Bible and does not analyze systematically all the verses concerning glossolalia. The prescriptions of 1 Corinthians on the correct use of the gift of tongues, for example, are mentioned quite hastily, and the episode of Ephesus (Acts 19) is only superficially treated, because it is not directly referred to the baptism in the Spirit. Sherrill's interpretative hypothesis is based on some simple considerations:

---

16 Sherrill does not mention the fact that Paul had prohibited women from publicly speaking in tongues (1 Corinthians 14). This prescription is of course never observed in Charismatic gatherings. It is instead used by Conservatives like Martella (1995) to show that Charismatic practices do not comply with the scriptures.

17 According to Leone (2010: 1), "[...] saints are among the most formidable communication media of Catholicism. Through saints, the Church proposes some narrative models of spiritual perfection. By embracing such models, believers are able to conform to certain religious values." The autobiographical account proposed by Sherrill has the same function: presenting in a persuasive way a model to gain spiritual perfection.

1. tongues have two functions: sign and gift (see above);
2. they can be classified in two types, both deriving from the Holy Spirit: comprehensible and existing tongues, and "spiritual tongues" that human beings can pronounce without direct comprehension;
3. everything that happened in the first Christian communities and everything that the Apostles did and lived in first person can happen again to ordinary people, if they let themselves be guided by the Spirit.

In Sherrill's account, the sacred text is always consulted in moments of difficulty or crisis. The biblical stories provide the criterion for evaluating the reality lived by the interpreter. The events narrated in the Bible constitute an ideal situation to be reproduced in the present. The source of today's problems is found in the distance from the condition of spiritual perfection of the origins. The interpreter, therefore, tries to imitate the actions narrated in the sacred text, to bring back to life rituals and practices allowing him to renew a direct relationship with God that were lost over the centuries. If the interpreter's imitation of the biblical events has the same effects experienced by the biblical characters, then the interpretation of the text is correct. Emotions and the achievement of supposedly supernatural experiences play a vital role in this type of verification of biblical interpretation. Rationalistic objections do not hold value in the face of such an interpretative style, which is nevertheless materialistic to some degree (i.e., measured on the base of concrete, "physical" results). Indeed, Charismatics' opponents accuse them of being "carnal," of preaching a Gospel of the immediate, immanent good (e.g., Martella 1995, Standridge 2001).

From a semiotic perspective, Sherrill's text portrays what could be defined as a "pragmatic interpreter," who bases his interpretation on facts more than on words. Facts experienced by the interpreter take the role of tokens of the types described in the Bible. In Sherrill's discourse, the problem for the interpreter is first and foremost to understand what kind of actions or facts are designated by specific biblical expressions (e.g., "baptism"), and what effects they had and can still have. The only way to find an answer is to experimentally recreate the biblical facts in the first person. The Bible becomes therefore a sort of scenario, a text to be put on stage, to be lived or *acted*. The instance of the "pragmatic interpreter" emerging from Sherrill's discourse assigns therefore to the scriptures a particular performative value. The Bible is read as a sort of handbook to acquire the power and the gifts of the Holy Spirit, to learn how to accomplish miracles, or simply how to overcome anguish and to live better. It is not surprising that its opponents often underline the similarity between Charismatic religion and magic. Moreover, the Charismatics' antagonists often argue that the identification with the role played by the Apostles and the proximity that Charismatics perceive between their experiences and what is narrated in the scriptures lead many to believe that they are the addressees of some sort of personal revelation (e.g., Martella 1995; MacArthur 1978).

Ethnographic research collecting further narratives of conversion, of baptism with the Holy Spirit, and of the receipt of tongues should verify to what extent Sherrill's discourse consists in an argumentative strategy or reflects an actual pattern. Indeed, given the importance of tongues as a sign of belonging to the community of the baptized with the Spirit, the group's direct influence plays a considerable role in the acquisition and performance of glossolalia.[18] In Charismatic groups, the individual study of the Bible is often a less determinant factor than social pressure in triggering conversion and the consequent reception of the charisma. In concrete practice, therefore, the individuals' search for the charisma is based both on the imitation of the community and on the imitation of the Bible itself, with an oscillating balance between these two poles. Goodman (1972), for example, reports 29 conversion stories, mainly from members of a Mexican Charismatic group. Some of these stories contain the motif of the imitation of the Apostles. Juan D.L., for example, says that he wanted to become a minister and was sent by his congregation to study at a biblical institute, where he prayed for three years for tongues, but in vain. The reason Juan gives for this prayer is that he and his community follow "the system of [...] the first ministers, as described in Matthew 7, that is, that a person, in order to become a minister, must be baptized by the Holy Spirit" (Goodman 1972: 28). Juan finally receives the baptism and the tongues after a bishop of his church imposes his hands upon him. Another man, Salvador, on the contrary, receives the tongues during a service without any knowledge of the biblical example:

> Before knowing anything about the Gospel, I started attending some services [...]. Neither did I know anything about the Holy Spirit. [...] It was only my third time of going to a service, and I was told that we would pray for two women so that they would receive the Holy Spirit. [...] I started praying for them. And seeing the manifestation of the Holy Spirit in them, it was given to me that I should sing the praise of the Lord in tongues [....] (Goodman 1972: 31)

In many cases, therefore, the performance of glossolalia is determined by social imitation and pressure more than by the desire to enact the Bible. However, the fact that Sherrill proposes the model of the pragmatic interpreter is significant,

18 The value of the tongues as the proof of both the baptism in the Spirit and the belonging to the community can sometimes entail pressure and coercion on the individual: this is one of the main arguments used against Charismatics, see e.g., MacArthur (1978) and Martella (1995). For an academic study of the community's role in encouraging and triggering conversion, glossolalia, and baptism, see Goodman (1972), Lofland and Skonovd (1981). See also below, § 6.

firstly because it is an index of the founding role that Charismatics assign to the sacred text, albeit maybe more from the theoretical-doctrinal than from the practical point of view; and secondly because it provides a discursive and argumentative model characterizing Charismatic semiotic style.

6 Conservative interpretative style

6.1 Argumentative style and interpretative principles: MacArthur

MacArthur lists and explains "five principles for sound biblical interpretation." The first and most important is the literal principle:

> *The literal principle* means understanding Scripture in its natural, normal sense. That is, what are the customary meanings of the words being used? If God wants to communicate His Word to us, He will do it in the most obvious and simple fashion possible [....] Once we abandon the literal interpretation, we discard all hope of achieving accuracy. Instead we have a free-for-all where only the imagination rules. (MacArthur 1978: 44)

The second is the "historical principle": interpretation must be based on an understanding of the historical context where the text was produced. The third is the "grammatical principle," i.e., the study of the meaning of each word and of the syntax, especially of the Greek text. MacArthur (1978: 46) partially reassures those who do not know Greek: "By this time perhaps you are saying, 'Good grief! I don't know Greek [...]. I'll never be able to study my own Bible.' Yes, you can – at your own level." This clearly establishes a hierarchy between the common reader and the more learned one. The fourth is the "synthesis principle," which can be identified with the non-contradiction principle and with "what the old reformers used to call *analogia scriptura* [...], based on the idea that no part of the Bible contradicts any other part" (MacArthur 1978: 46). The fifth is the "practical principle," according to which the believer applies what he reads in the Bible to his or her life. Finally, a correct interpretation of the Bible necessarily needs "the illumination of the Holy Spirit" (MacArthur 1978: 47).

Moreover, MacArthur categorically states that God's revelation is concluded, that no new revelation is possible until God speaks again in the end of times, and that "the canon" is perfectly inerrant and derives from an historical process guided by God. He is much concerned in defending the principle of *sola scriptura* and the unique authority of the Bible.

6.2 The interpretation of the biblical text: Martella

Martella's argumentation can be summarized as follows: the glossolalia of today's Charismatics is not a charisma and does not correspond to the original phenomenon described in the New Testament. Table 2 illustrates this:

Table 2: Glossolalia in Martella's argumentation.

New Testament glossolalia	Charismatics' glossolalia
was a clear and comprehensible language (Acts 2:8–1, 10:47, 11:17; 1 Cor. 4:6, 8–11; 1 Cor. 13:1).	is an ecstatic, psychotic, and inarticulate language.
did not manifest itself in all the baptized (1 Cor. 12:30).	is considered the indispensable sign of the baptism in the Spirit.
was not the only charisma received by the believers (Mark 16:16–17; Hebrews 2:3f).	is most often the only charisma received.
was the less important charisma, because it did not edify the church (1 Cor. 14).	is considered the most important charisma.
fades away at the end of the apostolic age (1 Cor. 13:8).	can have mediumistic or demonic characteristics.
is performed in order, with decorum, and only by men (1 Cor. 14).	is mostly performed in disorder, in ecstatic states, especially by women.

Herein, we will only focus on some key points of Martella's argumentation. The first is the centrality of Paul (see also Barr 1977), for example:

> Reading the NT we find these biblical elements: glossolalia was a language produced by the Spirit; it happened in a language that was unknown to the speaker; it was addressed to God, thus spiritually edifying the speaker. In public, it was only allowed to two or three people in turn (not simultaneously) and only if there was someone translating (1 Corinthians 14:27f.). (Martella 1995: 70)

This passage vaguely refers to "the NT" but is actually a summary of 1 Corinthians 14, although only one verse of that chapter is cited.

A second noteworthy element in Martella's interpretative style is his use of the historical method. Martella affirms that Mark 16:17–18 is often quoted by Charismatics, but that two of the most ancient manuscripts do not include the verses 9–20 and other manuscripts include them only as a gloss, i.e., as a marginal explanation added by a copyist in order to amend the abrupt end of the text. "This," Martella (1995: 71) argues, "should induce us not to use these verses to formulate doctrines." However, a few lines below, Martella cites without reservation the Letter to the Hebrews, the authenticity of which is also very uncertain (Corsani and Buzzetti 1996). Hebrews 2:3–4 is quoted together with many other verses, especially from Acts, because it bears testimony to the plurality of extraordinary events that took place during the apostolic age. By referencing these passages, Martella intends to prove both the exceptionality of the apostolic age and the fact that today's Charismatic emphasis on glossolalia is not justified by the scriptures.

A third point is the distinction between intelligible and ecstatic languages. According to Martella (1978: 72), "Paul rejects all ecstatic speaking as not being suitable for communication and for the Church's edification. The tongues spoken in the enthusiastic movements today are not tongues of the Pentecost type, but ecstatic, inarticulate and psychotic languages." Martella traces therefore a neat distinction between Charismatics' glossolalia and the xenoglossia of the apostles at Pentecost. This thesis finds however an obstacle in 1 Corinthians 14, where Paul refers to tongues with the same terminology used in Acts and describes the phenomenon as a charisma, even though he asserts that tongues are incomprehensible without translators. Martella (1995: 73) interprets 1 Corinthians 14 in light of the historical context of its production, emphasizing, e.g.,the influence played by "gnosis, mystery religions, Judaic mysticism" on the Corinthian community. When he stresses the difference between prophecy (comprehensible, edifying the church) and glossolalia, Martella proposes his view in a subtle way, by adding to Paul's words a dysphoric connotation. In Martella's interpretation, Paul's sentence "Those who speak in a tongue build up themselves" (1 Corinthians 14:4) becomes "Those who speak in tongues only think for themselves," while glossolalia "is not useful at all to the Church" (Martella 1995: 73).

The principle according to which Paul rejects all ecstatic speech undermines the whole discourse of Martella by casting an unresolved ambiguity upon it. This principle is questionable under several aspects. Firstly, although he assigns a preeminent position to prophecy and strictly restricts this practice, Paul says that he himself speaks in tongues and wishes this charisma for all his Christian fellows (1 Corinthians 18–19:5). Furthermore, Martella does not take into consideration the similarities between glossolalia and prophecy. For example, the prophecy episode narrated in Numbers 11:25 has many analogies with the Pentecost,[19] while in several passages prophecy is associated with an enthusiastic state.[20] Therefore,

19 "Then the Lord came down in the cloud and spoke to him [Moses], and took some of the spirit that was on him and put it on the seventy elders; and when the spirit rested upon them, they prophesied."
20 E.g., 1 Samuel 10:5–6: "[...] you will meet a band of prophets coming down from the shrine with harp, tambourine, flute, and lyre playing in front of them; they will be in a prophetic frenzy. Then the spirit of the Lord will possess you, and you will be in a prophetic frenzy along with them and be turned into a different person."

Martella's radical distinction is not totally justified on a scriptural basis. It is probably due to two practical reasons. Firstly, Conservatives are careful to underline the dangers of ecstatic phenomena that could come from evil entities cheating the believer who gives emotions and experience an excessive importance. Secondly, it is important for them to defend the authenticity and respectability of prophecies, because a significant part of their doctrine – especially as far as the Second Coming is concerned – is based on them (Barr 1977).

Another key concept in Martella's argumentation is that tongues ceased very soon. This affirmation is mainly based on a comparison between the Pentecost episode and the episode of the conversion in Cornelius's house. Martella attributes a particular importance to Acts 11:15, where Peter, who is narrating the second event, says: "And as I began to speak, the Holy Spirit fell upon them just as it had upon us at the beginning." Martella (1995: 72) associates the fall of the Spirit with the tongues described in Acts 10:44–48 and affirms that the phenomenon observed at Pentecost must be identical to the one in Cornelius's house, otherwise Peter would not order the baptism of the Gentiles (see § 1 above); the second step in Martella's reasoning is a generalization, based on the implication, "At the beginning ⇔ nevermore," where the double arrow should be read as "if and only if": if Peter says "at the beginning" referring to Pentecost, it means that the tongues are a transitory phenomenon, which only takes place in crucial moments in the mission of the primeval church and then nevermore.

Martella (1995: 74) introduces at this point another important distinction:

> It is now necessary to distinguish between the language spoken [...] at Pentecost, and the one Paul refers to in his epistle to the Corinthians. In the first case, it is not the common phenomenon of glossolalia (ecstatic language), but *xenoglossia*, i.e., speaking in a logical way a foreign language normally unknown. After Acts, the only place where the tongues are mentioned is 1 Corinthians, where the phenomenon is preeminently ecstatic; Paul does not approve it!

Therefore, according to Martella, in the short time between Pentecost and the moment of the writing of 1 Corinthians (barely more than twenty years) tongues completely ceased and were substituted by ecstatic and senseless glossolalia. Martella seems to consider only the canonical order of the texts, and not the historical order of their composition (1 Corinthians, Acts, Mark, Mark's ending). Martella's argumentation can be represented in a semiotic square[21]:

---

21 The semiotic square's components: S1 and S2 are contraries (two elements arbitrarily chosen, belonging to the same semiotic level but opposite and without common features); S1 and nonS1 are contradictories, they logically derive from the contraries; nonS1 and nonS2 are subcontraries (they are not totally opposed but have common traits); between S1 and nonS2 there is a relation of implication (Greimas 1970–1983).

Table 3: Martella's distinction of glossolalia from other types of language.

Glossolalia (S1)	Xenoglossia (S2)
Logical language (nonS2)	Ecstatic language (nonS1)

This square highlights some problematic points in Martella's discourse. Firstly, the opposition between glossolalia and xenoglossia is the result of an interpretation. Indeed, for Martella glossolalia is not a language, but a sequence of senseless sounds. However, the scriptures refer to both glossolalia and xenoglossia with the same terms.[22] Therefore, the distinction proposed by Martella is not based on a strict scriptural warrant. In order to overcome this problem, Martella counterposes the logical and ecstatic nature of the two phenomena (subcontraries). Martella stresses that xenoglossia means speaking in a logical way in a foreign language, but his accent on the contribution of reason introduces another important issue. Although the book of Acts does not specify to what degree the disciples were capable of understanding and controlling what they said in tongues, Martella opposes xenoglossia as a form of active speech to glossolalia as a form of passive speech, and he attributes an extremely dysphoric connotation to passivity. Concerning the contradictories, the contraposition between xenoglossia and ecstatic language seems to come from 1 Corinthians 14, where Paul says that glossolalia is produced by the spirit and not by the intelligence, and he stresses its incomprehensibility and disorder. However, between Pentecost and the Corinthians' glossolalia there is a striking similarity, which is expressed in Act 2:13 (where some of the bystanders think that the apostles are drunk) and 1 Corinthians 14:23 (where Paul warns that if uninitiated join the assembly during the speeches in tongues, they can think that the Christians are crazy). Significantly, Martella does not mention either of these verses.

In other passages, however, Martella is much more precise in the grammatical and semantic analysis of the Greek text's words. This is evident, for example, in Martella's interpretation of 1 Corinthians 13:8 ("Love never ends. But as for prophecies, they will come to an end [in the Italian version quoted by Martella: "will be abolished"]; as for tongues, they will cease; as for knowledge, it will come to an end"). According to Martella (1995: 74–75), the cessation of both prophecies

22 The most recurring formula in the New Testament is λαλεῖν γλώσσῃ. For a catalogue of the terms connected to the tongues see Scippa (1982: 17–18, 31–32).

and knowledge will take place in the eschatological future, when the Lord will directly teach the truth. This does not apply to tongues:

> Firstly, the text does not affirm that they will last until the advent of perfection, otherwise they would be listed among the things to be abolished; they will cease, i.e., they will fall into disuse. Secondly, the Greek verb is *pauomai* "cease," which is different from *abolish*. Thirdly, in Greek, the *voice* of the verbs used in the text is different ("abolish" is passive, "cease" is middle). Therefore, the meaning nuances will be different; [...] 1 Corinthians 13:8 should be translated as follows: "*As for the tongues, they will cease by themselves* (they will fall into disuse)," i.e., little by little. This is also confirmed by the Church's history. Paul relates the tongues to the Church's childhood and to the first phase of her adolescence.

In a footnote, Martella further explains:

> *Pauomai* is middle [...]; here this tense is used in an intransitive way, "stop, cease, desist, finish"; in an absolute way, it can mean "fall into disuse."

Martella emphasizes the reflexivity characterizing the middle tense in order to prove that tongues will cease "by themselves" instead of being abolished. Knowledge and prophecy are the subjects of the same verb (*katargeo*) in passive tense, while tongues are the subject of a different verb (*pauo*) in middle tense. This, according to Martella, proves that the first two will be eliminated by an external agent at the end of times, while tongues will not need an agent abolishing them, but will cease by themselves. Martella's interpretation, therefore, fills in a gap of sense left open by the text; this interpretation is based on the study of the words chosen by Paul and of their meaning, which is the subject of a differential analysis.

In MacArthur we find a very similar interpretative style. For example, MacArthur (1978: 16) proposes a doctrine of inspiration according to which "Scripture is not the works of men into which God puffed divine life. Scripture is the very breath of God! Scripture is God speaking [...]." The proof of this affirmation is supplied by the quotation of Timothy 3:16, a verse affirming that "All Scripture is inspired by God." MacArthur (1978: 16) refers specifically to the Greek word "*theopneustos*, which means 'God-breathed,'" but he omits that when the verse was written the canon had not been established yet. As a consequence, the helpfulness of this verse in determining which texts are truly inspired is highly doubtful. The author also quotes other verses, among which Jude 3, where Jude exhorts the Christians to "contend for the faith that was once for all entrusted to the saints." MacArthur interprets this passage as follows:

> In this statement, the Holy Spirit looks forward to the complete canon of Scripture. In the Greek text the definite article *the* preceding "faith" points to the *one* and *only* faith. There is no other. [...] Note also the crucial phrase *once for all* in Jude 3. The Greek word here is *hapax*, which refers to something done for all time, with lasting results, never needing

> repetition. Nothing needs to be added to the faith that has been delivered "once for all." [...] Also important in Jude 3 is the word *delivered*. In the Greek it is an aorist passive participle, which indicates an act completed in the past with no continuing element. In this instance the passive voice means the faith was not discovered by men but was *given to men by God*. (MacArthur 1978:17–18, emphasis in original)

This interpretative style is typical both of Conservative Evangelical literature arguing against glossolalia and of what Barr (1977) classifies as Fundamentalism. On the one side, the interpreter shows a great attention to the letter of the text, displaying a literalist interpretation mainly based on references to the grammar of the Greek text. On the other side, however, such linguistic considerations are combined with affirmations which appear arbitrary and not supported by the text itself. For example, it is not clear how MacArthur can be certain that in Jude 3 the Holy Spirit, which is not even mentioned in the text, "looks forward to the complete canon of Scripture."

It is therefore evident that the empirical application of the interpretative principles so clearly stated by Conservative Evangelicals is not as rigorous as a superficial reading could suggest. Everything, from the selection of the verses that are actually mentioned and interpreted in their discourse, to the relationship with the Greek text and to the application of some logical reasoning to short biblical passages, are interpretative operations that go far beyond the "plain reading" evoked by our authors. The flexibility by which the historical principle is applied (as we have seen for example in the case of the treatment of Hebrew), or the non-systematic way in which the Greek text is studied, are clues showing how the notions of originality and fidelity to the text, so clear when enunciated in principle, are problematic when compared to the actual interpretative practice.

7 Conclusion

Charismatics tend to approach the scriptures quite elastically, quoting a circumscribed number of verses and using different interpretative principles, all subordinated to an empirical test. Conservatives, on the contrary, carefully define their interpretative rules and often refer to such rules in order to show the validity of their reading of the scriptures. However, this does not mean that their works are particularly rigorous: generally, they do not apply their principles in a systematic or coherent way. Each author tends to follow now the principle of the historical analysis, now the grammatical principle applied to the Greek text, now a strictly literal reading, now a stylistic analysis aimed at pointing out and explaining the rhetorical figures; but rarely is there an attempt to apply all of these principles to the same passage, or a systematic treatment and equal consideration of all the verses that can be related to a certain subject. It seems ultimately that, in spite of their claim of considering the text only, Conservatives as well are influenced by the surrounding reality in their interpretative process. Indeed, their interpretative works have a strong apologetic character: their goal is to contrast the growth of the Charismatic movements and to defend the fundamentals of their doctrine. Such an apologetic goal leads them to read the text looking for determinate answers. In this context, as Crapanzano (2000) observes, literalism paradoxically ends up becoming a rhetorical device.

Conservative Evangelicals claim to possess an objective method of biblical interpretation and to be able to grasp the scriptures' true meaning. They tend to use arguments built in a logical and rational style; they believe Charismatics to practice a mysterious and esoteric religion; and they have a sharp sense of the "borders," especially of the distinction between saved (or true Christians) and unsaved. Contrarily, Charismatics are often persuaded to be able to speak mysterious, unknown, spiritual, or angelic languages, and they see this a-semantic form of expression as the most effective in order to communicate with the deity. Moreover, Charismatic movements tend to have an ecumenical perspective, i.e., they hope to reach a Christian union going beyond rigid doctrinal divisions. However, despite this apparent dichotomy, the distinction between the two groups is actually more nuanced.

As we have seen, the logical reasoning is often confined to a superficial (rhetorical) level of Conservative discourse. Moreover, Conservatives, on the one hand, minimize the supernatural by stressing the transcendent character of the divine, which does not manifest itself to mankind with sensible signs before the Second Coming. On this basis, they condemn potentially supernatural phenomena, such as glossolalia. Nevertheless, on the other hand, the supernatural dimension in Conservatives' discourse is not confined to the transcendent deity described in the Bible, but also includes magic. Martella (1995: 4–6, 75–80), for example, affirms that glossolalia can be caused and practiced by evil individuals or entities, such as witches and demons, which can take control over the incautious believer. A transcendent deity is therefore opposed to a series of contingent supernatural evil agents. Moreover, as we said, numerous Charismatic denominations share most of the "Fundamentalist" doctrine of the Conservative Evangelicals. In addition, despite its stress on emotion and spontaneity, Charismatic argumentation is not irrational or mysterious, but it is based on a particular logic (the logic of the "enactment" of the text, whose decisive test is empirical – albeit subjective – experience).

The main watershed between the two groups' interpretative styles is represented by their relationship with the sacred text. For the Conservative Evangelicals, the Bible is the one and only container of the Truth; it reports a set of historical and unrepeatable events, and a complete and ever-lasting revelation. As a consequence, it must be studied in its minimal details and its rules must be applied in the faithful's life. Charismatics tend instead to use the sacred text like a handbook, a source of *exempla* that can be imitated in all times in order to reach a more direct communication with God. This difference can be efficaciously illustrated by a comparison between a passage from MacArthur and a passage from Sherrill. According to MacArthur (1978: 61), "There are only two basic approaches to biblical truth":

> (1) the historical objective approach, which emphasizes God's action toward man as recorded in Scripture; (2) the personal subjective approach, which emphasizes man's experience of God. [...] Objective historic theology is Reformation theology. It is historical Evangelicalism. It is historical orthodoxy. We begin with God's Word [....] On the other hand, the subjective view is the methodology of historic Roman Catholicism. Intuition, experience, and mysticism have always played a big role in Roman Catholic theology. The subjective view has also been at the heart of liberalism and neoorthodoxy. The truth is what you think and feel and claim. The truth is what happens to you. The subjective view is historic Charismaticism [...].

In Sherrill, we can find an antithetical argument. Sherrill (2004 [1964]: 76) narrates the meeting between the Pentecostal leader David Du Plessis and a congregation of Episcopal priests:

> "Mr. du Plessis, are you telling us that you Pentecostals have the truth, and we other churches do not?" [...] "That is not what I mean." He cast about for a way to express the difference Pentecostals feel exists between their church and others – a feeling so often misunderstood – and suddenly he found himself thinking about an appliance he and his wife had bought [...].
>
> "We both have the truth," he said. "You know, when my wife and I moved to America we bought a marvelous device called Deepfreeze, and there we keep some rather fine Texas beef.
>
> "Now, my wife can take one of those steaks out and lay it, frozen solid, on the table. It's steak, all right, no question of that. You and I can sit around and analyze it [...]. We can weight it and list its nutritive values.
>
> "But if my wife puts the steak on the fire, something different begins to happen. My little boy smells it from way out in the yard and comes shouting: 'Gee, Mom, that smells good! I want some!'
>
> "Gentlemen, [...] that is the difference between our ways of handling the same truth. You have yours on ice; we have ours on fire."

The Charismatic "pragmatic" interpreter reads the sacred scriptures, especially the verses concerning the gifts, as a written text to be "enacted." By enacting the written text this model interpreter can reach an improved knowledge of the deity thanks to a direct experience. The written text is therefore reduced to a medium fostering a sensible encounter with God.[23]

For the conservative interpreter, the written text itself has a pre-eminent and exclusive role: "[...] the Bible is a verbalized, 'inscripturated' entity, the given form in which God has made himself known" (Barr 1977: 36). This also confers a special importance to the Bible as a material object, which represents the tangible presence of God. Ammerman (1987: 132), who studied U.S. Fundamentalist groups, observes: "For a Fundamentalist congregation, the pastor's uplifted Bible is as ritually significant as is the elevated host for someone partaking of the eucharist. [...] The Bible is for Fundamentalists the very presence of God in their midst." Since the label "literalist" derives from an erroneous stereotype (see Barr 1977, Crapanzano 2000) and does not correspond to the actual interpretative style of Conservative Evangelicals, we can define as "in-scriptural" the conservative interpreter, in contrast to the "pragmatic" Charismatic interpreter. As we have seen, these interpretative styles are connected to different argumentative styles: the one rational, grammatical, authoritative, and peremptory; the other colloquial, metaphorical, and personal.

It is probable that the reason for the lively controversy about glossolalia between Charismatics and Conservative Evangelicals does not derive from their incompatibility but rather from their very kinship. As we said, historical Pentecostalism originated from Conservative Evangelical denominations and it held conservative theological views, such as literalism and inerrancy. Moreover, despite the central and exclusive role that their doctrine attributes to scripture, Conservatives as well "often like a person to say that God actually spoke to him and told him or led him to do this or that: 'guidance' in this sense is very important" (Barr 1977: xvi). The idea of enacting and receiving precisely what is written in the Bible, as well as the utopia of actually coming back to the original conditions of the Apostolic age,[24] can be very attractive for Conservatives. This kinship leads Conservative apologists to be particularly aggressive and intransigent towards Charismatics, who threaten to shake their doctrine from the inside. This proximity and the flourishing of Charismatic movements worldwide lead Conservatives to defend their identity by clearly stating their doctrine and the difference between them and their competitors. However, Conservative practices connected to the concept of "guidance" also show that, while the borders

---

23 In its most extreme development, the stress on performance and on direct experience can lead to assigning a very scant importance to the Bible, as happens in the African Christian Church "Masowe weChrisanu," whose members define themselves as "the Christians who don't read the Bible" (Engelke 2004).

24 On originalism, see Barr (1977: 207–209).

between the doctrine of the two groups are mostly marked and neat, the domain of the actual religious practices is much more nuanced.

The problematic kinship between Conservatives and Charismatics also depends on the fact that Charismatic doctrine represents an extreme and peculiar interpretation of the concept of "sincerity." Sincerity, spontaneity, and earnestness are the qualities that Protestants have attributed themselves since the Reformation, in contrast to the dogmatism and ritual repetitiveness that they attributed to Catholicism and to other religions they got in touch with through colonization (Keane 1997, 2007; Yelle 2013a). Spontaneity assumes a new centrality and a new breadth in Pentecostal and Charismatic movements. This induces mainstream churches to set limits to it and to code their practices, thus assuming a position which is closer to the religions that were their initial targets. According to Shoaps (2002: 43), the spontaneity proposed by Charismatics contrasts with the "scriptedness" characterizing the practices of other religious groups, including Evangelical mainstream movements: "Scriptedness includes rote repetition, which has the danger of dulling the senses (so that the repeaters are not 'feeling' what they are saying) and canonized traditional prayers present the hazard of becoming confining formulae that do not allow individualized, spontaneous expression [...]."

Charismatics are therefore bringing to its extreme consequences the old Protestant argument against vain repetitions (Yelle 2013a: chap. 5; 2013b: chap. 4), and they are often using it against other Protestants. As literalism and its rational rigorous interpretative principles constitute for Conservative Evangelicals an interpretative style that is more shown-off than actually applied (a "rhetorical" device, to put it in Crapanzano's terms), so the "enactment" of the text as proposed by Sherrill is an interpretative principle often evoked to justify "spontaneous" practices. In the Assemblies of God congregations studied by Shoaps, for example, the main value of these practices does not reside in the fact that they conform with what is written in the Bible, but in their "earnestness." However, despite the claims for spontaneity and earnestness, Charismatic practices are ritualized – at least to some extent – and they follow implicit (i.e., not coded in written or official norms) but well-affirmed patterns, to the point that their breaking can cause ritual failure or infelicity. Coleman (2006), for example, reports the episode of a service where the members of a Swedish Charismatic group were disturbed by the unusual silence imposed by the pastor and finally abandoned the ritual, an action which is normally frowned upon but which in this case seemed justified by the subversion of implicit ritual rules. Similar episodes, as well as the consideration of glossolalia as the necessary seal of baptism and, consequently, of the individual's belonging to the community, are signs of a certain degree of "routinization" of charisma contrasting with Charismatics' claim for spontaneity (Weber 1956; Csordas 1997: chap. 2; Yelle 2013b: chap. 4).

In conclusion, the "in-scriptural" and the "pragmatic" interpreters should be considered as discursive models, as "instances" (à la Benveniste) placed at the ideal extremes of a continuum. Each empirical interpreter is not located in the extreme poles but in a more intermediate position, as the non-systematic application of the interpretative principles by the interpreters we studied clearly shows. The analysis proposed herein shows therefore that the practice of glossolalia, like all religious linguistic practices, has to be considered in the frame of a broader semiotic style, determined by a plurality of factors: doctrinal and theological presuppositions that influence the way in which the subjects interpret the sacred text and reality (e.g., the Conservatives' principle of inerrancy or the Charismatics' principle of the reception of the charismata); a peculiar interpretative style, consisting of particular interpretative processes carried out reading the sacred book (e.g., its grammatical and historical reconstruction, or the "acting" of the text as a way to understand and verify it); religious semiotic practices (such as rituals involving glossolalia for Charismatics, or the role of the Bible as a material object in Conservative services [Ammerman 1987; Leone 2012; Ponzo 2010]; a peculiar aesthetic sensibility (e.g., judging glossolalia as a beautiful chant or as a disharmonic cacophony); a determined communicative attitude toward others (openness and inclusion, or exclusion and refusal of dialogue); a determined rhetoric or argumentative style, based in one case on the appeal to the letter of the text, on logical reasoning, on the proposition of an objective truth, and in the other case on the appeal to emotion and experience, on "acting" the text.

References

Ammerman, Nancy Tatom. 1987. *Bible believers: Fundamentalists in the modern world*. New Brunswick: Rutgers University Press.

Barr, James. 1977. *Fundamentalism*. London: SCM Press.

Bartkowski, John. 1996. Beyond biblical literalism and inerrancy: Conservative Protestants and the hermeneutic interpretation of scripture. *Sociology of Religion* 57(3). 259–272.

Benveniste, Émile. 1966. *Problèmes de linguistique générale*, vol. 1–2. Paris: Gallimard.

Carlyle, May. 1956. A survey of glossolalia and related phenomena in non-Christian religions. *American Anthropologist*, New Series 58(1). 75–96.

Certeau, Michel de. 1996. Vocal utopias: Glossolalias. *Representations* 56. Special Issue: The New Erudition. 29–47.

Coleman, Simon. 2006. When silence isn't golden: Charismatic speech and the limits of literalism. In Matthew Engelke & Matt Tomlinson (eds.), *The limits of meaning: Case studies in the anthropology of Christianity*, 39–61. New York & Oxford: Berghahn.

Corsani, Bruno & Carlo Buzzetti. 1996. *Nuovo Testamento greco-italiano*. Greek text: Nestle-Aland. Rome: Società biblica britannica e forestiera.

Crapanzano, Vincent. 2000. *Serving the word: Literalism in America from the pulpit to the bench*. New York: New Press.
Csordas, Thomas. 1997. *Language, charisma and creativity: The ritual life of a religious movement*. Berkeley, CA: University of California Press.
Dixon, Amzi & Reuben Torrey (eds.). 1910–1915. *The fundamentals: A testimony to the truth*, 12 vols. Chicago: Testimony Publishing Co.
Eco, Umberto. 1995. *The role of the reader: Explorations in the semiotics of texts*. Bloomington: Indiana University Press.
Engelke, Matthew. 2004. Text and performance in an African church: The Book "live and direct." *American Ethnologist* 31(1). 76–91.
Goodman, Felicitas. 1969. Phonetic analysis of glossolalia in four cultural settings. *Journal for the Scientific Study of Religion* 8(2). 227–239.
Goodman, Felicitas. 1972. *Speaking in tongues: A cross-cultural study of glossolalia*. Chicago & London: Chicago University Press.
Greimas, Algirdas. 1970–1983. *Du sens: Essais sémiotiques*, vol. 1–2. Paris: Seuil.
Greimas, Algirdas & Joseph Courtès. 1979. *Sémiotique: Dictionnaire raisonné de la théorie du langage*. Paris: Hachette.
Harding, Susan. 1991. Representing Fundamentalism: The problem of the repugnant cultural other. *Social Research* 58(2). 373–393.
Harris, Harriet A. 1998. *Fundamentalism and Evangelicals*. Oxford: Oxford University Press.
Introvigne, Massimo & Pierluigi Zoccatelli. 2016. La seconda ondata: il risveglio carismatico. http://www.cesnur.com/la-seconda-ondata-e-il-risveglio-carismatico/(accessed 16 July 2016).
James, William. 1902. *The varieties of religious experience: A study in human nature*. New York: Longmans, Green & Co.
Jelen, Ted. 1989. Biblical literalism and inerrancy: Does the difference make a difference? *Sociological Analysis* 49(4). 421–429.
Jelen, Ted, Clyde Wilcox & Corwin Smidt. 1990. Biblical literalism and inerrancy: A methodological investigation. *Sociological Analysis* 51(3). 307–313.
Kay, William K. 2011. *Pentecostalism: A very short introduction*. Oxford: Oxford University Press.
Keane, Webb. 1997. From fetishism to sincerity: On agency, the speaking subject, and their historicity in the context of religious conversion. *Comparative Studies in Society and History* 39(4). 674–693.
Keane, Webb. 2007. *Christian moderns: Freedom and fetish in the mission encounter*. Berkeley, CA: University of California Press.
Leone, Massimo. 2010. *Saints and signs. A semiotic reading of conversion in early modern Catholicism*. Berlin: De Gruyter.
Leone, Massimo. 2012. Stile semiotico del fondamentalismo religioso. Preface to Jenny Ponzo, *Lingue angeliche e discorsi fondamentalisti. Alla ricerca di uno stile interpretativo*, 11–24. Rome: Aracne.
Lofland, John & Norman Skonovd. 1981. Conversion motifs. *Journal for the Scientific Study of Religion* 20(4). 373–385.
Luhrmann, Tanya M. 2012. *When God talks back: Understanding the American Evangelical relationship with God*. New York: Alfred A. Knopf.
MacArthur, John. 1978. *The Charismatics. A doctrinal perspective*. Grand Rapids: Zondervan.
MacArthur, John. 2001. *The battle for the beginning: The Bible on creation and the fall of Adam*. Nashville: W. Publishing Group.

Marsden, George. 1980. *Fundamentalism and American culture: The shaping of twentieth century Evangelicalism, 1870–1925*. New York: Oxford University Press.
Martella, Nicola. 1995. *Carismosofia: Paralleli fra occultismo e carismaticismo*. Rome: Punto Acroce.
Numbers, Ronald. 2006. The creationists: From scientific creationism to intelligent design. Cambridge, MA & London: Harvard University Press.
Peirce, Charles. 1931–1966. *Collected papers of Charles Sanders Peirce*. Edited by Charles Hartshorne, Paul Weiss & Arthur Burks. 8 vols. Cambridge, MA: Belknap Press.
Ponzo, Jenny. 2010. Alla ricerca di una meta-semiotica delle culture: analisi di segni e metasegni nella cultura e nello stile interpretativo fondamentalisti. *Lexia* 5–6. 275–292.
Ponzo, Jenny. 2012. *Lingue angeliche e discorsi fondamentalisti. Alla ricerca di uno stile interpretativo*. Rome: Aracne.
Propp, Vladimir. 1968 [1928]. *Morphology of the folktale*. Translated by Laurence Scott. Austin: University of Texas Press.
Robeck, Cecil. 2014. *The Cambridge companion to Pentecostalism*. Cambridge: Cambridge University Press.
Ruthven, Malise. 2007. *Fundamentalism. A very short introduction*. Oxford: Oxford University Press.
Samarin, William. 1972. *Tongues of men and angels. The religious language of Pentecostalism*. New York: Macmillan.
Scippa, Vincenzo. 1982. *La glossolalia nel Nuovo Testamento: Ricerca esegetica secondo il metodo storico-critico e analitico-strutturale*. Napoli: D'Auria.
Sherrill, John. 2004 [1964]. *They speak with other tongues*. Grand Rapids: Chosen.
Shoaps, Robin. 2002. "Pray earnestly": The textual construction of personal involvement in Pentecostal prayer and song. *Journal of Linguistic Anthropology* 12(1). 34–71.
Spittler, Russell. 1996. Glossolalia. In Stanley Burgess, Gary McGee & Patrick Alexander (eds.), *Dictionary of Pentecostal and Charismatic movements*. Grand Rapids, MI: Zondervan.
Standridge, Guglielmo. 2001. *Devo parlare in lingue?* Rome: Associazione Verità Evangelica.
Trevett, Christine. 1996. *Montanism: Gender, authority and the new prophecy*. Cambridge: Cambridge University Press.
Weber, Max. 1956 [1922]. *Wirtschaft und Gesellschaft. Grundriss der verstehenden Soziologie*, 2 vols. Tübingen: Mohr.
Yelle, Robert A. 2003. *Explaining mantras: Ritual, rhetoric, and the dream of a natural language in Hindu Tantra*. New York: Routledge.
Yelle, Robert A. 2013a. *Semiotics of religion: Signs of the sacred in history*. London: Bloomsbury.
Yelle, Robert A. 2013b. *The language of disenchantment: Protestant literalism and colonial discourse in British India*. Oxford & New York: Oxford University Press.
Youngblood, Ronald F. 1984. *Evangelicals and inerrancy*. Nashville: T. Nelson.

Kocku von Stuckrad

The place of language in discursive studies of religion

Looking Up in the Garden

These trees have no names
whatever we call them

where will the meanings be
when the words are forgotten

[...]

will the dream come back
will I know where I am

will there be birds

W. S. Merwin (2014: 19)

1 Introduction: The academic study of religion and its problem with language

Studying religion in a linguistic frame of analysis has a long tradition. In its modern form, this approach was strongly advocated by Friedrich Max Müller (1823–1900), one of the founding figures of the comparative study of religion. When the academic study of religion was established as an independent discipline at European universities before the end of the 19th century, language remained a cornerstone of its methodology, as well as a topic of heated debate. It has often been pointed out that the academic study of religion is too much focused on texts, textual studies, and philology; this has to do with a kind of Protestant hangover that influenced the way "religion" was studied around 1900, and in which texts and words were the major carriers of religious ideas and practices. Scholars approached religions mainly through written sources, and they constructed historical genealogies in analogy to the history of languages; this also means that religions that fell outside this focus were either

Kocku von Stuckrad, University of Groningen

https://doi.org/10.1515/9781614514329-013

disregarded or categorized as "primitive," "pre-historic," "magical," "superstitious," and so on.

But there is a deeper reason for the discipline's focus on language, as well. Following the speculations of Greek and Roman philosophers, and linking their ideas to Jewish, Christian, and Islamic hermeneutics, an influential cultural current emerged that can be described as Europe's obsession with language. What Hans Blumenberg (1986) called "the readability of the world" has been a driving force in philosophical, theological, and academic inquiry (see also Harrison 1998). The "text" of the Bible, or Torah, was not just regarded as a text but rather as the "texture" or "textile" (i.e., fabric) of the cosmos, which provided the key to unlock the divine mysteries; the Hebraists of the 16th and 17th centuries were interested in Hebrew as the language spoken in paradise, and scholars such as John Dee were curious to learn the language of the angels; the idea that the cosmos consists of letters, and that the essential meaning of the world can be decoded, read, and re-written, has been cherished by philosophers, theologians, and scientists alike, and it is still visible in the 20th-century "life sciences" (von Stuckrad 2010: 89–113; as to the subsequent impact of these ideas see Olender 2009).

In the course of the 20th century, the philological focus of the academic study of religion has come under fierce attack. The linguistic turn, the pragmatic turn, the "writing culture" debate, the cultural turn, and more recently the pictorial turn have changed the methodological assumptions of many disciplines in the humanities, including the study of religion. Many of these approaches, however, were still based on a prioritization of language, and while they criticized a philological approach in the study of religion, they ultimately reinforced a linguistic orientation of most cultural interpretations. New disciplinary approaches such as postcolonial studies, gender studies, media studies, ritual studies, animal studies, but also semiotics and aesthetics of religion have subsequently fostered an interdisciplinary conversation about religion that tries to move beyond the confines of texts and even language.

While today most scholars would agree that the study of religion needs to confront these challenges and should open up to non-textual sources and data, it is not at all clear what a sound methodology might look like that would not prioritize language as a major building block. One simple reason for this is the fact that humans, in a more obvious way than other animals, have developed language as an important medium of communication, and that the academic system seems entirely dependent on linguistic conversation and argumentation. This raises important questions: Is there a structural difference between linguistic and non-linguistic communication? Would it be possible to analyze a non-linguistic object – an image, for instance, or a ritual – without using the language games of academic argumentation? In other words, could the act of painting, reading a poem, or performing a ritual be considered a legitimate contribution to academic analysis? Even if we stick to linguistic communication, is there a valid reason to prioritize one genre (e.g., logical argumentation) over another (e.g., poetry)? One may think of Friedrich Nietzsche, who in his attempt to prioritize poetry and myth over reason still operated within the confines of language. And, to make it even more complicated, are the boundaries between these genres as clearly demarcated as most scholars want to believe? As Hayden White (1973) pointed out with respect to historiography, and Clifford Geertz (1988) with respect to anthropology, scholars are also authors whose narrative accounts of reality follow rules that are based on communication practices other than plain rational argumentation. In the end, it is not so easy to escape the linguistic structure of human communication, and criticisms of a linguistic bias sometimes overlook the complexities of what language is and does in its various forms.

This leads to the observation that if we want to study human language, we will have to look at non-linguistic dimensions as well, for instance at performative and social acts of communication. In philosophy, ever since Ludwig Wittgenstein's musings about language and language games, and since J. L. Austin's lectures on *How to do things with words* (1962), the problematic links between logic, language, truth, and representations of reality have repeatedly been discussed, if arguably still within the confines of linguistic communication. While philosophy thus still depends on linguistic frames of analysis, those new disciplines that study ritual and performative action have had a difficult time integrating language conceptually in their scholarly endeavors. One reason for this problem is the fact that those approaches do not simply coordinate other forms of behavior with language, whereas language itself is not monolithic: it is itself a highly variable and internally differentiated mode of performance that needs to be considered in combination with other modes of expression (such as the visual).

There are alternatives to these approaches. If we want to understand the conceptual link between language and human communication and action, it will be worthwhile to take into account the theoretical discussion that has been going on in discourse research for a long time, mainly in sociology and cultural studies. When it comes to the study of religion, discourse research has recently been the topic of much scholarly interest, as well (see, e.g., Wijsen and von Stuckrad 2016). In what follows, I will briefly describe the contours of a discursive study of religion; I will then discuss the place of language in discursive approaches to religion and look at the changes that discourse research can bring to our understanding of religion and the orders of knowledge that relate to it.

2 Discourse research and the study of religion

2.1 Literary studies and philosophy

At the beginning of what was to become discourse research, the study of language and texts was of crucial importance. In literary studies and in linguistic analysis, scholars were trying to define more concretely what constitutes meaning in language and texts. Texts do not exist without a context. Texts are documents with many different layers of meaning, and they are part of a larger communicational setting. For instance, a text can make explicit reference to another text (in a quotation or footnote), or it can contain a tacit reference to a text that readers may or may not recognize (such as reference to a biblical motif or verse). In the parlance of literary studies, this is called "intertextuality." But texts can also refer to non-linguistic objects, such as buildings, persons, or events. To understand the meaning of a text, interpreters have to look at the complete structure the individual text is part of.

Mikhail Bakhtin (1895–1975), one of the early theorists of discourse and language, pointed out that there is even an intertextual communication going on between the author, or speaker, and the expected audience, regardless of real readers or listeners. In Bakhtin's view, "the speaker himself is oriented precisely toward such an actively responsive understanding. He does not expect passive understanding that, so to speak, only duplicates his or her own idea in someone else's mind" (Bakhtin 1986: 69). This means that "the speaker talks with an expectation of a response, agreement, sympathy, objection, execution, and so forth (with various speech genres presupposing various integral orientations and speech plans on the part of speakers or writers)." In the line of this argument, Bakhtin formulates a "dialogical" and "interindividual" principle:

> A word (or in general any sign) is *interindividual*. Everything that is said, expressed, is located outside the soul of the speaker and does not belong only to him. The word cannot be assigned to a single speaker. The author (speaker) has his own inalienable right to the word, but the listener has his rights, and those whose voices are heard in the word before the author comes upon it also have their rights (after all, there are no words that belong to no one). (Bakhtin 1986: 121–122; emphasis original)

These structuralist approaches to texts were taken a step further when scholars critically addressed the question of what the links between texts, authors, and readers are. Can we speak of a text if there are no readers? Isn't a text that nobody reads just a collection of written words, stored in what Douglas R. Hofstadter calls "Tumbolia," i.e., in "the land of dead hiccups and extinguished light bulbs. It's a sort of waiting room, where dormant software waits for its host hardware to come back up" (Hofstadter 1979: 116)? And isn't the role of the author exaggerated in general? In his famous essay "The Death of the Author" (1967), Roland Barthes (1915–1980) argued exactly this:

> Thus is revealed the total existence of writing: a text is made of multiple writings, drawn from many cultures and entering into mutual relations of dialogue, parody, contestation, but there is one place where this multiplicity is focused and that place is the reader, not, as was hitherto said, the author. [...] [A] text's unity lies not in its origin but in its destination. (Barthes 1987: 148)

Michel Foucault (1926–1984) responded in his 1969 lecture "What is an Author" to Barthes' claims (although this intertextuality remains implicit, as Foucault does not mention Barthes). He argues that it is not enough to diagnose the disappearance of the author. "For the same reason," Foucault says, "it is not enough to keep repeating that God and man have died a common death. Instead, we must locate the space left empty by the author's disappearance, follow the distribution of gaps and breaches, and watch for the openings this disappearance uncovers" (Foucault 1998: 209). Foucault introduced the abstract concept of "author function" to the analysis of what constitutes the meaning of a text. Linking this to a broader concept of discourse, he claimed:

> [O]ne could find here an introduction to the historical analysis of discourse. Perhaps it is time to study discourses not only in terms of their expressive value or formal transformations but according to their modes of existence. The modes of circulation, valorization, attribution, and appropriation of discourses vary with each culture and are modified within each. The manner in which they are articulated according to social relationships can be more readily understood, I believe, in the activity of the author function and in its modifications than in the themes or concepts that discourses set in motion. (Foucault 1998: 220)

From here, it is only a short way to the understanding of discourse as a mechanism that creates meaning in social communication, rather than a linguistic unit with a clear message. Building on these approaches to language and communication, discourse research explores and analyzes the rules and dynamics of attributing meaning to texts or things and of establishing shared knowledge (explicit or tacit) in a discourse community; it also addresses the strategies and processes of legitimization, stabilization, and social organization of meaning and knowledge.

2.2 Discourse research in sociology and cultural studies

At the end of the 20th century, the discussions in literary studies and philosophy increasingly merged with conceptual frames in sociology, historiography, and cultural studies (overviews in Keller 2011a: 97–177; Keller 2011b: 13–58; Landwehr 2009: 60–90; as a reader collection see Angermuller, Maingueneau and Wodak 2014; Jaworski and Coupland 2014 [strangely avoiding Michel Foucault]). In sociological research, the influence of constructivist approaches to knowledge (Berger and Luckmann 1966) were particularly strong and led to what Reiner Keller calls the Sociology of Knowledge Approach to Discourse (SKAD; see Keller 2011b). This direction of discourse theory relates back to Ludwik Fleck's notion of *Denkstil* ("thought style," see Fleck 1935) and understands discourse research as a research perspective or research style that applies a spectrum of possible methods in order to answer its guiding research question (see Sarasin 2003: 8 and 30; Landwehr 2009: 100; Keller 2011b: 9). Consequently, scholars such as Dominique Maingueneau argue that the overarching theoretical framework is discourse studies, or discourse research, while discourse analysis is considered to be one of the disciplines or methods of discourse studies.

While all analytical methods in discourse theory have to take the linguistic dimension as an important point of reference, some methods – particularly what Norman Fairclough calls "textually oriented discourse analysis" (1992: 37–61) – place the linguistic analysis of discourse in the center of their interest (examples of such an understanding of discourse analysis are Schiffrin, Tannen and Hamilton 2015; Renkema 2009; Hjelm 2011). Within SKAD, as well as in the more historically oriented discourse theory, both leaning more heavily on Michel Foucault's work, the methods that are considered useful can range from philological methods to quantitative and qualitative methods, content analysis, etc. These approaches are also interested in studying discourses that legitimate the entire discursive production, such as philosophical, scientific, or religious discourses – something Dominique Maingueneau (1999) calls "self-constituting discourses."

Against this background, we can define "discourse" as communicative structures (comprising both linguistic and non-linguistic forms of communication) that organize knowledge in a given community. Discourses establish, stabilize, and legitimize systems of meaning and provide collectively shared orders of knowledge within a discourse community. Discourses form around specific topics, but they also get entangled with other discourses, or "discourse strands," which leads to the formation of a "discursive knot" (Jäger and Meier 2010: 47). It is in these changing constellations of various discourse strands that orders of knowledge transform and generate new meanings in a community. Michel Foucault argued that the scholarly work consists of the identification of discourses as a group, an identification and reconstruction that often goes against the dominant master narratives that are operative in a given community.

> The [...] purpose of such a description of the facts of discourse is that by freeing them of all the groupings that purport to be natural, immediate, universal unities, one is able to describe other unities, but this time by means of a group of controlled decisions. Providing one defines the conditions clearly, it might be legitimate to constitute, on the basis of correctly described relations, discursive groups that are not arbitrary, and yet remain invisible. [...] [I]t is not therefore an interpretation of the facts of the statement that might reveal [the relations], but the analysis of their coexistence, their succession, their mutual functioning, their reciprocal determination, and their independent or correlative transformations. (Foucault 2010: 29)

Following the critical deconstruction of a group of discursive knots, Foucault creatively considered new groupings, or unities:

> I [...] will do no more than this: of course, I shall take as my starting-point whatever unities are already given (such as psychopathology, medicine, or political economy); but I shall make use of them just long enough to ask myself what unities they form; by what right they can claim a field that specifies them in space and a continuity that individualizes them in time; according to what laws they are formed; against the background of which discursive events they stand out; and whether they are not, in their accepted and quasi-institutional individuality, ultimately the surface effect of more firmly grounded unities. I shall accept the groupings that history suggests only to subject them at once to interrogation; to break them up and then to see whether they can be legitimately reformed; or whether other groupings should be made; to replace them in a more general space which, while dissipating their apparent familiarity, makes it possible to construct a theory of them. (Foucault 2010: 26)

Foucault's project of suggesting new "groupings" of "things" is a constructive process that follows the interests of the researcher. Hence, it is important to point out that these discourses are not objectively given, as if a certain grouping would present itself as natural or logical. To be sure, it would be too simple to say that "facts" are "fabricated" in scholarly work, but the transition from historical "traces" to "sources" and "data" – and thus the establishment of facts *as* facts – is by no means an objective process (von Stuckrad 2010: 195–196). In many ways, the researcher is both the product of the discourse she or he describes and the producer of it through the attribution of meaning to things; I call this the double-bind of discourse research (on "Western esotericism" and "Pagan studies" as examples of such a double-bind, see von Stuckrad 2014: 152–158).

2.3 Reception in the academic study of religion

When we now turn to the academic study of religion, we can note that discourse research has been seriously picked up only recently, although Bruce Lincoln and Hans G. Kippenberg already in the 1980s explored the theoretical possibilities that discursive approaches have to offer (Kippenberg 1983; Lincoln 1989; see also Kippenberg 1992 and Lincoln 2005). The title of Kippenberg's 1983 article nails down precisely what is at stake here: "Discursive study of religion: Musings about an academic study of religion that is based neither on a generally valid definition of religion, nor on a superiority of science."

More recent publications indicate that there is a growing interest in the application of discourse theory to the study of religion (Heather 2000; Hjelm 2011; Wijsen 2013; Moberg 2013; von Stuckrad 2014; Neubert 2014; von Stuckrad 2015; Wijsen and von Stuckrad 2016). Many scholars collaborate in an interdisciplinary setting and explore the possibilities that discursive approaches have to offer to a field of research that is becoming ever more complex and multi-layered. Thinking more deeply about the status of language in discourse research is one of the important tasks, if we want to further develop the analytical power of discursive approaches in the study of religion. In the following sections I will address some of the relevant questions and gauge the potential of discourse research to better understand the role of language in religious communication.

3 Discourse and language

Thinking about the status of language in discourse research, it is useful to apply the differentiation, mentioned above, between discourse research as a field of study and discourse analysis as a specific method. While discourse research is interested in the multitude of ways that communities establish knowledge and attribute meaning to things, discourse analysis looks at the use of concrete concepts in linguistic communication and draws conclusions from that use. Hence, it is hard to imagine a discourse analysis in which language would not be the main tool for scholarly arguments. For instance, if you study the discourse on "climate change," you will start with investigating the usages of the term – and maybe related concepts, such as "global warming," to broaden your data set – in all kinds of communicative settings, from political declarations to scientific articles, juridical correspondence, surveys and interviews, or any other occurrence of the term. It would be unconvincing to use data that is not related to the relevant concepts under examination.

Studying the discourse on "climate change" or any other term, however, means to look deeper into the structures that generate knowledge in a communicative setting. If we want to find out how knowledge about the question of climate change is constructed, legitimated, and maintained, we will also look at the "infrastructure," or dispositives, that carry the discourse (Bührmann and

Schneider 2008). For instance, it makes a difference whether the term "climate change" is used in a governmental declaration, in an article by a Nobel Prize laureate, in a disaster film, as the title of a painting, in a university teaching program, or in a blog post by an anonymous author. Dispositives matter. Dispositives need to be distinguished from the discourses themselves, but they have a decisive influence on the establishment, legitimization, and maybe contestation of knowledge in a discourse community. Looking at the "carriers" of discourses, we also broaden the analytical spectrum and move beyond the analysis of language; at stake here are also communicative practices, the medium of communication, and the respective positions of the actors. Or, put slightly differently, "the enunciative *dispositif* [...] connects a textual structure and a social location" (Maingueneau 1996: 8; author's translation). This level of analysis can easily be combined with the praxeology of Pierre Bourdieu, in which the concepts of "social and symbolic capital," as well as the notion of "habitus," lend themselves to application in discourse research (see Schäfer, Seibert, Simoncic and Köhrsen 2016). In short, the study of discourse includes the language of communication and the social location and positioning of that linguistic communication.

The course of a discourse can also be radically altered by unforeseen events that are independent of language. "9/11" was such a discursive event that changed the way people worldwide think about "terrorism," "Islam," and related concepts. Similarly, any major event – such as a huge flood, the complete disappearance of the ozone layer, or Australia becoming uninhabitable because of the heat – would probably influence the discourse on climate change. Discursive events remind us of the fact that we are not the masters of discourse, or the masters of reality; our knowledge about the world is constructed and imperfect, which means that we are not in control of the world. There is a world out there that has impact on what we think is true, even though our knowledge will never be a "mirror of nature" (Rorty 1980) and discourse research is skeptical of a correspondence model of truth. But discourse research acknowledges the reality of things and is open to the possibility of nonhuman agency and the expansion of discourse communities across species and even objects. I will come back to this question.

We can say, therefore, that discourses are not limited to language and linguistic communication. But what about the question of whether there can be a discourse *analysis* – or, more generally, a meta-discursive communication – that would move beyond the limits of language and rational argumentation? Would, for instance, the performance of a ritual or the reading of a poem add something to scholarly understanding and interpretation of a discourse? In my view, the answer is positive. To begin with, all activities within academia (teaching a class, writing a peer review, giving a lecture at a conference, serving on a committee, etc.) are ritual performances beyond language that influence the discursive production of knowledge and the positioning of actors in a network of communication (this is very much in line with Bruno Latour's Actor-Network-Theory; see Latour 2005). But we can even go a step further: If a teacher includes the performance of a ritual in the classroom – for instance, a shamanic journey or a meditation – this would provide the students with a knowledge that is different from linguistically communicated knowledge, or even incommunicable in language. Some people would think that such knowledge is less "academic." Why? Because it is hard to have a rational debate about the content of these experiences? What discourse research makes clear is that rational debate is not the only way knowledge is established, confirmed, and maintained. From a discursive point of view, the issue at stake is not whether it is "academic" – academia is much more than rational argumentation – but whether it is part of academic communication that is openly reflected on and becomes an element in the production of knowledge. In fact, critical (self-) reflection may be the bottom-line of what it means to be academic. This critical reflection includes the dimension of performative action and non-linguistic communication; however, the analysis of how meaning emerges and is shared in the discourse community will always depend on language as well (in the example, the non-linguistic, performative actions are still linked to the concepts of "shamanism" and "meditation").

What about reading a poem then? Although reading a poem is of course not a performative act beyond language, poetry is usually not considered a genre that is suitable for rational argumentation. But again, generating knowledge is more than rational argumentation, and therefore poetry can provide important contributions to discourses and the attribution of meaning to things. By way of example, the poem "Looking Up in the Garden" by W. S. Merwin, which I quote as an opening to this chapter, is an excellent contribution to a discourse on language, meaning, memory, and nature. It offers meaning that the reader grasps directly. A rationalization of how the poem affects the reader and how it conveys meaning would necessarily limit the extent of knowledge that the poem offers in artistic form. In an academic setting that encourages pluralistic ways of acquiring knowledge there is no reason to discard the reading of a poem as non-scientific or subjective. Respecting the value of various knowledge systems does not necessarily mean that we have to integrate all of them in one overarching theoretical scheme; rather, we can honor their respective cultural locations (see von Stuckrad 2016: 218, with reference to Jay Johnston's discussion of cultural locations and her claim that discourse research needs to pay more attention to materiality; see Johnston 2016a). But even in their diversity they can be seen as contributions to a discourse, which then can be studied in its entirety.

4 New vistas, new narratives, and new orders of knowledge

Looking at religion and language from a discursive point of view offers a number of theoretical and practical opportunities that are worth exploring in more detail. I want to highlight just two of these opportunities here. One is the truly interdisciplinary nature of discourse research and its openness to include in its theoretical framework the possibility that things and non-human animals can be part of a discourse community. Another opportunity is the rethinking and restructuring of the religious and cultural fields along new parameters, or "groupings"; this can lead to a revisiting of what are often referred to as religious "traditions," opening up the underlying discourses to new interpretations.

Let us have a closer look at these implications.

4.1 Interdisciplinarity

Discourse research has emerged from disciplinary contexts as varied as literature studies, cultural studies, philosophy, historiography, sociology, political science, and anthropology. It is interdisciplinary in its core (see Angermuller, Nonhoff et al. 2014). Interdisciplinarity – in contrast to multidisciplinarity – means that the approaches and research results from various disciplines do not just exist side by side, but that they are brought into critical conversation with one another (Kocka 1987; Joas and Kippenberg 2005). Claims in historiography are contrasted to insights from the sociology of knowledge, anthropological claims are contrasted to insights from literature studies, and so forth.

Discourse research also includes the natural sciences. The practices and procedures in the natural sciences are themselves materializations of discourses. In their turn, they stabilize and legitimize the assumptions that have made them possible. By so doing, discursive structures steer the attribution of meaning to things and establish shared assumptions about accepted and unaccepted knowledge. Discourse analysis breaks down the borders between the natural sciences and the social or cultural sciences. Despite their different methodologies for producing accepted knowledge, the natural sciences are no less discursively structured and thus socially steered than the humanities (Latour and Woolgar 1986; Edwards, Ashmore and Potter 1995; Parker 1998; Potter and Hepburn 2008: 287–288; Nikander 2008: 413).

4.2 Discourses beyond the human species

Just as discourse research is interdisciplinary, discourses themselves span various cultural locations. Consequently, discursive changes become visible in different cultural locations and disciplines simultaneously. A good example of such a change is the emergence of animal studies. The establishment of this field of research is both the materialization of a discursive change and the stabilization of exactly the changes that made the field possible in the first place. As Jonathan K. Crane explains, "animal studies draws on history, anthropology, economics, philosophy, religious studies, political science, law, biology, psychology, and others. The field's diversity reflects the complexity of the subject matter" (Crane 2016: 20). Animal studies are part of a larger discourse that addresses the position of the human species in a global environmental setting, often with religious overtones that link environmental concerns with the veneration of nature as a living being (on the "Gaia hypothesis" and the global "greening of religion" see Taylor 2010).

Since the publication of Peter Singer's now classic *Animal Liberation: A New Ethics for our Treatment of Animals* in 1975, the field of bioethics and animal studies has continuously increased its influence. In a critical response to Aristotelian, Cartesian, and Kantian understandings of animals as "machines" that lack personality and agency, the privileging of the human species over other animals – a practice for which Singer popularized the term "speciesism" – has come under attack. The strongholds of belief in the extraordinary status of the human being fell one by one. Today, it is hard to escape the conclusion that the human animal is not fundamentally different from other animals. Nonhuman animals have language, personality, agency, theory of mind, a rich social life with individual characters, as well as ritual and inter-species communication (representative of the current discussion are Cavalieri 2004; Calarco 2008; Safina 2015). Paola Cavalieri has recently moved a step further and proclaimed "the death of the animal," i.e., the end of the distinction between humans and other animals (Cavalieri 2012). Similarly, Jonathan K. Crane notes that the "spiraling anthropocentrism that has long reigned in animal studies is increasingly found wanting, if not suffocating" (Crane 2016: 10). Leaving such anthropocentrism behind, Crane is part of a group of scholars who not only attribute agency and personality to nonhuman animals, but also see them as ethical agents in an inter-species dialogue.

Such an approach is in line with animism, like "paganism" a concept that theologians and scholars of religion used with negative connotations well into the 20th century. Recently these concepts have been adopted positively by religious practitioners and – in a shared discourse community – by scholars of religion. Following Graham Harvey's definition we can regard animists as "people who recognise that the world is full of persons, only some of whom are human, and that life is always lived in relationship to others. Animism is lived out in various ways that are all about learning to act respectfully (carefully and constructively) towards and among other persons" (Harvey 2005: xi). In this "new animism," relationship and, more abstractly, relationality are key terms because they emphasize the relative meaning that persons and actions achieve in a communicative network. This opens up new directions of research. As the editors of *The Relational Dynamics of Enchantment and Sacralization* note in their introduction: "What we, the editors, learned while co-composing this book, is that the point is not that everything is agentic; the point is that *how* something is agentic emerges as an effect of entangled networks of relational dynamics" (Ingman et al. 2016: 8; emphasis original). And the volume pushes the limits of discourse even further than communication between human animals and nonhuman animals. To do so, the authors make use of insights from "new materialism" (Coole and Frost 2010; Johnston 2016a; Ioannides 2016) and from Bruno Latour's Actor-Network-Theory (ANT), interpreting it as follows:

> The revolutionary claims that emerged from decades of ANT research were not that scientific facts had been revealed to be socially constructed, but rather, that even the highest, hardest and strongest of objects in the modern world (facts) were the emergent results of complex compositions that involved the agency of nonhuman actors. In other words, that said practices could not be adequately explained while maintaining a divide between "the social" and "the natural." [...] Once this realization sunk in, that the hard sciences actually needed to acknowledge the influence of nonhuman agency in order to legitimate their practices, the great divide between fact and fetish no longer appeared as given. To underline this ambivalence, Latour eventually coined the term "factish" (see Latour 2010, 2011). (Introduction to Ingman et al. 2016: 8–9)

Hence, agency is here extended beyond human and nonhuman animals to include "things" and "facts" as well. Science – and the laboratory life Latour and Woolgar examined – provides many examples of this, but I want to bring in literature again. A poem captures the meaning of what is at stake in a different, and perhaps even more apt, way than an academic description. Billy Collins' poem "Ode to a Desk Lamp" (Collins 2013: 223–224) clearly reveals the many layers of relationality with an "inanimate" object:

> Oh faithful light, under which I have written
> and read for all these decades,
> flying saucer with your underbelly softly aglow,
> rising on a stem from a heavy metal base,
>
> [...]
>
> Has anyone been with me longer?
> me without siblings or children,
> you with your kindly 60 watt frosted bulb,
> you who have not died like others I knew,

you nestled in a bath towel
on the floorboards of the car
as I backed it down the driveway of my marriage
and steered east then south down the two-then four-lane roads.

So may nights like this one,
me sleepless, you gazing down on the page
and now on a crystal rock, a tiny figure of a pig,
and an orchid dying in its blue China pot.

But that is more than enough
of the sad drapery of the past as I hold the present
between two fingers and the thumb
and a blue train whistles in the distance.

It's time to saddle up, partner,
once I unplug your tail from the socket,
time to ride out west,
far from the gaucheries of men,

the inconstancy of women,
and the rowdy mortality of them all,
until we find a grove of trees near a river –
just you and me with our bedrolls under a scattering of stars.

The dynamic relationality this poem describes stretches across human relationships, which have changed during a lifetime, and includes the relation with the desk lamp (and many other "objects" that are part of the relational network), as well as with trees, a river, and stars. This understanding of relationality brings us to Jay Johnston and her contribution to new materialism. Building her argument on poststructural philosophy, European art historical discourse, and what is known as the Western esoteric tradition, Johnston proposes an "Esoteric Aesthetics" that "enables a further reformulation and re-thinking of aesthetic relations *per se*. This approach has potentially radical implications for the concept of subjectivity, artistic agency and interpretations of the *role* of image or object *and* the viewer" (Johnston 2016b: 190–191; emphasis original). In an analysis of relational dynamics, things such as a magical amulet, a statue, and an image are considered both objects and subjects, subjects that perform their agency independently from human agency.

Discourse theory makes these poststructuralist extensions of its analytical tools possible because it allows for the inclusion of non-linguistic and non-rational ways of communication. A discourse community consists of more than human actors and may include dynamic objects, as well. When it comes to agency, though, it is important to keep in mind that agency, just like meaning, is always *attributed* to actors and things; agency is not just there. It is *we* who attribute agency to nonhuman animals or, as in new materialism, to things like images, stones, or a desk lamp. Empirical data suggests that nonhuman animals, too, attribute agency to other animals and presumably also to objects (similar to human toddlers who attribute agency to stuffed animals and other objects). It will be harder to prove, however, that agents such as images, stones, or desk lamps attribute agency to other members of the discourse community. Ingman et al. (2016) offer a solution to this challenge, arguing that agency is something that emerges in encounters. From that point of view, a desk lamp may or may not be able to attribute agency to others, but it could participate in encounters that distribute agency, exactly as it is expressed in Billy Collins' poem.

4.3 From traditions to discourses

The relationality that underlies cultural discourses allows for a fresh view of orders of knowledge that are often taken for granted. Indeed, if we follow Foucault's program and "accept the groupings that history suggests only to subject them at once to interrogation" (Foucault 2010: 26), we will be able to reinterpret the historical material and the genealogy of the present. In this sense, the notion of religious "traditions" is a problematic term because it reflects a certain order of historical material that is presented as evident and fixed; this fixed understanding is then projected back on historical material that would allow for quite different readings as well, only that those readings are made impossible due to the groupings that dominate contemporary orders of knowledge (for a critical analysis of "world religions," see Masuzawa 2005). I want to illustrate what is at stake here with two interrelated examples, one from the ancient Mediterranean and one from contemporary Europe.

During Greco-Roman times magic was a common religious activity and worldview. This kind of "ritual power" (Mirecki and Meyer 2002) flourished among Jews and Christians as well. There is no reason to sever magic from pious Jewish or Christian faith, as theological historiography used to do. As soon as we leave behind the grouping of discourses that artificially separates magic from religion, we can order the material in a different way. The Greek Magical Papyri, for instance, turn out to be one of the largest collections of ritual – and liturgical – texts from late antiquity, as Jonathan Z. Smith observed (1995: 21).

Sometimes, religio-magical practice could even involve devotion to planetary or other divine entities (von Stuckrad 2011). This contradicts the dominant discourse of monotheistic theology, according to which the veneration of stars – idolatry – was regarded as forbidden. This presumption has led some scholars to the conclusion that evidence of star cults can by definition not be evidence of Jewish authors. This, of course, is far too simple. Hans Dieter Betz argues that we cannot determine the religious background of the authors of magical spells in a general way. Instead, "the examples of Jewish magic present a complicated but illuminating picture, and [...] the question of the Jewishness of each particular spell may have to be answered from case to case, depending on the types of texts involved" (Betz 1997: 47). After having analyzed three spells of the Greek Magical Papyri, he concludes: "What makes them Jewish are the quotations from Scripture" (Betz 1997: 59) – nothing more. In a similar vein, Attilio Mastrocinque notes that "it must not be forgotten that magic texts were not part of a religion that can be labelled as 'magic', because there was no such thing. Those who practised magic worshipped Isis, Sarapis and Horus, or Hecate and Apollo, or the Hebrew god, or the saviour-Messiah, and frequently worshipped all these gods together" (Mastrocinque 2005: 45).

We can conclude that religious practice is much more nuanced than scholarly categories usually suggest. Neither does coercion exclude submission, nor does prayer exclude magic. It is a one-sided ordering of historical evidence to artificially distinguish magic from religion in this way. If we reconstruct the discursive constellation that led to this order of knowledge, we can also disentangle the discourse strands of religion, magic, prayer, liturgy, coercion, submission, etc. and "reassemble" or "regroup" them in a way that opens up new perspectives. We can critically revisit the groupings advocated by earlier generations of scholars, and future generations of scholars will surely do the same with our groupings of things. Discourse research is a hermeneutical, not an exact, enterprise, which is in line with Max Weber's apt remark: "It is not the 'factual' associations of the 'things' [*die 'sachlichen' Zusammenhänge der 'Dinge'*] but the intellectual associations of the problems [*die gedanklichen Zusammenhänge der Probleme*] that underlie the fields of scientific research" ("Die 'Objektivität' sozialwissenschaftlicher und sozialpolitischer Erkenntnis" [1904], quoted from Weber 1982: 166).

So, what's in a name? What does "magic," "religion," or "Christianity" mean without its situational and relational context? Jumping from antiquity to the 21st century, we are confronted with exactly the same questions. And again, discourse theory can help restructure the order of knowledge we share about those themes. What would happen if we let loose the groupings that "history suggests" (Foucault) and describe "Christianity" discursively? A discursive understanding of Christianity would identify discursive knots that are arranged around "Jesus" as their center; often, but not always, discourse strands of "Jesus" are entangled with "Messiah," "Christ," "Mary," "salvation," and a few others that constitute the core area of a Christian field of discourse. While the ancient Mediterranean material revealed the fact that Christian discourses were inseparably bound to Jewish and Roman discourses, a closer look at contemporary European and North American material suggests that Christian discourses have freed themselves from institutionalized Christian churches.

This is not the place to provide a detailed analysis of Christian discourse outside of the institutionalized churches or "traditions." My point is that contrary to a dominant narrative about secularization in Europe and parts of North America, Christian discourse is very much alive even in those areas that are deemed secularized. But to see this, we have to leave behind the traditional understandings of "Christianity" and look into Christian discourses instead. Every "esoteric" or "New Age" bookstore in Europe and North America has a section with channeled messages from Jesus, Mary, Mary Magdalene, or other sources that are linked to the Christian discursive field. A Google search for "channeling Mary," for instance, gives more than 720,000 hits (2 February 2016). In a relational network, it seems that these religious agents have been particularly eager in the past fifty years to get their messages across.

Here is an example of the Christian discourse that is usually not included in Christian "tradition": *A Course in Miracles*, written from 1965 to 1972 and published by Helen Schucman and William Thetford in 1976 (see the searchable version at http://courseinmiracles.com/), contains channeled messages from "Jesus Christ." *A Course in Miracles* consists of a 622-page textbook, a 478-page workbook, and an 88-page teacher's manual. Its teachings were subsequently interpreted and enhanced by authors such as Kenneth and Gloria Wapnick, Marianne Williamson, and Tara Singh. In 1992 Williamson discussed the book on *The Oprah Winfrey Show*, which resulted in the selling of an estimated two million volumes that year. The book has been translated into 22 languages and forms the basis of a global network of courses, centers, and initiatives. The Foundation for Inner Peace and the website www.acim.org function as the major hub and dispositive for this discourse.

5 Conclusion

I hope that these examples make it sufficiently clear what is gained by a discursive approach to religion and language. The interdisciplinary nature of discourse research, its openness to include communication beyond language and beyond the human species, as well as its openness to analyze new arrangements of knowledge that differ from what we habitually take for granted, provide an important contribution to a better understanding and interpretation of how language functions in religious practice.

Acknowledgments: I want to thank Alissa Jones Nelson for many discussions about the topics of this chapter. Her critical thinking helped me enormously to better understand the challenges and opportunities of discursive studies of religion.

References

Angermuller, Johannes, Dominique Maingueneau & Ruth Wodak (eds.). 2014. *The discourse studies reader: Main currents in theory and analysis*. Amsterdam & Philadelphia: John Benjamins.

Angermuller, Johannes, Martin Nonhoff, Eva Herschinger, Felicitas Macgilchrist, Martin Reisigl, Juliette Wedl & Daniel Wrana & Alexander Ziem (eds.). 2014. *Diskursforschung: Ein interdisziplinäres Handbuch*, 2 vols. Bielefeld: Transcript.

Austin, J. L. 1962. *How to do things with words: The William James Lectures delivered at Harvard University 1955*. Oxford: Clarendon Press & Oxford University Press.

Bakhtin, Mikhail. 1986. *Speech genres and other late essays*. Edited by Caryl Emerson & Michael Holquist. Translated by Vern W. McGee. Austin: University of Texas Press.

Barthes, Roland. 1987. The death of the author. In *Image, music, text*, 5th edn., 142–148. London: Fontana Press.

Berger, Peter L. & Thomas Luckmann. 1966. *The social construction of reality*. Garden City, NJ: Doubleday.

Betz, Hans Dieter. 1997. Jewish magic in the Greek Magical Papyri (PGM VII.260–71). In Peter Schäfer & Hans G. Kippenberg (eds.), *Envisioning magic: A Princeton seminar and symposium*, 45–63. Leiden: Brill.

Blumenberg, Hans. 1986. *Die Lesbarkeit der Welt*. Frankfurt am Main: Suhrkamp.

Bührmann, Andrea D. & Werner Schneider. 2008. *Vom Diskurs zum Dispositiv: Eine Einführung in die Dispositivanalyse*. Bielefeld: Transcript.

Calarco, Matthew. 2008. *Zoographies: The question of the animal from Heidegger to Derrida*. New York: Columbia University Press.

Cavalieri, Paola. 2004. *The animal question: Why nonhuman animals deserve human rights*. Oxford: Oxford University Press.

Cavalieri, Paola. 2012. *The death of the animal: A dialogue*. New York: Columbia University Press.

Collins, Billy. 2013. *Aimless love: New and selected poems*. New York: Random House.

Coole, Diana & Samantha Frost (eds.). 2010. *New materialisms: Ontology, agency, and politics*. Durham & London: Duke University Press.

Crane, Jonathan K. 2016. Beastly morality: A twisting tale. In Jonathan K. Crane (ed.), *Beastly morality: Animals as ethical agents*, 3–27. New York: Columbia University Press.

Edwards, Derek, Malcolm Ashmore & Jonathan Potter. 1995. Death and furniture: The rhetoric, politics and theology of bottom line arguments against relativism. *History of the Human Sciences* 8(2). 25–49.

Fairclough, Norman. 1992. *Discourse and social change*. Oxford: Polity Press.

Fleck, Ludwik. 1935. *Entstehung und Entwicklung einer wissenschaftlichen Tatsache: Einführung in die Lehre vom Denkstil und Denkkollektiv*. Basel: Benno Schwabe.

Foucault, Michel. 1998. What is an author. In James D. Faubion (ed.), *The essential works of Foucault 1954–1984*, vol. 2, *Aesthetics, method, and epistemology*, 205–222. New York: New Press.

Foucault, Michel. 2010. *The archaeology of knowledge. And the discourse on language.* Translated from the French by A. M. Sheridan Smith. New York: Vintage Books. First English edn. 1972.

Geertz, Clifford. 1988. *Works and lives: The anthropologist as author*. Stanford, CA: Stanford University Press.

Harrison, Peter. 1998. *The Bible, Protestantism, and the rise of natural science*. Cambridge: Cambridge University Press.

Harvey, Graham 2005. *Animism: Respecting the living world*. Kent Town, Australia: Wakefield Press.

Heather, Noel. 2000. *Religious language and critical discourse analysis: Ideology and identity in Christian discourse today*. Oxford: Peter Lang.

Hjelm, Titus. 2011. Discourse analysis. In Michael Stausberg & Steven Engler (eds.), *The Routledge handbook of research methods in the study of religion*, 134–150. London & New York: Routledge.

Hofstadter, Douglas R. 1979. *Gödel, Escher, Bach: An eternal golden braid*. New York: Vintage Books.

Ingman, Peik, Måns Broo, Tuija Hovi & Terhi Utriainen (eds.). 2016. *The relational dynamics of enchantment and sacralization: Changing the terms of the religion versus secularity debate*. Sheffield: Equinox.

Ioannides, George. 2016. The matter of meaning and the meaning of matter: Explorations for the material and discursive study of religion. In Frans Wijsen & Kocku von Stuckrad (eds.), *Making religion: Theory and practice in the discursive study of religion*, 51–73. Leiden & Boston: Brill.

Jäger, Siegfried & Florentine Maier. 2010. Theoretical and methodological aspects of Foucauldian critical discourse analysis and dispositive analysis. In Ruth Wodak & Michael Meyer (eds.), *Methods of critical discourse analysis*, 34–61. 2nd edn. London: Sage.

Jaworski, Adam & Nikolas Coupland (eds.). 2014. *The discourse reader*, 3rd edn. London & New York: Routledge.

Joas, Hans & Hans G. Kippenberg (eds.). 2005. *Interdisziplinarität als Lernprozeß: Erfahrungen mit einem handlungstheoretischen Forschungsprogramm*. Göttingen: Wallstein.

Johnston, Jay. 2016a. Slippery and saucy discourse: Grappling with the intersection of "alternate epistemologies" and discourse analysis. In Frans Wijsen & Kocku von Stuckrad (eds.), *Making religion: Theory and practice in the discursive study of religion*, 74–96. Leiden & Boston: Brill.

Johnston, Jay. 2016b. Enchanted sight/site: An esoteric aesthetics of image and experience. In Peik Igman, Måns Broo, Tuija Hovi & Terhi Utriainen (eds.), *The relational dynamics of enchantment and sacralization*, 189–206. Sheffield: Equinox.

Keller, Reiner. 2011a. *Wissenssoziologische Diskursanalyse: Grundlegung eines Forschungsprogramms*. 3rd edn. Wiesbaden: VS Verlag für Sozialwissenschaften.

Keller, Reiner. 2011b. The sociology of knowledge approach to discourse (SKAD). *Human Studies* 34(1). 43–65.

Kippenberg, Hans G. 1983. Diskursive Religionswissenschaft: Gedanken zu einer Religionswissenschaft, die weder auf einer allgemein gültigen Definition von Religion noch auf einer Überlegenheit von Wissenschaft basiert. In Burkhard Gladigow & Hans G. Kippenberg (eds.), *Neue Ansätze in der Religionswissenschaft*, 9–28. Munich: Kösel.

Kippenberg, Hans G. 1992. Pragmatic meanings as a particular source for the history of religion. In Shlomo Biderman & Ben-Ami Scharfstein (eds.), *Interpretation in Religion*, 53–67. Leiden: Brill.
Kocka, Jürgen (ed.). 1987. *Interdisziplinarität: Praxis – Herausforderung – Ideologie*. Frankfurt am Main: Suhrkamp.
Landwehr, Achim. 2009. *Historische Diskursanalyse*. 2nd edn. Frankfurt am Main & New York: Campus.
Latour, Bruno. 2005. *Reassembling the social: An introduction to Actor-Network-Theory*. Oxford: Oxford University Press.
Latour, Bruno. 2010. *On the modern cult of the factish gods*. Translated by Heather MacLean & Catherine Porter. Durham & London: Duke University Press.
Latour, Bruno. 2011. Fetish–factish. *Material Religion* 7(1). 42–49.
Latour, Bruno & Steve Woolgar. 1986. *Laboratory life: The construction of scientific facts*. Princeton: Princeton University Press.
Lincoln, Bruce. 1989. *Discourse and the construction of society: Comparative studies of myth, ritual, and classification*. Oxford: Oxford University Press.
Lincoln, Bruce. 2005. Theses on method. *Method and Theory in the Study of Religion* 17(1). 8–10. First published in *Method and Theory in the Study of Religion* 8 (3)[1996].225–227.
Maingueneau, Dominique. 1996. L'analyse du discours en France aujourd'hui. In Sophie Moirand (ed.), *Discours: Enjeux et perspectives. Numéro spécial Le Français dans le monde*, 8–15. Paris: Hachette.
Maingueneau, Dominique. 1999. Analysing self-constituting discourses. *Discourse Studies* 1(2). 175–199.
Mastrocinque, Attilio. 2005. *From Jewish magic to gnosticism*. Tübingen: Mohr Siebeck.
Masuzawa, Tomoko. 2005. *The invention of world religions: Or how European universalism was preserved in the language of pluralism*. Chicago: University of Chicago Press.
Merwin, W. S. 2014. *The moon before morning*. Port Townsend: Copper Canyon Press.
Mirecki, Paul & Marvin Meyer (eds.). 2002. *Magic and ritual in the ancient world*. Leiden & Boston: Brill.
Moberg, Marcus. 2013. First-, second-, and third-level discourse analytic approaches in the study of religion: Moving from meta-theoretical reflection to implementation in practice. *Religion* 43(1). 4–25.
Neubert, Frank. 2014. Diskursforschung in der Religionswissenschaft. In Johannes Angermuller, Martin Nonhoff, Eva Herschinger, Felicitas Macgilchrist, Martin Reisigl, Juliette Wedl, Daniel Wrana & Alexander Ziem, *Diskursforschung: Ein interdisziplinäres Handbuch*, vol. 1, 261–275. Bielefeld: Transcript.
Nikander, Pirjo. 2008. Constructionism and discourse analysis. In James A. Holstein & Jaber F. Gubrium (ed.), *Handbook of constructionist research*, 413–428. New York: Guilford Press.
Olender, Maurice. 2009. *The languages of paradise: Race, religion, and philology in the nineteenth century*. Translated by Arthur Goldhammer. Cambridge, MA: Harvard University Press.
Parker, Ian (ed.). 1998. *Social constructionism, discourse and realism*. London: Sage.
Potter, Jonathan & Alexa Hepburn. 2008. Discursive constructionism. In James A. Holstein & Jaber F. Gubrium (eds.), *Handbook of constructionist research*, 275–293. New York: Guilford Press.
Renkema, Jan. 2009. *The texture of discourse: Towards an outline of connectivity theory*. Amsterdam & Philadelphia: John Benjamins.

Rorty, Richard. 1980. *Philosophy and the mirror of nature*. 2nd printing, with corrections. Princeton: Princeton University Press.
Safina, Carl. 2015. *Beyond words: What animals think and feel*. 2nd edn. New York: Macmillan/ Henry Holt and Co.
Sarasin, Philipp. 2003. *Geschichtswissenschaft und Diskursanalyse*. Frankfurt am Main: Suhrkamp.
Schäfer, Heinrich Wilhelm, Leif Hagen Seibert, Adrián Tovar Simoncic & Jens Köhrsen. 2016. Towards a praxeology of religious life: Modes of observation. In Frans Wijsen & Kocku von Stuckrad (eds.), *Making religion: Theory and practice in the discursive study of religion*, 147–171. Leiden & Boston: Brill.
Schiffrin, Deborah, Deborah Tannen & Heidi E. Hamilton (eds.). 2015. *The handbook of discourse analysis*. 2nd edn. Oxford: Wiley-Blackwell.
Singer, Peter. 1975. *Animal liberation: A new ethics for our treatment of animals*. New York: New York Review/Random House.
Smith, Jonathan Z. 1995. Trading places: In Marvin Meyer & Paul Mirecki (eds.), *Ancient magic and ritual power*, 13–27. Leiden: Brill.
von Stuckrad, Kocku. 2010. *Locations of knowledge in medieval and early modern Europe: Esoteric discourse and Western identities*. Leiden & Boston: Brill.
von Stuckrad, Kocku. 2011. Astral magic in ancient Jewish discourse: Adoption, transformation, differentiation. In Gideon Bohak, Yuval Harari & Shaul Shaked (eds.), *Continuity and innovation in the magical tradition*, 245–270. Leiden & Boston: Brill.
von Stuckrad, Kocku. 2014. *The scientification of religion: An historical study of discursive change, 1800–2000*. Berlin & Boston: De Gruyter.
von Stuckrad, Kocku. 2015. Discourse. In Robert A. Segal & Kocku von Stuckrad (eds.), *Vocabulary for the study of religion*, vol. 1, 429–438. 3 vols. Leiden & Boston: Brill.
von Stuckrad, Kocku. 2016. Religion and science in transformation: On discourse communities, the double-bind of discourse research, and theoretical controversies. In Frans Wijsen & Kocku von Stuckrad (eds.), *Making religion: Theory and practice in the discursive study of religion*, 203–224. Leiden & Boston: Brill.
Taylor, Bron. 2010. *Dark green religion: Nature spirituality and the planetary future*. Berkeley & Los Angeles: University of California Press.
Weber, Max. 1982. *Gesammelte Aufsätze zur Wissenschaftslehre*, 5th edn. Tübingen: Mohr Siebeck.
White, Hayden. 1973. *Metahistory: The historical imagination in nineteenth-century Europe*. Baltimore: The Johns Hopkins University Press.
Wijsen, Frans. 2013. *Religious discourse, social cohesion and conflict: Studying Muslim–Christian relations*. Oxford: Peter Lang.
Wijsen, Frans & Kocku von Stuckrad (eds.). 2016. *Making religion: Theory and practice in the discursive study of religion*. Leiden & Boston: Brill.

Part III: **Media and materiality after the linguistic turn**

Seth L. Sanders

Words, things, and death: The rise of Iron Age literary monuments

> [W]hat we see in the construction of elite graves and royal tombs is the production of ideology in itself. Ideology [...] has no life outside the things that give it substance and that insert it into the world of action. In this sense then, archaeology is [...] a direct investigation of the real work of ideological production. (Adam Smith 2007: 165)

1 Introduction

Modern scholars have a tendency to assume that words, rather than things, are the best guide to ancient religion. The Indologist Gregory Schopen (1997) showed how a prejudice in favor of texts over archaeology shaped the study of Indian Buddhism, leading scholars to repeatedly prefer late, edited written sources over direct contemporary material evidence. For example, Schopen pointed out that while hundreds of inscriptions and excavated objects show that Indian monks owned and donated property, a number of scholars continued to insist this was not possible because it was prohibited in canonical texts. Similarly, while cemetary excavations testify to the fact that monks took elaborate care of their dead, some scholars still argued that we cannot be sure because the scriptures are silent on the matter.

Perhaps the clearest and best-known example of religion scholars preferring edited texts to contemporary artifacts comes from the ancient Near East, in the case of the Hebrew Bible. To this day the history of ancient Israel is usually presented as a retelling of biblical narratives with the miracles removed, merely supplemented by archaeological and nonbiblical written sources.[1] Despite repeated criticism, the periodization and main analytical categories for ancient Israel before the late Iron Age – the "patriarchal period," "Exodus," "conquest," "settlement," and "united monarchy" – represents a secularized sacred history, based in biblical narrative rather than ancient material evidence or documents.

1 On the use of Levantine archaeology in service of biblical texts see recently and incisively Pioske (2015), with earlier bibliography. For a detailed history of ancient Israel based entirely on contemporary material evidence, including inscriptions, see the first half of Liverani (2003) (and note the problematic second half, which attempts to compensate for the field's textual bias with an allegorical reading that tends to reinscribe the very problem pointed out in the first half).

Seth L. Sanders, University of California, Davis

https://doi.org/10.1515/9781614514329-014

Importantly, this is not because of any deliberate fundamentalist agenda but because of a set of underlying scholarly assumptions about the nature of different sorts of objects and how they signify – a semiotic ideology.

If the privileging of language prejudices our view of ancient evidence, it also shapes our theory about it, such as our choice of metaphors for understanding ritual objects. Famously, to interpret the meaning of the human material record eminent archaeological theorists like Ian Hodder chose writing as a dominant image for a comprehensible artifact. Hodder (1992) and others describe "reading" assemblages of grave goods or offering vessels as if they are books, with particular clusters forming "sentences."[2] But the problems of explanation produced by a language-centered view of culture are acute in archaeology, where so much of the evidence is not only nonverbal but not directly connected to any linguistic material at all.[3] Yet as an incisive survey by Rhodes (2013) shows, archaeological theorists typically continue to distinguish sharply between material things and linguistic signs.[4]

This linguistic bias in both our evidence and theory can be difficult to get outside of – a problem that also has an ancient – and biblical – history. In his response to a 2006 conference on ancient Near Eastern funerary ritual, the archaeologist Adam T. Smith argued against the privileged relationship of words

---

2 An extensive list of cases is given in Rhodes (2013). The past century of social theory has invalidated this opposition between privileged words and denigrated things, pointing out both evidentiary and ontological problems with it. On a large social scale, as Marx most prominently recognized, culture itself always depends on a material and economic basis. And on the scale of language structure and linguistic behavior, speech is intertwined with the material, the action of tongues, teeth, and hands as much as structures and minds. In these cases material existence makes possible and has an inescapable conditioning effect on consciousness (Marx's famous dictum [1971: 9] that "das Sein bestimmt das Bewusstsein"). Strictly materialist analysis retains the antinomy but merely reverses it by prioritizing things over words, arguing that it is the political-economic base that determines the cultural superstructure. A second set of arguments, from political theory (Althusser 1994) to anthropology (Irvine 1989) to archaeology (Preucel and Bauer 2001), undermines the antinomy itself: an ontological separation between words and things neither makes philosophical sense nor accounts for much of our data

3 For example, while there already are already rich textual corpora in Egyptian and East Semitic dealing with funerary ritual from the third millennium BCE (Morales 2016; Archi 2013) and cuneiform texts document a widespread pattern of tropes and rhetoric in royal funerary ritual language in the second millennium (Sanders 2012), the vast majority of funerary installations remain mute objects: the monuments themselves remain entirely nontextual through the early first millennium.

4 Rhodes' paper classifies different ways archaeological and anthropological theorists have claimed essential divides between language and material culture, including works such as Hodder (1992), Jones (2004), Layton (1989), Melas (1989), and Tilley (1989).

over things, because of how a culture's dominant ideals are actually enacted materially. "Ideology has no life outside the things that give it substance," Smith points out, following Althusser's famous argument that culturally dominant ideals are based in physical behavior. Why, then, has the study of ideology so often denied its material basis, privileging words over things in its analysis? The idea that discourse holds the key to culture's meaning and essence is in many ways a secularized version of an old Western theological assumption. We find a locus classicus in Saint Paul's essentializing the mind over the body and the spirit over the flesh (Galatians 5:13–18).[5] Just so, language is supposedly the privileged member of an opposition between words and things. There is a bad irony here: our theorizing *about* ancient religion should be more than the repetition of one particular ancient religion's own claims.

This paper introduces a pattern from the ancient Near Eastern archaeological record that lets us excavate the prehistory of this language-centered ideology, shining light on a specific way in which a culture reshaped its own relationship between language and the material realm. It investigates how ancient craftsmen changed the relationship between words, things, and death by beginning to inscribe instructions for funerary ritual on later Iron Age monuments (ca. 950–750 BCE). A comparison of earlier archaeological and written evidence for funerary ritual from the late third through the second millennium BCE suggests what changed. Up through about 1000 BCE a broadly shared practice held across Syria and Mesopotamia in which uninscribed monuments were animated by ritual. By performing two key tasks, naming the dead and feeding them, living participants indexed the presence of their ancestors relative to stone monuments. The ancestors' long-term presence was marked in space by objects, and renewed over time by short-term ritual acts.[6] Specifying how and when this changed lets us identify specific shifts in an ancient culture's semiotic ideology over time, and

---

5 For a broad historical theorization of this problem see Keane (2007). Schopen finds important further concrete cases of this viewpoint in the archaeology of Christianity, where "[...] the material remains that characterize the early Christian archaeology of North Britain cannot be, paradoxically, in any way essentially and historically Christian" because "they are independent of the Word" (Schopen 1997: 10–11). Schopen points out that this view of archaeology dovetails with classic Protestant views of religious language and concludes that "the old and ongoing debate between archaeology and textual studies is not – as is frequently assumed – a debate about sources" but rather "a debate about where religion as an object of investigation is to be located" and in this regard "It is possible, perhaps, that the Reformation is not over after all" (1997: 14).

6 For the best documented 3rd millennium Syrian cases see Porter (2002) (material evidence at Tel Banat) and Archi (2013) (archives and statuary at Ebla), for an introduction to the shifts in iconography and ritual see Bonatz (2000) and Porter (2002).

move our understanding beyond the ahistorical dead end of an essentialism of the linguistic or the material.

Archaeological data also offers a broader payoff for the study of religion. If we focus on that aspect of religion that facilitates interaction with physically non-copresent beings, we see that it naturally highlights the constant back-and-forth between words and things, as Webb Keane's early (1997) definition implies. In the ancient funerary ritual we will survey, human sacrificers and speakers interact with divine participants by engaging in dialogue with them, feeding them, and sometimes forming kinship relations with them. But taking the archaeological record and the materiality of religion into account requires us to expand a language-centered definition to include the creation of physical copresence itself.[7] As Keane himself later (2003) argued, gods become addressable persons and stone monuments become dead ancestors via a broader processes we can term objectification.

Because of their long-term durability and the extended context that can be preserved with them, stone funerary monuments afford remarkably rich evidence for *modes of objectification* in history, how different ideologies "enter into or are excluded from the processes by which things become objects" (Keane 2003). Textual evidence fleshes out the role these monuments played in two long-term ways that the dead were objectified and rendered present in Syrian and Anatolian ritual – via processes of naming and feeding – through the second millennium BCE. It is significant that this process of objectification is documented in two parallel genres of artifact forming two related streams of tradition during the first two millennia of written Near Eastern history: archival texts prescribing ritual speech, and uninscribed monuments indexing the presence of the dead. Seeing these as two intertwined streams of tradition, with each often assuming awareness of the other, helps relativize texts as their own kind of artifact, with their own patterning and assemblage.[8]

An especially interesting moment in the history of semiotic ideologies in Mesopotamia and the Levant comes when craftsmen first merge the two textual and material streams. The inscription of ritual instructions on the body of previously mute stelae created the first literary monuments in the alphabet, a new type of artifact entailing a different set of possible speaking and ritual roles (a participation

7 This is often done through formal, grammatically universal means in language (e.g., the use of deictics, pronouns, terms of address, but also via culturally specific forms such as Hindu *prāṇapratiṣṭhā*, as described in Yelle 2003: 30, 43, 52–53).

8 The structural parallels between the crafting of monuments and the crafting of bounded and defined pieces of discourse into texts on the one hand and text-artifacts on the other is laid out in Silverstein and Urban (1996).

framework in the terms of Goffman 1979). After the political disruption and new foundations of the Late Bronze (ca. 1400–1100 BCE) and early Iron Age (ca. 1100–900 BCE) the first funerary monuments are inscribed with messages to any reader who might encounter them. This new corpus represents the first alphabetic "historical" writing – prose narrative of political events, but they are as much demands for food and assertions of presence as they are narratives of history.

2 Burials as icons

The care of the dead had long been a defining element of ancient Near Eastern politics.[9] The best-known example of a stable, long-term mortuary ritual in the ancient Near East is the *kispu*, the food-offering to the dead, which is documented broadly in city-states and empires everywhere from early third-millennium Syria (Archi 2013) through the first-millennium Levant (Tsukimoto 1985; Greenfield 1973). But the particular relationship between funerary monuments, state forms, and writing has a more specific and volatile history beginning in the Iron Age. Placed together with earlier and contemporary data, this history illuminates how shifting political relationships between the dead and the living drove changes in semiotic ideology and practice.

The task of naming and feeding important dead through the *kispu*-offering seems to have been a role that second-millennium BCE rulers in West Semitic-speaking cultures were eager to fulfill. Making offerings to the prestigious dead was a privileged role for a ruler, with tangible rewards. But later monuments from Syria and Anatolia show Iron Age rulers had lost confidence in their heirs' desire or ability to feed them posthumously. A new uncertainty – and freedom – seems to have arisen in this period around the relationship of ancestor-making – a circumstance that led to creative new uses of writing.

9 For a rich Near Eastern survey see Laneri (2007); the fundamental theoretical statement on the political "dynamics of death," based on analysis of an early Amorite site, is Porter (2002). Porter points out (2002:4) that the funerary rituals of rulers often involve deliberate manipulation of ancestry: "Ritual attention to ancestors in the domestic context is also to be contrasted with the manipulation of ancestors in royal lineages and dynasties, which may be understood as the transformation and mediation of ancestor traditions appropriated in the legitimation and differentiation of power-holding groups." Not everybody gets to be remembered as an ancestor, a process that requires ritual and physical work (2002: 8), a point nicely formulated in van den Hout's deliberately paradoxical title, "Death as a Privilege" (1994). For mortuary politics in the context of Iron Age Anatolian monuments see Bonatz (2000), Gilibert (2011). For the question in the Iron Age southern Levant see Suriano (2010).

Preserved traces of mortuary ritual take two semiotic forms: monuments and archival texts. The archival texts give us a sense of what physical rituals were performed before the stelae, but before 1000 BCE stretching back to prehistory, stelae remained free of writing.[10] Traditions of landscape-making connected with funerary monuments go back to Syrian prehistory (Porter 2002). As in late antique Central Asia, they represented nodes in the geographical networks of mobile pastoralists. At sites such as Tell Banat on the Euphrates in the third millennium, monuments include burials plastered over for visual prominence in the landscape.

In a second-millennium Syrian ritual practice known from the sites of Mari and Emar, human participants visited specific stone stelae to make mortuary offerings.[11] Ritual texts prescribing their feeding suggest that these stelae served as sites of the presence of collective ancestors.[12] They index not only supernatural presence (written with a divine determinative marker in texts) but appetite:

---

10 There is a rare exception in the two memorial stelae for mortuary sacrifices, RS 6.021 and 6.028, discussed by Pardee (2000: 388–91). Crucially, their subject is not a deceased person but to commemorate the act of sacrifice itself. This places the only known written Late Bronze Age West Semitic monuments of mortuary activity in line with the texts known from Late Bronze Age archives in focusing on the ritual action rather than providing a physical presence and voice to the deceased by means of a written artifact. These two monuments are an exception that reinforces the rule, since both monuments are otherwise completely aniconic and undecorated, like giant writing tablets in the shape of tombstones.

11 For the texts, discussion and bibliography see Pardee (2000: 388–91) and Durand (2005). For an example of the erection of a ^{na4}*sikkanum ša* ^{d}*Dagan* "stele for Dagan," who is *bêl pagrê* "Lord of Mortuary Offerings" at Mari, see M.7014:3', 11' cited by Durand (2005: 62). Compare the statement from the Aqhat epic that a son will set up a *skn* for his father's *i͗li͗b* (probably "ancestral spirit") and eat his portion in the temple of the storm-god (*nṣb.skn.i͗li͗b...spủ.ksmh.bt.b*^{ʕ}*l* KTI (read: KTU) 1.17 i 26, 31).

12 It is also possible that they represent a collective of deities, though this is less likely because of Dagan's widespread association with both *sikkanū* and mortuary offerings. There are a number of certain cases of commemorative monuments for ancestors and gods already at Mari, often rather termed *humûsum* according to the texts cited in Durand (2005): e.g., Yahdun-Lim erects a *humûsum* in order to "establish his name," with the roots *šumu* + *šakānum* (2005: 93: ii, 19–20), and it appears as the funerary monument of a human individual in A.1073 (2005: 95), A.9 (2005: 97), and A.3605 (2005:99), but as a stele for a god in A.3194 (2005: 134) and A.618 (2005: 137). For the fundamental picture of stelae as representative of divine beings, either gods or ancestors, in West Semitic texts and cultures see Sommer (2009: 28–29), who insightfully concludes that "a deity's ability to be more than one person correlates with the ability to be more than one place." Is this what sets the dead Katumuwa apart from Hadad – that Hadad is many places and persons while Katumuwa, even with his person and being embodied in a stele and fed sacrifices, is only one?

they are anointed with blood and oil following the visit by a statue of a god and a shared human and divine meal at Emar.[13]

We can zero in on a period of change by comparing three written ritual artifacts from Syria and Anatolia: the earliest one is, like prior texts from the second millennium, a stand-alone written artifact; the second two are inscribed on massive stone sculptures, placing them among the first literary monuments of a new era. Together they suggest a shift in the role of royal funerary practices between the Late Bronze and Iron Ages, not only a media shift but a move from blessing to threat. The first is a Late Bronze Age ritual for Rāpiˀu, the eponymous lord of the king's high-status dead kin, from 13th-century Syrian Ugarit. Feeding Rāpiˀu confers success on the king because he will help the one who feeds him to become like him[14]:

> Now may Rāpiˀu, king of eternity, drink,
> May he drink, the god mighty and noble [...]
>
> To what you have requested he will bring you;
> Rāpiˀu, king of eternity, will bring you
> To your success, to what you have requested,
> By the power of Rāpiˀu, king of eternity,
> By the strength of Rāpiˀu, king of eternity,
> By his power, by his might,
> By his paternal care, by his divine splendor.
> Your strength will be that of the Rapaˀūma of the earth,
> As will be your power, your might,
> Your paternal care, your divine splendor.[15]

The text depicts a stable relationship of mutual benefit between king and departed ancestors. The speaker, a ritual expert, addresses the living, physically present king in the second person on behalf of the god Rāpiˀu. The ritual creates

---

13 See Emar VI 373, 34:34, 60, 167 ed. and tr. in Fleming (2000: 238–49) and Sanders (2013) for further discussion.

14 Compare the hopes of a royal hero in the Late Bronze Age, from the 13th-century BCE Ugaritic narrative poem of Aqhat:

> Bless him...
> So that he may have a son in his house, a scion within his palace:
> Someone to set up the stela of his ancestral god,
> in the temple the symbol of his clan;
> To send up his incense-smoke from the ground
> from the dust the song of his burial chamber.

KTU 1.17 i 25–28 (my translation, after Pardee 2003: 344)

15 RS 24.252 (KTU 1.108) 1–2, 19'-25' Edition and translation of Pardee (2002: 193–95).

a reciprocal relationship between living, dead and god.[16] Its explicitly stated goal is for the living king to gain the desirable aspects of his still-influential dead male relatives, the "Rapaʾūma of the earth/underworld." By means of the funerary deity Rāpiʾu, the eponymous king of eternity or posterity, he will resemble and benefit from those dead relatives in multiple (specifically, five) ways – in each instance, their powers become his. The ritual is a display not only of mourning, but of solidarity and power as he joins his male ancestors, the Rapaʾūma, in the underworld.[17]

By contrast, a very different type of artifact from few centuries later in the nearby Syrian site of Karkamish, displays a shift from promise to threat. Here we find a ritual demand engraved in hieroglyphic Luwian – a highly pictographic logo-syllabic script encoding an Anatolian language that is a later relative of Hittite. The inscription appears on a massive statue of the text's subject, the divinized founder of the Suhis dynasty, from the 10th or early 9th century BCE (Figure 1). He is rendered present in stone holding a mace and seems ready to enforce the text's words:

> He who does not [offer] an annual sacrificial meal of an ox and two sheep for this god Atrisuhas alongside the gods, may Atrisuhas come at him fatally! – KARKAMIŠ A4d (Hawkins 2000: 100–101)

The text, by the anonymous builder, ventriloquizes Atrisuhas to whoever might inherit ownership of the space the statue occupies. Atrisuhas is rendered present both deictically in the inscription and physically in the statue wielding a crushing mace. He offers no reciprocity. It makes no promises and names neither ancestors nor offspring: Atrisuhas will simply kill anyone who does not pay him tribute with the gods. While such tribute typically involved spoken ritual, the brief text does not bother to specify it. It contrasts with earlier funerary traditions from this culture. While the early Iron Age rulers of Carchemish claimed dynastic continuity and even specific royal titles with earlier Hittite kings, those dead Hittite kings had been ritually fed together with their ancestors.[18]

---

16 For Old Babylonian parallels, conducted directly between living and dead without the means of a specialized funerary deity, see the Genealogy of the Hammurapi Dynasty and Mari *kispu* rituals below.

17 The most coherent reading of the text is achieved by Suriano (2009), whose understanding of *tḥt* PN in lines 22–26 as "in PN's stead," rather than "under PN" manages to at once make better sense of the syntax and emphasize how the newly dead is stepping into the role of his ancestors.

18 For the regular appearance of the ancestral *huhhes hannes* "grandfathers and grandmothers" alongside the soul of the dead king and the gods – typically including the sun-goddess of the Earth and the god of the Good Day – in the royal funerary *šalliš waštaiš* ritual see the attestations

Figure 1: Statue of Atrisuhas.
Note: Photo courtesy of Alessandra Gilibert.

At Zincirli in Southern Anatolia, a parallel threat is inscribed in the West Semitic dialect of Samˀalian by the 8th-century king Panamuwa I on a monumental statue of the storm-god Hadad (Figure 2). The deixis is different: the dead man speaks to the future reader, anchored in the physically present image of the god "this Hadad" (statue). Like Atrisuhas he attempts to intertwine his own fate and feeding with that of the gods:

> But if any of my sons should grasp the sceptre and sit on my throne as king [...] and sacrifice [to this Hadad but not] remember the name of Panamuwa, saying "May Panamuwa's being {*nbš*} eat with Hadad! May Panamuwa's being {*nbš*} drink with Hadad!"[when he offers] his sacrifice, may he not accept it; what he asks, may Hadad not give to him [...] may he not allow him to eat because of rage, may he withhold sleep from him by night and may terror be given him![19]

---

in the edition of Kassian, Korolëv and Sidel'tsev (2002) (registered in the index, 798). Funerary sacrifice for a set of 44 named dead royal ancestors is attested in the texts edited by Otten (1951).
19 KAI 214 20–24 (my translation).

Figure 2: Panamuwa statue.
Source: https://upload.wikimedia.org/wikipedia/commons/4/41/Pergamonmuseum_-_Vorderasiatisches_Museum_045.JPG.

While Panamuwa does not aspire to be a god, he does demand to be fed with one. Rather than Atrisuhas' murderous assault, he threatens an inversion of the sort of blessings promised at Late Bronze Age Ugarit. Neglect of his naming and feeding will cause a breakdown in all the benefits of success and security that the royal dead promised to confer in the Ugaritic text.

All three of these texts come from a cultural sphere of interaction between Northern Syria and Southern Anatolia that was under the control of the Hittite empire during the Late Bronze Age and preserved vital elements of this legacy in the Iron Age. They also share an assumption that when living inheritors feed the royal dead they receive the blessings of rule and extended life.

What has changed in the two first millennium texts, such that they are both inscribed on large public monuments rather than tablets in a private archive, and that they both threaten the passing reader, demanding services that used to be assumed? The key difference seems to lie in the very different sorts of material world they assume: unlike the Ugaritic ritual, which assumes the physical presence of a trained ritual expert, a compliant royal heir, and a tacitly known ritual with accompanying offerings, personnel, and procedures, neither the Atrisuhas nor the Panamuwa monuments assume either. The only physicality they take for granted is their own; they stand in the open air and speak to whoever passes by: a public.

3 New foundations and funerary traditions in the Iron Age

What remains unclear after examining these three examples is exactly what the new monument-makers were afraid of, what they were hoping for, and whether they received it. The recently excavated monument of Katumuwa, a royal official from 8th-century BCE Zincirli, lets us put these pieces together.[20] In the inscription, written in the same local North-West Semitic dialect of Samʾalian as the Panamuwa inscription, the dead man visually represented on the monument also names the ritual acts to be performed, the form in which he remains present to receive them, and the space left to the inheritor in which he is present for the ritual. This lets us tie the text of an Iron Age Levantine funerary ritual to its context of performance, and this performance to zooarchaeological evidence of actual sacrificial practice.

The 8th-century southern Anatolian site of Zincirli represents a distinctive relationship between the use of writing and the development of a state in the Iron Age. First, the rulers of this area were among the first to create funerary monuments with inscriptions. An example of an older funerary image of the feast of the dead (*Totenmahl*) without an integrated inscription occurs on this 10th-century sarcophagus from Babylos (Figure 3); tellingly, to this sarcophagus a later inscription was added.

By contrast, the 8th-century inscription of Katumuwa integrates ritual instructions into the image of the dead man's postmortem feast (Figure 4). And alone of Syro-Hittite states of the region, the rulers of Zincirli chose to write their monumental inscriptions exclusively in the linear alphabet, in a variety of North-West Semitic dialects. This set them apart from their neighbors, who preferred the old and uniform Anatolian Hieroglyphic writing system emblematic of the Hittite empire. The choice to break with older Anatolian writing traditions is related to the unusual level of ritual detail the inscription gives[21]:

---

20 For the rapid and careful publication of the site background, the object in its archaeological context, and the inscription see Schloen and Fink (2009), Struble and Herrmann (2009), and Pardee (2009). For the name of the inscription's subject, written KTMW, see the evidence analyzed by Younger (2011).

21 The translation is mine (Sanders 2013), revising that of the original publication (Pardee 2009).

Figure 3: Detail of the Ahirom sarcophagus.
Note: Drawn by Porada (1973: 371 fig. 5). Illustration reproduced courtesy of the Jewish Theological Society.

Figure 4: Stele of Katumuwa.
Note: From Struble and Herrmann 2009: 27 fig. 4. Courtesy of the Oriental Institute of the University of Chicago. Drawing by K. Reczuch.

I am Katumuwa, servant of Panamuwa,
who acquired this stele for myself while alive
and set it up in the guest-chamber of my tomb
and ritually instituted this guest-chamber (thus:)
a bull for Hadad the Host,
and a ram for the Chief of Provisions,
and a ram for Shamash,
and a ram for Hadad of the Vineyard,
and a ram for Kubaba,
and a ram for my being[22] which is in this stele.
And as for any of my or anyone's offspring
if this guest-chamber becomes his
he must take an annual offering from the best of
this vineyard,
and make a slaughter where my being is,[23]
and apportion a thigh-cut for me.

While the area and culture of Zincirli displays unusually strong continuity between Late Bronze and Iron Age civilizations, they were nonetheless characterized by a series of new foundations and refoundings.[24] These breaks in urban settlement find correlates in other cultural areas. A particularly clear example appears in the new form of monuments, in the choice to inscribe them, and in a new form, breaking with the older heirloom script of Anatolian hieroglyphic.[25] Like the unique inventory of gods invoked in Katumuwa's monument, the

22 A more accurate but cumbersome rendering might be: "for my appetite and being, which are in this stele." The point is that the presence of the *nbš* makes ritually available two crucial capacities of Katumuwa's self: being fed and being identified.

23 Here a second dimension of the *nbš* may be at work: the earlier alimentary sense of "capacity for eating," in which the sacrifice may be ritually imagined as going into Katumuwa's gullet via the old Amorite practice of anointing the stone with its blood, and the later architectural sense of an inner chamber known from Qatabanian. In fact, it is plausible that from the point of view of the development of the ritual use of the term, the Katumuwa stele represents a turning point in which both potentialities are evoked. Further evidence would be needed to decide.

24 On the phenomenon see Mazzoni (1994); for the larger shift in power relations this tokens, Akkermans and Schwartz (2003: 368).

25 The earliest named founder of a dynasty at Zincirli is the Aramean Gabbar – yet he is named in a Phoenician inscription. In the monumental inscriptions of Kilamuwa, Panamuwa I, Panamuwa II, and Bar-Rakib, the name of the author only nominally agrees with the language in the last instance, and there the use of the now-international Aramaic may well be a sign not of Bar-Rakib's personal identity but of his capitulation to "my master Tiglathpileser." On language choice at Zincirli see the perceptive article of Young (2002) and the concluding note of Pardee (2009), which integrates the dialectal complexities of the Katumuwa inscrip-

decision to then write down the local variety of Samʾalian suggests a deliberate representation of elements unique to the time and place.[26] There seems to be a new relationship to both spatial and temporal concepts: a deliberate localization of written form in the representation of local language, as well as a sense of the dawning of a new era. This raises the question of whether choice in funerary ritual, like choice in writing, betokens a deliberately new relationship with the past.

4 Mortuary ritual and political authority between the Late Bronze and Iron Ages

For the Amorite kings of Babylon and Mari and the kings at Ugarit who inherited related ideologies, the inauguration and rule of a king was dependent on having the right relationship with the right ancestors. These relationships were maintained in two prominent ways in writing: lists of the names of kings and the ritual of feeding the dead known in Babylonian as *kispu*. In fact, at Babylon and Ugarit the two seem to have been fused into one, since the Old Babylonian sacrificial ritual known as the Genealogy of the Hammurapi Dynasty actually constitutes a king-list culminating in a command for all the dead to approach and eat:

> [...]The Amorites, the nomads ('tent-dwellers') the ones not recorded on this tablet, and the soldier(s) who fell while on perilous campaigns for their lord, princes, princesses, all persons from East to West who have neither caretaker (*pāqidu)* nor anyone to invoke your name: come! Eat this! Drink this! (And) bless Ammisaduqa, son of Ammiditana, king of Babylon. (My translation, after Finkelstein 1966)

tion into this picture. For the converse picture at Tell Ahmar see the comments of Bunnens (2006: 99).

26 The choice of linear alphabetic at Zincirli provides an illuminating contrast with the choice of cuneiform alphabetic at Ugarit. Ugaritic is created as choice in contrast to the logo-syllabic cuneiform of the Hittite and Babylonian empires; at Zincirli, use of the alphabet is a deliberate choice in the context of widespread Luwian. In both cases the script marks out a cultural realm, but at Ugarit this script is used to produce an extensive literature in one language variety while at Zincirli language choices appear to be mainly for monumental display, and to shift rapidly. Note well that the standardization of Ugaritic would be readily apparent even if not a scrap of clay were preserved, since it appears as well on axe heads, ivories, and mortuary stelae.

Similarly at Ugarit a number of the same dead Amorite rulers reappear in a ritual checklist as subjects of sacrifice.[27]

The goal for the king in mortuary ritual was to step into the role of ritual feeder and caretaker of politically important dead. If successful, the effect would be to actually *create* the right ancestors and allies to be related to, with the ensuing rootedness to the territory and kinship affiliations of these still-present dead.[28] By assuming this ritual role of caretaker (*pāqidu*) the Amorite king demonstrates that he is not only the heir of powerful ancestors and population groups, but a dutiful one.

Late Bronze Age West Semitic rulers in Syria continued to engage in these reciprocal relationships with the dead. The Old Babylonian ritual of the Hammurapi dynasty calls on the dead to approach, be present at the ritual to eat and bless the offerer. Similarly the beneficent dead ancestors known as *rapaˀūma* at Late Bronze Age Ugarit travel to reach a feast (Pardee 2011).

In all of these second-millennium cases – Old Babylonian Mari and Babylon, Late Bronze Age Ugarit – mortuary ritual creates reciprocal relationships between the living and collective groups of important dead ancestors.[29] And all three are based on data from archives. But as the nature of our sources shifts after the Late Bronze-Iron Age transition, so too does the ritual picture.

We do not fully understand what happened to this ideology in the transition to the Iron Age. To begin with a provocative literary text, in ancient Judah the relationship is sometimes represented as endangered or even severed. David's son Absalom is said to have set up a stele like Katumuwa – despite his being described elsewhere as having four children (2 Samuel 14:27):

> And Absalom went so far as to set up for himself, while alive, a stele in the valley of kings, for he said, "I have no offspring to invoke my name."

---

27 For analysis of the lists, with bibliography, see Pardee (2002: 195–204).

28 The way these rituals can work to claim or even generate ancestors, regardless of blood relation, is pointed up by the genealogically dubious *kispu* performed on Zimri-Lim's behalf: for Sargon and Naram-Sin, the two most prestigious dead Mesopotamian kings to whom Zimri-Lim could not possibly have been related, the *yarādu* (but not Simˀalite, Zimri-Lim's actual clan affiliation!) nomads, the Numheans, and "various others."

29 Interestingly, it is only at Emar that we find evidence of non-royal ritual practicioners, though everywhere except Ugarit seems to include non-royal dead among its ancestors.

But what was the relationship between death ritual, writing, and the state? The Iron Age monuments form a surprising picture: we simply have no West Semitic examples after the Late Bronze Age of dead ancestors being depicted as able to provide success. Our only explicit, archaeologically contextualized Iron Age texts prescribing mortuary ritual are the inscriptions of Panamuwa and Katumuwa, but other texts mentioning ritual for the dead fit this pattern: the deceased offer the living nothing positive.[30] There is no current Iron Age epigraphic evidence of reciprocity between the living and a dead dynasty or ancestor group.

This break between the Iron Age and earlier second millennium traditions is conditioned by political instability. In Anatolia, the divinized founder Atrisuhas is the most extreme example of this break: all he can do is threaten. He does not connect with his ancestors or promise things to his descendants.[31] Panamuwa's demand for feeding assumes a greater continuity: his request is to his sons, but he offers them nothing but to abstain from dethroning them. But Katumuwa shows no confidence that his sons – if they exist – will even inherit responsibility for his mortuary cult.

These new Iron Age rituals also share a larger religious problem: that of coordinating the co-presence of the dead and gods with the untrustworthy living inheritors. By making the divine participants (Atrisuhas, Hadad) or the dead (Katumuwa) present as monuments they invoke participation in new ways, Instead of ancestors in the past, these new funerary rites expand to include and emphasize the presence of gods. There is a move from sharing sacrifice with a temporally vertical series of ancestors, reaching back into the past, to one or more present gods. If ancestors are not thought of as able to provide, the gods can. A further instance of the immediate presence of divine beings in these Syrian and Anatolian rituals is provided by the configuration of an installation at Tell Halaf,[32]

---

30 Of course, implicit in the beneficent power of the ancestors described in the second millennium texts is the threat of losing their favor: as Greenfield already pointed out (1973, and in far greater detail Tsukimoto 1985), *kispu* is often represented in Babylonian (though interestingly, not West Semitic) contexts as done to placate the angry *eṭemmu*, the restless spirit of the dead. Yet this makes it no less significant that the texts of one large historical period consistently articulate the "reward" and a later set of texts consistently articulate the "punishment," or at best remain mute as to reward.

31 On the creation of new divine or semidivine beings in Iron Age Anatolia, compare the stele establishing the presence of and annual offerings for Tarhunzas of the Army (Bunnens 2006) with the stele establishing the presence of and annual offerings for Katumuwa's *nbš*; a similar process must have led to the creation and establishment of offerings for the divinized Atrisuhas. This process of creation of new supernatural beings is a further aspect of ritual creativity in Iron Age Anatolia that bears investigation.

32 For description of this burial with references see Struble and Herrmann (2009).

where the buried statue of a deceased male and female couple faces a statue of the storm-god around an offering-table.

How were the dead present in these rituals? As in the other detailed example from Zincirli, the Panamuwa inscription, the only active dimension of the dead mentioned is the one that eats and drinks; unlike gods or humans it is given no other actions or agency. What the Katumuwa stele adds is his immediate physical presence: it is "my being, which is in this stele." The mortuary tradition attested in detail for the first time here focuses in a new way on the dimensions of appetite and embodiment.

This suggests that Katumuwa was rendered present through his very need to be fed. As Greenfield (1973) and others have argued, ancient East and West Semitic cultures had available at least two basic ways of performing communion with the dead: a) invoking their name through address and memorialization, and b) sharing a meal with them. Both can be performatively effective, but within this ancient ideology the meal has a special kind of power to render someone's personhood present via need, and to perform the satisfaction of that need through feeding. The dead are imagined as hungry, the living present food to them and transfer that food's substance to them via burning or shared eating. Thus the effect of "eating" and "feeding" is produced. The living have thereby evoked and interacted with the dead person's being by summoning them to eat together and sharing the food with them.

We are also able to tell in our final example how this process was performed. Archaeozoology shows that the open-air courtyard adjacent to the room that held Katumuwa's stela also led onto a temple and contained a markedly high portion of bovid and caprid thigh-bones – precisely the cuts Katmumwa requested, along with the food he was supposed to share with his gods (Herrman 2014). A departed human could easily join the table to partake of the accepted cuisine of sacrifice to a god.

In these newly inscribed monuments we see new ritual and rhetorical devices for insuring both perpetuity and presence, but a narrower genealogical basis for doing so. Note the depth of named ancestors in Zincirli inscriptions: one in Panamuwa (KAI 214:1, 13, 14), none in Katumuwa. Compare this with the dozens of ancestors registered in the mortuary ritual of the Old Babylonian Hammurapi dynasty or the dozens registered in the mortuary ritual of the Late Bronze Age dynasty of Ugarit.

There is a strange line in the great art historian Alois Riegl's 1903 "Observations on the Origin and Nature of the Cult of Monuments," where he describes how a work becomes a literary monument once it is inscribed: "Monuments can be either artistic or literary, depending on whether the event to be remembered is brought to the viewer's consciousness by means of the visual arts or with the help of inscriptions" (1982: 21). The message is a command to any future viewer who may come across it, implicit or explicit, to enact the ritual of which the monument is a part, to become a participant along with the monument and its maker in commemoration.

This fits with another mostly forgotten line from a more popular German theorist, Max Weber, whose *Ancient Judaism* contains the apparently cryptic statment that alphabetic writing facilitated the creation of a literature "addressed to the reader" (Weber 1952: 195). This casual line was not banal: who else was literature for? Before the Iron Age, the idea of a general "reader" was inconceivable. Scribes and royal courts were the audience of essentially all written literature in the ancient Near East for the first two millennia of its existence. It is in the Iron Age Levant that we first find what Riegl would call literary monuments – intended not for a select audience but for any reader who came across them – in the alphabet, and not coincidentally the first literature intended for the reader – any who came across it.

The new literary monuments of the Iron Age draw on only a shallow past, but the result is newly creative. The design of these monuments stipulates the participants on the body of the monument itself. In the process they render explicit spatial relationships that Babylonian and Ugaritic scribes might not have thought of and would probably not have indicated: who is where, facing whom, within what. And in inscribing these monuments with the history and demands of the dead, a new genre is produced: the inscribed, self-identifying funerary monument that speaks from after death in the voice of the dead person yet addresses his needs in the present.

5 Conclusion: The new relationship between words and things in Iron Age funerary monuments

As the chronology of culture contact has become clearer in the Iron Age Levant, it is increasingly recognized that history-writing in the alphabet began with the rise of memorial inscriptions in West Semitic, which was conditioned by encounters with the Assyrian empire and its royal monuments (Mark Smith 2007; Sanders 2009). But the evidence of funerary memorial inscriptions in Syria and Anatolia suggests that this view must be expanded: more than one historical trajectory converged in the phenomenon of Iron Age monumental writing. One of these is that of mortuary ritual.

Here the new production of writing in memorial inscriptions also represents a new focus on rendering present in the Iron Age Levant. In earlier collective rituals, descendants speak to the dead, invoking them because they desire to gain the political role of caretaker. The new inscriptions and monuments actually speak on behalf of the dead and make demands for themselves. They are designed to produce the presence of the dead and demand their feeding, independently of initiative on the part of living kin. The literary portrait of Absalom's anxiety finds archaeological analogues in the monuments of Atrisuhas, Panamuwa I, and Katumuwa.

The monumentality of earlier funerary ritual objects – their claim on the present – could only be achieved by human ritual activity, on which the dead ancestor and the object itself were dependent for continued relevance. Funerary objects played varied roles as loci, monuments, or participants but were typically defined as things to which language was momentarily offered, not sites on which language was materialized.

Sometime early in the Iron Age, craftspeople and ritualists began a shift in semiotic ideology – the beliefs and practices by which people define a wide potential range of physical stuff into specific categories of meaningful object with particular cultural features. For the first time, craftspeople began to make language pointedly material. This was a literal inscription of a semiotic ideology: it made statements about the capacities and responsibilities of participants into permanent language; demands that words become things.

The inchoate genre of funerary memorial inscription worked to render the deceased present, without safely assuming participation from descendants or sharing with ancestors. They thus correlated with the new Syrian and Anatolian foundations of the earlier Iron Age, done by founders or establishers on their own behalf. The rise of the literary monument suggests a shift not only in the politics of death but in the semiotic production of the dead as objects. Thus the designers of these Iron Age monuments inscribed a certain type of thing – carved writing – and a certain type of language use – naming and ritual instructions for feeding – into the object with the result of building the object's reception – its monumentality – into itself via inscription. Words, when inscribed into things, made them monuments in a new way.

Acknowledgments: This paper was developed for the "Signifying the Social: Language, Objects, and Materiality" panel at the 2013 American Anthropological Association Meeting. I thank Catherine Rhodes for inviting me to participate, Courtney Handman and Robert Yelle for perceptive comments that improved the paper, and Tim Hogue, whose current UCLA Near Eastern Studies PhD thesis will be the first to show the full value of the notion of monumentality for the study of the ancient Levant, as well as its power to create dialogue with other times and places. It is based on philological and historical arguments first worked out in Sanders 2012 and 2013, where most sources are presented in more detail.

References

Akkermans, Peter M. M. G. & Glenn Schwartz. 2003. *The archaeology of Syria: From complex hunter-gatherers to early urban societies (c. 16,000–300 BC)*. Cambridge: Cambridge University Press.

Althusser, Louis. 1994. Ideology and ideological state apparatuses (notes towards an investigation). In Slavoj Žižek (ed.), *Mapping ideology*, 100–140. London & New York: Verso.

Archi, Alfonso. 2013. Ritualization at Ebla. *Journal of Ancient Near Eastern Religions* 13(2). 212–237.

Bonatz, Dominik. 2000. *Das syro-hethitische Grabdenkmal: Untersuchungen zur Entstehung einer neuen Bildgattung in der Eisenzeit im nordsyrisch-südostanatolischen Raum*. Mainz: P. von Zabern.

Bunnens, Guy. 2006. *A new Luwian stele and the cult of the Storm-god at Til Barsib-Masuwari*. Louvain: Peeters.

Durand, Jean-Marie. 2005. *Le culte des pierres et les monuments commémoratifs en Syrie amorrite* (Florilegium Marianum 8). Paris: SEPOA.

Finkelstein, J. J. 1966. The genealogy of the Hammurapi Dynasty. *Journal of Cuneiform Studies* 20(3/4). 95–118.

Fleming, Daniel E. 2000. *Time at Emar: The cultic calendar and the rituals from the diviner's archive* (Mesopotamian Civilizations 11). Winona Lake, IN: Eisenbrauns.

Gilibert, Alessandra. 2011. *Syro-Hittite monumental art and the archaeology of performance: The stone reliefs at Carchemish and Zincirli in the Earlier First Millennium BCE* (Topoi: Berlin Studies of the Ancient World 2). Berlin: Walter de Gruyter.

Goffman, Erving. 1979. Footing. *Semiotica* 25(1). 1–30.

Greenfield, Jonas. 1973. Un rite religieux araméen et ses parallèles. *Revue Biblique* 80. 46–52.

Herrmann, V. R. 2014. The architectural context of the KTMW Stele from Zincirli and the mediation of Syro-Hittite mortuary cult by the gods. In P. Pfälzner, H. Niehr, E. Pernicka, S. Lange & T. Köster (eds.), *Contextualising grave inventories in the Ancient Near East* (Qatna Studien Supplementa 3), 73–87. Wiesbaden: Harrassowitz.

Hodder, I. 1992. *Theory and practice in archaeology*. London: Routledge.

Hout, Theo van den. 1994. Death as a privilege: The Hittite royal funerary ritual. In J. M. Bremer, Th. P. J. van Den Hout & R. Peters (eds.), *Hidden futures: Death and immortality in ancient Egypt, Anatolia, the Classical, Biblical and Arabic-Islamic world*, 37–75. Amsterdam: Amsterdam University Press.

Irvine, Judith T. 1989. When talk isn't cheap: Language and political economy. *American Ethnologist* 16(2). 248–67.

Jones, A. 2004. Archaeometry and materiality: Materials-based analysis in theory and practice. *Archaeometry* 46(3). 327–338.

Kassian, Alexei, Andrej Korolëv & Andrej Sidel'tsev. 2002. *Hittite funerary ritual: šalliš waštaiš*. Münster: Ugarit Verlag.

Keane, Webb. 1997. Religious language. *Annual Review of Anthropology* 26(1). 47–71.
Keane, Webb. 2003. Semiotics and the social analysis of material things. *Language & Communication* 23(3). 409–425.
Keane, Webb. 2007. *Christian moderns: Freedom and fetish in the mission encounter*. Berkeley, CA: University of California Press.
Laneri, Nicola. 2007. *Performing death: Social analyses of funerary traditions in the Ancient Near East and Mediterranean* (Oriental Institute Seminars no. 3). Chicago: The Oriental Institute of the University of Chicago.
Layton, R. 1989. The political use of Australian Aboriginal body painting and its archaeological implications. In I. Hodder (ed.), *The meaning of things*, 1–10. London: Unwin Hyman.
Liverani, Mario. 2003. The rise and fall of media. In Giovanni Battista Lanfranchi, Michael D. Roaf & Robert Rollinger (eds.), *Continuity of empire (?): Assyria, Media, Persia* (History of the ancient Near East 5), 1–12. Padua: S.a.r.g.o.n.
Marx, Karl. 1971 [1859]. Zur Kritik der politischen Ökonomie. In *Karl Marx/Friedrich Engels: Werke*, vol. 13, 1–160. Berlin: Karl Dietz Verlag.
Mazzoni, Stefania. 1994. *Nuove fondazioni nel vicino Oriente antico: Realtà e ideologia: Atti del colloquio 4–6 dicembre 1991, Dipartimento di scienze storiche del mondo antico, Sezione di Egittologia e scienze storiche del vicino Oriente, Università degli studi di Pisa*. Pisa: Giardini.
Melas, E. M. 1989. Etics, emics and empathy in archaeological theory. In I. Hodder (ed.), *The meaning of things*, 137–154. London: Unwin Hyman.
Morales, Antonio. 2016. Text-building and transmission of pyramid texts in the Third Millennium BCE: Iteration, objectification, and change. *Journal of Ancient Near Eastern Religions* 15(2). 169–201.
Otten, H. 1951. Die hethitischen "Königslisten" und die altorientalische chronologie. *Mitteilungen der Deutschen Orient-Gesellschaft zu Berlin* 83. 47–71.
Pardee, Dennis. 2000. *Les textes rituels*. 2 vols. Paris: Éditions recherche sur les civilisations.
Pardee, Dennis. 2002. *Ritual and cult at Ugarit* (Writings from the Ancient World 10). Leiden & Boston: Brill.
Pardee, Dennis. 2003. The Aqhatu legend. In William Hallo & K. Lawson Younger (eds.), *The context of scripture*, vol. 1, *Canonical compositions from the biblical world*, 343–356. Leiden: Brill.
Pardee, Dennis. 2009. A new Aramaic inscription from Zincirli. *Bulletin of the American Schools of Oriental Research* 356. 51–71.
Pardee, Dennis. 2011. Nouvelle étude épigraphique et littéraire des textes fragmentaires en langue ougaritique dits "Les Rephaïm" (CTA 20–22). *Orientalia* 80. 1–65.
Pioske, Daniel D. 2015. *David's Jerusalem: Between memory and history* (Routledge studies in religion 45). New York: Routledge.
Porada, Edith. 1973. Notes on the sarcophagus of Ahiram. *Journal of the Ancient Near Eastern Society* 5. 355–372.
Porter, Anne. 2002. The dynamics of death: Ancestors, pastoralism, and the origins of a third-millennium city in Syria. *Bulletin of the American Schools of Oriental Research* 325. 1–36.
Preucel, R.W. & A. A. Bauer. 2001. Archaeological pragmatics. *Norwegian Archaeological Review* 34(2). 85–96.
Rhodes, C. 2013. Shifting perspective: from objects of material culture to cultural representation of the linguistic and non-linguistics. Paper presentation in panel entitled "Signifying the Social: Language, Objects, and Materiality." American Anthropological Association Meeting, Chicago, IL.

Riegl, Alois. 1982 [1903]. The modern cult of monuments: Its character and its origin. *Oppositions* 25. 20–51.
Sanders, Seth L. 2009. *The invention of Hebrew*. Champaign: University of Illinois Press.
Sanders, Seth L. 2012. Naming the dead: Funerary writing and historical change in the Iron Age Levant. *Maarav* 19.7–31.
Sanders, Seth L. 2013. The appetites of the dead: West Semitic linguistic and ritual aspects of the Katumuwa Stele. *Bulletin of the American Schools of Oriental Research* 369. 35–55.
Schloen, J. David & Amir S. Fink. 2009. New excavations at Zincirli Höyük in Turkey (Ancient Sam'al) and the discovery of an inscribed mortuary stele. *Bulletin of the American Schools of Oriental Research* 356. 1–13.
Schopen, Gregory. 1997. *Bones, stones, and Buddhist monks: Collected papers on the archaeology, epigraphy, and texts of monastic Buddhism in India*. Honolulu: University of Hawaii Press.
Silverstein, Michael & Greg Urban (eds). 1996. *Natural histories of discourse*. Chicago: University of Chicago Press.
Smith, Adam T. 2007. The politics of loss: Comments on a powerful death. In N. Laneri (ed.), *Performing death: social analyses of funerary traditions in the Ancient Near East and Mediterranean* (Oriental Institute Seminars no. 3), 163–166. Chicago: The Oriental Institute of the University of Chicago.
Smith, Mark S. 2007. Biblical narrative between Ugaritic and Akkadian literature, Part II, Mesopotamian impact on biblical narrative. *Revue Biblique* 114. 189–207.
Sommer, Benjamin D. 2009. *The bodies of God and the world of ancient Israel*. Cambridge: Cambridge University Press.
Struble, Eudora J. & Virginia Rimmer Herrmann. 2009. An eternal feast at Sam'al: The New Iron Age mortuary stele from Zincirli in context. *Bulletin of the American Schools of Oriental Research* 356.15–49.
Suriano, Matthew. 2009. Dynasty building at Ugarit: The ritual and political context of KTU 1.161. *Aula Orientalis* 27. 105–123.
Suriano, Matthew. 2010. *The politics of dead kings: Dynastic ancestors in the Book of Kings and ancient Israel* (Forschungen zum Alten Testament, 2. Reihe, 48). Tübingen: Mohr Siebeck.
Tilley, Christopher Y. 1989. *Metaphor and material culture*. Oxford: Blackwell Publishers.
Tsukimoto, Akio. 1985. *Untersuchungen zur Totenpflege* (kispum) *im alten Mesopotamien* (Alter Orient und Altes Testament). Kevelaer: Butzon & Bercker.
Weber, Max. 1952. *Ancient Judaism*. Translated and edited by Hans H. Gerth and Don Martindale. New York: Free Press.
Yelle, Robert A. 2003. *Explaining mantras: Ritual, rhetoric, and the dream of a natural language in Hindu Tantra*. London & New York: Routledge.
Young, I. 2002. The languages of Ancient Sam'al. *Maarav* 9. 93–106.
Younger, Lawson K. 2011. Two epigraphic notes on the new Katumuwa inscription from Zincirli. *Maarav* 16. 159–179.

Isabel Laack

The (poetic) imagery of "flower and song" in Aztec religious expression: Correlating the semiotic modalities of language and pictorial writing

Yca ye ninapanao tlaocolxochicozcatlon nomac ōmanian elcicihuilizchimalxochitlon nic ehuaya in tlaocolcuicatl oo nicchalchiuhcozcahuicomana yectli yan cuicatl nicahuachxochilacatzoa y nochalchiuhuehueuh ilh. ytech nictlaxilotia in nocuicatzin in nicuicani ye niquincuilia in ilh chaneque o çaquantototl quetzaltzinitzcantototl teoquechol in on tla'toa quechol in quicecemeltia in tloq, etc.

Cantares Mexicanos, folio 5r[1]

[I dress myself in a sad-flower-necklace; in my hands lie my sighing-shield-flowers. I raise a sad song; I turquoise-necklace-offer up a good song. I pull a sprinkle of flowers from my turquoise huehuetl. I, the singer, hold up my dear song to the sky; I take it from the sky-inhabitants: the zacuan-bird, the quetzaltzinitzcan-bird, the divine quechol–the quechol who sings, who entertains the Ever-Present, (the Ever-near.)][2]

1 Introduction

The people currently known as the "Aztecs"[3] lived in Central Mexico from the 13th to the 16th centuries CE. By building on the rich cultural history of Mesoamerica, the Aztecs developed within only two centuries a flourishing civilization abundant with intellectual, religious, and aesthetic achievements. These achievements included a complex cosmovision (*Weltanschauung*) – that is, a complex

1 This transcription of the manuscript is taken from Bierhorst (1985: 146).
2 This translation is taken from Tomlinson (2007: 68).
3 The name "Aztecs" was initially coined by Alexander von Humboldt (Humboldt 1810) and was made widely popular by William H. Prescott (1843). Since then, the term has generally been used to refer to the (largely) Nahuatl-speaking ethnic groups that formed the "Aztec empire" in the last centuries before the Spanish conquest. In particular, the name refers to the Nahuas who lived in Tenochtitlan-Tlatelolco, belonged to the ethnic subgroup of the Mexica, and controlled the "Aztec empire" both politically and militarily.

Isabel Laack, Ruprecht Karl University, Heidelberg

https://doi.org/10.1515/9781614514329-015

view of the world and sense of reality – and elaborate semiotic systems to express cultural knowledge, among the latter an extensive and elegant oral tradition and a refined writing system. Judged from the surviving sources, the Nahuas had an inclination for imaginary thinking dense with symbols, metaphors, and sensory imagery. One of the most famous examples for this kind of Aztec poetic expression is the image of 'flower and song' (*in xochitl in cuicatl*). This image was prevalent in songs from the oral tradition that were alphabetically transcribed in the early colonial (ca. 1550–1580 CE) documents known as the *Cantares Mexicanos* (Bierhorst 1985) and the *Romances de los Señores de la Nueva España* (Bierhorst 2009). The language of this rather small corpus of songs is largely intractable for modern readers and uses very unfamiliar semiotic modes. Nevertheless, the image of 'flower and song' (*in xochitl in cuicatl*) has confidently been interpreted in modern scholarship as a metaphor standing for an indigenous philosophical approach, which favored poetic aestheticism as the best way to gain and express insights about the ultimate, transcendent layers of reality. Since there is little contextual information available helping us to interpret the songs, scholars trying to reach any understanding of them are left with few options other than referring to rather general interpretations of the Aztec cosmovision. Accordingly, interpretations might differ so widely that one wonders whether they are talking about the same material and cultural context. Scholars in search of tight philological analyses might quickly get dispirited with this discussion. Nevertheless, it would be a shame to disregard the material completely for that reason.

In this paper, I would like to present an alternative interpretation of the image of "flower and song," an interpretation that is based on recent scholarly reconstructions of central facets of the cosmovision and ontology of Aztec culture in the time immediately before the Spanish conquest. Necessarily, this will be a rather abstract discussion, as well as truncated due to the required brevity of this paper.[4] In terms of epistemology, my alternative interpretation does not claim to have any better access to Aztec affect, sense, and thought than those interpretations offered before. It is simply a new attempt to search for cross-cultural historical semiotic understanding, a thought experiment inspired by reflection on potential Eurocentrisms in the earlier interpretations.

My core argument is that "flower and song" was used by the Aztec singers not as a metaphor referring to transcendent layers of reality but as a metonymic, indexical reference to sensorily experienceable, immanent principles of reality as Aztec culture perceived them. As the two elements "flower" and "song" were

4 Readers in search of a more detailed discussion are referred to my forthcoming book on the subject to be published in 2019 in the *Numen Book Series* (Brill).

considered as indexes of the same quality, the semiotic modalities of language and writing that deployed them were understood not as re-presentations but as direct presentations of the perceived principles of reality. Thus, the spoken and the written sign were ascribed the same ontological immediacy to reality. Based on this interpretation, to distinguish the ontological immediacy of speech from that of writing, or the poetic from the referential function of language, turns out to be an inappropriate division deriving from colonialism. Consequently, Aztec semiotic sense provides a fundamental challenge to dominant modern semiotic ideologies by resisting the dichotomy of rational versus poetic and performative discourse, as much as it resists the dominant modern dichotomy that sharply demarcates scientific from mythical, magical, or religious discourse. Readers open to an interpretational experiment of this kind are invited to follow me on the journey.

2 Introducing Aztec culture

The Aztec civilization rose quickly to political power and wide cultural influence in Mesoamerica, only to fall within just a couple of years through the Spanish conquest of Mexico. In the late 12th and early 13th centuries, Nahuatl-speaking groups had migrated from their semi-mythical home-place of *Aztlan* in the northern deserts into the Central Highlands and founded many small, increasingly competitive city-states. Among these were the twin-cities of Tenochtitlan and Tlatelolco, founded by the Mexica ethnic group around 1325 CE on a swampy island in the western part of Lake Texcoco in the Basin of Mexico, where Mexico City is now located.[5] Within the next century, the Mexica gained increasing influence in the valley of Mexico, based on their military prowess and strategic political skills. Allying with the two neighboring towns of Texcoco and Tlacopan, the Mexica established a strong new military confederacy in 1428 CE, the *excan tlatoloyan* or 'tribunal of three places' commonly called the "Triple Alliance" in English. Following many successful military campaigns within and beyond the valley of Mexico, the alliance soon rose to become a powerful hegemonic empire across large parts of Mesoamerica that controlled its subjects indirectly (Davies 1973: 62–85). The empire's main interest did not lie in political but in economic dominance, ensuring extensive tax or tribute payments and controlling an impressive market system (see Hassig 1985; Berdan and Smith 1996).

Within this socio-political context, the Mexica developed a rich culture, which combined their nomadic Chichimec legacy with traditions from the earlier Toltec

5 For the early history of the Aztec civilization, see Davies (1973: 3–85).

civilization. Thus, the new Aztec civilization was quintessentially Mesoamerican but had also acquired a characteristic, unique identity and a sense of mission as the People of the Sun (see Caso 1958). It was based on highly advanced political, economic, and educational systems and a complex social structure, which supported many intellectual professionals: scribes and historians; poets, orators, and interpreters of books; astronomers, astrologers and philosophers (Sahagún 1961). Its cosmovision was decidedly complex and diverse, placing its emphasis on aesthetic expression and pragmatic matters rather than on intellectual speculation. Believing themselves to be living in the unstable cosmos of the Fifth Sun, the Aztecs felt it their duty to constantly balance the dynamism of complementary forces in order to maintain the flow of cosmic energy. Humanity was nourished by the sun and the earth, and it needed to nourish the earth in return and to feed the sun to ensure its continuing movement (López Austin 2008b: 35). The Aztec cosmovision was heavily materialist, regarding human beings as part of the cosmos living in manifold interrelationships with the land, the skies, and their fellow inhabitants of the Fifth Sun, such as plants, animals, and the many deities dwelling in everything. In this way, what we would call "religion" was intertwined with every aspect of human life, including agriculture and diet, health and medicine, social structure and political motivations, historiography, and cultural identity. Many different forms of rituals formed an important part of everyday life, both on the level of small-scale personal rites and in form of the large-scale, public ritual performances held each month of the solar year (see, e.g., Quiñones Keber 2002).

The Aztec civilization knew many forms of cultural expression, among them was a very strong oral tradition. Elegant speech and rhetoric were taught in the *calmecac* and *telpochcalli* schools (see Calnek 1988), and the nobility were expected to show great virtuosity in the strongly formalized system of elegant speech (León-Portilla 1969: 27; Clendinnen 1991: 220; Lockhart 1993: 375). Classical Nahuatl was a complex language with refined linguistics and sophisticated rhetorical expression providing an extraordinarily rich reservoir of cultural and religious knowledge. It used many riddles and idioms and a high amount of metaphors and imagery. Some of the most beautiful formal speeches and prayers were recorded by Nahua intellectuals working with Fray Bernardino de Sahagún in the middle of the 16th century and survive in book six of Sahagún's *Florentine Codex* (Sahagún 1969). The alphabetical transcriptions of songs in the *Florentine Codex* and in the previously noted manuscripts *Cantares Mexicanos* and *Romances de los Señores de la Nueva España* are our main sources for the rich oral tradition of the Aztecs.

The Aztecs used many forms of visual communication including architecture, sculpture, jewelry, painting on linens, decoration of clothing and costumes, and feather working. They also used a complex writing system represented in the application of polychrome paints on flat surfaces, most importantly in screenfold books made from indigenous paper called *amatl*. Judging by comments in colonial sources (e.g., Díaz del Castillo 2008: 169), complete libraries were filled with works of writing. *In tlilli in tlapalli* 'the red and black [ink]', the indigenous expression for "writing" and "book," was regarded as the foundation of wisdom and cultural knowledge (Sahagún 1969: 258).[6] After the Spanish conquest, European literacy was introduced, including not only alphabetic writing but also a complete system of genres and forms of written expression. Following a phase of creative syncretism, such colonial systems gradually replaced indigenous semiotic modalities. Only a few manuscripts painted in the traditional style of the Central Highlands – called the "Postclassic International Style" (Boone and Smith 2003: 186–192) – have survived until the present day. Among them are tribute records and property plans, ethnic histories and genealogies, calendars and astronomical measurements, cosmologies, and handbooks for rituals and divination.[7]

In contrast to other Mesoamerican writing systems from earlier cultures or other regions (see Marcus 1992) – with Mayan writing the most famous among them – Aztec writing was not phonographic: rather than notating the sounds of language, it recorded visual imagery. Aztec pictorial writing was primarily based on the use of pictograms and ideograms. In brief, pictograms depicted material objects, such as a house or a stone, through iconic representations. Ideograms, on the other hand, visualized abstract concepts in a conventionalized form based on natural association or metonymy, either through the combination of several pictograms (a burning temple for "conquest," or a shield and spears for "war") or through conventionalized abstract signs (the concepts of "day" or "movement") (Boone 2000: 33; see Figure 1). These individual or compound signs were painted on the flat surface of the pages of codices made from paper, or on *lienzos* (large sheets of cotton) and *tiras* (long, mostly rolled pieces of animal hide or paper). They were arranged in an intricate manner, forming a visual grammar, and depicting narrative syntax and complex concepts of time and history (Leibsohn 1994; Boone 2000; see Figure 2). The surviving traditional manuscripts can be grouped into different genres: cartographic representations for migration stories, time-line frames for annals, event-based structures

6 See also the powerful Mexica legend about the loss of all books and thus all cultural knowledge during the migration (Sahagún 1961: 189–191).

7 Some of the most elaborate and beautiful manuscripts are from the so-called *Borgia Group* painted in the Mixteca-Puebla region (e.g., the *Codex Borgia*, the *Codex Féjerváry-Mayer*, and the *Codex Vaticanus 3773 B*), from the *Mixtec Group* (e.g., the *Codex Vindobonensis*, and the *Codex Zouche-Nutall*), from the *Aztec Group* (e.g., the *Codex Borbonicus*, the *Tonalamatl Aubin*, and the *Codex Boturini*), and the early colonial *Mapa de Cuauhtinchan No. 2* (see Cline 1972–1975).

Figure 1: Basic Aztec signs.
Note: Drawings by Isabel Laack after Codices Mendoza and Borbonicus.

for individual biographies, and table-style almanacs for divinatory purposes (Boone 2000: 64–86; see Figure 3).

This pictorial style of writing constitutes a highly evolved and complex communication system working with visual imagery, space, and colors. As such, many paintings are similar not only to European painting and graphic arts but also to European tables and figures, or mathematical or musical notion. The divination codices, for example, depict graphically the relationships within the sacred calendar between the different variables of the cosmos and the deities. They also show the correspondences between "units and cycles of time and the meanings that adhere to them" (Boone 2007: 3). According to art historian Elizabeth H. Boone (2007: 68), the structure of different sections of the divination almanacs is similar to graphics used in modern chemistry, logic, and statistical analysis: some are organized in sequential lists, others in tables constituted of multiplied and layered lists, and still others in diagrams formed in a particular shape (e.g., the shape of a deerskin; see Figure 4). Accordingly, Boone describes these almanacs as "equivalent to our books of philosophy, theoretical physics, astronomy, and astrology" (2007: 3). Like the notational systems of the modern European sciences, the almanacs simplified, abstracted, marked, labelled, and schematized the observed complex

Figure 2: Codex Borgia, folio 33.
Note: 1898 Loubat facsimile edition. Digital reproduction provided by the Metropolitan Museum of Art, Thomas J. Watson Library, New York City.

phenomena of nature. Several pictorial strategies were employed to depict this knowledge about the cosmos in lucid structures (Boone 2007: 238). In complex tables, “a great quantity of precise information” was presented “in a structure that facilitates ready inspection of individual data and quick comparison between potentially related phenomena.” This was a very efficient system of recording knowledge, which captured diverse nuances of cosmic relationships “impossible to render in words and sentences” (Boone 2007: 75). As such, the divination codices depicted the complex confluence of divine forces in form of a cognitive map of time, tide, place, and direction, which helped the diviner to navigate these currents and to guide proper living (Maffie 2014: 427).

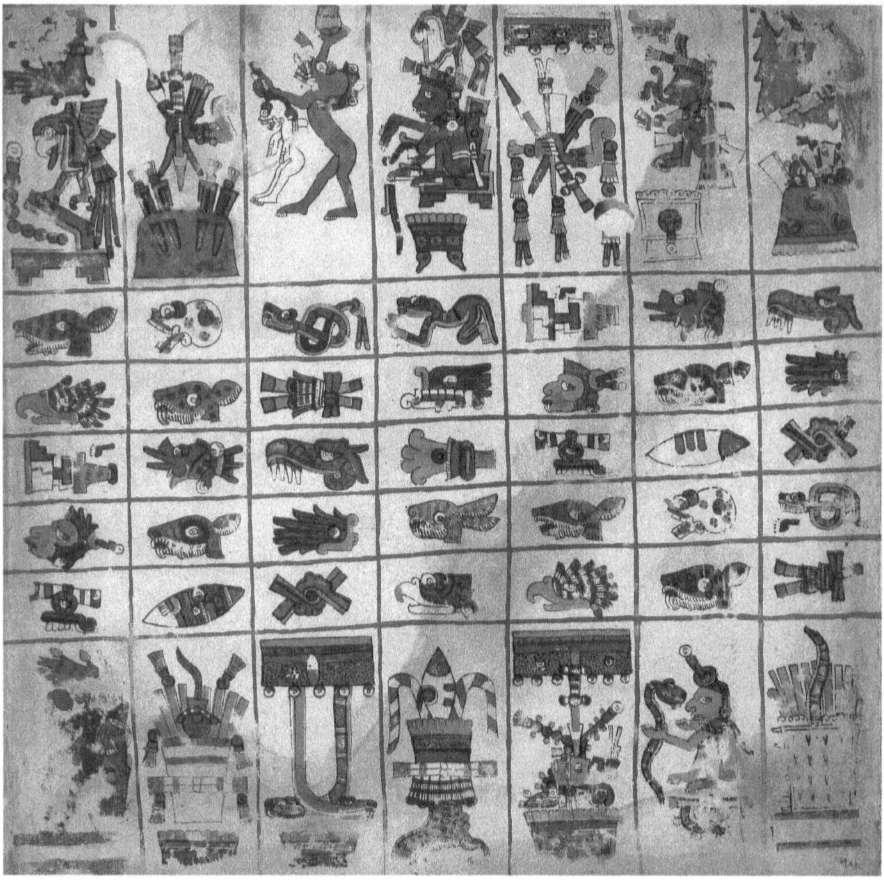

Figure 3: Divination Almanac, Codex Borgia, folio 6.
Note: 1898 Loubat facsimile edition. Digital reproduction provided by the Metropolitan Museum of Art, Thomas J. Watson Library, New York City.

3 The imagery of "flower and song" in the Aztec oral tradition

The two early colonial manuscripts, *Cantares Mexicanos* and *Romances de los Señores de la Nueva España*, are alphabetical transcriptions in Latin script of about 120 Nahuatl songs. Although the transcriptions lack information about the musical and performative aspects of the songs, they nevertheless tell us many things about the linguistic dimensions of the Nahuatl oral tradition.

Figure 4: Deerskin Almanac, Codex Borgia, folio 53.
Note: 1898 Loubat facsimile edition. Digital reproduction provided by the Metropolitan Museum of Art, Thomas J. Watson Library, New York City.

The original versions of the surviving copies of the two manuscripts stem from late 16th-century Central Mexico, with the *Cantares Mexicanos* compiled loosely and the *Romances* organized in a European-style anthology. The Nahuatl songs in the manuscripts were not only collected some decades after the conquest but also contain many references to post-conquest dates and Christian ideas. Whether they nevertheless present an "authentic" pre-Hispanic oral tradition that survived unchanged apart from some interpolations (León-Portilla 1992a and 2011: 196–208) or whether they are expressions of truly post-conquest sentiments within a nativist revitalization movement (Bierhorst 1985: 3–5), has been hotly debated in scholarship. Regardless of these different scholarly viewpoints, the post-colonial origin of the songs and some of their contents is beyond dispute, while fundamental characteristics in both style and subject clearly stem from the pre-Hispanic tradition (Lockhart 1993: 398–399; Gruzinski 2002: 150–179).

Reconstructing the songs' performative context from several sources permits the inference that they were most probably sung and danced as parts of larger rituals and ceremonies in both public and private settings. They were performed with drum and other musical accompaniments and embedded in multi-media performances. During these performances, the ritual participants also read manuscripts and sheets painted in the traditional writing style and – in their nature as material objects – handled them ritually (Bierhorst 1985: 72–80, 129; Bierhorst 2009: 44–45; Tomlinson 2007: 57–61, 87–90; Lee 2008: 136–142). The transcribed song texts contain many non-translatable syllables and vocables. For example the *yehuaya* and *aya* in the following lines:

> *Aquin nehua nipapatlantinemi yehuaya notlatlalia nixochincuicã cuicapapalotl aya*[8]
>
> [Who am I? I am soaring about, yehuaya! I compose; I flower-sing. It is a song-butterfly, aya.][9]

These vocables were most probably signs standing in a "liminal position between non-linguistic cry and semi-semantic word" and not only provided a "special rhythmic or melodic emphasis" but also had "exclamatory impact" and "substantial affective weight" (Tomlinson 2007: 84–85). In these vocables, the song itself is materialized: "The performer of the *cantares*, who so often sang a song about his song, could also sing the song sung about" (Tomlinson 2007: 87). According to Gary Tomlinson's analysis, the vocables point towards an indigenous language theory that regards sound as the (re)presentation of auditory layers of the essential principles of reality.

Regarding their format, the songs are divided in stanzas, strophes, and refrains, and show many pairings of verses (Tomlinson 2007: 54–61). Independent, self-contained, non-metrical verses of varied length are symmetrically arranged to form a coherent whole. There is generally no narrative element, nor any development of verses building toward a logical conclusion (Lockhart 1993: 394–396). Rather, verses are usually arranged around a center in terms of theme, feeling, or character: "The individual strophes often seem, indeed, to orbit around the theme or set of themes of the song they make up rather than pursuing a progressive elaboration, narrative or lyrical, of the topics at hand" (Tomlinson 2007: 61). Nahuatl linguist James Lockhart

---

8 *Cantares Mexicanos*, folio 11v. This transcription of the manuscript is taken from Bierhorst (1985: 166).

9 This translation is taken from Tomlinson (2007: 69).

characterized this type of structural organization as a "cellular-modular organization" (1993: 439), which, according to his analyses, was present not only in the language, but also in other parts of Nahua culture (Lockhart 1993: 419, see also 294–296, 437–441). This agglutinative, "conceptual parataxis" of Nahuatl at the level of its larger structural organization also manifests at the level of individual words and sentences; most characteristically in the use of a phenomenon called "hypertrophism" (Bierhorst 2009: 11), which forms many different ideas (and "words" in the European sense) into complex compounds. These compounds often combine subjects or objects with actions and colors and materials. In the example given above:

nicchalchiuhcozcahuicomana 'I turquoise-necklace-offer up' (Tomlinson 2007: 68)

tlaocolxochicozcatlon 'a sad-flower-necklace' (Tomlinson 2007: 68).

Other striking examples:

chachalchiuhquetzalitztonameyo 'the green-season-flower-songs turquoise-jade-shine' (Tomlinson 2007: 75)

mochipahualizichpochaçucenaxochicelticayotzin 'your pure and maidenly lily-flower freshness' [a salutation to Mary] (Bierhorst 2009: 11)

The language of the songs of the *Cantares Mexicanos* and the *Romances* is generally very dense in metaphors, symbolism, and imagery, with a certain set of stock images of flowers, songs, birds, and precious materials recurring "constantly through the corpus, mixed and varied in kaleidoscopic fashion" (Lockhart 1993: 394). The songs show also a strong incantational style with a high frequency of verbs referring to activities of spreading, descending, and summoning, in which "figures of authority," i.e., historical kings and military leaders, are called upon (Bierhorst 2009: 25–27, 44–45). The language of the songs is very similar to the *nahuallatolli* genre as it was recorded in the 17th century by Ruiz de Alarcón (1984) and Jacinto de la Serna (1953). The *nahuallatolli* was the strongly ritualized language of the shamans, diviners, and healers, and was used in ritual invocations (see López Austin 1967). It was "the language of the hidden," which addressed the hidden, yet very real and material nature of existing entities that was sheltered from everyday perception (López Austin 1988: 346). In its obscureness and rich complexity, this language was thought to reveal better than everyday language the essential quality of the entity addressed, and to be able to manipulate these forces (Gruzinski 1993: 158–161; Boone 2007: 4). The *nahuallatolli* is sometimes called a language of "magic" because of its strong formulaic character, invocational power, and manipulative intention. However, this European category is more misleading than helpful for understanding this phenomenon of Nahua culture. The *nahuallatolli* was believed to address directly the essential nature of things with the shamans being able to "work" on this "invisible substance" using their own "invisible and well-developed animistic bodies" (López Austin 1993: 153).

Nowadays, texts in the *nahuallatolli* remain almost untranslatable. The language used in the *Cantares Mexicanos* and in the *Romances* is similarly difficult to understand for non-native readers/listeners, since its rich imagery evokes a cultural habitus and an experience of life and of the world that is far from our reach (Lockhart 1993: 374–375; Rabasa 2011: 184). Some of the images, however, draw on cross-culturally understandable experiences and might give us an impression of how the imagery worked. The image of the (very beautiful) plumage of the Quetzal bird, for example, was used to refer to the concept of beauty; a necklace of precious stones was used for lineage and descent; and eagles and ocelots were images for brave warriors (León-Portilla 1980: 39). Many of these images come in pairs like "flower and song," but there were also quartets, quadruplets, and "necklaces of multiple images, all hovering luminously about the neck of a concept or thing" (Gingerich 1987: 97).

Regarding content, the main themes of ethnic pride, battle, martial glory, friendship, the refinements of nobility, and the divine were expressed with a lyricism of flowers, butterflies, birds, singing, music, and precious stones, and with many references to the ephemerality of everything that exists (Tomlinson 2007: 62–63). In some of the songs, the nature of music and song is explicitly reflected upon,[10] most prominently in the first four songs of the *Cantares Mexicanos*. Roughly sketched, "flower and song" or flower-songs (*in xochitl in cuicatl*) are created by the deities for human enjoyment as a compensation for the nourishment that humans provide to the deities through their death by war or sacrifice. Poets travel between the skies and bring the flowers down onto the earth, where they create a temporal flower land (*Xochitlalpan*). In this land, the flowers are sung as songs and soothe the sadness of Nahua nobles while these reflect on the deaths of their comrades and their own future sacrifice (Lee 2008: 164–167, 172):

> *Nocontimaloaya nocontlamachtiao xochiteyolquima cuicatlā poyomapoctli ic ye auian ye noyollo, nihualyolcuecuechahuaya nic ihnecuia ahuiacaxocomiqui in noyolia nic yhnecuia yectli ya xochitla netlamachtiloyan xochiyeihuinti noyolia.*

10 See, regarding the issue of this form of linguistic reflexivity, Aurélie Névot's chapter in this volume.

> [I exalt him, rejoice him with heart-pleasing flowers in this place of song. With narcotic fumes my heart is pleasured. I soften my heart, inhaling them. My soul grows dizzy with the fragrance, inhaling good flowers in this place of enjoyment. My soul is drunk with flowers.] (Bierhorst 1985: 140–141)

The imagery of "flower and song" (*in xochitl in cuicatl*) used so prevalently in many of the songs was interpreted by Garibay and his student Miguel León-Portilla as a root metaphor of Aztec culture, as a fundamental *difrasismo*[11] referring to the concept of "poetry." In León-Portilla's view (e.g., 1980: 44), the songs express a highly philosophical and spiritual sensitivity about the ephemerality of earthly life. Facing the evanescent nature of all things beautiful on earth, the minds of the melancholic poet-kings who wrote the songs are soothed exactly by this beauty of the flowers, called down with songs from the heavens, and by the grace of friendship among comrades. This beauty and grace can soothe them because it metaphorically speaks of the existence of an ultimate and everlasting realm. According to León-Portilla, the songs reflect on these philosophical issues and express a type of poetical aestheticism; that is, an epistemology of *in xochitl in cuicatl*, in which only poetry might truly capture and express this transcendent nature of reality.

Nahuatl specialist John Bierhorst, however, fundamentally challenged this interpretation of the imagery of "flower and song." In his view, it casts "a glow of humanism over Mexico's ancient past" (Bierhorst 2009: viii) and takes "the songs to be poetic ruminations of old kings stationed in flowery gardens – like shepherds stepped out of the *Eclogues* interlarded with firsthand reportage from pre-Cortésian battlefields" (Bierhorst 2009: vii). Bierhorst understood the songs as expressions of a post-conquest revitalization movement, in which the spirits of dead heroic ancestors are sung down from their dwelling places in the skies. The flowers and songs summoned from heaven to earth in many of the songs are only metaphors for the ghost spirits of the ancestors raining and whirling down, literally summoned down on earth through the performance (Bierhorst 1985: 3–5, 22–23). As part of complex musical and danced performances, the songs were thus actually a fully blown "ghost-song ritual" (Bierhorst 1985: 16–34). Most probably, Bierhorst was inspired for this interpretation by the 19th-century indigenous Ghost Dance movement in the North American Great Plains, with mock-battles remembering glorious past victories.

---

11 The term *difrasismo* (roughly translated in English as "two-phrases-device") was coined by the Nahuatl linguist Angel M. Garibay Kintana to refer to the very common stylistic device of paired images in Nahuatl. In his view, the two combined phrases metaphorically stood for a new, third meaning (1940: 112).

4 Visual imagery in Aztec pictorial writing

Aztec pictorial writing recorded visual imagery rather than the sounds of language; and the imagery used in spoken Nahuatl is directly visible in the pictorial texts. For example, the *difrasismo* 'water and mountain' (for *altepetl* or 'settlement/town') was depicted through the (stylized) visual appearance of water and a mountain (see Figure 5). The imagery used for the concept of "authority" was a ruler sitting on a mat. This image could not only be used as a figure of speech or a shorthand visual sign but could also be applied to express more complex thoughts, actions, or happenings. In an image painted in Sahagún's *Florentine Codex*, for example, the mat underneath a sitting ruler is woven from snakes disentangling and going off into different directions (see Figure 6). According

Figure 5: Altepetl, 'settlement/town'.
Note: Drawing by Isabel Laack after Codex Boturini.

Figure 6: Ruler sitting on serpent mat.
Note: Drawing by Isabel Laack after Sahagún 1979: 3, book 11, folio 84r.

to Emily Umberger's analysis, the image probably shows a ruler losing control of his subjects, with the individual serpents representing "the different strands of society that only a powerful ruler could coordinate" (Umberger 2007: 16). Similarly, imagery from important myths was used in historical narratives to express certain key concepts as they appeared in the myths; for example, the story of Huiztilopochtli and Coyolxauhqui provided imagery denoting political and social success and failure (Umberger 2007: 14). In this way, the imagery of "flower and song" is also used in the pictorial writings – though not as prominently as suggested by León-Portilla, who interpreted *in xochitl in cuicatl* as a poetic aestheticism and the one fundamental Aztec philosophical approach.

One of the most beautiful examples of the pictorial image "flower and song" is found on the second (surviving) page of the *Codex Borbonicus* (Anders et al. 1991), an early divination almanac from the Aztec tradition painted in traditional style (see Figure 7). Here, two human figures with animal features are depicted, most probably ritual participants incorporating deities. They are shown in a performative context surrounded by ritual implements and playing musical instruments such as the drum. From their mouths issue both simple speaking scrolls and elaborate ornate volutes that combine the pictorial signs for "flower" and "song." Most probably, this image presents a situation of performative singing as reflected upon in the songs of the *Cantares Mexicanos* and the *Romances*. As such, the concept of performative singing and "flower and song" is visually depicted in the pictorial writing system. In contrast to most forms of (modern and print) phonographic writing, the actual visual appearance of the signs and their spatial arrangement, as much as the particular combination of forms and colors, are highly relevant for the meaning of the respective image (Gruzinski 1993: 13; Leibsohn 2009: 7). Thus, the efficacy of each text depended not only on the "accuracy in recording concepts and facts," but also "its poetics, balance, and graphic execution" (Boone 2011: 197).

5 "Flower and song" as depictions of immanent reality

In the following section, I present an interpretation of the Nahuatl imagery of "flower and song" as used in the two semiotic modalities of language and writing that fundamentally differs from both León-Portilla's and Bierhorst's interpretations. In my view, this image does not refer to the summoned ghosts of heroic ancestors nor is it a metaphor for the idea of poetics as a form of philosophical aestheticism. Instead, I interpret it as an expression of an implicit cosmovision

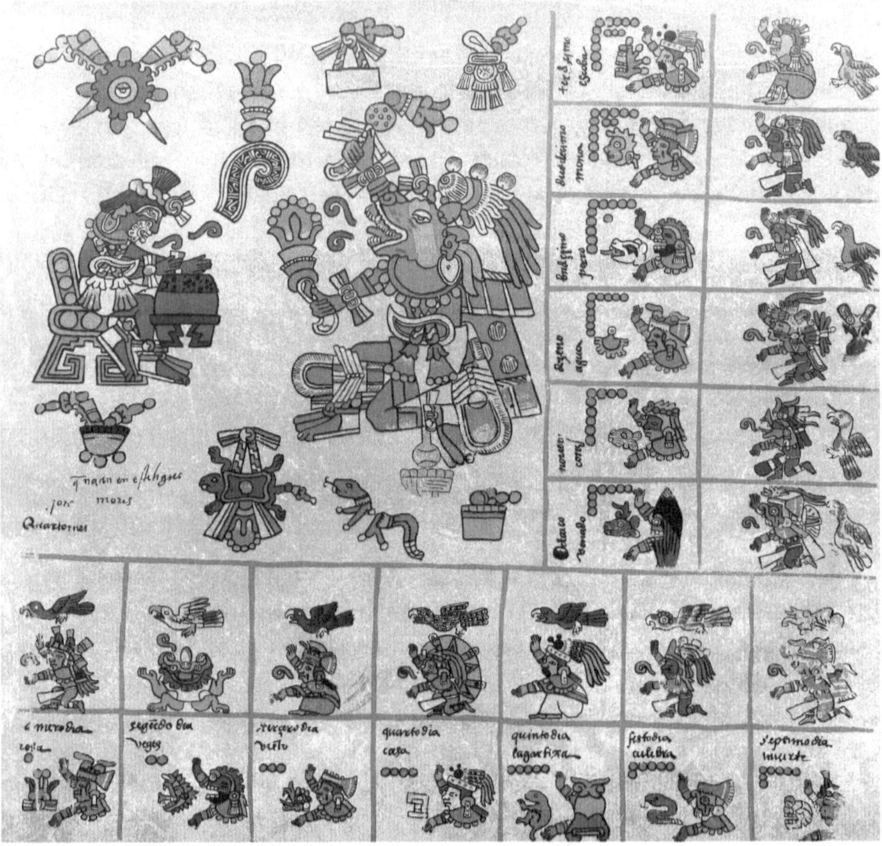

Figure 7: Codex Borbonicus, folio 2.
Note: 1899 Hamy facsimile edition. Digital reproduction by Isabel Laack.

and epistemology working not as a metaphor but as a metonymy or, more correctly, as an index. As such, the combination of "flowers" and "songs" points toward the Aztec idea that the many sensorily experienceable layers of reality were deeply interconnected and were manifestations of particular divine forces understood as the underlying principles of reality.

One of the greatest dangers in interpreting the meaning of "flower and song" is to bring in European horticultural associations, for instance by imagining settings of pastoral idyll and projecting European images of floral beauty (see Bierhorst 2009: 53–58). Botanical images and garden symbolism were important in Aztec and other Mesoamerican cultures, yet they worked differently than in Europe. Aztec culture pursued a defined "cult of brilliance" focused on sparkling light and blossoming, fragrant flowers. The image of the garden most fully expressed this love for things of extraordinary, blooming, flaming, brilliantly shining, and radiating beauty, and stood as an image for intensified reality; it expressed, that is,

> a transformational aspect of the here and now, a sacred aspect of reality that one called into being by manipulating this garden imagery in ritual contexts, particularly through song. In this symbolic garden, one came into direct contact with the creative, life-giving forces of the universe and with the timeless world of deities and ancestors. The garden is a shimmering place filled with divine fire; the light of the sun reflects from the petals of flowers and the iridescent feathers of birds; human beings – the souls of the dead or the ritually transformed living – are themselves flowers, birds, and shimmering gems. One's individual identity dissolves as one becomes part of the sacred ecosystem. This garden is not a place of reward for the righteous, existing on some transcendent plane of reality separate from the material world. It is a metaphor for life on earth, a metaphor that ritual transforms into reality by asserting that, in fact, this is the way the world is. (Burkhart 1992: 89)

Within this imagery, both flowers and songs were regarded as the "ultimate aesthetic achievement" of their respective realms (i.e., plant life and the use of language) (Knab 1986: 46) and were ontologically deeply interrelated, expressing the same principle of reality for different realms, according to indigenous understanding. In my reading, they were not, as Burkhart stated, understood as a *metaphor* for any transcendent, ultimate and imperishable spiritual world; rather, they were regarded as essentially immanent elements of the cosmos characterized by blossoming and withering, by earthly ephemerality. As such, the garden was considered metonymically as the quintessential expression of material reality and earthly life characterized by the continuing cycle of life and death, into which the Aztecs hoped to dissolve themselves. Let me explain in more detail how I reached this interpretation.

Jacinto de la Serna recorded a Nahuatl term that he translated as "metaphor": *nahualtocaitl*, a 'disguised, hidden name' (see Heyden 1986: 35). This term refers to the *nahuallatolli*, the language of the *nahualli*-shamans, and to the idea that language might reveal the inner quality of an entity. Based on analyses by Alfredo López Austin (1967, 1993: 153) and Serge Gruzinski (1993: 158–161), I think it is safe to say that the *nahuallatolli* was most probably regarded as a natural language with a strong "connection" between the linguistic signs and "that which they signify" and a "special relationship of fitness to their referents" based on iconicity (Yelle 2013: 61). In Tomlinson's view, the Aztecs regarded the signifier as closely connected with the signified, in a "metonymic circle connecting words to song, song to world, and world to words" (2007: 78, also 27). The act of singing was seen in unity with material things (Tomlinson 2007: 64), and the pictorial flowery song volutes manifested this "integrated, materialized indigenous world" (Tomlinson 1996: 275). While credit must be given to Tomlinson for revealing the Aztec belief in the naturalness of linguistic signs, I attempt to go much further with my analysis of Aztec ontology based on an interpretation of the fundamental ontological structure of the cosmos of the Fifth Sun. For this, I first need to refine our understanding of the use of "flower and song" as natural indexes.

This idea stands in stark contrast to common European understandings of metaphor, which have been applied to the Nahuatl *difrasismo*, for example by Garibay. According to these understandings, a metaphor does not express literal truths about the world and is thus generally not used in science, mathematics, or philosophy, but only in rhetoric and poetics. A metaphor merely compares the thing it designates with something else from a different domain that shows similar (but not identical) features; it projects one experiential domain onto a different one (see Lakoff and Johnson 1999: 119–122; Barcelona 2003: 3–4; Lakoff and Johnson 2011: 13, 179). In a metonym, by contrast, the thing it designates stands in a direct physical or causal relationship with the entity it names, as when a part of an entity is used to designate the whole (Lakoff and Johnson 2011: 47–51, 73).[12] The imagery of "flower and song" did not function as a metaphor for a third concept (the ultimate, transcendent layer of reality), comparing transcendency with flowers and songs because all share the feature of immateriality and thus are similar to one another. Rather, the relationship between flowers and songs was considered metonymical and based on contiguity; that is, flowers and songs were regarded as having a direct physical relationship because they shared the same essential quality. Thus, the Aztec imagery of "flower and song" was used not just as a rhetorical device (like a metaphor), but "flowers" and "songs" were both understood as natural indexes of the same essential quality. In terms of Peircean semiotics,[13] both flowers and songs were believed to be related by spatio-temporal contiguity. This relationship, rather than being a symbolic one based on similarity, was regarded as an existential, natural one, like smoke being a natural index of fire or like the turning weathervane being a natural index of wind.

This interpretation of Nahuatl imagery rests on a particular reconstruction of their general sense of reality and cosmovision.[14] The Aztecs believed themselves

---

12 The latter is usually considered a synecdoche.

13 I follow Robert A. Yelle's (2013: 28–29) reading of Peirce's semiotics.

14 This reconstruction abstracts from and generalizes the dominant cosmovision of the Nahua elite living in and around Tenochtitlan at the eve of the Spanish conquest in the early 16th century. Judged by the diversity of the material present even in the few surviving sources, the cosmovision

to be living in the cosmic era of the Fifth Sun, which was characterized by the constant movement of complementary forces through time and space (López Austin 1988: 52–68; see also López Austin 2008a: 43–44). Everything existing in the cosmos was influenced by this motion, including human beings in their physical materialities, personalities, emotional experiences, and concrete behaviors (López Austin 1988: 181–236; Martínez González 2011: 27–30). According to the interpretation of the leading Mesoamericanist, Alfredo López Austin (1988: 383), these forces were considered to be the fundamental principles of reality, both on a level graspable by human physical senses and on a level going beyond human sensory understanding. Appearing in complementary pairs that constantly counterbalance one another, these forces were also personified as deities within an impressively large and intricate pantheon. The many deities with their distinctive personalities were understood as the embodiments of particular forces and qualities as experienced by the Aztecs. As such, these deities presented, for example, the forces of elements such as rain, water, and the sun, the forces of life-spending and death-bringing energies, and the forces of human behavior patterns such as war or even individual emotions (see Nicholson 1971: 408–431). These divine qualities manifested in the many different layers and realms of reality: in the cardinal directions and natural elements; in the forms, materials, and consistencies of material objects; in distinct plant and animal species; in human characters and fates; and in anthropomorphic divinities. Every quality that could be perceived on one layer of reality (e.g., in the natural world) had its equivalent on another level of this same reality (e.g., in the human world); they were related through the *nahualli* or co-essence of qualities (see Monaghan 1998; Martínez González 2011).

Following this general sense of reality, the quality that characterized flowers in their radiating beauty also characterized the human aesthetic achievement of songs. Flowers and songs were regarded as manifestations of the same underlying principle of reality and thus as contiguous. Correspondingly, the sounds of language as much as the images of pictorial writing were regarded as natural indexes of the respective principle of reality, as direct depictions and expressions of respectively the sonic or the visual layer of reality. Rather than being arbitrary, secondary re-presentations of mental categories that merely mirror reality, language and writing were considered as presentations, as direct depictions of this reality. That is, they were not secondary depictions of reality, as re-presentations

differed across localities, social identities, and professions, and most probably even between individuals. See the discussion of this issue in my forthcoming book (Laack 2019), in the chapter titled "Living in Religious Diversity."

are, in which the signified (the presented) and the signifier (the representation) are separate from each other, but primary depictions of reality, in which the signified (the presented) and the signifier (the presentation) are considered as identical to each other.[15]

6 Expressing sensory knowledge in Aztec semiotic modalities

The Aztecs based this semiotic ideology on their culturally mediated, experiential, sensory knowledge about reality, which they expressed using strong sensory imagery. Aztec semiotic modalities of linguistic expression and pictorial writing transcended (or refused) not only the dichotomy of alphabetical versus pictorial writing but also the dichotomies of poetic versus rational discourse and religious versus scientific discourse. With respect to Aztec culture, it is extremely difficult to apply and distinguish the European categories of religion and science. A primary *definiens* for "religion" in substantialist approaches in the study of religion(s) has been a reference to transcendence or to the supernatural (famously criticized by Fitzgerald 2000) in contrast to the sciences, which refer to the natural world. The Aztecs, however, did not distinguish between these two layers of reality and had no concept of ontological transcendence. Rather, their ontology appears to have been fundamentally immanent and monistic.

In the surviving Aztec sources, there is no convincing indication that points toward the idea of a constitutional transcendence of the divine. The concept of the divine is present in the Nahuatl term *teotl* and manifested in many different personae usually called "deities" since the first Franciscan missionaries like Bernardino de Sahagún (1997) did so. *Teotl* is best described as a kind of force, energy, or power (see Hvidtfeldt 1958; Klor de Alva 1980: 68, 77–83; Gruzinski 1989: 22), which circulates through the cosmos and manifests in natural cycles. This was a constitutionally monistic concept referring to a "continually dynamic, vivifying, self-generating and self-regenerating sacred power, force, or energy [...] identical to reality per se and hence identical to everything that exists" (Maffie 2014: 21–22). This force was metaphysically homogeneous and non-hierarchical,

15 In this interpretation of "representation" and "depiction," I follow José Rabasa's adaption of Wittgenstein's differentiation between *Abbildung* 'depiction' and *Darstellung* 'representation' (from Wittgenstein's *Tractatus Logico-Philosophicus*) (Rabasa 2011: 37–41). According to Rabasa, the two concepts refer to two different kinds to present reality, one on a primary and the other on a secondary level.

with no divide between spiritual and material things (Maffie 2014: 22). The forces moving through the cosmos were not constitutionally separate from materiality (see also Maffie 2014: 47–62); rather, forces and materiality were simply different forms or faces of the same substance. Accordingly, the "deities" were perceived as highly immanent, as a "fully materialized sacral reality, a divine presence immanent in worldly things ranging from maize to all the special substances linked to song in the *cantares*" (Tomlinson 2007: 80). The Aztec divine did "not exist apart from or independently of the cosmos" but was "fully *copresent* and *coextensional* with the cosmos. [...] Teotl does not exist outside of space and time. It is as concrete and immediate as the water we drink, the air we breathe, and food we eat. Teotl is neither abstract nor transcendent" (Maffie 2014: 29, italics in the original).

Consequently, Aztec cultural knowledge about reality does not fit into the modern European categories that differentiate between scientific discourse, which expresses knowledge about the natural, immanent world, and religious discourse, which expresses knowledge about the supernatural, transcendent world. Neither did the Aztecs differentiate among methods for gaining knowledge about reality. Judging from the sources, they exerted considerable effort to understand and manipulate the underlying principles of reality – comprising both "natural laws" and the reasons for contingencies and chance happenings – in order to improve human life and to counteract diseases, starvation, social conflict, and other miseries. For this, they used ordinary human senses; Aztec culture had acquired ample knowledge about the world through close, long-term observations of nature. Additionally they attempted to expand this knowledge with the insights of religious and shamanic visions, which used senses beyond everyday waking consciousness and revealed the normally imperceptible realms of reality and the forces running through the cosmos. Thus, they applied and combined both "empirical" and "religious" methods, if we want to put it in European terms. The result was a rich cultural discourse about what the Aztecs believed were the underlying principles of (immanent) reality.

The most important feature of this reality was the close interrelationship of its different layers as apparent in the indigenous concept of *nahualli*. Although Nahua ontology was fundamentally monist, and maintained that everything that existed shared the same essential nature, the forces and energies circulating through the cosmos nevertheless realized themselves differently in the many varying qualities of things, in their distinct surfaces, forms, appearances, and – for animated beings – also in their behavior and their personalities. For human beings, these forces could be experienced through the senses as sounds, colors and light, smells and odors, different tastes and touches. The same quality could thus manifest on different layers of reality, so that "flowers" were expressions of the same quality as "songs." The Aztecs expressed their cultural knowledge about these interrelationships in their semiotic systems. For this, they particularly preferred the use of sensory imagery, in both language and writing. Thus, these semiotic systems very closely conformed to the culturally mediated sensory knowledge about the Aztec cosmos and were even regarded as direct depictions of this reality rather than re-presentations, as natural indexes rather than arbitrary symbols. The color used to paint a flower and the sound used to utter the term *xochitl* 'flower' were regarded as aspects of the visual and auditory layers of reality, in which the forces moving through the cosmos were understood to materialize in a way that is experienceable with the human senses. The image of the "flower" used pictorially or linguistically evoked a whole range of sensory experiences and thus activated the comprehensive knowledge about reality in the listener or reader by including all aspects of human cognition and of bodily, sensory, and emotional experience.

From the Aztec perspective, the differentiation between poetic and rational discourse, and the polemic assertion that only the latter is capable of expressing the truth about reality, do not play any important role. Aztecs used both language and pictorial writing to express their comprehensive cultural knowledge about reality and to make sense of this reality. They made meaning of their experiences with the help of abstract reasoning and cognitive rationality as much as with embodied cognition, body knowledge, sensory experiences, intuitive understandings, atmospheres, and emotion. Aztec linguistic and pictorial imagery could be understood as very effective forms of expressing the "embodied metaphors" (Lakoff and Johnson 1999: 128) with which people regardless of their culture make sense of the world, by relying on sensorimotor activities and experiences to produce "[m]ental images, image schemas, metaphors, metonymies, concepts, and inference patterns" (Johnson 1999: 82). In Aztec linguistic and pictorial imagery, these embodied concepts are used to comprehensively express the "felt qualities" of reality to "construct a rich, moving experience" in the act of expression itself (Johnson 2007: 221). As such, the Aztec listeners and readers did not exclusively "*think* about what is transpiring" so much as they did "*feel* and *experience* the qualitative whole that pervades and unifies the entire scene" (Johnson 2007: 224; italics in the original). In Aztec imagery, the "images, patterns, qualities, colors, and perceptual rhythms [...] are the principal bearers of meaning" (Johnson 2007: 234). In this respect, Aztec writing and reading includes aspects of understanding that modern European cultures typically allocate to separate categories of knowledge and forms of expression.

7 Against downgrading Aztec semiotic systems in evolutionary scales

When the Spaniards conquered Mexico in the first half of the 16th century, they brought the Aztec civilization to an end. The people and the lands were brutally exploited, and indigenous culture was violently suppressed. Within the first century of colonization, approximately ninety percent of the native population died as a result of military conflicts, the excesses of slavery, and devastating epidemics (see Stannard 1992; Lockhart 1993).

The Europeans, on the other hand, confronted with the existence of newly encountered peoples, made sense of their experiences by fitting them into their cultural frames of history and society. In close conjunction with the colonization and exploitation of the Americas, the American peoples were most often located somewhere on a level inferior to the Europeans. Particularly from the 18th century onwards, American civilizations were sorted into a historical timeline that represented the evolution of humanity through a "denial of coevalness" (Mignolo 2010: xi), meaning that the cultures of some presently living groups were depicted as anachronistic survivals from a distant past. This argumentation used several cultural aspects as markers for the degree of humanness and the evolutionary stage of the civilization: religion, the arts, the organization of society, and language as well as alphabetical writing and historiography in the European sense. In many cases, the particular cultural aspects used as markers were associated with "mental operations such as reasoning, memory, and the imagination" (Farago 1995: 6). One of the basic issues for the Europeans in this context was the question: Do the indigenous people possess rationality and intelligence?

The general devaluation of indigenous culture was voiced already by some early *conquistadores* and chroniclers in the 16th century (see Mignolo 2010: xi, 44, 133–134). The intellectual imperialism regarding forms of representation has continued well into the 20th century, with famous European writing theories (e.g., Gelb 1963; DeFrancis 1989; see also Ong 1967; Ong 1982; Goody 1986; Goody 1987) defining "real" and "full" writing as logographic and alphabetical, while largely ignoring indigenous American forms of recording knowledge. Similarly, many descriptions of Aztec culture present it as a primarily oral tradition, in which written/painted texts served only as mnemonic devices to stimulate the recitation of memorized cultural knowledge (León-Portilla 1992b: 70–71; León-Portilla 1992a: 317–319). Literary theorist Tzvetan Todorov presented one of the latest variants of this "epistemic violence" (Spivak 1988: 281) in his influential *The Conquest of America: The Question of the Other* (1984). In this publication, he combined writing theories with ideas from the orality–literacy debate and with a modernity theory that contrasts religious superstition with political rationality. His main argument explained the surprising victory of the few Spanish *conquistadores* against the impressive Aztec empire by referring to the superior semiotic system of the Spanish. According to Todorov, the Aztecs failed to defeat the Spanish because they acted based on a (pre-modern) ritualistic and inflexible oral tradition and were driven by religious superstitions and fatalism. The Aztec king Montecuhzoma II, constrained by this ritualized and overly fixed tradition, was unable to develop a successful strategy for how to deal with the arrival of the Spaniards, an event that was "absolutely unpredictable [...], surprising and unique" for the Mesoamerican experience (Todorov 1984: 84, see also 74–77, 81–84). He merely turned fatalistically to the stars in search for omens predicting the outcome of the political conflict with the Spaniards. Hernando Cortés, by contrast, (supposedly) used a praxeological approach to deal with the difficult political situation in the new lands. Because his consciousness had been shaped by a literate society, he was able to improvise and to act politically, strategically, and rationally, according to Todorov.

One of the cornerstones of Todorov's interpretation is the idea, derived from the orality–literacy debate, that people living in primarily oral societies show a different mentality and way of thinking from those in literate societies (Todorov 1984: 80). Within this theoretical frame, literate cultures using alphabetical writing are generally perceived as superior, because (supposedly) only alphabetical writing encourages sequential intellectual analysis, reflexivity, and rationality (Havelock 1982; Ong 1982). Todorov accordingly denied the Nahuas the capacity for strategic, rational thinking and acting. He asserted a clear correlation between the non-existence of (alphabetical, "true") writing in a society and superstition, ritualism, and historical fatalism; conversely, he presumed a correlation between logographic writing and the mental capacity for improvisation, rational thinking, and strategic action (see Todorov 1984: 252).[16]

In the judgment that Aztec civilization was inferior to European cultures, the linguistic rhetoric of the Aztecs also played a role, albeit a lesser one than that of their non-alphabetical writing system. After the destruction of Aztec intellectual culture in the first decades of colonization, knowledge of

16 By now, many Mesoamericanists have proven Todorov's interpretation of the conquest wrong and debunked it as a European projection of the orality-literacy theory that contradicts all indigenous perspectives on the conquest and all our knowledge about Aztec culture. For example, the depiction of Montecuhzoma II as unable to cope with the political situation while searching for omens was painted by a later generation of Natives some decades after the conquest trying to explain the inexplicable defeat of the mighty "Aztec" empire (see Lockhart 1994; Restall 2003).

the elaborate rhetorical registers in Nahuatl was increasingly lost among the indigenous people in the course of time. Europeans, on the other side, typically have had great difficulties in understanding classical Nahuatl with its rich, poetic, elegant, eloquent, and often formulaic diction, because of its flexible and complex linguistic structure and the many subtleties that are so different from European forms of expression. This difficulty was noted already by the first Spaniards in Mexico (Gingerich 1992: 357). After the first century of colonization, the interest of Europeans in this indigenous language continuously dwindled, until in the 19th century, knowledge of Nahuatl was minimal and it was simply devalued as a primitive language (Swann 1992: xiii-xiv). In the end, the ubiquitous use of a rich sensory imagery in Nahuatl texts, which mostly escapes European understanding, was regarded as a sign of an inferior developmental stage of linguistic expression.

The modern devaluation of Nahua thinking stands in a European tradition of theories of language that dismisses metaphors and imagery as emotional, irrational, and misleading. This tradition also supposes that only rational linguistic thought operates with logical propositions and is able to express objective truth about the rational structures of reality (see Johnson 1990 [1987]: x; Johnson 1999: 83–84; Lakoff and Johnson 1999: 98–102; Lakoff and Johnson 2011: 217–218). The European linguistic disenchantment fostered by Protestant literalism adopted this tradition and sharply criticized the performative and supposedly magical functions of language in rituals. The later European discourse of secular modernity even established the "ostensibly rational discourse of science and law [...] in opposition to poetry, rhetoric, and myth" (Yelle 2013: 4). Against this philosophical background, the linguistic obscurity (for European readers) of many Nahuatl texts and their strong "poetic" flavor using a large amount of imagery has been interpreted in the last two centuries as the expression of a pre-rational perspective on the world. Accordingly, the "Aztec civilization" has been judged as presenting a pre-literate, pre-rational stage of human development out of which Europe had long evolved (see Gingerich 1987: 101).

Thus, it was left to the Nahuatl scholars Garibay and León-Portilla to argue vehemently for the acknowledgement of Nahua "poetic" expression as an intellectually highly advanced philosophical discourse. They did so by implicitly referring to an alternative tradition within the European philosophy of language, in which poetry, including metaphor, was generally valued as enhancing knowledge about reality (see Lakoff and Johnson 2011: 218). In this way, Garibay and León-Portilla re-evaluated the rich imagery of Nahuatl positively by seeing it from a Western aesthetic perspective as lying at the heart of poetic beauty (see Tomlinson 1996: 23–24) and by declaring it as the expression of a highly advanced philosophy of poetic aestheticism.

There is the danger of taking my alternative interpretation of the Aztec imagery of "flower and song" as the starting point for a relapse into evolutionary thinking. I emphasized that the Aztec cosmovision subscribed to a natural, indexical connection among signifier and signified, in which language and writing stand in a natural, existential relationship to reality. This interpretation might be taken to imply that Aztec civilization represented a typical case of a ritualistic, pre-modern worldview, or even of "magic" as described by Edward B. Tylor and James G. Frazer. If we were to adopt Tylor's and Frazer's devaluation of magical thinking as a "mistaken application of the laws of association of ideas" (Yelle 2013: 27), we must surely see Aztec culture as an example of an inferior stage of human intellectual development. I would argue, however, that such a differentiation between rational and poetic language, combined with the evolutionary idea that a rational, scientific modernity has displaced earlier forms of pre-rational, ritualistic, magical cosmovision, is a stark example of epistemic violence, a projection of European historical developments and conceptual categories onto non-European cultures. In my view, the Aztec example thoroughly transcends these categories and ideas of the evolution of civilizations from pre-modern to modern stages, which are anachronistic and inaccurate as applied to the Aztecs.

8 Conclusion

In this paper, I argued for an alternative interpretation of the imagery of "flower and song," which was used frequently in the semiotic systems of linguistic expression and pictorial writing within the pre-Hispanic culture of the Aztecs in Central Mexico. The most famous interpretation thus far has been presented by León-Portilla, who regarded "flower and song" as a metaphor standing for an indigenous philosophical approach that favored poetic aestheticism as the best way to express insights about the ultimate, transcendent layers of reality. In contrast, I understand the image as an expression of Aztec comprehensive cultural knowledge about immanent principles of reality, as they sensorily experienced them within the frame of their culture. The rich imagery used in the two semiotic modalities of language and writing, understood as a natural index of this reality rather than as a metaphoric representation of it, refers to a form of cultural knowledge that combines abstract reasoning and cognitive rationality with embodied cognition, body knowledge, sensory experiences, intuitive understandings, atmospheres, and emotion. Thus, the imagery effectively activates a large range of human experience of reality. In the Aztec view, the imagery directly participated in this reality, because they regarded the linguistic and written signs as direct depictions of the auditory, visual, and experiential layers of reality. This semiotic theory and the very nature of Aztec pictorial writing as a non-logographic writing system point towards the limits of language for expressing cultural knowledge. The frequent use of imagery both in the Aztec oral tradition and in their form of recorded communication shows that the Aztecs did not reduce their experiential knowledge about reality to an abstract system of language alone but included other modes of expression to effectively communicate this comprehensive cultural knowledge.

With this interpretation, I challenge the historical downgrading of Aztec semiotic systems by Europeans based on their lack of alphabetical writing and the supposed lack of (modern) rational discourse by arguing that they indeed had comprehensive knowledge about the reality they lived in and expressed it in sophisticated ways based on a deliberate semiotic theory. Furthermore, I argue that this semiotic theory escapes the European differentiation between rational and poetic language as much as the differentiation between scientific and religious discourse. Apart from the Aztecs, many cultures of the world have emphasized other modes of sign relations than the ones of modern European semiotics, with its secular bias against symbolism and poetic performance, and its conviction in the arbitrariness of signs. Furthermore, many traditions claim to have special access to (a special) reality, while the ideas about the nature of (this) reality and the modes of accessing it differ considerably (see Yelle 2013: 5). The discussed European scholarly (d)evaluations of Aztec pictorial writing and linguistic expression and similar (d)evaluations of other cultures and their semiotic traditions should be recognized as cases of projecting polemics from the European history of religions onto cultural fields that are foreign to these considerations.

From my epistemological point of view, it is not the task of academic research to judge the respective, often incompatible truth claims of the semiotic traditions of other cultures, nor their experiences of reality. Thus, while the Aztecs would argue that there is a natural relationship between flowers and songs, and modern natural sciences would argue that both categories are, in fact, not causally or physically related but merely superficially similar, I would accept, for the context of academic research, neither truth claim. My intent, rather, is to describe and understand the Aztec sense of reality as earnestly as that of modern science(s). Accordingly, it is neither my intent to say that Aztec semiotic modes access reality better than those of secular European science nor that the Aztecs were more deeply in touch with reality. This would be a case of reverse colonialism and Othering, which projects romantic ideals onto the Noble Savage construed in opposition to Europeans. Rather, I wish to understand from an attitude of dialogue how the Aztecs understood reality and positioned themselves in it. Thus, when analyzing the dominant academic interpretation of the Aztec imagery of "flower and song," I found deep biases conditioned by European intellectual presuppositions, which I have endeavored to overcome. However, I am very much aware that my alternative interpretation most surely contains further misunderstandings, since the study of cultures is always a subjective affair. It is all the more so in the case of the discussed corpus of songs, because there is so little contextual information available to help modern readers reach a better interpretation. Nevertheless, critically reflecting on our intellectual parameters in dealing with different cultures will help us to refine our academic theories and to better understand the diversity in which humanity experiences reality and tries to make sense of it.

Acknowledgements: My thanks go to Robert A. Yelle and Christopher I. Lehrich for their very valuable comments on this paper, which helped me to clarify my semiotic concepts and to express my epistemological standpoint more precisely.

References

Barcelona, Antonio. 2003. Introduction: The cognitive theory of metaphor and metonomy. In Antonio Barcelona (ed.), *Metaphor and metonomy at the crossroads: A cognitive perspective*, 1–28. Berlin & New York: Mouton de Gruyter.

Berdan, Frances F. & Michael E. Smith. 1996. Imperial strategies and core-periphery relations. In Frances F. Berdan (ed.), *Aztec imperial strategies*, 209–225. Washington, D.C.: Dumbarton Oaks Research Library and Collection.

Bierhorst, John. 1985. *Cantares Mexicanos: Songs of the Aztecs*. Translated from the Nahuatl, with an introduction and commentary. Stanford, CA: Stanford University Press.

Bierhorst, John. 2009. *Ballads of the Lords of New Spain: The Codex Romances de los Señores de la Nueva España* (The William & Bettye Nowlin series in art, history, and culture of the Western hemisphere). Transcribed and translated from the Nahuatl by John Bierhorst. Austin: University of Texas Press.

Boone, Elizabeth H. 2000. *Stories in red and black: Pictorial histories of the Aztec and Mixtec*. Austin: University of Texas Press.

Boone, Elizabeth H. 2007. *Cycles of time and meaning in the Mexican Books of Fate* (Joe R. and Teresa Long series in Latin American and Latino Art and Culture). Austin: University of Texas Press.

Boone, Elizabeth H. 2011. Ruptures and unions: Graphic complexity and hybridity in sixteenth-century Mexico. In Elizabeth H. Boone & Gary Urton (eds.), *Their way of writing: Scripts, signs, and pictographies in Pre-Columbian America* (Dumbarton Oaks Pre-Columbian symposia and colloquia), 197–225. Washington, D.C.: Dumbarton Oaks Research Library and Collection.

Boone, Elizabeth H. & Michael E. Smith. 2003. Postclassic international styles and symbol sets. In Michael E. Smith & Frances F. Berdan (eds.), *The Postclassic Mesoamerican world*, 186–193. Salt Lake City: University of Utah Press.

Burkhart, Louise M. 1992. Flowery heaven: The aesthetics of paradise in Nahuatl Devotional Literature. *RES: Anthropology and Aesthetics* 21(1). 88–109.

Calnek, Edward E. 1988. The calmecac and telpochcalli in pre-conquest Tenochtitlan. In José J. Klor de Alva (ed.), *The work of Bernardino de Sahagún: Pioneer ethnographer of sixteenth-century Aztec Mexico* (Studies on culture and society 2), 169–177. Albany & Austin: State University of New York Press & University of Texas Press.

Caso, Alfonso. 1958. *The Aztecs: People of the sun* (The civilization of the American Indian series 50). Norman: University of Oklahoma Press.

Clendinnen, Inga. 1991. *Aztecs: An interpretation*. Cambridge: Cambridge University Press.

Cline, Howard F. (ed.). 1972–1975. *Handbook of Middle American Indians*, vol. 12–14, *Guide to ethnohistorical sources, part 1–4*. Austin: University of Texas Press.

Codex Borbonicus. Anders, Ferdinand, Maarten Jansen & Luis Reyes García (eds.). 1991. *Códice Borbonico: Facsimile of the Codex*. Graz: Akademische Druck- und Verlagsanstalt.

Codex Borgia. Anders, Ferdinand, Maarten Jansen & Luis Reyes García (eds.). 1993. *Códice Borgia: Facsimile of the Codex*. Madrid & Graz & Mexico City: Sociedad Estatal Quinto Centenario & Akademische Druck- und Verlagsanstalt & Fondo de Cultura Económica.

Codex Boturini. Lejarazu Rubin, Dinorah, Manuel H. Lejarazu, & Israel Heredia Arroyo (eds.). 1991. *Códice Boturini (Tira de la Peregrinación): Facsimile*. Mexico City: Taller de Artes Gráficas, Grupo Gisma.

Codex Mendoza. Berdan, Frances F. & Patricia R. Anawalt (eds.). 1992. *The Codex Mendoza*, vol. 3, *A Facsimile Reproduction*. Berkeley, CA: University of California Press.

Davies, Nigel. 1973. *The Aztecs: A history*. Norman: University of Oklahoma Press.

DeFrancis, John. 1989. *Visible speech: The diverse oneness of writing systems*. Honolulu, HI: University of Hawaii Press.

Díaz del Castillo, Bernal. 2008. *The history of the conquest of New Spain*. Edited by Davíd Carrasco. Albuquerque: University of New Mexico Press.

Farago, Claire J. 1995. Introduction: Reframing the Renaissance. In Claire J. Farago (ed.), *Reframing the Renaissance: Visual culture in Europe and Latin* America, *1450–1650*, 1–20, 301–305. New Haven: Yale University Press.

Fitzgerald, Timothy. 2000. *The ideology of religious studies*. New York & Oxford: Oxford University Press.

Garibay Kintana, Angel María. 1940. *Llave del Náhuatl: Colección de trozos clásicos, con gramática y vocabulario, para utilidad de los principiantes*. Otumba, Mexico: Imprenta Mayli.

Gelb, Ignace J. 1963. *A study of writing*, 2nd edn. Chicago: University of Chicago Press.

Gingerich, Willard. 1987. Heidegger and the Aztecs: The poetics of knowing in pre-Hispanic Nahuatl poetry. In Brian Swann (ed.), *Recovering the word: Essays on Native American literature*, 85–112. Berkeley, CA: University of California Press.

Gingerich, Willard. 1992. Ten types of ambiguity in Nahuatl poetry, or William Empson among the Aztecs. In Brian Swann (ed.), *On the translation of Native American literatures*, 356–368. Washington, D.C.: Smithsonian Institution Press.

Goody, Jack. 1986. *The logic of writing and the organization of society*. Cambridge: Cambridge University Press.

Goody, Jack. 1987. *The interface between the written and the oral*. Cambridge: Cambridge University Press.

Gruzinski, Serge. 1989. *Man-Gods in the Mexican Highlands: Indian power and colonial society, 1520–1800*. Stanford, CA: Stanford University Press.

Gruzinski, Serge. 1993. *The conquest of Mexico: The incorporation of Indian societies into the Western world, 16th-18th centuries*. Translated by Eileen Corrigan. Cambridge, MA & Cambridge, UK: Polity Press.
Gruzinski, Serge. 2002. *The mestizo mind: The intellectual dynamics of colonization and globalization*. New York: Routledge.
Hamy, M. E.-T. 1899. *Codex Borbonicus: Manuscrit Mexicain de la bibliothéque du Palai Bourbon*. (Livre divinatoire et rituel figuré.) Publié en fac-simile avec un commentaire explicatif du M. E.-T. Hamy. Paris: E. Leroux.
Hassig, Ross. 1985. *Trade, tribute, and transportation: The sixteenth-century political economy of the Valley of Mexico*. Norman: University of Oklahoma Press.
Havelock, Eric A. 1982. *The literate revolution in Greece and its cultural consequences*. Princeton: Princeton University Press.
Heyden, Doris. 1986. Metaphors, nahualtocaitl, and other "disguised" terms among the Aztecs. In Gary H. Gossen (ed.), *Symbol and meaning beyond the closed community: Essays in Mesoamerican ideas*, 35–43. Albany: Institute for Mesoamerican Studies & State University of New York Press.
Humboldt, Alexander von. 1810. *Pittoreske Ansichten der Cordilleren und Monumente americanischer Völker*. Tübingen: J. G. Cotta'sche Buchhandlung.
Hvidtfeldt, Arild. 1958. *Teotl and Ixiptlatli: Some central conceptions in ancient Mexican religion: With a general introduction on cult and myth*. Copenhagen: Munksgaard.
Johnson, Mark. 1990 [1987]. *The body in the mind: The bodily basis of meaning, imagination, and reason*, 2nd edn. Chicago: University of Chicago Press.
Johnson, Mark. 1999. Embodied reason. In Gail Weiss & Honi F. Haber (eds.), *Perspectives on embodiment: The intersections of nature and culture*, 81–102. New York: Routledge.
Johnson, Mark. 2007. *The meaning of the body: Aesthetics of human understanding*. Chicago & London: University of Chicago Press.
Klor de Alva, José J. 1980. *Spiritual warfare in Mexico: Christianity and the Aztecs*. Santa Cruz: University of California at Santa Cruz.
Knab, Timothy J. 1986. Metaphors, concepts, and coherence in Aztec. In Gary H. Gossen (ed.), *Symbol and meaning beyond the closed community: Essays in Mesoamerican ideas*, 45–55. Albany: Institute for Mesoamerican Studies & State University of New York Press.
Laack, Isabel. 2019. *Aztec religion and art of writing: Investigating embodied meaning, indigenous semiotics, and the Nahua sense of reality* (Numen book series). Leiden & Boston: Brill.
Lakoff, George & Mark Johnson. 1999. *Philosophy in the flesh: The embodied mind and its challenges to Western thought*. New York: Basic Books.
Lakoff, George & Mark Johnson. 2011. *Leben in Metaphern: Konstruktion und Gebrauch von Sprachbildern*, 7th edn. Heidelberg: Carl-Auer-Systeme.
Lee, Jongsoo. 2008. *The allure of Nezahualcoyotl: Pre-Hispanic history, religion, and Nahua politics*. Albuquerque: University of New Mexico Press.
Leibsohn, Dana. 1994. Primers for memory: Cartographic histories and Nahua identity. In Elizabeth H. Boone & Walter D. Mignolo (eds.), *Writing without words: Alternative literacies in Mesoamerica and the Andes*, 161–187. Durham, NC: Duke University Press.
Leibsohn, Dana. 2009. *Script and glyph: Pre-Hispanic history, colonial bookmaking and the Historia Tolteca-Chichimeca* (Studies in pre-Columbian art & archaeology 36). Washington, D.C. & Cambridge, MA: Dumbarton Oaks Research Library and Collection; distributed by Harvard University Press.

León-Portilla, Miguel. 1969. *Pre-Columbian literatures of Mexico*. Norman: University of Oklahoma Press.
León-Portilla, Miguel. 1980. Introduction. In Miguel León-Portilla (ed.), *Native Mesoamerican spirituality: Ancient myths, discourses, stories, doctrines, hymns, poems from the Aztec, Yucatec, Quiche-Maya and other sacred traditions*. Edited with a foreword, introduction and notes by Miguel Léon-Portilla. Translations by M. Léon-Portilla, J. O. Arthur Anderson, Charles E. Dibble & Mundro S. Edmonson. Preface by Fernando Horcasitas (The classics of Western spirituality. A library of the great spiritual masters), 1–59. New York & Ramsey & Toronto: Paulist Press.
León-Portilla, Miguel. 1992a. Have we really translated the Mesoamerican "ancient word"? In Brian Swann (ed.), *On the translation of Native American literatures*, 313–338. Washington, D.C.: Smithsonian Institution Press.
León-Portilla, Miguel. 1992b. *The Aztec image of self and society: An introduction to Nahua culture*. Salt Lake City: University of Utah Press.
León-Portilla, Miguel. 2011. Estudio introductorio a los *Cantares*. In Miguel León-Portilla (ed.), *Cantares Mexicanos I: Estudios. Paleografía, traducción y notas*, 151–296. Mexico City: Universidad Nacional Autónoma de México & Fideicomiso Teixidor.
Lockhart, James. 1993. *The Nahuas after the conquest: A social and cultural history of the Indians of Central Mexico, sixteenth through the eighteenth century*. Stanford, CA: Stanford University Press.
Lockhart, James. 1994. Sightings: Initial Nahua reactions to Spanish culture. In Stuart B. Schwartz (ed.), *Implicit understandings: Observing, reporting, and reflecting on the encounters between Europeans and other peoples in the early modern era*, 218–248. Cambridge: Cambridge University Press.
López Austin, Alfredo. 1967. Términos del Nahuallatolli. *Historia Mexicana* 17(1). 1–35.
López Austin, Alfredo. 1988. *The Human body and ideology: Concepts of the ancient Nahuas*, vol. 1. Salt Lake City: University of Utah Press.
López Austin, Alfredo. 1993. *Myths of the opposum: Pathways of Mesoamerican mythology*. Translated by B. R. & T. Ortiz de Montellano. Albuquerque: University of New Mexico Press.
López Austin, Alfredo. 2008a. Características generales de la religión de los pueblos nahuas del centro de México en el Posclásico Tardío. In Silvia Limón Olvera (ed.), *La religión de los pueblos Mexicanos* (Enciclopedia Iberoamericana de Religiones 7), 31–72: Granada: Editorial Trotta, Universidad de Granada.
López Austin, Alfredo. 2008b. Los mexicas ante el cosmos. *Arqueología mexicana* 16(91). 24–35.
Loubat, S. E. il Duca di. 1898. *Il Manuscritto Messicano Borgiano del Museo Etnografico della S. Congregazione di Propaganda Fide: Riprodotto in Fotocromografia*. Roma: Stabilimento Danesi.
Maffie, James. 2014. *Aztec philosophy: Understanding a world in motion*. Boulder: University Press of Colorado.
Marcus, Joyce. 1992. *Mesoamerican writing systems: Propaganda, myth, and history in four ancient civilizations*. Princeton: Princeton University Press.
Martínez González, Roberto. 2011. *El nahualismo* (Instituto de Investigaciones Históricas, Serie Antropológica 19). Mexico City: Universidad Nacional Autónoma de México.
Mignolo, Walter D. 2010. *The darker side of the Renaissance: Literacy, territoriality, and colonization*, 2nd edn. Ann Arbor: University of Michigan Press.

Monaghan, John. 1998. The person, destiny, and the construction of difference in Mesoamerica. *RES: Anthropology and aesthetics* 33(1). 137–146.
Nicholson, Henry B. 1971. Religion in pre-Hispanic Central Mexico. In Gordon F. Ekholm & Ignacio Bernal (eds.), *Handbook of Middle American Indians*, vol. 10, *Archaeology of northern Mesoamerica, Part 1*, 395–446. Austin: University of Texas Press.
Ong, Walter J. 1967. *The presence of the word: Some prolegomena for cultural and religious history*. New Haven: Yale University Press.
Ong, Walter J. 1982. *Orality and literacy: The technologizing of the word*. London & New York: Methuen.
Prescott, William H. 1843. *History of the conquest of Mexico: With a preliminary view of the ancient Mexican civilization, and the life of the conqueror, Hernando Cortés*. London: Bentley.
Quiñones Keber, Eloise (ed.). 2002. *Representing Aztec ritual: Performance, text, and image in the Work of Sahagún* (Mesoamerican Worlds: From the Olmecs to the Danzantes). Boulder: University Press of Colorado.
Rabasa, José. 2011. *Tell me the story of how I conquered you: Elsewheres and ethnosuicide in the colonial Mesoamerican world* (Joe R. and Teresa Lozano Long series in Latin American and Latino art and culture). Austin: University of Texas Press.
Restall, Matthew. 2003. *Seven myths of the Spanish conquest*. Oxford: Oxford University Press.
Ruiz Alarcón, Hernando de. 1984. *Treatise on the heathen superstitions that today live among the Indians native to this New Spain*. Translated and edited by J. Richard Andrews & Ross Hassig. Norman: University of Oklahoma Press.
Sahagún, Bernardino de. 1961 [1575–1578]. *Florentine Codex: General history of the things of New Mexico, Book 10: The people* (Monographs of the School of American Research, Santa Fe, New Mexico, Part XI). Translated from the Aztec into English, with notes and illustrations. Edited by Charles E. Dibble and Arthur J. O. Anderson. Salt Lake City: University of Utah Press.
Sahagún, Bernardino de. 1969 [1575–1578]. *Florentine Codex. General history of the things of New Mexico: Book 6 – Rhetoric and moral philosophy* (Monographs of the School of American Research, Santa Fe, New Mexico, Part VII). Translated from the Aztec into English, with notes and illustrations. Edited by Charles E. Dibble and Arthur J. O. Anderson. Salt Lake City: University of Utah Press.
Sahagún, Bernardino de. 1979 [1575–1578]. *Códice Florentino: Facsimile Edition*, 3 vols. Florence & Mexico City: Biblioteca Medicea Laurenziana & Archivo General de la Nación, Secretaría de Gobernación.
Sahagún, Bernardino de. 1997 [1559–1561]. *Primeros Memoriales: Paleography of Nahuatl text and English translation by Thelma Sullivan*. Completed and revised, with additions, by H. B. Nicholson, Arthur J. O. Anderson, Charles E. Dibble, Eloise Quiñones Keber & Wayne Ruwet. Norman, OK & Madrid: University of Oklahoma Press, Patrimonio Nacional & Real Academia de la Historia.
Serna, Jacinto de la. 1953. *Tratado de las idolatrías, supersticiones, dioses, ritos, hechicerías y otras costumbres gentílicas de las razas aborígenes de Mexico: Notas, comentarios y un estudio de don Francisco del Paso y Troncoso*. Seconda edición ampliada con importantes suplementos e indices. Madrid: Ediciones Fuente Cultural.
Spivak, Gayatri C. 1988. Can the subaltern speak? In Cary Nelson (ed.), *Marxism and the interpretation of culture*, 271–313. Urbana: University of Illinois Press.

Stannard, David E. 1992. *American holocaust: The conquest of the New World*. Oxford: Oxford University Press.
Swann, Brian. 1992. Introduction. In Brian Swann (ed.), *On the translation of Native American literatures*, xiii–xx. Washington, D.C.: Smithsonian Institution Press.
Todorov, Tzvetan. 1984. *The conquest of America: The question of the other*. Translated by Richard Howard. New York: Harper & Row.
Tomlinson, Gary. 1996. Unlearning the *Aztec Cantares* (Preliminaries to a postcolonial theory). In Margreta de Grazia, Maureen Quilligan & Peter Stallybrass (eds.), *Subject and object in Renaissance culture*, 260–286. New York: Cambridge University Press.
Tomlinson, Gary. 2007. *The singing of the New World: Indigenous voice in the era of European contact* (New perspectives in music history and criticism 15). Cambridge & New York: Cambridge University Press.
Umberger, Emily. 2007. The Metaphorical underpinnings of Aztec history. *Ancient Mesoamerica* 18(1). 11–29.
Yelle, Robert A. 2013. *Semiotics of religion. Signs of the sacred in history*. London: Bloomsbury.

Patrick Eisenlohr

Religious language and media: Sound reproduction and transduction

1 Introduction

There is a growing scholarly interest in the intersections of religion and media. This has resulted in a burgeoning literature, initially propelled by the investigation of religion in the public sphere. Directed against the Habermasian notion of the public sphere as secular, in recent years a considerable number of studies have shown that religious actors not only form an integral part of publics around the world, but that contemporary religious movements make full use of the techniques of mobilization and the cultivation of sociability among strangers characteristic of public spheres (Meyer and Moors 2006; Hirschkind 2006; see Eisenlohr 2012 for an overview). Moreover, this move has coincided with another reconsideration of the notion of the public sphere, criticizing its overly strong emphasis on deliberation. While scholars have pointed to the deliberative dimensions of religiously grounded interventions in public debate, they have also emphasized public spheres' embodied and visceral dimensions (Meyer 2004, 2008; de Abreu 2009; Oosterbaan 2009) as evident in entertainment, advertising, and religion, which in many cases also overlap. Another strand of research on religion and media has taken a different point of departure, i.e., the intrinsic connections between religion and media (de Vries 2001: 28; Stolow 2005). Religion is cast as a process of communication and interaction between human actors and non- or semi-human actors or forces located in a religious otherworld. Such interactions necessarily involve media, including their material and technical dimensions, as is evident from uses of scripture, sacred objects, images, and more recently also various forms of electronic and digital media that enable and enhance the interaction with the divine (Engelke 2010; Eisenlohr 2009, 2011; Morgan 2005; Schulz 2012).

In many, if not most religious traditions, language plays a pivotal role in making a religious otherworld accessible. Linguistic interaction and other forms of language use are ubiquitous in the interactions of humans with actors and forces in religious otherworlds, however conceived (Bauman 1983; Bowen 1993; Keane 1997, 2004; Eisenlohr 2011; Robbins 2001; Tomlinson 2004 and 2014). Despite this, research on religion and media and religion and language have

Patrick Eisenlohr, Georg August University, Göttingen

https://doi.org/10.1515/9781614514329-016

to date largely constituted separate literatures. In particular, much recent work on the materiality and aesthetics of religion has paid great attention to media (Hirschkind and Larkin 2008; Meyer 2010; Morgan 2010) but tends to reject language and language-based semiotics as analytical perspectives. This is surprising, not just considering the obvious materiality and aesthetics of language, whether in oral performance or textual form, but especially in light of the fact that key characteristics ascribed to media also apply to language. Even more to the point, some recent debates in media theory were already prefigured in 19th-century debates about the relative transparency of language as a medium, a situation that the German linguist Ludwig Jäger has described as media theory's "forgetfulness of language" (*Sprachvergessenheit der Medientheorie*) (Jäger 2000).

Paying attention to these intriguing parallels, in this chapter I discuss how contests about religious language have revolved around a contrast between, on the one hand, a preference for literalism, with its emphasis on reference and denotation; and on the other hand, a valuation of the poetic functions of language and its material properties. Turning to the issue of electronically mediated language in religious settings, I discuss how sound reproduction technology has become part of religious practices, drawing on my research on language and media among Mauritian Muslims. I analyze how electronic mediation of voice is intended to bring members of this community closer to the divine; and I show how the material dimensions of language, which I seek to capture under the logic of transduction, sustain religious interaction. Uses of sound reproduction aim to narrow the gap between Muslims and the divine by creating sonic presences that, in turn, provide affordances for particular ideas about religious language and media.

Media exist, because alterity exists. Mediation is the processes linking differing actors, objects, or social formations across qualitative, temporal, or spatial gaps. Such processes of mediation require, in order to unfold, some medium, which always has technical and material dimensions. Modern media theory has focused in particular on two aspects of media. On the one hand, theorists have highlighted the ways in which modern media enable the shrinking of space and time, so as to enable a relative immediacy in interacting with others (Harvey 1989; Tomlinson 1999). Here, in its overcoming of space and time, the medium functions so smoothly that awareness of it recedes into the background, giving way to the seemingly immediate presence of whatever it is that it mediates. On the other hand, media scholars have also analyzed how media forcefully assert their presence to such an extent that they constrain and override human agency. One of the fundamental insights of media theory, that the "medium is the message" (McLuhan 1964), stresses how the modalities and technologies of mediation have a shaping impact not only on their direct objects but also on a broad array of human relations. Some have regarded this propensity of modern media to transform social worlds and human subjectivities in their own image as a danger to established social contexts and human creativity (Baudrillard 1994). This has culminated in dystopian visions in which the perpetual acceleration of social life brought about by modern media turns humans into "invalids" that lose control of their lives to media machines that will in the end, in the guise of nanotechnology, even invade and colonize their bodies (Virilio 1998: 20, 179). Other media theorists have cast such developments in a far more positive light, celebrating a fusion of humans with machines that in the final instance will do away with human subjectivity and its attendant symbolic forms and meanings. "So-called man" will then be shaped by technical standards (Kittler 1997: 133) and eventually be liberated from the "yoke of subjectivity" (Kittler 1993: 181).[1]

It is clear that a great range of objects, apparatuses, or institutions can be treated as media, which leads to the danger that the notion of media may become too broad to be meaningful. Nevertheless, an overview of scholarship on media suggests that, among the manifold phenomena that have been designated under this category, there is perhaps one key quality that they have in common. This is the oscillation between great perceptibility, as in the assertion of their presence as they constrain and shape human agency and subjectivity, and their virtual disappearance in the act of functioning, enabling an air of immediacy across gaps of alterity (Bolter and Grusin 1999; Eisenlohr 2009; Krämer 2008).[2] Pointing to their interconnectedness, Jay Bolter and Richard Grusin have called these two states of media "hypermediacy" and "immediacy," respectively, stressing that "our two contradictory logics not only coexist in digital media today, but are mutually dependent. Immediacy depends on hypermediacy" (Bolter and Grusin 1999: 6). In order to operate successfully, media need to withdraw from experiential awareness, giving full presence to whatever it is they mediate. Whether working on a computer while looking at its screen, listening to reproduced sound, or making a phone call, if media operate successfully in expected ways, they, including the

1 Lacanian psychoanalysis is a likely influence in Kittler's perspective on subjectivity as a "yoke," whose removal is equivalent to liberation.

2 John Durham Peters (1999: 63–108) has shown how in the 19th and early 20th centuries desires for immediate "spiritualist" communication between humans and humans and the dead were closely connected to a fascination with emerging electronic media such as the telegraph and radio. In a related vein, Jonathan Sterne's (2003) history of the origins of sound reproduction has demonstrated how this technology grew out of a cultural milieu obsessed with the idea of hearing the voices of the dead. These "spiritualist" sensibilities are an important modern source of the connection between whatever counts as "new" media and desires for immediacy, or in Sterne's terms, the search for a "vanishing medium." For a related discussion, see Anderson Blanton's essay in this volume.

technical apparatuses and networks that constitute them, drop from awareness, while media users' perception is focused on the images, the sounds, or other phenomena mediated through them. In fact, the propensity of acts of mediation to temporarily erase themselves in the very act of mediation is one of the conditions of possibility for their success. However, if a computer malfunctions, and the screen image of the person in another part of the world with whom we are having a conversation disappears or freezes; if noise interferes with the enjoyment of recorded music; or if a cell phone call drops, the respective medium suddenly reenters awareness, and its users' perception redirects towards its obstinate material existence and infrastructure. Media therefore have the tendency to shift between states of perceptibility and disappearance. Desires for maximally performing, optimally transparent and therefore "vanishing" media notwithstanding, such oscillation is ultimately impossible to suppress and a fundamental characteristic of any medium. Wishes for immediacy go hand in hand with the development of ever more complex media apparatuses. These apparatuses become perceptible when they are experienced as overriding the control and agency of humans. Sudden reappearance, disrupting any impression of immediacy is also caused by the vulnerability of media, their inevitable tendency to periodically malfunction. In the underperformance or failure of media, the trace of the material suddenly thrusts itself into the awareness of the media user. "Noise" as understood by information theory is a trace of the materiality of the medium, "it protrudes into perception 'ecstatically,' haunting vision, hearing, or the sense of tactility and maintains itself 'in presence' to such a degree that it causes the mediality of the medium to 'break'" (Mersch 2002: 65–66; see also Krämer 2000).

For those familiar with 19th-century European debates about language, these deliberations about media strike a familiar note. In fact, the notion of media as transparent was prefigured in these earlier engagements with language. According to Hegel, language was of interest precisely because it seemed to be the medium of thought that was most transparent, in the sense that it left the least imprint of its own on what it mediates.

> Now the symbol is *prima facie* a sign. But in a *mere sign* the connection which meaning and its expression have with another is only a purely arbitrary linkage. In that case this expression, this sensuous thing or picture, so far from presenting *itself*, brings before our minds a content which is foreign to it, one with which it does not need to stand in any proper affinity whatever. So in languages, for example, the sounds are a sign of some idea, feeling, etc. But the predominant part of the sounds in a language is purely linked by chance with the ideas expressed thereby [....] (Hegel 1975 [1835]: 304)

For Hegel the linguistic sign (often referred to by him as the "word") is "by itself void of significance" (Hegel 1975 [1835]: 88), which enables "intelligence" to unfold in a "resistance-free element" (*in einem widerstandslosen Element*) (Hegel 1970 [1830]: 239 [§444 Zus.], see also Hegel 1970: 270, Bodammer 1969: 47–50, McCumber 2006: 118–119). These thoughts were further elaborated by Wilhelm von Humboldt, who characterized language as constituted by the connection between sound and idea (*Ton und Vorstellung*) (von Humboldt 1908: 581–583), a notion that anticipated the Saussurian formulation of the arbitrariness of the sign (Saussure 1983). Yet the notion that languages consist of arbitrary signs was already clearly formulated by Hegel, and can be traced even further back, to John Locke, who argued that the connection between words and ideas is based on a social contract (Bauman and Briggs 2003: 33–34; Peters 1999: 85). The Saussurian sign was a culmination of the dream of language as a transparent medium, in which the material forms and characteristics of the sound have no bearing whatsoever on the ideas and meanings conveyed. In Peircean terms, the Saussurian arbitrary sign would be a symbol, whose link to its object is defined by social convention, as opposed to indices and icons, which derive their meanings from relationships of contiguity and resemblance, respectively. The close parallels between theorizations of language as the medium providing the least resistance to thought and more recent discussions in media theory are striking but are rarely remembered.

The parallels between these earlier explorations of the mediality of language and more recent theorizing in media studies can also be brought to bear on the study of linguistic relativity in the tradition of Benjamin Lee Whorf and Edward Sapir. Whorf famously argued that linguistic categories, in particular grammatical categories, have a pervasive influence on habitual thought, including by reinforcing cultural stereotypes, and can therefore shape thought and cognition in distinct, although non-deterministic ways (Whorf 1956). According to him, language mediates thought in ways that bear testimony to particular formal features of the languages concerned. He distinguished between the "overt" and "covert" linguistic categories involved in such mediation. Overt categories have surface features that make them more readily discernible to their users, such as an always present formal marker of a particular grammatical category, as opposed to covert categories, such as gender in English, or noun classes in Navaho, which largely lack such features as formal markers, and therefore are less likely to enter their users' awareness (Whorf 1956: 88–91). Overt categories are just as involved in the mediation of thought as covert categories are. However, covert categories can influence thought in especially powerful ways, since in contrast to overt categories they largely operate on an unconscious level. A related perspective on the linguistic mediation of thought and the social has been developed by Michael Silverstein. Silverstein distinguishes linguistic forms that are maximally segmentable (like distinct words), can be referentially glossed, and have a relatively presupposed quality with respect to their contexts of use (such as when social etiquette makes one expect the use of such forms in a particular interaction), as for example Dyirbal "mother-in-law" vocabulary,[3] from those that lack these characteristics. Theorizing the "limits of awareness" in language, Silverstein has argued that the former are much more likely to be the focus of their users' attention and awareness, and also more likely to provide a basis for sociolinguistic stereotypes (Silverstein 2001 [1981]). In both of these approaches, work on linguistic relativity and the limits of awareness in language emphasizes a distinction between linguistic elements that function as media in highly perceptible and salient ways, and those parts of language that withdraw from experiential awareness in the process of mediating thought and social relationships.

The Protestant genealogy of a preference for a seemingly "transparent" linguistic medium whose own formal and material features retreat in the face of the meanings and pragmatic effects conveyed is well documented (Keane 2007; Yelle 2013). Hegel's philosophy of mediation, including its implications for the study of language, provides ample evidence for a Protestant bias towards language as a vehicle of spirit whose materiality is minimized.[4] Protestants also came to be known for their preference for "plain speech" (Bauman 1983) and literalism, that is, an emphasis on the referential content of language. Although Protestant language ideologies are not uniform, "[...] broadly speaking, the Reformation inspired a movement toward literalism, meaning both a valorization of the semantic content of language and a devaluation of its poetic and magical functions, which contributed to the rise of polemics against both ritual and mythological language" (Yelle 2013: 25). In religious contexts, the main "other" of such an approach to language was ritual and poetic language, especially in its Catholic

3 Dyirbal "mother-in-law language" is a register of avoidance and respect that speakers used to switch to when within earshot of their classificatory mother-in-law. Classificatory mothers-in-law used to be taboo relatives for users of Dyirbal. The register did not just involve the use of distinct honorific linguistic forms, such as the contrast between familiar T-forms and respect-indicating V-forms of address in many European languages, but the wholesale substitution of vocabulary by forms specific to the "mother-in-law" register. The register follows the same rules of grammar and phonology as everyday speech, but with few exceptions comprises specific alternate forms for every noun, adjective, verb, and time qualifier (Dixon 1990).

4 A good example for the links between the Protestant cultural milieu Hegel grew up in and his philosophy of mediation is the use of the Biblical term *Entäusserung* (from Luther's translation of Greek *ekkenoun* and Latin *exinanio* 'to make empty, to deprive') in the *Phenomenology of the Spirit*. There, Hegel uses this term to both refer to the incarnation of God in the Son but also in a related fashion as a general characterization of objectification as one of the necessary elements in the movement of spirit (e.g., Hegel 1986: 566–567, 570; English translation Hegel 1977: 472, 475). See also Eisenlohr (2009: 274–275, 290–291).

genres, but subsequently also extended to a wide array of religious others in the course of colonial expansion: "Poetry was held responsible for the personifications and polytheism of pagan mythology. The vain repetitions of Catholic and heathen prayers were labeled a form of rhetoric premised on the belief in an anthropomorphic deity, one susceptible to human persuasion and given to work magic in the world" (Yelle 2013: 9).

This suggests that the dialectics of mediation and seeming immediacy also apply to language. Protestant language ideologies have been described as focused on the referential function of language, interiority, sincerity, and a suspicion of ritual language or other genres that foreground the materiality of social and historical contexts (Bialecki and del Pinal 2011: 580; see also Shoaps 2002; Crapanzano 2000; Harding 2000; Engelke 2007; Robbins 2001; Bielo 2011). Such language ideologies seek to arrest one moment of a dynamic that is really an oscillation. Language, like other media, alternates between states of seeming transparency and those moments in which the obstinacy of its materiality foregrounds itself.

In religious contexts, one can distinguish a tension between two modes of employing language as a mediator between humans and actors in a religious otherworld. On one hand, there are forms of religious language that emphasize referential meaning in discourse. This perspective on language is close to the Hegelian and Saussurian notion of the arbitrary sign, in which the material and formal aspects of the linguistic sign stand in no inner relationship to signification. According to this semiotic ideology (Keane 2003: 419), the materiality of the sign should be sidelined in accounting for the meaning of discourse, including its pragmatic consequences, in fulfillment of a "project of immateriality" (Engelke 2007: 246) that also extends to language. On the other hand, there are numerous kinds of religious language that are precisely centered on the foregrounding of its material and formal characteristics, such as spells (Kang 2006), ritual registers (McIntosh 2005), which may sometimes be unintelligible to those performing them (Wirtz 2007), genres of ritual lament and wailing (Urban 1988), divination (Du Bois 1993), ritual prayer (Bowen 1993; Corr 2004; Mahmood 2001), and healing (Wilce 1999). The latter manifestations of religious language are indissolubly bound to the effects and uses of such linguistic genres. Even more so, the materiality of such religious discourse and genres is seen as indispensable for the production of its intended effects, namely to sustain desired interactions with a religious otherworld (Keane 1997; Kuipers 1990; Du Bois 1986). In some of these genres of ritual language, such as mantras (Staal 1989; see also Yelle 2003) the referential meaning of discourse may even be completely irrelevant.

The two overall types of religious language I discuss here are not always mutually exclusive. In some kinds of religious language, they may be combined in interesting ways. Yoonhee Kang has described how Petalangan ritual language in Indonesia is both informed by referentialist language ideologies and the valuation of the material and performative dimensions in ritual language (Kang 2006). Among anthropologists, Christian contexts have provided illustrations for the historical shift from a performativist to a referentialist language ideology (Keane 2007; Robbins 2001), a phenomenon also attested for Islamic modernist settings (Wilce 1998). In contrast to such permanent shifts from one mode of religious language to another, Petalangan and Sikh engagements with religious language, the latter as decribed by Myrvold (2015), provide evidence for a routine alternation between the principal two modes discussed here. Among Sikhs, the referential content of the *Guru Granth Sahib* is highly valued but the scripture is also a "living guru" whose presence is activated by chanting and singing the text. Another way of being close to the living guru is by ingesting sweetened water that has been consecrated by chanting hymns from the *Guru Granth Sahib* (Myrvold 2015), a practice that involves the transduction of religious language, a theme I will discuss at greater length below, providing discussions of the performative effects of religious language with a new twist.[5] Recitation of the Qur'ān is another very prominent example of combining attention to referential content with a stark foregrounding of the poetic patterning and performative dimensions of ritual language (Gade 2006). In Islamic settings, this alternation may also be mapped on different genres of religious language in different linguistic codes. In the Mauritian case I will discuss later in this chapter, referentialist sermons (*khutba*) in the main vernacular language, Mauritian Creole, stand next to Urdu na't, devotional poetry in honor of the Prophet Muhammad, with its characteristic emphasis on poetic form and performative effects. As in the case of Qur'ānic recitation, the alternation between referentialist and "formulaic," performative sensibilities towards language is often a matter of situational focus, potentially susceptible to rapid shifts.

In other words, religious uses of language clearly demonstrate that the mediality of language, here understood as bridging gaps between human actors and non- or semi-human actors and forces in an often imperceptible religious otherworld, feature a very similar alternation between salience and disappearance of the medium. Those kinds of religious language that heavily emphasize the referential content of language over its material form provide examples of a withdrawal of language as a medium. As there appears to be no necessary link between its material characteristics and its meanings or pragmatic effects, such

5 In a range of Islamic contexts a similar practice of "drinking the Qur'ān" is also common (El-Tom 1985; Wilkens 2013).

instances of religious language resemble the ideal of a "transparent" language, a perfect mediator that leaves no traces on what is being made accessible through it, thereby erasing itself in the act of mediation. In contrast, those linguistic interactions with a religious otherworld, where the materiality of the sign is intimately connected to its pragmatic effects, stand for a mode of mediation where language as an "in-between" between humans and the divine crucially shapes what is being mediated through it. As is the case in poetic forms of religious language, the formal and material dimensions of language are maximally foregrounded, leading to great salience of the medium. The oscillation between relative imperceptibility and salience of the medium thus seem to be constitutive of mediality as such, uniting language and other forms of media technology.

2 Sound reproduction as mediation

How do the medialities of sound reproduction and language relate to each other? To start with sound reproduction, the dream of a "vanishing medium" that perfectly and transparently conveys sounds, such as voices, has accompanied the development of this technology for a long time. Early on, the "fidelity" of reproduced sound and the concomitant suppression of "noise" played a prominent role in marketing strategies of the gramophone industry (Sterne 2003: 215–286), perhaps most famously captured in the 1899 advertisement image of The Gramophone Company (which subsequently became RCA), "His Master's Voice," featuring a dog approaching the funnel of a gramophone placed on what looks like the top of a coffin, supposedly emitting the recorded voice of its owner (Sterne 2003: 302). Jonathan Sterne has argued that the invention of sound reproduction technology was a response to a cultural milieu in late 19th-century North America and Europe fascinated with spiritism and the idea of listening to the voices of the dead (see also Schmidt 2000). At the time, many found the acousmatic voice (Chion 1994), meaning one separated from its source, thrilling and mystifying. While the novelty of acousmatic voices has long since vanished, their presence having become a banal feature of modern lifeworlds instead, the ability to technically reproduce voice and sound has added a key new dimension to the longstanding role of language in mediating between religious practitioners and religious otherworlds.

Religious practitioners in the most diverse contexts in the world today use technologies of sound reproduction, not just to enhance the social relationships that the circulation of religious language brings about (Greene 1999; Manuel 2008; Schulz 2008), but also to support attempts to reproduce authenticated religious discourse conforming to particular generic types, and thereby also to enter in proximity with the divine (Qureshi 1995; Hirschkind 2006; Brennan 2012). This may be done through entextualization, meaning the process of lifting a chunk of discourse out of a given context and reinserting it into new contexts (Briggs and Bauman 1992). The bounding and reproducing of a recognizable chunk of discourse turns it into a "text," but far from fixing it, entextualization as the lifting and grafting of discourse from one context to another emphasizes the processual qualities of texts. (See Paul Copp's paper in this volume for an illustration of this process.) Entextualization can be done in such a way that the gap between the context of origin and the target context is minimized, or it can result in a highlighting of what Briggs and Bauman have called "intertextual gaps."

In my research on media, voice, and Islam in Mauritius, sound reproduction, first in the form of audiocassettes, and more recently audio-CDs and mp3 files, was widely used in the circulation of Urdu devotional poetry in honor of the Prophet Muhammad. My interlocutors' interest in sound reproduction was in the saturation of new, everyday contexts with this genre of poetry that this technology enables beyond the boundaries of the ritual events where recitation normally takes place. Another field of deployment for sound reproduction was the preparation for such ritual events, where the circulated recordings of well-known and trained *na'‘t khwan* 'reciters of the na‘t genre' represented models of vocal performance to be emulated. Mauritian Muslims accord great importance to the appropriate vocal style for the success of the performance, which is intended to bring them closer to the Prophet, and ultimately to God, by expressing deep affection for the Prophet and asking for blessings to be showered on him. While listening to recordings of this devotional poetry featuring what my interlocutors felt were the right movements of pitch, volume, and vocal timbre, they prepared their own performances. That is, they used sound reproduction technology as an aid for the faithful and authentic entextualization of poetic discourse, in which any gaps between the context of the performance of origin and that of the target performance could be minimized (Eisenlohr 2006 and 2010). In semiotic terms, sound reproduction technology thus features as a device that supports the production of tokens that fit a type, here the generic conventions of the na‘t genre. The great care taken in the passing on and circulation of religious language is striking, as is the role of sound reproduction in these processes. The uses of sound reproduction are informed by a longstanding Islamic sensibility for the accurate transmission of religious texts. Accordingly, the validity and perceived authenticity of particular texts, such as *hadith*, the record of the deeds and words of the Prophet and his companions, is reckoned through a detailed examination of their chains of transmission (*isnad*) spanning centuries, and ideally linking present-day Muslims to those directly familiar with the Prophet and his companions through chains of reliable and morally trustworthy interlocutors (Graham 1993: 506–508). This paradigm of *isnad* also applies to the transmission of sacred objects, and can be extended to textual genres other than hadith. We could say that for many Mauritian Muslims, and Muslims elsewhere, sound reproduction technology has been domesticated into an established and powerful paradigm of language as mediating between Muslims and their Prophet, and ultimately God.

It is important to realize that such uses of technology in the linguistic mediation of the divine draw on particular assumptions about the medium employed. Using sound reproduction as a means to ensure the faithful and authentic entextualization of religious discourse mobilizes the notion of sound reproduction as a "vanishing" medium that leaves no traces on what it mediates, that is a mere "intermediate" rather than a "mediator" in Latour's terms (2005: 39). Such media ideologies drive the domestication of sound reproduction technology, including its latest digital versions in established ritual contexts, as in the cultivation of devotional poetry in honor of the Prophet Muhammad.

Another important way in which media technologies such as sound reproduction can shape the linguistic mediation of religious worlds is by refiguring participant roles in discourse. Ever since Goffman's explorations in that field, it has been clear that the "I" of discourse can take several forms that in turn can be assigned to particular participant roles and therefore forms of agency in discourse. To this effect, Goffman distinguished between composer or "ghostor" (akin to *ghostwriter*), the originator or sponsor who assumes responsibility for the speech act, and animator or relayer who is actually performing the act, all of which can be combined in a single person, or be taken up by different actors (Goffman 1974: 517–520; Levinson 1988; Irvine 1996). Most importantly, participant roles frequently shift depending on interactional context. In religious settings, the agency in discourse is of great significance, as for example particular forms of ritual language may be considered words of the ancestors or discourse uttered by deities, even if performed by human actors in a ritual setting. Here, the complex nature of the "I" in religious language is evident (Urban 1989), as well as the fact that actors in such settings can not only inhabit different participant roles in linguistic performance, but that the assignment of and expectations of such roles are of supreme importance for the efficacy and meanings of religious discourse. Uses of media such as sound reproduction can influence the assignment of participant roles, and thus reinforce established authoritative agencies in religious language, but can also result in anxieties about whose agency it actually is that is manifest in particular religious speech acts and discourses. In fact, the anxiety of and fascination with media regarded as "new" often lie in their propensity to reconfigure participant roles in interaction (Gershon and Manning 2014: 562–564).

For example, the perceived efficacy of na‘t recitations also lies in the assumed origins of the poetry as composed by renowned saint-poets, who composed na‘t in moments of spiritual intensity, such as when confronted by the presence of the Prophet himself. The poetry features an array of deictic makers, such as personal pronouns, spatial and temporal qualifiers, which together with the poets' pen names points to such authoritative contexts of origin. The recitation of poems preserves these indexical markers of a context that is located elsewhere in space and time. It is thereby an act of transposition (*Versetzung*), to use Karl Bühler's term (Bühler 1965 [1934]: 134–140; see also Haviland 1996; Shoaps 2002); that is, the insertion of a text into another discursive event in a way that indicates the former's origins in another spatial and temporal context. The performances also feature a discursive "I" expressing deep devotion and affection for the Prophet. Reciting performers therefore combine several participant roles. This is because the performers animating the poetry seek to align their agency with the authoritative saint-poets who were considered the composers of na‘t, and also with its responsible originators. This merger is unstable and requires constant support, notably through performing in ways considered appropriate and authentic. This dimension of authenticity does not just extend to the texts themselves, but very importantly also to the style and modalities of vocal performance. Mauritian Muslims take audio recordings of na‘t poetry by renowned na‘t khwan to be authoritative models of the vocal qualities that the performance should have, but that printed compilations of this poetic genre cannot provide. Audio recordings by esteemed performers are thus treated as a way to safeguard and authenticate na‘t performances in ways that align with and do justice to their assumed context of composition by saint-poets. Given the poetry's array of formal features pointing to these assumed origins, such uses of sound reproduction therefore become part of the indexical field of deictic reference (Hanks 1992). In this way, they also help to support the merger between the participant roles of composer, originator, and animator that those cultivating the genre aim for, which in turn enhances the performance of the poetry as a form of intercession with the Prophet, and thus mediates between Muslims and the divine. The question of media regimenting, or at least influencing the distributions and shifts of participant roles in religious language also has important implications for the larger question of the mediality of language in religion. As my example suggests, the appropriate regimentation of participant roles is crucial for the efficacy of religious language as a mediator of the divine, and uses of technology such as sound reproduction can intervene profoundly in this process.

Na‘t recitation also demonstrates that in religious language there is another kind of oscillation between salience and relative disappearance of the medium that is different from the modality I have discussed earlier. This mode is different from the relative perceptibility of linguistic forms as in "overt" and "covert" categories in Whorfian terms, or as in Silverstein's "limits of awareness." In fact, as far as the na't genre is concerned, its structure highlights the formal and material properties of language throughout, because of its web of metric, semantic, and phonetic parallelisms that is the hallmark of poetic language (Jakobson 1960). The additional dimension of the mediality of language I want to point at here relates to the faithfulness to established generic forms and norms of appropriateness in discourse, and the violation of such norms in certain linguistic performances. In technical terms these are matters of presupposed indexicality in the sense of being based on context-specific presuppositions of the co-occurrence of linguistic and non-linguistic signs, and departures from it as interactions unfold, as performers aim to perform language that corresponds to the expectations connected to the generic model of na't, or, put differently, to produce tokens of a type (the respective poetic genre). This requires a success in achieving the "correct" ways of entextualizing discourse and regimenting participant roles that actual performances of na't do not always meet. For example, according to many, the vocal style and timbre of na't recitation should not remind one of film songs. In Mauritius, however, Hindi film ("Bollywood") entertainment is extremely widespread, and its music sometimes influences the way some na't khwan recite the poetry. To an even larger extent, they have also shaped audiences' aesthetic sensibilities and expectations. Sometimes, recitations involve elements that are considered "film style" (*filmi taraz*), and that in turn renders the performance invalid for some, turning its perceived spiritual benefits into their opposite.

Following this example, I suggest that the mediality of language also consists in the alternations between the unfolding of the performance in expected ways, and moments where this is not the case.[6] This alternation does not just occur in relation to the expected relationships and correlations among the linguistic signs that make up the poetic text, but also involves relationships of co-occurrence between linguistic and non-linguistic signs of the performance, such as the participants' social identities and their bodily composure and spatial positions, qualities of the voice, and the features of the overall setting of the event. Instantiating all these complex sets of expected correlations and co-occurrences in performance is a delicate achievement always subject to

6 This alternation is similar to what Bauman and Briggs (1992: 149) have called a minimizing and maximizing of intertextual gaps. Bauman and Briggs have described these two movements as potentials of textuality that represent different strategies of establishing authority. I would go even further, suggesting that the two movements also represent the key modes of language's functioning as a medium of socio-cultural worlds, and point to features that language shares with other kinds of media.

failure. As long as performances unfold according to such situational and generic expectations, the linguistic medium draws little attention to itself as the mediator that enables interactions with the divine. However, the relative perceptibility and disappearance of language as a medium resembles an aggregate state in flux, which can change from one moment of a performance to another, as a performative event that unfolds in situationally expected ways suddenly departs from expectations. Then, the smooth functioning of language as a medium of the divine is disrupted, and reappears as an obstinate medium pushing itself into the awareness of those engaging with religious otherworlds. When, for example, the performance of na't blends with musical elements from Hindi films, the relative "transparency" of language as a medium evaporates, and attention will be redirected to the medium and its inappropriate formal and material aspects, as they suddenly stand in the way (at least for some listeners) of a rapprochement between practitioners and the divine. Such evaluations of appropriateness are of course perspective-bound, they may not be shared by all present. This is also the case in my example, because even though many Mauritian Muslims – and all *'ulema* concerned – reject *filmi taraz* in na't, other Mauritian Muslims see no harm in it. This implies that the mediality of language, at least as far as the dimension of presupposed indexicality and creative deviations from this are concerned, depends to a large extent on the shifting contexts and perspectives of such judgments of appropriateness.

3 Media, voice, and transduction

In the contemporary study of religion, the latter's material dimensions have lately gained much attention (Meyer 2014; Meyer and Houtman 2012); in fact 2005 saw the launch of a journal *Material Religion* specifically dedicated to exploring this key aspect of religion. While much of the work that has followed this direction of research has paid close scrutiny to media and its technical aspects, far less attention has been spent on the materiality of language in religious settings. How do we relate the material aspects of language with other media when it comes to the analysis of religion? In order to address this question, uses of sound reproduction technology in religious contexts, such as those I investigate in this chapter, may provide useful leads.

Sound reproduction can foreground the materiality of voice (Harkness 2014; Weidman 2014). In relation to both sound and voice, sound media open up a different perspective on the materiality of language since they involve transduction, the transfer of energy from one state into another. Media technologies convert discourse into different material modalities. For example, writing transduces sonically manifest language into a visual register, while sound reproduction technology transduces sound, which in case the medium through which it travels is air involves differences in air pressure, into electric signals that enter an analog or digital apparatus of storage, and are converted back into sound again when a recording is played. These transductions of energy into different states are very consequential in religious mediation through language, and are closely connected to religiously grounded notions about language.[7] We have seen that Mauritian Muslims value sound reproduction technology because they regard this as a means to faithfully reproduce sonic tokens that conform to their expectations of the na‘t genre, above all regarding the qualities of the reciting voice. Although written compilations of na‘t exist, they are treated as an aide-memoire only; since they reduce the poetry to its textual content, they cannot substitute the sonic power of the reciting voice that is regarded as crucial for the success of the performance. Therefore, those engaged in the performance of na‘t show a strong preference for the storage of sonic tokens in order to ensure the appropriate entextualization and transmission of this devotional genre, as opposed to their transduction into a visual register through writing. Mauritian Muslims who appreciate na‘t treat sound reproduction as a technical solution for the problem raised by the high value placed on the perceived authenticity of vocal qualities in religious performance.

The conversion of energy from one state to another that transduction effects can operate as a bridging of various gaps in the interaction with the divine. As Webb Keane has recently argued, forms of transduction such as writing can overcome gaps between different ontological realms, such as happens when a "message" from an imperceptible religious otherworld appears in writing or as a material object in the world where human religious practitioners find themselves. Transduction can thereby also bridge gaps related to differences in agentive capability, such as those between humans and gods (Keane 2013). Transduction, however, not only effects a connection between disparate realms and actors, but also engenders new phenomena along the way. According to Gilbert Simondon's (1992 [1964]) formulation of transduction as a process of "individuation" through

7 While all production of vocal sound and its perception revolves around physical processes of transduction, in my analysis I specifically use the notion of transduction as the core technical process in sound reproduction (Sterne 2003: 22, see also Helmreich 2007 on sound and transduction). Silverstein's use of the term in contexts of translation goes into a different, more metaphorical direction when he deploys the term to describe the rendering of non-referential meanings into another language (Silverstein 2003). See also Handman (2015: 227) for a related use of transduction as an analytical category.

which new entities, such as biological, social, and psychological phenomena emerge from an unstructured "pre-individual" milieu, transduction is a highly productive process. Simondon defines transduction as "a process – be it physical, biological, mental, or social – in which an activity gradually sets itself in motion, propagating within a given area, through a structuration of the different zones of the area over which it operates. Each region of the structure that is constituted in this way then serves to constitute the next one to such an extent that at the very time this structuration is effected there is a progressive modification taking place in tandem with it" (Simondon 1992 [1964]: 313). Sonic transduction provides a very concrete example of such a process, in which a domain through which sound propagates is reshaped in a manner analogous to the parts already touched by it. Such reshaping and restructuring then leads to the creation of new entities and phenomena. Here I suggest that shared "religious sensations" (Meyer 2008) may actually be the result of such sonic transductions. Given that sound impacts others who are present at the same moment in a religious setting, it can also generate ineffable feelings of religious community. "Speaking as a kind of sonorous touching" (Csordas 2008: 118) then opens up a perspective on language as sonic events that bodies encounter through processes of transduction. Such transduction goes beyond hearing in the strict sense of the term, as differences in air pressure are registered, not just by the hearing apparatus (which transduces sound waves into electrical impulses sent to the brain), but potentially by the entire body. As the flesh encounters language in such ways, we arrive at a very concrete understanding of language as embodied. The transductions that unfold when sound envelops and penetrates bodies may then be productive in several ways, including through the production of religious feelings and sensations.

The latter aspect, the role of language in the felt dimensions of religion, also points to the rhythmic qualities of language and its sounds, as is especially evident in poetry, as in my example of the na'tgenre. The rhythmicity of language, but also movement of vocal volume, pitch, and timbre, often result in suggestions of movement. Such movement, as in the coinciding of drumming, voice, and language in several Islamic settings in South Asia (Wolf 2014), has an impact on listeners through the logic of transduction. As a result, musically recited poetry has a special potential to generate bodily sensations though its rhythmic qualities and the bodily movements suggested by it. This is because such religious sounds modify the bodily economy of felt space through their movement (Eisenlohr 2018). As they impact bodies, the sensations generated by such sounds may be intertwined, in turn, with historically grounded religious traditions and their narratives. The rhythmicity and other dynamics of linguistic sounds therefore are another mode of mediating between human actors and the divine.

4 Conclusion

Language enables the circulating and sharing of religious forms and practices, often in conjunction with other media technologies, such as sound reproduction. I have discussed language as a materialization of religion that constitutes social relationships among religious practitioners, as well as relations between human and semi- or non-human actors in often imperceptible religious otherworlds. As language mediates and thereby shapes such interactions, it is often itself subject to further technological mediation. Examining the relationship between language and other media technologies, I have sought to show that both undergo similar oscillations between phenomenological disappearance and the reassertion of their presence as the trace of their materiality. This striking parallel between language and media, although frequently overlooked, is of great relevance for understanding the interplay of language, other kinds of media technology, and religion as interactions with the divine. Further, I have suggested that uses of sound reproduction in religious settings are closely geared to concerns religious practitioners have about processes of transmitting and entextualizing religious discourse, as well as the distribution of participant roles in interactions with the divine. While sound reproduction can support established ideas and paradigms of what language accomplishes in such interactions, its disruptive potential is equally present.

The vocal and sonic dimensions of language provide the most vivid illustrations of language as material and embodied. In ritual settings, they are often credited with the generation of strong religious sensations. I have suggested that the analytic of transduction can illuminate how sound, including vocal sound, can provoke such sensations that might undergird a religious tradition's sense of community. Transduction is also the key mode of operation of sound reproduction technologies. An important part of the sonic dimensions of religion is the rhythmicity of language, above all in poetic and musical genres. Rhythm is sensed in the performance of such genres as suggestions of bodily movement, enacting somatic relationships within religious traditions and with religious otherworlds.

References

Baudrillard, Jean. 1994. *Simulacra and simulation*. Ann Arbor: University of Michigan Press.

Bauman, Richard. 1983. *Let your words be few: Symbolism of speaking and silence among seventeenth-century Quakers*. Cambridge: Cambridge University Press.

Bauman, Richard & Charles L. Briggs. 2003. *Voices of modernity: Language ideologies and the politics of inequality*. Cambridge: Cambridge University Press.

Bialecki, Jon & Eric Hoenes del Pinal. 2011. Introduction: Beyond logos: Extensions of the language ideology paradigm in the study of global Christianities. *Anthropological Quarterly* 84(3). 575–593.
Bielo, James S. 2011. "How much of this is promise?": God as a sincere speaker in Evangelical Bible reading. *Anthropological Quarterly* 84(3). 631–653.
Bodammer, Theodor. 1969. *Hegels Deutung der Sprache: Interpretationen zu Hegels Äußerungen über die Sprache*. Hamburg: Felix Meiner.
Bolter, Jay David & Richard Grusin. 1999. *Remediation: Understanding new media*. Cambridge, MA: MIT Press.
Bowen, John R. 1993. *Muslims through discourse: Religion and ritual in Gayo society*. Princeton: Princeton University Press.
Brennan, Vicki L. 2012. Take control: The labor of immediacy in Yoruba Christian music. *Journal of Popular Music Studies* 24(4). 411–429.
Briggs, Charles & Richard Bauman. 1992. Genre, intertextuality and social power. *Journal of Linguistic Anthropology* 2(2): 131–172.
Bühler, Karl. 1965 [1934] *Sprachtheorie. Die Darstellungsfunktion der Sprache*. Stuttgart: G. Fischer.
Chion, Michel. 1994. *Audiovision: Sound on screen*. New York: Columbia University Press.
Corr, Rachel. 2004. To throw the blessing: Poetics, prayer, and performance in the Andes. *The Journal of Latin American Anthropology* 9(2). 382–408.
Crapanzano, Vincent. 2000. *Serving the word: Literalism in America from the pulpit to the bench*. New York: New Press.
Csordas, Thomas J. 2008. Intersubjectivity and intercorporeality. *Subjectivity* 3(1). 110–121.
De Abreu, Maria José A. 2009. Breath, technology, and the making of Canção Nova in Brazil. In Birgit Meyer (ed.), *Aesthetic formations: Media, religion, and the senses*, 161–182. New York: Palgrave Macmillan.
Dixon, R. M. V. 1990. The origin of "Mother-in-law vocabulary" in two Australian languages. *Anthropological Linguistics* 32(1/2). 1–56.
Du Bois, John W. 1986. Self-evidence and ritual speech. In Wallace L. Chafe & Johanna Nichols (eds.), *Evidentiality: The linguistic encoding of epistemology*, 313–336. Norwood, NJ: Ablex.
Du Bois, John W. 1993. Meaning without intention: Lessons from divination. In Jane H. Hill & Judith T. Irvine (eds.), *Responsibility and evidence in oral discourse*, 48–71. Cambridge: Cambridge University Press.
Eisenlohr, Patrick. 2006. As Makkah is sweet and beloved, so is Madina: Islam, devotional genres and electronic mediation in Mauritius. *American Ethnologist* 33(2). 230–245.
Eisenlohr, Patrick. 2009. Technologies of the spirit: Devotional Islam, sound reproduction, and the dialectics of mediation and immediacy in Mauritius. *Anthropological Theory* 9(3). 273–296.
Eisenlohr, Patrick. 2010. Materialities of entextualization: The domestication of sound reproduction in Mauritian Muslim devotional practices. *Journal of Linguistic Anthropology* 20(2). 314–333.
Eisenlohr, Patrick. 2011. The anthropology of media and the question of ethnic and religious pluralism. *Social Anthropology* 19(1). 40–55.
Eisenlohr, Patrick. 2012. Media and religious diversity. *Annual Review of Anthropology* 41. 37–55.
Eisenlohr, Patrick. 2018. *Sounding Islam: Voice, media, and sonic atmospheres in an Indian Ocean world*. Oakland: University of California Press.

El-Tom, Abdullahi. 1985. Drinking the Koran: The meaning of Koranic verses in Berti erasure. *Africa* 55(4). 414–431.
Engelke, Matthew. 2007. *A problem of presence: beyond scripture in an African church*. Berkeley, CA: University of California Press.
Engelke, Matthew. 2010. Religion and the media turn: A review essay. *American Ethnologist* 37(2). 371–379.
Gade, Anna M. 2006. Recitation. In Andrew Rippin (ed.), *The Blackwell companion to the Qur'ān*, 481–493. Malden, MA: Blackwell.
Gershon, Ilana & Paul Manning. 2014. Language and media. In N. J. Enfield, Paul Kockelman & Jack Sidnell (eds.) *The Cambridge handbook of linguistic anthropology*, 559–576. Cambridge: Cambridge University Press.
Goffman, Erving. 1974. *Frame analysis: An essay in the organization of experience*. New York: Harper & Row.
Greene, Paul D. 1999. Sound engineering in a Tamil village: Playing audio cassettes as devotional performance. *Ethnomusicology* 43(3). 459–489.
Graham, William A. 1993. Traditionalism in Islam: An essay in interpretation. *Journal of Interdisciplinary History* 23(3). 495–522.
Handman, Courtney. 2015. *Critical Christianity: Translation and denominational conflict in Papua New Guinea*. Berkeley, CA: University of California Press.
Hanks, William F. 1992. The indexical ground of deictic reference. In Alessandro Duranti & Charles Goodwin (eds.), *Rethinking Context*, 43–76. Cambridge: Cambridge University Press.
Harding, Susan F. 2000. *The book of Jerry Falwell: Fundamentalist language and politics*. Princeton: Princeton University Press.
Harkness, Nicholas. 2014. *Songs of Seoul: An ethnography of voice and voicing in Christian South Korea*. Berkeley, CA: University of California Press.
Harvey, David. 1989. *The condition of postmodernity: An inquiry into the origins of cultural change*. Oxford: Blackwell.
Haviland, John. 1996. Projections, transpositions and relativity. In John Gumperz & Stephen Levinson (eds.), *Rethinking linguistic relativity*, 271–323. Cambridge: Cambridge University Press.
Hegel, Georg Wilhelm Friedrich. 1970 [1830]. *Werke 10: Enzyklopädie der philosophischen Wissenschaften III*. Frankfurt am Main: Suhrkamp.
Hegel, Georg Wilhelm Friedrich. 1975 [1835]. *Hegel's aesthetics*: *Lectures on fine art*, vol. 1. Translated by T. M. Knox. Oxford: Oxford University Press.
Hegel, Georg Wilhelm Friedrich. 1977. *Hegel's phenomenology of spirit*. Translated by A. V. Miller. Oxford: Oxford University Press.
Hegel, Georg Wilhelm Friedrich. 1986. *Werke 3: Phänomenologie des Geistes*. Frankfurt am Main: Suhrkamp.
Hirschkind, Charles. 2006. *The ethical soundscape: Cassette sermons and Islamic counterpublics*. New York: Columbia University Press.
Hirschkind, Charles & Brian Larkin. 2008. Introduction: Media and the political forms of religion. *Social Text* 26(3), issue 96. 1–9.
Humboldt, Wilhelm von. 1908. Über Denken und Sprechen. In *Gesammelte Schriften VII.2*, edited by the Preussische Akademie der Wissenschaften, 581–583. Berlin: B. Behr.
Irvine, Judith. 1996. Shadow conversations: The indeterminacy of participant roles. In Michael Silverstein & Greg Urban (eds.), *Natural histories of discourse*, 131–59. Chicago: University of Chicago Press.

Jakobson, Roman. 1960. Closing statement: linguistics and poetics. In Thomas A. Sebeok (ed.), *Style in language*, 350–377. Cambridge, MA: MIT Press.
Jäger, Ludwig. 2000. Die Sprachvergessenheit der Medientheorie. Ein Plädoyer für das Medium Sprache. In W. Kallmeyer (ed.), *Sprache und neue Medien*, 9–30. Berlin & New York: De Gruyter.
Kang, Yoonhee. 2006. "Staged" rituals and "veiled" spells: Multiple language ideologies and transformations in Petalangan verbal magic. *Journal of Linguistic Anthropology* 16(1). 1–22.
Keane, Webb. 1997. *Signs of recognition: Powers and hazards of representation in an Indonesian society*. Berkeley, CA: University of California Press.
Keane, Webb. 2003. Semiotics and the social analysis of material things. *Language & Communication* 23(3). 409–425.
Keane, Webb. 2004. Language and religion. In Alessandro Duranti (ed.), *A companion to linguistic anthropology*, 431–448. Malden, MA: Blackwell.
Keane, Webb. 2007. *Christian moderns: Freedom and fetish in the mission encounter*. Berkeley, CA: University of California Press.
Keane, Webb. 2013. On spirit writing: Materialities of language and the religious work of transduction. *Journal of the Royal Anthropological Institute* 19(1). 1–17.
Kittler, Friedrich. 1993. *Draculas Vermächtnis. Technische Schriften*. Leipzig: Reclam.
Kittler, Friedrich. 1997. *Literature, Media, Information Systems*. Edited by John Johnston. Amsterdam: G and B Arts International.
Krämer, Sibylle. 2000. Das Medium als Spur und als Apparat. In Sibylle Krämer (ed.), *Medien, Computer, Realität: Wirklichkeitsvorstellungen und Neue Medien*, 73–94. Frankfurt am Main: Suhrkamp.
Krämer, Sibylle. 2008. *Medien, Bote, Übertragung. Kleine Metaphysik der Medialität*. Frankfurt am Main: Suhrkamp.
Kuipers, Joel C. 1990. *Power in performance: The creation of textual authority in Weyewa ritual speech*. Philadelphia: University of Pennsylvania Press.
Latour, Bruno. 2005. *Reassembling the social: An introduction to Actor-Network-Theory*. Oxford: Oxford University Press.
Levinson, Stephen C. 1988. Putting linguistics on a proper footing: Explorations in Goffman's concepts of participation. In Paul Drew & Anthony J. Wootton (eds.), *Erving Goffman: Exploring the interaction order*, 161–227. Cambridge: Polity Press.
Mahmood, Saba. 2001. Rehearsed spontaneity and the conventionality of ritual: Disciplines of *ṣalāt*. *American Ethnologist* 28(4). 827–853.
Manuel, Peter. 2008. North Indian Sufi popular music in the age of Hindu and Muslim fundamentalism. *Ethnomusicology* 52(3). 378–400.
McCumber, John. 2006. Sound-tone-word: Toward an Hegelian philosophy of language. In Jere O'Neill Surber (ed.), *Hegel and language*, 111–125. Albany: State University of New York Press.
McIntosh, Janet. 2005. Baptismal essentialisms: Giriama code choice and the reification of ethnoreligious boundaries. *Journal of Linguistic Anthropology* 15(2). 151–170.
McLuhan, Marshall. 1964. *Understanding media: The extensions of man*. New York & Toronto: McGraw-Hill.
Mersch, Dieter. 2002. *Ereignis und Aura. Untersuchungen zu einer Ästhetik des Performativen*. Frankfurt am Main: Suhrkamp.
Meyer, Birgit. 2004. "Praise the Lord": Popular cinema and pentecostalite style in Ghana's new public sphere. *American Ethnologist* 31(1). 92–110.

Meyer, Birgit. 2008. Sensational forms: Why media, aesthetics, and power matter in the study of contemporary religion. In Hent de Vries (ed.), *Religion: Beyond a concept*, 704–723. New York: Fordham University Press.
Meyer, Birgit. 2010. Aesthetics of persuasion: Global Christianity and Pentecostalism's sensational forms. *South Atlantic Quarterly* 109(4). 741–763.
Meyer, Birgit. 2014. An author meets her critics. Around Birgit Meyer's "Mediation and the genesis of presence: Toward a material approach to religion." *Religion and Society: Advances in Research* 5(1). 205–254.
Meyer, Birgit & Dick Houtman. 2012. Introduction: Material religion: How things matter. In Dick Houtman & Birgit Meyer (eds.), *Things: Religion and the question of materiality*, 1–26. New York: Fordham University Press.
Meyer, Birgit & Annelies Moors (eds.). 2006. *Religion, media, and the public sphere*. Bloomington: Indiana University Press.
Morgan, David. 2005. *The sacred gaze: Religious visual culture in theory and practice*. Berkeley, CA: University of California Press.
Morgan, David (ed.). 2010. *Religion and material culture: The matter of belief*. New York: Routledge.
Myrvold, Kristina. 2015. The scripture as a living guru: Religious practices among contemporary Sikhs. In Knut A. Jacobsen, Mikhael Aktor & Kristina Myrvold (eds.), *Objects of worship in South Asian religions: Forms, practices and meanings*, 163–181. Abingdon & New York: Routledge.
Oosterbaan, Martijn. 2009. Purity and the devil: Community, media, and the body: Pentecostal adherents in a favela in Rio de Janeiro. In Birgit Meyer (ed.), *Aesthetic formations: Media, religion, and the senses*, 53–71. New York: Palgrave Macmillan.
Peters, John Durham. 1999. *Speaking into the air: A history of the idea of communication*. Chicago: University of Chicago Press.
Qureshi, Regula Burckhardt. 1995. Recorded sound and religious music: The case of *Qawwali*. In Lawrence Babb & Susan S. Wadley (eds.), *Media and the transformation of religion in South Asia*, 139–166. Philadelphia: University of Pennsylvania Press.
Robbins, Joel. 2001. God is nothing but talk: Modernity, language, and prayer in a Papua New Guinea society. *American Anthropologist* 103(4). 901–912.
Saussure, Ferdinand de. 1983. *Course in general linguistics*. Translated by Roy Harris. La Salle, IL: Open Court.
Schmidt, Leigh Eric. 2000. *Hearing things: Religion, illusion, and the American enlightenment*. Cambridge, MA: Harvard University Press.
Schulz, Dorothea E. 2008. Soundscape. In David Morgan (ed.), *Key words in religion, media and culture*, 172–186. New York: Routledge.
Schulz, Dorothea E. 2012. *Muslims and new media in West Africa: Pathways to God*. Bloomington: Indiana University Press.
Shoaps, Robin A. 2002. "Pray earnestly": The textual construction of personal involvement in Pentecostal prayer and song. *Journal of Linguistic Anthropology* 12(1). 34–71.
Silverstein, Michael. 2001 [1981]. The limits of awareness. In Alessandro Duranti (ed.), *Linguistic anthropology: A reader*, 382–401. Malden, MA: Blackwell.
Silverstein, Michael. 2003. Translation, transduction, transformation: Skating glissando on thin semiotic ice. In P. Rubel and A. Rosman (eds.), *Translating cultures: Perspectives on translation and anthropology*, 75–105. Oxford: Berg.
Simondon, Gilbert. 1992 [1964]. The genesis of the individual. In Jonathan Crary and Sanford Kwinter (eds.), *Incorporations*, 297–319. New York: Zone.

Staal, Frits. 1989. *Rules without meaning: Ritual, mantras and the human sciences*. New York: Peter Lang
Sterne, Jonathan. 2003. *The audible past: Cultural origins of sound reproduction*. Durham, NC: Duke University Press.
Stolow, Jeremy. 2005. Religion and/as media. *Theory, Culture & Society* 22(4). 119–145.
Tomlinson, John. 1999. *Globalization and culture*. Chicago: University of Chicago Press.
Tomlinson, Matt. 2004. Ritual, risk and danger: Chain prayers in Fiji. *American Anthropologist* 106(1). 6–16.
Tomlinson, Matt. 2014. *Ritual textuality: Pattern and motion in performance*. Oxford: Oxford University Press.
Urban, Greg. 1988. Ritual wailing in Amerindian Brazil. *American Anthropologist* 90(2). 385–400.
Urban, Greg. 1989. The "I" of discourse. In Benjamin Lee & Greg Urban (eds.), *Semiotics, self, and society*, 27–51. Berlin & New York: Mouton de Gruyter.
Virilio, Paul. 1998. *The Virilio reader*. Edited by James Der Derian. Malden, MA & Oxford: Blackwell.
Vries, Hent de. 2001. In Media Res: Global religion, public spheres, and the task of contemporary comparative religious studies. In Hent de Vries & Samuel Weber (eds.), *Religion and media*, 3–42. Stanford, CA: Stanford University Press.
Weidman, Amanda. 2014. Anthropology and voice. *Annual Review of Anthropology* 43. 37–51.
Whorf, Benjamin. 1956. *Language, thought, and reality: Selected writings*. Cambridge, MA: MIT Press.
Wilce, James. 1998. Transforming laments: Performativity and rationalization as linguistic ideologies. In Gary B. Palmer & Debra J. Occhi (eds.), *Languages of sentiment*, 39–63. Philadelphia: John Benjamins.
Wilce, James. 1999. Healing. *Journal of Linguistic Anthropology* 9(1–2). 96–99.
Wilkens, Katharina. 2013. Drinking the Quran, swallowing the Madonna: Embodied aesthetics of popular healing practices. In Afe Adogame, Magnus Echter & Oliver Freiberger (eds.), *Alternative Voices: A plurality approach for religious studies: Essays in honor of Ulrich Berner*, 243–259. Göttingen: Vandenhoeck & Ruprecht.
Wirtz, Kristina. 2007. How diasporic communities remember: Learning to speak the "tongue of the *oricha*" in Cuban Santería. *American Ethnologist* 34(1). 108–126.
Wolf, Richard K. 2014. *The voice in the drum: Music, language, and emotion in Islamicate South Asia*. Urbana: University of Illinois Press.
Yelle, Robert A. 2003. *Explaining mantras: Ritual, rhetoric, and the dream of a natural language in Hindu Tantra*. New York: Routledge.
Yelle, Robert A. 2013. *The language of disenchantment: Protestant literalism and colonial discourse in British India*. New York: Oxford University Press.

Anderson Blanton

The "point of contact": Radio and the transduction of healing prayer

1 Introduction

With ears that could not bear to hear the rhetorical devices of rhythm, rhyme, and repetition during ritual performance, many early Protestant theologians attempted to mute the poetic play of language within the liturgical form. Enlivened through the new technology of typography and an antipathy toward divine communication that seemed to privilege rhetorical form over semantic content, Protestant prayer became characterized by an easily understandable vernacular language free from an excess of poetic embellishment (Yelle 2013: 115). Although this poetic economy of prayer persists in many Protestant contexts, it is interesting to consider how these older forms have been influenced by Pentecostalism and its performative resonance with technologies of the voice. This chapter examines a popular healing prayer mediated through the radio in order to track recent developments in the history of Christian language and ritual gesture.

Throughout the 1950s, millions of Americans gathered expectantly around their radios to hear Oral Roberts' *Healing Waters Broadcast*. Oral Roberts is perhaps the most famous healing evangelist in American history, and his performative techniques and fundraising methods have been replicated by Pentecostal and charismatic Christian organizations all over the world. During the "prayer time" of the broadcast, Roberts would instruct the audience to "put your hand upon the radio cabinet as a point of contact" to facilitate the communication of healing power. In addition to an extensive network of radio stations within the United States, this faith healing program encircled the globe through transmitters strategically located in Europe, Africa and India. The "point of contact" has now become a key descriptive phrase *and* technique of prayer within global charismatic Christian faith healing movements. Several recent studies of charismatic healing in religious studies and the anthropology of media, moreover, have emphasized the global resonance of this phrase.[1]

---

1 For other descriptions of the global performance of the point of contact, see (Bessire 2012; Brown 2011; de Witte 2012; Asamoah-Gayadu 2005).

Anderson Blanton, Yale University Institute of Sacred Music

https://doi.org/10.1515/9781614514329-017

The most important segment of the *Healing Waters Broadcast* occurred toward the end of the thirty-minute program, when, after several songs, some testimonies of miraculous healing by faith, and a brief sermon, Oral Roberts delivered the healing prayer during the prayer time of the program. As a specific technique of prayer, the prayer time was structured around what Roberts termed "the point of contact." In the early days of his ministry, Roberts developed this faith healing technique specifically in relation to the radio. According to Roberts, the radio as a point of contact allowed the patient to "turn loose" or "unleash" a standing reserve of faith that resided within the religious subject. Through numerous printed tracts, magazines, books and comics, the faith healer described how the point of contact focused the attention of the patient, allowing him or her to experience the presence of that which, under everyday sensory regimes, would persist undetected (Figure 1).

Roberts often used technological metaphors to explain this charismatic technique of prayer, comparing the point of contact to an electric light switch that when actuated through a manual gesture upon the object, allowed divine healing power to *flow* through the body of the patient (Reinhardt 2014).[2] It is not mere coincidence that Roberts was constantly invoking metaphors of technology to describe the point of contact, as the first explicit formulation of this new prayer-gesture emerged within the context of his popular radio broadcast. In an article entitled, "The Story Behind Healing Waters," published in the mass circulated *Healing Waters Magazine*, Roberts explains the basic ideas behind the radio as a point of contact:

> I conceived the idea of placing my hand over the microphone while people put their hands on the radio cabinet and by these two actions forming a double point of contact. From the very beginning of the Healing Waters Broadcast, I have felt led to offer a healing prayer at the close of each Program. [...] *At this time people gather around their radios and place their hands on their radio cabinets while I place mine over the microphone as a point of contact in lieu of placing my hands upon them* [...]. It has been amazing how many thousands of people have caught on to this idea and have turned their faith loose. Some very powerful miracles have been wrought through the broadcast and still even greater miracles are being wrought from week to week. (Roberts 1952b: 15)

Although Roberts claimed that his curative technique was divinely inspired when he fell into a deep trance-like state during his early ministry, it is interesting to consider earlier formations of this idea within the history of Evangelical

2 Recent contributions to the study of religious radio within the fields of anthropology and religious studies include (Bessire 2012; Blanton 2015; Hangen 2002; Larkin 2008; Klassen 2007; Schulz 2012).

Figure 1: The radio as point of contact.
Note: Roberts (1947: 38).

Christianity. The phrase "point of contact" became prominent within the context of late 19th-century debates about the proper pedagogical methods for "primary" and "beginner" classes within the Sunday school. The primary Sunday school department usually designated a class of children eight years old or younger. This phrase entered the debates in religious pedagogy full-force with the 1896 publication, *The Point of Contact in Teaching*, by the prominent advocate of progressive Sunday school education and editor of the *Sunday School Times*, Patterson Du Bois. Heavily influenced by the training methods of the Swiss educational reformer Johann Pestalozzi, Du Bois insisted that new methods of religious instruction in the Sunday school must begin with the immediate sensory experience of material objects that are “close at hand” for the child. Du Bois and other Sunday school reformers of the late 19th century were following broader educational trends that had been adopted in the public schools thirty years earlier. The “Object Lesson” became the catchphrase for this new pedagogical technique of inductivism. Criticizing established catechistical mnemotechnics that required children to retain and recite abstract theological concepts far removed from the child’s developmental plane of experience, Du Bois proposed object lessons that would mobilize the things of everyday life as a point of contact between the immediate sensory experiences of the child and the development of more abstract concepts. In the methodological section of his work entitled “applying the principle,” Du Bois recounts a story of how the point of contact was used to instruct a group of mischievous young boys who refused to pay attention to their Sunday school lesson on the Golden Rule. When it became painfully obvious to Du Bois, in his position of substitute teacher, that the usual methods of “scripture readings” or “ethical abstractions” would not quell the boisterous Sabbath school mob, he mobilized the object lesson.

> In less time than it takes place to tell it, I said to myself, “Get your point of contact; address them through their senses; get on to the plane of their common activity.” I immediately drew an ivory foot-rule out of my pocket and asked what it was. Silence and attention were immediate. Some called it a “ruler,” some a “measure,” and one finally said it was a “rule.” My next inquiry was to ascertain what it was made of. Some said ivory, some said bone. The class was in full control. It was easy then to lead them on to an imaginary rule, though keeping them in a certain suspense of meaning, until we had reached the Golden rule. Questioning then drew from them the relative value of ivory and gold, and of rules made from them – real or figurative. It is unnecessary to follow this process in more detail, but the class was conquered, for that day at least, and their disgraceful hubbub was turned into an exemplary discussion of eternal truth. Golden texts, theological doctrines, ethical abstractions from the Catechism or the Epistles, taken in themselves, would have been hurled at these bright minds in vain; but the contact with a single tangible object such as a boy would use, or, at all events, enjoys handling, was the successful point of departure for his spiritual instruction. (Du Bois 1896: 48)

It is important to note that the point of contact, as elaborated by Du Bois, was not merely a method that thematized the “raw” empirical data experienced by the child. The point of contact and its associated object lessons were designed to *train* the sensory faculties through exercises in observation and manual work. Thus, in his introduction to another influential treatise on religious pedagogy, Milton Littlefield’s *Handwork in the Sunday School* (1908), Du Bois emphasizes that the education of the child’s developing sensory faculties and motor energies is best achieved through a manual pedagogical method known as hand work.

Describing the manual techniques of coloring with crayons, sewing with thread, caressing the contour lines a relief map of biblical geography, or playing finger games, he states: “Give a boy a mode of Bible study which so *vivifies* the sacred page as to beget a love of it – as only manual methods can – and, in an otherwise Christian atmosphere, you have gone far toward making a Bible lover of him” (Littlefield 1908: xxi). Prefiguring the insights of Marcel Mauss' famous lecture on body techniques (Mauss 2006), he quotes a missionary from the coast of Labrador saying, “There is only one way to reach the soul, and that is through the body” (Littlefield 1908: xi). As an educational method, the point of contact should not be limited to a pedagogical exercise that merely highlighted certain empirical phenomena that had “given” themselves to immediate sense perception, but should rather be seen as a pious technique of the body that attuned the sense faculties and “vivified” the moral and spiritual character through a process of manual training.

By the late teens of the 20th century, the point of contact concept had become so ubiquitous within American Christian religious education that it was often mentioned as a key selling point in advertising catalogues issued by massive Sunday school printing factories such as the David C. Cook Publishing Company. Although I cannot go into more detail here, it might be a fruitful avenue of future research to consider how the pedagogical strategies of the point of contact and concomitant object lesson became closely articulated with the emergence of massive Evangelical Christian Sunday school factories and their promotion of pious paraphernalia such as the bible lesson picture card. With these earlier pedagogical resonances in mind, let us return to the point of contact within the context of mass mediated rituals of faith healing with an actual transcription of prayer from the *Healing Waters Broadcast*.[3]

2 *Healing Waters Broadcast*, March 15, 1953

> [23:33][4] And now comes that wonderful moment of prayer in the Healing Waters Broadcast when something like two million people this time each week gather around their radio

---

3 I would like to thank Steve Weiss and the archival technicians of the Southern Folklife Collection on the campus of the University of North Carolina at Chapel Hill for their generous assistance in helping me to digitize several rare radio transcription discs of the *Healing Waters Broadcast*. These rare radio discs are now housed within the Southern Folklife Collection and are accessible to researchers.

4 Translation Note: In an attempt to convey some of the sonic and poetic intensities that were sounded through Roberts' prayer, I have utilized italics. The italics are meant to convey to the

cabinets for my healing prayer. You come too unsaved man, unsaved woman. You sick people come. Some kneel, some raise their hands, *some touch their radio cabinets as a point of contact*. But I'm going to pray for God to save ya, for God to heal ya. Believe now. Just after they sing "Only Believe" I'm going to pray.

[24:07] song "Only Believe"
Only believe, only believe,
All things are possible, only believe.
Only believe, only believe,
All things are possible, only believe.

[24:32] Now Heavenly father, thousands and thousands of people are gathered around their radio cabinets for this healing prayer, for thy salvation, for thy healing, for thy deliverance. Grant me the miracle of their salvation. Grant me the miracle of their souls being transformed from sin, saved by thy power. And now, father, grant me the miracle of healing for the mortal bodies of every man, woman and child who is looking to thee right now with faith in God. Here, father, is a man who's been sick for years, a woman who's been bedfast, a little child who is crippled and afflicted. Hear my prayer, and grant their healing in the name of Jesus. Thou foul tormenting sickness, thou foul affliction and disease, I come against you in the name of the savior. In the name of Jesus of Nazareth, not by my name, but by the name and power of the son of God. And I take authority over you in the name of Jesus; and I charge you loose them. *Loose them*! *Come out*! *Come out* in the name of Jesus of Nazareth! And now neighbor, be thou made whole. Be thou made *whole*! In the name of Jesus, be thou *loosed* from thy *afflications*! Rise and praise God and be made whole. Amen, and amen. Believe now with all your heart.

[26:02] song "Only Believe"
Only believe, only believe,
All things are possible, only believe.
Only believe, only believe,
All things are possible, only believe.

Since the beginning of the *Healing Waters Broadcast* in 1947, hundreds of thousands of letters were sent to the Oral Roberts headquarters in Tulsa, Oklahoma by listeners claiming to have been miraculously healed during the prayer time of the program. Many of these testimonies were reproduced in Roberts' popular *Healing Waters Magazine*, and were intended to help cultivate a sense of belief in the reading audience. Indeed, these mass circulated testimonies helped to reinforce and replicate this technical gesture of prayer. In this way, the point of contact is sustained

reader a moment when the sound of the enunciation is characterized by an importunate urgency of the voice, as well as signal the percussive, visceral enunciation of a word during crucial moments of the healing prayer. It may be useful to actually read these transcribed prayers out loud, articulating the italicized words in a slower, more gentle tone, while the words in bold can be voiced in a more robust, louder staccato.

through a multi-mediated network that includes print (magazines, tracts, letters), radio, film and television (Figure 2). Perhaps ironically, the point of contact is predicated on a gesture of immediate face-to-face contact, yet its healing "effects" are consistently mobilized through the process of technological mediation. The following testimonies have been selected from the healing magazine and are representative of the general spirit of the curative narration and its relation to the radio as point of contact.

Figure 2: Cartoon illustration from *Oral Roberts' true stories* comic book for children.
Note: Roberts (1958: 21).

> "PLACES HAND ON RADIO AND HEARS AGAIN"
>
> Dear Brother Roberts,
>
> During your healing campaign in Jacksonville I was listening to your radio program. As you prayed for the sick I laid my hand and head upon the radio, and was healed of deafness in my left ear, which I had not heard out of in thirty years. I do praise God for what he has done for me. You may use this testimony in any way that others might believe God still hears.
>
> L. D. Lowery,
> 3019 Dillon St.
> Jacksonville, Fla (Roberts 1949: 9)

"NAZARENE MINISTER HEALED THROUGH BROADCAST"

Dear Brother Roberts:

For years I have been bothered with bad tonsils. I had been holding a revival near Mineral Wells, Texas and had developed a serious case of tonsillitis. I had been taking Sulfa drug but to no avail. My fever was high, pulse irregular and my throat was swelled so inside until I could hardly swallow. I was driving home that night after services and was suffering considerably. Brother Roberts' program was coming over my car radio and when he asked those in radio-land to lay their hand on the radio if they wanted healing, I did so. As he prayed, I prayed, and suddenly it seemed that something turned loose in my throat, and I swallowed and found the swelling was all gone. My temperature was normal and my pulse was regular. That has been nearly four years ago, and I have never had a sore throat since that time. Praise God for his healing power!

Rev. J. Royce Thomason
Nazarene Minister
Eldorado, Oklahoma (Roberts 1952b: 9)

3 There is no distance in prayer

Intimately related to the theological-technical term "point of contact," the healing campaigns of Oral Roberts also helped to solidify the phrase "there is no distance in prayer" within the vernacular language of global charismatic Christianity. Pentecostals often invoke the saying "there is no distance in prayer" to describe the collapsing of physical distance through the performance of prayer. Roberts popularized this phrase on a mass scale during the 1950s to explain the way that patients could be cured through his performances of healing prayer despite the fact that his actual physical presence remained unavailable to the dispersed magazine, radio, and television audience. On the one hand, this key descriptive phrase is based on the idea that "God is everywhere; therefore, there is no distance in prayer." This overt theological claim, however, elides the specific circumstances of technological mediation from which this descriptive phrase emerged. Roberts' description of this concept within his widely circulated healing magazine is revealing and worth quoting at length:

> A woman seriously ill in Norway heard my voice over Radio Luxembourg, the most powerful station in Europe. She couldn't understand a word of English. Two words stuck in her mind: my name, Oral Roberts. However, she later testified, that there was a power in my voice. Suddenly she sensed I was praying. She felt impelled to rush over to her radio and place her hands upon it. As my voice continued to utter prayer, she felt the surging of God's power enter her body, and in the flash of a second – she was healed![...] I prayed in Tulsa, Oklahoma. This prayer was put on Radio Luxembourg in Europe. A woman in Norway, who couldn't understand a word I was saying, felt God's power in my voice and was instantly

> and completely healed. There is no distance in prayer. God was with me in Tulsa when I prayed, was in Luxembourg in Europe when the program was released, was in Norway with the woman who couldn't understand English. God is everywhere; therefore, there is no distance in prayer. (Roberts 1955: 2)

As described by many practitioners of Pentecostal prayer, the negation of physical space between two distanced religious subjects and the concomitant unleashing of healing power are actuated by faith. During these performances of prayer, it is faith that bridges the distance between both the sacred and the everyday, and the patient and healer. This faith, in turn, requires a physical point of contact to enliven the efficacy of the prayer – what Roberts called "turning your faith loose." (See Figure 3.) This key component of the curative technique reinscribes the material supplement in the selfsame moment that it claims there exists *no* distance in prayer. In other words, a forceful aspect of the therapeutic rite is organized around an overt denial of the very material medium that allows for an experience of sacred presence to be sensed by the patient. To be sure, there is no distance in prayer; yet faith itself makes its appearance, or becomes sensible, through a structure of mediation that is contingent upon a material point of contact.

Figure 3: Woman feeling the resonance of prayer upon the loudspeaker.
Note: Roberts (1952a: 25).

The ubiquitous phrase "there is no distance in prayer" is thus an implicit commentary on prayer and the production of presence in an age of tele-technology.[5] More specifically, Roberts employed this phrase to describe the millions of written testimonies that claimed to have experienced the "presence" of Roberts himself in their private domestic spaces through the mediation of radio, television, and magazine. As in the account of the Norwegian woman healed through radio prayer, this experience of ritual presence often reverberates before or beneath the circuitry of representation. Here the radio is not merely a passive medium for the transmission of a discrete religious message, but an apparatus of belief that enlivens the voice with a presence in excess of any stable semantic content.[6] Even more than this, the machinations of the radio "loudspeaker" allow the religious subject to experience the vibrations of prayer entering through the hand and resounding throughout the body. In an age of mass mediated healing, the performative language of the Evangelical faith-cure becomes inextricably bound up with the specific capacities enabled through media technologies such as the radio. As a crucial medium in the technological history of prayer, the radio apparatus was interfaced with the healing performance, enabling Protestant ritual language to resonate on a new experiential register. Like so many other technological developments, the hand of the biblical reader was freed from the typographic structure of the printed prayer. In other words, the fingers of the hand no longer needed to "follow along" the printed line of the prayer book during the act of reading, but could actually feel the words through a new structure of mediation. This is certainly an oversimplification of a much larger history of print and the authorized practices of hearing the liturgy, yet this playful caricature challenges us to think about the specific ways in which the curative power of the Christian word is intimately intertwined with the physical media that allow it to circulate.

4 Conclusion: Ritual language and the apparatus of belief

Like Christ in the book of Mark putting his finger into the deaf man's ear and exclaiming "*Be opened!*," radio as a point of contact marks a new aesthetic

5 For more on the production of presence and its relation to what has been called the "materiality of communication," see Gumbrecht (2004).

6 For more on this notion of the materiality of language and the pressing question of how specific media enliven semantic content (or even "non-semantic" 'content') in particular ways, see the introduction to this volume.

formation in the history of Protestant ritual language. The vibrating electromagnetic diaphragm of the radio loudspeaker allowed for a new experience of the "prayer of faith," one that collapsed the gesture of manual imposition and the enunciation of prayer into a single sensation of tactility. With eyes closed and hand upon the apparatus, the patient could sense the prayer not only as a meaningful articulation of words, but as a non-semantic resonance, that, like glossolalia, signaled that the body had been quickened by an ecstatic presence from elsewhere. The radio apparatus itself opened up or extended the senses, allowing the hand to become an organ of audition. This special effect produced through the transductions of the radio loudspeaker organized a new sensational form (Meyer 2009) that interfaced classic prayer techniques from the Evangelical Christian tradition of the "faith cure" (Curtis 2007) and pedagogical methods in the Sunday school with the materiality of the radio apparatus.

In this analysis, the term transduction refers to the technical process whereby sound is converted into something else and that something else is translated back into sound (Sterne 2003).[7] Within the context of charismatic healing prayer and its concomitant rituals of manual imposition (the laying on of hands), the transduction of sound through the mouth of the radio loudspeaker organized new performative and somatic possibilities. The transductions of the radio apparatus amplified the poetic inflections of Roberts' prayer – those crucial moments within the ritual form when the healer voices words with a visceral, almost violent intensity – arming works to strike the illness causing demons within the patient with a percussive force. And this not merely on a metaphorical register, but through a reverberation of religious language that was "heard" through the palm of the listener like a hand placed upon the surface of a drum or the warm fleshly contours of the throat. Sounding what might be called a healing poetics of percussion, the ritual of faith-cure was transduced through the radio apparatus (Needham 1967). Through this technical translation, the boisterously voiced words "*Come out!*" "*loose!*" and "*whole!*" struck the distanced patient with visceral, palpable force. Like so many instances within the history of charismatic Christianity, the belief organized through this interfacing of prayer with a technical apparatus reverberates within the body with a sonic presence in excess of the mere semantic content of the word: speaking in tongues, rhythmic liturgical schema that open upon an ecstatic soundscape of unintelligible cacophony, tambourines, the guttural grunts of the preacher that signal the poetic anointing of

7 I would like to thank the ethnomusicologist David Novak for his helpful insights regarding the concept of transduction (personal communication). For more insightful research on sound, transduction and Protestant performance, see Handman (2015).

the Holy Ghost, clapping, etc. (Blanton 2015). In other words, through the transductions of an apparatus such as radio, there are instances of religious language when the praying voice of the loudspeaker usurps the function of the manually imposed hand – literally touching, pressing and palpating the patient with a warm presence.

Older forms of materialized prayer within the Pentecostal tradition such as the prayer cloth relied on exchanges of hand, postal economies and physical movement to produce an experience of belief through a temporal articulation characterized by delay and deferral (de Certeau 1985). The special effect of the radio, however, shifted away from this logic of circulation, organizing a new tactile attunement through the mechanical reproduction of the organs of hearing and vocalization. Belief became structured through a new form of immediacy that maintained a parasitical dependence upon the technical capacities of the radio as a specific medium of communication. Here the term “communication” should also resound with connotations of flow and touch that are foregrounded in performances of religious language such as the prayer gesture of radio tactility. Oral Roberts constantly evoked this apparatus of belief thorough his popular charismatic phrase, “get a point of contact and turn your faith loose!”

The point of contact reveals the specific ways in which new media have facilitated what Yelle (2013: 113) describes as “transformations in poetic performance.” More specifically, this apparatus of belief is an important recent development within a longer technological history of Protestant prayer. Just as the technology of moveable type facilitated changes in the structure and performance of the liturgy, the material affordances of the radio offered new possibilities and experiential spaces for the performance of healing prayer. In terms of media specificity within this genealogy of Protestant ritual language, we could also recall that Roberts skillfully translated the point of contact gesture for the televised tent revival. During these pioneering experiments with televisual healing, Roberts encouraged the dispersed members of the viewing audience to put their hand upon his hand during the performance of prayer. In this moment, Roberts pressed his healing hand upon a translucent pane of glass that remained unseen to the audience viewing the events of the revival from the privacy of their home. As the mechanical eye of the film camera zoomed in upon Roberts’ face and elevated palm, it looked as if the healer had actually pressed the flesh of his hand upon the glass tube of the television.[8] In addition to this special cinematic

8 During the same period that Roberts was experimenting with televised revivals, television advertisements for deodorant and other substances were also utilizing the translucent capacities of hidden studio glass to reveal specific textures and qualities of their products to the viewing audience. In both circumstances, the technical capacities of the medium were harnessed in order

effect, Roberts supplements his usual poetic enunciations of the prayer with greatly exaggerated facial expressions to "effect" the ritual performance through the televisual medium. The paradox of the point of contact as developed by Roberts is that it organizes a powerful experience of sacred immediacy through a specific structure of technological mediation. Indeed, part of the remarkable proliferation of charismatic healing around the world can be attributed to the creative ways in which earlier forms of ritual language have been performatively modulated to fit the material and sensory environments organized through new media technologies.

References

Asamoah-Gayadu, J. Kwabena. 2005. Anointing through the screen: Neo-Pentecostalism and televised Christianity in Ghana. *Studies in World Christianity* 11(1). 9–28.

Bessire, Lucas. 2012. "We go above": Media metaphysics and making moral life on Ayoreo two-way radio. In Lucas Bessire & Daniel Fisher (eds.), *Radio fields: Anthropology and wireless sound in the 21st century*, 197–214. New York: New York University Press.

Blanton, Anderson. 2015. *Hittin' the prayer bones: Materiality of spirit in the Pentecostal South*. Chapel Hill: University of North Carolina Press.

Brown, Candy Gunther (ed.). 2011. *Global Pentecostal and Charismatic healing*. London: Oxford University Press.

Certeau, Michel de. 1985. *What we do when we believe*. In Marshall Blonsky (ed.), *On Signs*, 192–202. Baltimore: Johns Hopkins University Press.

Curtis, Heather D. 2007. *Faith in the great physician: Suffering and divine healing in American culture, 1860–1900*. Baltimore: Johns Hopkins University Press.

Du Bois, Patterson. 1896. *The point of contact in teaching*. Philadelphia: J. D. Wattles & Co.

Gumbrecht, Hans. 2004. *Production of presence: What meaning cannot convey*. Stanford, CA: Stanford University Press.

Handman, Courtney. 2015. *Critical Christianity: Translation and denominational conflict in Papua New Guinea*. Berkeley, CA: University of California Press.

Hangen, Tona J. 2002. *Redeeming the dial: Radio, religion, and popular culture in America*. Chapel Hill: University of North Carolina Press.

Klassen, Pamela E. 2007. Radio mind: Protestant experimentalists on the frontiers of healing. *Journal of the American Academy of Religion* 75(3). 651–683.

Larkin, Brian. 2008. *Signal and noise: Media, infrastructure, and urban culture in Nigeria*. Durham, NC: Duke University Press.

Littlefield, Milton. 1908. *Handwork in the Sunday School*. Philadelphia: The Sunday School Times Company.

---

to *present* the miraculous qualities of the object in question. An example of Roberts' cinematic healing hand can be seen in my *Materiality of Prayer* collection, sponsored by the Social Science Research Council: http://forums.ssrc.org/ndsp/2013/04/10/tv-prayer/.

Mauss, Marcel. 2006. *Techniques, technology and civilization*. Edited by Nathan Schlanger. New York: Durkheim Press.
Meyer, Birgit. 2009. *Aesthetic formations: Media, religion, and the senses*. New York: Palgrave Macmillan.
Needham, Rodney. 1967. Percussion and transition. *Man (New Series)* 2(4). 606–614.
Reinhardt, Bruno. 2014. Soaking in tapes: The haptic voice of global Pentecostal pedagogy in Ghana. *Journal of the Royal Anthropological Institute*. 20(2). 315–336.
Roberts, Oral. 1947. *If you need healing, do these things*. Tulsa: Oral Roberts Evangelistic Association.
Roberts, Oral. 1949. *Healing Waters* 7(3). Tulsa: Oral Roberts Evangelistic Association.
Roberts, Oral. 1952a. *Healing waters* 6(7). Tulsa: Oral Roberts Evangelistic Association.
Roberts, Oral. 1952b. *If you need healing, do these things*. Tulsa: Oral Roberts Evangelistic Association.
Roberts, Oral. 1955. *Healing Waters* 10(3). Tulsa: Oral Roberts Evangelistic Association.
Roberts, Oral. 1958. *Oral Roberts' true stories* 110. Oral Roberts Evangelistic Association.
Schulz, Dorothea. 2012. Reconsidering Muslim authority: Female "preachers" and the ambiguity of radio-mediated sermonizing in Mali. In Lucas Bessire & Daniel Fisher (eds.), *Radio fields: Anthropology and wireless sound in the 21st century*, 108–123. New York: New York University Press.
Sterne, Jonathan. 2003. *The audible past: Cultural origins of sound reproduction*. Durham & London: Duke University Press.
Witte, Marleen de. 2012. The electric touch machine miracle scam: Body, technology, and the (dis)authentication of the Pentecostal supernatural. In Jeremy Stolow (ed.), *Deus in machina: Religion, technology and the things in between*, 61–82. New York: Fordham University Press.
Yelle, Robert A. 2013. *Semiotics of religion: Signs of the sacred in history*. London: Bloomsbury.

Jon Bialecki

"The Lord says you speak as harlots": Affect, *affectus*, and *affectio*

> Only chaos would result were anthropologists to classify social phenomena by the emotions which are supposed to accompany them, for such emotional states, if present at all, must vary not only from individual to individual, but also in the same individual on different occasions and even at different points in the same rite.
>
> Evans-Pritchard (1965: 44)

1 Introduction: Bad feelings about affect

I start out with the Evans-Pritchard quote not out of any fealty to the point made, but to observe that the claim is predicated on a set of presumptions: first, that producing variation in emotional states is something that is secondary or orthogonal to ritual, rather than central. The second presumption is that variance in emotional states with various ritual participants challenges the idea that ritual is supposed to work in uniform ways; variation would place into question, rather than confirm, the effectiveness of ritual.

There of course is a third presumption that is hidden in these two: that due to a presumption of interiority, variation in emotional states is something that cannot be determined from mere observation. Emotion is subjective, and subjectivity may not be beyond anthropological thought, but at least it escapes from the direct anthropological gaze.

Evans-Prichard's target here is, of course, the Durkheimian notion of collective effervescence; it was this vision of an energetics inhering in ritual that Evans-Pritchard was attempting to eclipse. It appears that Evans-Pritchard failed. Ritual is now often seen as doing the work of subjectification, triggering particular emotional states. This occurs either as a short-term phenomenon, or as a long standing constellation; the latter enduring forms can appear either as Geertzian "moods and motivations," as Harvey Whitehouse's emotionally inflected modes of ritually created cognition and memory, or as Foucauldian accounts of formations and dispositions effected through disciplinary or ethical processes (Geertz 1973: 87–125; Foucault 1992; Faubion 2001 and 2011; Laidlaw 2002 and 2014; Whitehouse 1995 and 2004).

Jon Bialecki, University of Edinburgh

https://doi.org/10.1515/9781614514329-018

It might even be safe to say that we as a field have come to a conclusion directly opposite to that of Evans-Pritchard; or at least contrary to his first two presumptions. In contemporary anthropology, many now see emotional states as central to an understanding of sociability. Or to be more exact, many see something *close* to or *preceding* emotional states as central; much of anthropology has adopted, almost without comment, affect theory, an account of subjectivity and sociability that has as its object the minute and visceral perturbations that are said to subtend emotion and exist outside of the linguistic materials from which earlier anthropological observations were made. Affect, in fact, is often explicitly framed as an analytic that is not just indifferent to language, but as a self-conscious rejection of the "linguistic turn" (see also Schaefer 2015).

In this essay, I will be making an argument that may not be all that surprising: that considerations of affect can have something to contribute to the anthropology of Pentecostalism and post-Pentecostal (or "charismatic") improvised ritual. This is a sort of low-hanging fruit "Me, as well" argument, and it may seem to be not much of a stretch, given the sort of peak frenetic displays associated with many forms of Pentecostalism.

However, this essay also has a second argument, with slightly higher stakes: that while the study of affect has a great deal of promise, methodologically many discussions of affect theory are problematic, and some are only nominally about affect at all. As it is treated in the discipline now, affect is often regarded as a form either of magic or of divination. This is not magic in the Malinowskian (1922: 6) sense of "the ethnographer's magic," though writerliness has a certain role in the thaumaturgy under discussion. Rather, affect is magic in that it is often a black box which mysteriously does its work without any investigation; or it is divination in the sense that those who use it proclaim a knowledge that they themselves say they should not know and cannot speak, given their definitions of the term.

By way of contrast, I'm going to argue that a discussion of affect makes better sense if we reimagine how it is that we think of, represent, and analyze affect; in short, I am going to argue that what is needed is a return to the geometrical methods that Spinoza first brought to this problem, though I will take this geometricization to the level of analysis and not just theorem proofs. In short, I claim that we make the study of affect the object not of an anthropological poetics, but of an ethnographic technics, one not dissimilar to the analytic mechanisms that stand at the center of so much linguistic anthropology. Such a move would also have the benefit of working towards a rapprochement of linguistic anthropology and affect theory.

Because we are thinking of affect theory not just in contradistinction to linguistic anthropology, but through the ethnographic lens of Pentecostal religiosities, we also need to consider the relation between affect theory and the anthropology of Christianity; though this will not take us as far from issues of linguistic anthropology as one might expect. One might think that when it comes to affect theory and the anthropology of Christianity, linguistic anthropology is more of a rival than a mentor. There are two reasons for this. The first stems from the fact that both linguistically- and semiotically-oriented anthropology has not only thrived when discussing Christianity, but has done particularly well with that "religion of talk," Protestantism. In fact, not only has linguistic anthropology proven its adequacy when it comes to Christian speech practices, but it has proven it three times over: at the level of semiotic ideology or metapragmatics, at the level of code, and at the level of the ethnomethodological, Christianities have been shown to be susceptible to linguistic-centered analyses.[1]

This brings us to our second reason to think that there may be an incommensurability between linguistic anthropology and affect theory. All this language work is a potential challenge to an affect-centered analysis because as commonly understood, affect as a category is a pre-linguistic phenomenon. Brian Massumi (2002), who has been one of the greatest influences on anthropological affect

1 "Language ideology" was originally a categorical and analytic term used to identify explicit discourses regarding efficient and ethical speech. Made to understand how various ethnic and national languages and genres of speech were set in hierarchical relation, it was also quickly adopted by anthropologists interested in Christianity, who were looking to account for the way that these religious actors prized certain forms of speech, and rejected others. There was particular interest in articulating a common Protestant concern for "sincere" speech, which often came hand in hand with a speech ethics that downplayed the material and collective nature of speech's inevitable mediation (Robbins 2001; Keane 2007; Bialecki and Hoenes del Pinal 2011; see Handman 2015 for an extension to issues of translation, institutional life, and social critique).

This interest in prescriptive statements about how proper religious language functions does not exhaust language in a Christian context. Language as code, a specific set of internalized lexical items and referents, has been put forward by Susan Harding (2000) as the engine of American Fundamentalist Baptist speech. This set of lexical features in the code facilitates some particular semiotic operations, such as typological reasoning; however, it is to large degree this form of speech's presence just as a language different from the language of a larger non-Christian world that does important boundary marking work for Harding. In a real way, for Harding conversion is allowing oneself to be fully coded over.

Conversation analysis and ethno-methodological approaches have also been useful in opening up Christian discourse. For instance, James Bielo's (2009) discussion of the debates that take place in Bible Study groups has been well received; Robin Shoaps's (2002) paper on sermons in the Assemblies of God has focused on how speakers use entextualization to present indirect speech (and at times, even consciously fictitious speech) as direct speech, all in the furtherance of a Protestant language ideology. Peter Stromberg (1993) has used the line by line parsing common to much conversation analysis to study the performative aspects of conversion narratives. Finally, Eric Hoenes del Pinal (2011) has used the same tool kit to identify important aspects of gesture as a communicative element in Mayan Charismatic prayer meetings.

theory, has presented affect as a mixture of embodied sensation and proprioception, a processual unfolding that precedes, both in temporality and emphasis, signification and coding; in fact, affect theory is explicitly presented by Massumi as being a corrective to the linguistic turn.

The relation between affect and language in Massumi's thought is made most clear in his essay on a scientific experiment conducted on children watching a German television video short. In this short, a snowman melting under an afternoon sun is relocated by his maker to the cooler climes of the mountains. His creator then says goodbye to the snowman and departs. Three versions of this were shown to the wee research subjects – a wordless one, as well as two overdubbed ones, a "factual" one with a dry voiceover account of exactly what was occurring on screen, and an "emotional" one, which true to its name struck the appropriate sentimental and touching notes as the narrative unfolded. Both core body states (heart-rate and breathing) and exterior (galvanic skin response) were measured during the viewing. The differences in the responses were notable. The "factual" one had the highest degree of arousal of interior bodily systems, but lowest galvanic skin response: children rated it as less pleasant, and it was subsequently shown to be not memorable. By contrast, the nonverbal version had the greatest galvanic response, though it also had a lower response from the core bodily indicators. The nonverbal version was also dubbed the most pleasant, even though all of the particular constituting scenes were individually described as "sad." The emotional one lay somewhere between the factual and the silent, in both galvanic and core body response, and in rated pleasure. (Interestingly, it was the version that was more easily recounted later on.)

Massumi notes that galvanic skin response is a measure of an automatic physiological reaction, while heart rate and breathing are associated with conscious states that are more open to self-monitoring. Massumi therefore considers the interior response as a measure of "emotion," the moment in which the autonomic response rises to the level of the conscious mind. The emotional here is something that is affected by the mode of signification that accompanies it, as seen by the different responses to the "emotional" and the "factual" versions, language can exacerbate or smother this kind of conscious response. By contrast, Massumi takes the surface skin response, which is understood as another index of arousal, as a measure of something else, something not conscious and not over-coded with signification. Because this mode of arousal escapes easy distinctions into pleasant and unpleasant (recall that for the children, it is both at once) he describes it as best thought of in terms of degrees and forms of intensity. This intensity, which escapes the verbal, is what Massumi calls affect.

This intensity called affect then is marked by what could be framed as alternately a pre-discursive or a-signifying nature, and also by what could be called a non- or a-subjective focus. For the same reasons, affect is often understood as being about a certain kind of immediacy and a lack of mediation. It's also seen as a kind of incipient possibility of divergence, a pluriform wealth of initial movements in different directions, which are often cognitively and linguistically vitiated and hence contained before they can be realized.

Massumi's invocation of affect has roots in early theories, of course; it also has been the object of much critique. We will turn to both of those issues in moment. Before we do so, I want to point out two things. The first thing I want to note is that this formulation, along with other quite similar theories from social critics like William Connolly and John Protevi, have been well received in anthropology. From Kathleen Stewart's genre-breaking monograph, *Ordinary Affects* (2007), to Yael Navaro-Yashin's (2012) discussion of the Turkish-Cypriot relationship with material items commandeered from the Greek-Cypriots, affect has become an established analytic category. There are two reasons for this. One is that attention to affect offers the possibility of a concordance between the human sciences that are laboratory based and those human sciences that are not, allowing for (in the words of Danilyn Rutherford 2013) a "science peace, not science war." The second reason affect has been embraced is that many anthropologists feel that, while affect is in no way particular to late modernity or neoliberalism, it has a special relation with contemporary forms of social organization (Mazarrella 2009; Muehlebach 2012; Richards and Rudnyckyj 2009; Rudnyckyj 2011). Affect, as a mode of distributed and almost atmospheric sea-changes that transform the subject from embodied and psychic states within and below rather than from a governing above, is often seen by these thinkers as perfect for political forms like neoliberalism that are centered on shaping subjects rather than building institutions.

Despite having all this to recommend it, strangely enough affect has not been taken up as a category very much in the anthropology of Pentecostal and Charismatic Christianity. There are, at least to my knowledge, only two concerted pieces that evoke Pentecostal affect as part of an explanatory mechanism. (Both Johnson 2018 and Willis 2018 came to my attention too late to address them in this essay, and modesty prevents me from discussing Bialecki 2017.) The first one, a book chapter by Gretchen Pfiel (2011), asks about the role of affect in a Portland, Oregon Charismatic Church. Here, however, it is clear that she is using affect in a manner that, at least in terms of Massumi's definition, is idiosyncratic. For Pfiel, affect is not on an axis apart from language, but is rather another signifying element, a way to index the Protestant ethos of spontaneity and sincerity (Keane 2007) that we saw in our discussion of Christian language ideology. Affect is sincerity's guarantor, since affect not only signals that the subject truly "feels" the affect-laden proposition, but is ideologically understood as operating a level that precedes the kind of self-consciousness that is necessary for any deliberate manipulation or mannerism. Here, particular affects are reduced to just another sign, and all of the substantive specificity of affect is subsumed. At best, this is affect as a complement to language, a form of multimodal communication (Clark 1996; Hoenes del Pinal 2011; Kendon 1990; Norris 2004).

That other invocation is at once more faithful to Massumi's vision, and bolder in articulating what the stakes are. Kevin Lewis O'Neill's work on Pentecostal Christianity in Guatemala is to my mind the sharpest and most ethnographically nuanced Foucauldian-inflected work in the anthropology of Christianity; O'Neill has focused on the relationship between the inner policing that Pentecostalism is often associated with, and the withdrawal of governmental powers associated with neoliberalism (see, e.g., O'Neill 2010). As part of this project, O'Neill has recently turned to the question of affect (2013). Attempting to break the "isomorphic relationship between space, place and religion" O'Neill suggests the use of "affective spaces" as "a flexible analytical tool" (2013: 1095, 1097). For O'Neill, affective spaces are moments when "affect serves as the medium through which spatial divisions and interconnections become legible" (2013: 1095). Piecing together a tripartite typology of nervous spaces, crowd spaces, and social imaginary spaces, O'Neill offers vignettes from his times in the field; these are offered, he says by way of a Kathleen Stewart quote, as "points of impact, curiosity, and encounter" (Stewart 2007: 5, in O'Neill 2013: 1105). We are given instances of a throng of worshippers reacting to a sermon in a movie-theatre that had been converted into a Pentecostal church, of a chaplain performing an exorcism in a notorious Guatemalan prison. Imagistic distillations of the field experience, these passages make for arresting reading.

Now, I want to be clear here, because there is a danger that what I say next will be misunderstood. O'Neill's argument for "affective spaces" makes sense to me. In fact, this paper is an attempt to continue his project. More importantly, I believe that he has properly identified the centrality, and possibly the primacy, of the affective in his vignettes. But this gets us to the nub of the problem. All I can do is believe him.

Consider this: Affect is presented as essentially a pre- or non-discursive phenomenon. And yet the mode through which O'Neill communicates these moments of affect is entirely narrative. His work is built out of passages along these lines: "His knees too weak to support his body, he asked for the Holy Spirit. I need the Holy Spirit, he whispered. The pastor echoed, He NEEDS the Holy Spirit, brothers! Do you?" (O'Neill 2013: 1108). But these passages are in essence a linguistic presentation of a non-linguistic phenomenon.

There are of course other examples where non-linguistic phenomena are transmitted through language; one can think of the rigors of formal phenomenological accounts that capture the immediately sensible, and convey it through linguistic mediation. But phenomenology is at least rich with method;

by contrast it appears that we are in danger that a relatively method-free affect theory might be in effect just the poor man's phenomenology. There is another problem with using this narrative mode to parse and communicate affect. Affect is supposed to be about the intersubjective and objectively observable, but a crypto-phenomenological account does not give us intersubjectivity, but rather experience from a single vantage point. We were promised a network, but are given a solitary node.

The difficulty lies in the fact that it is not clear that affect, as framed here, is susceptible to linguistic capture in the same way; its insurgent, incipient, and a-subjective nature make it hard to express. In fact, Massumi himself states that affect is something identifiable only through its "trace." O'Neill, following Kathleen Stewart's own pioneering of this technique in *Ordinary Affects* (2007), has chosen to express this trace through a poetics. This turn to poetics raises evidential difficulties. While I am certain that affect can be monumentalized through writing (Deleuze and Guattari 1994), how am I supposed to evaluate the transmission and translation of affect in an ethnographic scene? Also, if this takes the form of a poetics, how am I to know that I am dealing with an account of affect, and not an experiment in ethnographic writing that mistakes itself for such an account? It is probably no accident that much of this literature reads like experimental modernist writing, and affect theory has a genealogy that goes through aesthetic modernism. But we would not want to say that an entire genre of narrative fiction is reports of affect; and perhaps all discussions of affect do not have to be 20th-century high modernism either.

I am being unfair here to an extent. O'Neill does limit his account to specific instances, and he is clear about the actors and milieu that comprise each scenario. This could be compared to Stewart, who at times talks about lingering, non-*évènementiel* affects that seem to be long running states of affairs, rather than fleeting moments. This is also the case when we have discussions, following Michael Hardt (1999), of "affective labor," when the production and sustaining of certain affective tonalities is both the means and goal of some neoliberal regimes of production. While I again do not want to say that these ethnographers have misreported the state on the ground, or have failed to make important contributions to the discipline, it appears that the specificity of affect as a frame has disappeared, and we are now dealing with simply a synonym for emotion, one to be used only in a theoretical domain to index that one is working in the register of "theory."

This is also the case in discussions of affect and material culture, which are often blended together. An interest in materiality, and in Actor-Network-Theory in general, is no doubt at least partially rooted in the same disquiet about "discourse" that gave birth to anthropological affect theory. While it would be wrong to say that all material discussions of affect are exemplars of this disquiet, they are at least in dialogue with it. Here, we are told that these items (which are usually archaeological ruins, for reasons that could be the object of an entirely separate essay) have affective charge. It is worth noting that the exact manner in which these items transmit or produce affect is not explained – they just emit affect like plutonium emits radiation.[2] Again, this is not to say that I cannot imagine objects having affect-like causal effects that are not immediately and proximately dependent on discourse; we can think of Nancy Munn's discussion of qualisigns in *The Fame of Gawa* (1986) as an example of affect-like phenomena triggered by objects or experience, and which only later may be elaborated through linguistic practices such as spells. The problem is that we are not told how it is that affect is transmitted. Again, we are left with what ends up being effectively "gut-check anthropology."

There is the possibility that we are experiencing all this difficulty because there is something wrong with our initial, Massumi-derived formulation of affect. This theory of affect has been questioned on numerous fronts. Critical theorist Ruth Leys (2011) has questioned Massumi's reading of the science that he bases his account on, and further has claimed that there is a crypto-Cartesian divide between the mind and the body present here as well. Mazzarrella (2009) has also suggested that there is too much anxiety about mediation in affect theory. Further, drawing from Silverstein (2004), he has suggested that the split between discourse and affect may be particular to a Euro-American understanding of language.

Looking at both the methodological challenges, and these theoretical critiques, I would argue that there are three points here where we should make our incisions.

The first point is that this generalization of affect through methodological neglect and a lack of analytic rigor has caused part of our original definition of affect to drop out. Recall that originally affect also included both shifts in proprioception and bodily movement; but when we speak of affect without speaking of particular instances, more along the lines of talking about climate than talking about weather, these aspects of affect become hard to articulate, and eventually disappear.

The second point is that we do not see any quantification here. This is the result of a certain anthropological suspicion of quantitative data, which always brings with it questions about whose metrics, and what cultural values these metrics might be entangled with. (We should note the irony here, considering

---

2 See Fontein (2011) for a notable exception; it seems more than reasonable that human remains are material items that may contain or convey an affective charge.

that affect theory is supposed, at least by some, to mark a *rapprochement* of a sort with science.) Part of the problem has to do with intensity. Remember that, following Massumi, it is common to speak of affects as "intensities." Occasionally, these intensities are contrasted with extension – that is, classical Cartesian space, susceptible to measure. The implication is that intensities, unlike extension, are beyond quantification. In one way this is correct; but that does not mean we cannot think of differences in intensity that map on loosely to concepts of "greater" and "lesser." In a certain level of resolution, intensive forces are capable of measurement. Think for instance of temperature, a classic measure of a level of activity, and not of spatial extension. That is not to say that there is not something special about intensities – the first thing to notice about them is that division does not diminish them. If you take a meter (a measure of extension) and divide it in two, you get two half-meter units. By contrast, with temperature, if you divide something that is a hundred degrees Celsius, you do not get two fifty-degree units – you get (assuming that there is no heat leakage) two objects that are both one hundred degrees. But that does not mean that temperature cannot be measured. A relative ranking of intensities should not be too much of a problem, even if it means flattening some of the subtlety of the phenomenon (DeLanda 2002).

The third point has to do with the relationship between affect on one hand, and discourse and ideas on the other. Looking merely at Massumi's snowmen, we can see that this divide might be overstated: the galvanic conductivity of the children did not drop to nothing when watching the "emotional" video (which is probably a good thing, given that galvanic skin response presumably only zeros-out in death). We are faced not with an exclusive binary of either language or affect, nor even with a choice among language, affect, and emotion. This is something that Massumi admits, but does not emphasize; but he can be forgiven for this, for if he is attempting to set up affect as an intervention in the linguistic turn, it does little rhetorical work to start with affect and language being imbricated.

Rethinking the relation between language and affect takes some of the sting out of the previous critique. Narrative affective accounts are now not so strange, even though narration is still a form that runs opposed to the pre-subjective aspect of affect. But this then makes us ask a question: how do we distinguish affect from language, and what do we make of the claim that affect is "pre-linguistic"?

2 *Affectio* and *affectus*

I think turning to Massumi's inspirations might assist in reimagining the relationship between affect and language in a more productive way. Massumi cites his chief influences as Deleuze and Spinoza (specifically, the latter's posthumous 1677 book, *Ethics, Demonstrated in Geometrical Order*). The term "affect" is actually not that common in the Deleuzian corpus, and when it is found it is almost always in the sense that Spinoza uses the word; here, I'll be attempting a little cheat by condensing these two influences on Massumi and using a particularly Deleuzian-inflected reading of Spinoza (Deleuze 1978, 1988, 1990, 1992).

With Spinoza, affect is about one body interacting with another body, and the ensuing results. Or to be more exact, that is what the *affective* is about. Rather than use a single word, with Spinoza there are two Latin terms here – *affectio* and *affectus* – which are often translated as a single word, "affect." This choice of translation is, to quote Deleuze (1978), "a disaster"[3]: these two words are for two different concepts. *Affectio* can be parsed in (admittedly inelegant) English as "affection," the name for the force of one body upon another. Note that it is a formal category, unlike the "affect" of affect theory, which is substantively defined by a set of physiological reactions; a reason to favor a formal over a substantive category follows from Spinoza's dictum that we do not know what a body can do, and therefore to tie our definition of a physiological conception of affect is to limit ourselves in advance to what has been delineated by another discipline, a discipline which has employed a different set of methodologies to respond to a different set of questions.

Affectus, in contrast, is much narrower. It is the internal frisson that is a reaction to affection. One gloss given here by Deleuze (1978) is not particularly helpful: he frames *affectus*/affect as "every mode of thought as it is non-representational." The utility of this definition is that it allows us at least to distinguish affect from emotion as glossed in contemporary affect theory. Affect is different from emotion in that the latter is more prone to have representational aspects; emotion is usually an articulation of a relationship between two objects, rather than the immediate response bracketed off from the cause.

But determining how we can parse emotion from affect does not yet tell us what affect is. Another, less mentalist definition of *affectus*/affect is more useful: it is both the measure of and means through which human capacities are extended or reduced. Affect is the sensation that comes with an expansion of immediate modes of action, which Spinoza presents as becoming "more perfect" in one's essence. The term perfect is used here because someone with more immediate modes of action available is better situated to engage in all the possibilities inherent in one's form. We should note that this is not a unilinear expansion from a

3 This is taken from one of Deleuze's seminar lectures on Spinoza.

"less" to a "more" (or a more to a less). We can have at once the situated opening up for some capacities, and the closing of others. It is this play of expansion and contraction of possibility and powers that explains the wide variation in tonalities associated with the affective.

What does it mean to have an expansion of capacities? It means opening a space for more ideas. Ideas themselves come in one after the other in human beings; not a believer in free will, Spinoza uses the phrase "spiritual automaton" to describe humans as entities not in control of their cognition. What is the relationship between affect and idea? In one sense ideas both in their automaticity and in their representational nature clearly form a separate category from affects; but in another way ideas, when thought of as virtual capacities, are objects that can only appear in the space that is either dilated or constricted by affect, and hence have an intimate and derivative relationship with affect. Affect is not thought, but thought is one possible product of (or object for) affect.

This difference between affection as an outward encounter, and affect as a shift in powers, is also marked by their different temporalities. Affection is instant, it occurs at the moment of contact – and for Spinoza, who does not believe in Newtonian-like concepts of action at a distance, all contact is in some way bodily contact (even if mediated by other bodies, such as the air). The temporality of affect, though, is different. These dilations and contractions are always about a transition, and hence they have a duration that is a function of the speed of that transition.

But what is the relationship between this and language? Because we are dealing with more than two categories here, there is not a relationship between language and the affective, but relationships between language, affect, and affection. I will postulate that linguistic items are at once ideas, but drawing on Wittgenstein and speech act theory, I will further assume that language items are also actions, and hence affections for someone else. Since affection is what arises from one body acting on another body, though, not all affection is linguistic. Likewise, there is a non-linguistic supplement of affection in language. This means that full attention must be paid to all aspects of speech – not just the ideational load, but the volume, grain, pitch, and speed. And the impact of language-acts will in turn let loose affects, which produces more conceptions and more language.

What does this give us, analytically?

First, we now have a time frame for analysis – the gap between immediate affection and the duration of affect. We now have a "time limit" on affect – a flexible and immanent one, but a time limit nonetheless.

Second, we have a grammar, in that we split the affective atom, while still acknowledging the interrelation of the larger set of affective processes.

Third, we now can think of language, not as the antipode of the affective, but rather as at once something for which space is made by affect, and which has a double blow in affection, in that we must pay attention to the ideational but also the expressive, sonic, and sensual edges as well. We must also see what affects the full set of characteristics engenders; we can note parenthetically that this is a concept not completely unlike the indexical aspects of language as understood by one tradition in contemporary linguistic anthropology (Silverstein 1976, 2003).

Fourth, by having a definition of affect that is about shifts in capacities, we have a way out of the solipsistic box: we can look to shifts in speech and action after moments of affection, and thereby work back to the forms of affect that enabled them.

Fifth, we have a system that at once breaks with science, in that it is formal and not substantive, while not being in any way in opposition to "scientific" findings; the biological and physiological processes that have been central to much of affect theory are still articulable in this system, but we are not beholden to those other disciplinary frames or to their ontologies.

The formal aspects may seem to be too universal, but this formal system gives us a fuller capacity to think through difference than a substantive theory of affect does. The Spinozan dictum that "we not know what a body can do" (Deleuze 1990: 218) means that the question of what different capacities are found in bodies with different histories is an open one; unlike the scientific mode, there is no assumption that the western body either exhausts the form or sets a limit for other bodies with different social histories. Still, there is the possibility that this formal system is too dependent on a parochial opposition of subject and object that is too Cartesian, too western (see Course 2010), and if so, this should be reconfigured when it does not fit: I want to use Spinoza, and not have Spinoza use me. But attention to this geometrical framing means that we now have, in principle, a method of presenting field data that is capable of being collectively appraised, rather than working on a subjectivist faith in a gut-check. While not falsifiable in the Popperian sense, this model has the feature that if it does not meet ethnographic data, we can at least see where the data stresses the model to the point that the seams start to show.

3 "People can I have attention for just a moment, I think we have a word"

There is one more thing that I want to wring out of a Spinoza-inflected affect theory, but I want to get to that point by way of the city of Anaheim in Orange County, California. The city of Anaheim, that is, in 1985.

We will also be turning our attention to a large man in several senses of the word – he is John Wimber, the head of the Vineyard, originally a Southern Californian but now a global Evangelical Christian movement that practices Pentecostal charismata like speaking in tongues, prophecy, and performing deliverances from demons (Bialecki 2009 and 2017; Luhrmann 2012). Wimber himself is an interesting figure – he was (at different times) both the founding director of the Department of Church Growth at the Fuller Institute of Evangelicalism and Church Growth, and a session player for the Righteous Brothers. Wimber is best known, though, for taking his knowledge of the spiritual practice of Global Pentecostal and Charismatic Christian practices, and bringing it to the Vineyard, becoming a founding figure of the movement (Bialecki 2015).

The meeting is being held in the main Vineyard church of that time, but it is not a church meeting; this is in the last day of a *Signs and Wonders* conference, an admixture of the technical and supernatural, a hands-on course on how to use Supernatural Pentecostal practices to achieve numerical church growth. This course was originally offered at Fuller Seminary, one of the leading Evangelical intellectual centers in the United States. At Fuller it was wildly successful, and also widely controversial; despite begin called "the most famous seminary course in America," elements of Fuller Faculty had it shut down, anxious that their Evangelical school was becoming too closely associated with both these Pentecostal practices, and with John Wimber (Bialecki 2015). The course persevered, though in a different form; he began to offer it as a conference to ministers and other interested parties, whether or not they were Vineyard affiliated. While the substance was fundamentally the same, the transition from course to conference meant that a whole semester's worth of material was condensed to a single week.

The day I would like to focus on was a Friday, the terminal day of the conference, during a session in the latter part of the afternoon. Normal sessions are organized as standard lectures; you should note that this is not a normal session, however. In fact, it is so unusual that I encourage you to view it if possible (*Signs and Wonders* 1992: DVD 12).[4] The conference schedule is being broken. It starts with John Wimber, wearing a blue blazer, allowing a man to relay a word of knowledge: that is, a prophetic message received from God.

A few notes about the video itself. It has been around in various forms, some more official than others, but it was originally an in-house production by the Vineyard's media arm, and was meant to be purchased by churches for training

4 This is also available on Youtube as John Wimber Vineyard Signs & Wonders Conf 1985 12/12. https://www.youtube.com/watch?v=Com-MyVEkOc, accessed 30 January 2005.

purposes. This is an edited piece, which was, as far as I can tell, taken from a two-camera recording of the proceedings. While there are edits as we switch vantage from one camera to another, it appears that most of the visual editing is trying to track changes both on stage and in the audience. But it would seem that all we are going to see unfolds in real time, and that the soundtrack is a continuous recording.

If I were conducting a traditional linguistic analysis of this video, there could be multiple analytic frames. One might concern itself with how language is valued. It would focus on identifying moments of "sincere" speech; alternately it would be concerned with moments where speech was seen as valuable because it is the antithesis of sincere speech, divine words that are just transversing the speaker. A code-focused discussion would identify particular lexical items and metaphors – focusing on the phrase "I have a word," and the formulas used in faux-Biblical language. Conversation analysis would shift its attention to turn-taking in speech, tracking how each speaker in the series attempts to reframe the speaking event as falling into the particular speech genre and deictic relative positioning that they prefer to occupy at that moment.

If this were a "traditional" affective analysis, we would either focus on a poetics of description, attempting to formulate language evocative enough to hint at the always-receding affective traces. Alternately, we would speak of the generaltonalities of this scene, perhaps even speaking about *typical affects* found in this manner of prayer, transforming its specificity into a generic form.

Again, I am certain that all these methods would produce different forms of knowledge; I am not questioning their value *tout court*. But language-based techniques end up reducing everything in one way or another to a semiotic logic, and most affect-theory discussions are either unclear as to what is meant by "affect" in a particular instance, or unclear about how they transform affect into first person quasi-phenomenological accounts, or unclear about the means through which affect operates. By way of contrast, what I am going to try to present now is a reading of the *affections* that occur, and the expansions, contractions, and shifts in *affect* (i.e., *affectus*) that give rise to the capacity for different speech acts to occur. The gambit is that a switch to a formal system will enable us to speak about what is not necessarily a subjective or conscious phenomenon, and will also allow us to identify the specific evidence we draw on.

What the matter before us will present is a movement-by-movement account of how the various affections build on one another during the course of the video. It will begin with John Wimber breaking from his normal introduction to allow someone to present a prophetic word that he had received: the message, delivered by a young man referred to as "Mike," is that

> You [the various pastors present at the conference] were doing this task [professional ministry] of quote-unquote serving God, and the way God looks upon your heart, because of how you treat the things you are doing, you speak to your associates in the coffee house or restaurant after the service or whatever, the attitude of your heart when you're talking about it is like a harlot, like a prostitute talks about the trick that she just turned. (*Signs and Wonders* 1992: DVD 12)

It ends with the speaker asking that "leaders repent" of this right now. Wilber then gives some commentary on this prophecy, suggesting that this is characteristic of a wider movement, and that "this is not the first time that this word has come forth." He then calls on pastors to come to the stage and "repent."

At this point, forty or more men come to the stage; immediately, one of them starts crying loudly. What this does is open up a moment in which people start publicly praying and wailing at an ever-increasing volume that goes on for thirteen minutes, until Wimber brings it to a close by leading everyone present in singing a hymn.

There are words, punctual prophecies that are called out as this occurs, but what is doing the work is not the content of these words, since often the general din makes it unclear who is speaking, or what exactly is being said. What is important is rather the volume and speed of both the words, and the various sobbing and groaning as well, that takes place as this scene unfolds; even more important is the affective strain that is communicated by their sonorous qualities.

What I have tried to list below, with each event tied to a rough time stamp (which starts the second that the title card is removed and Wimber first appears), are not the moments of specific speech acts, as they would appear on a standard transcript in many linguistic anthropological analyses (compare with, say, the transcript in Silverstein 2004). Rather, what I have tried to isolate are the specific *points of inflection*. These are the moments where volume (measures relative to other moments in the video) or speed (expressed here when possible in beats-per-minute, or BPM, based off of the rhythm of language or other bodily sounds) is transformed by and through language that has a certain "affection," and increases ("affects") the general expressed capacity of everyone in the room to engage in this cacophonous "repentance." This is in short an attempt to borrow some traditional linguistic-anthropological techniques, and apply them strictly to the affective aspects of the various sound-images that constitute speech, along with the various kinesthetic and proprioceptive rhythmic and punctual turning in points that occur.

00:32 After slowly dragging the lectern back (suggesting he knows that the stage-space might be used), we have John Wimber bringing the meeting to order in a very matter-of-fact way with the phrase, "People can we have your attention for just a moment? We have a word."

00:40 Mike appears, he has to repeat his opening lines "He told me" when someone shouts "Louder." He is speaking faster than Wimber, but not that fast, when he gets to indirect reported divine speech he slows down. He has a slow circling motion he makes with his head.

1:30 At "the trick that you just turned," he switches to short, sharp statements, he has a downward tone in his phrases. The emphasis is always at the end of the phrase.

1:49 Switches to first right hand down chopping, then left, with index finger, then right with index finger.

2:30 We're back to Wimber, slower, shorter phrases, three to eight word phrases. Switches to less charged words (hirelings) and phrases about absent emotional states (callous and insensitive) and more gender appropriate language (gigolo).

3:35 Wimber, after invoking Ezekiel, longer phrases, an acceleration in speech with much shorter gaps between phrases, though volume steady.

4:00 Inserts himself into the narrative, claiming that "several months ago, actually several years ago," which he uses to slow down, makes slow half-circles, constantly decelerating speech. It's the offering of Wimber as a model for identification, but also an opportunity for those in the audience to mirror his tone.

4:30 More doubling of phrases in speech, shorter repetitive two words, larger upward arc in tone, language accelerates when it shifts to an erotics ("lovers, bridegroom to the bride, some of us have been gigolos").

5:00 Really speeds up, with talk of taking church positions for career advancement, then slows down sharply, with "we're very much like professional gigolos" down sliding tone.

5:30 Taking fingers and jabs them down with the phrase "if you're here today, and you have any reason." His hands grasp each other at belt level when he says "public repentance."

5:53 Clapping at the second that people get up. People leap up at a sprightly pace.

6:08 General applause breaks into patterned clapping at the incredibly fast pace of about 190 bpm.

6:17	A man in pink shirt starts crying; general crying is roughly doubled in volume by 6:25.
6:30	Every one kneels in a roughly ten second period. Wimber whispers *sotto voce* into microphone "forgive me Jesus, forgive me Lord."
6:40–7:10	A few chuffles – low, snuffling-like staccato sounds somewhere between laughing and crying – by Wimber into microphone. People are spaced apart from each other by a gap less than the distance of the elbow to the hand. This is closer than I would suspect is the average zone of American private space, even considering that this can vary with class and religion; this spacing is even less generous when kneeling.
7:57	Wimber, arms open, chest bared, hands outstretched but just short of shoulder height (a vulnerable looking position). Most are doubled down crying, mumbling under their breaths; good chance that these are "private" tongues (glossolalia).
8:20	One or two sobs that are transmitted through someone's body microphone, three voices continuing moaning increases in volume and speed.
8:55	Crying in a dissonant harmony, volume sharply increases at this point.
9:00	Introduction of loud, warbling wailings as background so punctual sobs (wailing will continue for about three minutes and forty seconds). "Mike" who has his hands outstretched, takes them down.
10:30	A lot of bobbing up and down by people kneeling, doubled over. Almost all are face down.
10:40	Slow clapping (at 75 bpm) immediately heads into [...]
10:50	[...]someone screams out "by his stripes shall be healed, by his stripes," temporarily pausing clapping, which resumes, slightly louder, at a relatively slower 71 bpm. Continuous wailing in the background, not unlike a "ghost in haunted house" sound effect.
11:00	"We're at war go [indiscernible]" other than the persistent background wail, most of the punctual sobs have stopped. Wimber stands up, hands at side.
11.22	Mike and Wimber with outstretched hands.
11:24	Wimber "Lord hear our cry" two to three second gap between each "we're sorry" phrase, but gaps become shorter.

11:30	Long gap then Wimber breaks with "we're sorry" thematic with "forgive us oh god" downward tone, with emphasis at beginning of phrase (at "we're sorry").
11:45	Wimber after a seven second gap "Hear our cry" with quivering voice, flat emphasis.
12:20	Some shouted words by "Mike."
12:09–12:30	A woman rocks back and forth 12 times, at 40 bpm, then face changes, raises up hands and shakes four times, holds them still, right hand clinches into a fist for a second; holds position for ten seconds until camera switches.
12:50	At this point, we now have God being quoted via prophecy as direct speech: speaking in first person in words – long phrases, high volume – are presented by Mike. The wailing increases, then stops entirely.
13:40	Mike: "So the country suffered! So with my church!" "As the rulers of the people bring their ears back to me, miracle working power, authority power, destruction."
14:00	Two voices – "it's breaking" over and over, going from 40 bpm to around 60 bpm (probably the wailing voice); then a lower voice at a clipped rate speaking under the repeated "it's breaking" phrase.
14:40–14:50	Shouted second voice to the fore, "I am coming and I will restore my church, and the whole world will know my glory!"
14:50	Applause for one second then forming patterned clapping at 160 bpm, running until 15:06.
15:18	After three seconds of silence a female voice – quiet – "How long have I waited for this day I rejoice in your company."
15:30	Sharp rise in ambient sound for about three second as speakers switch.
15:46	People still sobbing on stage.
15:50–16:13	Another higher pitched, louder voice, slightly faster (women), decelerates sharply at end.
16:30	Inaudible, sharp, highly pattered speech.
16:54	"I called you by birth" (a male voice) a series of high pitched sobs.

17:27–17:37 Four times "we're going home" at home hands wave outward, with increasing velocity and distance; with each repetition the hands are raised higher.

17:50 A female African American speaker, using the most "biblically coded speech" as it is presented in a style that is particularly thorough in the degree of iconicity of the King James Bible. This is the fastest speaker yet – bursts of acceleration, sparking at about 30 bpm, climbing up to about 50 bpm at time-mark 19:00 with concluding phrase "my name my name my name not yours my alone I'm God and I am a jealous God" again, a shift to explicitly emotion/relational terms.

18:50 Clapping outbreak, preceding another scream that occurs at the nineteen-minute mark.

19:25 Closing claps at 170 bpm; Wimber asks everyone to join him in a hymn.

Again, this transcript is not an exact capture of what occurred, and it is in no way a substitute for viewing the video of the event itself. But it helps us track not just a general flow of things, but also the way that specific affections give rise to affects, which in turn trigger actions that stand as affections for other bodies. The overarching pattern is clear: we see Wimber, starting out speaking in a measured way, and being careful to engage in what we might think of as a monologue-driven (Tomlinson 2014) form of turn-taking in public speech, give the floor to Mike, who recounts prophetic words in a more punctuated and rhythmic (though still conversational) style. When Mike is done and Wimber speaks again, Wimber attempts to decelerate what occurred, using less loaded terms, but also shorter phrases delivered at a slower pace; we can see Wimber taking the force let loose by Mike and controlling it as he relays it. But Wimber does not desire to stop what is occurring. He works instead to give its expression shape, and open it up for the audience to not just have affects, but produce affections.

Starting around the four-and-a-half minute mark, Wimber's doubling of terms marks the shift to a poetics of speech built around patterns, but also an accelerating drum-beat, a crescendo that runs all the way to when he repeats the word "gigolos" for a final time. He starts up again, though, when he calls people pastors to come to the stage for public repentance; this return to an accelerating rhythm in movement and speech, at the tail end of the previous crescendo, creates the effect that a new upward movement has begun, and that the monological moment is over.

Both the general applause and the sound of pastors leaving their chairs to stand on stage create a wash of something like a white noise, a force without a tempo. But as people carry out affections through clapping and are affected by clapping, an immanent rhythm emerges, with rather fast, though uneven count of beats per minute. This sound is joined by someone who breaks into loud crying, a sobbing which has its own rhythm. We do not know the exact trigger, of course – it may possibly have been that this man would have broken out at tears at this moment if everyone had silently remained seated. But the shift to the front of the stage, and continuing tom-tom like clapping, and the force of Wimber's words were likely building up; and once this tipping point is reached, his tears appear to be autocatalyzing as the volume of the crying quickly grows louder.

This is when people, exposed to the volume, pressed on bodily by those next to them, fall face down. Their heads are lowered, and many have their eyes closed: the only thing to coordinate them is sound, which is increasingly the sound of sobs and moans. A plateau is hit here, and it is easy to see this as a self-sustaining cycle, where the sounds of others in mourning bring out a mourning in them. Of course, Evangelicals are good at public lamenting, but that doesn't mean that this is not genuine. It means that these are bodies that are trained to respond in one particular tonality to certain recognizable affections, and that these bodies have been conditioned such that affective tipping points are calibrated for much lower thresholds (see, e.g., Hirschkind 2006).

And as these thresholds are hit, like that first sobbing man, those present start acting in idiosyncratic ways. They twitch rhythmically, going through moments of repeated contraction and release (see, e.g, the action described at 12:09–12:30 above), people start shouting out short phrases (11:24, 11:30, 11:45, 12:20, 14:00). This roughly marks another point of inflection, as people also start shouting out phrases that are in the grammatical first person (12:50, 13:40, 14:40–14:50, 15:18 16:54, 17:50). The biblical register that is often relied upon shows that they are clearly the animator, but not the author or principle (Goffman 1981), as they appear to be prophetically relaying God.

Why does this turn in speech occur then, and not earlier? I would suggest that the intensification of the affections comprising the extended bath of sound resulted in a shift in the "speed" of the affect of those who prophesize – that both the associations informing speech and the production of speech had been given an immediacy such that the individual did not consciously review his or her impressions and then formulate them as reported speech. Here, we are obviously speaking about trends in a population, as not everyone spoke in this manner, but for those who are obviously predisposed to understand subjective events as God speaking to them, such as Mike, the manner of presenting those subjective events, and the volume and strain with which they are produced, is obviously not the same as it was in the initial moments of the exercise in repentance. Assuming that reviewing and presenting these subjective events are two different and sequentially ordered processes, we see that the elaborating and rephrasing of them for an audience (something like what Freud [1965] called "secondary revision" in his theory of dreams) is rushed through under the impetus of the force of affections and the qualities of the affect. Stimulus and response are threaded together by this speed, and in the rush the work of disarticulating the divine and human voice is temporarily left by the wayside.

4 Conclusion: Food or poison

This experiment is not quite at its end. I promised that I would argue for an additional benefit from a Spinozian framing. It is time to make good on that promise.

One thing that was not discussed earlier was the question as to why it was that certain affections produce expansions or contractions of possibilities. Spinoza's gambit was that each affection either accorded with an expanded the set of constitutive relations that comprised the person, or it interfered with these internal relations, breaking them down. The encounter in its purest form is a choice between food and poison, though there are few moments that crystalline. Hence Spinoza's claim that ultimately affects, in their architectonic form, asymptotically run in the direction of either sorrow or joy.

It would take too long to discuss why Spinoza thought that affect was particular to living things, and that is a point that would probably be granted anyway without argumentation. But it is worth asking if non-biological entities have essences – that is, if entities other than singular persons, such as institutions, have sets of virtual capacities that are inherent in their form, provided that the right affective economy, the right arrangement of affection and affect, comes about. It is obvious we can speak about the affects of those persons that together constitute these collectives, but can we speak of the affects and capacities of the collectives as being in some way autonomous?

Whatever Spinoza says, I would say that there are entities that have a range of potential organizations, topological forms that could be actualized in different ways. This is another way of saying that forms entail capacities, but they may be realized in multiple separate and distinct ways, or not at all. This is worth noting because in our discussion, we have focused on the web of affections and the transformations of affects that occurred at the level of constitutive individuals. But we can consider what occurred here not just as a release of individual capacities, but as a collectivity doubling back on itself, engaging in self-affection in what, in a biological entity, would be considered a will to increase capacities, to come closer to realizing its essence. In a sense, then, this video was a moment of the Vineyard as an entity with an essence realizing itself in a patterned manner – which seems to be the perfect definition of ritual (Stash 2011). Not all affective instances are ritual, and there may be moments where an institution realizes itself more without a vast amount of affection and affect from constant human bodies. Lastly we can suspect that we will encounter situations where something may be food for an institution, but poison for the institution's constituents. But this does suggest, at least, that we have come full circle to where we began, the issue of arousal and ritual.

It is my hope that I have done something similar to realizing a swath of essence, to have ever so slightly assisted a section of socio-cultural anthropology to have an incrementally more nuanced capacity to think through an issue that has been central to it for well over a decade now. But of course, it's for you collectively to judge whether, as Spinoza would put it, I have just served up food or poison.

References

Bialecki, Jon. 2009. *The Kingdom and its subjects: Charisms, language, economy, and the birth of a progressive politics in the Vineyard*. University of California, San Diego dissertation.

Bialecki, Jon. 2015. The Third Wave and the Third World: C. Peter Wagner, John Wimber, and the pedagogy of global renewal in the late twentieth century. *Pneuma* 37(2). 177–200.

Bialecki, Jon. 2017. *A diagram for fire: Miracles and variation in an American Charismatic movement*. Berkeley, CA: University of California Press.

Bialecki, Jon & Eric Hoenes del Pinal. 2011. Introduction: Beyond logos: Extensions of the language ideology paradigm in the study of Global Christianity(-ies). *Anthropological Quarterly* 84(3). 575–593.

Bielo, James. 2009. *Words upon the Word: An ethnography of Evangelical group Bible study*. New York: New York University Press.

Clark, Herbert H. 1996. *Using language*. Cambridge: Cambridge University Press.

Course, Magnus. 2010. Of words and fog: Linguistic relativity and Amerindian ontology. *Anthropological Theory* 10(3). 247–263.

DeLanda, Manuel. 2002. *Intensive science and virtual philosophy*. London & New York: Continuum.

Deleuze, Gilles. 1978. *Lecture transcripts on Spinoza's concept of affect*. http://www.gold.ac.uk/media/deleuze_spinoza_affect.pdf (accessed 5 February 2014).

Deleuze, Gilles. 1988. *Spinoza: Practical philosophy*. San Francisco: City Lights Books.

Deleuze, Gilles. 1990. *Expressionism in philosophy: Spinoza*. New York: Zone Books.

Deleuze, Gille. 1992. Ethnology: Spinoza and us. In Jonathan Crary & Sanford Winter (eds.), *Incorporations*, 625–633. New York: Zone.

Deleuze, Gilles & Félix Guattari. 1994. *What is philosophy?* New York: Columbia University Press.

Evans-Pritchard, E. E. 1965. *Theories of primitive religion*. London: Oxford University Press.

Faubion, James. 2001. Toward an anthropology of ethics: Foucault and the pedagogies of autopoiesis. *Representations* 74(1). 83–104.

Faubion, James. 2011. *An anthropology of ethics*. Cambridge: Cambridge University Press.
Fontein, Joost. 2011. Graves, ruins, and belonging: Towards an anthropology of proximity. *Journal of the Royal Anthropological Institute*. 17(4). 706–727.
Foucault, Michel. 1992. *The history of sexuality*, vol. 2, *The use of pleasure*. London: Penguin.
Freud, Sigmund. 1965. *The interpretation of dreams*. Translated by James Strachey. New York: Avon.
Geertz, Clifford. 1973. *The interpretation of cultures: Selected essays*. New York: Basic Books.
Goffman, Erving. 1981. *Forms of talk*. Philadelphia: University of Pennsylvania Press.
Handman, Courtney. 2015. *Critical Christianity: Translation and denominational conflict in Papua New Guinea*. Berkeley, CA: University of California Press.
Harding, Susan F. 2000. *The book of Jerry Falwell: Fundamentalist language and politics*. Princeton: Princeton University Press.
Hardt, Michael. 1999. Affective labor. *Boundary 2*, 26(2). 89–100.
Hirschkind, Charles. 2006. *The ethical soundscape: Cassette sermons and Islamic counterpublics*. New York: Columbia University Press.
Hoenes del Pinal, Eric. 2011. Towards an ideology of gesture: Gesture, body movement, and language ideology among Q'eqchi'-Maya Catholics. *Anthropological Quarterly* 84(3). 595–630.
Johnson, Jessica. 2018. *Biblical porn: Affect, labor, and pastor Mark Driscoll's Evangelical empire*. Durham, NC: Duke University Press.
Keane, Webb. 2007. *Christian moderns: Freedom and fetish in the mission encounter*. Berkeley, CA: University of California Press.
Kendon, Adam. 1990. *Conduction interaction: Patterns of behavior in focused encounters*. Cambridge: Cambridge University Press.
Laidlaw, James. 2002. For an anthropology of ethics and freedom. *The Journal of the Royal Anthropological Institute* 8(2).311–332.
Laidlaw, James. 2014. *The subject of virtue: An anthropology of ethics and freedom*. Cambridge: Cambridge University Press.
Leys, Ruth. 2011. The turn to affect: A critique. *Critical Inquiry* 37(3). 434–472.
Luhrmann, Tanya Marie. 2012. *When God talks back: Understanding the American Evangelical relationship with God*. New York: Alfred A. Knopf.
Malinowski, Bronislaw. 1922. *Argonauts of the western Pacific: An account of native enterprise and adventure in the archipelagoes of Melanesian New Guinea*. London: G. Routledge & Sons; New York: E.P. Dutton & Co.
Massumi, Brian. 2002. *Parables for the virtual: Movement, affect, sensation*. Durham, NC: Duke University Press.
Mazzarella, William. 2009. Affect: What is it good for? In Saurabh Dube (ed.), *Enchantments of modernity: Empire, nation, globalization*, 291–309. New Delhi: Routledge.
Muehlebach, Andrea. 2012. *The moral neoliberal: Welfare and citizenship in Italy*. Chicago & London: University of Chicago Press.
Munn, Nancy. 1986. *The fame of Gawa: A symbolic study of value transformation in a Massim (Papua New Guinea) society*. Cambridge & New York: Cambridge University Press.
Navaro-Yashin, Yael. 2012. *The make-believe space: Affective geography in a postwar polity*. Durham, NC: Duke University Press.
Norris, Sigrid. 2004. *Analyzing multimodal interaction: A methodological framework*. New York: Routledge.
O'Neill, Kevin Lewis. 2010. *City of God: Christian citizenship in postwar Guatemala*. Berkeley, CA: University of California Press.

O'Neill, Kevin Lewis. 2013. Beyond broken: Affective spaces and the study of American religion. *Journal of the American Academy of Religion* 81(4). 1093–1116.
Pfiel, Gretchen. 2011. Imperfect vessels: Emotion and rituals of anti-ritual in American Pentecostal and Charismatic devotional life. In Martin Lindhardt (ed.), *Practicing the faith: The ritual life of Pentecostal-Charismatic Christians*, 277–305. New York: Berghahn Books.
Richards, Analiese & Daromir Rudnyckyj. 2009. Economies of affect. *Journal of the Royal Anthropological Institute*. 15(1). 57–77.
Robbins, Joel. 2001. God is nothing but talk: Modernity, language and prayer in a Papua New Guinea society. *American Anthropologist* 103(4). 901–912.
Rudnyckyj, Daromir. 2011. Circulating tears and managing hearts: Governing through affect in an Indonesian steel factory. *Anthropological Theory* 11(1). 63–87.
Rutherford, Danilyn. 2013. Affect: provocation. http://culanth.org/fieldsights/60-affect-provocation (accessed 31 January 2014).
Schaefer, Donovan O. 2015. *Religious affects: Animality, evolution, and power*. Durham, NC: Duke University Press.
Shoaps, Robin. 2002. "Pray Earnestly": The textual construction of personal involvement in Pentecostal prayer and song. *Journal of Linguistic Anthropology* 12(1). 34–71.
Signs and wonders and church growth. 1992. Placentia, CA: Vineyard Ministries International. DVD.
Silverstein, Michael. 1976. Shifters, linguistic categories, and cultural description. In K. Basso & H.A. Selby (eds.), *Meaning in anthropology*, 11–55. Albuquerque: School of American Research & University of New Mexico Press.
Silverstein, Michael. 2003. Indexical order and the dialectics of sociolinguistic life. *Language and Communication* 23(3–4). 193–229.
Silverstein, Michael. 2004. "Cultural" concepts and the language-culture nexus. *Current Anthropology* 45(5). 621–652.
Stasch, Rupert. 2011. Ritual and oratory revisited: The semiotics of effective action. *Annual Review of Anthropology* 40. 159–174.
Stewart, Kathleen. 2007. *Ordinary affects*. Durham, NC: Duke University Press.
Stromberg, Peter G. 1993. *Language and self-transformation: A study of the Christian conversion narrative*. Cambridge: Cambridge University Press.
Tomlinson, Matt. 2014. *Ritual textuality: Pattern and motion in performance*. New York: Oxford University Press.
Whitehouse, Harvey. 1995. *Inside the cult: Religious innovation and transmission in Papua New Guinea*. Oxford: Oxford University Press.
Whitehouse, Harvey. 2004. *Modes of religiosity: A cognitive theory of religious transmission*. Walnut Creek, CA: AltaMira Press.
Willis, Laurie Denyer. 2018. "It Smells Like a Thousand Angels marching": The Salvific Sensorium in Rio de Janeiro's Western Subúrbios. *Cultural Anthropology* 33(2). 324–348.

Contributors

Leslie Arnovick, Professor of English, University of British Columbia, specializes in English language studies with particular interest in historical pragmatics and medieval English. She is the author of *Written reliquaries: The resonance of orality in medieval English texts* (John Benjamins, 2006), which analyzes the oral performance of spoken acts recorded in Old English and Middle English texts by reconstructing their original cultural and linguistic contexts. The analysis combines methodologies from oral theory and historical pragmatics to explore curses, proverbs, promises, prayers, gibberish, and performative silence. Her other publications include *Diachronic pragmatics: Seven case studies in English illoctutionary development* (John Benjamins, 1999) and *The English language: A linguistic history* (rev. 3rd edn., Oxford University Press, 2017), a textbook for upper-division undergraduate courses in the history of the English language, co-authored with Laurel J. Brinton.She is currently at work on a monograph exploring the interaction among early English vernacular forms (e.g., sermons, charms) and orthodox prayers taken from Catholic liturgy.

Jon Bialecki, JD, PhD, is a Fellow in the School of Social and Political Science at the University of Edinburgh. His academic interests include the anthropology of religion, anthropology of the subject, ontology and temporality, religious language ideology, and religious Transhumanist movements. His work has been published in several edited volumes, as well as in academic journals such as the *South Atlantic Quarterly, American Ethnologist, Anthropological Theory* and the *Journal of the Royal Anthropological Institute*; his ethnographic monograph, *A diagram for fire: Miracles and variation in an American Charismatic movement*, was published in 2017 by the University of California Press.

Anderson Blanton is Associate Research Scholar at the Yale University Institute of Sacred Music. His major research interests include media ethnography, the digital humanities and studies of the Human/Technological interface. He is the author of *Hittin' the prayer bones: Materiality of spirit in the Pentecostal South* (University of North Carolina Press, 2015), as well as curator of the *Materiality of Prayer* website sponsored by the Social Science Research Council. He is currently curating a large collection of printed religious ephemera that will be featured on the *Material and Visual Cultures of Religion* website hosted by Yale University.

Paul Copp is Associate Professor in Chinese Religion and Thought at the University of Chicago. His research focuses on the intellectual, material, and visual cultures of Chinese religion, ca. 700–1200 CE, and the paleography and material culture of Dunhuang and the eastern "silk roads." He is the author of *The body incantatory: Spells and the ritual imagination in medieval Chinese Buddhism* (Columbia University Press, 2014), as well as articles such as "Anointing Phrases and Narrative Power: A Tang Buddhist Poetics of Incantation," and "Manuscript Culture as Ritual Culture in Late Medieval Dunhuang: Buddhist Talisman-Seals and their Manuals." At present, his main project is a study of the worlds of anonymous 9th- and 10th-century Chinese Buddhists whose practices, ritual and scribal, are evidenced by manuscript handbooks and liturgies discovered among the cache of materials from Dunhuang. Its working title is "Seal and Scroll: Material Religion and the Ritualist's Craft at Dunhuang."

https://doi.org/10.1515/9781614514329-019

William Downes is a Senior Fellow in the School of Politics, Philosophy, Language and Communication Studies at the University of East Anglia, Norwich, UK. Educated at Queen's University in Kingston, Ontario, the University of Toronto and University College London, he taught at Glendon College, York University, Toronto, and in England at the London School of Economics and the University of East Anglia. He has been a Northrop Frye Fellow at Victoria College, Toronto, and in 2014, Fellow at the Institute of Advanced Study at Durham University. He has written numerous articles employing linguistics as a method, broadly understood to include cognition, pragmatic theory and the philosophy of languge, in order to understand culture. He is the author of *Language and society* (2nd edn., Cambridge University Press, 1998) and a study in the cognitive phenomenology of religion, *Language and religion* (Cambridge University Press, 2011).

Patrick Eisenlohr is Professor of Anthropology, Chair of Society and Culture in Modern India at the University of Göttingen. He obtained a PhD from the University of Chicago in 2001 and previously held positions at Utrecht University, Washington University in St. Louis, and New York University. He is the author of *Little India: Diaspora, time and ethnolinguistic belonging in Hindu Mauritius* (University of California Press, 2006), and *Sounding Islam: Voice, media, and sonic atmospheres in an Indian Ocean world* (University of California Press, 2018). He has conducted research on transnational Hindu and Muslim networks in Mauritius and India, the relationships between religion, language, and media, the sonic dimensions of religion, the links between media practices and citizenship, as well as language and diaspora.

Courtney Handman is Associate Professor of Anthropology at the University of Texas at Austin. She received her PhD from the University of Chicago in 2010 and previously taught at Reed College. Her work focuses on the religious publics produced through missionary discourses and ambivalences about institutions in Protestant practice. Her book *Critical Christianity: Translation and denominational conflict in Papua New Guinea* was published by the University of California Press in 2015.

Naomi Janowitz, Professor of Religious Studies at the University of California, Davis, is the author of numerous articles on Judaism, Christianity and Graeco-Roman religions in late antiquity including "Re-creating Genesis: The Metapragmatics of Divine Speech" in *Reflexive language: Reported speech and metapragmatics* (Cambridge University Press, 1993). She has also authored *The poetics of ascent: Rabbinic theories of language in a late antique ascent text* (SUNY Press, 1988), *Magic in the Roman world: Pagans Jews and Christians* (Routledge, 2001), *Icons of power: Ritual practices in late antiquity* (Penn State Press, 2002), and most recently *The family romance of martrydom in Second Maccabees* (Routledge, 2017).

Isabel Laack is Senior Researcher at the Institute for the Study of Religion, Ruprecht Karl University, Heidelberg. She received both an MA and a PhD in the Study of Religion, Anthropology, and Musicology, and recently held a Marie Curie International Outgoing Fellowship (European Research Council) including a two-year-long research stay at the Department of Anthropology at Harvard University. Her work focuses on Mesoamerican religions and contemporary European religiosity with main theoretical research interests in the aesthetics of religion, including indigenous semiotics, embodiment, visual and auditory religion, and material text practices. She is author of *Religion und Musik in Glastonbury: Eine Fallstudie zu gegenwärtigen Formen religiöser Identitätsdiskurse* (Vandenhoeck & Ruprecht, 2011) and of a Habilitation thesis that is forthcoming in the Numen Book Series, *Aztec religion and art of writing: Investigating embodied meaning, indigenous semiotics, and the Nahua sense of reality* (Brill, 2019). She has published articles in several journals including *Method & Theory in the Study of Religion*, *Journal of Religion in Europe*, and *Zeitschrift für Religionswissenschaft*. She has also written book chapters in volumes published by Brill, Vandenhoeck & Ruprecht, and Springer.

Christopher I. Lehrich graduated from the University of Chicago (BA 1992, MA 1994, PhD 2000). He is the author of *The language of demons and angels: Cornelius Agrippa's occult philosophy* (Brill, 2003); *The occult mind: Magic in theory and practice* (Cornell University Press, 2007); and numerous articles; and the editor of *On teaching religion: Essays by Jonathan Z. Smith* (Oxford University Press, 2012). He is a former ACLS Fellow.

Naphtali S. Meshel received a PhD from the Hebrew University of Jerusalem (Department of Bible) in 2010. Following postdoctoral research in Mysore, India (Sanskrit grammatical texts) and at the University of Pennsylvania (Akkadian texts), he served as Assistant Professor at Princeton University (Department of Religion and Program in Judaic Studies, 2010–2016). He returned to Jerusalem with his family in 2016, and is jointly appointed in the Department of Bible and in the Department of Comparative Religion at the Hebrew University of Jerusalem. His research focuses on the Hebrew Bible in its ancient Near Eastern contexts and on its early interpreters. He has a special interest in Levitical legal literature, and in the use of intentional ambiguity as a poetic device in Wisdom Literature and in prophecy. Within the field of religion more broadly, he is interested in the development of theoretical frameworks for the analysis of complex ritual systems, and in the processes through which formal tools for logical deduction are forged within ritual contexts. His first book, *The grammar of sacrifice* (Oxford, 2014), examines the ancient intuition that sacrificial rituals, like languages, are governed by "grammars." He is currently working on ancient models for the "science of ritual" and on their explanatory power for systems of purity and impurity. Meshel previously taught at the Russian State University for the Humanities, and was a member of the Institute for Advanced Study (Princeton, NJ).

Aurélie Névot is a researcher at the French National Center for Scientific Research (CNRS), Research Center on Modern and Contemporary China (CECMC, EHESS). As an anthropologist, her research focuses on a Chinese minority: the Sani branch of Yi nationality. She studies in particular its scriptural shamanism based on a secret writing exclusively reserved for shamans called "Masters of Psalmody" (*bimos*). Névot has published three books on this topic: *Comme le sel, je suis le cours de l'eau. Le chamanisme à écriture des Yi du Yunnan (Chine)* (Société d'ethnologie, 2008), *Versets chamaniques. Le livre du sacrifice à la terre (textes rituels du Yunnan, Chine)* (Société d'ethnologie, 2013), and *The masters of psalmody (*bimos*). Scriptural shamanism in southwestern China* (Brill, forthcoming). Developing an anthropology of transmission, she has also directed a book about the master-disciple relationship: *De l'un à l'autre. Maîtres et disciples* (Éditions du CNRS, 2013). Another aspect of her research concerns the interplay between religion and politics, as well as the inculturation and acculturation phenomena introduced by Christianity. The recent institutionalisation of the Sani scriptural shamanism prompts Névot to question the process of patrimonialisation as implemented in China since 2003 and monitored by UNESCO. In *La couronne de l'orient. Le centre du monde à Shanghai* (Éditions du CNRS, 2014), she highlights the fact that the Chinese Pavilion built during the World Expo Shanghai 2010 shows the new cosmological orientation of China regarding the international constellation. It re-elaborates ancient representations in order to edify a new era where China ensures universal Harmony.

Jenny Ponzo is Associate Professor of Semiotics at the University of Turin (Italy). She is also the Principal Investigator of the ERC project NeMoSanctI, "New Models of Sanctity in Italy (1960s–2010s) – A Semiotic Analysis of Norms, Causes of Saints, Hagiography, and Narratives" (grant agreement No. 757,314). Between 2014 and 2017 she was a postdoctoral researcher at the Ludwig Maximilian University, Munich, where she carried out a project about religious themes in fiction and taught courses in semiotics of religion. Previously, she worked at the University of Lausanne (Switzerland) and at the University of Turin. In 2014, she was awarded both a PhD in Italian Literature (University of Lausanne, Switzerland) and a PhD in Semiotics (University of Turin, Italy). Her doctoral research – a semiotic study of the representation of national identity in Italian 20th-century fiction about the Risorgimento – was awarded grants from the Swiss "Fondation pour des bourses d'études italo-suisses" and "Fondation Zerilli-Marimò", as well as the "Prix Société Dante Alighieri." She is the author of two monographs and of academic articles on issues such as civil religion, fundamentalism, and semiotics of literature. She is now working at her third monograph, *Religious narratives in Italian literature after the Second Vatican Council: A semiotic analysis* (under contract with De Gruyter).

Seth Sanders, Professor at the University of California, Davis, earned a BA at Harvard College and a PhD at The Johns Hopkins University. His interests include Pentateuchal composition, the conditions of possibility of Hebrew literature, and journeys to heaven. He is the author of *The invention of Hebrew* (University of Illinois Press, 2009) and *From Adapa to Enoch* (Mohr Siebeck, 2017); and editor or coeditor of *Cuneiform in Canaan* (Israel Exploration Society, 2006), *Margins of writing, origins of cultures* (Oriental Institute Press, 2005), and *Ancient Jewish sciences and the history of knowledge in the Second Temple period* (NYU Press, 2014). His current projects include: rethinking the origins of biblical literature, supported by NEH and Guggenheim fellowships; Mesopotamia and the Bible (under contract with Oxford University Press).

Mustafa Shah is a Senior lecturer in the School of Languages, Cultures and Linguistics at the School of Oriental and African Studies (SOAS), London University, where he completed both his BA and PhD degrees in the field of Arabic linguistics and Islamic Studies, respectively. His principal research and teaching interests include early Arabic linguistic thought, theology, *ḥadīth* and Qur'ānic exegesis. He has recently edited a four-volume collection of published articles on the Prophetic traditions entitled *The ḥadīth* (Routledge, 2010) and a further collection entitled, *Tafsīr: Interpreting the Qur'ān* (Routledge, 2013). He is joint editor of the *Oxford handbook of Qur'ānic studies* and editor of the *Oxford handbook of Hadith studies* (both forthcoming). He serves as series editor of *Themes in Qur'ānic studies* published by Equinox.

Kocku von Stuckrad is Full Professor of Religious Studies at the University of Groningen, the Netherlands. He has published extensively on topics related to the cultural history of religion in Europe, method and theory in the study of religion, discursive study of religion, the diversity of knowledge systems, esoteric and mystical traditions in European intellectual history, the history of astrology, religion and (philosophies of) nature, as well as on religion and secularity. His most recent monograph is *The scientification of religion: An historical study of discursive change, 1800–2000* (De Gruyter, 2014). He served as President of the International Society for the Study of Religion, Nature, and Culture (ISSRNC) and as President of the Dutch Association for the Study of Religion (NGG). He also was a founding board member of the European Society for the Study of Western Esotericism (ESSWE). He was co-chair of the Critical Theory and Discourses on Religion Group, as well as of the Religion in Europe Group, of the American Academy of Religion.

Paolo Visigalli teaches at Shanghai Normal University, College of Humanities and Communication, and is scholar in residence at the Center for Global Asia, NYU Shanghai. He holds a PhD in Asian and Middle Eastern Studies from the University of Cambridge, an MA in Religious Studies from the Universities of Padua and Venice "Ca' Foscari", and a BA in Oriental Languages and Cultures from the University of Rome "La Sapienza." Combining close textual analysis with wider theoretical concerns, Paolo's research explores early India's intellectual and religious life, focusing on Hindu and Buddhist texts. He is also interested in early Chinese thought and comparative philosophy. Paolo's research languages are Sanskrit, Pali, and, increasingly, Classical Chinese. He is the author of several book chapters and articles that have appeared in *Philosophy East and West*, *Journal of Indian Philosophy* and *Indo-Iranian Journal*. His current major project is a monograph on etymological theory and practices in early Hindu and Buddhist texts.

Laurence Wuidar (PhD in Musicology from the Université Libre de Bruxelles) teaches the History of Medieval Philosophy at the Dominican *Studium* of Bologna (affiliated to the Pontifical University San Tommaso d'Aquino in Rome) and is a research associate in musicology at the University of Geneva (FNS). She published several books on music within the scientific, philosophical and theological traditions from late antiquity to the 17th century. On music in history of science and theology, these books include *Musique et astrologie après le concile de Trente* (Brepols, 2008); *Fuga Satanae. Musique et démonologie à l'aube des temps modernes* (Droz, 2018); on patristic litterature and music metaphor, *L'uomo musicale nell'antico Cristianesimo. Storia di una metafora tra Oriente e Occidente* (Brepols, 2015); *La simbologia musicale nei Commenti ai Salmi di Agostino* (Mimesis, 2014); and on music within the philosophical and hermetic tradition, *Canons énigmes et hieroglyphes musicaux dans l'Italie du 17ème siècle* (Peter Lang, 2008); *L'angelo e il girasole. Conversazione filosofico-musicali* (ESD, 2010). Her articles appeared in journals covering various fields of research from art history to history of medicine, history of philosophy, musicology and theology. She is currently working on music in medieval mysticism.

Robert A. Yelle is, since 2014, Professor for the Theory and Method of Religious Studies and Chair of the Interfaculty Program in Religious Studies at Ludwig Maximilian University, Munich. He studied at Harvard College (BA in Philosophy 1988), the University of California at Berkeley (JD 1993), and the University of Chicago Divinity School, where he received a PhD in the

History of Religions (2002) based on research conducted in Calcutta, India, on a Fulbright-Hays Fellowship. Prior to arriving in Munich, Yelle was Associate Professor at the University of Memphis. He has received fellowships from the University of Toronto, the University of Illinois at Urbana-Champaign, New York University School of Law, and the John Simon Guggenheim Memorial Foundation. Yelle is presently Editor of the American Academy of Religion/Oxford University Press book series *Religion, Culture, and History*, and was previously Executive Secretary of the North American Association for the Study of Religion (2007–2011). His monographs include *Explaining Mantras* (Routledge, 2003), *The Language of Disenchantment* (Oxford University Press, 2013), *Semiotics of Religion* (Bloomsbury, 2013), and *Sovereignty and the Sacred* (University of Chicago Press, 2019).

Index

Note: Locators with letter 'n' refer to notes

ʿAbbād ibn Sulaymān 179
ʿAbd al-Jabbār 175–176, 180–181
ʿAbd al-Qāhir al-Jurjānī 175
Absalom 345
Abū Hāshim 180–181, 183
– theory of states 169n23
Abū Manṣūr al-Māturīdī 163
academia: as ritual performances 312–313
Achema 117–118, 129–132
Adolph, Robert 264
Aelfric of Eynsham 87, 89–92, 100
affect 436–437
– *affectio* (affection) *vs. affectus* (affect) 24, 427, 431, 438
– a-signifying nature of 421–422
– and discourse 425–426
– and immediacy 422
– and language 421, 423, 425–426, 428–429
– as linguistic turn 419, 424
– as magic 419
– material culture 424
– measuring of 24
– and neoliberalism 422
– points of inflection 432
– and ritual 439
– temporality of 428
– as term 427
– time limit on 428
– typical affects 431
affect theory 419–420, 425–427, 431
– aesthetic modernism 424
– linguistic turn, as corrective to 421
Africa 280n7, 404
African Christian Church 299n23
agency 104, 106, 109, 317, 343, 383, 385, 393
– and discourse 392
– divine 146, 173, 178, 185
– moral 160
– nonhuman 312, 315–316, 318
– and subjectivity 384
Agni: Altar of Fire (documentary) 64
Ahituv 144
Alarcón, Ruiz de 359
al-Bāqillānī 170–172, 176–177, 183n40, 183–184
Alfonso, Pedro 152
algebra 269
– abstract thinking 268
– algorithms 268
– quadratic formula 268
ʿAlī ibn Abī Ṭālib 162n9
Allāh 217n9
alterity 383–384
Althusser, Louis 140, 329
– Christian religious ideology 139
– theory of divine names 23
American Fundamentalist Baptist 420n1
Amitābha 73, 77
Ammerman, Nancy 299
Amoghavajra 77
Anatolia 331, 333, 335–336, 339–340, 342, 342n31, 344–345
Ancient Judaism (Weber) 344
Ang, *bimo* 130
Anglo-Catholics 263
Anglo-Saxons 89. *See also* Pater Noster; Lord's Prayer
– Apostles' Creed, used by 100–101, 106
– charms 23, 88, 92–93, 103, 110–111
– healing rituals 100
– infant baptism 102
– leeches 104
– prayers, use of 87
Animal Liberation: A New Ethics for our Treatment of Animals (Singer) 315
animal studies 305, 315
animism 315–316
Anquetil-Duperron, Abraham Hyacinthe 209
anthropocentrism 315
anthropology 1, 24, 57, 271, 306, 314–315, 404, 422
– affect theory, adoption of 419
– "gut-check" anthropology 425

https://doi.org/10.1515/9781614514329-020

anthropology (continued)
- linguistic anthropology 5, 420, 429
- socio-cultural anthropology 439
- symbolic anthropology 18
Anthropology of Christianity movement 4, 423
Āpastamba-Śrautasūtra 52–53
Apollo 133
Apostles' Creed 87, 89, 99, 102
- baptism, birthright of 91
- baptismal elements 102
- and charms 92, 100–101, 103–104, 106, 109–110
- Christian right of initiation 100
- declaratory Creed, reciting of 103
- de-institutionalization of liturgical context 88
- English, translation into 101
- folk medicine 106
- folk ritual, co-opting of 107
- and healing 104, 111
- and incantations 109–110
- institutional setting, belonging to 107
- and instrumentality 107
- as liturgical 106–107
- medicinal herbs 96
- and Nicene Creed 100
- speakers, transformative effect on 103
- as speech act, illocutionary force of 100
- as subjective 107, 109–110
- traditional referentiality 100
Apostolic age 299
Aqhat 333n14
Aquinas, Thomas 227
Arabia 176
Arabic 14, 166, 169, 177, 182–183, 185, 187
archaeozoology 343
Aristotle 245, 315
Asad, Talal 18
Ash'arī 172–173, 180, 183
Ash'arīs 161–162
Ash'arī school 163, 170, 181
Ashcroft, Richard 263–265
Asia 51–53, 69, 84, 280n7, 332, 397
Assemblies of God 300
Assyrian empire 344
Athanasius of Alexandria 215, 233–234
Atharva Veda 58–60. *See also* Vedas
Athenagoras of Athens 220
Atrisuhas 334–336, 342, 342n31, 345
Aubrey, John 15
August, Karl 203
Augustine 89–90, 101–103, 106, 215, 217, 219n11, 223–225, 230–231, 234, 243
Aurelius, Marcus 236
Austin, John Langshaw 23, 139, 154, 306
- and naming 140
- speech act theory 140, 142, 144, 154
autonomy 19, 258–259
Avesta 209
Aztecs 372n16, 374. *See also* "flower and song" (*xochitl in cuicatl*); Nahuatl songs
- abstract reasoning of 370
- *amatl* books 353
- botanical images, importance to 364–365
- *calmecac* and *telpochcalli* schools 352
- complex social structure of 352
- cosmovision of 349–350, 352, 366–367
- cult of brilliance 364–365
- culture 22, 24, 350–351, 361, 364–366, 372–373
- deities, as immanent 369
- *difrasismo* "water and mountain" depictions 362, 366
- divination codices 354–355
- divine, concept of 368–369
- embodied metaphors, expression of 370
- Fifth Sun 352, 366–367
- "flower and song" 350, 361, 363–367
- ideograms 353
- imaginary thinking, inclination toward 350
- inferiority, claim of 372–373
- knowledge, and nature, observations of 369
- language and writing, as depictions of reality 367–368
- linguistic signs, naturalness of 366
- *nahualli* (co-essence of qualities) indigenous concept of 367, 369
- ontology of, as immanent 368–369
- oral tradition 350, 352, 356, 371, 375
- as People of the Sun 352
- pictorial writing 24, 353–355, 362–363, 367, 370, 375

- poetry 24, 350, 372–373
- as pre-rational, claims of 372–373
- semiotic ideology of 368, 370, 375
- shamanic visions 369
- surprising victory over 372
- and *teotl* 368
- writing system 350, 352, 353

Babylon 340, 341
Babylos 337
Bacon, Francis 16, 266
- and Baconianism 16, 267, 269
Bakhtin, Mikhail 307
baptism 103, 109–110
- and exorcism 104
- healing rites 106
- as indexical 145
- original sin 102
Bar-Rakib 339–340n25
Barr, James 280, 296
Barthes, Roland 308
Bartholomaeo, Paulinus a Sancto 210n35
Bauman, Richard 391, 394n6
Baxter, Richard 64–65
Beauzée, Nicolas 210
Bede (Venerable) 91n6, 101, 103
Bengal 209
Bentham, Jeremy 16
Benveniste, Émile 109, 301
Bernard of Clairvaux 230
Betz, Hans Dieter 319
Bhagavaddharma 76, 78
Bible 2, 13, 99, 220, 284–285, 288–289
- acrostics 10
- *Authorized King James Version* 263
- Bible Study groups 408, 420n1
- Christian Biblicism 1
- as Container of Truth 297
- divine speech 219
- gospel, as plain speech 14
- Hebrew Bible 3, 10, 33, 36, 39, 44, 62, 305, 327
- inerrancy of 278–279, 280n11
- interpretation of 23, 281, 287, 290
- language, prohibitions against 3
- as material object 299, 301
- parallelism in 15
- Third Commandment 3
- translation of 17–18, 261
- as unique 278–279
- as Word of God 282
Bielo, James 420n1
Bierhorst, John 361, 363
bimos (Masters of psalmody) 115–116n4, 119n7, 130–133
- blood sacrifice, as transubstantiation 121–122
- celestial speech 119
- chanting of 114–116, 118, 121–122
- chants, as secret speaking 115
- chants, as visual 119
- co-dehiscence 117
- and dance 126
- divine speech, as vehicle of 124
- master-father, as transubstantial process 120
- *midje* manuscript 123–124
- multiple identities of 123
- orality, interiorization of writing 121
- oral writing 115, 117
- psalmodic chimera 117, 124
- and psalmody 118, 120, 123
- reflexivity of 125–126
- and ritual 123
- ritual book, chanting of 121
- ritual language 114, 117
- ritual language, as sacrificial 116
- ritual speech, and reflexivity 117
- sacrificial animals 122
- scriptural shamanism 117
- *se*, theme of 122
- secret speaking, and consubstantiality 117
- secret writing of 114, 116
- shamanistic identity, and blood 120
- shamanistic speech 117
- and shamans 121–124, 127–128
- sharing blood 116
- and spirits 115
- stem-family 116
- syllabic writing 114
- *teu* (read aloud) 118, 122
- texts, memorization of 121
- textual immersion 121

bimos (Masters of psalmody) (continued)
– writing, as depository of speech 119
– writing-blood 115–117, 115–116n4, 121–122, 134
Bingen, Hildegard von 218
bioethics 315
Black, Max 271
Blumenberg, Hans 305
Boethius 216–217
Bollywood 394
Bolter, Jay 384
Book of Common Prayer, The 14–15, 263
Book of the Name, The (Eleazer of Worms) 151
Book of Nature 220
Boone, Elizabeth H. 354
Bourdieu, Pierre 312
Boyle, Robert 264–265
Brahmanism 16
– Brahmins 196, 200n17, 209–210, 210n35
Bredesen, Harald 283–285
Bṛhaspati 193–194
Briggs, Charles L. 391, 394n6
broad church 263
– high church 263
– low church 263
Bronze Age 331, 332n10, 333, 336, 339, 341–343
Brooke, John H. 257
Brothers Grimm 14
Browne, Thomas 246–249
– informative intent in 248
– plain style of 249
– poetic devices, use of 248, 249
Bry, Johann Theodor de 219
Bücher, Karl 64
Buddha 8, 75, 81, 83
Buddhism 81, 83
– Buddhist ritual practice 72
– Chinese 68–69, 72–73, 75, 77
– esoteric Buddhism, growth of 70–71
– Indian 327
– Mahāyāna 73
– Shingon 13
Bühler, Karl 393
Burchard of Worms 91
Burke, J. G. 245
Burkhart, Louise M. 365
Butler, Judith 140, 140n3
– divine naming 139

Caitanya 17
California 24
Calvinism 262–263
Calvin, John 252, 262
Cambridge Platonists 267, 270
Cameron, M. L. 98
cantares 358, 369
Cantares Mexicanos 349–350, 352, 356–357, 359, 363
– flower-songs in 360–361
Canterbury Psalter 101
Cao clan 70
Cardona, George 197
Carismosofia: paralleli fra occultismo e carismaticismo (Martella) 281
Carter, Michael 184
Catholicism 255, 300
Cavalieri, Paola 315
Cavanaugh, William 259–261
Caxton, William 261
Celestial Hierarchy, The (Dionysius) 226–227
Certeau, Michel de 119
cessationism 280, 280n12
Chancery English 261
Charismatic movement 276, 282–283, 285, 296, 299, 414–415
– and affect 422
– charismatic healing 416
– charismatic practice, and healing touch 24
– direct experience, importance of 279
– ecumenical perspective 297
– glossolalia, as characterizing trait of 278–279, 291–292, 301
– as neo-Pentecostal movement 279
– opponents of 280–281, 288, 289n18
– point of contact 404–405
– sacred text, as handbook 289–290, 298
– sincerity, interpretation of 300
– spontaneity, centrality of 300
– spread of 280
– “there is no distance in prayer” phrase 411
Charismatics, The: A Doctrinal Perspective (Sherrill) 280

charm healing
- oral performances 93
- performance pragmatics 92
- utterances, as sung 93
charms
- baptismal elements 104
- charm performance 88, 94n8, 99
- charm rites 88–89
- de-institutionalization of 107, 110n14
- as discursive performance 106, 110
- divine assistance 111
- and exorcism 104–105
- and healing 110
- and incantations 107
- and instrumentality 107
- performative ends of 98
- performing of 110
- personal voice 110
- power of 110
- water, as restorative 104
chemas 117, 129
- after voicing 134
- and ancestors 133
- ancestral cave (*fei*) 130–132
- echo (return of voice) 132
- matrilineal process 128
- return, idea of 132
- trans-gender medium 133
Chézy, Antoine-Léonard de 209
chiasmus 3–4, 10–11, 22, 58–59, 61–62
China 23, 69–71, 75–76, 78, 80, 115–116n4, 120
- Buddhist practice in 68, 84
- chanting 68
Chinese Buddhism 73, 75, 77. *See also* Dunhuang manuscripts
- external framing 72
- internal framing 72
- manuscript liturgies 68–69
- ritual practice 68–69, 72
Chinese language 195–196
Christianity 89, 161n8, 223, 261, 285, 319, 329n5, 419–420, 420n1, 423. *See also* Bible; Protestantism
- incarnation, doctrine of 172n28
- infant baptism 102
- pagan techniques, incorporated into 90
Christin, Anne-Marie 119
Chrysostom, John 224–225
Chün-fang Yü 77
Church of England 263
- Anglican preaching 262
Church Fathers 216–217
- creation, as musical instrument 221
Cicero 243
City of God 219
Clement of Alexandria 215, 232–233
Codex Borbonicus 363
Codex Borgia 355–357
Codex Boturini 362
Coleman, Simon 300
Coleridge, Samuel Taylor: Romantic theory of imagination 256
Collins, Billy 316, 318
colonialism 351
- reverse 375
colonization 371–373
communication theory 10
Confessions (Augustine) 224
Confucianism: names, rectification of 16
Confucius 22
Connolly, William 422
Conquest of America: The Question of the Other, The (Todorov) 371–372
Conservative Evangelicals 276, 278, 282, 293, 296, 299, 301. *See also* Evangelical Christian movement
- Bible, centrality of 279, 297
- Charismatics, opponents of 279
- scriptedness of 300
- spread of 280
constructivism 309
Cook, Michael 160n7
Copernican revolution 207
Corpus Dionysiacum, The 229
Cortés, Hernando 372
Counter-Reformation 8
Course in Miracles, A (Schucman and Thetford) 320
Coyolxauliqui 363
Crane, Jonathan K. 315
Cranmer, Thomas 14–15
Crapanzano, Vincent 297, 300
Cratylism 207

Cratylus (Plato) 179, 207
Cross, Stephen 204
Cudworth, Ralph 267
Cummins, Fred 63–65
Cuthbert, St. 103
Cyprian 224n17
Cyril of Jerusalem 102–103

Darwinian revolution 270–271
David C. Cook Publishing Company 408
Dead Sea Scrolls 148n33
De Andia, Yasabél 229n23
"Death of an Author, The" (Barthes) 308
Decretum (Burchard) 91
Dee, John 305
Deleuze, Gilles 426, 427
De mutatione nominum (Philo) 234–235
De opificio mundi (Philo) 222
Derrida, Jacques 1, 5, 119
Descartes, René 253, 315, 425–426, 429
– algebra, innovation of 268–269
– conic sections 268
– deductive system 267
– doubt, method of 270
– new philosophy 267
determinism 164
dhāraṇīs 75
Dharmakṣema 81
Dialogue with Trypho the Jew (Justin) 225
Diamond Sutra 70, 73
– chanting of 83
– liturgies for 78–83
– texts, sets of 83
Dionysius 215, 225, 227–229, 231
– angelic hierarchy 226
discourse
– and affect 425–426
– as communicative structures 309
– discourse knots 309–310
– discourse strands 309
– kinship systems 139
– and language 307–308
discourse analysis 5, 23–24, 306–307, 309, 312, 314, 319–320
– animal studies 315
– double-bind of 310
– and habitus 312
– as interdisciplinary 314–315
– and language 311, 313
– natural sciences 314
– openness of 314
– performative action 313
– production of knowledge 313
– textually oriented 309
discourse theory 317, 319
– and agency 392
– *vs.* discourse analysis 311
– discursization and pragmaticalization 99
– interactional context 392
– study of religion, application to 311
Divine Logos 220–221
divine names 139, 140, 147, 155
– and blessing 148
– deferential avoidance 150
– and divination 388
– divine name ideology 149
– dwelling formula 145
– empty space aniconism 143
– iconic aniconism 148
– immanent theory of divine representation 145
– as indexical 148
– performativity, mode of 142
– power of 149
– secret names 151–152
– and taboos 153
– Tetragrammaton 3, 20, 150
Divine Names, The (Dionysius) 228–229
Donne, John 262
Dr. Faustus (Marlowe) 245–246
Druze 161
dualism 60
dual-modalities 154
Du Bois, Patterson 406
– hand work 407–408
– point of contact 407
Duffy, Eamon 255
Duncan, Isadora 20
Dunhuang manuscripts 68–71, 77–78, 81, 83–84
Du Plessis, David 283, 298
Dura Europos synagogue 146, 148, 148n30, 150
Durand, Jean-Marie 332n12

Durkheim, Émile
- collective effervescence, notion of 418

Eadwine 101
East India Company 204
Ecclesiastical Hierarchy, The (Dionysius) 226–227
Ecgbert, Archbishop 90
Eclogues (Virgil) 361
ecumenism 279
Egypt 18
Eight Lectures (Pāṇini) 194, 198
Eleazer of Worms 151–152
Eligius, St. 89, 90
Elisha 236
Elizabeth I 260
Emar 332, 341n29
emic practice 5
empiricism 266, 270
- and skepticism 271
Enarrationes in Psalmos (Augustine) 224, 230
England 3, 23, 110n14, 243, 255, 257, 259, 261, 267, 270–271. *See also* Great Britain
- Deist period in 15
- English Reformed tradition 263
Enlightenment 16, 258
entextualization 99, 391, 398, 420n1
- of religious discourse 392
enunciation theory 281
Erasmus 247
Eshel 144
Essay towards a real character and a philosophical language (Wilkins) 266
Ethics Demonstrated (Spinoza) 427
etic system 5
Euclid 266–267, 270
Eurocentrism 350
Europe 5, 16, 195, 258, 280, 318, 320, 364, 373, 390, 404
- differentiation between rational and poetic language 375
- language, obsession with 305
- nation-states, rise of 257
- pagan folk traditions, persistence of 89
Evangelical Bible Institute 281
Evangelical Christian movement 405, 413, 430. *See also* Conservative Evangelicals
- point of contact 406
- public lamenting 437
Evans-Pritchard, E. E. 83, 418–419
Excitable Speech (Butler) 139
exorcism 104–105, 107–108
Ezra 171

Fairclough, Norman 309
faith healing 405
- point of contact 408–411
Fame of Gawa, The (Munn) 425
Ficino, Marsilio 245, 255–256
Filliozat, Jean 209
Fleck, Ludwik 309
Fleming, Luke 140
Flexion Group 205
Florentine Codex (Sahagún) 352, 362
"flower and song" (*xochitl in cuicatl*) 375–376
- as aesthetic achievement 365
- Aztec culture, as root metaphor of 361
- ghost-song ritual 361
- as immanent images 365
- as indexical 350–351, 363–364
- as metonymic 350, 366
- as natural indexes 366–367, 374
- as performative 363
- post-conquest revitalization movement, as expressions of 361
- spatio-temporal contiguity 366–367
- themes of 360
Fludd, Robert 219
Foley, John Miles 94
Foucault, Michel 1, 308, 319, 418, 423
- things, groupings of 309–310, 318
Foundation for Inner Peace 320
France 203, 209n34, 268, 270
- French Imperial Library 209
Francis of Assisi 218
Frazer, James G. 374
Freud, Sigmund 438
Fu Dashi 81
Fuller Institute of Evangelicalism and Church Growth 430
Fuller Seminary 430
Fundamentalism (Barr) 280

funerary rituals 333–334, 336–337, 344–345
– address and memorialization, invoking of 343
– appetite and embodiment, dimensions of 343
– archival texts 332
– feeding the dead, ritual of (*kispu*) 331, 340–341, 341n28, 342n30, 343
– models of objectification 330
– and monuments 332
– presence of gods, emphasizing of 342
– sharing of meals 343

Gabbar 339–340n25
Galen 186
Galileo 267
Gardner, Robert 64
Garibay Kintana, Angel M. 361, 361n11, 366, 373
Gazali 217n9
Geertz, Clifford 18, 306
Gelasian Sacramentary 102–103
gender studies 305
Genealogy of the Hammurapi Dynasty 340
generativists 43
Genette, Gérard 207
German Idealism 206
Germany 202–204
Gerold, Théodore 219n11
Ghaylān al-Dimashqī 164n15
Ghost Dance movement 361
Gihwa 81
Gioia, Ted 64
Glorious Revolution 259
glossolalia 13, 23, 278, 284–285, 287–289, 289n18, 291–293, 299–301, 430
– condemnation of 297
– Holy Spirit, as gift of 276–277
– opposition to 279
– as sequence of senseless sounds 294
Goffman, Erving 330–331
– "ghoster" and relayer 392
Golden Rule 407
Goodman, Felicitas 289
Goody, Jack 14
Gorgias (Plato) 244
Grace Community Church 280
grammar 36, 47
– comparative grammar 203n23
– as generative 35
– grammars of ritual 49
– of language 48
– mathematical modeling, amenable to 35
– operative categories, grouped into 35
– rigorously applied 35
– and Sanskrit 197–199, 200–203, 205–206, 208–211
– as term 49
– as unconsciously internalized 35
Grammar of Sacrifice, The (Meshel) 36, 51
– critique of 50
– operative categories 37
– hierarchics 37
– jugation 37
– praxemics 37
– zoemics 37
GRAMMUR (Generative, Rigorously Applied Mathematically Modelled Unconscious Rules) 31, 49
Gramophone Company 390
Grassi, Ernesto 256
Great Britain 280. *See also* England
Great Commentary (Patañjali) 193, 195, 198–199, 201–202, 211
Greek Magical Papyri 318–319
Greenblatt, Stephen 247
Greenfield, Jonas 342n30, 343
Gregory of Nyssa 233
Grusin, Richard 384
Gruzinski, Serge 365
Guanshiyan 75
Guanyin (Bodhisattva) 71, 73, 76
Guanziza 75
Guatemala 423
Guru Granth Sahib 389

Habermas, Jürgen: public sphere 382
Hadad 335, 342
ḥadīth (prophetic tradition) 166, 171, 174, 183, 391
Halbertal, Moshe 148n34
Hamilton, Alexander 208–209
Hammurapi dynasty 341, 343

haṃsa mantra 57, 60–61, 63. *See also* mantras
– Great Sayings 59
– meaning of 58
– as mirror 62
Han (Chinese) 120
Handwork in the Sunday School (Littlefield) 407
Hanslick, Eduard 21
Harding, Susan 420n1
Hardt, Michael 424
– affective labor 424
Harmonia Mundi 219
Harré, Rom 271
Harvey, Graham 315–316
Hasedera Temple 77
al-Ḥasan al-Baṣrī 162n10
Ḥassān ibn Thābit 176
Havelock, Eric 14
healing prayer 411
Healing Waters Broadcast 404–405, 408–409
Healing Waters Magazine 405, 409
Heath, Malcolm 245
Hebrew 3, 10–11, 14, 15
Hebrew Bible 3, 10, 33, 36, 39, 44, 62, 305, 327
Hebrew sacrifice 32, 34, 36–42, 44–49, 51, 145, 147. *See also* sacrifice, in ancient Near East
– logic of 46
– and salt 46–47
Hegel, Georg Wilhelm Friedrich 388
– linguistic sign 385–386
– and mediation 387, 387n4
Heidelberg school of ritual dynamics 50
Heine, Heinrich 203n24
Heisenberg, Werner 271
Henry VIII 259, 263
Herbert, George 262
Herder, Johann Gottfried 206–207
Herodotus 21
Herrick, James A. 245–246
hierarchics 37, 48, 50–53
Hindi films 394–395. *See also* Bollywood
Hinds, Martin 167n19
Hinduism 57, 61, 63. *See also* mantras; Sanskrit; Tantras; Vedas
History of the Royal Society (Sprat) 264
Hittites 334, 336
Hobbes, Thomas 14–16, 259–260, 265–266
– as *bête noir* 267
– Euclidian deductivism 267
– materialism of 268–269
Hodder, Ian 328
Hoenes del Pinal, Eric 420n1
Hoffmann, E. T. A. 21
Hofstadter, Douglas R. 307
Holy Roman Empire 258–259
Homer 245
Homo Ritualis (Michaels) 50
Horvat Teman 142
Houseman, Michael 127
Huichang suppression 69
Huiluan 73
Huiztilopochtli 363
Humboldt, Wilhelm von 196n9, 386
Hundley, Michael 145n21, 145n22
Hydriotaphia, Urne-Buriall: or a discourse of the sepulchral urnes lately found in Norfolk (Browne) 248

Ibn al-Nadīm 169–170
Ibn Fāris 182–183, 185, 187
Ibn Ḥazm 186
Ibn Kullāb 168–170, 172–173, 179, 183
iconicity 57–58, 60, 65–66
– diagrammatic icon 61
– indexical icon 62
– sequential iconicity 61
iconoclasm 9, 17
idolatry 145–146, 148
iʿjāz al-Qurʾān
– doctrine of 174–176, 178
– roots of, in Qurʾān 173
ʿilm al-kalām 160
imagination 256–257
Imrūʾ al-Qays 176
Incantation of Great Compassion 72
– chanting of 77
– *dhāraṇī* 75–77
– liturgies for 73–77

incantations 93–94
- agency of 109
- de-institutionalized incantations 106
- as discursive act 110
- first-person directives 107–109
- and intertextuality 94
- second-person directives 107–108
- and subjectivity 108
- traditional referentiality 94
India 4–7, 16, 64–65, 71, 195, 197, 203, 209, 211, 404
- as cradle of civilization 203n24, 204
indigenous culture: devaluation of 371
individuation: process of 396–397
Indology 194
Indonesia 6–7, 389
Indra 193
inerrancy 280, 280n11, 299, 301
information theory: and noise 385
Ingman, Peik 318
Ingold, Tim 119
Institutes (Calvin) 262
interdisciplinarity 314
interiority 388, 418
intersubjectivity 424
intertextuality 22, 57, 60, 65, 307–308
- oral-performance texts 94
Iron Age 24, 327, 331, 333–334, 336–337, 339, 341–342, 344, 346
- Iron Age drawings 142
- Iron Age monuments, carved writing 345
Isḥāq ibn Ibrāhīm 165–166. *See also* Muḥammad; *na't* devotional poetry
Islam 159n3, 160, 312, 391
- atomism, theory of 169–170n26
- *imām*, infallibility of 161
- Islamic theological thought 158
- Shī'ī camp 161
- Sunni camp 161–163, 163n14, 185
Ismael 183
Ismā'īlī 161
isnād (transmission) 391–392
Israel 327
iṣṭilāḥ, 178, 180–185
Italy 280

Jackson, Bernard 11
Jäger, Ludwig 383
al-Jāḥīz 175
Jahm ibn Ṣafwān 164, 168
Jakobson, Roman 4, 6, 10–12, 246, 248
Jameson, Fredric 4
James, William 279
Japan 77, 84
Jerome 217–218
Jerusalem 147, 171
Johnson, Cale 154
Johnston, Jay 313
- esoteric aesthetics 317
joint speech 57, 66
- authenticity, and resonance, distinction between 65
- Catholic repetitions 64
- characteristics of 63
- work songs, converging with 64
Jolly, Karen 109
Jones, Richard Foster 263–264
Jones, William 194, 205, 210
Jubbā'ī 184
Judaism 161n8
jugation 37–39, 41, 48, 50, 52–53
- jugational patterning 40, 42–43
Justin 223–224, 236

kalām 159–160
kalām nafsī 172, 183
Kang, Yoonhee 389
Kant, Immanuel 253, 315
Karkamish 334
Katumuwa 337, 339–343, 339n22, 339n23, 339–340n25, 342n31, 345
Kātyāyana 196
Kautsa 16
Kawada, Junzo 134n30
Keane, Webb 4, 8, 262–263, 330, 396
Keller, Reiner 309
al-Khalīl ibn Aḥmad 179, 182
Khara-Khoto (Mongolia) 69
al-Khaṭṭābi 175
Khawārij (seceders) 165n9, 169n10
Kilamuwa 339–340n25
Kimelman, Reuven 148n30

kinesics 20
Kippenberg, Hans G. 310–311
kispu 331, 340–341, 341n28, 342n30, 343
Kitāb al-Mughnī 175–176, 180
Kittler, Friedrich 384n1
Koichi Shinohara 70–71, 84
Kopf, Lothar 183n40, 187
Kripke, Saul 141
Kroll, Richard 263–265
Kuna 121

Labrador 408
Lacan, Jacques 384n1
Lacnunga 87, 92, 95, 97–98, 103–105, 108
Language. *See also* individual languages
– and affect 421, 423, 425–426, 428–429
– arbitrary signs, consisting of 386
– as binary 5
– capacity of 141
– as code 420n1
– colonial oppression, as tool of 19
– and communication 308
– credal language 107
– critique of 7
– dialogue in 57
– and discourse 307, 313
– discourse research 311–312
– diversity of 18
– divinity of 199, 229, 233
– ecstatic languages 292, 294
– and education 247
– effective language 139, 140
– as embodied 397
– European theories of 373
– forms of 64
– and glossolalia 291, 293
– grammars of 34–35, 49, 51
– indexical capacity of 141
– indigenous languages, theories of 358
– as ineffable 218
– and knowledge 236, 250, 264
– language games 306
– language ideology 23, 154, 345, 371, 420n1
– limits of 48
– “limits of awareness” of 387
– linguistic bias 328–330
– magical power of 195–196, 200, 211, 245
– and materiality 20–21, 387, 394
– and media 398
– mediality of 386, 389, 393–394
– as mediator, between humans and actors 388
– music as 215–217, 222–226, 228, 230, 234–235, 237–238
– national languages, creation of 261–262
– origins of 158–161, 173, 178–179, 182–184, 187, 205
– paratextual 82–84
– as performative 219–220, 313, 413
– plain language 255, 265, 267
– plainness, style of 243
– and poetics 245, 252–256, 265, 269, 272, 404
– power of 139, 155
– pragmatic theory of 246
– and praxis 19–20
– Protestant models of 19
– referential function of 388–389
– and religion 2, 8, 60, 305–306, 314, 320, 382–383, 389, 398
– religious language 164, 243, 388–393, 396, 414–415
– rhythmic qualities of 397–398, 432
– and ritual 8, 22, 32, 47–48, 61, 114, 116–117, 121, 197–198, 201–202, 345
– ritual language 263, 271, 413–416
– secret language 122
– semiotic modalities of 350–351, 363, 374–375
– sound and idea, connection between 386
– sound reproduction 390, 398
– spiritual language 277–278, 297
– spoken language 65
– study of 304
– and thinking 260
– transparency of 385–386, 388, 395
– vernacular language 123, 127, 411
– and writing 19, 21, 370, 374
Latin 2, 12–14, 91, 96–97, 101
Latour, Bruno 19, 392
– Actor-Network-Theory (ANT) 313, 316, 424–425

Lee, Benjamin 141
Leechbook 87, 103, 105, 108
Leone, Massimo 155, 287n17
León-Portilla, Miguel 361, 363, 373–374
Levant 24, 330–331, 337, 344
Leviathan (Hobbes) 259
Lévi-Strauss, Claude 6, 60
Leys, Ruth 425
Liang Dynasty 81
Liao 69
Life of Moses 223
Lincoln, Bruce 310–311
linguistics 31, 35, 105, 194, 201, 203, 271, 352
– cognitive registers 243–244
– and glossolalia 277
– historical linguistics 195, 207, 211
– linguistic anthropology 1, 420
– linguistic iconoclasm 16
– linguistic ideology 57, 64, 66, 150–151
– linguistic turn 9, 305
– structural linguistics 1–2, 6
literalism 280, 299–300, 383, 387
literary monuments 344
literary studies 308–309
– and intertextuality 307
Littlefield, Milton 407
Locke, John 8, 386
Lockhart, James 358–359
Logos 221–222
"Looking Up in the Garden" (Merwin) 304, 313
López Austin, Alfredo 365, 367
Loraux, Nicole 132
Lord, Henry 65
Lord's Prayer 87–89, 91, 94, 95, 101. *See also* Pater Noster
– charm performance 99
– and charms 106, 110
– "deliver us from evil," as petition 98
– and healing 94
– and incantations 97
– and sickness 95
– strength of 97
Lowth, Robert 10
Luther, Martin 252, 261, 387n3
Ma'bad al-Juhanī 164n15
MacArthur, John F., Jr. 280–282, 290, 295–296, 298
Madelung, Wilferd 168–169n22, 170n27
magic
– and prayer 319
– ritual power of 318
Mahābhāṣya (Patañjali) 32
Mahākāśyapa 81–82
Mahāparinirvāṇa Sutra 81
Mahmood, Saba 18–19
Maimonides, Moses 32–33n5, 33–35, 52
Maingueneau, Dominique 309
Malinowski, Bronislaw 12, 115, 419
al-Ma'mūn 165–67
mantras 4, 11–13, 15, 17, 22, 65, 80–81, 83, 388. *See also dhāraṇīs*; *haṃsa* mantra
– power of 16
Margalit, Avishai 148n34
Mari 332, 340–341
market capitalism 269
Marlowe, Christopher 245–246
Martella, Nicola 281–282, 287n16, 291–292, 295, 297
– semiotic square 293, 293n21, 294
Marx, Karl 328n2
Massumi, Brian 420–427
Mastrocinque, Attilio 319
material domain 24
materiality 7, 313, 388, 390, 398, 424, 425
– and language 20–21, 387
– and media 9, 22
– of sign 388
Material Religion (journal) 395
materia sacra 51, 53
Māturīdīs 161–162
Mauritius 394
– Muslim community 383, 391–393, 395–396
– *na't* genre 391, 393, 395–396
Mauss, Marcel 408
Mayan writing 353
Mazzarrella, William 425
McDannell, Colleen 18
McKinnon, James 219n11
media 387
– hypermediacy 384
– and immediacy 384

– materiality of 9, 22, 385
– perceptibility, and disappearance 385
– and subjectivity 384
– as transparent 385
media studies 305
media theory
– forgetful of language 383
– human agency, overriding of 383, 385
– space, shrinking of 383
melisma 238
Melos amoris (Rolle) 231
Merleau-Ponty, Maurice 120, 127n15
Merton, Robert 264
Merwin, M. S. 304, 313
Meshel, Naphtali S. 31, 50–51, 201–202
Meshel, Zeev 144
Mesoamerica 351, 372
– botanical images, importance to 364–365
Mesopotamia 329–330, 349
metaphors 7, 16, 57, 60, 116, 118, 164, 168, 225, 256–257, 271–272, 299, 350, 359, 363–366, 373–374, 414, 431
– concept of 185
– denseness of 2, 8
– embodied metaphors 370
– God, expression of 222–223, 225, 228–229, 231–233, 236–238
– metaphorical language 23
– musical instrument, man as 215, 218–219, 221–223, 228, 231–234, 236–238
– ritual objects 328
– technological metaphor 405
– veil of analogy 228
Metapragmatics 420
Mexica ethnic groups
– Chichimec legacy, and Toltec civilization, combination of 351–352
– Triple Alliance 351
Mexico 349, 351, 357, 361, 371, 373–374
Michaels, Axel 32–33n5, 33, 33n6, 50–52
Middleton, Conyers 13
miḥna 167, 179
Miller, Perry 262
mimesis 8
Mirandola, Gianfrancesco Pico della 256
Mishna 33
Mitchell, W. Fraser 262
modernity 4, 6, 37, 424
– epistemological authority, reorganization of 264
– religious superstition *vs.* political rationality 371–372
Mongolia 69
monism 60, 62
monotheistic theology 146, 318
Montanists 278n5
Montecuhzoma II 372, 372n16
More, Henry 267
Morgan, Thomas 15
morphology 23, 48, 51, 53, 207–208
Morris, Christopher W. 258
Morrissey, Mary 262–263
Muʿāwiya ibn Abī Sufyān 162n9
Muḥammad 17, 158–159, 186
– first revelations of 159n2
Muḥammad ibn Aḥmad ibn Sālim 172
Müller, Friedrich Max 2, 16, 304
– Semitic languages 206n27
multidisciplinarity 314
Munn, Nancy 425
music
– angelic music, and liturgical music 227
– apophatic (negative) theology, as mirror of 218–219
– dangers of 217
– as divine language 23, 217–230, 237–238
– divisions of 216
– as ineffable 218, 238
– internal and external, distinction between 217
– mathematics, ruled by 215, 217
– and mystics 218
– as non-discursive language 230
– profane music 216–217
– prophetic discourse 234–238
– *quadrivium*, as part of 215
– rhetoric, sister of 219
– sacred music 216
– and silence 228–229, 229n23
– sounding number, as science of 219
– as spiritual medicine 216
al-Muʿtaṣim 167

Mu'tazila 163–165, 167–168, 170, 172
– absolute fideism, disapproval of 162
– on divine names 182
– i'jāz al-Qur'ān, doctrine of 173
– and Mu'tazilites 184–185
Myrvold, Kristina 389

nahuallatolli genre
– and iconicity 365
– language of magic 359–360
Nahuas. *See* Aztecs
Nahuatl songs 356–357
– conceptual parataxis of 359
– cosmovision 363–364, 366
– "flower and song" 363–367
– and hypertrophism 359
– incantational style 359
– as indexical 363–364
– language, devaluing of 373
– narrative, lack of 358
– performative context 358
– Quetzal bird 360
– structural organization of 358–359
names, personal. *See also* divine names
– and baptism 141
– and blessing 144
– building-as-name ideology 145
– and deference 146
– and deictics 141
– divine names 142
– indexical capacity of 141
– linguistic role of 141
– recontextualization, resistance to 141
– rigid performativity 141
– social use of 140
– and taboos 140, 142
Naram-Sin 341n28
na't devotional poetry 24, 389, 391, 393, 395
– indexicality of 394
– poetic language, as hallmark of 394
– reciting voice, power of 396
naturalism 270
Navaro-Yashin, Yael 422
naẓm: concept of 175
al-Naẓẓām 175
Nebuchadnezzar II 171
neoliberalism 422–423
neo-Platonism 218, 244, 249, 255–257, 265
– magic, aligned with 245–246
New Guinea 18
new materialism 316, 318
– and relationality 317
New Philosophy 264–265
New Song 221
New Testament 291
– speaking in tongues 277, 291
Newton, Isaac 257, 267, 269, 428
Nicene Creed, Triune God 100
Nichiren 17
Nicholas of Cusa 245
Nicodemus 281
Nietzsche, Friedrich 7, 306
Niles, John 92–93
9/11: as discursive event 312
Noble Savage 375
North America 320, 390
North Britain 329n5
Novak, David 414n7
Nuer practices 83

"Ode to a Desk Lamp" (Collins) 316–318
Odes of Solomon (Rolle) 232
Oedipus 60
On Christian Doctrine (Augustine) 243
On the excellency and grounds of the mechanical hypothesis (Boyle) 264–265
On the Language and Wisdom of the Indians (Schlegel) 193, 195, 202–204, 205n26, 207–208, 209n33, 211
Oldham-Appleby, Joyce 259
O'Neill, Kevin Lewis 424
– affective spaces 423
oral writing
– and orality 117
– orality-literacy debate 371–372, 373n16
– and shamans 129
Orator (Cicero) 243
Ordinary Affects (Stewart) 422, 424
Origen 13, 233, 233n38, 234
Orsi, Robert 18
Othering 375
Otto, Rudolf 12, 21

paganism 315
Panamuwa I 335–337, 339–340n25, 342–343, 345
Panamuwa II 339–340n25
panentheism 62
Pāṇini 32, 194, 198, 208
Pardee, Dennis 332n10, 339–340n25
Parham, Charles 278, 283, 286–287
Parmentier, Richard J. 155
Patañjali 32, 32–33n5, 43, 200n17
Pater Noster 99, 103. *See also* Lord's Prayer
– audience participation 95
– baptism, birthright of 91
– charm incantations 96–97
– and charms 92, 94, 106
– curative formulas, integral role in 95
– de-institutionalization of 106, 110n14
– Eucharistic liturgy, role in 95
– folk rites 106
– as good medicine 97
– and healing 111
– and incantations 93–94, 110
– incantations, as frame for 110
– incantations, as requests 97
– medicinal herbs 96
– power of 96
– strength of 97
– as subjective 107, 110
– unique status of 97
Paul the Apostle 3, 217–218, 277–278, 283, 286–287, 291–295, 329
Peirce, Charles Sanders 5, 61, 366, 386
– icon 6
– signs, modalities of 20
Penitential of Theodore 90–91
Pentecostalism 23–24, 278, 283, 285, 299, 404, 419–420, 423
– and affect 422
– and prayer 415
– spontaneity, centrality of 300
performative actions
– and meditation 313
– and shamanism 313
performativity
– and divine names 142
– and speech act 148
Persia 146
Pestalozzi, Johann 406
Peters, John Durham 384n2
– spiritualist communication 384n2
Petrus, Alfonsi 152, 153
Pfiel, Gretchen 422
Phaedon (Plato) 235
Phaedrus (Plato) 244
Philo of Alexandria 215, 221–225, 223n15, 234–237
Phrygia 278n5
phúsis vs. thésis 179
plainness 272
– abstract concepts, and understanding mysteries 253–254
– and algorithms 265
– biblical literalism 261
– charismatic authority 251
– cognitive principle of relevance 246
– corpuscular philosophy 265
– as cultural innovation 257–258
– dimensions of 244
– emergence of 257–258
– empirical or scientific plainness 252
– and *endoxa* 251, 271
– genuine authority 251–252
– and gospels 262
– implications, avoiding of 251
– inferential directness 244
– informative intent 250
– irrational literalism 260
– linguistics of 246–247
– literalist plainness 252
– low complexity, striving for 250
– and mathematics 267
– maxims of 250–251
– as norm 244
– ontic logos 257
– ostensive-inferential communication 246
– plain speech 14, 23
– plain style 243
– poetic-aesthetic attempt 253
– poetic effects 253
– poetic language 252
– principles of 249–250
– referentiality, dominated by 246
– role authority 251
– scientific versions of 269

plainness (continued)
- as semipropositional 253
- sincerity condition 249
- transparency of 244, 246
- truth evaluation condition 249, 251, 260
Plato 7, 179, 179n34, 207, 216n4, 219–220
- mimesis, attack on 8
- Orpheus, antipathy toward 21
- Platonic ideas 253
- and poetics 244
- rational dialogue 245
- and rhetoric 244
- transcendence of the One, notion of 223
Platonism 256. *See also* neo-Platonism
- folk Platonism 256
Plotinus 218, 225, 229
poetry 388
- and dialectic 245
- expressive function 246
- felt space 397
- meta-representational function 246
- and parallelisms 121, 127
- phatic function 246
- poetic-aesthetic cognition 245, 264
- poetic function 246
- reading of 313
- recited poetry, and bodily sensations 397
- referential function 246
- as revelatory 245
- and representation 255–256
- and ritual 11
point of contact concept 408, 416
- advertising catalogues, use in 408
- American Christian religious education, ubiquitous within 408
- poetic performance, transformations of 415
Point of Contact in Teaching, The (Du Bois) 406
Pons, Jean François 193, 209, 209n34, 210
Popper, Karl 429
Porter, Anne 331n9
Porter, Mark 65
Postclassic International Style 353
postcolonial studies 305
poststructuralism 317
praxemics 37, 48, 50–53
Propp, Vladimir 5
Protestantism 8, 17, 256, 261, 300, 415, 420
- Anglican Latitudinarians 263
- language, referential function of 388
- literalism of 3, 262, 373, 387
- plain speech, preference for 387
- prayer, vernacular language of 404
- ritual language 413–414
- "scripture alone" (*sola scriptura*) 262
- sincere speech, concern for 420n1, 422
- and spontaneity 422
- transparent linguistic medium, preference for 387
- vain repetitions, critique of 4, 64–65
Protevi, John 422
pseudo-Dionysius the Areopagite. *See* Dionysius
public sphere 382
Puritans 15–17, 262, 263
Pythagoras 216

Qatabanian 339n23
qiyās (analogical reasoning) 181
Quakers 263
Quis rerum divinarum heres (Philo) 234–235
Qur'ān 23, 160, 160n6, 161n8, 167, 175, 389
- content of 158
- as created 164–166, 168, 170, 173, 178–179, 182, 184, 187
- eternal status, notions of 164, 166, 169, 172
- God, uniqueness of 159, 159n2
- iʿjāz al-Qur'ān, doctrine of 173–174
- inlibration, schema of 172
- *iṣṭilāḥ*, and *tawqīf* 178–185
- *kalām nafsī* (internal speech) 170
- linguistic inimitability of 158–159, 161, 176–177
- *muklūq* 165
- origin of language, debate on 183–184, 186–187
- origins of 158
- and poetry 176–178
- recitation, act of 158–159, 171–172
- speech of God 159, 165, 168–173, 183
- text, created *vs.* uncreated, debate over 168, 173, 178, 187
- as uncreated 158, 164, 166, 168, 170–173, 183–184, 187
- uniqueness of 175

radio
- faith-cure, as healing poetics of percussion 414
- immediacy of 415
- poetic inflections, amplification of 414
- as point of contact 24, 405
- radio prayer 413–414
- tactility of 415
- transductions of 414–415
Rāpiʾu 333–334
Rāpaʾūma 334
rationalism 266
Reformation 3, 13, 259–260, 300, 329n5. *See also* Protestantism
Reformed theology 206
Relational Dynamics of Enchantment and Sacralization, The (Ingman et al.) 316
relationality 317–318
relativism 271
relevance theory 249
- contextual implications 246–247
Religio Medici (Browne) 248
religion 319
- academic study of 304–305, 310–311
- archaeological data 330
- and language 305–306, 314, 382–383
- linguistic aspects of 1
- material aspects of 395
- and media 382–383
- religious language, ideologies of 8–9, 22
Rémusat, Abel 196n9
reproduction technology 383
Republic, The (Plato) 244–245
requests
- and incantations 97
- mands, as type of speech 97–98
Restoration 259, 263–264
rhetoric 11, 16, 64, 94, 97–98, 173, 175–176, 187, 236, 249, 257, 262–263, 270–272, 276, 296, 301, 308, 352, 372–373, 426
- conative-expressive rhetoric 246
- music, as sister of 216
- and poetics 244, 247, 256, 366
- rhetorical devices 297, 300, 343, 404
- transcendental reality 256
Rhetoric as Philosophy (Grassi) 256
Rhodes, C. 328, 328n2
Riegl, Alois 343–344
Rig Veda 58–60, 196. *See also* Vedas
ritual 119
- and affect 439
- grammar of 33, 48, 51–52
- and performance 312, 313
- and poetry 11
- and repetition 11
- ritualization 11–12
- ritual lament 388
- ritual language 4, 8, 22, 48, 388–389
- ritual performance 65
- ritual prayer 388
- ritual systems, grammar of 31–32, 33n6, 33–36
- and subjectification 418
- as type of communication 4
ritual programs
- chanting scriptures 72
- ritual frames, creation of 71
- texts, adaptation of 71
- xylograph liturgies 71–72
ritual studies 305
Roberts, Oral 24, 404–405, 409–410, 414, 415–416n8
- point of contact 415–416
- "there is no distance in prayer" phrase 411, 413
- "turning your faith loose" 412
Rocher, Rosane 208, 211
Rolle d'Hampole, Richard 226, 230–232, 234
Roman Catholic Church 17, 260, 263
- Eucharist 63
- Roman Catholic literalism, poetic-aesthetic within 254–255
Romances de los Señores de la Nueva España 350, 352, 356–357, 359–360, 363
Roman Empire 278n5
Romanticism 204
Rome 146
Routley, Erik 219n11
Royal Society 249
Rufinus of Aquileia 99–100
al-Rummāni 175
Rutherford, Danilyn 422

sacrifice 32, 201
– in ancient Near East 330, 334, 337, 339–342
– Aztec 360
– Christian 254
– Hebrew 32, 34, 36–42, 44–49, 51, 145, 147
– Vedic 59
– Yi 116–118, 121–122, 125, 127, 129, 131–132, 134
Sahagún, Bernardino de 352, 362, 368
Sāḥībī (Fāris) 187
Sahlins, Marshall 120
saja' (rhyme) 177
Sales, Anne de 120, 125
Sālimiyya 172
saṃskṛ 201
Sanders, Seth 144
sandhi 51
Sanis 114–115, 115n3, 117–119, 123, 126, 130, 130n20, 133
– agnatic ideology of 120
– and echo 131
– mythology, cave, recurrent element in 129n18
– patrilineality in 120
Sanskrit 193
– as artificial language 210, 210n35
– *vs.* Chinese 196, 196n9
– divine 204
– and grammar 197–199
– grammar, and religious merit 199–200
– grammatical transparency of 203
– morphological transparency of 194–195, 197, 209, 211
– as perfect language, illusion of 209, 211
– religious knowledge, primordial patrimony of 195
– ritual, and grammar 200–202
– ritual, and magical power of language 200
– as sacred language 195
– transparency of 194, 201–202, 205–206, 208–210
Sapir, Edward 386
ṣarfa 175
Sargon 341n28
Sarum Missal 102
śāstra 199, 200
Saussure, Ferdinand de 2, 5–6, 8, 386
– arbitrary sign 386, 388
Sāyaṇa 197
Scandinavia 102
Schelling, Friedrich Wilhelm Joseph 206
Schlegel, August Wilhelm 203, 203nn23–24
Schlegel, Friedrich 23, 193, 195, 196n9, 202, 205n26, 206n27, 208–211
– comparative grammar, popularizing of 203n23
– flexional languages 205
– grammar, emphasis on 207
– grammatical transparency of Sanskrit 203, 205–206, 208–211
– historical comparative grammar 203
– India, as cradle of civilization 203n24, 204
– morphology, role of 207–208
– organic and generative, opposition between 205–206
– on origins of languages 205
Schmid, Neil D. 83
Schmidt, Brian 142, 143
Schopen, Gregory 327, 329n5
Schopenhauer, Arthur 204
Schucman, Helen 320
science: rise of 258, 263
scientism 264
Scotus, Johannes Eriugena 229
Scripture of the Incantation of Great Compassion 73, 83
– Eight Great Diamond Spirits 79–82
– *fayuanwen* 78
– "Mantra of Offerings to the Bodhisattva Xukong" 81
– "Mantra for the Purification of Spoken Karma" 81
– *qiqingwen*-like prayer 78, 80
Searle, John 23
Second Coming 293, 297
semiotic ideology 6, 9, 20–21, 24, 328–331, 345, 368, 388, 420
serial cereal offerings 37–39, 44–45
Serna, Jacinto de la 359, 365
Severi, Carlo 121, 124–127
Shakespeare, William 245–246
shamans 115–116, 119, 121–124, 127–128
– oral writing, as specialists of 129

Sherrill, Elizabeth 280
Sherrill, John 280–283, 285–290, 298, 300
Shīʿī 161
Shklovsky, Viktor 5
Shoaps, Robin 300, 420n1
Sībawayhi 182
ṣifa 183
Ṣiffīn 162n9
signs: and referents 61
Sikhs 389
Silk Road 68
Silverstein, Michael 6, 62–63, 154, 386, 393–394, 396n7, 425
– limits of awareness 387
Simondon, Gilbert 396–397
Singer, Peter 315
Singh, Tara 320
Sissa, Giulia 132–133
Skeris 219n11
Skinner, Quentin 258
Smith, Adam T. 327–329
Smith, Jonathan Z. 20, 318
Smith, Morton 146
sociability 419
Sociology of Knowledge Approach to Discourse (SKAD) 309
Socrates 179n34, 244–245
Soka Gakkai movement 17
Somenzi, Chiara 229n23
Song state 69, 75, 77
Sophists 244
sound production 384n2
– acoustic voice 390
– deictic reference, indexical field of 393
– and language 390, 398
– participant roles 392
– religious texts, transmission of 391–392, 398
– voice, materiality of 395–396
speaking in tongues. *See* glossolalia
speciesism 315
speech acts 23, 154n46, 432
– de-institutionalization of 110
– performativity of 142, 144, 148, 154
speech act theory 139–140, 142, 144, 428
Spells, Images, and Mandalas: Tracing the Evolution of Esoteric Buddhist Rituals (Koichi) 84
Sperber, Dan 246, 257
Spinoza, Baruch 24, 419, 426–427, 429, 438–439
– spiritual automaton 428
Sprat, Thomas 264–266
Staal, Frits 32, 32–33n5, 33, 47–48, 52, 64, 201–202
Sterne, Jonathan 384n2, 390
Stewart, Dugald 210n35
Stewart, Kathleen 422–424
Stowe Missal 105
Stromberg, Peter 420n1
structuralism 1–2, 4–5, 12–13
Structuralists 43
subjectivity 18–19, 106–110, 317, 384, 419
Sufi tradition 217n9
Suhis dynasty 334
Sunday school 406, 408
– object lesson 407
Suriano, Matthew 334n17
syncretism 353
syntax 35, 48, 51, 53, 187, 290, 353
Syria 329, 331–333, 336, 341, 344–345

al-Ṭabarī *165*
Taittirīya Saṃhitā, 197–198
Tambiah, Stanley 11
Tang empire 69–70, 75
Tantras 13, 57, 60–62
Tarhunzas of the Army 342n31
tawqīf 178–187
Taylor, Charles 257
Tell Banat 332
Tell Halaf 342–343
Tempest, The (Shakespeare) 245–246
Tenochtitlan 351
teotl (kind of force) 368
Tertullian 235–236
Texcoco 351
Thetford, William 320
They Speak with Other Tongues (Sherrill) 280–281

Timaeus (Plato) 216n4, 219
Tlacopan 351
Tlatelolco 351
Todorov, Tzvetan 372n16
– orality-literacy debate 371–372
Toltec civilization 351–352
Tomlinson, Gary 358, 365–366
Toulman, Stephen 259
Tractatus in Psalmos (Origen) 233–234
transduction 383, 389, 396, 396n7, 398, 414
– as process 397
– religious sensations 397
– sonic transduction 397
Transoxiana 163
transparency 201–203, 208
– language, magical power of 195
– and ritual 195
Triple Alliance 351
Tylor, Edward B. 374

Ugarit 333, 340–341, 343–344
– Ugaritic sacrificial system 52
Umberger, Emily 362–363
United States 278, 280, 404, 430
Upaniṣads 200, 209
Urdu 389, 391
ʿUthmān 158
Utriusque Cosmi, maioris scilicet et minoris metaphysica (Flood) 219

Vandermeersch, Léon 116
Vedas 58, 196, 198–199, 205
– recitation of 16
– and Tantras 57, 60–62
Vedic India 203
Vial, Paul 114, 126, 130
Vickers, Brian 257
Vijayanāgara 197
Vineyard movement 430–431, 438–439
vyākaraṇa (Sanskrit grammar) 196, 202
vyākṛ, 197–198

Walker, D. P. 245, 255–256
Wapnick, Gloria 320
Wapnick, Kenneth 320
Wāṣil ibn ʿAṭāʾ, 162n10
al-Wāthiq 167
Weber, Max 319, 344
Weiss, Bernard 183
Weiss, Steve 408n3
"What is an Author" (Foucault) 308
White, Hayden 306
Whitehouse, Harvey 418
Whorf, Benjamin Lee 386, 393, 394
Wicca 11
Wiccan Rede 11
Wilkins, John 266
Williamson, Karina 229n23
Williamson, Marianne 320
Wilson, Deirdre 246
Wimber, John 430–436
Wittgenstein, Ludwig 306, 428
Woolgar, Steve 316
Wormald, Patrick 111
Wu, Emperor 81
Wulfstan 91, 101, 103

xenoglossia 277–278, 294
Xuanzang 79

Yelle, Robert 261–263, 415
Yi people 114, 134
Yoruba 20
Young, Ching-chi 119n7
young-earth creationism 280, 280n10

Zagorin, Perez 263–265
Zaydī 161
Zeno's paradox 47
Zhai Fengda 79, 83
Zhang clan 69–70
Zhili 77
Zimri-Lim 341n28
Zincirli 335, 337, 339, 339–340n25, 340n26, 343
zoemics 37, 48, 50–53

www.ingramcontent.com/pod-product-compliance
Lightning Source LLC
Chambersburg PA
CBHW031409230426
43668CB00007B/253